Colonizing the Realm of Words

SUNY series in Hindu Studies

Wendy Doniger, editor

Colonizing the Realm of Words

The Transformation of Tamil Literature in Nineteenth-Century South India

SASCHA EBELING

SUNY
PRESS

Published by State University of New York Press, Albany

Printed in the United States of America

For information, contact State University of New York Press, Albany, NY
www.sunypress.edu

Production by Eileen Meehan
Marketing by Michael Campochiaro

Library of Congress Cataloging-in-Publication Data

Ebeling, Sascha.
Colonizing the realm of words : the transformation of Tamil literature in nineteenth-century South India / Sascha Ebeling.
p. cm. — (Suny series in Hindu studies)
Based on the author's thesis (doctoral)—Universität zu Köln, 2005.
Includes bibliographical references and index.
ISBN 978-1-4384-3199-4 (hardcover : alk. paper)
ISBN 978-1-4384-3200-7 (pbk. : alk. paper)
1. Tamil literature—19th century—History and criticism. 2. Literature and society—India, South—History—19th century. I. Title.

PL4758.E24 2010
894.8'1109004—dc22 2009052829

10 9 8 7 6 5 4 3 2 1

Meinen Großeltern
Emmy Ebeling (1915–2001)
und
Aloys Heller (1918–2007)
in tiefempfundener Verehrung
und Dankbarkeit

Contents

List of Figures and Tables xi

Preface and Acknowledgments xiii

List of Abbreviations xix

Note on Transliteration, Pronunciation, and Translations of Tamil Primary Sources xxi

1 Introduction 1

Colonizing the Realm of Words: Literature and Colonialism 4

Tamil Literature in Nineteenth-Century South India 12

How to Ignore a Century of Literary Production 15

A Century of Cultural Change 19

In Search of a Lost Literature: The Chapters of This Book 27

2 Mapping the Universe of the Pulavar: Ti. Mīṉāṭcicuntaram Piḷḷai (1815–1876) and the Field of Traditional Literary Practices 33

Pulavar Education and Pre-Modern Tamil Poetics 37

The Pulavars' Genres: *Pirapantam* Works and Temple Myths (*talapurāṇam*) 55

Scholarship in the Name of the Lord: Monasteries as Patrons 57

When One's Fame Rises to the Heavens: The Pulavars' Economy of Praise 62

"Addressing the Assembly of Poets" (*avaiyaṭakkam*) 74

The Public Premiere (*araṅkēṟṟam*) 76

Occasional Poems (*taṉippāṭal*) and Epistolary Poems (*cīṭṭukkavi*) 79

The Spoken and the Written Word: Composition, Performance, and Transmission 84

Of Gods and Kings: Themes and Contents of Pulavar Literature 87

The Uses of *Akam* Poetics in the Nineteenth Century: The *Kuḷattūrkkōvai* (1853) 90

Makāvittuvāṉ Ti. Mīṉāṭcicuntaram Piḷḷai: A Poets' Poet 101

3 Pulavars and Potentates: Structures of Literary Patronage at the Zamindars' Courts and Beyond 103

Literature and Rituals of Courtly Representation 106

The System of Literary Patronage at the Zamindars' Courts 111

A "Who Is Who" of Nineteenth-Century Royal Patrons and Their Poets 116

Thanjavur 117

Pudukkottai 121

Ramnad and Sivagangai 122

Smaller Zamindaris 128

Of Beauty and Benevolence: Themes of Courtly Literature 132

Kāma's Arrows Whizzing Past the King: Royal Panegyrics and Eroticism in the *Cētupati viṟaliviṭutūtu* 144

The Pulavar in the Age of Mechanical Reproduction: Changes in Patronage 159

4 Toward the Modern Tamil Author: The Colonial Critique of the "Vernacular" and Māyūram Vētanāyakam Piḷḷai (1826–1889) as an Agent of Change 165

Māyūram Vētanāyakam Piḷḷai: A Biographical Reconstruction 171

Writing for "the moral improvement of the Natives of India": The *Nītinūl* (1859) 180

Law, Women's Education and Devotional Poetry: Vētanāyakam Piḷḷai's Other Writings 193

5 The Emergence of the Tamil Novel 205

The History of Prathapa Mudaliar (1879): An "approximation to a novel"? 208

The History of Suguna Sundari (1887): A "longwinded moral tale, weary and unprofitable"? 225

The Fatal Rumor or The History of Kamalambal (1893–1895): "Vedanta through fiction"? 232

Further Comparisons 237

6 Epilogue 247

Appendices

1 The Dating of the *Cētupati viṟaliviṭutūtu* Revisited 253

2 Chronological Table of the Earliest Tamil Novels Published Before 1900 257

3 Original Tamil Texts Quoted and Annotations 263

Glossary 295

References 299

Index 341

List of Figures and Tables

Cover Illustration and Figure 1.1	His Highness Dambadas Ramachandra Tondaiman Bahadur (1829–1886), painting by Raja Ravi Varma (1879), reproduced with kind permission from Mangharam (2003: 163).	
Figure 2.1	Ti. Mīṉāṭcicuntaram Piḷḷai (1815–1876), late nineteenth-century portrait, reproduced with kind permission from Paula Richman. *Extraordinary Child. Poems from a South Indian Devotional Genre*. Honolulu: University of Hawaii Press, 1997. Page 115. © 1997 School of Hawaiian, Asian & Pacific Studies.	35
Figure 2.2	A *pyal* school, late nineteenth-century photograph (in: Gehring 1906: 105).	37
Figure 2.3	A *kōmūttiri* verse (in: Taṇṭapāṇi Tēcikar 1965: 228).	47
Figure 2.4	A *caruppatōpattiram* verse (drawing based on Taṇṭapāṇi Tēcikar 1965: 72).	48
Figure 2.5	An *aṭṭanākapantam* verse (in: Taṇṭapāṇi Tēcikar 1965: 232).	50
Figure 3.1	U. Vē. Cāminātaiyar (1855–1942), early twentieth-century portrait.	161
Figure 4.1	Māyūram Vētanāyakam Piḷḷai (1826–1889), late nineteenth-century portrait, author's collection.	171
Figure 5.1	Title page of the second edition of *The History of Prathapa Mudaliar*, author's collection.	207
Figure 5.2	Advertisement for a re-edition of *The History of Suguna Sundari* (in: Vētanāyakam Piḷḷai 1917, back of front cover).	224

Figure 5.3	Pi. Ār. Rājam Aiyar (1871–1898), late nineteenth-century portrait, (frontispiece in Rajam Iyer 1905).	231
Table in Appendix 2	Chronological Table of the Earliest Tamil Novels Published Before 1900	258

Preface and Acknowledgments

Colonialism transformed many things, inexorably, decisively. But what about ways of narrating and listening, of reading and writing, of using one's imagination to do things with words? What about literature? How can the realm of words, the language we use and what we do with it, be colonized? During the course of the nineteenth century, all of India's literatures were thoroughly transformed under the impact of colonialism and Western modernity. This book examines the complexities of this momentous transformation by focusing on the case of Tamil, India's second oldest classical language besides Sanskrit. Based on extensive archival research and a wealth of textual material, this book tackles a variety of issues pertinent to Tamil elite literary production and consumption during the nineteenth century: the functioning and decline of traditional systems of literary production in which poet-scholars were patronized by religious institutions, landowners, and local kings; the anatomy of changes in textual practices, genres, styles, poetics, themes, tastes, and audiences; and the role of literature in the politics of social reform, gender, and incipient nationalism. By concluding with a discussion of what was at the time the most striking new genre—the Tamil novel—this book illuminates the larger picture of nineteenth-century Tamil literary culture.

Many of the questions discussed below are of course not limited to Tamil literature alone, but rather equally concern other literatures of South Asia or even other regions. In what follows, I have therefore tried to point to parallels and analogies as much and often as the scope of this book permitted. But I am aware that what I could only allude to or mention in passing would require a much more detailed comparative discussion—a discussion that could not be the aim of the present work and that, in any case, would presuppose in-depth studies of other literatures that we do not yet possess. Also, Tamil presents a special case. As the only living Indian language with over two thousand years of documented literary activity, it provides us with a particularly rich archive—an archive that scholars have only just begun to explore. Many areas on the map of Tamil literary history are still blank. In writing about the nineteenth century, I am exploring one such largely uncharted terrain, a terrain that, for a long time, has been actively dismissed as "the dark period" of Tamil literature and that has only recently begun to receive due attention. I will return to that problem in the Introduction. In order to be able to discuss here what one may call the most "representative" works, I have surveyed over four hundred Tamil texts written during the nineteenth century. Still, the question of which authors and texts to include, the problem of selection and judgment any literary historian faces, has remained a vexing one. Given the limited space of a single volume, it seemed a good idea to focus on a few select texts and authors illustrating my arguments most clearly. To compensate, at least in part, for what had to be passed over, I have included a substantial number of notes intended to point readers to the available primary and secondary literature. In these notes, I have tried to be as comprehensive as possible with regard to nineteenth-century Tamil literature.[1]

Since this is a book about the destinies of other books, it seems appropriate to dwell for a moment on its own destiny. A few sections of Chapters 4 and 5 appeared in earlier versions as my afterword in: Vedanayakam Pillai, Mayuram. 2005. *The Life and Times of Pratapa Mudaliar*. tr. by Meenakshi Tyagarajan. New Delhi: Katha. This material has been revised for the present book. This book began, in a sense, more than a decade ago, when my Tamil teacher, Thomas Malten of the University of Cologne, Germany, first initiated me to the works of Māyūram Vētanāyakam Piḷḷai and the wonders of nineteenth-century Tamil literature. I am profoundly grateful for his unceasing support, encouragement and advice during all these years. During my time at the London School of Oriental and African Studies (SOAS), I was fortunate to have the opportunity to study with Stuart Blackburn, who was at the time himself working on nineteenth-century Tamil, and who greatly encouraged me in my interests and kindly shared his materials. I am grateful that he has remained interested in my project even after I left SOAS. Eventually, I submitted a PhD dis-

1. I am currently compiling an encyclopedia of nineteenth-century Tamil literature that will include entries on individual authors, works, genres, publishers, etc., and that will hopefully one day serve as a reference companion to this book. The footnotes here are meant for the interim.

sertation to the University of Cologne, which might be seen as this book's earlier avatar. The work on the dissertation received generous funding and support from various agencies at different points of time. I would like to thank the *Studienstiftung des deutschen Volkes* (German National Academic Foundation), the *Deutsche Akademische Austauschdienst* (DAAD, German Academic Exchange Service) and the *Käthe Hack Stiftung* at the University of Cologne for their support, as well as the *Deutsche Morgenländische Gesellschaft* (German Oriental Society) for honoring this manuscript with their research award in 2007. Special thanks are also due to the late Margarethe Klenk and her sons and grandchildren for kindly sharing with me the most congenial living atmosphere of their charming villa in Köln-Lindenthal where much of this book was written. Finally, a generous award by the Whiting Foundation for excellence in Undergraduate Core teaching at the University of Chicago provided me with a very welcome sabbatical year during which I was able to make the final revisions to this book. As R. G. Collingwood remarked with characteristic clarity: "The duties of a professor may not be very arduous, but they do not encourage a state of mind favourable to the writing of books" (1972: viii). Thus, I thank Martha Roth, Dean of the Humanities Division of the University of Chicago, and Mario Santana, Master of the College, for granting me this leave.

To Dieter B. Kapp, my mentor and the supervisor of my dissertation, I owe a debt of gratitude. During the period of my studies in Cologne, he has been both teacher and friend, and much I have learned from him was not taught formally in a classroom. Ulrike Niklas, who first taught me Classical Tamil language and literature, has been an ever-generous teacher, friend, host, and ally in many projects as well as in life in general. Daud Ali, also at SOAS in London, taught me many things, and I am glad that he, respected teacher, friend, roommate, and accomplice on so many book raids in South India, continues to share his ideas and insights with me. When during an extended research period in South India in the year 2000 I was desperately trying to find a Tamil scholar to discuss a number of questions regarding the complex works of the nineteenth-century Tamil poets, I had great trouble finding someone competent and willing to read and discuss these works with me. Invariably, the answer I received was that those works were too difficult and that I should try someone else. At last, the late Pandit T. V. Gopal Iyer and his brother, the late Pandit T. S. Gangadharan, both of the École Française d'Extrême-Orient (EFEO) in Pondicherry, graciously opened an entire library of "sealed books" for me by initiating me to the works

I was curious to understand and by never refusing to discuss any text about which I would ask them. Without their constant generous help and those many weeks of discussions, this study would not have been possible. Pandit Gopal Iyer passed away on April 1st, 2007, and Pandit Gangadharan followed him on December 30, 2009. Their absence will continue to be felt by all of us who had the privilege of working with them.

I furthermore wish to thank the staff at various libraries and research institutions in India and around the world, viz. the Tamil Nadu Archives, the U. V. Swaminatha Iyer Library, the Roja Muthaiah Library, the Connemara Public Library, all in Chennai; the libraries of the French Institute and the EFEO as well as the National Archives in Pondicherry; the British Library and the SOAS Library in London; and finally the Regenstein Library at the University of Chicago. Access to the precious book and manuscript collections of the Tiruvavatuturai Atinam has been graciously granted by His Holiness the 23rd Mahasannidhanam Seer-vala-Seer Sivaprakasa Desika Paramacharya Swamigal and Ramji. Moreover, I wish to express my appreciation to the Honourable Judges of the Madras High Court for generously granting permission to consult the administrative records in the High Court Archives. Megan Macken and her most helpful staff at the Visual Resources Collection of the University of Chicago have kindly assisted me with the illustrations for this book. I am also grateful to my editors at SUNY Press, Nancy Ellegate, Eileen Meehan, and Michael Campochiaro, for their fine work and for making the experience of working jointly on this book such a pleasure.

While I was working on this book, many friends and colleagues have supported me in different ways by sharing their own research, sending papers, responding to my lectures, providing information, criticism, time for discussion, food, shelter, affection, and so much more. I wish to thank Thomas Anzenhofer, V. Arasu, Annemarie Backs, Nick Barnard and Galla Cassettari, Hanne M. de Bruin and P. Rajagopal, Jean-Luc Chevillard, Björn Christlieb, Whitney and Suzanne Cox, Jean Deloche, Dominic Goodall, Ronald Inden, S. Innasi, Arunajeet Kaur, Suma Kommattam, the late Bhavana Krishnamurthy, Gyanesh Kudaisya, Thomas Lehmann, Heike Liebau, Nora Melnikovová, Sanghamitra Misra, S. Muthaiah, R. Nagasamy, John J. Paul, Sivasubramaniam Pathmanathan, Rochelle Pinto, Sheldon Pollock, Rajesh Rai, the late Father S. Rajamanickam SJ, Bhavani Raman, Sita Anantha Raman, Sumathi Ramaswamy, Peter Reeves, Thadshayani Sadagopan, A. Ma. Sami, Peter Schalk and Gerd Falk Schalk, Charlotte Schmid, Tina Schöpper, Nirmal Selvamony and his family, S. R. S. Sharma, David Shulman, Eszter Somogyi, the Sunderraj family (especially my "Akka" Sabrina and Angie), Takanobu Takahashi, S. P. Thinappan, Torsten Tschacher, A. R. Venkatachalapathy, G. Vijayavenugopal, and Eva Wilden.

Daud Ali, Yigal Bronner, Steven Collins, Whitney Cox, Richard Fox, Nisha Kommattam, Srilata Raman, David Shulman, Torsten Tschacher, Uthaya Veluppillai, and Eva Wilden all have read one or more chapters as drafts. I am very grateful to all of them and to the two anonymous readers for SUNY Press for their invaluable comments and perceptive criticism. When I was writing the dissertation that led to this book, my friends in Cologne, Mats Exter, Daniel Kölligan, Jörg Neuheiser, Thomas Neuner, and Henrike Zillhardt, though slogging away fearlessly at their own research projects, always had time for elaborate lunches in the Mensa of the University of Cologne and for extended coffee (or rather [ˈfrəʊzn]) afterward, often amounting to hours of talking about everything under the sun. I miss these endless conversations laced with affectionate comradeship very much.

Special thanks also go to my colleagues and friends at the University of Chicago for providing the most collegial and congenial working environment: Muzaffar Alam, Dan Arnold, Elena Bashir, Yigal Bronner, Dipesh Chakrabarty, Steven Collins, Wendy Doniger, Philip Engblom, Jason Grunebaum, Yuming He, Berthold Höckner, James Lindholm, Rochona Majumdar, Kaley Mason, James Nye, Thomas Pavel, Valerie Ritter, Mario Santana, Clinton Seely, Ulrike Stark, Kotoka Suzuki, Gary Tubb, and Christian Wedemeyer. I am particularly grateful to Alicia Czaplewski, Wendy Doniger, Steven Collins, Claude Grangier, Clinton Seely, Ben Schonthal, and Paula Saward for doing whatever they could to make settling in and taking up work in Chicago a truly pleasant experience, helping to see me through the first difficulties of a continental move, both physically and emotionally. Moreover, I thank Richard Fox for constantly providing me with the finest substances for intellectual and culinary consumption, while remaining himself a consummate anti-substantialist, and for listening to numerous endless disquisitions on this book's content while swimming, thus assisting me, quite literally, in keeping my *mens sana* and my *corpus sanum*. While discussing my work with him—whether in the University swimming pool or outside of it—I have often been saved by the buoyancy of his thought. Thanks also to Judith and Zachary Fox for being there. MeLinda Morton's friendship, taste in movies, fascination with gadgets, and advice on virtually everything have become much cherished, indispensable parts of my life. I hope we will continue our conversations, over steaks and shakes, for many years.

This study would never have been conceived without Tharmarajah Suppiah ("Rajah") and his family who opened my eyes to the beauties and miracles of Tamil when I was still a young boy and without whom I would never have pursued the study of Tamil through my later days. I am grateful that these friends have so profoundly influenced the course of my life. Michael Goeke has also profoundly influenced my life, perhaps more so than he knows, and I am truly grateful for the privilege of his friendship through all these many years. A *fuerte abrazo* goes to Eva Fernández Casaña for making his life so happy.

What I owe to Nisha Kommattam is difficult to put into words. I wish to thank her for being with me in times of both *khushi* and *gham* as my harshest critic and most ardent supporter. Only she knows all the secrets behind these lines. Miffy, too, provided all the support that I could possibly expect from a young Beagle puppy. He has effectively taught me to look at life *sub specie canis,* and he and his bunny brother Mop have to be commended for their merciful decision not to eat my manuscript before I could send it to press.

Finally, this book would never have been completed without the ongoing encouragement which, expressed in so many wonderful ways, I continue to receive from my family: my parents Teja and Renate Ebeling, and my sister Mareike (whom I have too often unduly bothered by using her room, computer, printer, and e-mail). Crucial to my years as a student, and indeed to all my life, has also been the constant and generous loving support offered by my grandfather Aloys Heller and my grandmother Emmy Ebeling, two extraordinary human beings. Both carried in them the wisdom of almost an entire century, but they wrote no books, composed no operas, painted no paintings. The traces they left are what lives in those few of us who had the privilege of knowing them and of sharing their lives. Both have given me everything, and both have always been curious to know how my work progressed. Sadly, neither of them lived to see the printed book. To their memory this study is dedicated as a token of my heartfelt admiration and lifelong gratitude.

Chicago, 6 January 2010

List of Abbreviations

Abbreviated Titles of Sources

All references are to page numbers unless otherwise indicated.

EC	*Eṉ carittiram* = Cāminātaiyar (2000).
ETL 2	*Encyclopaedia of Tamil Literature,* vol. 2 = Hikosaka / Samuel (1992).
ETL 3	*Encyclopaedia of Tamil Literature,* vol. 3 = Hikosaka / Samuel (1996).
SMPC I	*Śrī Mīṉāṭcicuntaram Piḷḷaiyavarkaḷ carittiram,* vol. 1 = Cāminātaiyar (1933).
SMPC II	*Śrī Mīṉāṭcicuntaram Piḷḷaiyavarkaḷ carittiram,* vol. 2 = Cāminātaiyar (1940).
SMPT	*Śrī Mīṉāṭcicuntaram Piḷḷaiyavarkaḷ pirapantattiraṭṭu* = Cāminātaiyar (1926). Reference is to number of poem.
TCC	*Taṉicceyyuṭcintāmaṇi* = Kantacāmikkavirāyar (1908).
TPT 2	*Taṉippāṭal tiraṭṭu,* vol. 2 = Irāmacāmippulavar (1964a). Reference is to number of poem.
TPT 3	*Taṉippāṭal tiraṭṭu,* vol. 3 = Irāmacāmippulavar (1964b). Reference is to number of poem.
TPT 4	*Taṉippāṭal tiraṭṭu,* vol. 4 = Irāmacāmippulavar (1964c). Reference is to number of poem.
TPTC	*Taṉippāṭaṟṟiraṭṭu* = Cuppiramaṇiyappiḷḷai (1939).

Other Abbreviations

b.	born	ftn.	footnote	pp.	pages
ch.	chapter	Mal.	Malayalam	r.	ruled
chs.	chapters	Mar.	Marathi	Skt.	Sanskrit
d.	died	MS	Manuscript	st.	stanza(s)
Engl.	English	MSS	Manuscripts	Tam.	Tamil
esp.	especially	p.	page		

Note on Transliteration, Pronunciation, and Translations of Tamil Primary Sources

Besides certain obvious exceptions (such as well-known place names or proper names), I have used the standard transliteration system for Tamil as explained in Beythan (1943) so as to satisfy specialist readers and enable non-specialist readers to pronounce the unfamiliar words they encounter. Similarly, words from other Indian languages have generally been transliterated following the standard conventions for the language in question. The pronunciation of Tamil is approximately as follows:

Vowels

The vowels *a, i, u, e, o* are pronounced as in Italian and short unless marked by a macron which denotes long vowels (*ā, ī, ū, ē, ō*). It is important always to pay attention to that distinction. *ai* is pronounced as in Engl. *stray*, *au* as in *house*. Word-initial *e/ē* and *o/ō* are pronounced with a glide [je]/[je:] (as in *Yemen* and *Yeats*) and [wo]/[wo:] (as in *wombat* and *woe*). Word-final *u* is pronounced short with the lips spread [ɯ], not rounded.

Consonants

The consonants are pronounced approximately as in English with the following exceptions. Double consonants *tt, mm, pp* etc. always have to be pronounced distinctly. *ṭ*, *ṇ*, and *ḷ* are retroflex sounds pronounced with the tip of the tongue curved back to touch the hard palate [ʈ], [ɳ], [ɭ]. Intervocalically and after nasals, *k*, *t*, *ṭ*, *p* become voiced, e.g., Vētanāyakam [ve:da'na:jagam], Kampaṉ ['kamban]. Intervocalical *k* can be softened to *h* as in *akam* ['aham]. *ḻ* is pronounced like the *r* in American Engl. *purr; ṉ* as in Engl. *pin*. *c* and *cc* are pronounced [tʃ] as in Engl. *match*, but word-initial and intervocalical *c* is often pronounced [s] as in Engl. *sea*, e.g., *Caṅkam* ['saŋgam]. *ṅ* is the velar nasal *ng* [ŋ] in Engl. *sing;* followed by *k* it is pronounced [ŋg], e.g., *iṅkē* "here" rhymes with English *sing gay*. *ñ* is pronounced as in Spanish [nj] or like Engl. *ny* in *banyan*. *r* and *ṟ* are both trilled as in Spanish, but *ṟṟ* is pronounced somewhat like *tr* in English *tree*, and *ṉṟ* like *ndr* in *laundry*.

Unless indicated otherwise, all translations are mine. While this book is primarily a historical study of the uses of literature, it is also meant—in its reliance on Tamil primary sources—to be philologically grounded. Many of the texts I discuss below are little known and not easily accessible even to Tamil specialists. I have therefore decided to include quotations from Tamil primary sources at some length. The translations from Tamil I give here do not lay any claim to literary status. Rather than "sounding nice," they are intended as philologically accurate renderings of the original Tamil text. However, given the present state of affairs in the field of Tamil studies, to attempt such renderings is fraught with many difficulties, particularly when we translate pre-modern texts, such as the works of the poets discussed here. In far too many cases, we still do not really understand these texts well enough and thus cannot afford to change texts in translation simply to make them sound better in English. Also, some of the texts discussed here are literary in a very self-conscious way. Their very essence is to play with language and poetic conventions, to mislead and surprise the reader, to obfuscate and to be ambiguous. Consequently, rather than glossing over these problems, I have decided to address them directly whenever possible. As such discussions of textual minutiae might distract the reader from the general historical argument of the book, they have been kept to a minimum and relegated to a separate appendix where the original Tamil texts of all the primary sources used may be found together with brief annotations. These hopefully fulfill a major philological requirement: to illustrate the translation process and to make my decisions transparent, so that the reader can see why I adopted a particular reading and discarded others. All the original quotations are numbered, and this number is found in square brackets [ ] in the main text of this book so as to allow for easy reference.

However, when my analysis deals with the language of a particular text (as in the discussion of *cittirakkavi* stanzas in Chapter 2), the original Tamil text had to be quoted in the main text. In the most puzzling of these cases, I have inserted the original Tamil words into the English translation between braces { } in order to show accurately how the original maps onto its English shadow and to reduce some of the violence inherent in any act of translation. I am not sure whether—in adhering to these general guidelines—I have always managed to steer clear of what some have called "Translatorese" or "Indologese" (see e.g. Doniger/Smith 1991: lxxiii). I can only say that I have very much tried to do so. But on the other hand, we still know so little about the semantic and morphological niceties of pre-modern Tamil. Therefore, I am convinced that in cases of doubt greater precision ultimately warrants a slightly less "sexy" translation.

Figure 1.1. His Highness Dambadas Ramachandra Tondaiman Bahadur (1829–1886), painting by Raja Ravi Varma (1879).

1

Introduction

The cover of this book and Fig. 1.1 show the imposing figure of His Highness Dambadas Ramachandra Tondaiman Bahadur (1829–1886) who ruled the South Indian princely state Pudukkottai from 1839 until his death.[1] We see the raja, a seasoned quinquagenarian potentate, clad in a typical Indian royal outfit, the long, richly embroidered overcoat, the ornate crown, the sword, cane, and fine jewelry—all-in-all a sight familiar to students of British India from many paintings and photographs.[2] The South Indian locale is also depicted rather unambiguously by the temple tower (Tam. *kōpuram*) in the background. At first glance, this seems to be a rather stereotypical image of what the British used to call a "native ruler." On closer scrutiny, however, the image is complicated by a small detail: the book the king is holding up with his left hand. It bears on its spine three words, all of them proper names, all of them far from innocent signifiers: Homer, Iliad, London. What is Homer's *Iliad* doing in a small kingdom in nineteenth-century South India? Why is the book there? The portrait was painted in December 1879, and by that time book printing had already spread widely throughout Southern India. Local rulers and landlords had a long-standing tradition as patrons of the arts, and as the new medium was gaining ground, they often sponsored the expensive printing process. At one level, then, the raja is here portrayed as a typical patron, a lover of arts and letters, a generous donor who embraces a new cultural medium. The newness of the book as a medium, even as a commodity, is important in this context, and it is connected to the remaining question: why Homer's *Iliad* out of all possible texts?

1. For more on the kingdom of Pudukkottai and Ramachandra Tondaiman, see the monographs by Dirks (1987) and Waghorne (1994), which both have further portraits (including photographs) of this much-depicted ruler. See also Chapter 3.

2. Compare for instance the portraits found in Bayly (1990) or Worswick/Embree (1976).

If the book, the physical object, is already a clear, unmistakable sign of Western-style modernity, London as its place of publication and the identification of the text serve to underscore the message. In other words, it is hard not to read this portrait as a striking allegory of Empire, or more precisely, of the cultural effects sparked by the colonial encounter. Here we see an Indian king embracing not only Western literature but the very pinnacle of Western cultural traditions, the West's "classic" foundations. The raja as bibliophile is presented to us as simultaneously Western, modern,[3] and well-read, perhaps we may say enlightened. For, if the heroic tale of the *Iliad* was appropriate reading for any *Western* ruler, it demonstrates beyond doubt that the Raja of Pudukkottai was a man of style, literary gusto, and classical education. Now, if I have uncovered the allegory successfully, there is of course another question which immediately suggests itself: Why would the Raja of Pudukkottai want to be portrayed like this? The long answer to this question is a story of many cultural transformations taking place in nineteenth-century South India—and this story is the subject of this book.

From our distance as spectators of the twenty-first century it is impossible to tell whether Raja Ramachandra himself suggested the precise details of his portrait. It is likely that the artist who painted the king influenced the decision, for the artist was none other than Raja Ravi Varma (1848–1906), one of India's most celebrated modern painters.[4] Varma was an expert painter of Indian royalty who always crafted the composition of his paintings with great care. Note, for instance, how here the brightness of the flower bouquet directs our attention to focus on the book—a good reason to assume that the

3. I follow Stuart Blackburn in my use of the terms "modern" and "modernity" in this book to refer "broadly to that condition which a diverse range of changes, from rationality and hygiene to the novel, were thought to create [in India], often in imitation of European models but always as a break with 'tradition,' a set of beliefs and practices, including language and literature, thought to represent authentic Indian culture" (2003: 3). Analogously, texts, practices, etc., existing before or not affected by these changes will be referred to as "pre-modern" or "traditional." The expression "colonial modernity" links these changes explicitly to the colonial situation. Outside of my literary-historical use of these terms, there is a considerable body of literature discussing the implication of using the terms "modernity" and "modern" in the Indian context. Here I can only mention the discussions by Washbrook (1997; 1998) and van der Veer (1998), Chakrabarty (2002, esp. in the introduction), Menon (2004), and the special issue on "Multiple Modernities" of the journal *Daedalus* (Winter 2000).

4. On Ravi Varma see Mitter (1994, ch. 5), Guha Thakurta (1986), Arunima (2003), Neumayer/Schelberger (2005) and the beautiful, lavishly illustrated volume by Parsram Mangharam (2003).

painting's symbolism was at least in part carefully calculated. While Varma portrayed several men and women with books in their hands or on tables following a general Western fashion of his times, this is the only painting I have seen in which we find a classical Western literary text in such a prominent position, i.e., in the hand of an Indian ruler.[5] Thus, the allegory of Raja Ramachandra, or India embracing classical Western culture, seems indeed unique amongst Varma's paintings. Now, if this painting points to the story of South India's cultural transformations, Ravi Varma's life and all his art, which India's Viceroy Lord Curzon saw as "a happy blend of Western technique and Indian subject" (Mitter 1994: 180), could also be examined as an example of how Indian cultural traditions were transformed under colonial influence. For the purposes of this book, however, we need to remain in the realm of words rather than colours. The year of 1879, the year in which Ravi Varma painted the ruler of Pudukkottai, is no insignificant moment in the literary histories of either the British colonizers or colonized South India. In this year, the religious reformer and famous editor of classical Tamil texts Āṟumuka Nāvalar (b. 1822) passed away, as did, far away in Britain, George William MacArthur Reynolds (b. 1814), the forgotten popular novelist whose long-running serialized novel *The Mysteries of London* (1844) was avidly read all over India and influenced the development of many modern Indian literatures. Fellow novelist Sir Henry Rider Haggard (1856–1925), known for his adventure novel *King Solomon's Mines* (1885), was at the time involved in the Anglo-Zulu war, an event that altered perceptions of the British Empire at home and abroad. While Józef Konrad Korzeniowski (1857–1924), better known as Joseph Conrad, was still learning the English language which he would later so profoundly enrich with his writings, Edward Morgan Forster (d. 1970) was born. His novel *A Passage to India* (1924) influenced the destinies of many who thought about India in the West. In September of 1879,

5. In Mangharam's (2003) catalogue of Varma's paintings we find eleven portraits that include books. The portrait that comes closest in composition to Raja Ramachandra's is the one of Maharaja Sayajirao III of Baroda at his Investiture dated 1882 (Mangharam 2003: 146), which includes a copy of Adam Smith's *The Wealth of Nations*, thus forming a rather different sort of imperial allegory. Sir T. Madhava Rao, the Dewan of Baroda, is painted with various volumes of administrative reports by his side (153), while the Englishman P. S. Melville, an agent to the Governor General, stands next to "Scott's Poetical Works" and a volume labeled "Shakespere [sic]" among others (155). Maharani Lakshmi Bayi of Travancore is depicted in 1883 with two interesting titles: *Near Rome or Europe Described* and *The Young Ladies' Book* (85; see also Neumayer/Schelberger 2005: 301).

the celebrated Tamil politician and social reformer Ī. Vī. Rāmacāmi Nāyakkar (better known as "E.V.R." or "Periyar," d. 1973) was born. Still in the same *annus mirabilis*, several months before a man named Thomas Alva Edison invented the electric lightbulb, a man named Māyūram Vētanāyakam Piḷḷai (1826–1889) invented the Tamil novel. While much has already been written about the former invention, the latter takes up a good part of the following discussion. However, the story of how the Tamil novel emerged cannot be told without also telling the story of the raja's new books: of how traditional systems of literary production—in which poet-scholars were patronized by religious institutions, landowners, and local kings—gradually declined; of how textual practices, genres, styles, poetics, themes, tastes, and audiences changed; and of the role literature played in the politics of social reform, gender, and nationalism—in short, by telling the larger story of nineteenth-century Tamil literary culture. The aim of this book, then, is to examine how a literature was transformed under colonial influence. Before we look at the particular case of Tamil literary culture, the terms "literature" and "colonialism," heavily overdetermined as they are, require further reflection.

Colonizing the Realm of Words: Literature and Colonialism

Scholars have for some time pointed to the importance of texts in general and literary texts in particular for "colonial" enterprises around the world and at various times.[6] As Elleke Boehmer (2005: 14) has emphasized, "empire was in itself, at least in part, a textual exercise" depending on a wealth of writings, such as official reports, admin-

6. I use quotation marks here to suggest that "colonialism" itself is not a straightforward and undisputed term that could be used without further qualification. Skeptical of large-scale generalizations rather common in the field of Postcolonial Studies, I would like to emphasize the trivial but often neglected problem that "colonialism," the "colonial encounter," etc., did not mean the same thing everywhere and at all times. In the remainder of this book, then, the terms "colonial," "colonialism," etc., will be used without quotation marks to refer to colonial India during the period examined here, the nineteenth century, unless indicated otherwise (as for instance in the present section and in the Epilogue where somewhat broader claims are made). For a critique of the concept of and the historiography employing the term "colonialism," see Washbrook (2004). Cooper/Stoler (1997) as well as Dodson (2007) have also emphasized the complexity of "colonialism" and cautioned against using the term indiscriminately for historically diverse processes. See also Osterhammel (1997) for an attempt to disambiguate the terminology.

istrative papers, newspapers, political treatises, pamphlets, diaries, popular verse, letters, etc. Ania Loomba specifies that "literary texts [. . .] encode the tensions, complexities and nuances within colonial cultures. [. . .] Literature written on both sides of the colonial divide often absorbs, appropriates and inscribes aspects of the 'other' culture, creating new genres, ideas and identities in the process" (1998: 70). In other words, the transformations must be seen as mutual; colonial encounters transform both the literature of the colonizer and the literature of the colonized. Drawing on the terminology suggested by Mary Louise Pratt (1992) in her study on travel writing, Loomba further explains that "[l]iterature is an important 'contact zone,' to use Mary Louise Pratt's term, where 'transculturation' takes place in all its complexity" (1998: 70). For Pratt, 'contact zones' are "social spaces where disparate cultures meet, clash, and grapple with each other, often as highly asymmetrical relations of domination and subordination" (1992: 4) or spaces "in which peoples geographically and historically separated come into contact with each other and establish ongoing relations, usually involving conditions of coercion, radical inequality, and intractable conflict" (6). "Transculturation," then, refers to the mutually transformative processes happening in this "contact zone."[7] Pratt elaborates that a

> "contact" perspective emphasizes how subjects are constituted in and by their relations to each other. It treats the relations among colonizers and colonized [. . .] not in terms of separateness or apartheid, but in terms of copresence, interaction, interlocking understandings and practices, often within radically asymmetrical relations of power. (7)

Viewing literature as a "contact zone" allows us to examine how colonialism affected practices centered around the production and consumption of what we call "literary" texts on both sides of the colonizer/colonized divide without forgetting that such a divide was never fixed and given but historically shifting, therefore requiring our critical analysis. As we shall see in the discussion below, negotiations within this contact zone of literature could reach very far. They could reformulate both literary "form" (genres, styles) and "content" (themes, ideas), as well as thinking about texts in terms of aesthetics or poetics.

7. In a similar sense, Daniel Jeyaraj uses the term "inculturation" (*Inkulturation*) in his study of the Danish Halle Mission in eighteenth-century South India (see Jeyaraj 1996).

These complex processes of queries, adjustments, and reformulations taking place within the contact zone of literature are what I would like to refer to with the shorthand expression "colonization of literature."

Proceeding from the insight that colonial interaction obviously affected the literature of the colonizer, a large number of critical studies have examined this literature—British literature in particular.[8] Notably the works of a number of 'colonialist' writers, such as the above-mentioned Joseph Conrad, E. M. Forster or Henry Rider Haggard (and we have to add Rudyard Kipling, 1865–1936) have received extended and repeated critical attention.[9] Their works are now part of a veritable canon of colonial, or colonialist, writing that haunts departments of English and Comparative Literature. Furthermore, we also possess a better understanding of those English authors who did not explicitly respond to imperial developments, but who "participated in the representation of British global power mainly by taking it for granted" (Boehmer 2005: 24). Indeed, as Gayatri Chakravorty Spivak has cautioned, "it should not be possible, in principle, to read nineteenth-century British literature without remembering that imperialism, understood as England's social mission, was a crucial part of the cultural representation of England to the English" (1999: 113). Edward Said, focusing more specifically on the novel, has highlighted that "imperialism and the novel fortified each other to such a degree that it is impossible [. . .] to read one without in some way dealing with the other" (1994: 84). While in his work Said offers an important argument about the history of the novel in *Western* literature, we may look beyond the novel's history in the West and note that it was precisely during the colonial encounter that Indian authors produced what they called 'novels' in various Indian languages. We will return to this point in Chapter 5.

While the transformations of the colonizers' literatures have attracted considerable attention (with still no end in sight), the literatures of the colonized have not fared equally well.[10] As far as I can see,

8. This literature is too vast to allow the citation of individual works here. For a good overview see Boehmer (2005) and the short but very informative chapter by Theo D'haen (2002).

9. I use the term "colonialist" in Elleke Boehmer's sense to refer to literature "which was specifically concerned with colonial expansion. On the whole it was literature by and for colonizing Europeans about non-European lands dominated by them" (2005: 3).

10. One of the few studies to examine both the literatures of the colonizer and of the colonized, the reception of English literature in India, and the representation of India in English literature, in conjunction is Trivedi (1993). From a different angle, Joshi (2002) studies both the reception of novels from England and the writing of novels in English in colonial India.

this observation is true for colonial South and Southeast Asia as well as Africa and possibly for other areas too. As Rosinka Chaudhuri has observed in 2002, "Postcolonial studies, following Said's *Orientalism*, [. . .] has still not adequately articulated the response of the 'East' in its encounter with the forces of colonization" (2002: 9). Already in the 1980s, Aijaz Ahmad had criticized Edward Said's *Orientalism* (1978), a foundational text for the field of Postcolonial Studies, of ignoring the responses and perspectives of the colonized:

> A notable feature of *Orientalism* is that it examines the history of Western textualities about the non-West quite in isolation from how these textualities might have been received, accepted, modified, challenged, overthrown or reproduced by the intelligentsias of the colonized countries: not as an undifferentiated mass but as situated social agents impelled by our own conflicts, contradictions, distinct social and political locations, of class, gender, region, religious affiliation, and so on—hence a peculiar disjuncture in the architecture of the book. (Ahmad 1992: 172)

While I agree with Laurie J. Sears that this was somewhat inadequate as a critique of Said's particular project and its achievements,[11] it is intriguing that, as Rosinka Chaudhuri remarks, despite this critique much work after Said has "continued in the same vein, emphasizing the deconstruction of Western colonialist discourse rather than the complexities in the situation of the colonized" (2002: 9). The problem with this approach is not only that it presents merely one side of the coin. More importantly, by systematically ignoring the side of the colonized it runs the risk of reiterating and cementing the very Western cultural hegemony it professes to call into question. To say this more explicitly: The question of how literatures were colonized, through mutual processes of transculturation, cannot be answered by

11. Sears writes: "Said clearly states that his purpose is to show how the Orient has been produced in European and American texts. Had Said's *Orientalism* not focused on European discourses, it is doubtful whether it would have received the attention that it did. In effect, his work presents a clear challenge to Asians and Middle Easterners, and those who write about them with empathy, to explore the reception of and resistance to the discursive formations of Orientalism" (1996: 14, ftn. 31). Also, in the 1970s when Said was writing his book, still so little was known about non-Western literatures in the West that it would simply not have been possible for a single author to produce a study with the level of insight of *Orientalism* while doing equal justice to the literatures of colonizer and colonized. It is, in fact, still doubtful whether such a project could be undertaken even now, three decades after Said.

examining merely the literature of the colonizer. This might seem a trivial observation indeed, but very few critics so far seem to have realized it. The few attempts that have been made to explore the literatures of colonial India have focused on Indian writing *in English* rather than on writing in the many indigenous Indian languages.[12] Again, we find a number of much-discussed, 'canonical' authors, in particular Mulk Raj Anand (1905–2004), R. K. Narayan (1906–2001), and Raja Rao (1908–2006), who have come to represent the voices of the colonized in literature departments in the West. In contrast, the rich literatures produced in the colonized countries in many different languages other than English still remain largely unexplored, one might say marginalized. This is again particularly true for India. The largest amount of work on non-English colonial Indian writing has been done on Bengali, notably on the works of Bankimchandra Chatterjee (1838–1894), Michael Madhusudan Dutt (1824–1873), and Rabindranath Tagore (1861–1941).[13] This body of work is followed by a few studies on colonial North India,[14] while the South—with its major languages Tamil, Telugu, Kannada, and Malayalam—has only just begun to receive due attention.[15]

Given that many postcolonial critics originally set out precisely to query or destabilize the hegemony of the center and the agency

12. On Indian writing in English, see the recent surveys by Mehrotra (2003) and Rege (2004) and the literature cited there. Chaudhuri (2002) is an illuminating study of English poetry written in colonial Bengal.

13. While there exists a considerable secondary literature in Bengali, I only point to the more recent among the studies in English: Kaviraj (1995), Chatterjee (1995), Roy (1995), Banerjee (1998), Sarkar (2001), Raychaudhuri (2002), Bhattacharya (2005), and Ghosh (2006) and the literature cited there.

14. Important monographs in English, some of which focus not on literature proper but on language history and politics or book history, include King (1994), Dalmia (1997) and Orsini (2002) for Hindi materials, Russell (1972), Pritchett (1994), and Stark (2007) for Urdu, Naregal (2001) for Marathi, Dwyer (2001) for Gujarati, Mohapatra (1997) for Oriya, and Pinto (2007) for print in Goa. Bhatia (2004) discusses theater in colonial North India.

15. On Telugu see Leonard (1970), Sai Prasad (1991), Schmitthenner (2001), Vijayasree (2002), Mantena (2002; 2005), Mitchell (2005; 2009), Rajagopal (2004; 2005), Katten (2005), and Velcheru Narayana Rao's introduction and afterword in Apparao (2007). On Malayalam, see Panikkar (1996), Arunima (1997; 2004), Menon (1997; 2002; 2004), Kumar (2002), and the essays in Ravindran (2001). On Kannada, see Padikkal (1993; 2002), Ramachandran (2001), and Amur (2001). Significantly, Stuart Blackburn's and Vasudha Dalmia's recent volume on nineteenth-century Indian literatures contains only four (out of fourteen) essays which deal with South Indian materials (two essays on Tamil, one on Telugu, and one on Malayalam). See Blackburn/Dalmia (2004).

of the colonizer, this is a somewhat peculiar development. Though avowing time and again that the "Empire" is writing back and that Western critics should take literary production in the "Third World" more seriously, what has happened is predominantly a large-scale amplification of the colonizer's writing, of the center, not the periphery. In circles of endless introspection, the colonial center continues to look at its own navel. If the "provincialization" of Europe, and, one might add, of North America—the renewal of European and North American thought "from and for the margins" which Dipesh Chakrabarty (2001: 16) has called for—is an ideal to aspire to or at least a caveat to heed in critical inquiry in the twenty-first century, the study of literature under colonialism does not so far appear to show much interest in this approach.[16] As Ania Loomba observed already a decade ago:

> [Our contemporary] globality is often reduced to discussions of literatures written or translated into English, reminding us that in many ways postcolonial studies is simply a reworking of the older concepts of "Commonwealth literatures" or "Third World literatures." But even these literatures cannot be adequately discussed outside of the difficult interplay between their local and global contexts, an awareness that is all too often erased as we celebrate the hybridity or polyphony or magic realism of these texts! (1998: 257)

Thus, what we need as scholars of non-Western literatures as well as Comparative Literature is quite simply a more sustained shift of emphasis. We need to examine the literatures produced in the colonized languages more systematically and with both greater depth and breadth. We need to study the individual colonized literary cultures in India, Southeast Asia, or Africa in much greater detail, paying attention to their own complex histories before, during, and after colonial contact. To determine how indigenous literary cultures fared in the colonial contact zone, we need to be prepared to engage with them with the same amount and finesse of close reading that we have applied to Western colonial texts. The present book attempts a small step in that direction by studying the transformation of literary

16. There are, of course, exceptions, such as the work of Patrick Colm Hogan (e.g., 2000a; 2000b; 2004) who has striven for over a decade to enrich Western academic debates on literature with non-Western categories, examples, and approaches.

practices under colonialism through a particular detailed case study, that of Tamil literature.

As such, the present study may be viewed as a contribution to very recent debates raised by those scholars who attempt to explore the phenomenon of colonialism in India through an analysis of the transformation of indigenous cultural practices under its impact. Theoretically and methodologically, attempts to explore the colonial transformations of cultural practices have been nourished by the ever-increasing body of secondary literature that is devoted to identifying ways in which "colonial knowledge" was constructed—"those forms and bodies of knowledge that enabled European colonizers to achieve domination over their colonized subjects around the globe" in Phillip Wagoner's words (2003: 783).[17] If one works from this definition, the diverse indigenous cultural practices, such as elite and folk literature, music, dance, and so on can, of course, not easily be subsumed under the label 'colonial knowledge.' But there are ways in which they intersect with and inform the epistemological strategies employed to construct this knowledge, for instance when the nature and quality of indigenous literary production was debated in antiquarian concerns to recover Indian history, or in the debate about the Dravidian family of languages, as Thomas R. Trautmann has shown (1999a; 1999b; 2006). More specifically, as I will discuss further below, the interest of missionaries and colonial officials in the Tamil language and literature was certainly part of the larger process of colonial

17. The literature which explores the construction of "colonial knowledge" in India is copious, so that merely a few important studies can be cited here. These may be classified, following Phillip Wagoner (2003) into two broad categories: The first category which largely subscribes to the view that the role played by the colonized subjects in the production of "colonial knowledge" was negligible, and which Wagoner labels "postcolonialist," consists of a number of influential works which have helped us to see that European colonial conquest depended not exclusively on military, economic or political power, but to a decisive extent also on the power of knowledge. These are among others: Said (1978), Inden (1986; 1990), Cohn (1987; 1992; 1996), Dirks (1989; 1993; 2001), Metcalf (1994), and Viswanathan (1989). The second category, which has grown out of the first and which Wagoner calls "collaborationist," insists that indigenous agents contributed actively to the process of knowledge formation. This position has emerged notably through the following works: Irschick (1994), Bayly (1999), Trautmann (1999a; 1999b; 2006; 2009), Peabody (2001; 2003), Pinch (1999), Eaton (2000), and Tavakoli-Targhi (2001). Specific "cultural technologies of rule," as Dirks (2001: 9) has called them, have also been addressed in numerous studies: On the census, see Cohn (1987, ch. 10) and Appadurai (1993). The geographical survey is discussed in Edney (1990), while public health regulations are treated in Arnold (1986; 1993), and colonial anthropology in Dirks (1997). Architecture and town planning form the subject of Oldenberg (1984) and Dossal (1991).

knowledge production on India in general. In recent scholarship on colonial constructions of knowledge, the occupation with language and literature has been viewed in relation to similar disciplines, e.g., geography and ethnology.[18] Establishing these disciplines was one of the essential mechanisms through which colonial domination operated. Domination through science meant an attempt to control the bewildering, alien variety of peoples, languages, and behavior patterns which the colonizers initially found on the Indian soil. As Veena Naregal has argued, scientific classification was "the cognitive predilection that the European mind had developed for responding to the unfamiliar" (2001: 44). While it may not be a specifically European strategy, the colonial classificatory program was certainly far-reaching, highly systematic, and potentially all-encompassing. Much of the administrative labor during the nineteenth century centred around researching into and documenting law codes and regulations, mapping the geographical dimensions of the empire, counting its people, determining races, castes, religions, languages, and so on. All these activities were "appropriation techniques" applied in order to come to terms with and ultimately control Europe's alien 'Other.'

Thus, the colonial situation provided a specific background for the development of Tamil literary activities as the activities of the colonized. A study such as the present one, which attempts to recover indigenous cultural practices under the impact of colonialism, will by definition tend to amplify the voices of the colonized, and will show the *agency* on the part of indigenous groups. It will serve to demonstrate that Indians were not simply 'helpless' subaltern victims who were forced to surrender to an external cultural hegemony, but that indigenous agendas were fashioned and re-fashioned in a situation of cross-cultural dialogue.[19] In such an insistence on indigenous agency, it will become clear that not only colonial knowledge in a strict sense of the term, but also cultural practices were reformulated "through a complex form of collaboration between colonizers and colonized, and an attendant process of epistemic confrontation and adjustment between European and indigenous knowledge systems" (Wagoner 2003: 783). It is no secret that the colonial encounter affected Indian

18. See e.g., Naregal (2001: 45).

19. In using the term "dialogue" here, which partially rests on Irschick (1994), I certainly do not wish to explain away the violent and exploitative side of colonialism. But unlike Sanjay Subrahmanyam, who considers the term altogether inappropriate (2001, ch. 1), I do think that it helps to explain *some* of the complex and varied cultural interactions between India and the West.

literatures, music, dance, and other cultural forms. But it did so not in a unidirectional way by simply imposing European norms and standards onto existing ones. Neither does a simplistic dichotomous model of "Western impact" and "indigenous response" capture the full historical reality.[20] As becomes apparent when one actually confronts the cultural artifacts—the texts, songs, paintings produced during the colonial period—the situation was much more complex than this, and it is these complex inter- and intra-cultural processes of multifaceted, multilateral "epistemic confrontation and adjustment" that the present study is concerned with.

One further clarification is perhaps required, when one speaks about confrontations between "European and indigenous knowledge systems." As David Washbrook has emphasized, "European culture never became entirely synonymous with *British* colonial rule" (2004: 493, emphasis added). From the sixteenth century onward, the European presence in South India comprised Portuguese, Dutch, Danish, French and Germans, so that not all "Europeans" were British. Washbrook rightly points out that "[e]ngaging with European knowledge, therefore, did not have the immediate effect of implying subordination to colonial authority" (ibid.). We will have to bear this in mind, when we try to address the question to what extent and in what ways Indian authors and intellectuals engaged with European ideas. The fact that those ideas were not *eo ipso* perceived as the ideas of the colonial oppressors, and that the 'West' was not automatically "British," accounts for the openmindedness with which some social reformers and authors assessed and responded to Western knowledge.

Tamil Literature in Nineteenth-Century South India

Another clarification concerns the historical period examined here. I am using the term 'nineteenth century' to refer loosely to the period under discussion rather than as a strict delimitation. The one hundred years between 1800 and 1900 are merely the *focus period* for what follows, and I will have to transgress these temporal boundaries occasionally, as cultural phenomena more often than not refuse to conform to the constraints of artificial time limits. I wish to emphasize that it is first of all merely the time period in which most of the texts, people, and events discussed here are located. My aim is not to try to establish a specific "epoch" within the history of Tamil literature, which could

20. See e.g., Das (1991).

be posited (in a more or less essentialist way) as something internally coherent, clearly circumscribed, and monolithic. The reason for this caution is that, given our current knowledge of nineteenth-century Tamil texts, we are simply not (yet) in a position to say which (or if any) factors may ultimately produce such internal coherence.[21] Also, strictly speaking, the colonization of Tamil literature in the sense elaborated above did of course not simply stop at the turn of the century. For a comprehensive view, one would have to include the period from 1900 up to India's Independence in 1947. However, given the enormous literary production during that period and given how little research has been done on it so far, I could not do more than allude to a few trends and developments at the end of Chapter 5 and in the Epilogue. Doing full justice to this period would require a separate monograph.

The next clarification of the subtitle of this book, the one concerning the expression "Tamil literature," will require some more consideration, as the term disguises somewhat its own linguistic, aesthetic, geographical, and socio-political dimensions. The present study focuses on South India, or, more specifically, on the Tamil-speaking areas of what was during the nineteenth century the Madras Presidency. Although occasionally Sri Lankan scholars and authors are mentioned, I have had to exclude for reasons of space a detailed discussion of the literature(s) produced not only in Sri Lanka, but notably in Singapore and Malaysia where a rapidly increasing literary production in Tamil started during the nineteenth century.[22] From a linguistic point of view, the term "Tamil" may seem clear enough, but we should bear in mind that no language lives in isolation or as a single, monolithic entity. There were, in fact, many "Tamils" during the period discussed here. The idiom used by the first novelists, for instance, was a heavily sanskritized Tamil, which was newly fashioned to be capable of expressing modern Western ideas and concepts. The missionaries, too, struggled to create a language that would reach the

21. See, however, the recent volume on nineteenth-century Indian literatures edited by Stuart Blackburn and Vasudha Dalmia which, in the editors' words, "attempts to look at the colonial century as a whole, as an historical period in its own right" (2004: 8).

22. On nineteenth-century Tamil literature in Sri Lanka, see Kaṇapatip Piḷḷai (1967), Celvarācaṉ (1967), Vithiananthan (1969), Vimalachandra (1969), Young/Jebanesan (1995), Civaliṅkarājā/Civaliṅkarājā (2000), and the literature cited there. Most of what is available on Tamil literature in Malaysia focuses on the twentieth century, see Dhandayudham (1973), Venugopal (1999), and Irāmaiyā (1978). Singapore Tamil literature is discussed in Tiṇṇappaṉ (1993) and Tiṇṇappaṉ/Civakumāraṉ (2003).

masses, but still convey Christian ideas with appropriate accuracy.[23] Additionally, English found its way into the Tamil language, not only through new lexical items, but also at the level of syntax, when sentences first "thought" in English were formulated in Tamil. In trying to capture the contemporary spoken language of the city of Madras and elsewhere, nineteenth-century playwrights often used not only individual English terms, but entire phrases in their Tamil plays.[24] Furthermore, the Madras Presidency was clearly a multiethnic and multilingual environment. In colonial Madras city speakers of Tamil, Telugu, Hindustani, Persian, Gujarati, and Marathi, as well as Armenian, Portuguese, and English lived side by side, and "society was accustomed to a multiplicity of 'tongues,' " as David Washbrook observes (1991: 180).[25] At the court of the Maratha rulers in Thanjavur, scholars and poets composed works in Telugu, Sanskrit, Tamil, and Marathi.[26] Entire genres, such as the *kuṟavañci*, were borrowed from one language by another or developed simultaneously, and we also find genres and individual texts which employ more than one language.[27]

Having thus qualified the term 'Tamil,' we are left with the question of what "literature" is supposed to refer to. This question is important, since the present study does not cover the entire spectrum of texts that would (ideally) be included in a conventional handbook

23. Writing in 1900, the missionary and Professor of Tamil George U. Pope observed: "There exists now much of what is called Christian Tamil, a dialect created by the Danish missionaries of Tranquebar; enriched by generations of Tanjore, German, and other missionaries; modified, purified, and *refrigerated* by the Swiss Rhenius and the very composite Tinnevelly school; expanded and harmonized by Englishmen, amongst whom Bower (a Eurasian) was foremost in his day; and, finally, waiting now for the touch of some heaven-born genius among the Tamil community to make it as sweet and effective as any language on earth, living or dead" (1995: xii, original emphasis).

24. See e.g., the social plays *Ṭampāccāri vilācam* (c. 1867) by Caitāpuram Kācivicuvanāta Mutaliyār (?1806–1871) and *Piratāpa Cantira vilācam* (1877) by Pa.Va. Irāmacāmi Rāju (1852–1897).

25. For South India as a multilingual environment, see Washbrook (1991). Washbrook has also pointed out that certain languages became associated with particular functions: "Persian, Marathi and Telugu were ubiquitous languages of state; 'Hindustani' the *lingua franca* of war; Gujarati, Armenian and Telugu were languages of commerce" (2004: 495).

26. See the discussion of the Thanjavur Maratha court in Chapter 3.

27. The "language question" became politically important during the late colonial period, when extended debates over the coining of technical and scientific terms for educational purposes took place in connection with the non-brahmin movement. These debates have been examined by Venkatachalapathy (1995). For the nexus between the Tamil language and formulations of Tamil identity, see also Ramaswamy (1997).

on Tamil literary history. In what follows, I have had to focus on what we may term *elite* literary production, excluding those texts which could variously be labeled "folk," "non-elite," or "popular" literature. The main reason for my choice to focus on elite literature is that, unlike the popular literature of this period, it has not yet received the attention it deserves. Nineteenth-century Tamil literature as a whole has only comparatively recently begun to interest scholars.[28] And while Stuart Blackburn and A. R. Venkatachalapathy have discussed popular and particularly 'oral' texts,[29] the compositions of the *pulavars*, the traditionally educated pre-modern Tamil literary scholars-cum-poets, have not yet been critically examined. The works of the modern authors, and particularly the early Tamil novels, have so far only been treated rather superficially. Furthermore, my focus on elite literary production has also meant that, with few exceptions, I had to pass by most of the non-Hindu literature, i.e., works produced by Christian and Muslim authors.[30]

How to Ignore a Century of Literary Production

Why is it that, as I observe in the Preface, nineteenth-century Tamil literature has only very recently begun to receive due scholarly attention? The lack of interest is quite remarkable, for anyone who bothers immediately finds a great wealth of sources, both literary and non-literary. Many of the printed books, pamphlets, journals, and magazines are still available in libraries around the world, while the colonial archive, the extensive volume of records of British colonial knowledge, may be used to complement our reading of the literary sources. Additional materials may occasionally be found in private archives and family collections, so that the problem for the literary historian becomes this very overabundance of sources, while specialists of earlier periods generally bemoan the dearth of sources in their field. This *embarras de choix* is, however, not the main reason for the

28. A remarkable exception is Mayilai Cīṉi Vēṅkaṭacāmi's pioneering monograph published as early as 1962 which is outdated in parts, but—in its wide scope—has not yet been superseded. The work by Civakāmi (1994) primarily provides (valuable) lists of works and authors, while only the introduction contains some historical-analytical observations.

29. See Venkatachalapathy (1999) and Blackburn (2003; 2004).

30. For a short of overview of Christian Tamil literature, see Rajarigam (1958). On the Tamil works produced by Muslim poets and authors, see Shu'ayb (1993) and Tschacher (2001; 2002) and the literature cited there. For a general background on Christians and Muslims in nineteenth-century South India, see Bayly (1989).

widespread scholarly aversion to study nineteenth-century texts. The main reason may be seen in the fact that literary historians have generally considered the nineteenth century to be merely a "transitional" period, which lacks true poetic originality or literary innovation.[31] As Stuart Blackburn observes,

> as the high-tide of colonialism, the nineteenth century is generally viewed with suspicion, as a time of decline and loss, its literature uninspired, lacking the splendour of the courtly cultures that preceded it, as well as the dynamism of the nationalism that followed. [. . .] Dismissal of nineteenth-century literature as transitional is certainly well established in Tamil literary studies. (1998: 157)

While the earliest modern works, such as the first novels or stage plays, are usually found to be lacking in "maturity,"[32] the earlier verse compositions of the pulavars are maligned as unnecessarily difficult, "artificial," "prurient," and "decadent." The latter prejudice may be regarded as a direct continuation of British colonial diatribes against "vernacular" literary production. This colonial critique of Tamil literature, sparked initially by European colonial administrators but quickly imbibed and disseminated by Indian intellectuals, will be discussed in Chapter 4. Suffice it here to say that around mid-nineteenth century, an increasing number of essays, colonial reports, newspaper articles, etc. began to criticize the existing body of Tamil literature—i.e., nearly two millennia of literary production—for being immoral, superstitious, unrealistic, repetitive, unoriginal, and useless poetry as opposed to useful prose. What the American Methodist minister Rev. Peter Percival (1803–1882), who as Professor of Vernacular Literature at the Presidency College in Madras had dedicated his life to the study of Tamil, wrote in 1854 is symptomatic of this critique. While in his wide-ranging survey of Indian culture, *The Land of the Veda*, Percival had many good things to say about "the Hindus" and about the Tamil language in particular, he finds himself pressed for words to describe the character of Tamil literature:

> Even the beautiful story of Nala and Damyanti [sic], that in the hand of India's illustrious dramatic bard is so inimitable, and free from objection as it exists in its original form [in

31. Characteristically, in his *Introduction to Tamil Literature* the historian N. Subrahmanian titles his chapter on the literature of the nineteenth century "The Age of Experimentation and Transition" (1981). Kamil Zvelebil also speaks of "the transition period of the second half of the 19th cent." (1975: 5).

32. For such critiques of the early novels, see the discussion in Chapter 5.

> the Skt. *Mahābhārata*], has been so interlarded with poetic license and licentiousness, that on expurgating one of its versions [probably the *Naiṭatam*] for the use of a select class, I was obliged to expunge upwards of five hundred out of eleven hundred stanzas. It is not meant that the Hindus are exclusive in this sort of taste; the dramatists and novelists of Europe, even of England, furnish evidence to the contrary. But the Hindu exceeds the Westerns in his utter transgression of all bounds of decency. No conception can be formed of some of the productions of the Hindus; they are grossly extravagant in the fertility of licentiousness. Gross obscenity, dark superstition, an extravagant and horrible marvellousness with frequent references to idolatry, form the principal ingredients of that seasoning which renders the popular literature of the Hindus palatable to the taste of the public. (1854: 122)

Percival's utter discomfiture is evident here. He seems indeed unable to form any "conception" and almost appears traumatized when in his search for an adequate description he repeats key terms of hyperbole: "gross," "extravagant," as well as "licentiousness." A clash of Indian and European epistemes, of what Gayatri Spivak (1999), drawing on the work of Michel Foucault, has called "epistemic violence" becomes apparent in his words.

We still find observations as dismissive as Percival's at the beginning of the twentieth century expressed by both Europeans and Indians.[33] But the initial wholesale dismissal of Tamil literature began

33. The French scholar Julien Vinson (1843–1926), like Percival a professor of Tamil (in Paris), in the introduction to his *Manuel de la langue tamoule* published in 1903, dismisses not only nineteenth-century works, but Tamil literature in its entirety: "[L]a littérature tamoule est secondaire. A part peut-être les recueils de sentences morales, il n'est pas un poème de quelque importance dont une traduction complète puisse être lue sans fatigue par des Européens. Les descriptions y sont diffuses, monotones, pleines de mauvais goût et d'exagérations choquantes, conformes d'ailleurs à un type uniforme donné. Les poèmes d'amour ne sont pas plus variés, et les poèmes de guerre se ressemblent tous; ce sont proprement jeux d'esprit, des amplifications de rhétorique sur une formule générale et sur un canevas minutieusemenet réglé" [Tamil literature is secondary. With the exception perhaps of the collections of moral adages, there is no poem of some importance whose full translation could be read without tedium by Europeans. The descriptions we find there are diffuse, monotonous, full of bad taste and shocking exaggerations, and they follow a given uniform type. The love poems are not very varied, and the war poems all resemble each other. They are actually witticisms, rhetorical amplifications of a general formula and on a canvas that is strictly regulated even in its details.] (1986: XLIVf). For another example, see the quotation from Srinivasa Aiyangar's monograph *Tamil Studies* (published in 1914) which I have prefixed to Chapter 2 (Srinivasa Aiyangar 1982: 183).

to be revised during the last two decades of the nineteenth century, when the recovery and nationalist reassessment of the earliest known Tamil texts, the *Caṅkam* poems, served to rehabilitate a part of classical Tamil literature as a valuable heritage. I will return to this point in the next section. Further revaluations in the 1940s and 50s, notably in the immensely popular historical novels by Ra. Kiruṣṇamūrtti 'Kalki' (1899–1954) which glorified a South Indian and particularly Tamil Cōḻa past, pushed the threshold of respectability, even veneration, further toward the present.[34] Yet, this rehabilitation and revaluation ended somewhere shortly after the period of the medieval Cōḻas, the last dynasty thought to testify to a glorious past that was quintessentially Tamil. Consequently, the period from approximately the fifteenth to the nineteenth centuries remained—and for some scholars still remains today—the "dark period" of Tamil literature, a period of decadence and decline for which the old accusations of immorality and uselessness have not yet been dispelled. Thus, the eminent literary historian Mu. Arunachalam writes of the *viṟaliviṭutūtu*, a popular genre of the eighteenth and nineteenth centuries which I will discuss below in Chapter 3:

> This poem, by introducing the *viṟali*, a woman singer-cum-dancer to the patron, who was in those days a petty chief of the degenerate times, seeks to pander to his amorous nature. These patrons were mostly uneducated, uncultured rustic men, to whom only the vulgar, the sensuous and the bizarre had the greatest appeal. Their morals were not high and hence even a little gifted poet, unless he was spiritually inclined, could not help pandering to the tastes of such men. (1974: 249)

Though Percival wrote over a century earlier, we still seem to hear his startled ghost speaking through Arunachalam's statement and condemning the courtly literature of the period as "vulgar," "sensuous," and "bizarre." In a similar vein, the well-known literary historian

34. In *Pārttipaṉ kaṉavu* ("Parthiban's Dream," serialised between 1941 and 1943) and *Civakāmiyiṉ capatam* ("Shivakami's Vow," 1944–1948), Kalki evoked the grandeur of the ancient South Indian Pallava dynasty of the seventh century. His bestselling novel *Poṉṉiyiṉ Celvaṉ* ("Ponni's Darling"), a majestic historical romance, glorifies the Cōḻa kings of the tenth century. It was serialised between October 1950 and May 1954 and subsequently published in five volumes. *Pārttipaṉ kaṉavu, Civakāmiyiṉ capatam,* and *Poṉṉiyiṉ Celvaṉ* are all available in English translation (see Venkataraman 2003, Kalki 2008, and Karthik Narayanan 1999–2003). On Kalki, see also Ramnarayan (2006).

Mu. Varadarajan writes as late as 1988 about nineteenth-century Tamil literature:

> The literature of this period is full of the frigid conceits and the pedantic exercises of the grammarians, and the simplicity, the directness and the restraint characteristic of the early literature are now lost. Most of the poets of this age seem imitative and repetitive not only in their narrations but also in their descriptions. Taste in poetry has become sophisticated and poets are judged by the jingle of their alliteration and the acrobatics of their metre. We come across with really talented writers capable of original productions but they are only a very few. Even the works of these eminent poets evince a childish delight in riotous imaginations and hyperbolic utterances. There is, in many works of this period, not so much of art as of artificiality, and, therefore, many of these works have fallen into oblivion. (1988: 52)

Excoriating remarks such as these may be found everywhere in the existing scholarship on Tamil literature. One of the aims of the present book, then, is to dispel the myth of the nineteenth century as a "dark period" in Tamil literary history.

A Century of Cultural Change

In fact, I would argue that the nineteenth century must be considered a period of paramount importance within the historical development of Tamil literature and Tamil culture in general for a number of reasons. First of all, as both Stuart Blackburn and A. R. Venkatachalapathy have demonstrated in their recent research, the nineteenth century saw the advances of the printing press and its mass products, such as newspapers, magazines, pamphlets, and books.[35] The role that the various uses of print played in contemporary society can hardly be overestimated. As Blackburn has pointed out,

> print increased literacy, multiplied the copies and widened the distribution of traditional texts, reached new audiences with new types of information, encouraged new literary

35. See Venkatachalapathy (1994a) and Blackburn (2001; 2003; 2004).

> forms; [. . .] through all these innovations, print facilitated public debate on everything from vernacular education to child marriage and nationalism. (2003: 12)

Already before mid-century, we find the first Tamil authors of printed books, the first classical Tamil texts in print, the first Tamil publishers, and commercial publishing (ibid., 6). During the second half of the nineteenth century, Tamil society witnessed a sudden rise and quick growth of newspapers, journals, and magazines. Amongst them are the well-known English language newspaper *The Hindu* and its Tamil counterpart *Cutēcamittiraṉ*, both founded by Ka. Cuppiramaṇiyam (better known as G. Subramania Iyer, 1855–1916). Many of these journals and newspapers targeted at the urban metropolis of Madras, but a number of papers were also available in the mofussil, the hinterland, like *Jaṉavinōtiṉi*, *Tiṉavarttamāṉi*, or *Ñāṉapāṉu*.[36] These new media were indeed the vehicles for "public debate on everything."[37] They contributed to the emergence of a new public sphere in which debates on contemporary socio-political issues could take place. Among these debates we find e.g., the "modernization" of Tamil language and literature; the uses of English, religious, and inter-caste tensions; the question of the social position of women—women's education, child marriage, widow re-marriage, and the abolition of widow-burning (or *sati*)—as well as (re-)formulations of Tamil identity and nascent nationalism.[38]

While the development of Tamil journalism depended on the printing press, it also helped to fashion a "modern" Tamil prose. In the final decades of the century, prose was increasingly used for literary

36. For a history of Tamil journals and journalism, see Samy (2000), Campantaṉ (1987), and Caktivēl (1997).

37. On the role of the press as a vehicle of public debates in the Madras Presidency, see Sadasivan (1974, esp. pp. 60–67).

38. Based on the classic study by Habermas (1991), the notion of the "public sphere" has been discussed for the Indian context by Naregal (2001) and Orsini (2002) among others. Christopher A. Bayly has postulated what he calls an "information revolution," which consisted in the "creation of new, knowledgeable institutions: the army, the political services, the revenue, legal and educational establishments" and the "emergence of an attenuated sphere of public debate in which European expatriate ideologues and a handful of Indian spokesmen attempted to critique government and society through the press and public meeting" (1999: 143). The development of public opinion in the Madras Presidency is traced by Sadasivan (1974) and Raman (1999). The literature on the genesis of Tamil nationalism is considerable; see in particular Suntharalingam (1974), Kiruṣṇaṉ (1984), Rajendran (1994), Pandian (1994), Ravindiran (1996), Rösel (1997), Vaitheespara (1999), and Blackburn (2003, ch. 5).

purposes, replacing what had previously been a tradition of poetry.[39] In tandem with the rise of prose, the genre of the novel was appropriated for Tamil. But the novel was not the only genre employed to express colonial modernity and social reform.[40] Modern Tamil drama was born when playwrights decided to address contemporary social problems in a language that people could easily understand and that drew upon English words and colloquialisms rather than employing the difficult, often hermetic style of the pulavars. With the arrival of prose and the novel, Tamil literary culture expanded beyond its primary mode of orality: Private, individual reading and independent publication gradually emerged from the older modes of public recitation in front of large audiences and systems of literary patronage.[41] Formerly, the literary compositions of the scholarly poets, consisting of ornate and complex poetry, were publicly recited. The performances often took place on a number of days in front of a large audience. The whole event was sponsored by wealthy citizens, and the poet was honored with generous gifts. Such elaborate performances were also used as major opportunities to negotiate and display economic wealth and social prestige. These social activities were severely disrupted by the advent of the novel—in the form of the printed book—which was meant for private and silent consumption. Although often enough the early novels were read out by literate persons to a number of listeners who sat down around them (a practice that is still found today in rural areas in Tamilnadu), such readings remained confined to individual households and did not involve a wider audience. The "print revolution" that took place in nineteenth-century South India even inspired playwrights to compose works that were never meant to be performed. In the year 1891, Rao Bahadur P. Cuntaram Piḷḷai (1855–1897), professor of philosophy in Trivandrum, published his historical drama *Maṉōṉmaṇīyam*. In his preface he stated explicitly that this play was primarily meant to be read but not to be enacted.[42]

39. For the development of modern Tamil prose, see Paramacivāṉantam (1966), Chengalvaraya Pillai (1966), Zvelebil (1973, ch. xvii; 1995: 573–576), Pillay (1957), Asher (1972a), and the remarks in Baker (1978).

40. For a description of how various social issues were reflected in literary works, see Subramanian (1978).

41. On the changing reading practices, see Venkatachalapathy (1994b). A more elaborate argument may be found in his recent Tamil monograph (Vēṅkaṭācalapati 2002).

42. See Zvelebil (1995: 190–192). Cuntaram Piḷḷai's drama also became an influential text in the development of Tamil nationalism. See Meenakshisundaram (1974b) and Thirunavukkarasu (1971).

Thus, with an increasing number of new texts becoming available, a "reading public" consisting of educated middle-class readers with sufficient leisure time emerged in tandem with a growing market for books.

Moreover, the nineteenth century saw a process of systematic recovery, publication, and public recognition of what form today the earliest extant strata of Tamil literature, commonly referred to as *Caṅkam* poetry (c. 100 BCE to 250 CE). During the course of centuries, these ancient texts had become marginalized (although they had never fully disappeared from the cultural memory of Tamil society, as some critics think).[43] When during the second half of the nineteenth century scholars such as Āṟumuka Nāvalar (1822–1879), Ci. Vai. Tāmōtaram Piḷḷai (1832–1901), and U. Vē. Cāminātaiyar (1855–1942) searched for palmleaf manuscripts and collated, edited, and published the ancient texts, their importance was realized and Tamil suddenly emerged as a truly "classical" language. The drastic impact that this reassessment of *Caṅkam* literature had on the entire contemporary society is aptly described by Kamil Zvelebil: "The Tamils rediscovered their age-long heritage, their cultural independence and indigenous integrity, their separate nationhood" (1992: 144). It has to be noted, however, that what is condensed by Zvelebil into one sentence was in fact a long and complex process. Scholars have referred to this process as the "Tamil Renaissance," stressing its similarity with events that took place in Northern India.[44] Tamil was found to be a second "classical" language besides Sanskrit, and the only living Indian language which has a continuously documented tradition of more than two thousand years.[45] The antiquity of Tamil literature was soon deployed in a systematic fashion to combat the hegemonic position and linguistic elitism of Sanskrit and with it North Indian culture. During the following decades, Tamil literature was invoked to create a shared Tamil past, the foundations upon which modern nationalist thoughts and

43. This process of reassessment, collating and editing has become generally known as the "rediscovery" of *Caṅkam* literature. The term is unfortunate, as the poems were never entirely lost or forgotten. The full history of this fascinating process still remains to be told. See also Zvelebil (1975, ch. I) and Zvelebil (1992, ch. 6).

44. See Nambi Arooran (1980), Zvelebil (1973, ch. xviii) and Zvelebil (1992, ch. 6). For the impact of the "Tamil Renaissance" on Hinduism, see Ryerson (1988).

45. It was, however, not until the year 2004 that the Central Government in Delhi officially recognized Tamil as a classical language besides Sanskrit. On October 31, 2008, Union Culture minister Ambika Soni announced that Telugu and Kannada were now also granted official classical language status pending the outcome of a public interest litigation filed in the Madras High Court (*The Hindu*, 1 November 2008; *The Telegraph* (Calcutta), 1 November 2008).

sentiments could be developed. Ancient Tamil tradition could now be used as a safe "proof" of cultural uniqueness and therefore the right and necessity to form an independent nation. Thus, what was initially only a *literary* discovery became highly consequential in the wider socio-political sphere.[46]

Simultaneously, the joint labors of British, French, German, and American missionaries and colonial administrators enabled the Western world for the first time to obtain a wider knowledge of Tamil language and culture. The efforts of Robert Caldwell (1814–1891),[47] George Uglow Pope (1820–1908),[48] Francis Whyte Ellis (c. 1778–1819),[49] James Henry Nelson (1838–1898),[50] Charles E. Gover (d. 1872),[51] Arthur Coke Burnell (1840–1882),[52] Jean Antoine Dubois (1766–

46. The role that the *Caṅkam* poems played in the development of Tamil language devotion and nationalism is discussed in Ramaswamy (1997, esp. 34ff.). See also Baker (1978: 5f.).

47. Caldwell became famous for his *Comparative Grammar of the Dravidian or South Indian Family of Languages* published in 1856. He also wrote a *Political and General History of Tinnevelly* (1881), and a pamphlet on a South Indian caste, *The Tinnevelly Shanars* (1849), besides various smaller publications. For his biography, see the short sketch by Thompson (1961), Meenakshisundaram (1974a: 34–38), and the useful Tamil biography Cētuppiḷḷai (1964). Caldwell's own *Reminiscences* were published by his son-in-law (Wyatt 1894). See also Ravindiran (1996).

48. Initially a Wesleyan methodist minister and later professor of Tamil and Telugu at Balliol College, Oxford, Pope was a prolific writer. He published several monographs on Tamil language and literature, among them his three *Catechisms of Tamil Grammar* (1842, 1844), his multivolume *Handbook of the Tamil Language* (1855ff.), richly annotated translations of the *Tirukkuṟaḷ* (1886, see Pope 1992), the *Nālaṭiyār* (1893) and the *Tiruvācakam* (1900, see Pope 1995), a translation of the treatise on *puṟam* poetics *Puṟapporuḷveṇpāmālai* together with several poems from *Puṟanāṉūṟu* (reprinted in Pope 1997), and numerous articles. For his biography, see Thangiah (1952), Meenakshisundaram (1974a: 55–59), and the biographical notes reprinted in Pope (1997).

49. Ellis was one of the founders of the College of Fort St. George and author of a partial translation of the *Tirukkuṟaḷ* and few essays on South Indian culture. His important contribution to the theory of the Dravidian language family has been emphasized by Meenakshisundaram (1974a: 38–40) and in Thomas Trautmann's comprehensive studies of Ellis (1999a; 1999b; 2006).

50. Nelson's magisterial manual *The Madura Country* published in 1868 set the standard for other colonial district gazetteers and handbooks. See also Chapter 4.

51. Gover is remembered today mainly as a folklorist. His *magnum opus* is *The Folk-Songs of Southern India* published in 1871 (Gover 1983).

52. Known for his research in palaeography (Burnell 1874) and lexicography (as one of the authors of the famous *Hobson-Jobson* dictionary, see Yule/Burnell 1994). See also the literature cited in Chevillard (2004: xxiii).

1848),[53] Julien Vinson (1843–1926),[54] Louis Savinien Dupuis (1806–1874), Louis-Marie Mousset (1808–1888),[55] August Friedrich Caemmerer (d. 1837),[56] Karl Graul (1814–1864),[57] Peter Percival (1803–1882),[58] and Miron Winslow (1789–1864),[59] to name only some of the more impor-

53. Abbé J. A. Dubois of the Mission Étrangères in Paris has become famous for his general encyclopaedic account of South Indian culture *Description of the Character, Manners, and Customs of the People of India; and of their Institutions, Religious and Civil,* first published in an English translation in 1817 (see Dubois 1817) and 1825 in the original French *Moeurs, institutions et cérémonies des peuples de l'Inde* (Dubois 1825). For his biography, a valuable study of his works and further literature, see the German edition by Thomas Kohl (2002).

54. Born in Karaikkal, Vinson became professor of Tamil and Hindustani in Paris. He published a Tamil language manual in 1903 (Vinson 1986) and translated parts of the *Cilappatikāram,* the *Maṇimēkalai,* and the *Cīvakacintāmaṇi* (Vinson 1900), as well as two episodes from Kampaṉ's *Irāmāyaṇam* (Vinson 1861). In 1894, he published a partial translation of Āṉantaraṅkap Piḷḷai's famous diaries (Vinson 1894). See also Meenakshisundaram (1974a: 65f.).

55. The catholic missionaries Mousset and Dupuis published a Tamil-French dictionary (1st vol. 1855, 2nd vol. 1862) and a French-Tamil dictionary (1873). In 1863, Dupuis published his *Grammaire française-tamoule;* in 1865 a French-Tamil conversation manual. See also James (2000: 194–198). On the French scholars in general, see also the literature cited in Chevillard (2004).

56. Caemmerer translated the first two parts of the *Tirukkuṟaḷ* into German in 1803. See also Nehring (2003).

57. Graul, a Lutheran missionary from Leipzig, published his series *Bibliotheca Tamulica* between 1854 and 1865. It contains translations of texts on Vedanta philosophy, his *Outline of Tamil Grammar* (1855), a German translation of the *Tirukkuṟaḷ,* and a text edition and Latin translation of the latter work. Graul also translated Nampi's poetological treatise *Akapporuḷ viḷakkam* (Graul 1857) as well as selections from Tāyumāṉavar's poems, the *Civavākkiyam, Nālāyirativviyappirapantam,* and *Puṟapporuḷveṇpāmālai* (Graul 1865) into German. He assembled a Tamil library for the Leipzig Mission the catalogue of which he published in 1853 (Graul 1853). Moreover, he wrote a large number of articles on various aspects of South Indian culture. On Graul's life and achievements, see Lehmann (1964) and in particular the masterful study by Nehring (2003), which also contains a bibliography of his writings (pp. 371–378) and further secondary literature. On German contributions to Tamil studies in general, see Lehmann (1961) and Mohanavelu (1993).

58. The American Methodist minister Peter Percival was Professor of Vernacular Literature at the Presidency College in Madras and editor of the magazine *Tiṉavarttamāṉi* (1855ff.). He compiled an English-Tamil and a Tamil-English dictionary (1861), as well as a collection of Tamil proverbs (1843, 3rd ed. 1877). In 1854, he published his general survey of Indian culture *The Land of the Veda* (Percival 1854). See Zvelebil (1992: 154, ftn. 27), Meenakshisundaram (1974a: 54f.), and James (2000: 174 et passim).

59. Winslow has become famous for his Tamil-English dictionary published in 1862 (Winslow 1995). See also Meenakshisundaram (1974a: 66).

tant researchers, led to a far-reaching and unprecedented growth of knowledge on South India in general and Tamil language and literature in particular.[60] During earlier centuries, the reports of missionaries and traders had only been sporadic. To a certain extent, the work of the nineteenth-century researchers was based on what had been accomplished by their predecessors, notably the often misspelled German Lutheran Bartholomäus Ziegenbalg (1682–1719), Johann Philipp Fabricius (1711–1791), and the Italian Jesuit Costanzo Giuseppe Beschi (1680–1747), but scholarly activities had never before been so thorough and systematic. Scholars engaged in a number of related endeavors, all focusing on the description and analysis of Tamil language sources: literary history, epigraphy, the study of folk literature, the translation of Tamil works into European languages, the preparation of text editions and grammars, comparative linguistics, and the diachronic analysis of the Tamil language.[61] We may therefore say that during the nineteenth century what could be referred to as "Tamil philology," in the broadest sense of the term, was thoroughly transformed on the model of a European-style scholarly discipline.[62] In all these efforts, Tamil became an "object" which was collected, compared, measured, counted, and which, above all, gained a historical dimension in this classifying and ordering process. It is important to emphasize at this point that Tamil philology was by no means an exclusively European pursuit. Both Indian and Western philologists collaborated in manifold ways under the umbrella of the various language-based disciplines. They jointly built their storehouse of knowledge, an archive which, to a certain extent, continues to be utilized by Tamil scholars today.

Thus, while Tamil was canonized and historicized, its speakers witnessed a number of decisive changes in the wider social and economic spheres. Not only new technologies, such as the steam engine, railways, hot air balloons, the postal system, and a centralized water supply, but also changes in judicial administration and the educational system, social and religious reform movements, and Western missionary activities in tandem with an increasing influence of English and

60. For a general overview of the contribution of Western scholars to Tamil studies, see also Meenakshisundaram (1974a). European efforts in the field of Tamil lexicography are discussed in James (2000).

61. For the development of Tamil literary historiography, see also Zvelebil (1992: 1–11).

62. I explore the transformation of Tamil philology during the nineteenth century and in particular the role of the Madras College of Fort St. George in this transformation in Ebeling (2009b).

Western ideas were factors which produced a need to "refurbish" the Tamil language in order to keep pace with the diverse manifestations of modernity.[63] New Tamil words and expressions were called for as the influence of English, the idiom of "the Modern," became increasingly palpable. Tamil now had to be available for a number of new purposes: administration, Western-style education, journalism, and a newly created "vernacular literature" in prose. Naturally, foremost amongst the advocates of linguistic modernization was the English-educated elite. This consisted to a large extent of people who worked in various positions as government officials or traders and bankers. They had benefited initially from both traditional Tamil and English education. As we shall see, all these diverse socio-cultural changes influenced the fate of Tamil literature. In sum, what Christopher A. Bayly has observed with regard to North India is certainly true for the South as well: "[T]he simultaneous introduction of public instruction, the printing press, public debates in newspapers, the English language, libraries and dense archives transformed Indian society in the nineteenth century more thoroughly than colonial capitalism transformed its economy" (1999: 9).

This very short sketch of nineteenth-century Tamil cultural history may suffice to show that the nineteenth century was indeed an important period within the larger development of South Indian culture. As the foregoing discussion suggests, the nineteenth century entailed new regimes of imagination and new technologies of knowledge production. As a time of far-reaching social transformations, the nineteenth century cannot be easily ignored. It should also have become clear that all the processes of social reform and cultural change outlined above were intimately interwoven and cannot be seen in isolation. The massive transformation of Tamil literature and the entire literary sphere, which forms the subject of the present study, was firmly embedded in and partially triggered by this tapestry of wider social changes.[64]

---

63. Changes in the educational system are discussed in an important contemporary publication, Satthianadhan (1894), and in Raman (1996). For the missionary impact on Tamil society, see Nørgaard (1988), Grafe (1990), Bugge (1994), and Hudson (2000). On the social and religious reform movements, see Jones (1989, ch. 6), Subrahmanian (1979), and Paramarthalingam (1995).

64. Summaries of the development of Tamil literature in tandem with other social changes may also be found in Subramanian (1978), and in Visswanathan (1984) who assumes a wider perspective that includes the first half of the twentieth century.

In Search of a Lost Literature: The Chapters of This Book

Mikhail M. Bakhtin once observed that the "development of literature is not merely growth and change within the realm of unshakable boundaries of a specific definition; it affects the boundaries themselves."[65] This may remind us that the task of the literary historian is not a simple one, as not only the object of inquiry but also its social moorings are subject to change. It is essential for the historian to address the changing ideas of what "literature" might mean to those who produced and "consumed" it, as well as the question of what exactly happened outside its immediate boundaries, what people *did* with their texts. More specifically for a South Asian context, Sheldon Pollock (2003b) has recently formulated a set of goals and caveats, which anyone striving to reconstruct South Asian literary traditions and practices will have to bear in mind. While no single (and single-authored) volume can hope to be responsive to all of Pollock's observations, they help us to recognize and to re-think the chances and limitations of the approaches we choose toward South Asian literary cultures. In the present study, I have attempted to work from what Pollock has called a "historical-anthropological spirit," in addressing the question of "what the texts of South Asian literature meant to the people who wrote, heard, saw, or read them, and how these meanings may have changed over time" (2003b: 14). This perspective is important, since it prevents us from falling victim to an attitude which has until very recently hampered the study of nineteenth-century Tamil texts. Instead of prematurely dismissing them, simply because they do not correspond to our own tastes and standards, we may attempt to illumine their historicity, their specific "social logic," their "site within a highly particularized and local social environment" (Spiegel 1990: 78). In other words, we can begin to take nineteenth-century Tamil literature seriously, once we understand "that verbal discourse is a

65. My translation of Bakhtin's famous words (Бахтин 1975: 476): "Становление литературы не есть только рост и изменение ее в пределах незыблемых границ спецификума; оно задевает и самые эти границы." The currently available English translation by Michael Holquist and Caryl Emerson (Bakhtin 1981) through which Bakhtin has become known in the English-speaking world is often rather free and occasionally inaccurate. Their version reads "the growth of literature is not merely development and change within the fixed boundaries of any given definition; the boundaries themselves are constantly changing" (Bakhtin 1981: 33). To say that the "boundaries themselves are constantly changing" perhaps comes close to what Bakhtin actually meant, but it is not what he wrote.

social phenomenon—social throughout its entire range and in each and every of its factors, from the sound image to the furthest reaches of abstract meaning" (Bakhtin 1981: 259).[66] As such social phenomena, our texts are also historical. The question then is "[*h*]*ow* a given form of literary work appeared as it did, *where* it did, and *when* it did," to quote Hayden White's lucid formulation (1975: 99).

My emphasis in what follows, then, will be on the *texts* produced by poets and modern authors, unlike the existing body of scholarship on nineteenth-century Tamil literary culture, which has mainly been concerned with the wider institutional background of literary production, in order to write the history of Tamil book publishing. I seek to determine to what ends nineteenth-century Tamil literary texts were deployed in contemporary society, to examine the specific ways in which literary producers and audiences related themselves to what they sang and heard or wrote and read. As Gabrielle Spiegel has remarked, such a quest for the social logic of texts makes it necessary to examine both "their relation to their site of articulation—the social space they occupy, both as products of a particular social world and as agents at work in that world—and to their discursive character as articulated 'logos,' that is, as literary artifacts composed of language and thus requiring literary (formal) analysis" (1993: 9). Seeing literary texts as "agents," which actively participated in the ongoing life of their times, prevents us from falling victim to a widespread prejudice concerning pre-modern Indian texts: that they "bore little direct relation to the contemporary temporal setting" (Chandra 1979: 209). In Chapters 2 and 3, I will attempt to show that the opposite was true. As all literature is fundamentally a "social phenomenon," the pre-modern Tamil compositions were by no means fossilized, anachronistic artifacts, as scholars have often thought, but they naturally performed very specific functions in contemporary society. Similarly, the modern texts produced around and after mid-century, the essays, novels, dramas, etc., all had their own social logic, which is explored in Chapters 4 and 5. The second important point Spiegel makes is her insistence that literature also requires "literary (formal) analysis."

66. Again, Michael Holquist's and Caryl Emerson's translation of Bakhtin is free and interpretive. Bakhtin's original formulation is: "Форма и содержание едины в слове, понятом как социальное явление, социальное во всех сферах его жизни и во всех его моментах —от звукового образа до отвлеченнейшнх смысловых пластов" (more literally: "Form and content are one in (verbal) discourse understood as a social phenomenon, social in all spheres of its life and in all its moments—from the sound image to the most abstract semantic layers") (Бахтин 1975: 72).

While such literary analysis is my preoccupation throughout, I examine the essentially pre-modern aesthetic and poetological underpinnings of nineteenth-century Tamil literature at some length in Chapter 2. Their transformation after mid-century is discussed in Chapter 4. Furthermore, with a view to reconstruct the "particular social world" of the texts, i.e., in order to arrive at an understanding of the specific conditions of Tamil literary production and reception during the nineteenth century, I had to focus my analysis on individual people: poets, authors, patrons, audiences. Though I have chosen to construct a narrative with a multiplicity of actors (and this is reflected in the catalogue of poets and patrons given in Chapter 3), it was impossible to give equal consideration to all of them. Consequently, I have decided to focus on detailed case studies of two men who were perhaps the most eminent men of letters of the nineteenth-century Tamil scene: Makāvittuvāṉ Ti. Mīṉāṭcicuntaram Piḷḷai (1815–1876) who epitomizes the life of the pulavar, the poet-scholar, and Māyūram Vētanāyakam Piḷḷai (1826–1889), a colonial official and social reformer who became one of the first "modern" Tamil authors. The two were close friends, and, as we shall see, their friendship in a way symbolizes the transformation of Tamil literature that forms the subject of this study.

Following major events in the life history of Mīṉāṭcicuntaram Piḷḷai, Chapter 2 addresses the systems of literary production of the pulavars: the texts and genres, their pre-modern poetics and aesthetic features, their themes and contents, the composition, performance and transmission of literary works, the education of a pulavar, the audiences and patrons. I argue in particular that the pulavars operated within what I call an "economy of praise" where praise was "traded" in the form of verses to serve pulavars, patrons, and audiences in specific ways. This economy accounts for the particular purposes that the texts of the pulavars were made to serve. To illustrate form and content of a typical pulavar composition, I discuss in greater detail Mīṉāṭcicuntaram Piḷḷai's poem *Kuḷattūrkkōvai*, composed in 1853. Chapter 3 addresses the literary production of the pulavars under the patronage at the courts of zamindars and native kings. Again, the focus is on the nature of the texts produced in a late pre-modern courtly environment, the patrons and their motives, the audiences. I examine the specific function of literature in such an environment and, in particular, the role that texts played in the zamindars' ritualized remembrance of former glory. By way of collecting the data necessary for an assessment of nineteenth-century courtly literature, I have included a survey of the most important courts of zamindars and kings and their poets (Thanjavur, Pudukkottai, Ramnad, and Sivagangai as well as smaller zamindaris). As in the previous chapter, I also discuss an exemplary text, Tuvātrīm Tacāvatāṉam Caravaṇap Perumāḷ Kavirāyar's *Cētupati viṟaliviṭutūtu,* which shows major characteristic features of nineteenth-century Tamil courtly literature. The final part of Chapter 3 addresses the decline of the traditional systems of literary patronage and the changing occupations of the pulavars, who under the impact of the colonial state, found new jobs as book publishers, editors of texts, and Tamil teachers. Chapter 4 discusses how British company officials and missionaries criticized the existing Tamil literature and language as "backward," "superstitious," and generally unfit to express colonial modernity. They called for a "new vernacular" and a new literature with moral content that could be used in the newly refurbished educational system. This critique further affected the pulavars and Tamil poets, as their literature was devalued and ultimately became obsolete. Also in Chapter 4, I reconstruct the biography and discuss the works of Vētanāyakam Piḷḷai, the first modern Tamil author to take up the colonial critique of the "vernacular" and to write works accordingly, in what may be called a gradual movement of literary modernization. The story of Vētanāyakam Piḷḷai's evolution as an author symbolically reflects the development of Tamil literature. He began his literary career with a book on moral conduct written in verse, then wrote prose essays on women's education, and toward the end of his life two novels, one being the first Tamil novel, which appeared in 1879. While Chapter 4 focuses on the content of Vētanāyakam Piḷḷai's earlier works and on the question of how they reflect contemporary socio-political debates, Chapter 5 is devoted to the emergence of the Tamil novel. By comparing three early novels, two by Vētanāyakam Piḷḷai and one by B. R. Rājam Aiyar, I attempt to illumine the factors which led to the development of this genre. I also attempt to show how the new educative and social reformist function, which Tamil literature was required to perform, shaped these texts. Drawing upon Mikhail Bakhtin's (1975; 1981) influential theorization of the novel as a genre with dialogical capacities, I examine the early Tamil novels as multivocal texts, as sites of *dialogues* between tradition and modernity, reality and imagination, didacticism and entertainment, the self and the colonial other, the written and the spoken word, as well as Tamil and English. The appendices, which follow a short Epilogue in Chapter 6, contain first a re-assessment of the date of the *Cētupati viṟaliviṭutūtu,* the sample text which is discussed at some length in Chapter 3. Appendix 2 contains a chronological table of the earliest Tamil novels, i.e., those which were published before 1900. Appendix 3 provides the original Tamil versions of all the quotations from

Tamil primary sources not already incorporated into the main text of the present study.

In their recent volume on nineteenth-century Indian literary history, Stuart Blackburn and Vasudha Dalmia have emphasized three premises which inform their attempt at "a new framework for understanding the literature of the period" (2004: 22). Firstly, they observe that the "initial task of a new literary history of nineteenth-century India [. . .] is to identify pre-colonial forms and assess their continued vitality" (ibid., 8). Secondly, such a new literary history must also pay attention to the specific colonial situation in which Indian and Western literary cultures met. It therefore has to "engage with the deep and pervasive influence of European literary practices, including colonial policies and institutions" (ibid.). Thirdly, a new literary history of nineteenth-century India needs to "reach beyond obvious literary genres and conventional concepts" (ibid., 9). In the present attempt to examine nineteenth-century Tamil literary culture, I have heeded the first two of these premises. But particularly in my discussion of "pre-colonial forms" and "their continued vitality" I have had to explore a hitherto largely uncharted terrain. Therefore, I have thought it wise to focus on what Blackburn and Dalmia call the "obvious literary genres" instead of reaching beyond them. After all, one has to know what the "obvious" actually is in order to be able to progress beyond it. The widespread dismissal of nineteenth-century Tamil literature discussed above has bequeathed us an urgent need to collect basic data, to identify the important (and less important) literary works and their producers. In order to address this need, I have provided as many clarificatory and informational notes as possible on the following pages. But rather than laying out here merely a positivist cemetery of materials, I have endeavored to arrange them into a larger narrative of cultural transformation. In constructing this narrative, I have followed Bakhtin's advice to show not merely the "growth" and "change" of literature, but to address the relocation and renegotiation of boundaries. In sum, the aim of the present study is to examine a crucial moment in the history of Tamil literature: the momentous transformation of the entire system of Tamil elite literary production and consumption that took place in South India during the course of the nineteenth century.

2

Mapping the Universe of the Pulavar

Ti. Mīṉāṭcicuntaram Piḷḷai (1815–1876) and the Field of Traditional Literary Practices

> Learning was then confined to a class of indolent men or religious fanatics, who had no other work than this sort of exercise in prosodial gymnastics and who depended for their precarious subsistence on the bounties of kings and noblemen. Their object was to display their skill in versifying and to scare the ordinary readers by making their stanzas obscure by the use of obsolete and ambiguous words.
>
> —M. Srinivasa Aiyangar, 1914[1]

In his condemnation of late pre-modern literary practices, Srinivasa Aiyangar was certainly not alone. His view may be seen as representative of what many twentieth-century literary histories want to make us believe.[2] In fact, as has been pointed out above, this dismissive attitude is still prevalent among present day literary historians and it accounts for the dearth of studies of nineteenth-century Tamil literature. Aiyangar's remark also strikingly demonstrates how thoroughly the impact of colonial modernity had managed to alter the opinions about what were legitimate literary practices at the beginning of the twentieth century, i.e., merely two generations later. Contrary to this view, the present chapter will attempt to take these "indolent men or religious fanatics" seriously, to take a closer look at "their precarious subsistence" and their "exercise in prosodial gymnastics." Far from

1. Srinivasa Aiyangar (1982: 183).

2. See Chapter 1 for a discussion of similar views.

indolent, these men produced a large number of literary works many of which are fascinating tokens of profound erudition, great skill, and vivid imagination. And regardless of the tastes of later generations, they played an important role in their own society.

In their path-breaking study of Nāyaka politics and culture, Velcheru Narayana Rao, David Shulman and Sanjay Subrahmanyam have emphasized the importance of two major institutions within pre-modern South Indian society: the temple and the royal court (1998: 170, et passim). One may say that both these institutions clearly continued to be important political agents during the nineteenth century, if we understand the term "temple" in a wider sense as "religious institution," comprising both various kinds of Hindu "monasteries" and temples proper, and if we take the term "royal court" to include the zamindaris into which earlier "kingdoms" were converted during this period. Besides other functions, the royal courts and the religious institutions were the main patrons to sponsor literary activities. Consequently, our analysis will focus on each of the two. While the literary culture that grew around temples and monasteries shall be discussed here, the literary activities at various royal courts will form the subject of the following chapter.[3] Here, in order to explore the complex field of traditional literary practices prevailing throughout the nineteenth century, we will follow the career of one particular poet who was the most outstanding example of his day.

---

3. A. R. Venkatachalapathy points out a third group of patrons besides the religious institutions and the kings and zamindars (1994a, ch. 1): A poet's activities could also be sponsored by wealthy landlords, tahsildars, traders, farmers, or caste leaders. A large number of Mīṉāṭcicuntaram Piḷḷai's works were commissioned by members of this group, particularly his *talapurāṇams*. His *Tirukkuṭantaip purāṇam* was sponsored by the tahsildar of Kumbakonam, one Civakurunāta Piḷḷai (Cāminātaiyar 1933: 259f.). Rich Ceṭṭiyārs sponsored the *Kaṇṭatēvip purāṇam* (1867) (ibid., 280) and the *Vīravaṉap purāṇam* (1868) (ibid., 308), Mutaliyārs the *Tirutturuttip purāṇam* (1867) (ibid., 294ff.), and Cāliyars the *Taṉiyūrp purāṇam* (1868) (ibid., 300ff.). The *talapurāṇams* on Āṟṟūr, Viḷattoṭṭi, and Tiruvāḷoḷipuṟṟūr were sponsored by local Śaiva Vēḷāḷars (ibid., 215). Among his *pirapantams*, the *Maṅkaḷāmpikai piḷḷaittamiḻ* (1866) was sponsored by a textile merchant in Kumbakonam named Kaṉakacapaip Piḷḷai (ibid., 276f.), and the *Kuṭantait tiripantāti* (1866) by one Ampalavāṇa Ceṭṭiyār who paid 300 Rs. on the occasion of its premiere function (ibid., 278). Moreover, also works with nonreligious contents could be commissioned by patrons, as e.g., Aḻakiyacokkanātap Piḷḷai's *kātal pirapantam* which was composed in praise of one Muttucuvāmiyā Piḷḷai from Tirunelveli (see Aḻakiya-cokkanātap Piḷḷai 1868). In his autobiography, U. Vē. Cāminātaiyar also describes how itinerant bards and scholars were paid in villages out of common funds administered by the village headman (2000, ch. 17).

Figure 2.1. Ti. Mīṉāṭcicuntaram Piḷḷai (1815–1876), late nineteenth-century portrait.

No description of Tamil literary production during the nineteenth century could ignore the eminent figure of Makāvittuvāṉ Tiricirapuram Mīṉāṭcicuntaram Piḷḷai who has become immortalized less by the large number of his own works than by a massive two-volume biography titled *Tiruvāvaṭuturaiyātīṉattu Makāvittuvāṉ Tiricirapuram Śrī Mīṉāṭcicuntaram Piḷḷaiyavarkaḷ carittiram* ("The Story of Ti. Mīṉāṭcicuntaram Piḷḷai, Mahāvidvān of the Tiruvāvaṭuturai monastery") written in the 1930s by his most illustrious pupil Uttamatāṉapuram Vēṅkaṭarāmaṉ Cāminātaiyar (1855–1942).[4] This biography, together with Cāminātaiyar's autobiography *Eṉ carittiram* ("My Story"), figures among the most important sources for our knowledge of this period.[5]

4. See Cāminātaiyar (1933) and Cāminātaiyar (1940). An abbreviated English version of these two volumes is provided by Guruswamy (1976). This is useful for the mere "story line," but necessarily lacks many of the details of the original which are of interest to the cultural historian.

5. See Cāminātaiyar (2000), henceforth referred to as *EC* followed by the page number. This autobiography is available in a full English translation by Kamil Zvelebil (1990b; 1994).

Following the biography of Mīṉāṭcicuntaram Piḷḷai will enable us to gain insights into the complex world of elite literary practices of the first three quarters of the nineteenth century, the world of the pulavar, the "traditional," pre-modern literary scholar-cum-poet. As we move along with Mīṉāṭcicuntaram, we will also be able to discuss some of the key concepts of pre-modern Tamil poetics, the characteristics of genres, the thematic content of the literature, its impact in courtly and religious circles, and other topics which are essential for an understanding of these pre-modern literary practices. Whereas most other sources we have for studying nineteenth-century Tamil literature focus on the colonial metropolis of Madras, Mīṉāṭcicuntaram Piḷḷai's life history opens up new, important vistas on literary practices of the mofussil, and thus serves as a counterpoise to re-assess our commonly held assumptions about the overwhelming impact of urban elite culture on nineteenth-century literature in general.

On Thursday, April 6th of 1815, Mīṉāṭcicuntaram Piḷḷai was born in the village of Atavattūr, west of the town of Tiricirapuram (Tiruchirappalli, or in colonial English: Trichinopoly) and south of the river Kāvēri.[6] He was named after the goddess Mīṉāṭci, the tutelary deity of his family, by his father Citamparam Piḷḷai, a native of Madurai, who worked as a teacher in the village, and his mother Aṉṉattācci. They belonged to the Vēḷāḷar community, a powerful non-brahmin *jāti* (sub-caste) of paddy cultivators, which had become very influential as wealthy landowners or religious and cultural patrons. As we shall see below, several nineteenth-century intellectuals were Vēḷāḷars, not only Mīṉāṭcicuntaram Piḷḷai's friend M. Vētanāyakam Piḷḷai, but also other celebrated fellow literati, such as H. A. Kiruṣṇa Piḷḷai and Āṟumuka Nāvalar.[7] Significantly, Mīṉāṭcicuntaram Piḷḷai composed a poem (*Cēkkiḻār piḷḷaittamiḻ*) on the Śaivite saint Cēkkiḻār, author of the epic *Periyapurāṇam* (12th c.), and fellow Vēḷāḷar, in which he praises the community and highlights its preeminent role in society.[8]

6. For tracing the story of Mīṉāṭcicuntaram Piḷḷai's life, I follow the narrative as presented in the two volumes of his biography (Cāminātaiyar 1933; 1940), which are referred to here as *SMPC* I and *SMPC* II, respectively, followed by the page number. The information given there will be supplemented by various other sources. Two very condensed biographical accounts are Mātavaṉ (2000) and Mōkaṉaraṅkaṉ (1991). Cutler (2003) also discusses the role of Mīṉāṭcicuntaram Piḷḷai in nineteenth-century Tamil literary culture.

7. The Christian poet Henry A. Kiruṣṇa Piḷḷai (1827–1900) is remembered today for his epic poem *Iraṭcaṇiya yāttirikam* (1894), a Tamil version of John Bunyan's *The Pilgrim's Progress* (1678/84). For his biography and his works, see Hudson (1970), Masillamani (1969), Yesudhas (1969), and Ñāṉacikāmaṇi (1998). Āṟumuka Nāvalar is discussed below.

8. For a discussion of this poem, see Richman (1997, ch. 5).

Figure 2.2. A *pyal* school, late nineteenth-century photograph.

Pulavar Education and Pre-Modern Tamil Poetics

A few months after Mīṉāṭcicuntaram Piḷḷai's birth, the family moved to the nearby village Cōmaracampēṭṭai, where the villagers admired Citamparam Piḷḷai as an erudite Śaivite devotee, and above all a gifted poet. There, another son, Cokkaliṅkam, and one daughter, Mīṉāṭci, were born. The young Mīṉāṭcicuntaram attended his father's traditional school from the age of five onward. This village or *pyal* school (*tiṇṇaip paḷḷi*) consisted of a group of usually fifteen to twenty-one students who met on the sheltered platform in front of the schoolmaster's or village leader's house (see Figure 2.2).[9] There, each student was trained individually in Tamil language and literature, ethics, mythology, common folklore, arithmetics, and practical (e.g., agricultural and business) issues. The students practiced writing by first drawing letters with their fingers on the sandy ground. Later, they were taught how to write on small portable blackboards (*palakai*) or palm leaves (*ōlai*), but the main way of storing knowledge was learning by heart what the teacher recited in front of the children. Every day the students noted

9. My description of the functioning of these village schools is based on Gover (1873) and U. Vē. Cāminātaiyar's recollections of his own school days (*EC*, ch. 10). Hudson (1970, ch. 4) discusses the information given by Gover with regard to the life history of the nineteenth-century Christian Tamil author Henry A. Kiruṣṇa Piḷḷai (1827–1900).

down on their boards the lesson for the next morning in order to take it home and learn it. Gradually, they thus memorized a considerable amount of literary and scientific texts, a knowledge which could then be drawn upon to compose new works or to interpret the existing ones. Thus, the students were from the beginning brought up in what was an essentially *oral* culture. Poetic training and linguistic versatility were achieved by memorising literary works (mostly of devotional nature), grammars (such as *Naṉṉūl*), and *nikaṇṭus* ("dictionaries" of synonyms in verse form). The Indian official and member of the Royal Asiatic Society, Charles E. Gover (d. 1872), in his account of the village schools of the Madras Presidency published posthumously in 1873, describes the typical curriculum thus:

> Only four subjects are taught in a Pyal school, whatever its character. These are reading, writing, arithmetic, and memoriter work in the high dialect and Sanskrit. Taking the first-named subject, it must be noted that all the text-books are in the high dialect, and that ordinary modern Tamil, &c., is not taught at all. The books used in almost every Tamil school are:—The Kural of Tiruvalluvar; Attisudi of Auveiyar; Krishman-thudu; Panchatantra; Ramáyana of Kamban; and Kada Chintamani. The grammatical portion of study is drawn from the Nannul, and the Nighantu.[10] (1873: 54)

More critically, he also remarks that "much time is often given to construing beautiful but obscure poems written in the high dialect, and, except as moral teachers, of little use in the concerns of daily life" (52). These "obscure poems," however, were in fact the hallmark of the literary and linguistic education in a pyal school that served to familiarize the students with the tradition of elite literary production.

10. Most of the texts Gover enumerates will be easily recognized by students of Tamil literature and therefore need no further comment. His "Krishman-thudu" is most probably the *Kiruṣṇaṉ tūtuc carukkam*, a part of Villiputtūrār's Tamil version of the *Mahābhārata* (c. 1400 CE). Various nineteenth-century collections of folk narratives (*katai*) assembled for educational purposes were known by the name "Kada Chintamani" (*Katācintāmaṇi*). The most popular book with this title was probably by one Ātimūla Mutaliyār who also helped the missionary Miron Winslow (1789–1864) in compiling his *Comprehensive Tamil and English Dictionary* (1862) (see also Murdoch (1968: 193) who may be referring to the same book). Another example of these collections (though published later than Gover's account) is Chandrewarnam Mudaliyar (1875). The identity of Gover's "Nighantu" is also uncertain.

When Gover complains that "the books read are all in the high dialect, and hence, both in the collocation and the form of the words themselves, are altogether different from the language the lads must speak and hear in their after-life" (55), he overlooks the role that the pyal school played in making accessible the *literary* language and in thus opening up and preserving the literary heritage. In the diglossic situation that existed with regard to the literary language (or "high dialect") and the everyday language people actually spoke, such an institution was required to ensure that the literary texts would not fade into oblivion. While the colloquial language was rather effortlessly picked up outside the school, the literary texts could not be understood without a teacher's commentary that would explain difficult words or obscure mythological allusions of which the literature of the preceding centuries abounds. David Shulman has recently argued that during the thirteenth to fifteenth centuries Tamil literary production is characterized by an "intra-linguistic turn," where language "turns back on itself, examines and toys with itself as a primary subject of the poet's attention," so that such kind of linguistic experimentation "becomes an autonomous, axiomatic goal" (2004: 158f.). Accordingly, such texts employed increasingly sophisticated techniques of word play and lexical ambiguitiy, of phonaesthetic effects and intriguing metrical patterns. Some of these techniques became codified in poetic treatises as figures of speech or, in the Tamil terminology, *collaṇi* "embellishments of the word" and *poruḷaṇi* "embellishments of the meaning." If we move further in time, this intra-linguistic sensibility can be shown to extend into the poetic world of the nineteenth century, which was in many ways the culminating point of this tradition. Consequently, the students were actively encouraged to make themselves familiar with the far-reaching whimsicalities of the literary language. This was done by various technical practices. Students would have to compose a poem ending exactly with a line previously given by the teacher. Or one boy would recite a verse, then another boy would make up a verse that began with the last word of the former boy's verse, and so the chain would go on in order to practice the poetic technique, or figure of speech, known as *antāti* (see below). In Cāminātaiyar's words: "In the olden days students were first taught *antātis* as this was thought useful to them for practicing the segmentation of words, building up a good vocabulary and also for memorization" (*EC* 185f.).

The technique of *maṭakku* (or *yamakam* < Skt. *yamaka*) was practiced by making the student use the same word, syllable, metrical foot, or phrase in successive lines, each time with a different sandhi split yielding a different meaning. This ranked among the more difficult poetic skills, as it required a large, prestructured lexical knowledge to draw upon in composition. To illustrate this, we may look at a stanza from the *Puliyūryamakavantāti*, an *antāti* poem which consists of 100 *yamaka* stanzas in praise of Śiva in Chidambaram (also known as Puliyūr "Tiger Town"), by the Srilankan poet Mātakal Mayilvākanappulavar (1779–1816).[11] The twelfth stanza, for instance, runs like this in the original metrical version:

maiyalaṅ kāram payilkaṇṭar vaṇpuli yūrarvaitta
maiyalaṅ kārampa mākip peruki varakkuḷirā
maiyalaṅ kāram pakaittiṭa vāṭai varuttiṭattiṉ
maiyalaṅ kāram paṭaravev vāṟuyir vāḻparicē. (Nallaiyāpiḷḷai 1882: 10f.)

Here the first two feet of every line are identical. When we split the sandhis, however, we can see that it would not make sense to split these first two feet in the same way in every line. Instead, each time different words are used:

mai alaṅkāram payil kaṇṭar vaṇ puliyūrar vaitta
maiyal aṅku ārampam āki peruki vara kuḷirā-
mai alaṅku āram pakaittiṭa vāṭai varuttiṭa tiṉ-
mai alam kār ampu aṭara evvāṟu uyir vāḻ paricē.

So the first line has to be split as *mai alaṅkāram*, the second as *maiyal aṅku āram(pam)*, while the third and the fourth lines use enjambment: *kuḷirāmai alaṅku āram* and *tiṉmai alam kār am(pu)*. Poetic conventions generally require the poet to find a different sandhi-split sequence for each of the four lines of a stanza, i.e., no split may be repeated.[12] As to the content of the stanza, it is a typical example of personal devotion (*bhakti*) being expressed by the conventional imagery of love poetry:

The beautiful one of Tiger Town,
whose throat is adorned by blackness,
has stirred up [in me]

11. I have not been able to gather further information about Mayilvākanappulavar. For his dates and a list of (some of) his works, see Zvelebil (1995: 434).

12. Those who find such wordplay bewildering may consider an example from the English language. In the following limerick, the last line achieves a *yamaka*-like effect when spoken aloud: There once was a woman from Ryde / Who ate too many apples and died. / The apples fermented / inside the lamented / and made cider inside her inside.

an infatuation which began there
and keeps growing.
Without their coolness,
my shaking pearls annoy me,
the cool north wind
makes me grieve.
I have no strength!
While the black ocean roars,
how can my soul live on?

The devotee is imagined as a woman in love with the beautiful deity, Lord Śiva, whose throat is black as he swallowed the poison created by the churning of the milk ocean.[13] To describe the woman's yearning, the poet uses familiar images which express her suffering. As so often in Tamil (or in other Indian) love poetry, we find the idea that the intense infatuation (*maiyal*) creates a feeling of insufferable heat which cannot be cooled by anything. The lady's pearl necklace, which is usually cooling on the skin, has become hot because of her love and thus annoys her. The chilly north wind has no soothing effect on her. Suffering thus, she has lost all her strength and wonders how she might survive.

In his later days, Mīṉāṭcicuntaram Piḷḷai also composed a *yamakavantāti* on Chidambaram, the *Tiruttillaiyamakavantāti,* where roughly half the lines contain *yamaka* sequences, as well as poems on two other temples, the *Tiruccirāmalaiyamakavantāti* and the *Tuṟaicaiyamakavantāti* (see *SMPT* 1709–1809; 1811–1922; 1925–2026). Apart from constituting entire genres, such as the *yamakavantāti, yamaka* sequences are often included in pulavar compositions, where they may occur in combination with other "embellishments," particularly *cilēṭai* (a device which is discussed below).[14] Incidentally, *yamaka* poems perhaps best indicate how much of the pulavars' knowledge has already faded into oblivion only a century later. While such verses were commonly read (though never considered easy to understand) until the beginning of the twentieth century, nowadays even erudite readers find it extremely difficult to figure out the appropriate sandhi splits without a commentary. And unfortunately commentaries do not exist for the major part of the extant *yamaka* poems.

13. For this and other allusions to Śiva mythology found in the texts discussed in this book, see Doniger (1973; 1975).

14. See also the discussion of Māmpalak Kaviccinka Nāvalar's *Cantiravilācam,* which uses *yamaka* and *cilēṭai,* in the following chapter.

A similar, though somewhat less challenging technique is known as *tiripu*. Here, the first syllable of a line is changed while some of the following syllables remain the same. In a stanza addressed to his wealthy patron Poṉṉuccāmit Tēvar, the Ramnad court poet Māmpaḻak Kavicciṅka Nāvalar (1836–1884) asks him for a garment. In its original metrical version the stanza looks like this:

> *kaṟpōrvai tikarevaruṁ kalituṟantu putuvaivayaṟ kaḷaṅkaṭōṟu*
> *neṟpōrvai kiyapaṭinaṉ ṉitippōrvait tiṭavutitta nipuṇānāḷum*
> *poṟpōrvai vēlararuḷ pūttapoṉṉuc cāmimaṉṉā pukaḻukkēṟṟa*
> *naṟpōrvai yiṉṉameṟku nalkavillai paṉivarutta naviloṇātē.*
> (Paḻaniccāmi 1908: 47)

At first sight, here only the first syllable of the first metrical unit in each line makes the difference. A split of the sandhi, however, reveals that instead of repeating the word *pōrvai* four times, different words are used for the *tiripu*:

> *kaṟpōr vaitikar evarum kali tuṟantu putuvai vayal kaḷaṅkaḷ-*
> *tōṟum*
> *nel pōr vaikiyapaṭi nal niti pōr vaittiṭa utitta nipuṇā nāḷum*
> *poṟpu ōr vai vēlar aruḷ pūtta poṉṉuccāmi maṉṉā pukaḻukku*
> *ēṟṟa*
> *nal pōrvai iṉṉam meṟku nalkavillai paṉi varuttam navil oṇātē.*

> O learned man born to amass heaps of righteous wealth,
> so that all the threshing grounds near the fields of Putuvai
> abound in paddy,
> and the poverty of all the scholars and brahmins well-versed
> in the Vedas is dispelled,
> o king Poṉṉuccāmi whose grace equals that of the one with
> the sharp spear whose
> beauty is always realized by all [Lord Murukaṉ],
> you still have not given me a good upper cloth that suits
> your fame!
> I cannot express the pain I suffer during the cold season.

This technique of *tiripu* is clearly one of the most common devices in premodern Tamil poetry to be found in almost every work. Consequently, the Tamil teachers of the nineteenth century could not spare their students the pain of learning it well. To this end, the students needed to memorize words and their different combinations as well as metrical patterns, or what I have called above prestructured lexical knowledge which helped them to distribute the syllables accordingly.

As we shall see below, practicing *tiripu* and *yamakam* were just the very basics for the young students. Besides the works already mentioned above, the young Mīṉāṭcicuntaram studied in his father's school various smaller works, such as *Aruṇakiriyantāti*, *Mīṉāṭciyam-maipiḷḷaittamiḻ*, and also the sixteenth-century poem *Naiṭatam* (*SMPC* I: 9f.). But studying at school was not enough for the young boy who also spent his spare time imitating the works of famous poets. He listened attentively to the frequent discussions that his father had with other scholars who came to visit him. In turn, when he and his father were invited to someone else's house, he entertained everyone by reciting poetry and explaining its meaning. One of the poems of the "early" Mīṉāṭcicuntaram, composed while still in his teens, may serve to further illustrate not only what these young poet apprentices had to accomplish, but also how the clever manipulation of language, the essential part of nineteenth-century Tamil poetics, actually worked. When once visiting a wealthy *mirāsdār* (owner of hereditary land) in his village Muruṅkaipēṭṭai, the boy was asked to improvise a *veṇpā* stanza ending with the words "Say the meaning of this song! (*ippāṭṭuk karuttañ col*)" (*SMPC* I: 13f.). Adding one more word to it, so as to suit the metre, the boy came up with the following verse:

oṇkamalam vāḻntaṉṉa māki yuralaṇaintu
taṇkayanīrt tūṅkit takumēṟūrn teṇkatiriṉ
mēyavitat tāṉmūva rākum viḷampiyateṉ
tūyavippāṭ ṭukkaruttañ col.

What was so remarkable about this short stanza, even to the young boy's contemporary audience, was that it displayed a mastery of one of the most important and typical structuring principles in pre-modern learned poetry, viz. the *cilēṭai* (< Skt. *śleṣa*), a kind of pun, "double entendre" or paronomasia, which draws on lexical ambiguity or the language's capacity to express two (or more) different meanings at the same time.[15] A closer look at the above poem will explain how this worked. What we find is a riddle cast into an extended *cilēṭai* on (a) the three gods of the Hindu trinity, Brahmā, Viṣṇu, and Śiva, taking up commonly known mythology, and (b) the word "paddy"on the other hand. The first line presents a *cilēṭai* on Brahmā and paddy:

15. For a definition of the term and a masterful study of its application in various art forms of pre-modern India, see Bronner (2010).

oṇkamalam vāḻntu aṉṉam āki may mean (a) with reference to Brahmā, "residing on a brilliant lotus flower [and] becoming a goose." The first epithet refers to Lord Brahmā appearing on a lotus flower which has sprouted from the navel of Lord Viṣṇu, while the second is a reference to the well-known myth of Brahmā transforming into a goose (*aṉṉam*, Skt. *haṃsa*) to fly up to the top of the gigantic fire *liṅga* that Śiva became to test the greatness of Brahmā and Viṣṇu.[16] But these two epithets may also be read with reference to paddy, as (b) "living in clear water, [and] becoming (cooked) rice/food." Next, *ural aṇaintu taṇ kayam nīr tūṅki* contains a *cilēṭai* with Lord Viṣṇu and paddy, thus (a) "being tied to a mortar [after stealing butter Viṣṇu as the young boy Kṛṣṇa was tied to a mortar as punishment by his foster-mother Yaśodā], [and] sleeping on the cool deep ocean," and (b) "being put into a mortar [for pounding it into rice], [and] staying in cool deep water [while growing on the field]." Then, in *takum ēṟu ūrntu eṇ katiril mēya* we get a *cilēṭai* with Lord Śiva and paddy: (a) "riding on a befitting/worthy bullock [i.e., Nandi], [and] living near the mighty sun," and (b) "being carried/walked on [for thrashing] by a suitable bullock[-cart], [and] living in a thick sheaf of grain." Then the verse continues for five words unambiguously, *vitam tāṉ mūvar ākum viḷampiyatu* "like this are the three [Gods], it is said" only to finish off with another pun: *eṉ tūya i-p-pāṭṭu karuttam col*, (a) "Say the meaning of my pure song!," or (b) "the meaning of my pure song is 'paddy' (*col*)."[17] To reassemble this mind-boggling linguistic experience into a fixed form again:

(a) Residing on a brilliant lotus flower and becoming a goose,
  (b) Living in clear water and becoming food,
(a) Being tied to a mortar and sleeping on the cool deep ocean,
  (b) Being put into a mortar and remaining in cool deep water,
(a) Riding on a befitting bullock and living near the mighty sun,
  (b) Being carried by a suitable bullock and living in a thick sheaf of grain—

16. See Shulman (1980: 42) and the sources for this myth cited there.

17. The third line may also be read as *vitam tāṉ mūvar ākum—viḷampiyatu eṉ*, i.e., "of this kind are the three [Gods]—why is this said?" as an introduction to the following riddle "Say the meaning of this pure song of mine!" This poem is complex indeed.

Of this kind are the three [Gods], it is said.
(a) [Now,] say the meaning of this pure song of mine!
(b) The meaning of this pure song of mine is "paddy."

Note how nicely the last line may be read as both the question of the riddle and its answer. Such complex verbal feats, here so brilliantly demonstrated by the young Mīṉāṭcicuntaram, belonged to a tradition that may be traced back to medieval Indian poetics.[18] Over the centuries, as more and more emphasis was laid on the poet's skill and wit, it had become more widespread, so as to finally become part of the "basic" education of a young pulavar apprentice in the nineteenth century.[19] Yet, Mīṉāṭcicuntaram's early talents were quite extraordinary, and they were acknowledged by his contemporaries. The *mirāsdār* was so impressed by the young boy's ability and sharp wit that he gave a wagonload of paddy as his reward. This was, in fact, not the only occasion when his poetic talents had earned him material reward (*SMPC* I: 12f.), and this to a certain extent foreshadows the later instances of support given by wealthy patrons on which the poet depended throughout his entire life.

In 1830, when Mīṉāṭcicuntaram Piḷḷai was fifteen years old, his father Citamparam Piḷḷai, who had always done everything to encourage his child prodigy, passed away. The villagers continued to support the boy and his studies. They also arranged Mīṉāṭcicuntaram's marriage with the eleven-year-old Kāvēriyācci.[20] In order to be able to continue his education with other scholars, the boy moved to the town of Tiruchirappalli, where he stayed in a small house south of the East Street on the Rock Fort (for a rent of 25 annas per month). There, he studied with one famous scholar after the other, such as Uṟaiyūr Muttuvīra Vāttiyār, author of the grammatical treatise *Muttuvīriyam*, or Marutanāyakam Piḷḷai, who taught Śaiva Siddhānta philosophy and was the first to edit and publish the canonical texts of that school (*Meykaṇṭacāttiram*). But he also spent considerable time teaching others what he had learned so far. Whenever he was free, he

18. See Bronner (2010). For an overview on the use of *cilēṭai* in Tamil literature, see Nākarācaṉ (1983) and Tamiḻaraci (1980).

19. See also the following chapter for a discussion of how the Ramnad court poet Māmpaḻak Kavicciṅka Nāvalar employs *cilēṭai* in his poem *Cantiravilācam*.

20. The custom of child marriage was still prevalent throughout the nineteenth century, but it became one of the most fiercely disputed social issues against which Vētanāyakam Piḷḷai and other social reformist literati fought (see below, Chapter 4).

used to travel around in order to obtain a particular text as a palm-leaf manuscript, copy it down, and study it. Thus, he read not only *Kamparāmāyaṇam*, the famous medieval Tamil version of the *Rāmāyaṇa* epic, or the *Taṇṭiyalaṅkāram*, a medieval treatise on poetics, but also various religious works by Kumarakuruparar and others, and he learned the art of *cittirakkavi*. Requiring considerably stronger formal limitations than *tiripu* and *yamakam*, *cittirakkavi* belongs to the most difficult types of figures of speech. The term *cittirakkavi* or "picture poem" refers to a poem in which the lines or syllables are arranged so as to fit into a fanciful picture or diagram (*cittiram*) if written down.[21] As Indira Viswanathan Peterson has remarked, in this kind of pure word play "the focus is on the patterned arrangement of the syllables in a stanza" (2003a: 150). Although this technique may be traced back to the seventh-century Śaivite poet Tiruñāṉacampantar, it became increasingly popular during the development of medieval literature, so that the nineteenth-century poet could be put to test by asking him to compose such a stanza. These pictorial poems are far from frequent in the works of Mīṉāṭcicuntaram Piḷḷai and his contemporaries. Nonetheless, it appears that many of the *cittirakkavi* compositions now known were composed during the nineteenth century.[22] In the biographies of the poets, such verses are usually embedded into anecdotes that emphasize the poet's mastery of language. Mīṉāṭcicuntaram Piḷḷai's magnum opus *Amparppurāṇam* (1869) has one entire chapter containing more than thirty stanzas which rehearse the various possibilities of *cittirakkavi*.[23] The following four examples from this chapter shall suffice to show Mīṉāṭcicuntaram's mastery over this form of *collaṇi*. All the stanzas of this chapter describe the beautiful nature of the Naimica forest (Skt. *naimiṣāraṇya*), a sacred place where ascetics and sages perform their penance and which forms the conventional backdrop for the story of the *purāṇam*.[24]

---

21. The classical treatise on *cittirakkavi* is *Cittirakkavi viḷakkam* by Vi. Kō. Cūriyanārāyaṇa Cāstiriyār (1870–1903), see Palarāma Aiyar (1939). For a modern overview of various types and works see Mātavaṉ (1983). For a recent discussion of the phenomenon in Sanskrit *kāvya*, see Peterson (2003a) and the literature cited there.

22. In the list of 62 poets who composed *cittirakkavis* provided by Mātavaṉ (1983: 240–2), about one third belong to the nineteenth century.

23. Further *cittirakkavis* are also found in his *talapurāṇam* on Nākapaṭṭiṉam named *Tirunākaikkarōṇappurāṇam* (1869) in the *Nantinātappaṭalam* (see Mīṉāṭcicuntaram Piḷḷai 1970).

24. On the meaning of the Naimiṣāraṇya, see also Hiltebeitel (1998).

The first stanza (276) follows a *cittira* structure called *kōmūttiri* (< Skt. *gomūtra* "cow urine") which refers to the zigzag pattern that cows leave behind on the ground when urinating and walking at the same time. The syllables of the first and second, and the third and fourth lines of the poem below may be connected crosswise so as to yield the same syllabic structure (see Figure 2.3).

āya vāḻai kurāvata vāruva,
nēya māḻai marānita mōruva,
pāyakāñci palavu nirampuva,
tūyatāñcupa mēvupa rampuva (Taṇṭapāṇi Tēcikar 1965: 71).

Banana trees, bottle-flower trees and fig trees are
growing opulently,
The wish-fulfilling mango trees and the *marā* trees are
daily being marveled at,
Wide-spreading *kāñci* trees and jack trees abound —
[A feeling of] dwelling in pure bliss pervades everything.

As in the other verses of this chapter, the poet paints here a charming picture of the sylvan idyll of the Naimiṣāraṇya. The next *cittirakkavi* form to be considered here is called *caruppatōpattiram* (< Skt. *sarvatobhadra*), which means "good/auspicious from all sides." This is a double palindrome where the syllables can be connected forward and backward both horizontally and vertically so as to yield the same

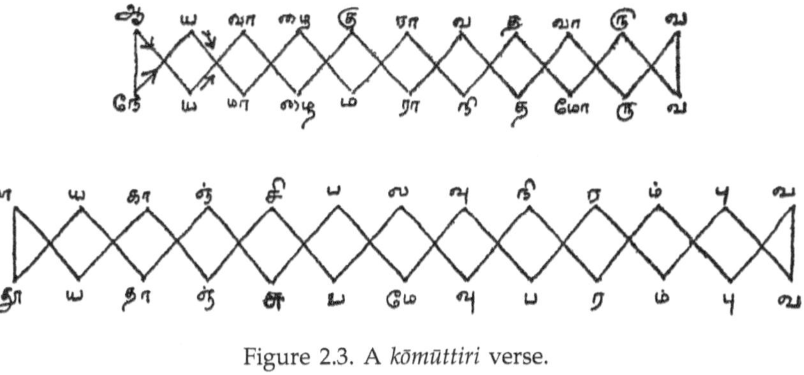

Figure 2.3. A *kōmūttiri* verse.

mā	vā	yā	vī	vī	yā	vā	mā
vā	yā	vō	vā	vā	vō	yā	vā
yā	vō	vā	mā	mā	vā	vō	yā
vī	vā	mā	mē	mē	mā	vā	vī
vī	vā	mā	mē	mē	mā	vā	vī
yā	vō	vā	mā	mā	vā	vō	yā
vā	yā	vō	vā	vā	vō	yā	vā
mā	vā	yā	vī	vī	yā	vā	mā

Figure 2.4. A *caruppatōpattiram* verse.

sequence.[25] Stanza 282 of the *Amparppurāṇam* (Taṇṭapāṇi Tēcikar 1965: 72) follows this complex pattern illustrated in Figure 2.4. A version of the text with split sandhi is included below the original for easier reference:

māvāyāvī vīyāvāmā
vāyāvōvā vāvōyāvā
yāvōvāmā māvā vōyā
vīvāmāmē mēmā vāvī.

mā ā yā vī vīyā, vā mā
āyā, ōvā āvu-ō, yā vāyā,

25. In her discussion of a Sanskrit *sarvatobhadra* verse from the *kāvya* epic *Kirātārjunīya*, Indira Peterson remarks that "Mathematically the verse has the dihedral symmetry called D_4 in group theory, the symmetry of a square that can be flipped about a horizontal axis, flipped about a vertical axis, or rotated through ninety degrees" (2003a: 151).

ō, āmā mā vāvu ōyā,
vīvu-ām ām ēm-ē mā vāvī.[26]

The flowers of the mango tree, the ebony tree and the *yā* tree do not wither,
The leaping does do not suffer, the cows do not leave, what does one lack here?
Oh, the wild cows [and other] animals do not stop their frolicking!
The large ponds provide the pleasure of water which is final dissolution.

In the last line, when the poet speaks of water being destruction (*vīvu*), he refers to religio-philosophical ideas of the dissolution of the self. Note how in all these stanzas Mīṉāṭcicuntaram Piḷḷai connects motifs of beautiful nature and scenery to philosophical and spiritual ideas: "bliss," "destruction," and in the following stanza "the realization of spiritual knowledge" (*pōta nāṟal*). His stanzas are much more than mere wordplay. Below this shiny rhetorical surface, he also manages to convey a sense of the sacred forest as the abode of the sages. Nature and spirituality at the content level are as intricately interwoven as the syllables at the formal level. Complex textures such as these hopefully disprove the common prejudice that meaning shrivels when form is blown up and that *cittirakkavi* poems *always and per se* have to be mere "verbal jugglery."

The next *cittirakkavi* verse to be discussed here is an example of *aṭṭanākapantam* (< Skt. *aṣṭa-nāga-bandha*), or "structure of eight snakes." It is one of the most fanciful patterns where the syllables of the poem may be fitted into a picture of eight intertwined snakes (as illustrated in Figure 2.5, next page). Besides this snake pattern, there are many other *pantams*, where the syllables yield natural (often devotional) objects, such as *śivaliṅgas*, peacocks, scorpions, oil lamps, drums, or just abstract geometrical patterns.[27] Stanza 292 of the *Amparppurāṇam* follows the figuration of the eight snakes (see Taṇṭapāṇi Tēcikar 1965: 75):

26. For *ōvā āvu-ō* read *āvu-ō*{clitic *ō*} *ōvā*. *Yā vāyā* is literally "which ones are not available?." According to Mīṉāṭcicuntaram Piḷḷai's autocommentary, the following *ō* is supposed to be an expletive (*acai*), but I kept it as an interjection in the translation. The last line is: *vīvu-ām*{"dissolution" plus *ām* = *ākum* "being"} *ām*{"water"} *ēm-ē*{"pleasure" plus clitic *ē*} *mā*{"large"} *vāvī*{< vāvi "pond" with a lengthened final syllable}.

27. Many of these are illustrated in Murugan/Mathialagan (1999).

Figure 2.5. An *aṭṭanākapantam* verse.

cūta mēyavan tīntaḻai tuṉṟuva
cīta māmalar cīrtuṟṟa māṇpiṉa
ēta meṉṟatoṉ ṟiṉṟuṇṭu tīviya
pōta nāṟaliṉ māṟaṭum poṅkarē.

The lovely sweet buds are crowded on the mango trees,
The beautiful cool flowers are of special excellence,
Everything is faultless, there are [only] sweet things,
In this forest where the enemy is subdued by realization
of spiritual knowledge.

Another form, often subsumed under the label of *cittirakkavi*, are verses which are not connected to visual images, but which attempt to create peculiar sound effects. Some of these only use a limited set of consonants or vowels. Again in the *Amparppurāṇam*, we find a stanza which has *t* as its only consonant (*takara varukkac ceyyuḷ*). I give the original, a version with split sandhi and a translation:

> *tittittatētūt tottuttutaitēt*
> *tuttattu tēttī tuttatta tōta.* (Taṇṭapāṇi Tēcikar 1965: 70)
>
> *tittittatē tū tottu tutai tēttu*
> *tattu tēttī tuttattu atu ōta.*
>
> It was sweet{*tittittatē*} that the honeybees{*tēttī*}
> buzzing{*tattu*} in the narrow buds{*tutai tēttu*} of pure
> white{*tū*} flower bunches{*tottu*}
> were singing{*ōta*} the second note{*tuttattu atu*}.

Apart from this, there are stanzas without nasal consonants (*anācikam*) or without labials (*nirōṭṭakam*). With a final one, a combination of these two, which, additionally, employs only *a* as a vowel, we shall finish our tour through the realm of the embellished word. To demonstrate that Mīṉāṭcicuntaram Piḷḷai was not the only nineteenth-century pulavar to compose *cittirakkavi* poems, we now leave the Naimica forest. The following stanza comes again from the stylus of Māmpaḷak Kavicciṅka Nāvalar. The framing anecdote here is that one day his patron Poṉṉuccāmit Tēvar ordered the poet: "Within ten minutes time compose for me a *veṇpā* which does not use either labials, nasal consonants nor the *kāl, kompu* and *viciṟi* [i.e., vowel] marks [other than short *a*] and which extols the greatness of Lord Śiva!" (Irāmacāmippulavar 1953: 117).[28] Needless to say, the result was quickly heard:

> *alaka kacaṭa taṭara ḷakaṭa*
> *kalaka cayaca kataṭa—calaca*
> *taraḷa carata tarata tatala*
> *karaḷa caraḷa kaḷa.*
>
> *alaka kacaṭatu aṭar aḷam kaṭa*
> *kal aka caya caka taṭa—calaca*
> *taraḷa cara tata rata tatala*
> *karaḷa caraḷa kaḷa.*

---

28. The verse (plus the same commentary) is also found in Irāmacāmippulavar (1964: 247).

O you with measure{*alaka*} dwelling inside the mind{*aka*}
of the educated{*kal*},
overcoming{*kaṭa*} the concentrated{*aṭar*} thickness{*aḷam*}
of defects{*kacaṭatu*}!
O victorious one{*caya*}! O expanse of the earth{*caka taṭa*}!
O water-born{*calaca*},
Who is strong{*tatala*} as a chariot{*rata*} from which fast-
moving{*taraḷa*} arrows{*cara*}
shoot forth{*tata*}!
O throat{*kaḷa*} in which poison{*karaḷa*} [is spreading]
unobstructedly{*caraḷa*}![29]

The reader may have noticed that all the poet could do was to create a series of vocatives which, omitting the final personal marker -*ṉ* or -*r*, conveniently end in -*a*. Such linguistic limitations are then obviously reflected at the level of meaning. In other words, here indeed form deftly dominates over content, so much so that these and other verses were quickly discarded by later generations as "exercises in prosodial gymnastics," if we remember M. Srinivasa Aiyangar's unfavorable statement quoted at the beginning of this chapter.

But, of course, content was not the main point in these verses. On a continuum between emphasis of meaning at one end and emphasis of form at the other, some poems, such as Mīṉāṭcicuntaram Piḷḷai's, hold the balance, while in the last poem quoted form has actually become the content. Here, more than anything, the verse was composed to show the poet's intelligence and skill in manipulating language. In any case, the sources we have for the nineteenth century tell us that such verbal complexities were never easily understood. Even fellow pulavars were to some extent dependent on the *urai*, the explanatory commentary provided either by the poet himself or by one of his amanuenses. It is thus no coincidence that for the *cittirakkavi* part of the *Amparppurāṇam* we have an autocommentary by Mīṉāṭcicuntaram Piḷḷai, which is marked as such in the printed edition. For the audience to be able to savor the stanzas, the commentary had to be part of the recitation.

The complicated figurations of *cittirakkavi* were very much the tip of the rhetorical iceberg, extremes calculated to display the poet's

29. My reading of line three does not follow Irāmacāmippulavar's commentary which may be translated as: "O trembling Śarabha! O you having the stability of a spreading chariot!" Moreover, this time in accordance with the commentary, I take both *alaka* and *aka* in the first line as vocatives of the personalized nouns *alakaṉ* and *akaṉ*. While *akaṉ* literally means "the one who is inside," the sense of *alakaṉ* "one who has a measure (*alaku*)" is slightly unclear to me. What does the epithet refer to in this poem?

genius and to provide intellectual stimulation for the listeners. On the other hand, they were important enough for the fifteen-year-old Mīṉāṭcicuntaram Piḷḷai to learn and practice them. The other devices of *cilēṭai*, *yamakam/maṭakku*, and *tiripu* were much more common, although here as well one finds a hierarchy of forms in which *tiripu* is the most and *cilēṭai* the least frequent. Besides being employed in a particular work as ornamented language, these poetic devices often constituted entire genres, such as *yamaka-antāti* or *cilēṭai-veṇpā*, which were quite popular. Occasionally, such a formally defined genre could even be pressed into more restricted boundaries, when a combination of devices was attempted. The poet Vēmpattūr Piccuvaiyar (1850–1910), known to his contemporaries by his telling title *cilēṭaippuli* (lit. "tiger of the *cilēṭai*" or "master punster"), composed a *Maturai-nirōṭṭaka-yamaka-vantāti* where the lines are not only arranged in *yamakam* formations and *antāti* linkage, but also contain no labial consonants.[30]

What emerges from the examples seen above is a possible generalization to characterize the aesthetics of pre-modern Tamil literature composed during the nineteenth century. These compositions betray an overall concern with ornamentation or "embellishment" (*aṇi*), with language that attracts the reader's/listener's attention to itself, that pushes itself into the foreground. We find parallels not only in Sanskrit, but in many other Indian literatures.[31] It may be noted that this is precisely what was important about poetry in general to Western structuralist and formalist critics, such as Roman Jakobson who viewed poetry as "a province where the internal nexus between sound and meaning changes from latent to patent and manifests itself more palpably and intensely" (1960: 44). As Jakobson has famously put it, the poetic function of language promotes "the palpability of signs" (ibid., 25). The poetic character of a composition is revealed when "words and their combinations, their meaning, their exterior and interior form are not indifferent references to reality, but when they obtain their own weight and value."[32] As has been said, such a

30. For further information on this poet, see the following chapter.

31. See, for instance, Ingalls (1989) for parallels in Sanskrit and Velcheru Narayana Rao's essay in Pollock (2003a) for parallels in Telugu.

32. My translation from Jakobson's Czech essay "Co je poezie? (What is poetry?)" (1933), where he defines poeticity (*básnickost*) thus: "Ale v čem se projevuje básnickost?—V tom, že slovo je pocit'ováno jako slovo a nikoli jako pouhý reprezentant pojmenovaného předmětu nebo jako výbuch emoce. V tom, že slova a jejich skladba, jejich význam, jejich vnější a vnitřní forma nejsou lhostejnou poukázkou na skutečnost, nýbrž nabývají vlastní váhy a hodnoty" (1972: 414).

concern originated for Tamil sometime during the intra-linguistic turn of the medieval period. Then Tamil grammarians had started to adapt some of the formal rhetoric practices (*alaṃkāra*) of the Sanskrit *kāvyas* and their theoreticians. That this process was truly one of adaptation and not mere imitation is demonstrated by the fact that the pulavars quickly found ways to thoroughly exploit the specific capacities of the Tamil language. Yigal Bronner has pointed out that Tamil *cilēṭai* poems often function through linguistic traits not found in Sanskrit, for instance when Tamil phonology creates homophones from originally different Sanskrit words, as in Skt. *śaṅkha* and *saṃgha,* which both become *caṅkam* in Tamil (2010: 296n54). In one of the poems discussed below we will find a further example of this type where Skt. *śeṣa* "the snake king" and *ceṭa* "slave" both become *cēṭaṉ* in their tamilized form.[33] Since in Tamil, no written distinction is made between voiced and voiceless or aspirated and unaspirated consonants, the Sanskrit vocabulary metamorphoses—as loan-words—into a rich treasury of homophones. Unfortunately, the complex process of mutual influences between Sanskrit and Tamil poetics is still too poorly understood to venture further conclusions. The point here is that whatever emerged from the encounter persisted into the nineteenth century.

While the literary production of the pulavars continued to follow rules of the medieval period, theoretical discussions of poetics continued along the same lines. Although the historical development of Tamil poetics is still far from clear, we can say here that nineteenth-century scholars continued to write grammars that by and large followed their medieval predecessors. We know of at least three significant poetic treatises that were newly written during this period. All of them form part of larger books that deal with all the five aspects of Tamil grammar (*aintilakkaṇam*), viz. *eḻuttu* (phonology and orthography), *col* (morphology, syntax, etymology), *poruḷ* (semantics, literary content), *yāppu* (prosody and poetics), and *aṇi* (rhetoric). The first of these grammars, the *Muttuvīriyam* composed by Mīṉāṭcicuntaram Piḷḷai's teacher Uṟaiyūr Muttuvīra Vāttiyār, has already been mentioned above. In both content and form, this grammar comes perhaps closest to the works of the medieval period. As earlier grammars, it is written in *nūṟpā* (Skt. *sūtra*) form, and it uses the (archaic) grammatical language of works like *Tolkāppiyam* or *Iṟaiyaṉār Akapporuḷ*.[34] Unfortunately, we do

33. See the discussion of one of Vētanāyakam Piḷḷai's poems [2.6] below on page 66f.

34. See, for instance, the second *nūṟpā* of the part on *poruḷ* (*Poruḷatikāram, Akavoḻukkiyal* 2): *"akapporuḷ kaikkiḷai yaintiṇai peruntiṇai / yeṉaveḻuvakaippaṭu meṉmaṉārpulavar"* (Muttuvīra Upāttiyāyar 1889: 147). Other stanzas use similar expressions.

not know anything about its author, nor when exactly the work was written. The first two parts were first printed in 1881. The complete grammar was first published in 1889 with a short commentary by one S. Pulney Andi who had obtained the manuscript from its author.[35] Before that time, the work must have been available to other pulavars in manuscript form. The second work is another fivefold grammar named *Cuvāminātam* as it was composed by one Cuvāmi Kavirāyar from Kalliṭaiyūr. Formally, it is rather exceptional as it is written in 202 four-line *āciriyappā* stanzas, but content-wise it corresponds to the other works on poetics. The first full edition was only brought out as late as 1975 by the linguist Ce. Vai. Caṇmukam.[36] The third grammar is called *Aṟuvakai Ilakkaṇam* ("grammar of six kinds") as it adds a sixth category to the traditional five, viz. *pulamai* "erudition"or "poetic genius." It was written by the wandering ascetic Taṇṭapāṇi Cuvāmikaḷ (1839–1898), arguably one of the most eccentric poets of the nineteenth century.[37] *Aṟuvakai Ilakkaṇam* consists of 786 *nūṟpās* and like *Cuvāminātam* does not use the archaic language of the earlier grammars, but again in content it takes up the long-standing poetic rules. This is not the place to study how precisely such poetic manuals related to actual literary practice. What is important here is to see that not only the literary production of the nineteenth-century pulavars continued existing traditions, but also their poetic manuals.

The Pulavars' Genres: *Pirapantam* Works and Temple Myths (*talapurāṇam*)

Let us now continue to follow the footsteps of Mīṉāṭcicuntaram Piḷḷai in order to discuss another formal aspect of nineteenth-century pulavar literature: the various literary genres employed. Traveling around with fellow pulavar apprentices to visit various temples, Mīṉāṭcicuntaram Piḷḷai came to compose his first fully-fledged *pirapantam* works. The term *pirapantam* (< Skt. *prabandha*) refers to what Kamil Zvelebil has called a "hypergenre," which subsumes a motley group of traditionally

35. See the "Publisher's Note" in Muttuvīra Upāttiyāyar (1889).

36. See Caṇmukam (1975) and his introduction where he compares *Cuvāminātam* to earlier grammars.

37. Though an itinerant ascetic, Taṇṭapāṇi Cuvāmikaḷ was married and had a son who composed a verse biography on his father's life. He was also amazingly prolific. According to Zvelebil, his "total output was 49,722 stanzas of poetry" (1995: 651). See also Subramania Aiyar (1970: 49–53).

96 different genres in verse form as described in the so-called *pāṭṭiyal* grammars (lit. "nature (*iyal*) of poetry (*pāṭṭu*)") written from about the tenth century until the end of the nineteenth century.[38] Some of these genres may be defined by their specific form (especially stanzaic structure), e.g., *antāti* or *iraṭṭaimaṇimālai*, some by their content, e.g., *ulā*, *kātal* or *paraṇi*, and some by a combination of both content and form, e.g., *piḷḷaittamiḻ*, *kōvai*, or *kuṟavañci*. Their length varies also, and some of them (e.g., *kōvai* or *ulā*) are older than others (e.g., *kuṟavañci*, *kātal*, or *noṇṭināṭakam*).[39] This diversity, however, has not prevented the grammatical tradition from lumping all of them together under a single term, of which *ciṟṟilakkiyam* "small/minor literature" is a common synonym. Despite its name, this "minor literature" came to play an increasingly important part in the literary production from the late medieval period onward, and it may be said that almost the entire pre-modern literary production of the nineteenth century consisted of *pirapantams*. In the course of this study, we will examine a number of such works.

Looking back to Mīṉāṭcicuntaram Piḷḷai and his literary debut, we find that his earliest surviving work is a specific type of *pirapantam*. Having arrived at the temple of Ūṟṟattūr, he recited the *Tiruvūṟaippatiṟṟuppattantāti*, i.e., a poem of the *patiṟṟuppattantāti* genre on the "sacred [town of] Ūṟai [= Ūṟṟattūr]." The genre denotes a poem of 100 stanzas, every ten in a different metre, in the so-called *antāti* (< Skt. *anta* + *ādi*, "end (and) beginning") arrangement, again a very popular poetic device of the time, which refers to the repetition of the last letter, syllable, metrical foot, word, or phrase of one stanza as the first part of the following stanza.[40] Cāminātaiyar points out how

---

38. However, the actual total number of different *pirapantams* listed in the various *pāṭṭiyals* is more than 200. See Zvelebil (1974: 193f.) for a more detailed discussion of the characteristics of this hypergenre. Furthermore, see Muilwijk (1996) for discussions of the features of *pirapantams* and of the *pāṭṭiyal* works. At least one of the *pāṭṭiyals* known to us today can be quite safely assigned to the nineteenth century, viz. the *Pirapantatīpikai* written in 1849 by one Vēmpattūr Muttuvēṅkaṭa Cuppaiya Nāvalar. The editors of this treatise, Ca. Vē. Cuppiramaṇiyaṉ and Annie Thomas, have arrived at this date on the basis of the *śaka* year 1771 and *caumiya āṇṭu* given in the last stanza of the work (see Cuppiramaṇiyaṉ/Thomas 1982).

39. For a description of how the various *pirapantam* genres are treated in the *pāṭṭiyals*, see Ceyarāmaṉ (1981). The characteristics of individual *pirapantams* are discussed in Cuppiramaṇiyaṉ/Vijayalaṭcumi (1980), Cuppiramaṇiyaṉ/Pakavati (1983), and Caṇmukam Piḷḷai (1982).

40. Thus, in the *Tiruvūṟaippatiṟṟuppattantāti* the first stanza ends with the metrical foot "kariyāṉē" and the second stanza starts with "ariya"; it ends with "reṇṇamiṉṟē" and the third stanza begins with "eṇṇam," and so on (*SMPT* 2441ff.).

Mīṉāṭcicuntaram included in his work ideas from the Śaivite *bhakti* works *Tiruvācakam* and *Tēvāram*, as well as the *Tirukkuṟaḷ*. Moreover, he also drew on the *talapurāṇam* (Skt. *sthalapurāṇa* or *mahātmya*, "temple myth") of the temple, a work containing the localized legends of a particular sacred place which explain its origin and claims to its sacred character. These works could be written in Sanskrit or Tamil, and thus, more specifically, the term refers to a particular genre that contains these legendary accounts and is often a combination of myths and local historical accounts.[41] Having once embarked on the enterprise of versifying a temple legend, Mīṉāṭcicuntaram Piḷḷai spent his entire life composing what grew into a large number of *talapurāṇams* on many different shrines, often by framing the existing local Sanskrit written and Tamil oral traditions into complex and ornate verse compositions. The *Amparppurāṇam* discussed above is a typical example of these. In his biography, Cāminātaiyar lists twenty-two *talapurāṇams* of Mīṉāṭcicuntaram Piḷḷai most of which he and Tiyākarāca Ceṭṭiyār later edited and printed (*SMPC* II: 283). For the Sanskrit texts, he usually relied on the assistance of Sanskrit pandits with whom he studied the texts. Occasionally, he even had the Sanskrit *sthalapurāṇa* translated into Tamil prose and then used this prose text as a source for his own work.

Scholarship in the Name of the Lord: Monasteries as Patrons

While in his early twenties, Mīṉāṭcicuntaram Piḷḷai visited for the first time the Tiruvāvaṭuturai *maṭam* (< Skt. *maṭha*), one of the leading non-brahmin Śaivite monasteries of the time.[42] Apart from their main function of serving as residences for Śaivite or Vaiṣṇavite devotees and managing rest houses (choultries and chattrams) for pilgrims, these *maṭams*, especially the non-brahmin ones, ranked among the most important patrons for pulavars. From their emergence during the medieval period onward, they had played an important part in contemporary society as centres of religious power as well as major locales of traditional education, religious art, and erudition, and also

41. For a comprehensive discussion of this genre, see Shulman (1980), and more specifically on the Tamil material Kiruṣṇacāmi (1974) and Mātavaṉ (1995).

42. The colonial English term for *maṭam* was "mutt" (see Yule/Burnell 1994: 605). Though *mutt* is often used in the secondary literature and hence quite familiar to scholars of colonial India, I have avoided it here for its ambiguity in English.

as considerable political and economic forces, since they often managed large temples and possessed enormous stretches of cultivated land.[43] This landed property was mostly endowed to them by local rajas and wealthy zamindars, while the temples yielded additional income. Thus, the *maṭams* had gradually amassed enormous riches, so that their economic power was quite unparalleled during the course of the nineteenth century. The Tarumapuram monastery, for instance, a sister institution to Tiruvāvaṭuturai, collected an annual income of "about a lac of rupees" from land and other properties according to an article in the *Hindu* newspaper from 1900.[44] The total annual income of Tiruvāvaṭuturai itself was estimated in 1906 to be twice as much, i.e., 200,000 rupees (Hemingway 1906: 232). Moreover, the Tiruvāvaṭuturai *maṭam* or rather *ātīṉam* (i.e., a central institution that administers other subordinate *maṭams* and temples) controlled 130 smaller *maṭams*, and the value of its library was placed at Rs. 30,000 (Baker 1975: 73). The bigger temples, even if not related to a particular *maṭam*, were often just as wealthy and played similar roles in contemporary society.[45] As Baker aptly summarizes,

> owning lands, commanding vast incomes, often controlling markets and credit, dispensing valuable jobs and contracts [to local priests, administrators, craftsmen, suppliers for all kinds of temple activities, etc.], organising festivals, patronising art and learning, maintaining charities and regulating social status, the temples unsurprisingly were drawn into local politics. [. . .] The temple was thus a fount of power and a symbol of dominance in the rivalries for local resources and status which were what politics in the locality was all about. (74)

---

43. In his analysis of the social role of non-brahmin Śaivite monasteries in Tanjore District in the nineteenth century, Geoffrey Oddie states that "[b]y late nineteenth century Thiruvavaduturai [Tiruvāvaṭuturai] was endowed with 25,000 acres of land in the Tinnevelly district, 1,000 acres in Madura and 3,000 acres in Tanjore" to which "thousands of acres of temple land and other endowments in the Madras Presidency and elsewhere" have to be added (1984: 41).

44. *The Hindu*, 19 October 1900, quoted in Oddie (1984: 48, ftn. 47). The Tarumapuram *ātīṉam* possessed 2,500 acres in Tanjore District and 12,500 outside it, and it administered twenty-seven temples (Baker 1975: 73).

45. The most spectacular example is the famous temple in Tirupati (Chittoor District, now in Andhra Pradesh) which could boast of an annual income of no less than five lakhs during the late nineteenth century (Baker 1975: 71).

But the enormous power of the religious institutions extended well beyond their immediate vicinities. It was most palpable for the common people when religious dignitaries, notably the heads or pontiffs of the monasteries or other priests of high rank, toured the country. They went in processions, which frequently entailed much pomp and magnificence. The following description by the nineteenth-century historian of Madurai, James Henry Nelson (1838–1898), refers to the seventeenth century, but two centuries later the religious dignitaries would fashion themselves in similar ways as they were

> carried in gorgeous palanquins or on the backs of elephants, preceded by heralds and bands of musicians and dancing girls, and accompanied by enormous crowds who testified their loyalty and love by loud shouts of joy, by words of praise and endless prostrations, [and] by strewing the road with new clothes. (1868: 79)

Such splendor intentionally equaled the carefully orchestrated display of *royal* processions. As shall be elaborated in the next chapter, the two most powerful institutions within pre-modern South Indian society, the *maṭams* and the royal courts, used essentially the same techniques to impress their importance on the minds of those under their control. Similarly, the major religious festivals were celebrated on a grand scale, as becomes apparent from U. Vē. Cāminātaiyar's descriptions. For Tiruvāvaṭuturai, the so-called *guru puja*, the annual festival in honor of its founder, was (and still is) an occasion of special importance. In S. K. Guruswamy's words,

> Conferences of learned men, discourses, concerts by the leading musicians of the day, performances by batch after batch of pipers and drummers, processions, displays of fireworks and above all, sumptuous feeding of the thousands who gather there for the occasion, from the highest to the lowest—all these make the day a memorable occasion for men of all sorts and conditions. (1976: 89)

In his autobiography, U. Vē. Cāminātaiyar describes how he first witnessed *guru puja* in January of 1872, after he had become Mīṉāṭcicuntaram Piḷḷai's student about a year earlier. Naturally, the young boy of sixteen years was overwhelmed by the masses of people who had come from all over South India, the musicians, the Sanskrit scholars and their Vedic chanting, the *Tēvāram* singers, the pilgrims, poor people and brahmins who came for the public distribution of food (*annatāṉam*).

To the present day, the monasteries work as charitable institutions accepting money and other donations and redistributing them to those in need, so that one is reminded of Pierre Bourdieu's observations on the economic power of such religious institutions. They objectively function as a kind of bank, but their functioning rests on the fact that they must not be considered one.[46] Their patronage of Tamil (and Sanskrit) scholarship included commissioning religious works for certain temples and occasions, and providing the general meeting point for pulavars and itinerant poets who came from all over South India. Though historically their main function was the study and propagation of the religio-philosophical ideas of Śaiva Siddhānta, they did not turn down scholars with different predilections, but offered them large (manuscript) libraries containing Śaivite as well as Vaiṣṇavite literature. They also employed a limited number of very gifted pulavars as permanent *ātīṉavittuvāṉ*s or "official monastic scholars." As the monasteries represented, in Geoffrey A. Oddie's words "a natural extension or further institutionalization of the *guru*-disciple model" (1981: 1), they also fostered the poets' educational activities. They became important acculturating institutions for young pulavar apprentices, where besides Mīṉāṭcicuntaram Piḷḷai and his disciples U. Vē. Cāminātaiyar and Pūvaḷūr Tiyākarāca Ceṭṭiyār (1826–1888) a large number of nineteenth-century scholars were educated. The remuneration given to the poets consisted of money, food, and honorary titles. Thus, the two scholars from Jaffna Āṟumuka Nāvalar (1822–1879) and his student Capāpati Nāvalar (1844–1903) had obtained their title (*nāvalar*, "eloquent one") from Tiruvāvaṭutuṟai. The latter also earned the title *makāvittuvāṉ* "pre-eminent scholar" (< Skt. *mahā-v.*) from the Tiruñāṉacampantar Maṭam in Madurai (Civakami 1994: 25), while Mīṉāṭcicuntaram Piḷḷai was given the same title by the pontiff of Tiruvāvaṭutuṟai. U. Vē. Cāminātaiyar (1996: 141) lists the following *maṭams* as important literary patrons during the nineteenth century: Tiruvāvaṭutuṟai Maṭam, Tarumapuram Maṭam, Tiruppaṉantāḷ Maṭam, Kāñci Ñāṉappirakācar Maṭam, Maturai Tiruñāṉacampantar Maṭam, Tirunelvēli Ceṅkōl Maṭam, and the Vīraśaiva *maṭams* at Kumpakōṇam, Citamparam, Tiruvaṇṇāmalai, Tuṟaiyūr, and Mayilam. Among these,

46. "Thus, the temple functions objectively as a sort of bank, but one which cannot be perceived and thought of as such, in fact, provided that it is never understood as such" (Bourdieu 1998: 114).

the Tiruvāvaṭuturai *ātīṉam*, which traces its history back to the fourteenth century, ranked first.[47]

When Mīṉāṭcicuntaram Piḷḷai first arrived there, he marveled at the sight: The place was teeming with Śaiva ascetics with their *rudrākṣa* beads and their saffron robes, humble devotees and wealthy men coming from far and near. There were groups of pulavars showing each other the gifts they had obtained as remuneration for their compositions, and the attendants were faultlessly pursuing their duties, arranging flower garlands and fruits for the offerings. He was sure there was no other place in the world where the spirit of both Lord Śiva and Tamil learning could be imbibed so thoroughly (*SMPC* I: 33f.). The pontiff of the *ātīṉam* was at the time the fourteenth in succession named Vēḷūr Śrī Cuppiramaṇiya Tēcikar, himself a well-known scholar of Sanskrit and Tamil, a master of the *Śaivāgamas*, the *Meykaṇṭacāttiram* and the works of the Cittar poets, and an eloquent speaker (*SMPC* I: 34).[48] He examined the young boy to see which works he had mastered so far, and soon he became fond of him, realizing his great potential. Mīṉāṭcicuntaram was taught by Cuppiramaṇiya Tēcikar for just a few days before he had to leave again, but these few days were sufficient to instill in him an ardent desire to come back. And indeed this first visit led to a lifelong attachment to the monastery to which he returned whenever possible.

In 1854, the acting *ātīṉavittuvāṉ* Tāṇṭavarāya Tampirāṉ recommended Mīṉāṭcicuntaram Piḷḷai, by then famous everywhere for his poetic talents, as his successor to the new junior head of Tiruvāvaṭuturai also named Cuppiramaṇiya Tēcikar (*SMPC* I: 167f.).[49] It was however not before the year 1860 that Mīṉāṭcicuntaram actually obtained the post, due to Cuppiramaṇiya Tēcikar's intercession with the acting pontiff Śrī Ampalavāṇa Tēcikar.[50] He had just moved to Māyūram, in order to be closer to the monastery, which he cherished as a place of scholarly and religious inspiration, when he received the happy

47. For the history of the Tiruvāvaṭuturai ātīṉam, see Makāliṅkam (2002).

48. He was pontiff from 1789 to 1845 (Makāliṅkam 2002: 20f.).

49. Apart from what we learn from Cāminātaiyar's writings, not much is known about the junior head Mēlakaram Cuppiramaṇiya Tēcikar. He became the sixteenth pontiff of Tiruvāvaṭuturai in 1869 and died in 1888. He was known by his contemporaries for his liberal patronage of the arts and his generous administration of the monastery's charitable institutions. Apart from his sponsorship, he maintained close links to many of the leading intellectuals of his time.

50. Ampalavāṇa Tēcikar was the fifteenth pontiff in succession from 1845 to 1869 (Makāliṅkam 2002: 21).

news. As the official *ātīṉavittuvāṉ* he was not only free from financial worries, but he also had two personal attendants to look after him. A spacious cowshed opposite the main building of the *maṭam* was converted into his residence with ample space for both himself and his students. Shortly after his appointment, he composed a *pirapantam* work, a *kalampakam*, to honor the pontiff. At the first public recital of this poem, Ampalavāṇa Tēcikar conferred on him the honorary title *makāvittuvāṉ* ("great scholar") and gave him a shawl and other gifts appropriate for the occasion (*SMPC* I, ch. 20). Both his appointment as *ātīṉavittuvāṉ* and this title may be considered the crowning achievements of his life. And Tiruvāvaṭuturai remained the centerpoint for all of his many activities until his death sixteen years later.

To continue our tour through the universe of the nineteenth-century pulavars, we should turn back at this point to the *young* Mīṉāṭcicuntaram Piḷḷai. Encouraged by his first encounter with the Tiruvāvaṭuturai ātīṉam, he went on practising his art as a poet by composing further *pirapantams*. To these early works of his belong *Tiruppaiññīlittiripantāti* with 101 stanzas, *Tiruvaṉaikkāttiripantāti* (now lost), *Tiruccirāmalaiyamakavantāti* (100 stanzas), and *Akilāṇṭanāyaki Piḷḷaittamiḻ* (114 stanzas on the goddess Akilāṇṭanāyaki in the town Tiruvaṉaikkā). In this latter work, we can see how the young pulavar introduced poetic innovations within the traditional genres he employed. Unlike any other *piḷḷaittamiḻ*, here we find no less than twelve invocatory stanzas to deities and saints (*kāppu* or *kaṭavuḷ vāḻttu*). The *Akilāṇṭanāyaki Piḷḷaittamiḻ* was admired by everyone for its perfection. It was also the first work of his that he had printed, in 1842, at age twenty-seven, during his first visit to Madras that a wealthy friend of his had sponsored. There he met, among others, the famous scholar Maḻavai Makāliṅkaiyar who was so impressed by the work that he funded its printing. When the small book came out, it contained not only the *piḷḷaittamiḻ* itself, but—according to common pulavar practice—several *ciṟappuppāyiram* stanzas composed by different poets.

When One's Fame Rises to the Heavens: The Pulavars' Economy of Praise

A *ciṟappuppāyiram* (lit. "special preface," also called *cāṟṟukkavi* "praise poem") is a kind of congratulatory verse which in rather standardized terms praises a literary work and its contents, the poet, his standing and scholarly lineage, and generally also the patron who commissioned the work. If longer, it also contains some information about the time, place, and cause of the composition of the work.[51] It was generally written by the poet's guru, his colleagues and friends, or his disciples. Also the commentator on a book could write a *ciṟappuppāyiram*. Such verses varied in length from a typical four-line *viruttam* or *kaṭṭaḷaikkalittuṟai* stanza to the much longer *akaval*, which could have more than one hundred lines. They also varied in sophistication and could be more or less ornate and original. In fact, length and originality of the *ciṟappuppāyiram* often depended on how much one wished to honor and impress the author concerned and, by extension, one's fellow pulavars. We learn from Cāminātaiyar that in later days Mīṉāṭcicuntaram Piḷḷai's own *ciṟappuppāyirams* were always carefully calculated so as to correspond to the poet and his abilities:

> The *ciṟappuppāyirams* he wrote were composed so as to fit the repute of the author of the work. Whenever they obtained a *ciṟappuppāyiram* from him, the authors gained much prestige. Therefore they tried in many ways to get him to write *ciṟappuppāyirams* for themselves. He used to write them in *akaval, viruttam* and *taravu koccakam* stanzas. If the work was particularly good, he would write an *akaval* or many *viruttams*. If not, he would write one or two verses merely stating that such and such a book was written by such and such a person. (*SMPC* II: 282f.)

A typical example of the latter type is the following stanza that Mīṉāṭcicuntaram Piḷḷai wrote for a *veṇpāmālai* on the deity of the Trichy Rock (Tiricirāmalai) composed by one Cupparāya:

> May the garland of *veṇpās* that the honorable pulavar
> Cupparāya
> has sung always live on well, so that the exquisite love
> for the
> cause of all wisdom, which rests on the Trichy Rock,
> where sweet waterfalls spring forth, may blossom!
> (*SMPT* 5088) [2.1]

Here, the reader does not really learn much about the work. Other poets could be equally laconic. Among the verses Mīṉāṭcicuntaram

---

51. The *ciṟappuppāyiram* as a poetic practice seems to be quite old, as it is mentioned already in Nakkīrar's commentary on *Iṟaiyaṉār Akapporuḷ* (see Buck/Paramasivam 1997: 1–4).

himself obtained for his *Akilāṇṭanāyaki Piḷḷaittamiḻ*, we find a rather unadorned and straightforward *veṇpā* composed by Nārāyaṇacāmi Nāyakar from Peṉṉelūr:

> A sweet *piḷḷaittamiḻ* with pure words the great and noble
> Mīṉāṭcicuntaram has composed, wishing that the learned
> may enjoy it, plunging into the ocean of love
> of the heavenly lady *Akilāṇṭa* in Tiruvaṉaikkā. (*SMPT* 272) [2.2]

Often, however, the stanzas were much more elaborate and original. For an example of how clever poets could be, we may look at the verses composed by the district munsiff Māyūram Vētanāyakam Piḷḷai when Mīṉāṭcicuntaram Piḷḷai premiered his *Cīkāḻikkōvai* in 1859. The *kōvai* is one of the older *pirapantam* genres which consists of approximately 400 stanzas that tell the story of an anonymous young couple in love. We will take a closer look at this genre below, when we discuss another *kōvai* written by Mīṉāṭcicuntaram Piḷḷai. For the moment suffice it to say that this particular poem honors Lord Śiva in the town Cīkāḻi (sometimes just Kāḻi in the poems). Vētanāyakam Piḷḷai, a good friend of our poet, starts his eulogy by a clever extended metaphor in which he presents Mīṉāṭcicuntaram as a reincarnation of the ninth-century poet Māṇikkavācakar, author of the first fully-fledged *kōvai*, the *Tiruccirrampalakkōvai* or just *Tirukkōvaiyār* praising Śiva in Chidambaram (Tillai).[52] As this venerable predecessor could not possibly be overtly insulted by claiming that the later *kōvai* is better, Vētanāyakam finds his way around this problem:

> The same Māṇikkavācakar who composed the *Tirukkōvaiyār*
> and was born long time ago in Vātavūr
> has now been born again in Trichy
> as the rising sun bearing the excellent name Mīṉāṭcicuntaram,
> and he has written a *kōvai* for Kāḻi.
> Although by age the faultless *kōvai* on Tillai is older,

52. I say "first fully-fledged *kōvai*" as we do possess a possibly earlier poem named *Kōvai*, the *Pāṇṭikkōvai*, which has been reconstructed from the sample verses given in the poetic treatise *Iṟaiyaṉār Akapporuḷ* (Buck/Paramasivam 1997). However, this poem differs greatly from later works, not only because it is fragmentary. As we shall see below, later *kōvai* works generally refer or allude to the *Tirukkōvaiyār* as the first text in the tradition they continue.

by the beauty of its imagination this new *kōvai* is
superior.
What the world [of scholars] says is true: When the great
scholars
compose verses daily, they will achieve maturity in their
words! (*SMPT* 1685) [2.3][53]

As "Māṇikkavācakar" had several centuries to practice before being born again, his new *kōvai* was of course more refined than his first one. Through this witticism Vētanāyakam Piḷḷai also managed to provide two kinds of intertextual references, one to the "first" *kōvai* (as the authority and touchstone of the genre), and another one to the realm of myths and legends. Such references are actually characteristic of *ciṟappuppāyiram* stanzas in general, as they set the praised poet into relation with an already established venerable tradition. The next *ciṟappuppāyiram* stanza makes this reference to legends even more explicit. The first three lines present *in nuce* the legend of Māṇikkavācakar's demise as found in the *Tiruvātavūrarpurāṇam*.[54] The following lines contain the same idea of the saint poet's rebirth, but finish off with a humorous *cilēṭai*:

Delighted by his beautiful *kōvai,*
the Lord of Chidambaram [Śiva] who has no comparison
took the man from Vātavūr [Māṇikkavācakar] with him.

53. I cannot refrain from a word on this and the following translations, which I consider particularly hopeless specimens when compared to the original verses. Above all, I have not been able to avoid that these English versions turned out much longer than their Tamil equivalents. Vētanāyakam Piḷḷai's stanzas all have only four lines and, in their extreme concision, are incredibly rich and heavily textured. They were one of the main reasons for me to include the original Tamil text (with brief annotations) in a separate appendix (referred to by the number in square brackets), so that readers may develop their ideas of what this poetry is really like, should they so desire.

54. The legend has it that the saint poet Māṇikkavācakar attained salvation after composing his *Tirukkōvaiyār*: One day while he was staying in a hut near the temple in Chidambaram, Lord Śiva visited him in the guise of a Śaivite saint and asked him to recite all his works, as he wished to copy them down on palm leaves. He also asked him to compose a *kōvai.* Māṇikkavācakar obliged, and when he had finished, Śiva deposited the manuscript in the sanctum of the temple. When the next day the temple priests opened the door, they found the manuscript and by its style realized that the work must have been written by none other than Māṇikkavācakar. They went to his hut and asked him to explain the work to them. The poet led them back to the sanctum, pointed at the icon, and with the words "The Lord himself is the meaning" he disappeared. For a more elaborate version of this legend and other details about the poet, see Pope (1995: xxxii).

As later the Lord desired another *kōvai*,
he had the same man reborn in the fertile Cirapuram [Cīkāḻi],
gave him the name Mīṉāṭcicuntaram and made him compose a *kōvai*
on Kāḻi. [Thus,] it is true that this was the son of Citamparanātaṉ. (*SMPT* 1686) [2.4]

Citamparanātaṉ does not only denote Śiva as the "Lord of Chidambaram," but it is also, as we may recall, a slightly altered form of the name of Mīṉāṭcicuntaram Piḷḷai's real father Citamparam Piḷḷai. On closer scrutiny, this is not the only *cilēṭai* we find in this stanza. The poem starts with the phrase *tiru amar kōvaiyai* which may be read as (a) "the *kōvai* in which beauty resides" (abridged for reasons of concision to "beautiful *kōvai*" in my translation above), or (b) "the *kōvai* which begins with [the auspicious first word] *tiru*," as indeed the *Tirukkōvaiyār* does. Another *cilēṭai* may be found in the expression I translated as "[Śiva] who has no comparison." The original *poruvil*, means (a) "without comparison" (*poru il*), but also (b) "[with] the fighting bow" (*poru vil*), which is an allusion to Śiva occasionally using the mythical mountain Meru as his bow. Moreover, in this and the following stanzas, Vētanāyakam employs several of the traditionally twelve different names for Cīkāḻi. Here, we find Cirapuram besides Kāḻi, but later he also uses less common names, such as Piramapuram, Pukali, Puṟavam, Caṇpai, and Koccai.

Apart from legends, the other stanzas draw on Śaivite and Vaiṣṇavite mythology which was of course so popular that Vētanāyakam Piḷḷai, though himself a catholic Christian, knew it well and could allude to it. Two stanzas take up the image of the thousand-headed serpent king who carries the whole world on his head (Skt. Śeṣa or Ananta). While in the first one the idea is rather simple (Mīṉāṭcicuntaram's *kōvai* is so beautiful that it moves even the celestials), the second one again uses *cilēṭai*-paronomasia.

Those who listen to the excellent *kōvai* which the great man Mīṉāṭcicuntaram
has lovingly composed on the Lord of Piramapuram will be delighted.
I alone am afraid that it will come to the ears
of the King of Snakes:
If he nods approvingly the ground will tremble, the mountains will tremble,

the oceans will tremble, the trees will tremble, the houses
will tremble,
all living beings will tremble
and come to grief. (*SMPT* 1687) [2.5]

As Ananta desired to learn the cool Tamil[55] from you
but had no means to recompense you,
he became your slave{*cēṭaṉ*} and thus got his name.
As Agastya began to hate Tamil like his enemy,
when it refused him and instead desired your company,
he obtained the name "Tamil hater."
Hence, who in this world will be equal to you,
o great Mīṉāṭcicuntaram in whose garlands bees dwell?
When you sing this *kōvai* on the fertile Puṟavam,
who will marvel at you? (*SMPT* 1692) [2.6]

The last stanza quoted shows two instances of *cilēṭai*. The first one with Ananta as a slave is a fine example illustrating Tamil's own *cilēṭai* creativity as independent from Sanskrit pointed out by Bronner (quoted above). As already remarked, another Sanskrit name for the Sanskrit Ananta is Śeṣa "residue." This becomes *cēṭaṉ* in Tamil, which may also mean "slave" from the Sanskrit word *cēṭa*. Only in Tamil the two words are homophones, which makes the pun possible in the first place. Secondly, Agastya is usually referred to as a *tamiḻ muṉivaṉ* "Tamil sage," but this could also mean "one who hates Tamil." The next two mythological stanzas again display Vētanāyakam Piḷḷai's sense of humor:

O Lord of Pukali, praised by Brahmā, the incomparable
Viṣṇu
and many others, you may have obtained many a
garland of verses
containing praise by celestials and humans, [but] have
you got
any [poem] like this *kōvai* by the scholar Mīṉāṭcicuntaram
of experienced intellect?
You know that I am the judge of this place, Sirkali,
[so] you will tell the truth before me! (*SMPT* 1697) [2.7]

55. Describing Tamil as *taṇ* "cool" (and therefore pleasant) is a standard trope in classical Tamil literature.

The raincloud, embodiment of *dharma*, bearing the name
Mīṉāṭcicuntaram
who has drunk the ocean of cool Tamil
has rained in Cirapuram which is surrounded by
devotees,
and he has poured forth the pure ambrosia named *kōvai*,
so that the shores of this world and the heavenly world
flow over, the waves dashing against them.
Seeing this, God, the Lord of Pukali which is
worshipped,
would drown, were he not one who possesses a boat.
(*SMPT* 1700) [2.8]

The word employed for boat in the last line is *tōṇi*, an allusion to another name for Cīkāḻi, viz. Tōṇipuram "Boat town." But not all of Vētanāyakam Piḷḷai's twenty stanzas are so inspired. Some can be quite unabashedly and hyperbolically flattering as the following one.

O you poets who grieve as you have studied
so many books without benefit,
the noble Mīṉāṭcicuntaram who understands all the good
books
has written a *kōvai* on Kāḻi!
If you study just one single foot{*cīr*} of one line of one
verse of this book,
you will shine as scholars who know every book,
masters of this world and the next. (*SMPT* 1690) [2.9]

Most interesting for our purpose here, however, are the stanzas in which Vētanāyakam Piḷḷai measures his own verses against those of his friend. Here, as in the previous poem, we find pulavar flattery at its best, but we also witness another popular *ciṟappuppāyiram* technique: The praiser humiliates himself in order to make the qualities of the praised more salient.

O great leader Mīṉāṭcicuntaram who has composed a
kōvai in sweet verses,
I will also make a poem in your meter. Those who see
my verse
will not think of it again, but praise the works composed
by
the noble scholars of yore. Those who understand your
verses

will discard the works of the elders as secondary and
  dislike them,
[now] say who is a good man: you or I? (*SMPT* 1693)
  [2.10]

O great man with a bow [Murukaṉ or Kāmadeva],
Mīṉāṭcicuntaram, you are like the ascetic who ascended
  to heaven [Agastya],
even if I have no ability to praise the *kōvai* composed by
  you
and which rises to the respect [of scholars], as your fame
which is spreading in this world and rising to heaven
is on the tongues of the erudite,
please accept also my praise which is full of blunders,
so that the evil eye may not fall on you! (*SMPT* 1694)
  [2.11]

The belief regarding the evil eye referred to in the last verse has it that something consummately beautiful must not be without any blemishes, small though these may be, as it would attract the evil eye (*kaṇṇēṟu*). Of course, these "blunders" form part of a severe understatement. Vētanāyakam Piḷḷai certainly knew how dexterously his verses were composed—as did the audience. He was just responding to a poetic convention, one of the acknowledged techniques of inter-pulavar communication.[56] Then, making up for nineteen stanzas of extended flattery and praise, the final one of Vētanāyakam Piḷḷai's poems contains the factual information the audience also would expect from a *ciṟappuppāyiram*.

In the current year 1859 in the month of *Puraṭṭāci*,[57]
the great man Mīṉāṭcicuntaram of supreme intellect
premiered the *kōvai* on Pukali, pure as rain,
in the Valampuri maṇṭapam which gives wealth causing
  benefits,
before the Lord of the sacred Kāḻi,
  where lovely gardens are dripping with honey,
and the celestials showered their rain of flowers,

56. And Mīṉāṭcicuntaram Piḷḷai was likewise a master of this technique. Though it was uncommon to directly *respond* to somebody else's *ciṟappuppāyiram*, we have one stanza in which he in turn says that he could not compose even one single stanza to match Vētanāyakam's verses (see *SMPC* I: 177).

57. This Tamil month corresponds to the period of mid-September to mid-October.

> while many rich people assembled and showered many
> a rain of gold,
> when the group of pulavars praised and opulently
> showered their rain
> of verses, and while many musical instruments were
> sounding. (*SMPT* 1704) [2.12]

This stanza refers to the so-called *araṅkēṟṟam*, the first public recitation before a large audience, of Mīṉāṭcicuntaram Piḷḷai's *kōvai*, which was celebrated on a grand scale during a number of days in the Valampuri maṇṭapam located in the Piramapurēcar (Śiva) temple in the town of Cīkāḻi. On this occasion, also Vētanāyakam Piḷḷai's *ciṟappuppāyiram* verses were recited. From Mīṉāṭcicuntaram Piḷḷai's biography we learn that each day's recitation was concluded with one stanza by Vētanāyakam, so according to U. Vē. Cāminātaiyar there must have been more than these twenty verses plus similar eulogies by other pulavars who attended the functions (*SMPC* I: 176f.). Those are, however, no longer extant, but they are alluded to in the above stanza as the pulavars' "rain of verses." Similarly, the reference to "many rich people" who "assembled and showered many a rain of gold" is perhaps hyperbolic, but not entirely dreamed up. Cāminātaiyar notes that from the many wealthy people and dignitaries in the audience Mīṉāṭcicuntaram received gifts ranging from 50 to 300 rupees for his work (177).

Thus, as in the above case, poets used to obtain *ciṟappuppāyirams* as a gift and token of recognition from colleagues. Or they actually asked renowned teachers or colleagues for their verses in order to be associated with their authority and thus share their prestige. Here, the underlying meaning of such a stanza reveals itself. As A. R. Venkatachalapathy has remarked: "In a feudal society where education and knowledge was the preserve of a restricted social stratum, authority naturally derived from being recommended by somebody already in possession of the requisite qualifications" (1994a: 7). This is reflected in the fact that the *ciṟappuppāyirams* were often put *before* the actual work, when pulavars began to first print their poems around mid-century. In a context where "literary works, produced by a small group of privileged scholars, circulated within a circumscribed social sphere," Venkatachalapathy argues, the *ciṟappuppāyiram* was "a stamp of approval, a gatepass for entry into the world of letters" (8). True as this is, it highlights only one aspect of the functioning of *ciṟappuppāyirams*. Viewed from a wider perspective, they were more than this.

Of course, as a means of authentication, a "stamp of approval," a *ciṟappuppāyiram* stanza clearly served the interest of the poet praised. But the bond thus created between one poet and another worked as a mutual obligation. The fact that a particular poet wrote a *ciṟappuppāyiram* for someone else in turn demonstrated his high status and authorizing capabilities. Importantly, the *ciṟappuppāyiram* provided a space, though conventionalized, for a pulavar to show his poetic skills and wit, which underwrote his claim to high esteem, as we have seen in the case of Vētanāyakam Piḷḷai. Furthermore, the whole process of a work's introduction by means of ritualized praise did not work without an audience, a reading (or initially listening) public which witnessed the eulogy. Part of this audience were the pulavars themselves, always the most skeptical critics of each other engaging in protracted competitions. The annals of Tamil literary history abound with anecdotes of envious pulavars trying to surpass each other in eloquence and poetic effects. To take just one example: the blind poet Māmpaḻak Kaviccinka Nāvalar at the royal court of Ramnad whose work we have already met above. He felt insulted when another pulavar, Vicuvanāta Pārati, remarked to the king that he could not compose verses when a blind person was present as this was inauspicious.[58] The king, however, asked him to proceed. As soon as Vicuvanāta Pārati had finished his recitation, Māmpaḻak Kaviccinka Nāvalar stood up and explained to everyone that this poem had actually been written by himself for some other patron. He thus accused his colleague of plagiarism. To support his claim, he recited the entire poem again word by word. The court was stunned. Though the king was very much embarrassed, he finally asked the two poets to tell the truth so that the matter could be settled in an honorable way. Promptly, Māmpaḻakkavi admitted that he possessed the special capacity of being able to repeat any poem on hearing it just once and that he wanted to teach his colleague a lesson for insulting him. He had of course seized the opportunity to both take revenge and display his talent. What else could the king do but smile and remunerate both of these pugnacious poets?

Thus, a poet's status was constantly contested as he was criticized by his colleagues. Within these circles of unending renegotiation and inter-pulavar competition, securing the friendship and support of a fellow pulavar meant a lot. Networks of praise and accompliceship had to be set against the many voices of disapproval, and this was what the *ciṟappuppāyirams* signalized. As U. Vē. Cāminātaiyar reminds us, any poet who obtained a *ciṟappuppāyiram* from Mīṉāṭcicuntaram Piḷḷai's teacher Kāñcīpuram Capāpati Mutaliyār also was sure to get

58. This anecdote may be found in Subramania Aiyar (1970: 37f.).

one from Mīṉāṭcicuntaram himself, as he could count on the established networks of approval (*SMPC* I: 69). Conversely, we know of several cases when Mīṉāṭcicuntaram Piḷḷai categorically refused to furnish a stanza, as with the poet and musician Kōpālakiruṣṇa Pāratiyār (1811–1881), nowadays famous for his *Nantaṉār Carittirak Kīrttaṉai*, a composition telling in prose passages and songs the story of the Śaivite saint Nantaṉār alias Tirunāḷaippōvār.[59] As the *kīrttaṉai* was written in a rather simple and colloquial style, Mīṉāṭcicuntaram Piḷḷai decided that he could not compose a *ciṟappuppāyiram* for a work that contained ungrammatical expressions and was not written in high Tamil, although Kōpālakiruṣṇa Pāratiyār had repeatedly asked for it. One day, however, while Mīṉāṭcicuntaram was having a nap after lunch, Pāratiyār came and sat down on his veranda in front of the house. He started singing a few songs from his *Nantaṉār Carittirak Kīrttaṉai*. Soon he was lost in his music and sang with great emotion of Śiva in Chidambaram. Hearing the line "Seeing the Lord in his golden hall one day would end all misery!," Mīṉāṭcicuntaram woke up and was greatly moved by the sweet words reaching his ears. Tears were streaming down his cheeks. When he went out to see who this gentleman was, he realized that this was Kōpālakiruṣṇa Pārati. Ruefully, he welcomed him and immediately composed a four-line verse to praise both the poet and his work (*SMPC* I: 193–5).[60]

---

59. U. Vē. Cāminātaiyar has written a small biography of Kōpālakiruṣṇa Pārati who was both his teacher and his father's friend (Cāminātaiyar 1936b). See also Ramaswami Aiyar (1932) and Kurumūrtti (2003).

60. Despite his emotional reactions, his verse reflects to a certain extent his initial discontents, as it is brief and rather routinely crafted:

> *kōmēvu tiruttillai naṭarācap perumāṉṟāḷ kūṭi yuynta*
> *pūmēvu pēraṉpar tirunāḷaip pōvārtam puṉitac cīraip*
> *pāmēvu palavakaiya vicaippāṭṭā liṉimaiyuṟap pāṭi yīntāṉ*
> *ēmēvu kōpāla kiruṭṭiṉapā ratiyeṉṉu micaival lōṉē* (SMPC I:193).

> The gifted musician Kōpālakiruṣṇa Pārati in whom happiness dwells{*ēm mēvu*}
> has sweetly sung in different kinds of beautiful{*pā mēvu*} songs of the sacred fame
> of the great devotee Tirunāḷaippōvār who dwells in this world, redeemed
> by joining Lord Naṭarāja's feet in the magnificent{*kō mēvu*} holy Tillai.

Incidentally, this verse also illustrates the problems which Tamil polysemy often creates. The epithet *kō mēvu* which qualifies *tiruttillai* "holy Tillai" may be translated variously as "where cows dwell," "where there are *kō* [jujube] trees," or "where greatness abides" (hence my translation as "magnificent"), depending on how we decide to interpret the word *kō*. As we do not have any further context for this stanza, a satisfactory decision cannot be made. For the poem, see also Cāminātaiyar (1936b: 56–59).

Thus, praise bound poet to poet and poet to audience. In more general terms, Arjun Appadurai has argued that praise in Hindu India created "a 'community of sentiment' involving the emotional participation of the praiser, the one who is praised, and the audience of the act of praise" (1990: 94). But one may shift the focus of analysis and emphasize what was actually at stake for both praiser and praised besides emotions. At least in part praise served to secure a poet a place with a patron on whom he depended to earn his living. In other words, praise was directly convertible into economic welfare. To that end, praise was circulated or "traded" in a hypostatized, palpable form—the lines of the poets' verses. Therefore, I would like to argue that this "community of sentiment" functioned within what one may call an overall *economy of praise*.[61] And this may be seen as one characteristic feature of the world of the pulavars in nineteenth-century South India. Their entire literary production was firmly embedded in this economy of praise which included poets, audiences, and patrons, each with their respective interests. They were all served in different ways. The *ciṟappuppāyirams* worked to negotiate the status of a particular poet vis-à-vis his fellow poets and before a literary audience. The systems of patronage in either monastic or royal contexts which form the subject of the present and the next chapter served to link poets to patrons, again before an audience. And there were further important institutions within this economy, such as the public premiere of a work (*araṅkēṟṟam*), the correspondence between pulavars via epistolary verses (*cīṭṭukkavi*), or the *avaiyaṭakkam* stanza, a kind of *captatio benevolentiae* most works contained. The key term operating within all of these various institutions was *pukaḻ* which, depending on the context, may mean both "praise" and its result "fame." The pulavars' verses tell us about a person's "unending fame rising up to the sky" (*tavāta pukaḻ vāṉ mēl vayaṅka*) or his "ever-increasing fame"(*peruku pukaḻ*), and we find various synonyms for the meaning "fame," such as *cīr*, *kīrtti*, *cīrtti*, *icai* or *pēr*. As an essential quality of both poet and patron, *pukaḻ* was much more than an abstract concept. The various institutions through which *pukaḻ* was negotiated and made public shall be discussed, one by one, in what follows.

61. Though I have not used his terms, my formulation of an *economy of praise* is indebted to Pierre Bourdieu's model of an *economy of symbolic capital*. According to Bourdieu, symbolic capital (honor or prestige) is acquired through the exchange of other sorts of capital: social (membership of a social group), cultural (education, academic titles), and economic (what may be directly converted into money). In my description of the pulavars' universe, I have attempted to pay attention to these various factors and their interplay. For a useful introduction to Bourdieu's model (plus a critique of its utility), see Droste (2001).

"Addressing the Assembly of Poets" (*avaiyaṭakkam*)

While the *ciṟappuppāyiram* was a peritext closely associated with the original work but not originally a part of it, the *avaiyaṭakkam* may be seen as a trace which the pulavars' economy of praise left *within* the literary text itself. Its literal meaning is "addressing/appeasing the assembly [of pulavars]." At least since the early medieval epic *Cīvakacintāmaṇi* it has become part of the conventional incipit of premodern Tamil texts besides the *kaṭavuḷ vāḻttu*, the invocation of certain Hindu deities. The *avaiyaṭakkam* section of a text consists of one or more stanzas in which the poet apologizes for the shortcomings of his work in front of the learned assembly of other poets. He humiliates himself by claiming that he has failed to do justice to his subject or to produce a formally appropriate work. This is usually done in a more or less elaborate simile (*uvamai*) in which the poet compares himself or his work (or both) to some inferior person or kind of writing.[62] This poetic convention is similar to the *captatio benevolentiae* topos of Western literatures. Like the *ciṟappuppāyiram* stanzas seen above, an *avaiyaṭakkam* stanza could be simple and straight to the point, as in the following example taken from Māmpaḻak Kavicciṅka Nāvalar's Tamil rendering of a Sanskrit erotic work, the *Śṛṅgārarasamañjarī* (Paḻaniccāmi 1908: 2).

> Like a mute without the slightest intelligence
> from the day of his birth,
> running around in a frenzy and
> beginning to compose
> an elaborate commentary
> on all the arts that have been explained [*śāstras*],
> that I should begin to recite the *Śṛṅgārarasamañjarī*
> composed in accomplished Sanskrit
> before the experts of Tamil
> which is praised in this sea-girt world —
> what an act of presumption! [2.13]

Here the analogy is clear: Both the mute foolishly attempting to comment on all the *śāstras* and the poet beginning his translation in front of the venerable Tamil scholars commit an act of presumption or audacity (*tuṇivu*). They are equally mad. While here not much

62. For details of the historical development of the *avaiyaṭakkam* and an extensive collection of sample stanzas from various works, see Cauntarapāṇṭiyaṉ (1988).

more is said about the poet or his work, an *avaiyaṭakkam* stanza may refer in more sophisticated ways to genre conventions or allude to features of the work concerned.[63] The following delightful poem is Mīṉāṭcicuntaram Piḷḷai's *avaiyaṭakkam* to his *Akilāṇṭanāyaki Piḷḷaittamiḻ* on the goddess in Tiruvaṉaikkā (see *SMPT* 155).

> If you ask: what is it like,
> the *piḷḷaittamiḻ* I composed on
> our Lady of the beautiful Tiruvaṉaikkā
> where the sweet budding mango trees grow densely,
> their red fire shining everywhere,
> while the young, soft, small, fresh southern wind
> carrying pollen of the *puṉṉai* flowers
> begins to blow, rising from fragrant Mount Potiyam
> where he who drank up the water of the bulging waves
> [= Agastya] resides?
> It is like the babbling gift of a small child
> who hears the lectures on books expounding
> *meypporuḷ* [the nature of things]
> in the assembly of those following the divine
> *Śaiva* path,
> the path of the elders with the right knowl-
> edge in their minds,
> and who gets up, milk dripping from his red
> *kumutam*-flower mouth,
> slowly toddles with searching steps
> and before this assembly
> takes a small palmleaf
> in his hands. [2.14]

Besides being considerably more elaborate than Māmpaḷak Kaviccinka Nāvalar's verse, this stanza achieves a humorous effect by presenting the poet as a young prattling baby listening to the lofty philosophical debates of the "real" poets. A baby naturally is the epitome of innocence and humility and thus marks a stark contrast vis-à-vis the august assembly of pulavars. But the effect of this verse further rests on its allusion to a generic convention. The *pirapantam* genre known as *piḷḷaittamiḻ* (lit. "Tamil [for] a child") has as its subject the depiction of the deity (or person praised) as a baby in which the poet

63. David Shulman has discussed a few "classic," highly personalized *avaiyaṭakkam* verses from the medieval period by Pukaḻēnti, Kampaṉ, and Cēkkiḻār (2001b: 109–113).

adopts the voice of a mother.[64] Thus, the poet referring to himself here as a baby (instead of a mother) before the other poets is a form of self-humiliation particularly appropriate for this genre. Note also how the poet describes the sacred abode of the deity praised in his work, Tiruvaṉaikkā with its flowering mango trees and the mild and fragrant southern wind, by means of a *locus amoenus* (beautiful place or "pleasance") topos common in classical Tamil literature.[65]

Viewed from our perspective of the economy of praise, one thing is important about the *avaiyaṭakkam* stanza as a conventional component of a literary text: The literary text itself contained an obligatory slot for status negotiations among the poets. The fact that this negotiation was conventionalized does not mean that it lacked force. While on the one hand the poet overtly, and sometimes ostentatiously, displayed his talents in front of an audience, he attenuated and belittled his own efforts in a few words. Needless to say, these seemingly humble words often achieved the opposite effect. As in Mīṉāṭcicuntaram Piḷḷai's verse seen above, it was yet another display of the poet's ingenuity. Furthermore, the "assembly of scholars" invoked in all *avaiyaṭakkam* stanzas was not merely a virtual one, not merely a genre convention. Historically, it referred to a very real performative situation. Pre-modern Tamil literary works were rarely, if ever, silently read by an individual. Rather they were publicly performed, recited in front of a mixed audience which usually consisted of the poet's students and pulavar colleagues, the person(s) who commissioned the text and his followers, and finally a number of interested people attracted by the spectacle of such a performance.

The Public Premiere (*araṅkēṟṟam*)

This leads us to another institution which formed part of the economy of praise: the so-called *araṅkēṟṟam* (lit. "ascending the podium"), the ritualized first public performance of a literary work. Drawing on Mīṉāṭcicuntaram Piḷḷai's biography, A. R. Venkatachalapathy (1994a: 6) provides a comprehensive description of a typical *araṅkēṟṟam*:

> The event was usually fixed on an auspicious day, and the news passed on to the local people and persons of

64. For a study of another *piḷḷaittamiḻ* by Mīṉāṭcicuntaram Piḷḷai, the *Cēkkiḻār Piḷḷaittamiḻ*, and of the *piḷḷaittamiḻ* genre in general, see Richman (1997).

65. For the term *locus amoenus* and a discussion of its significance in Western literary traditions, see Curtius (1963) and the entry in von Wilpert (1989: 535).

> importance in neighbouring localities. Organized by the patron of the work, the arangettram was the occasion when he derived social prestige and cultural authority by making public his patronage. Consequently, it was often a very pompous affair. The arangettram was usually held in a public place, especially the local temple, thereby giving religious sanction and authority to the event and the text. [. . .] The mantapam or the hall would be decorated with traditional festoons and the arangettram would begin at an appropriate muhurtam (auspicious time). The palmleaf manuscript would then be placed before the presiding deity of the temple, and worship would be offered. The text would then be placed in the hands of the author, who, after accepting the prasadam (usually, sacred ash and flower-garlands) would proceed with the arangettram. Often the text would be read out by one of the author's disciples, while the author himself would elaborate on the meaning of the verses and explain the literary and mythological allusions to the devout audience. These sessions could continue for a number of days (usually in the late afternoons), depending on the length of the composition, its terseness, the ability and inclination (the latter being proportionate to the value of the patronage) of the author.

Such public events almost invariably attracted large crowds. Often, the recitation was accompanied by musicians who also played and sang during the intermissions. Occasionally, the daily recitals of the *araṅkēṟṟam* could continue, with intervals, for up to a year.[66] Sometimes, the poet did not even provide the explanatory comments (*avatārikai*) himself, but one of his students had to comment on his master's text. The student's ability to do this well, adducing parallels from other texts, was seen as yet another token of the poet's genius, this time as imparted to others. In such cases, the poet was merely physically present, not heard but seen—and admired.

The effect these recitations had on the audience is vividly painted in Cāminātaiyar's account:

> As they were listening to the sublime quality of the composition and to the beauty with which he explained its meaning, drawing upon the best verses of many other works so that

66. Thus in the case of Mīṉāṭcicuntaram Piḷḷai's *Tirunākaikkarōṇappurāṇam* (1869), see *SMPC* I (319).

> one could understand well, everyone felt being afloat on the ocean of supreme bliss. And they exclaimed: "What penance did we perform to be allowed to see this scholar and to listen to his excellent sweet words!" (*SMPC* I: 173)

Though this description is perhaps slightly hyperbolical, the degree of enthusiasm and excitement that such performances created with the audience is difficult to gauge for a reader of the twenty-first century. The audience certainly took an active part in every performance, not only through their applause but also by asking questions whenever something needed to be clarified or repeated. It is in the context of a performance culture that we have to see the pulavars and their compositions. Many of the poetic devices and other stylistic features of pre-modern Tamil poetry can only be truly appreciated when the text is recited or sung. And to be able to read was a privilege of the educated higher echelons of society. Thus, the spoken word mattered, and everything was geared toward showing the grandeur of the poet and by extension also of the patron.

Particularly the concluding day (*pūrttiviḻā*) of an *araṅkēṟṟam* provided an occasion for grand display. It was the day that the poet received his official reward in the form of money, precious shawls and other clothes, flower garlands, or a palanquin. Not only did large masses gather to follow the spectacle, it could also be "made public" in another way. In the case of Mīṉāṭcicuntaram Piḷḷai's *Tirukkuṭantaippurāṇam* (1866) the palmleaf manuscript was placed with great éclat on the back of an elephant and taken on a procession around the town (*SMPC* I: 274f.). His *Tirupperuntuṟaippurāṇam* (1874) went on a similar parade in a palanquin, the spectacle equaling a king's marriage procession, as Cāminātaiyar observes (*SMPC* II: 192). This observation is not at all far-fetched. Usually, the gods or a king would go on a procession around the village or the town. That a palmleaf manuscript could be taken on parade in a similar way shows the concern that its importance be perceived by a large group of people. The aim of such processions was the dissemination of news, something everyone needed to know. The great fame of both poet and patron crucially depended on the fact that it was made public in every possible way. A maximum number of people had to know about it, otherwise it would have been of little use for gaining social recognition. Given the great prestige both poet and patron gained during the *araṅkēṟṟam*, it is hardly surprising that, besides the poet's own disciples and his friends, competing and envious pulavars formed part of the audience. They served as watchful arbiters or suspicious critics of the new work. In fact, accounts of fierce disputes between pulavars over new verses abound everywhere in our sources.

Although I said earlier that large crowds of people were attracted to such public performances, we should not be mislead to think that this was indicative of a mass culture. The difficulty and scholarly nature of the literature recited presupposed an educated audience which had to know the poetic traditions well in order to be able to enjoy fully what they heard. As such profound literary erudition was almost impossible to achieve for a non-pulavar, a new work and its particularly interesting aspects had to be commented upon and explained, but even such exegesis was geared toward literary connoisseurs. Consequently, the *araṅkēṟṟams* as described above and similar performances were very much elite enterprises. The average people could, and were encouraged to, witness them, but they remained accessory figures, by-standers who were entertained more by the colorful panoply, the music, and the overall pompous display than by the lofty content of the verses. At the same time, they were an essential part of the game. After all, representation always depends on a context against which it unfolds. What mattered, what created the elite in the first place was their difference vis-à-vis the common people. Public events such as *araṅkēṟṟams* served to create and reinforce this difference. They were institutionalized instruments of social distinction.

Occasional Poems (*taṉippāṭal*) and Epistolary Poems (*cīṭṭukkavi*)

For a last factor within the economy of praise discussed here, one has to look at another group of literary texts, which may be subsumed under the larger generic term *occasional stanzas* (*taṉippāṭal*). This leads us back from the sphere of rituals and performances to textual practices. A glance at the available anthologies[67] suggests that the composition of occasional poems was an important aspect of a pulavar's occupation throughout the nineteenth century. What has come down to us is a large number of single stanzas composed on various special occasions, notably the death of one's patron or fellow pulavar, or general eulogies on kings or deities. It is important to take these stanzas seriously as literature, for they were composed and functioned according to the same poetic rules as the longer works. While royal panegyrics will be

67. Most useful for nineteenth-century occasional poetry are the volumes of Cu. A. Irāmacāmippulavar's *Taṉippāṭal tiraṭṭu* (*TPT* 2, 3 and 4) and *TCC*, as well as *TPTC* for its detailed commentary (*patavurai*). For a discussion of *taṉippāṭals* in comparison with their Sanskrit and Telugu counterparts, see Narayana Rao/Shulman (1998).

dealt with in the following chapter, the use of occasional stanzas for inter-pulavar "communication" is what interests us here.

When in November 1879 the famous scholar and editor of classical Tamil texts Āṟumuka Nāvalar (b. 1822) passed away, Ci. Vai. Tāmōtaram Piḷḷai (1832–1901), himself a well-known scholarly editor, wrote:

> Had Āṟumuka Nāvalar not been born, in the town of Nallūr, say,
> where would [our] praised Tamil be, where the *śruti* [Vedas]? — All famous
> *Purāṇas* and *Āgamas* where? Where his public lectures?
> Our knowledge about God, where would it be? (*TPT* 2: 752) [2.15]

> The power of the Vedas has faded, the power of the excellent *Śaivāgamas* has faded,
> the power of the three times six *Purāṇas* that the mighty Cūtamuṉi sang has faded,
> the power of the precious Śaiva religious knowledge has faded, the words spoken by the great
> sage on the golden Mount Potiyam [Agastya] have faded — Āṟumuka Nāvalar,
> loved so much in this world, has attained unity with our Lord. (*TPT* 2: 753) [2.16]

Tāmōtaram Piḷḷai enumerates the various fields of learning which Āṟumuka Nāvalar pursued and extols him as an editor of classical religious texts, *purāṇas* and *āgamas*. When twenty years later, in 1901, Tāmōtaram Piḷḷai himself passed away, the scholar Vi. Kō. Cūriyanārāyaṇa Cāstiriyār (1870–1903), head pandit at the Madras Christian College and one of the leading figures of the 'Pure Tamil Movement' (*taṉittamiḻ iyakkam*), praised him thus:

> Like a bee dancing in the forest, collecting honey from fragrant blossoms,
> Tāmōtaram Piḷḷai has edited many good books of the sublime Tamil we praise.
> To take up his excellence and praise it—who has
> the stature among you well-versed pulavars of the cool Tamil? (*TPT* 2: 756) [2.17]

Here, the stylistic similarities between such a single stanza and longer works become obvious. The bee simile is a conventional topos, and the name Tāmōtaram is cleverly woven into a *yamakam* employed in all the four lines, culminating in the last line in the new syllable split *(evar) tāmō taram uṭaiyār* "who has the stature?"[68]

One could quote many more verses composed along the same lines by one pulavar for another. What is important to note here is that the addresser's sweet words of praise ("loved so much in this world," "well-versed pulavars of the cool Tamil") at the same time enabled him to write (or rather sing) himself into the memories of a larger audience that would appreciate his talents. But even when there was only a small or no audience, the pulavars' versification would not stop. A special case of the occasional poem was used as a means of communication between pulavars. *Letters* sent by one poet to another or to his patron were more often than not written in verse form. This particular form of versified letter was known as *cīṭṭukkavi* (lit. "letter verse"). The verse was dictated to a student or servant who wrote it down on a palmleaf and then took it to its addressee. U. Vē. Cāminātaiyar and other students repeatedly acted as messengers for Mīṉāṭcicuntaram Piḷḷai. Needless to say that a pulavar's *cīṭṭukkavi* could be as elaborate and sophisticated as a proper literary composition. In other words, it usually contained *cilēṭai,* original allusions or creative similes, and other figures of speech. A stanza composed by Vētanāyakam Piḷḷai may serve as an example of a typical *cīṭṭukkavi.* Once during a rapidly spreading cholera epidemic, Vētanāyakam Piḷḷai asked the head of the Tiruvāvaṭuturai monastery Mēlakaram Cuppiramaṇiya Tēcikar to donate some money for medicine. One of his stanzas ran thus:

> Science prescribes half a *māttirai* for *mey;* without even this much
> many have died of the disease produced in excrements{*malam*}.
> Bestow your grace to avert this ravaging disease, o Cuppiramaṇiya,
> happiest and purest, who stays in this world as a wise teacher
> to eradicate the disease of the three *malams*! (*EC* 382) [2.18]

68. Tāmōtaram Piḷḷai had been one of Cūriyanārāyaṇa Cāstiriyār's examiners and a benevolent supporter of his activities. For Cūriyanārāyaṇa Cāstiriyār (who tamilized his name as Paritimāl Kalaiñar) and for a short overview on the Tamil purist movement, see Kailasapathy (1979).

Here, the three words left untranslated form part of an extended *cilēṭai*. *Māttirai* refers to (a) a measurement of time in prosody, and (b) a "medicinal pill," while *mey* means both (a) "consonant," and (b) "(human) body." The word I have translated as "science" is in Tamil *ilakkaṇam* which first of all means "grammar," but it may also be read as "science" (or *śāstric* teaching) in a wider sense. Thus we may read the first line as either (a) "Grammar prescribes half a time unit for a consonant," or as (b) "Science prescribes half a pill for the body." Both these meanings may be applied to the next phrase, "without even this much many have died," that is to say (a) "without even half a pill" and (b) "without the (very short) time unit of a consonant," i.e., "in no time." *Malam* in the last line refers to "impurities of the soul" (which is what Cuppiramaṇiya Tēcikar's philosophical teachings tried to abolish), but it is also the word used in the second line for "excrements" (through which cholera is spread). Here, the poet does not speak explicitly of the addressee's fame (*pukal̲*), but of course the obligatory token of the economy of praise is not absent. The eulogy here consists of calling the addressee "the happiest and the purest" (*ānanta nin̲malan̲ē*) and "wise teacher" (*vittakan̲*). Given the brevity of the original four short lines, these two simple epithets had to perform the job. As may be expected, Tēcikar understood the message. The wittily versified petition did not fail. From the money that Tēcikar gave Vētanāyakam bought a large amount of medicine and distributed it in the villages.

An example of a *cīṭṭukkavi* that displays the pulavars' sense of humor is a verse epistle sent by Mīn̲āṭcicuntaram Piḷḷai to Vētanāyakam Piḷḷai's younger brother Ñān̲appirakācam Piḷḷai. It consists of one short *kuṟaḷ veṇpā* and two *viruttam* stanzas (*SMPC* I: 312f.):

> O great man bearing the name Ñān̲appirakācar, the generous,
> consider this letter!
>
> I need a quadruped with great strength and beauty.
> When I say "a spotless quadruped," 'tis not an elephant, nor a horse, nor a strong bull,
> nor a milk cow, freed from anger, [for] it is the nature of all these to move around.
> Never leaving the one who obtained it, it should stay where it is placed.
> If you send one such thing, I shall sit on it and derive much pleasure.
> You also, exceling in the most sublime qualities, will be shining with great fame.

You wise man, pray, make it happen in this way!
It would be good to hand this well-cleaned thing over to
the man who will come. [2.19]

The humorous effect here rests on the use of the word *nāṟkāli*, lit. "quadruped" which may refer to an animal with four legs, but is more commonly used in its meaning "chair" (or "stool"). Mīṉāṭcicuntaram Piḷḷai had become ill and could neither sit nor lie down properly, so his doctors recommended that he rest on a reclining chair. He sent a servant with this note to his friend Ñāṉappirakācam Piḷḷai who worked at the law court in the nearby town of Taraṅkampāṭi (Tranquebar). Ñāṉappirakācam responded without hesitation by purchasing a chair immediately. He sent the man back to his master who kept this precious gift for the rest of his life. If we believe our poet, sending this chair as a gift was done for mutual benefit. Mīṉāṭcicuntaram points out that obliging him would make both of them happy. While the poet's benefit was clearly material, the reward for the poet's benefactor was to "be shining with great fame{*cīrtti*}." This fame would form an additional adornment to someone who was already glorified as "the liberal{*vaḷḷal*}," "excelling in the most sublime qualities{*uttama nal kuṇattil uyar*}," and a "wise man{*vittaka*}."

What the above examples clearly show is that in their *cīṭṭukkavis* the pulavars drew upon the same language of praise and flattery as in their elaborate literary works. A verse epistle was a poet's business card that had to express his wit and talent *in nuce*. It also shows the pulavars' attitude to language. Whenever Tamil was used, it had to be adorned and polished, as one's way of speaking (or writing) itself gives token of one's character and skills.

To sum up the discussion of the economy of praise within which pulavars, patrons, and audiences all played their specific parts, it may be noted that positing this economy as an analytical category to understand the literary system within which the pulavars functioned is by no means an anachronistic invention. The uses of praise to specific ends were theorized in the contemporary grammatical literature itself. Though dating from the medieval period (c. 1200), the treatise known as *Naṉṉūl* had remained during the following seven centuries *the* standard grammar with which every young student had to familiarize himself. Its popularity is confirmed by the large number of commentaries available, at least four of which were written during the nineteenth century.[69] In this grammar, we find a discussion of how

69. These four are by Mukavai Irāmāṉucak Kavirāyar (c.1785–1853), Tiruttaṇikai Vicākapperumāḷ Aiyar (b.1798), Āṟumuka Nāvalar, and Caṭakōpa Irāmāṉucāccāriyār (1871–1910). I discuss the *Naṉṉūl* boom during the nineteenth century in Ebeling (2009b).

books should be composed. From *cūttiram* 52, we learn that an author must not praise himself even though he may be a master of all the sciences.[70] But in the next *cūttiram*, we find exceptions to this rule. A pulavar may praise himself (*taṉṉaip pukaḻtal*) when seeking the favor of a king by presenting to him a palmleaf which details the poet's many attainments and skills (*ōlaittūkku*), before those who do not realize his abilities, when defending himself and his work before an assembly of pulavars, and finally when challenged and ridiculed by a fellow poet.[71] That these exceptions were explicitly listed in *Naṉṉūl* clearly shows how serious pulavars took their eulogizing business and the status and rank it implied. It also shows the fluidity and fickleness of the whole process of status negotiation. Being challenged and having to defend oneself was not an occasional threat but a constant part of a poet's life. Māmpaḻa Kaviccinka Nāvalar's clever tirade against his fellow poet who wanted him to be removed from the court was thus not only less extraordinary than it may seem to a reader of the twenty-first century, it was also sanctioned by the long-standing rules of Tamil poetics. Finally, one might add that the economy of praise is by no means exclusively found in Tamil literature. We see similar structures at work in other literary cultures throughout South Asia. In Sanskrit, for instance, we find the *kavipraśaṃsā* (praise of poets), verses at the beginning of a poem containing some sort of appreciation of earlier poets. The Urdu *musha'ira*, the assembly where poets come together to recite and criticize their verses, also shows many parallels to poetic competition in South India.[72] Further research is required to examine these social structuring mechanisms from a comparative perspective.

The Spoken and the Written Word: Composition, Performance, and Transmission

As the existence of such institutions as the *araṅkēṟṟam* shows, the pulavars' works were clearly intended to be recited and publicly

70. *tōṉṟā tōṟṟit tuṟaipala muṭippiṉun*
tāṉṟaṟ pukaḻtal takuti yaṉṟē (Āṟumuka Nāvalar 1963: 41).

71. *maṉṉuṭai maṉṟat tōlait tūkkiṉun*
taṉṉuṭai yāṟṟa luṇarā riṭaiyiṉum
maṉṉiya avaiyiṭai velluṟu poḻutiṉun
taṉṉai maṟutalai paḻitta kālaiyun
taṉṉaip pukaḻtalun takumpula vōrkkē (Āṟumuka Nāvalar 1963: 41).

72. For a discussion of the *kavipraśaṃsā* see Pollock (1995). The institution of the *musha'ira* is discussed by Rahman (1983) and Naim (1991).

performed. In fact, the works themselves betoken the importance of the spoken word, as many of the poetic devices and other stylistic features of the pulavars' poetry can only be perceived when the text is sung or recited. Yet, despite the importance of performance, it would be misleading to place the pulavars into a context of a *primarily* oral culture. While for a long time prominent in scholarly discussions of literature, the simple dichotomy of oral vs. literate has not infrequently aroused suspicion. As Sheldon Pollock has pointed out, the relationship between literature and orders of oral, manuscript, and print cultures may be more complex than this simple opposition suggests.[73] Despite their emphasis on performance, the pulavars not only knew how to read and write, but also created large manuscript libraries, and, as we shall see below, after mid-century also became primary agents of book publishing. We therefore have to consider what was indeed a complex interplay of orality, memorization, and performance, as well as literacy, writing, and printing, when trying to describe the pulavars' work.

The factors that point to an oral culture were the public performance of texts, text memorization, and modes of composition. Besides the *araṅkēṟṟam*, poetic texts were generally performed or recited on specific occasions, such as temple festivals and important holidays. Poetic recitals were also arranged in order to instruct the listeners who could be young pulavar apprentices in the *maṭams* or a more general audience that gathered for public lectures. Furthermore, as part of their specific education, pulavars would generally strive to memorize not only a large mass of literary texts, but also grammatical treatises and lexical works. As we have seen above, this memorization was essential for a poet's ability to compose verses himself or to comment on other poets' works. The composition of the pulavars' texts was often equally oral, in the sense that a poet would sit down and recite his verses to his students who acted as scribes and copied down on palmleaf what the master said. We learn from U. Vē. Cāminātaiyar that his teacher Mīṉāṭcicuntaram Piḷḷai was particularly famous for being able to dictate different works simultaneously with great speed and ease.[74] Mīṉāṭcicuntaram would sit down in front of a group of students and dictate to each one a different text, so that manuscripts could be quickly produced. We also know that when

73. See Pollock (2003b: 15, 21f.). Other essays in the same volume also problematize the dichotomy oral-literate (see Pollock 2003a).

74. U. Vē. Cāminātaiyar remarks that his master could even continue conversations with visitors while dictating his verses (*EC* 355).

still a student himself, Mīṉāṭcicuntaram Piḷḷai used to copy manuscripts from whatever source he could find in order to study new texts. This is of course where literacy comes into play. The palmleaf manuscripts produced by the pulavars and their disciples served as *aide mémoires* for recitations and for pedagogical purposes. But even during the process of composition the manuscripts that the disciples produced could be used by the poet to once again go through and amend his verses.[75] A pulavar's composition thus became a relatively fixed "work," also firmly associated with the poet's name and fame, unlike folktales and ballads, which would vary from performance to performance and were mostly anonymous. Even when basing his performance on manuscripts, the performer of folk literature usually tailored the text to his specific needs, and scribes took greater liberty when copying folklore manuscripts.

Additionally, a manuscript was also important as a physical object. It could be collected and stored, as in the large monastery libraries, in order to preserve precious knowledge. It could also be honored in religious rituals, such as in private pujas or when it was taken on grand procession around the town on the occasion of an *araṅkēṟṟam*. Cāminātaiyar records instances of manuscripts being worshipped on domestic altars (*EC* 558). Ironically, doing worship did not always mean the best for the manuscripts. In a chapter of his autobiography titled "Tamil cast into the floods," Cāminātaiyar laments that occasionally manuscripts were cast into rivers or burned for religious reasons (*EC* 683f.). But often palmleaf manuscripts seem to have been treasured in the same way that later printed books became valued objects: We frequently find on nineteenth-century palmleaf manuscripts the name of the manuscript's owner inscribed on one of the last leaves. Typically, the owner would refer to his manuscript using the Sanskrit term *pustakam,* which was later employed for printed books.

The increasing spread of printed books during the course of the nineteenth century will form the subject of Chapter 4, but it is worthwhile at this point to note how little attention Mīṉāṭcicuntaram Piḷḷai apparently paid to what was going on in the world of print. He did edit a few works, most notably the infamous, complicated eleventh-century *akam* poem *Kallāṭam,* which was printed in 1868

75. U. Vē. Cāminātaiyar recalls how his master dictated to him his *Tirupperuntuṟaippurāṇam* in May 1873. After writing down what his teacher said, he read out what he had just written for revision and corrections, and finally produced another manuscript with the new, revised version (*EC* 333).

(without commentary),[76] and there were plans for editions that never materialized.[77] But he never showed much enthusiasm for having his own works printed. It was his student Tiyākarāca Ceṭṭiyār who already during his master's lifetime started to publish his works. In this respect, Mīṉāṭcicuntaram was surely atypical and more conservative than many of his fellow pulavars who became the first editors of Tamil books, as we shall see below.

Of Gods and Kings: Themes and Contents of Pulavar Literature

So far our discussion of the literature produced by the pulavars during the nineteenth century has been primarily centered around formal aspects: pre-modern poetics and modes of composition and performance. What still remains to be commented upon is the thematic content of this literature. In other words, what did the pulavars write *about*? If one were to answer in a single word, this answer could be *praise*. Given what we saw above about pulavar practices and their engagement in what I have called an "economy of praise" this is perhaps not very astonishing. Praise, in its various manifestations, may be called the one unifying element, the common thematic thread running through almost all of these works. If we remember now that the two most important literary patrons, during the nineteenth century (as well as earlier), were religious institutions and royal courts, praise as a subject of literature may be divided accordingly into two groups: praise of a particular deity, saint, or sacred place (temple or town), and praise of a *human* patron, e.g., a king, wealthy trader, one's guru, or some other person under whose sponsorship literature was created. Viewed thus, these two groups suggest the common dichotomy of "religious" versus "secular" so often applied in the study of Western

76. According to U. Vē. Cāminātaiyar, the *Kallāṭam* was during the nineteenth century a measure for testing a pulavar's erudition—due to its complexity. He mentions the popular byword: *kallāṭam kaṟṟavarōṭu collāṭātē!* "Don't argue with those who have studied the *Kallāṭam*!" (*EC* 363). Mīṉāṭcicuntaram Piḷḷai's edition of 1868 was printed in Madras by the Athenaeum and Daily News Press.

77. When Cāminātaiyar discovered for himself the Jaina epic *Cīvakacintāmaṇi*, he met Puracai Aṣṭāvatāṉam Capāpati Mutaliyār (d. 1886) in Madras who told him that Mīṉāṭcicuntaram Piḷḷai had planned to edit the work in collaboration with his student Cōṭacāvatāṉam Cupparāya Ceṭṭiyār (d. 1894), but found it too complicated and gave up (*EC* 583f.).

literatures. But in the literature discussed here there is no such clear-cut distinction. Gods and saints are always present in pre-modern nineteenth-century works, if only in allusions, metaphors, or similes. In fact, as we shall see later, this is one of the important features to distinguish these works from the modern literature produced under Western influence after mid-century where the realm of the religious and mythological was treated in very different ways. Thus, if one wished to stick to the label "religious," one could differentiate between religious works *sensu strictu* and "less religious works"—admittedly a rather poor categorization. Therefore, I have thought it wiser to distinguish between the subject of praise. While works written for and about kings and rich landlords form the subject of the next chapter, the works composed to extol gods, saints, or sacred places will be discussed here, since most of Mīṉāṭcicuntaram Piḷḷai's literary output belongs to this latter category.

Praise of deities and sacred places was usually woven into verses by drawing upon narrative materials from the *purāṇas* and other mythological sources. These could be adduced to praise in varying detail the holy acts of a deity, its name(s) and various forms or incarnations, feet, vehicle (*vākaṉam*) and other attributes, birthplace or major places where holy actions were performed, or the devotees and their actions. Often such praise was further linked to extended descriptions of natural beauty—forests, hills, and gardens with lovely trees and flowers and animals—as manifesting the divine (as seen above in the verses quoted from Mīṉāṭcicuntaram Piḷḷai's *Amparppurāṇam*). How precisely puranic and other material could be treated largely depended on the restrictions that particular genres imposed. As already briefly discussed above, the pulavars' works were usually cast into different *pirapantam* genres, classifiable according to their length into the longer *talapurāṇams* telling the legends of a particular shrine, and into other, shorter genres. The particular genre a poet chose depended often on the amount of money or other gifts he obtained from his patron(s), as he had to make a living from what his versification earned him. Longer works, particularly the *talapurāṇams*, often required many months of intensive work. Thus, the quality of patronage could be directly reflected in the quality of the poem. One day, Mīṉāṭcicuntaram Piḷḷai was asked by his student Tiyākarāca Ceṭṭiyār why the *Amparppurāṇam* he was writing at the time was less well executed than the *Uṟaiyūrppurāṇam* composed twenty years back. He replied that the reason why he was able to write that work so well was the generosity of his erstwhile patron, adding "If anyone would put me up and sponsor me now in the same way, how much could I achieve!" (*SMPC* I: 122). In contrast, shorter works such as *antātis* or *mālais* were sometimes composed on the spot as a token of the poet's devotion when he visited a particular temple. The available listings of nineteenth-century Tamil works in Vēṅkaṭacāmi (1962), Civakāmi (1994), or Ceyarāmaṉ (1983) bear testimony of the large number and variety of genres involved here.[78] Typical titles of such works include *Vināyakar patikam, Tiruñāṉacampantar piḷḷaittamiḻ, Tiruppaḻani veṇpā, Tirukkaḻukkuṉṟam Tiripuracuntari mālai, Tiruvōttūr Iḷamulai Ampikai antāti,* and *Maturai Mīṉāṭciyammai ūñcal,* to name only some of the most popular genres. The deities of particularly famous and important temples, such as Śiva (as Naṭarāja) in Chidambaram, accumulated a considerable number of *pirapantams* by many different poets throughout the century.

While the content of *patikams, mālais,* or *antātis* was not fixed, several of the *pirapantam* genres already predetermined the content by its conventions. A *piḷḷaittamiḻ,* for instance, describes the actions and sports of the deity while still a baby, whereas the *ulā* depicts a procession of the deity or its icon and the reactions of the female spectators. With the *ulā* genre, we come to another important theme of nineteenth-century pulavar literature—love and eroticism. From the large number of *pirapantams* available, our poets not seldom chose such which required that their story about a god or saint be linked to *erotic* descriptions. The *ulā* describes the varied reactions of women of seven different ages falling in love with an exceedingly beautiful god or king while he goes out in a procession. We will briefly return to the *ulā* genre in the next chapter. Mīṉāṭcicuntaram Piḷḷai composed an *ulā* on Śiva in Tiruviṭaimarutūr in 721 *kaṇṇis* (couplets) which was premiered in the temple in 1870 (*SMPC* I: 330).[79] Other genres, such as *tūtu* ("messenger") or *kātal* ("love") equally deal with love as their primary topic. The way love is depicted in these works may be considered, at a general level, as a late reworking of the thematic conventions known as *akam* in ancient Tamil *Caṅkam* poetry. The most typical genre that explicitly takes up these ancient *akam* conventions is called *kōvai,* literally "string" or "arrangement." To see how the *akam* traditions extend into the nineteenth century, i.e., nearly two

78. According to the listings in Civakāmi (1994), the most popular pre-modern genres during the nineteenth century, with the number of works listed given in brackets, were *patikam* (1,237), *mālai* (374), *antāti* (281), *veṇpā* (153), *talapurāṇam* (104), *piḷḷaittamiḻ* (76), *catakam* (69), *kōvai* (62). Although the tendency is probably correct, the actual numbers here should be treated as preliminary.

79. The text is contained in *SMPT* as 1705–1706.

thousand years after their first codifications, and to provide a more in-depth discussion of the content of the pulavar literature, we will now look at one of Mīṉāṭcicuntaram Piḷḷai's *kōvai* works, his first one titled *Kuḷattūrkkōvai*. It is one of the few works of his that were written to honor not the gods, but one of his many friends and fellow pulavars.

The Uses of *Akam* Poetics in the Nineteenth Century: The *Kuḷattūrkkōvai* (1853)

Mīṉāṭcicuntaram Piḷḷai composed his *Kuḷattūrkkōvai* in 1853 in honor of his good friend Māyūram Vētanāyakam Piḷḷai, an extraordinary man of letters who we have briefly met above and who, as we shall see below, became an important force in the Tamil literary field after mid-century. At the time Vētanāyakam, still a young man of twenty-seven, had just been reinstated to his office as Foujdaree Translator in the Civil and Session Court of Tiruchirappalli from which he had previously been dismissed by accident. He certainly was all the more delighted also to be honored by a long poem which mentions his name in every stanza. The specific occasion for receiving such a great gift was that he had previously helped Mīṉāṭcicuntaram Piḷḷai in an important court case. The *Kuḷattūrkkōvai* was thus written as a token of the poet's gratitude.[80] As was briefly stated above, the *kōvai*, or to be more precise *akapporuḷ-kōvai* (i.e., "*kōvai* whose subject is *akam* (love)"), one of the oldest *pirapantam* genres, consists of approximately 400 quatrains (in the *kaṭṭaḷaikkalitturai* meter) telling the story of two anonymous lovers.[81] Here, the individual erotic vignettes found in the ancient *Caṅkam* anthologies are spun into a chronological sequence. This makes up a largely linear narrative starting with the first accidental

80. For details of the case, see *SMPC* I (150–2).

81. Those who prefer a definition in technical terms may refer to one of the *pāṭṭiyal* treatises. For instance, the first stanza of the *Pirapantatīpam* (perhaps written in the nineteenth century) gives the following definition: "If we examine the *akapporuḷ-kōvai*, / [it is] singing four hundred poems in *kaṭṭaḷaikkalitturai* [metre] / showing the nature of *kaḷavu*, of *kaṟpu* and of *varaivu* [and] having / two kinds of *mutal-poruḷ*, twice seven [kinds of] *karu-poruḷ*, / five times two [kinds of] *uri-poruḷ*, and the constitutive elements of love poetry{*akappāṭṭuṟuppu*}" (Cuppiramaṇiyaṉ 1980: 1–3, my translation). As we see, this definition employs the technical terms of the earlier *akam* treatises (*Tolkāppiyam*, *Iṟaiyaṉār Akapporuḷ*, and *Akapporuḷ Viḷakkam* alias *Nampiyakapporuḷ*). The definition given in *Muttuvīriyam* (*yāppatikāram*, *oḻipiyal* 81) is similar (Muttuvīra Upāttiyāyar 1889: 319). For further details regarding the historical development of *akam* poetics, see Parthasarathi (1990) and Manuel (1997).

meeting when the male protagonist spots a beautiful girl. Once they have realized each other's intentions, they unite four times, overcoming various obstacles with the help of his and her friends. Then, she desires to get married, something he is not too happy about. In any case, their relationship has to be revealed to their parents. When those disapprove, the young couple elopes. Then they return, get married, and enjoy a happily wedded life. Before long, however, he leaves her for various reasons and she is devastated. When compressed into these few words, such a plot may perhaps seem rather stereotyped and concatenative. Indeed the emphasis of what happens in a *kōvai* is not on narrative cohesion. In other words, what counts are still the individual scenes as miniature descriptions redolent of the *Caṅkam* poems. True, they are woven into a larger tapestry, but this to a certain extent remains a patchwork quilt rather than forming an integrated portrait.[82] Certainly more than at the level of content, the integrating forces may be seen at the level of form: In every *kōvai* poem all the individual stanzas follow the same rigid pattern. Each stanza encapsulates one particular moment in the lovers' lives, e.g., their first accidental meeting, his doubting whether she is human or a goddess, his concluding that she must be human, etc. In the various traditions of *akam* poetics, these individual scenes are referred to as *tuṟais* or *kiḷavis*, which I will render as "situations," simplifying Norman Cutler's (1987: 82) term "narrative situations."[83] The sequence of

82. That the single stanza remains in the poet's focus is further demonstrated by the fact that *kōvais* usually enumerate *several* reasons for the hero leaving his wife at the end. According to the poetic treatises, these reasons are generally viewed as alternatives, so that here, at last, the narrative linearity becomes blurred.

83. Rather than a single consistent *akam* theory, we have today various traditions or schools of *akam* poetics which developed away from each other at different points of time. Therefore, with regard to the structure of themes and "situations" we find in the *kōvai* genre, the Tamil terminology is rather confusing. To avoid this confusion one may look at the actual work first and explain the theory from that perspective. We can distinguish between three structural levels of a *kōvai* poem: At a first level, a *kōvai* can be divided into three "parts," viz. *kaḷavu* "pre-marital meetings of the two lovers," *varaivu* "the marriage" and *kaṟpu* "married life." At a second level, these parts each have several "chapters" or rather "thematic sections." In the *Kuḷattūrkkōvai* (as in several other nineteenth-century *kōvais*), *kaḷavu* has 18 thematic sections: *kaikkiḷai* "He first sees her and falls in love," *iyaṟkaippuṇarcci* "The first accidental union," *vaṉpuṟai* "He assures her that he will not leave," *teḷivu* "She realizes that he will come back after leaving," *pirivuḻimakiḻcci* "He feels happy to see her again after their first separation," *pirivuḻikkalaṅkal* "He feels distressed at the place where he left her," *iṭantalaippāṭu* "He again reaches the same place to meet her," *pāṅkaṟkūṭṭam* "The lovers meet with the help of his friend," *pāṅkimatiyuṭaṉpāṭu* "Her confidante comes to know," *pāṅkiyiṟkūṭṭam* "The lovers meet with the help of her confidante," *orucārpakaṟkuṟi* "Tryst during daytime,"

these situations is always the same, the only variation consisting in the possibility to leave out a particular stanza or to describe the same scene in two (or more) stanzas.[84]

Following these genre conventions, the *Kuḷattūrkkōvai* starts with the thematic section called *kaikkiḷai* or "prelude."[85] Here, the first situation is called *kāṭci* ("sight"), i.e., the moment when our hero first sees the lovely young girl. Kuḷantai is another name for Kuḷattūr, Vētanāyakam Piḷḷai's birthplace.

---

pakaṟkuṟi iṭaiyīṭu "Obstacles to this tryst during daytime," *iravukkuṟi* "Tryst during nighttime," *iravukkuṟiyiṭaiyīṭu* "Obstacles to this tryst during nighttime," *varaital vēṭkai* "She wants to get married," *varaivu kaṭātal* "Her confidante appeals to him to marry her," *oruvaḻittaṉattal* "The two lovers separate temporarily," and *varaiviṭai vaittupporuḷ vayiṟpirital* "He leaves her to acquire wealth for the wedding." The part on *varaivu* includes eight thematic sections: *varaivumalivu* "Excitement at the prospect of the wedding," *aṟattoṭuniṟṟal* "Telling the truth [to their parents]," *uṭaṉpōkku* "Elopement of the lovers," *kaṟpoṭupuṇarntakauvai* "People's reaction to the elopement," *mīṭci* "Return of the lovers," *taṉmaṉaivaraital* "Marriage in his home," *uṭaṉpōkkiṭaiyīṭu* "Obstacles to the elopement," *varaital* "The wedding." The part on *kaṟpu* is divided into seven thematic sections: *ilvāḻkkai* "Happy domestic life of the lovers," *parattaiyiṟpirivu* "He leaves her to seek the company of prostitutes," *ōtaṟpirivu* "He leaves in order to study," *kāvaṟpirivu* "As he is a king, he parts from his wife to defend his country," *tūtiṟpirivu* "He leaves his beloved as he goes on a mission for an allied king," *tuṇaivayiṟpirivu* "He has to leave her to help another king in battle," *poruḷvayiṟpirivu* "He leaves to earn wealth." Note that this sequence of thematic situations is also the one given in the poetic treatise *Akapporuḷ Viḷakkam* alias *Nampiyakapporuḷ*, perhaps 13th to 14th c. (see Kōvintarāca Mutaliyār 1966, esp. st.123, 172, 180, 201). Finally, at a third level, these various thematic sections each contain one or more "situations," each forming a single stanza of the entire poem. In some poetic traditions (going back to *Tolkāppiyam*), these situations are called *kiḷavi*, while the thematic sections are known as *kiḷavittokai* or *kiḷavikkottu*. Other traditions use the term *tuṟai* for the situation and *kiḷavi* for the larger thematic section (thus, e.g., U. Vē. Cāminātaiyar in his commentary on Civakkoḻuntu Tēcikar's *Kōṭīccurakkōvai*, see Cāminātaiyar 1932). Unfortunately, no research has been done so far that would help us to distinguish clearly the historical development of different theories of *akam* poetics. Hence, the application of Tamil poetic terms to actual literary texts often does not illuminate the texts but rather raises new questions. To avoid any further confusion I have decided to use the English terms instead.

84. Nineteenth-century *kōvai* works generally seem to follow *Akapporuḷ Viḷakkam* in their sequence of thematic sections and situations. However, Mīṉāṭcicuntaram Piḷḷai's three *kōvais*, as well as Civakkoḻuntu Tēcikar's *Kōṭīccurakkōvai*, all contain additional situations not found in *Akapporuḷ Viḷakkam*. Whether these "new" situations follow other poetic treatises or whether they are individual inventions of the poets remains to be discovered through further research.

85. The term *kaikkiḷai* refers *sensu strictu* to "one-sided love" in *akam* poetics, but it has come to be employed to denote the prelude in the *kōvai* genre, the time when the hero first falls in love with the heroine.

The beautiful red lotus, the blue nelumbo of exceeding
   charm, the blossoming jasmine,
the lovely *kōṅkam*, and the alluring red *kāntaḷ* —
endowed with all these [different blossoms],
   near Kuḷantai, [the town of] the great man
      Vētanāyakam who studies
         the beautiful pure Tamil,
   on the grandiose, big mountain
there stood a fragrant creeper. (*SMPT* 4611) [2.20]

To unravel the heavy symbolism at play here, we may start with the very basics. What we (and the anonymous protagonist) find on this mountain near Kuḷattūr is a mysterious plant, a single creeper or liana which bears five different blossoms at the same time. As also in other Indian literatures, this creeper (*koṭi*) is a young girl, but why this surrealist flower metaphor? The initiated, as for instance fellow pulavars, knew that the blossoms mentioned here were not arbitrarily chosen. To those familiar with *akam* poetic conventions, these five flowers immediately conjure up the five poetic categories (*tiṇai*) of classical Tamil love poetry: The red lotus (*kañcam*) stands for *marutam*, the blue nelumbo (*nīlam*) for *neytal*, jasmine (*taḷavu*) for *mullai*, *kōṅkam* for *pālai*, and *kāntaḷ* for *kuṟiñci*. These poetic categories, famously referred to as "interior landscapes" by A. K. Ramanujan, each comprise a particular love sentiment that is usually expressed in a particular (imagined) landscape. Thus, the *kuṟiñci-tiṇai* evoked by the *kāntaḷ* flower describes clandestine, premarital love taking place in the hillside. In the *neytal-tiṇai*, symbolized by the blue nelumbo, the landscape is the seashore, and the sentiment expressed is the one of the heroine separated from her lover and anxiously waiting for his return. We need not go into further details of these complex poetic systems here.[86] What is important for us is that such allusions and symbols are present in the poem in the first place. The mountain near Kuḷattūr itself is significant. Rather than pointing to a real mountain, it is an important poetic convention. As we have said, the mountainside is the place of action for *kuṟiñci*, which depicts the first secret union of the two lovers. And their lovemaking is precisely what is described (or rather alluded to) in some of the following stanzas.

86. The systems of *akam* poetics are conveniently outlined in Ramanujan (1996, afterword) and Zvelebil (1973, chs. 5–7), and in greater technical detail in Manuel (1997). For further details on the relation between *kōvai* and the *Caṅkam* poems, see Cutler (1987, ch. 4).

Further, as the phase of love depicted here is *kaikkiḷai*, love which is still unrequited, the poem starts with the appropriate flower for *marutam* (representing *ūṭal* "love quarrel") and ends with the one for *kuṟiñci* (representing the much desired "union" of the two lovers). Then, according to the rules of *akam* poetics, *pālai* has to be inserted between *mullai* and *kuṟiñci*. Thus, the respective plant, here *kōṅkam*, is found between *taḷavu* and *kāntaḷ*. As may perhaps be expected, in addition to this symbolism the poem is not even free from *cilēṭai* word play. What I translated above as "the beautiful pure Tamil" is in the original *maṉ pūtta centamiḻ*. It may be variously read as (a) "the pure Tamil which has{*pūtta*} beauty{*maṉ*}" or (b) "the pure Tamil which made the [three Tamil] kings{*maṉ*} flourish{*pūtta*}." Another convention is that the genre distinguishes between two "heroes," the anonymous lover called *kiḷavittalaivaṉ* or "hero of the narrative" in Norman Cutler's words (1987: 83), and the *pāṭṭuṭaittalaivaṉ* "hero of the composition" (ibid.) whose praise is sung by the poem. By poetic rule, the name of the *pāṭṭuṭaittalaivaṉ* must be present in every stanza, and indeed in the 438 stanzas of the *Kuḷattūrkkōvai* we find the name Vētanāyakam 438 times.

But there is still more to this stanza. At the level of intertextuality, the educated audience hearing it will be reminded of the first stanza of Māṇikkavācakar's famous *Tirukkōvaiyār*, the ninth-century poem on Śiva in Chidambaram (Tillai). This stanza may be translated thus:

> The radiant lotus, the glorious water lilies, the
> resplendent
> flowering *kumiḻ* in the Lord's Tillai, the *kōṅku*, and
> the luxuriant *kāntaḷ*—consisting of these, a garland full of
> divine fragrance rising high, lithe as a liana,
> with the [graceful] gait of the goose,
> shines like the beautiful Love God's victory banner.
> (Cōmacuntaraṉār 1970: 6) [2.21]

Obviously, Mīṉāṭcicuntaram Piḷḷai's stanza is modeled on this verse.[87] Here, we have again five blossoms united into a lithe, fragrant garland. Besides the different *pāṭṭuṭaittalaivaṉ*, only the symbol of premarital love is different. Instead of a meaningful mountain, the scene is set in Tillai, Śiva's town Chidambaram. But the intention is nonetheless clear,

87. For possible translations of *Tirukkōvaiyār* 1, see also Cutler (1987: 150) and Ramachandran (1989: 1). For a discussion of the poem, see also Shulman (2002) and Cutler (2008).

as we are told that this flower-garland shines like the victory banner of Kāmadeva, the God of Love.[88] Besides such parallel construction, this *Tirukkōvaiyār* stanza may even help us to further illuminate the flower symbolism at work. Traditional exegesis of the *Tirukkōvaiyār* tells us that the five blossoms refer to particular parts of the girl's beautiful body: lotus = face, water lilies = eyes, *kumiḻ* = nose, *kōṅku* = breast, *kāntaḷ* = hands (Ramachandran 1989: 1–2). By extension, this also applies to Mīṉāṭcicuntaram Piḷḷai's poem.[89] Thus we can see how a nineteenth-century pulavar engages with earlier textual traditions and practices. The following stanzas of the *Kuḷattūrkkōvai* are equally in line with the *Tirukkōvaiyār*. The second stanza expresses the *kiḷavittalaivaṉ*'s bewilderment at such an unwonted sight. In this and the following translations, the heading gives the situation and in parentheses the speaker of the poem.

Doubt (HE)

Is it heaven, or the world where Brahmā resides, or the
  world chosen by Viṣṇu
with Lakṣmī on his chest, or the shining world of the
  snakes, or the earth
girded by the cool ocean?
    The ground on the hill of the generous Vētanāyakam
        who is ornamented by tolerance
    has performed great penance to be touched
    by these beautiful, much-admired feet of hers.
  (*SMPT* 4612) [2.22]

As the hero wonders where such a beautiful creature could come from, he refers to the various divisions of heaven in Hindu mythology. *Cattiyalōkam* (Skt. *satyaloka*), the world where Lord Brahmā resides is generally considered to be the highest. Viṣṇu's heaven is called *vaikuṇṭam* (Skt. *vaikuṇṭha*). *Nākalōkam* (Skt. *nāgaloka*, "snake world"), is the most beautiful of all the heavenly worlds offering all imaginable sensuous pleasures. Hence, it is also called *kāmaloka* "kingdom of love" (Walker 1995: 388). This is of course appropriate for the theme of *akam*. Overly beautiful as she is, the "creeper" could well be from that world. However, as he keeps looking at her, he is soon convinced that she must be human.

88. On the mythology of Kāmadeva, see Benton (2006).

89. Apart from the "literary" interpretation of the *Tirukkōvaiyār* I am attempting here, there exist also *theological* readings of the text by Śaiva Siddhāntins which superimpose allegorical meanings onto the erotic elements (Cutler 1987, ch. 5).

Conclusion (HE)

The girl whose body is softer than flowers
is a daughter of this world:
Like those who do not approach the young man Vētanāyakam
whose liberal hands excel the *kalpaka* trees [in generosity]
and ask him "Please support us!," the garlands in her hair are fading.
As if inviting [me] "Come hither!," her shining eyes are blinking. (*SMPT* 4613) [2.23]

The withering flower garlands in her hair and her blinking eyes indicate that she is human. The eyes of the Gods never blink, nor do their garlands wither. The simile for Vētanāyakam Piḷḷai's generosity may be explained thus: While the wish-fulfilling *kalpaka* tree gives only when asked, Vētanāyakam supports the needy even without being asked. But our hero is still not sure what to make of this. In what is a form of soliloquy common in classical Tamil poetry, he addresses his own mind (*maṉamē*):

Finding out about her intentions (HE)

On the hill of the generous Vētanāyakam who resides in Kuḷantai
where the fields yield superior paddy,
and where the gander joyfully feeds the [tastier] shrimps to his
female which [usually] eats carps,
her soft eyes send out two glances—one confusing, the other inviting—
like the ocean which gives both ambrosia and maddening poison.
O mind, examine [both of these]! (*SMPT* 4614) [2.24]

Here we also find a double praise of Kuḷattūr. Firstly, it is the place where superior paddy grows. Secondly, the ganders find superior kinds of fish for their females. That even the animals take delight in giving to others serves to underline Vētanāyakam Piḷḷai's generosity. The two ambivalent glances her eyes send out are, of course, a well-known *akam* topos (see e.g., *Tirukkuṟaḷ* 1091). This stanza ends the prelude. The next thematic section describes the first accidental union of the two (*iyaṟkaippuṇarcci*) through which the increasingly impatient lover is finally rewarded. But before this first union, we may witness the usual dalliances. First, he has to summon up the courage to actually talk to her. Remembering an adage from the *Tirukkuṟaḷ* does the job. What I have rendered below as "Begging is [. . .] a nice thing" (*irappum or ēr uṭaittu*) is a direct quotation from *Tirukkuṟaḷ* 1053: *karappilā neñciṟ kaṭaṉaṟivār muṉṉiṉ / ṟirappumō rēer uṭaittu*, i.e., "Standing before those who do not hide anything and in their hearts know their duty—begging to those is a nice thing [lit. possesses beauty]." Then, having overcome his fears, he becomes rather outspoken about his desires.

Thinking of standing behind her, submissively beseeching her (HE)

On the hill, where there are gardens,
in Kuḷantai of the illustrious Vētanāyakam
who is as dear as their own eyes to everyone,
don't be afraid my heart, just dispel the sorrow that attacks your mind!
"Begging is indeed a nice thing, if they refuse to give anything,
it is their own sin"—this [truth] you have understood,
so let us go closer and entreat her. (*SMPT* 4615) [2.25]

Standing behind her to beseech her (HE)

On the hill of the Love God alias Vētanāyakam,
the tall Viṣṇu with strong shoulders that [scholars] measure,
I have determined the way of doing service:
You who are like goddess Śrī, your hair [shining] like sapphires,
to still my cruel hunger for love,
please grant me the nectar of your mouth,
red [like the fruit of the] *kovvai* creeper,
so that I may eat
after bathing in the tank of your *alkul*
which is bedecked with jewels. (*SMPT* 4616) [2.26]

The expression "bathing in the tank of your *alkul*" is clearly an overt reference to the sexual act, as the term *alkul* refers to a woman's private parts.[90] The analogy used here for the act and kissing is that one

90. *Alkul* is a very common term in classical Tamil literature, but rather difficult to translate precisely, as both the texts themselves and their commentators often yield controversial opinions. As may be easily imagined, the word has a long history of being edited out of texts, expurgated, circumscribed, and mistranslated. Hence, it is currently impossible to decide whether the word actually denotes the *pudendum muliebre* in its entirety or a part thereof, or whether it is best rendered by a more general term, such as "lap." Given this lack of clarity, I have decided to leave the term untranslated.

usually takes a bath before eating a meal, due to religious ideas of purity. Here, the hero rather frankly communicates what he expects from his new acquaintance. It is important, however, to note that although we find such clear references to the physical dimension of love throughout the poem, a *kōvai* never contains any graphic descriptions of the sexual act in the manner of certain Sanskrit erotic poetry (or, as we shall see in the following chapter, the *viṟaliviṭutūtu* works composed in courtly circles). The next stanza shows that the girl does not remain entirely indifferent to his behavior. He notices that she has ceased to pursue any of the activities usual for young maidens. Playing ball, swimming, gathering flowers, or playing on a swing are typical topoi used in medieval Tamil love poetry to describe the occupations of an innocent young girl. Losing interest in these is a conventional sign of incipient love.

Coming in front of her (HE)

On the hill of the eminent Vētanāyakam,
this ocean of learning, well-known [to everyone],
you have stopped all this: swimming in the mountain pond
with your praised group of female friends, plucking flowers,
and moving, rocking hard, on the praised swing.
Is it because of the great penance I have performed
that you are standing here all alone?
Please tell me! (*SMPT* 4617) [2.27]

Having thus put her on the spot, he ventures a little further. The following situation extends a well-known conceit common to both Tamil and Sanskrit love poetry. According to classical Indian ideals of female beauty, ladies have to have opulent, pendulous breasts but a delicate waist. The usual conceit then is that the lady's breasts pose a threat to her waist, as the breasts' weight might cause the waist to break. Here, the poet expands this conceit further. The hero thinks that the bees searching for honey in the flower garlands which adorn her hair form an additional burden, so they have to be chased away.[91]

Driving away the bees and touching her waist (HE)

O you group of bees in regular division
  on the hill of our friend, the famous Vētanāyakam
    with a compassionate mind,

91. This situation called *vaṇṭōccimaruṅkaṇaital* is not found in *Akapporuḷ Viḷakkam*, but in all three *kōvais* by Mīṉāṭcicuntaram Piḷḷai. However, it is apparently not Mīṉāṭcicuntaram's invention, since it is also found in Civakkoḻuntu Tēcikar's *Kōṭīccurakkōvai*.

the ocean of learning, wish-fulfilling gem to the
learned,
the beautiful *kalpaka* tree, liberal as the black raincloud,
you must not stay in the five rows of garlands that
adorn the hair of this girl,
sucking honey, lest her slender waist break. (*SMPT* 4618)
[2.28]

And thus the flirtations continue for quite some time and take the new couple through the ups and downs of love. After much sulking, quarreling, reconciling, etc., the tale is concluded, and the *Kuḷattūrkkōvai* ends on a cheerful note:

What he said being with her when he joyfully saw the [coming of the] rainy season

The breasts of her with the bow-shaped eyebrows
were adorned with sandal paste and swelled, as we
united.
As if hovering above the liberal hands of the generous
Vētanāyakam of Kuḷattūr, who lives in a mansion
where Lakṣmī dwells, as if on the golden Mount Meru,
pour forth and prosper, cool rain clouds! (*SMPT* 5048)
[2.29]

In *akam* poetry, the rainy season (*kārpparuvam*) comprises the Tamil months of *Āvaṇi* and *Puraṭṭāci* (mid-August to mid-October). It is the time when lovers rejoice, since men may stay at home and look after their wives without having to fight battles or being otherwise called away. In the poem, the hero asks the rainclouds to continue their benevolent duty for long, so that the two lovers may spend much time together. But not only the lovers' embrace forms an appropriate happy ending to the *Kuḷattūrkkōvai*. Also at the formal level the poem is concluded as poetics would recommend it. The last four words of the original Tamil (*poḻi* "pour forth," *vāḻiya* "prosper," *taṇ* "cool," *mukilē* "rain cloud(s)"), comprising the entire last line in my translation, are all auspicious words. Moreover, mentioning Mount Meru and goddess Lakṣmī further adds to the auspicious note that pervades this final stanza of the poem.

Now, before we conclude our discussion of the *Kuḷattūrkkōvai*, let us for a moment return to the idea of *praise* as the typical content of the pulavars' compositions. In the last stanza of the poem, just as in the preceding stanzas we have seen, the *pāṭṭuṭaittalaivaṉ* or "hero of the composition," Vētanāyakam Piḷḷai, is cleverly woven into the erotic scenario. The *kiḻavittalaivaṉ* asks the clouds to pour forth their rain as if they were located above the generous Vētanāyakam into whose hands their rain would fall. Generally, *kōvais* flatter their *pāṭṭuṭaittalaivaṉs* by praising them as generous, compassionate, and knowledgeable persons. We may recall the penultimate stanza discussed above which nicely exemplifies this when Vētanāyakam Piḷḷai is referred to as: "famous," having a "compassionate mind," an "ocean of learning (*kalvikkaṭal*)," a "wish-fulfilling gem (*cintāmaṇi*)," the wish-fulfilling *kalpaka* tree, and "liberal as the black raincloud (*kār*)." Similar adulatory epithets are found in every stanza of the *kōvai*, praising the *pāṭṭuṭaittalaivaṉ*'s physical beauty (e.g., by comparing him to the Love God), his good qualities (knowledge, tolerance, compassion), and his wealth. To incorporate such eulogies into their compositions served the pulavars well, as the *pāṭṭuṭaittalaivaṉ* was frequently the patron who paid the poet for his service. Following the distinction between *kiḻavittalaivaṉ* and *pāṭṭuṭaittalaivaṉ*, we can distinguish two levels of the text: the level of the erotic narrative and the level of (hyperbolic) eulogy. The two levels are intricately interwoven in every stanza of a *kōvai*, but the eulogy grounds the tale of love in a reality which may be "historical" as in our text (referring to historical persons) or "devotional" whenever a deity becomes the *pāṭṭuṭaittalaivaṉ*.

Blending the two levels of erotic narrative and eulogy in the *kōvai* genre has been discussed in terms of an interplay between *akam* and *puṟam* poetic conventions (Cutler 1987: 82f.). Given how little we still know about the historical development of both these conventions, it is difficult at present to decide how to best theorize the influences earlier poetic traditions exercised on the *kōvai*. What we can say at the moment is that a number of *akam* elements known to us from the *Caṅkam* anthologies (the cast of unnamed characters, images, similes, motifs, lexical items) are still found in the *kōvai* texts of the nineteenth century. Thus, the nineteenth-century *kōvais* may be seen as continuing poetic traditions which extend over two thousand years. What characterizes these late works is above all their far-reaching intertextuality, the way they allude to and play with older texts and textual conventions. The *Kuḷattūrkkōvai* quotes other texts, such as the *Tirukkuṟaḷ*, bases itself on the first poem of the tradition, the *Tirukkōvaiyār*, extends classical conceits, etc. In the foreword to his edition of Mīṉāṭcicuntaram Piḷḷai's *Cīkāḻikkōvai*, U. Vē. Cāminātaiyar alludes to this incorporating, ingesting quality of the *kōvai* texts. He praises the text as containing beautiful rhythms, quotations from the *Caṅkam* poems,[92] ideas from the Śaiva *śāstras*, and puranic stories about Śiva and the canonical Śaivite saints (Nāyaṉmār) used as similes (1903: 1). And though Cāminātaiyar emphatically insists that such beauty cannot be found in any other work, similar things could be said about the other two *kōvais* written by Mīṉāṭcicuntaram Piḷḷai. They are, in fact, characteristic of pulavar literature as a whole, which was always scholarly, even scholastic—a literature for the initiated.

Makāvittuvāṉ T. Mīṉāṭcicuntaram Piḷḷai: A Poets' Poet

When compared to the works of his contemporaries, Mīṉāṭcicuntaram Piḷḷai's compositions were often seen as particularly skilfull and erudite, so that he has been called "a poets' poet" (Guruswamy 1976). The superiority of his poetry and learning notwithstanding, Mīṉāṭcicuntaram Piḷḷai in many ways epitomizes both the lifestyle and literary activities of the nineteenth-century pulavars. He was at the heart and center of a scholarly community, which functioned according to its own mechanisms, which I have attempted to elucidate in this chapter. We have looked at how a young pulavar was educated and which texts he studied, which genres the pulavars employed to what ends, and how much depended on oral performance and memorization. We have seen how the pulavar's literary production took place within an economy of praise, driven by networks of patronage where poets, patrons, and audiences all played their specific roles.

When on Tuesday, February 1, 1876, Mīṉāṭcicuntaram Piḷḷai passed away at the age of sixty, the universe of the pulavars had lost one of its brightest stars. He died peacefully and in the company of his disciples and friends in the Tiruvāvaṭuturai ātīṉam, protected

92. It is interesting that Cāminātaiyar explicitly acknowledges quotations/examples from the *Caṅkam* poems (*caṅkacceyyuṭpirayōkaṅkaḷ*) in Mīṉāṭcicuntaram Piḷḷai's *kōvai*, whereas I have not found any other source in which he tells us anything about how much of the *Caṅkam* literature Mīṉāṭcicuntaram Piḷḷai and his fellow pulavars actually knew. His remark may be taken as a hint that we have to revise our current theories about the somewhat miraculous "rediscovery" of *Caṅkam* literature by Cāminātaiyar and others (as outlined in Zvelebil 1992, ch. 6, based on Cāminātaiyar's own writings). Another hint is presented by the fact that when educated in Tamil as a young boy in Jaffna, Āṟumuka Nāvalar studied the Jaina epic *Cīvakacintāmaṇi* that Cāminātaiyar apparently did not know about (Ambalavanar 2006: 185; 187). Would this indicate, as Ambalavanar suggests, that scholars in Sri Lanka had a wider sense of what constituted Tamil literary tradition?

from the hustle and bustle of the annual *guru puja* celebrations that were in full swing. U. Vē. Cāminātaiyar, at the time a young man aged twenty, recounts how he was reading out a decade from the *Tiruvācakam* when his teacher closed his eyes. The obsequies were performed elaborately and presided over by the head of the monastery, Mēlakaram Cuppiramaṇiya Tēcikar, a close friend of Mīṉāṭcicuntaram. His sacred remains were adorned with ashes and *rudrākṣa* beads and taken on a solemn procession to the sound of firecrackers with multitudes of priests, pupils, and fellow pulavars standing by, shedding their tears. The body was cremated on the banks of the river Kaveri. Mīṉāṭcicuntaram Piḷḷai's son Citamparam Piḷḷai lit the funeral pyre. Cāminātaiyar remembers how he and others went home afterward, took a copy of their favorite works composed by their teacher and read stanza after stanza to drive away their sorrow.[93]

If we believe Cāminātaiyar's biography, Mīṉāṭcicuntaram Piḷḷai lived a life of studying and teaching, of reading and composing verses without much noticing the social and political changes taking place around him. It is striking how few references to these momentous transformations one finds in Cāminātaiyar's writings about his teacher. The poet's disciples, however, were facing a different reality where the impact of colonial modernity became increasingly palpable. But before we address these changes, we have to consider a second traditional sphere of the pulavars' literary activities. While Mīṉāṭcicuntaram Piḷḷai's life was centered around religious institutions, many of his fellow pulavars moved in a very different world—the courts of the zamindars and native rulers.

93. See *SMPC* II (244–255), for an account of Mīṉāṭcicuntaram Piḷḷai's death. U. Vē. Cāminātaiyar records that many fellow pulavars, friends, and acquaintances sent letters of condolence or poems. Most of them, however, are now lost.

3

Pulavars and Potentates

Structures of Literary Patronage at the Zamindars' Courts and Beyond

With ten bags full of pearls and diamond pendants
You have supported me and made me happy,
O great king, you know the pleasures of amorous talk
And playful caresses on a soft cushion!

—Kaṉam Kiruṣṇaiyar

Right at the beginning of the nineteenth century, British colonial impact severely altered the worlds of the local rulers and native kings (poligars, Tam. *pāḷaiyakkārar*) who had emerged as free agents during the Nāyaka period. After the so-called "Poligar Wars" of 1800–1801, the erstwhile independent kingdoms became *zamindaris* or revenue estates and, as such, part of the Madras Presidency.[1] They

1. On the Poligar Wars, see Rajayyan (1974). The fascinating history of the zamindars is traced into the twentieth century by Baker (1976). Since the publication of Nicholas Dirks' (1987) famous study of the kingdom of Pudukkottai about two decades ago, a considerable number of historians have engaged in what has become an extended debate on the so-called "little kings" and the extent and nature of their power. It is, of course, beyond the scope of the present study to contribute to this debate from a theoretical point of view. A useful overview of the arguments involved may be found in Frenz (2000, ch. 3.2) and the English version Frenz (2003, ch. 2), while the historical development of theories on "little kingdoms" and the Indian state is outlined in Schnepel (1997, ch. 1). Dirks' formulation of the "hollow crown" has been variously criticized and re-assessed, notably in Pamela Price's insightful study of Ramnad and Sivagangai (1996), which I have drawn upon repeatedly in order to formulate my own argument. A critique of Dirks' theorizations on royal gift-giving has been provided in Norbert Peabody's study of the kingdom of Kota in Rajasthan (2003). Barbara Ramusack's recent monograph on the Indian princely states deals mostly with northern India, and what

had to pay a fixed regular revenue (peshkash) to the British East India Company according to the so-called Permanent Settlement of 1801–1803. At a general level, this policy brought, whether desired or not, the infamous benefits of a *Pax Britannica* which stopped the incessant warfare between local kings rampant during the eighteenth century. On the other hand, British intervention gradually drained the royal treasuries (or granaries) and curtailed the power of the former rajas. This happened, at least in part, because—once again—British colonial administrators misinterpreted historical reality. As Christopher Baker points out: "For the British administrator, the role of the zamindar floated somewhere between that of a tax-farmer and that of a country gentleman" (1976: 9). But until 1803, the poligars had been something quite different. They were above all political leaders overseeing their respective territories with the aid of their military forces. Land management had never been any of their concerns, but was in the hands of village communities. "The poligars levied dues, but these were essentially taxes to cover military and administrative costs and tributes, not rents" (ibid.). The plans of the government in Madras, however, envisioned the zamindars as landholders and revenue collectors at their service. "To this end, they liberally endowed them with titles and medals, invited them to play an important part in imperial occasions, constantly looked to them to act as spokesmen of rural society, and set up the Court of Wards to protect the estates during sickness, minority, or hard times" (ibid., 10). Thus forced to metamorphose into tools of British colonial ambition, it is perhaps no great wonder that in the following decades the zamindars did not play their new role very well.

Baker has shown that the zamindars generally had left the control of what was a very localized and meagre economy in their respective areas to a complex quasi-administrative network. Involved were wealthy peasants (raiyats), village headmen, and village accountants (Tam. *karṇam*), all with their own (at times conflicting) interests. In Ramnad (Tam. Irāmanātapuram), the largest zamindari, the king had

---

she has to say about princely patronage of literature is limited to a short paragraph on collecting and editing Sanskrit manuscripts (2004: 145).

I have avoided the use of the term "little king" throughout, since I find it entirely inappropriate in the present context. As David Shulman has pointed out, the "little kingdom" is "little only in our name for it, certainly not in its complexity, its sophistication, its creative impulses, or its outrageously grandiose pretensions" (2001a: 92). I have instead followed the language use of the literature discussed here in speaking of "king," "raja," "ruler," etc.

appointed an estate collector, a sheristadar and manager, and an office of over a hundred people, which in turn oversaw a large number of subordinate administrators, so as to yield a total number of 454 men employed to look after accounts and legal issues (ibid., 17). Needless to say, such an administration became a labyrinthine scenario awash with conflicting ambitions and dubious bookkeeping, so that ultimately "the zamindars had little chance of becoming attentive managers of the welfare of their estates, even should they have so desired" (ibid., 20). Consequently, their central concern remained, as in earlier centuries, questions of political status and personal honor. In fact, recent research suggests that these questions became increasingly important during the course of the nineteenth century. Pamela Price reminds us of the royal duties of late precolonial times: "One who would be king entered into a number of activities of protection—military, ritual, distributive—which, if successfully and properly performed, gave an aura of legitimacy to claims on honour, privilege, and rank" (1996: 29). Now, at the beginning of the nineteenth century, the poligars were irrevocably deprived of one of these arenas where royal status was negotiated during earlier times—the battlefield. Due to the policies of the East India Company, warfare with other kingdoms no longer served to underline a ruler's authority and claims. In response to this, the arena of the—still incessant—royal litigations shifted during the course of the century from the battlefield to the law courts established by the colonial government, as Pamela Price has shown in her study of the kingdom of Ramnad (1996). Additionally, what remained—apart from the negotiations of royal status at the law courts—were the tasks of ritual performances (as audio-visual statements of royalty) and distribution (or regulation of access to the resources of the "kingdom"). And this is indeed what the zamindars and native princes took to, focusing their attention on public *display* of royal status through rituals. During the course of the century, the rajas' economic resources and in tandem their distributive power dwindled further, so that, in the end, they were unable to afford even many of their ritual activities, such as parades or courtly musical and literary events. All in all, however, the nineteenth century is characterized by a production of a courtly literature which is by no means quantitatively inferior to that of earlier periods. In fact, as we shall see, nineteenth-century court poets created a remarkable corpus of works following poetological and thematic conventions that may be traced back to Nāyaka times. The variations, fractures and shifts of emphasis that we may discern in these works vis-à-vis their predecessors are so subtle that one is tempted to think of nineteenth-century Tamil courtly poetry as being thoroughly anachronistic. It is striking that the pulavars continued to write about royal splendor in those self-obsessed, ostentatious modes we find in the Nāyaka period, although they were functioning in an entirely different social environment.[2] In the present chapter, I would like to argue that this kind of "cultural conservatism" was not at all anachronistic, but that it was in fact purposefully pursued by the zamindars. At a time when the rajas' former prerogatives (military and economic power) were more and more curtailed, an emphasis on royal rituals was one of the few things which remained. Ritual activities of various kinds were an important way of hearkening back to former glory and of fashioning an essentially "royal" self which could still be respected and admired in a changing sociosphere. The zamindars' ritual activities comprised various royal ceremonies, festivals, and parades, as well as patronage of the arts. Thus, literature came to play an important part in what Baker has aptly called the zamindars' "ritualized remembrance of their past glory" (1976: 43).

Literature and Rituals of Courtly Representation

For many of their royal rituals, the zamindars and princes looked back to earlier traditions established by their predecessors during the late precolonial period, the Nāyaka period, or even earlier.[3] In the native state of Travancore (in modern-day Kerala), for instance, the rulers continued to celebrate the pompous festivals of royal consecration which gave the raja the status of a twice-born (Mal. *hiraṇyagarbham*), weighing the body of the raja against an amount of gold to be distributed to brahmins (Mal. *tulāpuruṣadānam* or *tulābhāram*), and every six years, the fifty-six days long *murajapam* to ensure the general safety and fertility of the country, all established by the state's founder Mārttāṇḍa Varmma during mid-eighteenth century (Kawashima 1998: 18–23). Such festivals involved large masses of people, not only the ruler's extended household and those who were in charge of the ceremonies (priests, musicians, and their various assistants), but also a large audience before which the spectacle could take place. Not

2. For the courtly literary culture of the Nāyaka period, see Narayana Rao et al. (1998).

3. We do not have a *longue durée* study of the royal representational practices at Indian courts. But a comparative look at the concerns expressed in nineteenth-century courtly literature and e.g., the courtly literature of the medieval Cōḷa kings suggests that such a study may be fruitful.

surprisingly, these rituals cost enormous amounts of money. For the *murajapam* of 1875–76 the raja paid no less than Rs. 182,009, and as late as 1911 the estimated cost for this ceremony equaled about 4 percent of the entire state expenditure (ibid., 22). In the Tamil-speaking area, the most important annual festival was *Navarāttiri* ("nine nights," also known as *Daśarā* or *Mahānavamī*), a ritual to celebrate the Goddess (Durgā or Kālī) and to ask her protection of the realm, which may be traced back to the Vijayanagara period. The splendors of the *Navarāttiri* festival have been repeatedly discussed in the secondary literature, and there is no need to reproduce the discussion here.[4] We may add, however, some information from a literary source which has generally been overlooked. In the writings of U. Vē. Cāminātaiyar we are told that during the 1870s in the kingdom of Pudukkottai scholars of Sanskrit and musicians received gifts of up to Rs. 100 on the occasion of the *Navarāttiri* festival (1957, ch. 6). Given the large masses of people who gathered on these occasions, such generosity could easily lead to enormous costs. We know that for the celebrations of the year 1892 (September 22 to October 5), the raja of Ramnad Pāskara Cētupati (Bhaskara Setupati, 1868–1903), spent almost one lakh rupees (Breckenridge 1978: 79).

Besides these large-scale celebrations, there were, of course, a number of other rituals, such as smaller temple festivals, or processions. Especially the processions were major ceremonial activities—events which united ruler and ruled in a common act of representation. During the procession the ruler displayed his status geographically while people could observe the king, i.e., take *darśana* of him. We shall see below how the depiction of royal processions became an important topic of courtly literature.[5] Furthermore, we find that processions were utilized to disseminate news, to *publicize*, in a very real sense of the word, whatever the raja had to show or say. How this age-old

4. An important source for the modalities of the *Navarāttiri* festival during the late nineteenth century is an anonymous eyewitness account of the 1892 celebrations in Ramnad which was first serialized in the newspaper *Madras Times* during the month of October 1892 and later published in pamphlet form (Pandiyaji/Venkataram Aiyangar 1896). This source has been discussed in detail by Breckenridge (1978). Pamela Price (1996, ch. 5) has re-assessed this material and added a discussion of *Navarāttiri* as celebrated in 1863 in the neighboring kingdom of Sivagangai based on the account by Shortt (1867–1870). Burton Stein has discussed the festival during the Vijayanagara period (1984), while Burkhard Schnepel has examined the *Daśarā* festival in Orissa (1997, esp. ch. VI).

5. On the significance of royal processions in medieval India, see also Ali (2004b), while Leslie Orr (2004) discusses medieval South Indian temple processions.

tradition was employed for the uses of colonial modernity becomes clear from the following case of the zamindar of Eṭṭaiyapuram (in Tinnevelly District) Sri Rajah Jagavira Rama Venkateswara Ettappa Nayakar Bahadur (b. 1878). In 1901, the raja arranged a durbar to celebrate the occasion of the coronation of King Edward VII in faraway London. He delivered a speech which betokens his loyalty to the future Emperor of India and his recognition of the "innumerable benefits" the Raj had brought about. He lamented that he could not be among the visitors in London to partake of

> the grand and gorgeous spectacle they enjoy this day. As it is, I could but make a feeble attempt at what I thought the only best way of commemorating the event, by planting trees and topes [gardens], sinking wells, feeding and clothing the poor, and conducting a procession of the Emperor's portrait round the streets of this town and holding a Durbar like this, here. (Vadivelu 1984a: 176)

While King Edward himself was probably little aware that his portrait was being paraded through the streets of a loyal South Indian town that day, the raja celebrated the occasion in his own terms, not forgetting the apposite 101 gun salutes. Thus, nineteenth-century royal rituals entailed, in Baker's terms, "an expensive display of pomp and circumstance, and careful attempts to underline the special relationship between the zamindar and the [British] government" (1976: 20).

At the local level as well, the ruler's status vis-à-vis the leading raiyats had to be ascertained. Links to the lower levels of society were maintained by direct support (in cash or shares of the harvest) and the funding of charitable institutions. Here again, the Ramnad zamindari provides a good example. Baker explains that the raja had "a long list of functionaries paid either in cash or in shares of the harvest, including messengers, irrigation overseers, paddy measurers, various guards and watchmen, potters, carpenters, smiths, washermen, shoemakers, and shepherds" (1976: 37). The charitable institutions comprised, among others, choultries and chattrams, but also houses where the poor and needy were fed. All these activities were financed by revenues from the royal estate. In addition to sponsoring these institutions, the zamindars' concern with status also meant that they continued, and sometimes extended, their earlier patronage of temples and other religious endowments, and also of the arts, particularly music and literature.

Besides other functions, music and literature served to provide amusements at the many large-scale festivals the kings organized. As their negotiations of status and authority acquired a very different character under colonial impact, courtly patronage of literature was one of the venerable traditions the king could revert to. Viewed from such a wider perspective, the zamindars had, of course, "inherited" the institution of maintaining poets at their courts. Already during the medieval period, poets and their compositions played an important role in the context of wider royal representational practices of which they were an integral part.[6] As the ruler's royal status was one that was constantly threatened, from both inside and outside the kingdom, the king's power needed to be demonstrated again and again to show that he was still a justified ruler. Even regardless of any threats, kingship in medieval South India entailed that royalty was overtly displayed and made palpable for the court, the king's entire realm, and also his enemies. In order to do to this, the king relied upon a whole *sign system* of courtly representational practices which included not only courtly poetry and general patronage of the arts, but also royal processions, the systematic and calculated giving of gifts (Skt. *dāna*), or religious and secular festivals. All these were highly ritualized undertakings linked to occasions on which the ruler would show himself before his people and thus communicate his claims to authority. While festivals were organized as a token of the ruler's grandeur and/or religious attachments, and processions served to delineate, at least symbolically, the geographical extension of the realm, literature, as the concern with refined and carefully "embellished" language, formed part of the ruler's endeavor to distinguish himself from the ordinary, to fashion his royal self as ornamental, and led to the institution of court poets who could immortalize the king and his fame in their verses. Such acts of display—whether perceived primarily through the eye or the ear—would seek to establish a contact between the ruler and the ruled through a common representational idiom, a common repertory of signs with which both parties needed to be familiar. In this system of communication much depended on the royal body (clothes, ornaments, insignia) as the physical manifestation of royal power, as well as on the king's demeanor, gestures, and rhetorics.[7]

But what was said before and *about* him was no less important. Besides the obvious function of entertaining and amusing the court, courtly poetry served as a vehicle to underscore the king's authority by

6. See Shulman (2001a) for an outline of the historical development of royal patronage from the Caṅkam age to the Nāyaka period.

7. For a study of royal representational practices in early medieval India, see Ali (2004a). The importance of the royal body during the nineteenth century is discussed in Waghorne (1994).

praising his generosity, valor, wisdom and erudition, and particularly his physical beauty and sexual prowess. Poets actually *did things* with the words they used, and they did them not only to the ruler but also to the audience. As other ritualized forms of courtly behavior (e.g., festivals, hunting expeditions, processions), the performance of literature created and reinforced a group identity and thus had an integrating function for those at court and a separating function toward those outside. The audience was part of a "community" which included the poet as perfomer as well as the king himself, for speaking of the king and his qualities was also to speak about those who surrounded him. A *common* act of representation always implies that the identities of both ruler and subjects are constituted. Courtly literature, then, did not simply portray life at court in a *re*-presentation of what was already constituted as a given reality. Instead, Indian court poetry to a decisive degree structured and constituted the inner makeup of the people at court and thus influenced their ideas of the world. As a quasi-heuristic device, courtly poetry determined how people at court perceived and interpreted what they saw around themselves.[8]

This reality-constituting potential of courtly literature was true for the medieval and perhaps also the Nāyaka periods. But was it still true for the nineteenth century, a time where so much had changed? In their discussion of the Maratha rule in Thanjavur (mid-1670s to 1855), Velcheru Narayana Rao, David Shulman, and Sanjay Subrahmanyam highlight the striking continuities with earlier cultural formations: "In poetry, music, and erudition, in devotional forms, in the rampant symbolism of the royal court, the Nāyakas' power could still be felt" (1998: 317). They further name the identification of the king as an avatar, his consumptive and erotic excess, and the earlier "experimentation with new [literary] genres" as continuing courtly features (315–17). On the other hand, they add that throughout the Maratha period "[f]or many reasons, royal rhetoric sounds increasingly empty" (315). Now, Pamela Price's work on Ramnad has already shown that "empty" is certainly too negative a term to describe the considerable impact which the royal families and their practices had

8. Despite India's great wealth of courtly literatures, historians have only very recently begun to ask questions regarding the function of literature in a courtly environment and its relation toward other forms of courtly representation. Important in this respect is Ali (2004a) who deals with a variety of (mostly Sanskrit) sources from the early medieval period. In the absence of further literature dealing with Indian contexts, my argument also draws on current research done on medieval European societies where we are faced with comparable problems. For a useful discussion of literature as a specific medium of courtly representation, see e.g., Ortmann/Ragotzky (1990).

on nineteenth-century South Indian society (1996). But in order to be able to assess how "royal rhetoric" was related to the zamindars' historical reality, we will have to take a closer look at the actual texts and the imaginary worlds court poets conjured up during this period. Before we can discuss the content of courtly literature, however, we need to further describe the institutional moorings in which such literature was produced—the system of courtly patronage.

The System of Literary Patronage at the Zamindars' Courts

How then were the zamindars and their poets bound up in a system of patronage? What did this system include, and what role did the audience play? How was a court poet expected to behave vis-à-vis his patron? And what could the patron do? Surprisingly, I have not been able to find a comprehensive theory of literary patronage anywhere, despite its importance in a large number of literary cultures at different times and places.[9] While it cannot be the task of the present study to fill such a theoretical lacuna, we may extract some important points from the existing body of theoretical musings on patronage in general, in order to arrive at a fuller understanding of what happened in the nineteenth-century South Indian context. Barbara Stoler Miller and Richard Eaton view patronage as a specific form of socio-political organization, or as "a multi-dimensional, sometimes loosely codified network of exchanges involving not only the production of art and literature, but also its performance, transmission, reinterpretation, and preservation" (Stoler Miller 1992: 3). This definition is useful in that it stresses multidimensionality, instead of a bilateral person-to-person relationship between patron and poet, and in that it includes whatever happens to the work *after* its creation. What is missing here, for our purposes, is first a specification of the actors in the network between whom the exchanges actually take place. As we shall see, the actors involved in the system of royal patronage consisted of the king as patron, the poet as beneficiary as well as fellow pulavars and peers who also received sponsorship, and—importantly—the court (or sometimes even a larger "public") as the audience without which the display of royal generosity would have remained unnoticed. Secondly,

9. Early studies of literary patronage, such as Schirmer/Broich (1962), are generally remarkably devoid of theoretical reflections. The absence of theoretical considerations in the field of literary patronage studies is also lamented by Griffin (1996: 13).

the definition fails to specify the nature of the exchanges that took place between the three actors. Here, another attempt at a definition might come in. In his study of literary patronage in seventeenth- and eighteenth-century England, Dustin Griffin has defined it, in rather general terms, as "a systematic economic arrangement, a complex exchange of benefit to both patron and client" (1996: 13), while he modifies the term "economic" by talking of "cultural economics" to "suggest that patronage is not simply money and housing in exchange for printed dedications" (ibid.). Griffin further emphasizes that what is actually at stake for the patron besides material gifts is what Pierre Bourdieu has famously called "symbolic capital," i.e., he links patronage to questions of hierarchical status and authority. This, then, is the point where we may, once again, draw on the concept of the "economy of praise" developed in the previous chapter. Like those pulavars who were patronized by religious institutions, wealthy individuals or caste groups, court poets, too, negotiated "praise" with their patrons and amongst each other. So, at one level, surely, royal patronage consisted in remunerating poets for composing works on religious or erotic themes or as courtly panegyrics. Poets would receive material gifts in the form of money, food, clothes (including honorary shawls), jewels and other ornaments, palanquins, and even land for their services. But if court poetry was employed to negotiate "praise," its function was more complex than a single-sided elevation of the king. The poet himself acquired distinction and gained prestige as he (and not someone else) was patronized by the king. And patronage of poets and other artists was not an *option* that a king could choose. Since largesse was one of the important characteristics of royal behavior, the king was obliged to be a patron, whether he wanted to be one or not. As may be expected in such a scenario, this compulsory generosity was amply exploited by poets who received gifts even for mediocre verses. In his autobiography, U. Vē. Cāminātaiyar recalls his encounter with a pompous, dimwitted poet who arrived in the village in a palanquin and with an entourage of disciples and servants. He announced himself as the court poet of Piratāpa Cimma Makārāja and poet laureate (*varakavi*), but quickly turned out to be a man "without the slightest training in grammar or literature. He would earn money by singing old stanzas into which he inserted here and there the name of wealthy men whom he visited, thus pretending that the poem was newly composed just for them" (*EC* 98). To make it worse, he also recited curses on those who refused to give money. As those curses were taken very seriously, he usually succeeded in "making" new patrons.

Another striking example of how the pulavar could manipulate his patron is provided by the lines quoted at the beginning of this chapter. Again in Cāminātaiyar's autobiography we find the story of the famous poet and musician Kaṉam Kiruṣṇaiyar who one day felt that his art was not sufficiently appreciated by his princely patron, the zamindar of Uṭaiyārpāḷaiyam, Kaccik Kalyāṇaraṅka Uṭaiyār.[10] He composed a song to voice his complaint in the form of a concubine addressing her careless lover:

> Ten bags full of pearls and diamond pendants
> And bag after bag full of money you have pretended
> To give me for the songs that I sang and my dancing!
> Enough, now I have realized what I got! [3.1]

As expected, the zamindar was greatly moved. He knew that the poet could have left him to go to some other court and live in royal luxury, had he wanted to. But he had never asked for any favors other than the zamindar's affection. Remorsefully, the zamindar thought "We forgot how famous we have become because of him!" and he apologized for his behavior. Having obtained what he wanted, Kaṉam Kiruṣṇaiyar instantly altered the song slightly:

> With ten bags full of pearls and diamond pendants
> You have supported me and made me happy,
> O great king, you know the pleasures of amorous talk
> And playful caresses on a soft cushion! [3.2]

As he sang thus, the zamindar smiled: "How music and verse always serve you as you please!" And when the poet replied with a laugh "Am I a zamindar? Who else do I have to serve me? Who will bow to my command?" the zamindar said: "Here you have me! And there are a thousand people who would bow their heads at your command of music." The four lines of this song emblematically reflect the patronage at South Indian royal courts. The poet does not only enumerate some typical gifts given by patrons, but he also praises the patron as a skilled lover. The theme of the king as an erotic paragon, or in more general terms the nexus between royal status and eroticism, was, as we shall see in a moment, a standard, traditional topic to be taken up in nineteenth-century Tamil courtly literature.

While thus a king could not easily refuse the poet's services, the poet, as the remorseful zamindar realized, was relatively free to choose his patron. Poets could take both their skills and reputation with them

---

10. *EC* (25f.). Cāminātaiyar has also written a small biography of Kaṉam Kiruṣṇaiyar which recounts this incident; see Cāminātaiyar (1936: 55–58).

and seek the favor of some other ruler if they were dissatisfied with their condition. As we shall see, this is indeed what happened during the course of the century when the zamindars found themselves increasingly financially limited and pulavars found new occupations as book editors and language teachers. In any case, poets frequently traveled from one court to another, thus seeking various patrons to accumulate gifts. There was, of course, the possibility to become an official, permanent court poet (*camastāṉa vittuvāṉ*), but these positions of high rank and honor were, as may be expected, rather limited.[11] As the extant body of courtly literature shows, most nineteenth-century Tamil poets composed works on more than one patron. The zamindari courts were swarmed by various pulavars and musicians who traveled from patron to patron.

The poets not only chose their patrons to gain material benefits from them. They also obtained honorary titles as markers of their high status and specific "symbolic capital." These honorary titles were many, such as *varakavi* "(divinely) gifted poet," *nāvalar* "eloquent one," *makāvittuvāṉ* "great scholar," *kavicciṅkam* "lion among poets," *kavirattiṉam* "jewel among poets," or *kaviccakkaravartti* "emperor among poets," but it is difficult to determine their specific significance, or why a particular title was given to a particular poet.[12] What is clear, however, is the distinction that such a title would convey, so that the poets typically responded with a poem celebrating the generosity of their patron. Thus, the Ramnad court poet Māmpaḷak Kaviccińka Nāvalar upon receiving the title *kaviccińkam* from his patron Poṉṉuccāmit Tēvar, praised him with the following verse:

> He with the shining spear surrounded by kites,[13] the
> golden Mount Meru,
> The merciful raincloud, Poṉṉuccāmi, the lord of the
> flourishing Southern Putuvai,
> Has given me the title "lion among poets" whose power
> is coveted everywhere,

11. From the available sources it is difficult to estimate how many poets were *camastāṉa vittuvāṉs* at a particular court at any given time. All we can say is that the large and more powerful kingdoms, such as Ramnad, Tanjore, or Pudukkottai, tended to employ more poets and give more lavish gifts than smaller zamindaris could afford to.

12. Note that also the colonial government participated in the game by conferring titles, such as *'makāmakōpātyāyar'* and others. Perhaps the most famous recipient of this distinction was U. Vē. Cāminātaiyar.

13. The implication of this conceit is that kites surround the spear as they are attracted by the pieces of flesh sticking to the blade after it has been used in battle to kill one's enemies.

And also beautiful, supreme garments praised [by all]
which display his kindness,
And thus he has patronized me (Paḻaniccāmi 1908: 47)
[3.3].

Such verses served the double purpose of extolling *both* patron and poet, royal generosity and poetic excellence, at the same time. They also projected a special bond between the two used to demarcate specific positions at the royal court. What mattered was how one was perceived by others in a hierarchically organized society.

The poets, in turn, had a large number of standardized epithets for their patrons, praising them variously as *vaḷḷal* "patron," *māl* "great man," *caratamāl* "lord of truth," *mativallōṉ* "man of mighty intellect," or with various, often Sanskrit, synonyms for "king," e.g., *maṉṉaṉ* "lord of the earth," *pūpālaṉ* or *pūpaṉ* "earth-protector," *narēntiraṉ* "lord of mankind," *taḷaciṅkam* "warrior lion," *turaicciṅkam* "lion of nobles," *ceyaciṅkam* "lion of victory," or *rajēntiravuttamaṉ* "highest among lords of kings." These epithets were applied in a highly conventionalized manner to refer to the protagonist of courtly literary genres. As we have seen in the case of the *Kuḷattūrkkōvai*, Mīṉāṭcicuntaram Piḷḷai's composition for his friend, the judge Vētanāyakam Piḷḷai, they ultimately served to praise any kind of patron, not just real kings.[14] But whenever they did refer to a real king, they were audible tokens of royal status in the overarching sign system of courtly representation.

At another level, these epithets highlight the fact that the texts themselves bear traces of the patron-client relationship. From a very early point onward, the patronage system must have been so powerful that it resulted in the poetic convention of incorporating the patron as a second "hero" of a poem, or *pāṭṭuṭait talaivaṉ*, besides the protagonist or *kiḷavit talaivaṉ*.[15] Typically, the story of a narrative *pirapantam* work unfolds against the backdrop of the *pāṭṭuṭait talaivaṉ*'s country

14. Consequently, when Pamela Price (1996: 93) argues that Poṉṉuccāmit Tēvar's concern to style himself *maṉṉar* or *pūpālaṉ* "king" and *vaḷḷal* "liberal patron" becomes apparent from one of the poems written on him by his court poet Cantiracēkara Kavirāyar, too much is read into what was in fact a poetic convention. The argument may even be reversed: If at all Poṉṉuccāmi had such aspirations, he could style himself "king" only because of the poetic tradition which allowed this cipher to be taken up by him.

15. The distinction between *pāṭṭuṭait talaivaṉ* and *kiḷavit talaivaṉ* depends on the arrangement of *akam* themes into a linear sequence as in the *kōvai* genre, and it seems that it was first made in Nakkīrar's commentary on *Iṟaiyaṉār Akapporuḷ* which uses the earliest extant *kōvai* work, *Pāṇṭikkōvai*, as an example (see Paramasivam/Buck 1997). The distinction is further elaborated in the thirteenth-century treatise on *akam* poetics *Akapporuḷ Viḷakkam* alias *Nampiyakapporuḷ*. For further details regarding the historical development of *akam* poetics, see Parthasarathi (1990) and Manuel (1997).

or town. If he is a king or some other powerful chief who actually rules a particular stretch of land, this of course makes sense. But as we have seen in the case of the *Kuḷattūrkkōvai*, where the lovers meet on Vētanāyakam's (nonexistent) hill, it may sometimes result in mere insistence on the rules of poetics. In any case, the locale of the *pāṭṭuṭait talaivaṉ* is always described employing the picturesque Indian counterpart of a *locus amoenus* topos. We hear of the country's fertility and luxuriant vegetation where the southern wind carries the fragrance of beautiful flowers and bushes swarmed by bees over gliding rivers and lotus ponds. In a similar vein, the town is prosperous with ample streets of decorated houses and golden pavillions inlaid with precious stones. The poets frequently refer to the realm of the gods to find similes for the beauty depicted. Thus, the town is likened to the splendors of the city of Kubera, the god of riches, or the country to Śiva's abode Mount Kailāsa. All these lavish descriptions of nature are fraught with a heavy symbolism of kingly splendor and opulence, often connected to the erotic mood of poetry (Skt. *śṛṅgāra rasa*).

In addition to these depictions of the local setting, there are set places in the overall structure of a *pirapantam* where descriptions of the patron may be inserted. One of these is a more or less standardized tableau: the section on "the ten limbs" or ten constituents of a kingdom (*tacāṅkam*). The *tacāṅkam* is also known as a fully-fledged *pirapantam* genre in itself, but originally it was found as part of other works, notably the *ulā* literature which describes the varied reactions of women of different ages seeing a royal procession. The ten constituents generally depicted are the king's mountain, river, country (as habitable land, *nāṭu*), town, horse, elephant, garland, war drum, banner, and scepter. Such a systematic enumeration—as a stereotyped element of a larger composition—serves as a blueprint for a standardized mode of extolling the king. It is a checklist with readymade slots that the poetic tradition provides for the poet to fill in. But it is also a very real list of royal emblems as *signs* of nobility and power, some of which appear as standard insignia, e.g., in royal processions. These emblems *re*-present as visible tokens the totality of royal power in its various aspects, such as fertility and wealth, protection of the subjects, physical beauty, and prowess in warfare.

A "Who Is Who" of Nineteenth-Century Royal Patrons and Their Poets

To demonstrate the extent and variety of the zamindars' patronage of Tamil literature during the nineteenth century it will be useful to briefly survey the activities of the most important rulers. Although there exists a considerable literature on several of the estates and "kingdoms" in the Tamil-speaking area, specific information on literary patronage is generally very hard to come by. Therefore, I have attempted to provide as many prosopographical details as the scope of this chapter allowed. In what had to remain a preliminary survey, I have identified the most important men who were either temporarily sponsored or permanently employed as court poets (*camastāṉa vittuvāṉs*).[16] While this section focuses primarily on the patrons and the poets they sponsored, the content of nineteenth-century courtly literature will be discussed in depth in a separate section.

Thanjavur

One may begin a systematic overview of the various courts which were involved in literary sponsorship with the largest and perhaps most famous court: that of the Maratha rulers in Thanjavur (Tanjore, Tam. Tañcāvūr, Tañcai) which flourished from the mid-1670s to 1855.[17] The period under analysis here—the last fifty years prior to the kingdom's final annexation to British India by Lord Dalhousie—may be regarded as the final flourish of a courtly culture which had developed through the centuries, sponsoring literature in various languages (Marathi, Sanskrit, Tamil, Telugu), music, drama, and dance as well as natural sciences and medicine. The atmosphere at the court had always been a multilingual, even multicultural one. But it has to be

16. The preliminary nature of this survey is due to the problem that the two major extant kinds of sources for prosopographical data have not yet been systematically analyzed. Firstly, information can be culled from the elaborate genealogical details on title pages of nineteenth-century printed books. Secondly, the *ciṟappuppāyiram* stanzas published in these books or in later collections of solitary stanzas (*taṉippāṭal*) are also valuable sources, as are the *taṉippāṭal* collections themselves (particularly *TCC* and *TPT*). Due to the sheer amount of materials available, my survey could not be comprehensive.

17. On the general history of the Maratha rulers in Thanjavur see the classical accounts by Hickey (1988) and Srinivasan (1944), as well as Subramanian (1988). Two publications in Tamil which both contain English summaries may be added: Vēṅkaṭarāmaiyā (1984; 1987). The two general histories of Tamil Nadu, Rajayyan (1982) and Subrahmanian (1984, esp. ch. 6), also provide valuable information. The transition from the Nāyakas to the Marathas is briefly outlined in Narayana Rao et al. (1998: 313–318), while the court's fiscal decline during the eighteenth century is discussed in Subrahmanyam (2001, ch. 5). The events that led to Serfoji's loss of power vis-à-vis the British in 1799 form the subject of Rajayyan (1969). Seetha (2001) provides an overview of the important musical activities at the court. The courtly literature composed in Marathi is briefly discussed in Tulpule (1979, chs. 31 and 32). On Telugu court literature, see Narayana Rao and Shulman (2002) and Venkata Rao (1978, ch. 2.II).

said very clearly that the Maratha court was by no means a typical example of nineteenth-century court culture. Its exceptional position was largely due to the unparalleled pursuits of the most celebrated of its rulers, King Serfoji II (1777–1832, Tam. Carapōji, Mar. Sarfojī). He ruled from 1798 until his death and had profited as a young boy from a European education imparted by the German missionary Christian Friedrich Schwartz (1726–1798).[18] He was noted not only as one of the greatest sponsors of the arts and (indigenous as well as European) sciences, but also as an enlightened personality who deeply impressed his contemporaries. In sharp contrast to his political power, Serfoji's efforts to sponsor and promote the arts and sciences were so remarkable that a relatively large amount of secondary literature has tried to capture and document it.[19] However, with regard to the specific question of sponsorship of Tamil poets, the literature becomes scarce.[20] Perhaps the most important Tamil poet at Serfoji's court was the protestant Vētanāyaka Cāstiri (1774–1864) who was appointed court poet in 1830. Due to his specific role as a Christian writer and since he has been well-served in Indira Peterson's recent work, I venture to pass him by.[21] The second important poet was Koṭṭaiyūr Civakkoḻuntu Tēcikar (c. 1770–1860) who became the head pulavar at Serfoji's court and librarian of the king's famous Saraswati Mahal library. Unfortunately, very little is known about his life.[22] Like other pulavars employed by the king to cater to his curiosity in the

18. On Schwartz, see Anonymous (1901), Frykenberg (1999), and Jeyaraj (1999).

19. See the literature cited in Peterson (1999a; 1999b; 2003; 2004) and Nair (2005).

20. Efforts have been made to systematically catalogue and describe the Tamil literature produced under the Thanjavur Maratha kings (see Aṟivuṭainampi 1994), but the series has not progressed beyond the first volume. Given such absence of comprehensive surveys, the manuscript catalogues of the Saraswathi Mahal Library published from 1925 onwards (see e.g., Olaganatha Pillay 1964) and the library journal remain valuable sources of information. All in all, it seems that among the extant works produced at the Thanjavur court there are more texts in Sanskrit, Telugu, and Marathi than in Tamil, and more texts were produced during the seventeenth and eighteenth than during the nineteenth century, notably under the patronage of King Śāhāji (r. 1684–1712).

21. See Peterson (2002; 2004) and the literature cited there. Additionally, see Hudson (2000, ch. 8), Dayanandan Francis (1998), Cuntararācaṉ (1996, ch. 6), and Pākkiyamaṇi (1999).

22. We know that his father was a certain Taṇṭapāṇi Tēcikar. Civakkoḻuntu Tēcikar himself lived till the age of ninety, had two wives, two sons, and five daughters. His second son, Cāmināta Tēcikar, was a student of Mīṉāṭcicuntaram Piḷḷai's and in 1864 became Tamil pandit in Kumbakonam College. For a biographical sketch, see also Irāmacāmip Pulavar (1955b: 16–19). On Civakkoḻuntu Tēcikar's work as a pandit in the college of Fort St. George, see the discussion below.

field of medical sciences, Civakkoḻuntu Tēcikar wrote medical works: *Carapēntirar vaittiya muṟaikaḷ*, *Carapēntirar caṉṉirōka cikiccaikaḷ* (written in 1826), and *Carapēntirar vaittiyam*. Moreover, he also composed various *pirapantam* poems. The three most popular of these were edited with commentaries and analyses in 1932 by U. Vē. Cāminātaiyar: *Kōṭīccurakkōvai* is a typical *akapporuṭkōvai* text in 444 stanzas which closely resembles Mīṉāṭcicuntaram Piḷḷai's *Kuḷattūrkkōvai* discussed in the previous chapter. The *pāṭṭuṭaittalaivaṉ* is Śiva as Kōṭīccurar, the deity in Civakkoḻuntu Tēcikar's birthplace Koṭṭaiyūr.[23] The second text, the *Tañcaip peruvuṭaiyārulā*, describes in 313 couplets (*kaṇṇis*) the splendid parade of Śiva as Bṛhadīśvara, the deity of the Great Temple in Thanjavur. As Lord Śiva is the hero of the work, the patron king Serfoji does not feature prominently in the poem. He is only obliquely mentioned in one stanza as "the king of the charming great city of Thanjavur wielding his sceptre upon the entire beautiful four-fold earth."[24] As a matter of course, such conventional epithets do not tell us much about historical realities. More interesting from the point of view of royal patronage is the *Carapēntira pūpāla kuṟavañci nāṭakam*, a fortune-teller "dance drama" (*kuṟavañci*) which describes how the beautiful courtesan Mataṉavalli falls in love with king Serfoji as she sees him in procession. She pines for him and suffers until her love is finally fulfilled through the intercession of her confidante. A female fortune-teller predicts this happy ending.[25] The play was regularly enacted during the *brahmotsava* festivals in Thanjavur and is said to have been premiered in the Great Temple (Seetha 2001: 245f.). The text abounds with lavish descriptions of the king, his parade and court, as well as typical topoi of erotic poetry (e.g., the love-sick heroine being unable to bear the cooling rays of the moon or the soothing breeze). Interestingly, the text reflects the multilingual atmosphere at Serfoji's court, when the fortune-teller, boasting about her many customers who reward her generously, recounts how women come to her from far and near asking her in various languages to read

23. See also the analysis in Cāminātaiyar (1932).

24. "*cantamuṟu / nāṉilamuñ ceṅkō ṉaṭattu meḻirrañcai / mānakara maṉṉaṉ*" (Cāminātaiyar 1932: 238, st. 56f.). See also the discussion of the work in Aṟivuṭainampi (1994: 53–89).

25. The text is also discussed in Aṟivuṭainampi (1994: 150–177) and by Jāṉ Ammaiyār (1967). The new edition by Cīṉivācaṉ (1988) may be considered for its prefatory matter. An edition with musical notation has been prepared by Kulēntiraṉ/Kiṭṭappā (1994). For an in-depth analysis of the *kuṟavañci* genre, see Muilwijk (1996). For the historical development of the genre, see Peterson (1998). On landscape and place in the *kuṟavañci*, see Peterson (2008).

their palms. In song 46, the phrase "Look at my hand!" is repeated in Telugu, Marathi, Kannada, Hindustani, and English. The stanza with the English version reads:

> An English lady with a bright forehead
> Said "Look [at] my hand!"
> I came running and looked at the lines in her palms,
> And she remunerated me with this girdle.
> (Cāminātaiyar 1932: 337f.) [3.4]

Civakkoḻuntu Tēcikar's other works known to us are two *sthalapurāṇas, Tiruviṭaimarutūrppurāṇam* and *Āccāpurattalapurāṇam* (see *ETL* 3: 7), and the *Kōṭīccurarulā* (*Koṭṭaiyūrulā*), which is no longer extant. In 1885, U. Vē. Cāminātaiyar published a work titled *Śrī Mattiyārccuṉa māṉmiyam*, a prose version of Civakkoḻuntu Tēcikar's *talapurāṇam* on Tiruviṭaimarutūr (alias Mattiyārccuṉam).[26]

Finally, if we omit from the list of the Thanjavur pulavars given in Aṟivuṭainampi (1994: 8–16) those who were exclusively involved in collating and editing medical texts, we are left with Umaiyammāḷpuram Aṉantapārati Aiyaṅkār (1786–1846)[27] as a court poet of Serfoji's, and Aruṇācalakkavi,[28] Nārāyaṇakkavi,[29] Kiruṭṭiṇakavi,[30] Pūraṇap Piramāṉanta Yōki,[31] and Nārāyaṇacāmi Nāvalar[32] as court poets under Serfoji's successor Sivaji II (r. 1832–1855). Among these, Aṉantapārati Aiyaṅkār is the only poet about whom we have some information.

---

26. See Cāminātaiyar (1943) and *EC* (563f.). Civakāmi (1994: 311) erroneously lists a *Mattiyārccuṉa māṉmiyam* alias *Marutavaṉa purāṇam* among Civakkoḻuntu Tēcikar's works.

27. Author of *Tiruviṭaimarutūr noṇṭināṭakam, Uttararāmāyaṇa kīrttaṉai, Pākavata tacamaskanta nāṭakam, Tēcikappirapantam* (authorship ascribed), *Yāṉaimēlaḻakar noṇṭiccintu, Marutūr veṇpā, Muppāṟṟiraṭṭu, Iṭapa vākaṉakkīrttaṉai*, and *Kallaṇai vaipavakkīrttaṉai*. See also Zvelebil (1995: 37f.), Casie Chitty (1982: 7), Māṇikkam (1974: 41), Irāmacāmip Pulavar (1955d: 114f.) and *ETL* 2 (237). His *Tiruviṭaimarutūr noṇṭināṭakam* contains a benediction of his fellow court pulavar Civakkoḻuntu Tēcikar (see Cāminātaiyar 1932: viii).

28. Author of *Mataṉacuntarappiracāta cantāṉa vilāca nāṭakam*, which has been edited by Jagannathan (1950). See also the MS 646 No. 600 listed in Olaganatha Pillay (1964: 527ff.).

29. Author of *Pāṇṭiya kēḷī vilāca nāṭakam* also edited by Jagannathan (1950). See the MS 640 No. 170(a) listed in Olaganatha Pillay (1964: 520ff.). He is also listed in Irāmacāmip Pulavar (1960a: 734).

30. Author of *Pārata ammāṉai*. See also the MSS 621–25 Nos. 59–63 listed in Olaganatha Pillay (1964: 501ff.).

31. Author of *Pirammāṉantayōki carittiram*.

32. Author of *Tirukkaṇṇapuram purāṇam* and school teacher.

Pudukkottai

Another important royal center of patronage was the kingdom of Pudukkottai (Tam. Putukkōṭṭai). The kingdom and its rulers have been the subject of two influential monographs by Nicholas Dirks and Joanne Punzo Waghorne who both have examined how royal power and practices were transformed under colonial influence.[33] Yet, we know very little about the patronage of Tamil literature at the Pudukkottai court. Joanne Waghorne relies on oral sources about palace life, when she explains:

> Members of the old families of Tamil scholars protest to this day that at the time of Ramachandra Tondaiman a process began that ended the power and position of the Tamil poets at court and replaced these ancient scholars with Sanskrit-trained Brahman pandits. They charge that while traditionally the raja in durbar honored Tamil scholars and poets with shawls, those special gifts were later given to the Brahmans. (1994: 73)

Irāmaccantirat Toṇṭaimāṉ (1829–1886), whose portrait by master painter Ravi Varma has been discussed above in the Introduction, occupied the throne from 1839 to 1886. While I have not found any sources which would prove that Tamil poets really had manifest "power and position" during earlier times, there is another source which mentions the sponsorship of Sanskrit scholars. In 1877, the brahmin A. Cēṣaiyā Cāstiri, who had formerly served as dewan (manager of estate) in the native state of Travancore and who was held in high esteem by the British, became dewan of Pudukkottai.[34] U. Vē. Cāminātaiyar recounts how, under Cēṣaiyā Cāstiri's dewanship, on the occasion of the Navarattiri festival scholars of Sanskrit and music were examined as to the extent of their knowledge and subsequently honored with gifts of up to 100 Rs. (1957, ch. 6). It is not clear from Cāminātaiyar's account whether Tamil poets were honored too.[35] In the available

33. See Dirks (1987) and Waghorne (1994), as well as an earlier version of the latter (Waghorne 1989). For the general history of the kingdom, see also Radhakrishna Aiyar (1916) and Cirañcīvi (1981b).

34. For biographical information on Cēṣaiyā Cāstiri, see Kamesvara Aiyar (1902) and Menon (1903).

35. We do know for sure, however, that Cēṣaiyā Cāstiri sponsored the publishing ventures of several pulavars, notably Ci. Vai. Tāmōtaram Piḷḷai's and U. Vē. Cāminātaiyar's editions. See the discussion below.

literary histories, I have found a single Tamil poet who is generally recognized as a court poet of Pudukkottai during the nineteenth century. This is Paṉaiyañcēri Murukēcak Kavirāyar (1792–1888), the son of one Paracurāma Piḷḷai, who is credited with various shorter *pirapantams*, viz. an *āṉantakkaḷippu*, a *pañcarattiṉamālai*, a *cintu*, a *carittira akaval* on a deity called Ulakanātacāmi, and a number of occasional stanzas.[36] Furthermore, in the biography of his teacher, U. Vē. Cāminātaiyar mentions that on one occasion Mīṉāṭcicuntaram Piḷḷai stayed in the palace of Pudukkottai for an entire month. He composed five stanzas on the generosity of the first queen, Janaki Subbamma Bai Sahib, but these verses are no longer extant (*SMPC* II: 202).[37] Finally, Mayilai Cīṉi. Vēṅkaṭacāmi tells us that a certain Maḻavarāyaṉēntal Citampara Pāratiyār (alias Ciṉṉaccāmi Pāratiyār, d. 1897) frequently received gifts from the king of Pudukkottai as well as from the zamindars of Ramnad and Sivagangai (1962: 221f.). His works are *Amparīṭa carittiram, Kucēla carittiram, Turuva carittiram, Urukkumaṇi kaliyāṇam, Ñāṉāṉantap pēriṉpak kīrttaṉai, Periyapurāṇak kīrttaṉai, Tirukkōkarṇam Pirakatāmpāḷ palacantak kummi, Maturai Mīṉāṭciyammai palacantak kummi, Mayūrakirinātar vaṇṇam*, and *Kuṉṟakkuṭikkumaraṉ vaṇṇam*.[38]

Ramnad and Sivagangai

In the standard accounts of nineteenth-century Tamil literature, the rulers (*cētupatis*) of Ramnad (Irāmanātapuram) figure most prominently as patrons of art and literature.[39] Emphasizing continuity with earlier royal traditions, A. V. Subramania Aiyar remarks, that the

36. See Vēṅkaṭacāmi (1962: 196), Civakāmi (1994: 358), and Irāmacāmip Pulavar (1958a: 59f.). His *pirapantams* were first published in Madras in 1866 (see Murukēcak Kavirāyar 1866). His occasional stanzas are collected in *TCC* (409–411).

37. Cāminātaiyar also mentions one Kaṇapati Kavirāyar as a Pudukkottai court poet (ibid.), but he is listed nowhere in the available reference works. It is possible that he is the same Kaṇapati Kavirāyar who was a court poet of the Cēṟṟūr zamindar and who is discussed below.

38. See also Paḻaniyappaṉ/Paḻani (1984: 408), Irāmacāmip Pulavar (1956c: 54–56), and Civakāmi (1994: 311).

39. See for example Civakāmi (1994: 23). There is a considerable literature on the history of the Ramnad kingdom. See Thiruvenkatachari (1959), Kadhirvel (1977), Cirañcīvi (1981a), Breckenridge (1978), the works by the Ramnad court historian Es. Kamāl (1987; 1989; 1992; 2001; 2002; 2003), Kamāl/Mukammatu Cerīpu (1984), and finally the pathbreaking study by Pamela Price (1996). In a fine art-historical study, Jennifer Howes (2003) has examined the Ramnad Palace architecture and notably the wall paintings inside the palace. For Ramnad's "interaction" with the Dutch East India Company in the eighteenth century, see Bes (2001).

"Sethupathys had maintained a continual line of Court poets whose number and work is legion" (1969: 82). In a similarly enthusiastic vein, S. Thiruvenkatachari points out that "[b]esides maintaining scholars and poets in their own courts as Asthana Vidwans, the Setupatis patronized Tamil scholarship wherever it was found in the Tamil country" (1959: 104).[40] This long tradition of literary and scholarly patronage is reflected in the considerable amount of literary works connected in some way or other to the Ramnad court, which have been preserved to the present day. Ramnad's literary patronage during the nineteenth century, then, rested firmly on a tradition of more than a century before.[41] Three men were particularly important patrons: the Raja of Ramnad named Muttu Rāmaliṅka Cētupati (1841–1873), Poṉṉuccāmit Tēvar (1837–1870), his elder brother and manager of estate (dewan), and the son of the latter, Pāṇṭitturait Tēvar (1867–1911), the zamindar of Pālavaṉattam.[42] While the raja Muttu Rāmaliṅka Cētupati himself composed several *pirapantam* works in Tamil as well as songs in Sanskrit and Hindustani,[43] his manager Poṉṉuccāmit Tēvar was the more active patron of music, poetry, and Tamil scholarly endeavors.[44] Pamela Price discusses Poṉṉuccāmi's ambitions to secure royal status for himself, caught up as he was in the imbroglios of royal succession

40. The *cētupatis'* contributions to Tamil literature and culture are also briefly summarized in Seshadri (1979) who copied much from Thiruvenkatachari's chapter on literary patronage (1959: 95–106), including numerous mistakes. A classical essay by one of the pulavars associated with the court is Irākavaiyaṅkār (1928). See also the essays in Muttuccāmi (1994).

41. Christopher Baker has highlighted the special role of the Ramnad kingdom vis-à-vis the other estates: "More than any other zamindar, the raja of Ramnad needed to maintain the memory of his family's historical role and the raja's attentions had always focused less on economic welfare and more on the trappings of his ancestral 'royalty' " (1976: 36). The patronage of Tamil literature and scholarship, and in particular the creation of a body of "courtly" literature, played a decisive part in refreshing the collective memory of the humbler members of his territories.

42. For a biography of Poṉṉuccāmit Tēvar and his son Pāṇṭitturait Tēvar, see Irākavaiyaṅkār (1951). See also Irāmacāmip Pulavar (1965: 78–97) on Poṉṉuccāmi, and Irāmacāmip Pulavar (1956a: 61–63) on Muttu Rāmaliṅka Cētupati.

43 Irākavaiyaṅkār (1951: 34f.) mentions the titles *Murukaraṉupūti, Pirapākaramālai, Vaḷḷimaṇamālai* (in 208 *veṇpā* stanzas), *Caraca Callāpamālai, Nītipōtakaveṇpā,* and the two books of *kīrttaṉais Kāyakappiriyā* and *Rasikarañcaṉam.* Vēṅkaṭacāmi (1962: 195, 201) adds *Caṭākkara Cārappatikam* and *Pālapōtam.* No less than 308 *taṉippāṭals* of his are collected in *TCC* (284–336). See also *TPT* 2 (276–88).

44. Poṉṉuccāmit Tēvar is said to have composed a work named *Alaṅkārak kōvai,* which is no longer extant (*ETL* 2: 439f.). His occasional stanzas are contained in *TCC* (451–461) and *TPT* 4 (127–131).

disputes. She interprets his lavish patronage as his effort to "go outside the arena of [royal] ritual to show his grandeur" (1996: 92). As has been stated above, however, patronage of arts and literature itself had always been an integral part of royal ritual, and a look at the poets' compositions suggests that the literature composed for Poṉṉuccāmi is not much different from what was written in praise of Muttu Rāmaliṅka Cētupati or, in fact, in praise of any other royal patron. Thus Poṉṉuccāmi's patronage of literary and scholarly activities was, in the semantics of courtly ostentation, a typically royal endeavor, or, in other words, a deliberate *sign* of his royal status.

In order to broaden his own knowledge of Tamil literature, Poṉṉuccāmi frequently engaged in learned disputes with his court poets and scholars, amongst whom we find Māmpaḻak Kaviccinka Nāvalar (1836–1884), Tuvātrīm Tacāvatāṉam Caravaṇap Perumāḷ Kavirāyar alias Ciṟiya Caravaṇap Perumāḷ Kavirāyar (d. 1886 or 1888), Tillaiyampūr Cantiracēkara Kavirāyar (d. 1883), and the Sanskrit poet Makāmakōpātyāyar Rajū Cāstirikaḷ.[45] Māmpaḻak Kaviccinka Nāvalar, certainly the most famous of the Ramnad court poets, was a blind poet who regularly stunned his courtly audience by his verbal feats and expertise in composing ornate poems and thus obtained the title *kavicciṅkam* "lion of poets" from his patron Poṉṉuccāmit Tēvar. What we know about his life is not much:[46] He was born in Paḻaṉi as the second son of one Muttaiyā Āccāri and his wife Ammaṇiyammāḷ in 1836. He lost his eyesight while suffering from smallpox at the age of three, but his father insisted that he obtain a decent education and taught him Tamil by writing out the alphabet with his fingers on his son's back. Later on, the young boy was further educated in Tamil by one Mārimuttuk Kavirāyar and in Sanskrit by Cupparāya Pāratiyar and Irāmacāmi Aiyar. Due to his great talent and abilities in both languages, the child prodigy quickly attracted wealthy men who sponsored him. The first of these sponsors was one Veṅkaṭacāmi Nāyakkar from Pāppampaṭṭi on whom he composed a number of praise poems, including a *kuṟavañci*. When Māmpaḻak Kaviccinka Nāvalar heard of the lavish patronage pulavars enjoyed at the Ramnad court, he knew that this was where he wanted to be. But since blind people were considered inauspicious at the court, it was not easy for him to

45. See Irākavaiyaṅkār (1951: 39–48).

46. My account is based on what is told by Paḻaniccāmi (1908) and on the later biographical sketches by Irāmacāmip Pulavar (1953: 97–119) and Cāmpacivaṉ (1961, ch. 4), which are both largely based on the former. A curiosity is Caravaṇapavāṉantar (1970b) who has written a short biography of Māmpaḻak Kaviccinka Nāvalar consisting of prose passages in poetic style interspersed with songs.

be admitted. According to his biographers, his great moment arrived when one day Poṉṉuccāmit Tēvar wanted his court poets to "translate" a Sanskrit *stotra* (praise poem) on goddess Lakṣmī into a Tamil *veṇpā*. As Māmpaḻak Kaviccinka's verse was the only one to satisfy the dewan, the poet had found his way into the courtly world of letters, and subsequently was employed permanently as court pulavar. What we know about his life at the Ramnad court is restricted to a series of anecdotes which provide frames for his pyrotechnical poetic feats. These cover the whole gamut of pulavar brilliance discussed in the previous chapter, including not only *yamaka*, *tiripu*, and *cilēṭai*, but also *cittirakkavis* and poems in which single words are repeated several times or poems which avoid certain consonants and vowels. From his occasional stanzas we know that he was given his title "*kaviccinkam*" by Poṉṉuccāmit Tēvar and that he also received upper cloths, shawls, turbans, a parasol, and other gifts from both Poṉṉuccāmi and the Raja Muttu Rāmaliṅka Cētupati. We do not know when and why he left the Ramnad court, but we are told that he married at the age of twenty-seven and lived in Paḻaṉi until his death in 1884. Again, from his extant verses we can say that while staying in Paḻaṉi, he must have enjoyed the patronage of a number of rich men and zamindars.[47] His *magnum opus*, a Tamil *śleṣa-kāvya* titled *Cantiravilācam*, was not written in praise of the Ramnad king, but for one Vēlappak Kavuṇṭar, the zamindar of Vēḷukkuṟicci (in modern-day Salem District).[48] At the age of twenty-one, he composed the *Tēvāṅka purāṇam*. On the request of some wealthy men in Salem town, he translated a Sanskrit *kāmaśāstra* (erotic) text, the *Sṛṅgāra-rasa-mañjarī*, into Tamil.[49] His elaborate *pirapantam* compositions and occasional stanzas were later collected and published in one volume (Paḻaniccāmi 1908).[50]

Tuvātrīm Tacāvatāṉam Caravaṇap Perumāḷ Kavirāyar alias Ciṟiya Caravaṇap Perumāḷ Kavirāyar (i.e., "C.P.K. the Younger") was born into a family of court poets, as his grandfather Aṭṭāvatāṉam Caravaṇap Perumāḷ Kavirāyar alias Periya Caravaṇap Perumāḷ Kavirāyar (i.e., "C.P.K. the Elder") had also been patronized by the Ramnad kings. Due to their name, the two have often been confused by literary historians. I have

47. In Paḻaniccāmi (1908), we find poems in praise of one Englishman named Manuel who was the tahsildar of Tiruccenkōṭu in Salem District, of the Madras High Court lawyer Kurumūrtti Ayyar, of the zamindar of Pōṭiyanāyakkaṉūr Vaṅkāru Tirumalaippōṭaya Turai, the zamindar of Maruṅkāpuri, and of many others.

48. See the discussion below.

49. I have not been able to identify the original Sanskrit source.

50. See also *TCC* (501–530) and *TPT* 2 (564–650).

dealt with this problem in Appendix 1 where I also propose a new date for Ciriya Caravaṇap Perumāḷ Kavirāyar's most important work, his *Cētupati viṟaliviṭutūtu,* which is discussed in detail below. Apart from his masterpiece, he also composed several other pirapantams, viz. *Maturaic cilēṭaiveṇpā, Kuṉṟaic cilēṭaiveṇpā, Kantavarukkac canta veṇpā, Tiruccuḻiyal ōreḻut-tantāti, Kaḻukumalai ōreḻuttantāti, Makaravantāti, Paṉacait tiripantāti, Maturai yamakavantāti, Kayaṟkaṇṇimālai, Maturai Mīṉāṭciyammaṉ Cōmacuntarakkaṭavuḷ pēril aṭimaṭakkāciriyaviruttam, Irāmāyaṇavaṇṇam* and *Puvaṉēntiraṉ ammāṉai.*[51] Tillaiyampūr Cantiracēkara Kavirāyar alias Cantiracēkara Kavirāca Paṇṭitar is remembered today chiefly for his pioneering anthology of occasional poetry published in 1878 under the title *Taṉippāṭaṟṟiraṭṭu* which he had compiled on behalf of Poṉṉuccāmit Tēvar who also sponsored its printing at the Kalāratnākaram press in Madras.[52] Besides this book, only a few occasional stanzas have survived some of which we will see below. He also composed a *mummaṇik kōvai* on the pontiff of the Tiruvāvaṭuturai ātīṉam Cuppiramaṇiya Tēcikar, and a *Tulukkāṇattammai patikam* (Civakāmi 1994: 306), and he is the author of important commentaries on older works, such as *Naṉṉūl, Yāpparuṅkalakkārikai,* and *Taṇṭiyalaṅkāram.*[53] Additionally, the available anthologies of occasional stanzas contain a large number of verses in praise of Poṉṉuccāmit Tēvar and Muttu Rāmaliṅka Cētupati by numerous other poets.

The story of Pāṇṭitturait Tēvar's munificent patronage is really the story of how the study of Tamil literature and literary history came into its own at the beginning of the twentieth century, as are the sponsoring activities of the later Ramnad zamindar Pāskara Cētupati (1868–1903).[54] Suffice it to say here that Pāṇṭitturait Tēvar continued and even extended the good work of his father, while he also composed poems himself.[55] Pāṇṭitturait Tēvar is today remembered as

51. His occasional stanzas are collected in *TCC* (346–356) and *TPT* 2 (50, 289–318). See also Irāmacāmip Pulavar (1956a: 76–79).

52. The first edition is Cantiracēkara Kavirāca Paṇṭitar (1878). Many later editions of the work followed both with and without commentaries which were newly written.

53. For a biographical sketch, see Irāmacāmip Pulavar (1955d: 61–64).

54. A very short sketch of Pāṇṭitturait Tēvar's patronage is given in Subramania Aiyar (1970: 117–119). See also Pālacuppiramaṇiyaṉ (1998: 139–157). For a biography of Pāskara Cētupati, see Kamāl (1992).

55. A few stanzas are collected in *TCC* (600–608), *TPT* 2 (725–727), and *TPT* 3 (101f.). He also composed a *Irācarācēcuvari patikam* and a *iraṭṭaimaṇi mālai* on the eighteenth-century philosopher and scholar Civañāṉacuvāmi alias Civañāṉamuṉivar. The latter was published in 1905 (Pāṇṭitturait Tēvar 1905). His essays appeared in *Centamiḻ,* the journal of the Madurai Tamil Sangam. Moreover, he was also the compiler of several anthologies of poems, viz. *Paṉṉūṟṟiraṭṭu* (first edition in 1898), *Caivamañcari* (1904), etc.

the founder of the *Maturai Tamiḻc Caṅkam*, a scholarly association for the promotion of Tamil learning which, named after the legendary Tamil Sangams, was established in May 1901 and from 1903 onward published its well-known journal *Centamiḻ*. The journal quickly became the leading forum for Tamil scholarly discussions, and a large number of Tamil literary "classics" were printed by the Sangam. Its fascinating history—which is also the history of the many pulavars involved—still remains to be written.[56] Pāṇṭitturait Tēvar's court poets were Nārāyaṇa Aiyaṅkar (1861–1947),[57] Eṭṭaiyapuram Vīrācāmi Aiyaṅkar, Cuntarēcuvara Aiyar, and others.[58] The Srilankan poet Uṭuppiṭṭi Civacampup Pulavar (1829–1910) composed a *nāṉmaṇimālai* on Pāṇṭitturait Tēvar as well as a *nāṉmaṇimālai* and a *kallāṭak kalitturai* on Pāskara Cētupati.[59]

The zamindars of the nearby estate of Sivagangai (Civakaṅkai)[60] patronized "Cilēṭaippuli" Vēmpattūr Piccuvaiyar (alias Piccupāratikaḷ or Muttuveṅkiṭa Cuppayyar, 1850–1910), who is said to have become the court poet of Muttuvaṭukanātaturai on whom he composed a *kātal pirapantam*. He was a student of Vaṉ Toṇṭar, one of Mīṉāṭcicuntaram Piḷḷai's disciples. His other works are *Tirupparaṅkuṉṟam Murukaṉ ānantakkaḷippu, Paṉaṅkuṭip Periyanāyaki ammai patikam, Caṅkarācāriyār patikam, Poṉmāric cilēṭai veṇpā, Maturai nirōṭṭaka yamakavantāti*, and *Kuṉṟakkuṭi Caṇmukanātar ulā*.[61] The zamindar Turaiciṅka Tēvar also sponsored one Villiyappa Piḷḷai who composed a work titled

---

56. For a short sketch of the history of the Madurai Tamil Sangam, see Zvelebil (1992: 199–201). For the importance of the Tamil Sangam with regard to Tamil language devotion, see Ramaswamy (1997, esp. 220–222).

57. For his biography, see Irāmacāmip Pulavar (1955e: 58–63).

58. See Irākavaiyaṅkār (1951: 76).

59. Vēṅkaṭacāmi (1962: 217) gives his dates as (1830–1909) while Paḷaniyappaṉ/Paḷani (1984: 426) give the name as Civacampulavar and 1830 as his year of birth. Irāmacāmip Pulavar (1955a: 1f.) has the dates 1852–1910. Muttucumaraswamy (1992: 29–33) has 1829 and 29 September 1910 as his dates and lists several other works composed on behalf of Pāskara Cētupati which I have not seen. According to Civakāmi (1994: 311), he composed a *iraṭṭaimaṇi mālai* on Pāskara Cētupati, but this may be a confusion with the *nāṉmaṇimālai*. His *pirapantams* have been collected in Cevvantināta Tēcikar (1939).

60. On the history of Sivagangai, see Kamāl (1997) and Maṉōkaraṉ (1994).

61. See Paḷaniyappaṉ/Paḷani (1989: 355f.), Irāmacāmip Pulavar (1956b: 13–24), Vēṅkaṭacāmi (1962: 236), and Civakāmi (1994: 346). His occasional stanzas are collected in *TCC* (683–687), *TPT* 2 (705–706, 844–846), and *TPT* 3 (261–263). Irāmacāmip Pulavar (1956b: 17) also mentions that one Muttuvīrappap Piḷḷai was a court poet in Sivagangai, but we only find one poet with the same name in *TCC* (362) and *TPT* 2 (319–328) who is said to have been a court poet in Ramnad.

Pañcalaṭcaṇat tirumukavilācam (premiered in 1899), an intriguing satire on the great famine in South India in 1876.[62] The critic Rakunātaṉ details his futile search for biographical information on Villiyappa Piḷḷai. What he could find out was that the poet passed away at the age of sixty-seven around the year 1905 (which means that he would have been born in the 1830s or 1840s). His father was one Ayyamperumāḷ Piḷḷai from Piramaṉūr, and his Tamil teacher was Vayalcēri Caravaṇak Kavirāyar. He worked as a treasurer for the Sivagangai zamindars (Rakunātaṉ 1980: 214f.).[63] For his *Pañcalaṭcaṇat tirumukavilācam*, he received *ciṟappuppāyirams* from famous fellow pulavars, such as Tuvātrīm Tacāvatāṉam Caravaṇap Perumāḷ Kavirāyar and Vēmpattūr Piccuvaiyar. With great irony the poet portrays the reactions of various social groups (astrologers, goldsmiths, prostitutes, moneylenders) to their aggravating conditions. When the starving people pray to Lord Cuntarēcuvara (Śiva) in Madurai, the god admits that he is unable to do anything and gives them a letter addressed to the Sivagangai zamindar Turaiciṅka Tēvar, asking him to relieve their suffering. David Shulman has seen this work as marking the limit of a historical development in which the relationship between "king" and "god" was renegotiated to the extent that poets assert their patron's superiority over the deity (2001a: 91). The *Pañcalaṭcaṇat tirumukavilācam* certainly displays one of the boldest forms of hyperbole in Tamil royal panegyrics.

Smaller Zamindaris

Besides the larger courts of Thanjavur, Pudukkottai, Ramnad, and Sivagangai there were a number of smaller zamindaris whose patronage was nonetheless significant throughout the century. Irutayālaya Marutappatēvar, the zamindar of Ūṟrumalai (in modern-day Tirunelveli District) was famous for his patronage.[64] U. Vē. Cāminātaiyar devoted a chapter of his autobiography to a description of how he spent a few days at Marutappatēvar's court (*EC*, ch. 113). He was impressed not only by the faultless daily routine with which everything worked at

62. For a study of this poem, see Rakunātaṉ (1980, ch. 5).

63. See also Irāmacāmip Pulavar (1958b: 151–153).

64. The Ūṟrumalai zamindars sponsored Tamil literature during earlier centuries as well. The eighteenth-century court poet Kaṭikaimuttup Pulavar, famous for his complicated *cilēṭai* poem *Camuttiravilācam* on which Māmpaḷakkaviccinka Nāvalar's *Cantiravilācam* was modeled (as we shall see below), wrote his *Mataṉavittāramālai* to praise one of Marutappatēvar's ancestors. For a discussion of a document on the family history (*vamcāvaḷi*) of the Ūṟrumalai zamindars, see Dirks (1982).

the court, but also by the depth of Marutappatēvar's learning. When he met him, the zamindar was engaged in a study of a *talapurāṇam* together with four of his scholars, two of which Cāminātaiyar remembers as Muttuvīrap Pulavar and Aṇṇāmalai Pulavar. The first, better known as Puḷiyaṅkuṭi Muttuvīrak Kavirāyar, was one of the zamindar's regular court poets. Not much is known about him, but a few of his panegyric verses are still extant.[65] We also know that Marutappatēvar's wife Mīṉāṭcicuntara Nācciyār sponsored his *Caṅkara Nārāyaṇakkōyil Kōmatiyampikaip piḷḷaittamiḻ* (Mātavaṉ 1994: 25).[66] The other scholar was none other than Ceṉṉikuḷam Aṇṇāmalai Reṭṭiyār (1861–1891), famous for his poem *Kāvaṭiccintu* which he composed on behalf of Marutappatēvar.[67] The *Kāvaṭiccintu* is a collection of twenty-two stanzas in popular folk metres on Murukaṉ in Kaḻukumalai to be sung by devotees who march in procession carrying the *kāvaṭi* pole. Drawing heavily on *akam* conventions, the poem describes a female devotee's intense love for the god. Due to its beautiful imagery, particular rhythms, and assonances, the poem has become very popular and continues to be sung to this day.[68] Moreover, Taṇṭapāṇi Cuvāmikaḷ wrote his *Vīrakēraḷamputūr Navanītakiruṭṭiṇaṉ kalampakam* on Marutappatēvar's family deity Kṛṣṇa in Vīrakēraḷamputūr (Vīrai).[69] In the introduction to his edition of this text, Vē. Irā. Mātavaṉ mentions Vācutēvanallūrk Kantacāmippulavar, Tirukkamavak Kavirāyar, and Puṉalvēli Irāmacuvāmi Pāratikaḷ as further court pulavars. Hardly anything is known about them.[70] 'Cilēṭaippuli' Vēmpattūr

65. See Irāmacāmip Pulavar (1960a: 935), and *TPT* 3 (221) where one poem is printed. He also composed two *ciṟappuppāyiram* stanzas on Māmpaḷakkavicciṅka Nāvalar's poem *Cantiravilācam* (see Irāmacāmi Piḷḷai 1952: 29–31). See also Mātavaṉ (1994: 13–26).

66. For an edition of this *piḷḷaittamiḻ*, see Muttuvīrak Kavirāyar (1968). Mātavaṉ lists the title as *Caṅkara Nārāyaṇakkōyil Kōmatiyammaip piḷḷaittamiḻ*.

67. For Aṇṇāmalai Reṭṭiyār's biography, see Cīṉivācaṉ (1984). See also Māṇikkam (1974: 25–27), Irāmacāmip Pulavar (1958c: 110–130), *ETL* 2 (175–177), and the literature cited there. His other works known to us are *Karuvai mummaṇikkōvai, Karuvaiyantāti, Kōmatiyantāti, Caṅkaranārāyaṇakkōyil tiripantāti, Vīraiccilēṭaiveṇpā, Vīraittalapurāṇam, Vīrai navanīta kiruṭṭiṇaṉ piḷḷaittamiḻ, Vīrai navanīta kiruṭṭiṇacāmi patikam, Vīraiyantāti*, and a few stray verses which may be found in *TCC* (587–97), *TPT* 2 (724) and *TPT* 3 (259–60).

68. On the *Kāvaṭiccintu*, see *ETL* 2 (175–177) and the literature cited there, as well as Zvelebil (1974: 223). The *cintu* genre is discussed in detail by Muttappaṉ (1983) and Tirumurukaṉ (1991).

69. The text has been edited by Mātavaṉ (1994).

70. According to Irāmacāmip Pulavar (1959: 195), Kantacāmippulavar composed a *Vaṭapaḻani vaṇṇamañcari*, a collection of thirty *vaṇṇam* stanzas on Murukaṉ in Vaṭapaḻani. One stanza is quoted there. According to Mātavaṉ (1994: 24), Irāmacuvāmi Pāratikaḷ composed an *orutuṟaikkōvai*. One *taṉippāṭal* of his praising Marutappatēvar is given in Irāmacāmip Pulavar (1959: 106).

Piccuvaiyar[71] was also sponsored by Marutappatēvar as was Cevar̲kuḷam Kantacāmippulavar (1849–1922).[72]

The zamindars of Eṭṭayapuram (in modern-day Tuticorin District) are today above all remembered for their patronage of the famous poet and social activist Ci. Cuppiramaṇiya Pārati (Bharati, 1882–1921) toward the end of the nineteenth century.[73] But throughout the century the zamindars had fostered Tamil literature. Two of the court poets known today were Mukavūr Mīn̲āṭcicuntarak Kavirāyar (d. 1895), who worked in Eṭṭayapuram for fifteen years and later migrated to the Cēr̲r̲ūr zamindar's court, and Karuttamuttup Piḷḷai (1816–1895). Mīn̲āṭcicuntarak Kavirāyar was born in the village of Mukavūr near Cēr̲r̲ūr, where his father was employed as court poet. While he was educated as a pulavar by his father, he himself later taught Aṇṇāmalai Reṭṭiyār. He composed a few *pirapantams*, viz. a *vaṇṭuviṭutūtu* and *Payōtarappattu* on Irācavallipuram Muttucāmippiḷḷai, a *piḷḷaittamiḻ* and *Utāracōtan̲ai mañcari* on the Eṭṭayapuram zamindar Āṇṭiyappap Piḷḷai, an *orutur̲aikkōvai*, *Murukar an̲upūti*, *Kaḻukumalait tiripantāti*, *Tirupparaṅkirip patikaṅkaḷ*, *Kutiraimalaip patikam*, and several solitary stanzas.[74] Karuttamuttup Piḷḷai (1816–1895), about whom we know nothing certain, is said to have composed three *paḷḷus* (*Kaḻukumalaip paḷḷu*, *Vēḷāḷar paḷḷu*, and *Ten̲kācaip paḷḷu*), three *antātis* (a *kalittur̲aiyantāti*, a *patir̲r̲uppattantāti*, and a *veṇpāvantāti*) on Murukan̲ in Tiruccentūr, *Civakirikkumarakkaṭavuḷ piḷḷaittamiḻ*, *Civatattuvacitāniti* (translated from Skt.), *Tiruppuvan̲appurāṇam* (based on the Skt. *sthalapurāṇa* of that place and composed for the head of the Tarumapuram ātīn̲am), *Viruttaparācariyam*, and *Vilvavan̲appurāṇam* (a Tamil rendering of the Sanskrit *Marutūrpurāṇam*).[75]

71. See above under the discussion of Sivagangai.

72. Kantacāmippulavar, son of the Eṭṭayapuram court poet Muttuvīrappak Kavirāyar, composed a work named *Tūtukkaṇṇi* on Kṛṣṇa in Vīrakēraḷamputūr in addition to several single stanzas and songs. For a biographical sketch, see Irāmacāmip Pulavar (1958b: 71–82). His single stanzas are collected in *TPT* 3 (860–67); see also Paḷaniyappan̲/Paḻani (1984: 42f.). He also composed a *cir̲appuppāyiram* on Māmpaḻakkaviccinka Nāvalar's poem *Cantiravilācam* (see Irāmacāmi Piḷḷai 1952: 31). Single stanzas in praise of Marutappatēvar by other poets can be found in Irāmacāmip Pulavar (1959: 127, 245, 258) and *TCC* (532–37; 629f., nos. 70–72).

73. On the history of the zamindari, see Ganapathi Pillai (1890) and Vadivelu (1984a). On the patronage Bharati enjoyed at the court, see the biography by Subrahmanian (2000).

74. A biographical sketch is contained in Irāmacāmip Pulavar (1955c: 88–90). His solitary stanzas are collected in *TCC* (532–68).

75. See Paḻaniyappan̲/Paḻani (1984: 73f.), Irāmacāmip Pulavar (1958a: 120–127), Vēṅkaṭacāmi (1962: 210), and Civakāmi (1994: 297). According to Paḻaniyappan̲/Paḻani, Karuttamuttup Piḷḷai was not employed as a court poet but worked as an accountant and envoy (*tān̲ātipati*) of the zamindar.

The zamindars of Uṭaiyārpāḷaiyam (in modern-day Tiruchirapalli District), Kacciraṅkappa Uṭaiyār (r. 1801–1835) and his son Kaccik Kalyāṇaraṅka Uṭaiyār (r. 1842–1885) patronized not only the poet and musician Kaṉam Kiruṣṇaiyar we briefly met above, but also the ancestors of U. Vē. Cāminātaiyar as court musicians (see *EC*, chs. 5–8).[76] Kantacāmikkavirāyar (d. 1871) who was employed as *vittuvāṉ* by the Tiruvāvaṭuturai monastery, composed a *kōvai* on Kacciraṅkappa Uṭaiyār.[77]

The zamindars of Cēṟṟūr (in modern-day Kamarajar District) employed Mukavūrk Kantacāmikkavirāyar (1823–1887), the father of Mukavūr Mīṉāṭcicuntarak Kavirāyar mentioned above.[78] In his youth, he was educated by the head of the Tiruvāvaṭuturai monastery Cuppiramaṇiya Tēcikar and by the monastic scholar Tāṇṭavarāyattampirāṉ.[79] Together with his younger brother Irāmacāmikkavirāyar (b. 1830)[80] he composed the *Cēṟṟūr Muttuccāmiturai kuṟavañci* on the zamindar Muttuccāmit Tēvar. Irāmacāmikkavirāyar was also employed as a court pulavar to teach Muttuccāmit Tēvar's son Cuntaratācat Tēvar (d. 1896).[81] The poet Kalpōtup Piccuvaiyar (d. 1888) composed an *orutuṟaikkōvai* on Cuntaratācat Tēvar.[82] One Kaṇapati Kavirāyar is also mentioned as a court poet in the secondary literature. He composed a work known as *Kurucāmi Nāyuṭu mītu marutavilācam*.[83] Civakāmi (1994: 304f.) lists Irācapāḷaiyam Caṅkaramūrttikavirāyar as a

---

76. On the Uṭaiyārpāḷaiyam zamindari, see Vadivelu (1984b), and the essay titled "Uṭaiyārpāḷaiyam" by U. Vē Cāminātayar (2005).

77. See Palaniyappaṉ/Paḷani (1984: 37), Vēṅkaṭacāmi (1962: 202), and Civakāmi (1994: 295).

78. On the history of the Cēṟṟūr zamindari, see Vadivelu (1984b).

79. For a short biographical sketch, see Irāmacāmip Pulavar (1956a: 70–72). Three occasional stanzas of his are collected in *TCC* (531–2).

80. I have not (yet) been able to determine the date of his demise, but we learn from Vadivelu that when he wrote his book around 1907, Irāmacāmikkavirāyar was still alive (1984b: 337).

81. A biographical sketch of Irāmacāmikkavirāyar is given in Irāmacāmip Pulavar (1956b: 109–120). His single stanzas are collected in *TCC* (617–31). Among them we also find verses on other zamindars, e.g., Pāskara Cētupati, Irutayālaya Marutappatēvar, the zamindar of Civakiri Caṅkilivīrappa Ciṉṉattampi Paṇṭiyaturai, as well as functionaries of the Cēṟṟūr court. He also composed a *ciṟappuppāyiram* on Māmpaḻakkavicciṅka Nāvalar's poem *Cantiravilācam* (see Irāmacāmi Piḷḷai 1952: 31). See also Māṇikkam (1974: 243f.). For a stanza sung by Muttuvīrap Pulavar, author of the grammar *Muttuvīriyam* (see Chapter 2 above), in praise of the zamindar Cuntaratācat Tēvar, see *TPT* 2 (35).

82. See Paḻaniyappaṉ/Paḻani (1989: 355), Irāmacāmip Pulavar (1955e: 129–134) and Civakāmi (1994: 346). He also composed a *Tiruvāṭāṇai antāti*. For his single stanzas, see *TCC* (280–284) and *TPT* 2 (698–704).

83. See Irāmacāmip Pulavar (1959: 178) and Paḻaniyappaṉ/Paḻani (1984: 17f.).

court pulavar, but he most probably belongs to the eighteenth century. He composed a *Cēṟṟūrp paḷḷu* on behalf of Irāmaliṅkat Tēvar.[84]

Finally, Mutturāmaliṅka Tēvar, the zamindar of Ciṟuvayal employed Tirumāṉūr A. Kiruṣṇaiyar who became his court poet and scholar in 1889.[85] The zamindars of Ariyilūr,[86] Civakiri,[87] Maruṅkāpuri,[88] Nāmakkal,[89] and Vēḷukkuṟicci[90] were also known as patrons of Tamil literature during the nineteenth century.

Though still far from being a comprehensive catalogue, what has been said above about the various zamindars and their court pulavars surely shows the extent and diversity of courtly patronage during the nineteenth century. A considerable number of poets frequented the courts where they found either temporary or permanent patronage. The patrons needed them as they needed their patrons.

Of Beauty and Benevolence: Themes of Courtly Literature

The two most important themes that nineteenth-century courtly literature was concerned with are the patron's generosity and his physical

84. He also composed an *aintiṇaikkōvai* on Kaṉṉivāṭi Malaiyāṇṭi Appaiya Nāyakkar and is supposed to have studied under Civaññāṉa Yōkikaḷ (?1725–1785) at the Tiruvāvaṭuturai monastery. A biographical sketch may be found in Irāmacāmip Pulavar (1960b: 30–39). See also Paḷaniyappaṉ/Paḷani (1984: 273f.), Irāmacāmip Pulavar (1959: 320), *TCC* (259–261) and *TPT* 2 (34).

85. See *EC* (667, et passim) and Irāmacāmip Pulavar (1962: 166).

86. U. Vē. Cāminātaiyar mentions that, during mid-century, his father was sponsored as a court musician by the zamindar of Ariyilūr, while one Caṭakōpa Aiyaṅkār was a scholar of Tamil and music there (*EC*, ch. 8). See also *EC* (ch. 12).

87. Irāmacāmi Piḷḷai (1952: 32) gives a *ciṟappuppāyiram* stanza on Māmpaḷakkaviciṅka Nāvalar's poem *Cantiravilācam* composed by a certain Eṭṭiccēri Tirumalaivēluppulavar who is mentioned as a court *vittuvāṉ* of Civakiri. He seems to be the same person as Tirumalai Vēṟkavirāyar (c. 1868–1944) listed in Civakāmi (1994: 339) and Irāmacāmip Pulavar (1958d: 98–107). He was also patronized by the zamindars of Ūṟṟumalai and Cēṟṟūr.

88. Civakāmi (1994: 23f., 363) mentions that the Maruṅkāpuri zamindar patronized Veṟimaṅkaipākak Kavirāyar whose known works are *Cokkaliṅka Nāyakar varukkakkōvai, Tirukkōṭṭiyūrp paḷḷu*, and an *ulā*, a *kōvai*, and *kuṟavañci* on Maruṅkāpuri. Further information on him may be found in Irāmacāmip Pulavar (1958a: 35–37). A few stanzas by Māmpaḷakkavicciṅka Nāvalar in praise of the zamindar Raṅkakiruṣṇa Muttuvīrappūccayaturai are collected in *TCC* (528f.). See also *EC* (691).

89. The poet Ve. Irāmaliṅkam Piḷḷai (1888–1972), famous as Nāmakkal Kaviñar, recalls in his autobiography that the zamindar of Nāmakkal, Turaicāmi Reṭṭiyar, sponsored Tamil poets (Irāmaliṅkam Piḷḷai 1977: 135).

90. The *Cantiravilācam*, which Māmpaḷakkavicciṅka Nāvalar wrote for the Vēḷukkuṟicci zamindar, is discussed below.

beauty-cum-desirability. Other characteristics, such as prowess in battle, were also commented upon but they were clearly secondary. Depending on both genre constraints and the occasion for which a particular text was composed, these two themes could be treated in a variety of ways by the pulavars. As has become apparent from the discussions of patrons and poets above, with regard to literary genres, the corpus of nineteenth-century courtly literature can be broadly divided into firstly a large number of occasional stanzas which are currently available in anthologies (notably *TCC* and *TPT*), and secondly a considerable number of individual *pirapantam* works. In what follows, I examine what seem to me representative examples of both these two groups.

To begin with the most simple kind of verse, we note that in praising his patron's largesse, a poet could be straight to the point, as in the following stanza by Poṉṉampalam Piḷḷai (d. 1762) which praises the Cēṟṟūr zamindar Civappirakācat Tiruvaṇātatturai:

> Food in one hand, gold in the other,
> Whenever one comes, gracious words—
> Thus is the nature of our noble king Civappirakācaṉ,
> A wealthy man of ever-increasing fame. (*TPT* 2: 651) [3.5]

The zamindar is praised for freely giving food (*aṉṉam*) and gold (*coṉṉam*), but the stanza lacks the embellishment and *finesse* typical of other pulavars' works.[91] We may note the presence of a key term of the pulavars' economy of praise: "ever-increasing fame" (*peruku pukaḻ*)—two words sufficient to conjure up the image of a widely acclaimed ruler. Furthermore, we find what is definitely a characteristic feature of our poetry, though here still restrained and, as it were, *in*

---

91. Cāminātaiyar narrates a framing anecdote for this poem which places it in a humorous context: One day, the zamindar was just having a meal when Poṉṉampalam Piḷḷai came to see him. Excited to see the poet who was very dear to him, Civappirakācat Tiruvaṇātatturai immediately stopped eating and quickly washed his hands. When he welcomed the poet, there was still some rice sticking to his right hand, while on his left hand he was wearing a golden ring that he had removed from his right hand before eating but forgotten to put back into place. The poet laughed when he realised this, and thus produced the poem which could also be read as "Rice on one hand, a gold[en ring] on the other." When the zamindar finally realized why the poet was pulling his leg, he laughed, washed his hands again, and placed the ring back on his right hand. Poṉṉampalam Piḷḷai thereupon observed that even though the zamindar had now changed the things on his hands, there was no need to change the meaning of the poem. So, in the end, the usual (and surely expected) flattery prevailed (Cāminātaiyar 1957: 175f.).

statu nascendi. Hyperbolic expressions ("whenever one comes . . . ," "ever-increasing fame"), euphemisms and other modes of distortion are usually employed to extol the king. An excessive use of these, well beyond the limits of the credible, combined with a taste for the "ornamental" is a stylistic feature inherited from the Nāyaka period, and we will see striking examples below. Thus, compared to what was usual, the blunt and unadorned flattery expressed in Poṉṉampalam Piḷḷai's poem quoted above was rare. More often, a poet would highlight his patron's munificence by comparing him to traditional symbols of liberality and abundance: the wish-fulfilling *kaṟpaka* tree (Skt. *kalpa-vṛkṣa*), gem (Tam./Skt. *cintāmaṇi*) or cow (Skt. *kāmadhenu*), the golden Mount Meru, the god of wealth Kubera or the generous king Karṇa, all known from mythology, and finally the raincloud which showers forth its cooling and nourishing rain and thus makes the country prosperous. We may recall the poem by Māmpaḻak Kaviccińka Nāvalar quoted above praising Poṉṉuccāmit Tēvar as a "merciful raincloud," or we may take the following stanza by Aḻakiya Cokkanāta Piḷḷai on his patron Muttucuvāmi Piḷḷai:

> The hands of the beautiful, eminent Muttucuvāmi
> Resemble the clouds in the heavens, because
> They continually provide rice and shower forth gold/
> plenty of water,
> So that all calamity leaves the country. (*TPT* 2: 687) [3.6]

The patron provides rice as he distributes money and food (particularly on ritual occasions, such as the *aṉṉatāṉam* ceremony), whereas the raincloud provides rice in the sense that it waters the paddy fields. The second part of the comparison depends on an instance of wordplay. The word *kaṉakam* "gold" may be split up as *kaṉa(m) kam* "plenty of water," so that the comparison between Muttucuvāmi's hands and the rainclouds nicely hangs on this one word. Note how the patron is further described as "beautiful" (*cuntaram cēr*), a feature which leads us to the second important theme to be found in royal panegyrics. Physical beauty is perhaps the most often repeated feature characterizing a patron in the pulavars' poems. We may speak of "beauty" in a wider sense, as sometimes additional "adorning" features come into play, as in the poem on Poṉṉuccāmit Tēvar by a poet simply known as Maturaic Campanta Maṭattut Tampirāṉ:

> The flocks of peacocks await the black rainclouds,
> The charming *cakōra* birds long for the moonlight,

O king Poṉṉuccāmi whose arms are garlanded with
jasmine,
The sweetness of your words shining with your excellence
My ears await. (*TPT* 2: 558) [3.7]

In a charming analogy, the *tampirāṉ* praises the sweetness of Poṉṉuccāmi's speech (*vacaṉac cuvai*), which also reflects his preeminent character, his "excellence" (*cīr*). In the same way that peacocks eagerly await the coming of the monsoon and the *cakōra* birds await the moonlight (on which they are believed to subsist), the speaker's ears crave for a sound uttered by the patron. The garlands of jasmine flowers around Poṉṉuccāmi's arms further serve to aestheticize his image; the "king's" beauty matches the beautiful and heavily suggestive surroundings. And he matches them not only visually, but also at a symbolical level. To the literary connoisseur the jasmine flowers are more than just nice-looking, fragrant adornment. They evoke the *mullai tiṇai* of ancient Tamil *Caṅkam* literature, a specific "interior landscape" which symbolizes the heroine's anxious waiting for the return of her lover. The peacocks and *cakōra* birds are also purposefully inserted into this landscape. The coming monsoon is a sign for the heroine that her beloved will soon come back to her. From a poetological point of view, we find here the coalescence of elements pertaining to both Tamil *akam* and Sanskrit *śṛṅgāra-rasa* conventions—a typical feature of the Tamil courtly literature of the period discussed here. Finally, the fact that we have a first-person speaker here ("*my* ears") is also noteworthy. There are different ways in which poetic subjectivity may manifest itself in the text of which the first person is only one. But here the use of the first person is significant. The poem becomes a personal, intensified statement, charged with emotion. This emotional quality of the text and the *akam* and *śṛṅgāra* elements make one thing very clear: The patron is praised not in the sober enumerations of his glorious deeds or the repetition of his noble qualities, but in a love poem. The subtle shift of emphasis away from the patron's largesse and toward his beauty has led the poet to a language of longing and desire, to the language of love. And this is not an exceptional case, but as we shall see below, it is the predominant mode of nineteenth-century Tamil court literature. Panegyrics and eroticism go together. The ways of weaving the two into poetry are manifold and dependent on poetic conventions as well as the tastes of poets and patrons. They account for the variety we find in the actual literary production and which I survey in the remaining part of this chapter.

A poem which manages to encapsulate both the patron's largesse and his attractiveness was composed by the Ramnad court poet Tillaiyampūr Cantiracēkara Kavirāyar:

What her foster-mother said

The generous donor who cannot be compared to hands
Giving wealth [like] rainclouds, to a wish-fulfilling cow,
To a wish-fulfilling gem, to Karṇa, nor to the rainclouds
Of the *kārttikai* month, Poṉṉuccāmi, came in procession
On a black hill whose trunk was full of *matam*.[92]
Who will have mercy and help the girl, who saw him
And fell in love, that she does not die? (*TPT* 2: 343) [3.8]

In the first half of the stanza, the poet has included a manual-style inventory of typical comparisons expressing largesse (the wish-fulfilling cow, gem, Karṇa, etc.), while the second half of the text again takes up the age-old tradition of *akam* poetics. A young girl has seen Poṉṉuccāmi riding in procession on an elephant, and now she is pining away, weakened by her lovesickness. Unlike the *tampirāṉ*'s verse, this stanza does not have a first-person speaker. The modern-day editor of the poem has prefixed a note on the speech situation (*kūṟṟu*) which I have rendered (paying hommage to A. K. Ramanujan's famous style of translation) as "What her foster-mother said."[93] And indeed, the stanza could be spoken by a concerned foster-mother, one of the familiar speakers of Old Tamil *Caṅkam* poetry. The focus here is clearly on the lovesick maiden. But we also learn that the mere sight of Poṉṉuccāmi obviously has a strong impact. Though his physical charms are only indirectly expressed, the reader/listener gets a sense of the patron's "beauty" or rather desirability. A mere glimpse of this paragon of beauty is enough to ensorcel female consciousness. The language the poet employs is excessive. Poṉṉuccāmi's generosity is entirely beyond comparison, and the girl is about to die from her lovesickness. Strong words indeed, but of course, we are dealing here with a specific kind of language use that strives to go beyond the ordinary and quotidian. The praise of kings requires more than realistic words.

92. *Matam* refers to the exudation from a rutting elephant's temples.

93. That this note on the speech situation was not originally prefixed to the poem but forms part of later (i.e., twentieth-century) interpretive endeavors becomes apparent from the version of the same poem published earlier in *TCC* (369) where this note is missing. The *kūṟṟu* notes on the other poems quoted below are equally later additions.

Similar poems thematizing the impact of the beautiful "king" in procession abound throughout the nineteenth century. Cantiracēkara Kavirāyar has another verse, which describes Poṉṉuccāmi's charms, this time in a less personalized tone:

So that everywhere their fame may increase, thrice seven
  donors
Made gifts and praised the good-natured one:
"Because of his generosity fame will surely stay with
  him!"
[Thus blessed] Poṉṉuccāmi rode one day on an elephant.
Those who saw him parading through the streets
Fell in love, lost their shell bracelets and jewel girdles,
Their minds became vexed, and they lost their sense of
  shame as well. (*TPT* 2: 350) [3.9]

Again we find the juxtaposition of the patron's generosity (*īkai*, lit. "gift, the act of giving") and his allure. Again we see the tokens of the poets' economy of praise, as both the fame of Poṉṉuccāmi and of those who present their gifts to him is foregrounded. The effect becomes even more patent in the affirmative, insistent repetition of the original Tamil (*"taṅkum taṅkum ivaṟkē pukaḻ"*) which is only insufficiently rendered in my "fame will surely stay with him." That the women lose their bracelets and girdles is again a typical symptom of lovesickness known from *Caṅkam* literature. In the two following verses, Aḻakiya Cokkanāta Piḷḷai describes the same scene through the voice of the heroine's confidante, again a typical speech situation known from Old Tamil literature:

What the confidante said

O illustrious Muttucāmi surrounded by maidens,
A girl saw your parade coming, and fell in love!
Her thirst grew daily, her garments became loose,
She forgot about her weak body—this to say I came
  (*TPT* 2: 685) [3.10].

She whose bright forehead resembles the rainbow
Is forever mad with desire. As the moon spreads his fire
At night, ever grieving, she calls you, king Muttucāmi,
"Come!"—[So] please do join her! (*TPT* 2: 686) [3.11]

That the moonlight, which is usually perceived as cooling, is felt to be a hot fire is yet another standard symptom of the heroine's lovesickness. The moon and the corpus of myths and beliefs about it that Paula Richman has aptly referred to as "moonlore" (1997: 27) play a crucial role in the depiction of the heroine's unrequited love in courtly poetry. As the discussion of Māmpaḻak Kavicciṅka Nāvalar's poem *Cantiravilācam* below will further illustrate this point, let us now briefly dwell on the erotic aspect of the last-quoted stanza. The language of the verse suggests that the heroine's desire is by no means only spiritual. The request to "join her" is a somewhat indirect expression, but what is meant is clearly something physical. We have a verse by Cantiracēkara Kavirāyar which is more explicit. Here, the heroine has perhaps really lost her "sense of shame," when she asks her friend to intercede:

What she said to her confidante

My girl,
the devotee who worships
  the highest one
    who has burned with his eye
    the body of the arrow-shooting god of love,
    and who is praised by Tirumāl, by the Lord of the
      flower [Brahmā],
    and by those without blemish,
the generous Poṉṉuccāmi, the manager of the Cētupati
  king's palace—
if you find a way to make him sleep with me and
  become my companion
in passion, then I will live happily in this world! (*TPT* 2:
  353) [3.12]

The crucial term here is the verb *maruvu* "to unite," which clearly refers to the sexual act though by no means in vulgar terms. The "highest one" is Lord Śiva who once burned the love god Kāmadeva with his third eye and who is praised by both Viṣṇu and Brahmā. We also note, in passing, an instance of language use which firmly anchors the poem in a colonial environment influenced by the English language. The word used for "manager" is the tamilized English word *māṉēcar* which is cleverly woven into the *yamaka* at the beginning of each line.[94] According to the medieval grammarians, the language to be used for literary compositions could only contain Sanskrit words (*vaṭaccol*) and regional/dialect words (*ticaiccol*). The introduction and

94. See the original Tamil text below in Appendix 3 [3.12].

skillful poetic manipulation of an English word nicely shows us the multilingual environment in which a nineteenth-century pulavar functioned. As in other stanzas quoted above, the patron is depicted as both a generous person (*vaḷḷal*) and as a desirable lover.

For the moment, one last example shall suffice to illustrate how the patron was imagined as an erotic paragon. Drawing on the device of *cilēṭai* paronomasia, Aḻakiya Cokkanāta Piḷḷai lets a somewhat outspoken girl declare:

> O prince, my gift is greater than yours here,
> Beautiful monarch Muttucāmi!—If you first
> Give me one handful of gold, I swear
> I shall give the two handfuls of my breasts. (*TPT* 2: 683)
> [3.13]

The word used for both "gold" and "breast" is *taṉam*, another instance of the specific *cilēṭai* capacity of the Tamil language which fuses the original Sanskrit *dhana* and *stana*. The humorous effect rests on the wordplay when the girl says that she would give *iru kait taṉam* for *oru kait taṉam*. Again, we face a typical scenario: The patron is generous with regard to material wealth, but he is also given to erotic excess. Caresses in exchange for money of course also point to the institution of the courtesan, but this is a point to be taken up below.

As we have seen above, the "king" on parade is a significant topos in courtly poetry. It is, in fact, such a standardized scenario in courtly literature that it merits further consideration. At least from the times of the medieval Cōḻa kings onward (if not earlier), royal processions have continued to fascinate court poets. While pulavars have devoted some genres in their entirety to the description of these processions (such as *ulā* and *pavaṉikkātal*),[95] they have also been "incorporated"into other genres (such as *kuṟavañci* or *vilācam*). The "procession genre"*par excellence* is the *ulā* (lit. "procession," connected to the verbal root *ulā(vu)*- "to move about").[96] But despite its name, the genre does not

95. The *pavaṉikkātal* seems to be one of those "theoretical" *pirapantam* genres which exist in the *pāṭṭiyal* treatises, but of which we have no actual texts (left). See Ceyarāmaṉ (1981: 392–394) and Aḻakapparācu (1983: 133f.) for a discussion.

96. On the *ulā* genre in general, see Ceyarāmaṉ (1966) and Caṇmukam Piḷḷai (1982: 12–47). An interesting discussion is also found in Shulman (1985: 312–324). A chapter on the *Tirukkayilāyañāṉavulā* (also known as *Ātiyulā*) is contained in Balasubramanian (1980). On *ulās* composed during the Cōḻa period, see Thirumavalavan (1991), while Ali (1996, ch. iv) deals specifically with the *Vikkiramacōḻaṉulā*.

focus on a description of the actual procession. Instead, it describes the varied reactions of women of seven different ages falling in love with the exceedingly beautiful king (or god) on parade. This particular focus is significant, as Daud Ali has argued. The fact that—in tandem with the narrative focalization—the eyes of the audience dwell on the beautiful women crowding the streets, implies that "the *ulā*, [. . .] sets up a circulation of desire in which the hearer is obliged to insert himself (or herself) in the place of the languishing female devotee" (1996: 214). As the gazing women are offered "as ciphers to be entered by those at court" (ibid., 215), the courtly audience is forced into an act of identification. We can see similar processes at work in some of the stanzas quoted above, when the admiration for the "king" is expressed in terms of a girl falling in love with him. Such identification processes are the subtle manipulations through which courtly literature exerted its powerful reality-building influence. The listeners are united into a "community of sentiment," and it is this community which *creates* the court in the first place.

Among the genres which "incorporate" the subject of the royal procession, we may mention the *kuṟavañci*, the *vilācam*, and the *kātal*. As in the *ulā*, in the *kuṟavañci*, and the *vilācam* genres, the royal procession provides the point of departure for the entire plot. The heroine falls in love with the king, as she sees him one day riding in procession. She would probably not have been able to see him otherwise, as access to the court was usually limited. But unlike the *ulā*, which provides a classified inventory of possible emotional reactions to the fateful encounter, the *kuṟavañci* and the *vilācam* focus on an individual poetic persona and her specific emotions. In Civakkoḻuntu Tēcikar's *Carapēntira pūpāla kuṟavañci nāṭakam*, which was briefly mentioned above, the young (and of course excessively charming) Mataṉavalli falls in love with King Serfoji II of Thanjavur. How exactly this happens is described in the poem with the following words:

> In the vicinity
> Of the ever-valiant hero [King Serfoji]
> And his army commanders,
> Kāmadeva—who is worshipped
> As the commander of women—
> Shot forth his flower arrows,
> Ere Mataṉavalli saw the beauty
> Of King Serfoji, the ruler
> Of our exalted city of Thanjavur,
> And with her pure heart
> Fell in love. (Cāminātaiyar 1932: 303, st. 15) [3.14]

As so often in Indian poetry, the Love God and his flower arrows are ultimately to blame. Again the language is the language of royal hyperbole ("ever-valiant hero," "exalted city," "pure heart"). As this longer genre leaves more space for description, the excellence of Serfoji, his town, and his rule are detailed and extolled in a separate verse which precedes this stanza (ibid., 296ff., st. 9), and they are thematized or alluded to throughout the poem. Yet, despite all this talk about him, King Serfoji is only obliquely present in the poem. As in the *ulā* genre, the patron remains a typical *pāṭṭuṭait talaivaṉ*, impassively in the background. He does not figure as an active character within the story. But the overall impression and message of the poem is similar to what the audience is made to think through the shorter stanzas quoted above: Beauty, generosity, righteous rule, etc.

Similarly, the *vilācam* genre takes as its starting point the "sight," the *darśana*, of the king in procession.[97] Only two specimens of this genre are extant today.[98] One is the eighteenth-century poem *Camuttiravilācam* (lit. "Address to the Sea") composed by the Eṭṭayapuram court poet Kaṭikaimuttup Pulavar (c. 1665–1740),[99] and the other one is Māmpaḻak Kavicciṅka Nāvalar's masterpiece *Cantiravilācam* ("Address to the Moon") composed in praise of Vēlappa Kavuṇṭar, the zamindar of Vēḷukkuṟicci (in modern-day Salem District). At the beginning of the *Cantiravilācam*, the "plot" is conveniently summarized in the following elaborate stanza:

Seeing the glamor of his procession: the mighty man
  called Vēlappaṉ,
    who worships
      Lord Arttanārīcuraṉ[100] of Tirucceṅkōṭu, the
        embodiment of grace,
      our mother Periya Nāyaki,

97. There are many different works which bear the title *vilācam*, but which must in fact be seen as belonging to different genres. Poets employed the term not only for the "address" poems discussed here, but also for other poetic compositions and notably (following a Sanskrit tradition) for theatre plays. The available secondary literature has not always realized these distinctions and often lumped *vilācams* of a very different kind together. See e.g., the discussions in Nākarācaṉ (1980) and Iḷaṅkumaraṉ (1985: 246f.).

98. Nākarācaṉ (1980) mentions a work named *Pūtara vilācam* which supposedly also belongs to this genre, while Iḷaṅkumaraṉ (1985: 246) speaks of a *Nati vilācam* by Cēṟai Kaṇapatik Kavirāyar. I have not been able to find these works.

99. On Kaṭikaimuttup Pulavar, see Zvelebil (1995: 341f.).

100. Arttanārīcuraṉ (Skt. Ardhanārīśvara) refers to Lord Śiva in his androgynous form, as half man and half woman.

the goddess of Attaṉūr,
and the one with the spear [residing on] the Kūvai hill [Murukaṉ],
who came to dispell the confusion of his devotees,
and who multiplies his wealth,
the famous ruler of Vēḷukkuṟicci, the lord of Parañcai town,
the raincloud of a noble lineage pouring forth a rain of wealth,
the refined one, son of Nañcayacāmi,
one *cittiṉi* [girl][101] among the clear-minded women remained solitary,
as her desire grew; unable to bear the [sight of the] rising full moon
she became angry, and strung many words together.
(Irāmacāmi Piḷḷai 1952: 9) [3.15]

Yearning for the ever-absent patron, the young girl sits awake at night and tells her love pangs to the moon—hence the poem's title. *Mutatis mutandis*, the story we find in the *Camuttiravilācam* is the same, but instead of the moon it is the ocean which is made to listen (and the royal patron, of course, is different). It is important to note at this point that this "plot" is only given in one particular stanza of the entire work which, so to say, sets the scene for the reader's understanding: The bulk of the two works consists of verses in which the heroine expresses her lovesickness in elaborate imagery and particularly *cilēṭai* and *maṭakku*. Hence, unlike in the *kuṟavañci*, there is no "real" plot here, but rather an intended "frame" or narrative background for the individual poems. The poet's emphasis is clearly not on the narrative, but rather on an impressive display of his command over *collaṇi* and *poruḷaṇi* devices of verbal ornamentation. Nonetheless, the poems do thematize the king in procession, and his praise is woven into the love poems. In the *Cantiravilācam*, we find prefixed to the girl's love laments two stanzas of explicit eulogy:

101. It is intriguing that the heroine is classified as a *cittiṉi*, the tamilized version of Skt. *citriṇī*. This term forms part of the classification of women into types which we find in post-*Kāmasūtra* treatises on erotics (e.g., *Ratirahasya* or *Anaṅgaraṅga*), but I have never come across this usage of the term in Tamil literary texts. For further details on the classification of women in erotic texts, see Kapp (1975; 2003).

Generous as a rain cloud,
Kubera with exalted fame,
Preeminent scion of the Ganga [= Vēḷāḷar] lineage,
Whose horses have gilded ornaments,
Lord of all mankind,
Virtuous, happy one,
Noble scholar of Tamil which has many beauties,
Whose shoulders are ornamented with garlands
  crowded with excellent bees,
A man of lasting victory,
Beloved son of valiant Nañcayan̲,
Endowed with exquisite ancient fame,
Never neglecting the words of the elders,
Paragon of good conduct—
[All this] is king Vēlappan̲! (ibid., 5) [3.16]

Having them all in the right place,
The Lady of the flower [Lakṣmī] on his chest,
  Which is beautiful and anointed with fragrance,
Sarasvati on his radiant face,
And joyful Kor̲r̲avai [Durgā] on his mighty shoulders,
So that the wide world worships him,
He is a man of outstanding moral conduct.
His mind shines forth, never swerving from the two feet
  Of dear Lord Murukan̲ [dwelling on] the Kūvai hill.
He is wealthy and joyful Vēlappan̲ of Vēḷai
  [Vēḷukkur̲icci] town,
  Surrounded by groves where many rain clouds abide.
And as he has been given a nature to resemble Indra,
Throughout many lives, happiness prevails and fame
  remains.
There is not the slightest enmity (ibid., 7) [3.17].

Such eulogy is very similar to what we read in other poems about other patrons. The patron's devotion, generosity, moral integrity, benevolence, wealth, and erudition are all standard qualities. His beauty and desirability form the subject of the remaining verses. But again, as in the *kur̲avañci*, the king remains impassive, almost reduced to a mere excuse for the detailed *fantasia* on the heroine's emotions.

By way of concluding our discussion, we have to mention one final courtly genre which is related to the *ulā*, the *kur̲avañci,* and the *vilācam* in that it eulogizes the king by highlighting his achievements as a consummate lover. The *kātal* (or *kātaṟ pirapantam*), which has "love" as its name, is again a narrative poem in that it details how the king and the heroine meet on the occasion of a hunting expedition. A subtle, yet important difference this genre introduces vis-à-vis the other genres, lies in the fact that the king actively takes part in the story as a "romantic," conquering hero, so that the older distinction between *pāṭṭuṭait talaivaṉ* and *kiḷavit talaivaṉ* becomes blurred. In David Shulman's words: "The two have coalesced into a single figure, the patron/erotic paragon; the old distinction, with its suggestive tension and built-in distance between the framework of patronage and the imagined world of the poem, has been obliterated" (2001a: 97). To transpose the patron as an active figure into the world of the poem—rather than merely having fictional characters praise his "inaccessible" beauty from afar—is perhaps the most consistent and resolute way of depicting the patron as the consummate lover and the target of all desires.[102]

To sum up, two important themes of nineteenth-century courtly literature have been discussed: the patron's generosity and his beauty and role as exemplary lover. In what follows, the nexus between royal panegyrics and eroticism shall be explored further by examining in detail a longer *pirapantam* work.

Kāma's Arrows Whizzing Past the King: Royal Panegyrics and Eroticism in the *Cētupati viṟaliviṭutūtu*

Apart from its reflexive mode of courtly panegyrics,[103] court literature also had to entertain the patron and his extended "household." Part of this entertainment was provided by the infamous erotic content of some of these works. A stunning example may be found in a work named *Cētupati viṟaliviṭutūtu*, a long poem in 1,245 *kaṇṇi*s (couplets),

102. For the plot of the *kātal* genre and further details, see David Shulman's illuminating discussion of Cuppiratīpak Kavirāyar's poem *Kūḷappa Nāyakkaṉ kātal* from the eighteenth century (2001a: 92–97). See also the useful commentary on this work in the edition by Aruṇācalam (1943). For a theoretical discussion of genre features and a list of works, see Aḻakapparācu (1983). The most important nineteenth-century *kātal* text is probably Aḻakiyacokkanātap Piḷḷai's poem on one Muttucuvāmiyā Piḷḷai from Tirunelveli (see Aḻakiyacokkanātap Piḷḷai 1868).

103. Narayana Rao, Shulman, and Subrahmanyam talk about "reflexive circles" enveloping the king, since he constantly hears his titles, his fame, sees images of himself in the mirror or on paintings, etc. Having to listen to the poets' praise also forms part of these circles. "Life in the court is a montage of endless self-replication" (1998: 60).

composed some time during the first half of the nineteenth century (possibly between 1845 and 1862) by the poet Tuvātrīm Tacāvatāṉam Caravaṇap Perumāḷ Kavirāyar (d. 1886 or 1888) at the Ramnad court.[104] A *viṟaliviṭutūtu*, yet another type of *pirapantam*, is a subtype of the genre of the *tūtu* or "messenger" poems, similar to the Sanskrit *dūta kāvyas*.[105] The messenger who is sent with a message of love may be a bee, parrot, goose (*aṉṉam*), peacock, raincloud, the south wind, the poet's heart, a tobacco leaf, paddy, a deer, money, etc., so that a large number of subgenres arise, each with its own conventions. In the *viṟaliviṭutūtu*, a dancing girl (*viṟali*) acts as a messenger on behalf of a somewhat naive brahmin who wishes to appease his wife after having an affair with a prostitute. The genre seems to become popular from the end of the sixteenth century onward; at least the earliest surviving example, the *Teyvaccilaiyār viṟaliviṭutūtu*, is datable to that period.[106] In these poems, we find an intriguing amalgamation of royal panegyrics with overt eroticism which goes far beyond the symbolism of the stanzas examined above. Untypically with regard to other Tamil narrative poems, the story is told in the first person, a strategy that not only underscores the immediacy of the erotic passages but also identifies, if only obliquely, the poet with the somewhat naive brahmin protagonist. As we shall see, the poem reflects the status of and relationship between poet and patron within the larger courtly sociosphere.

The story of the *Cētupati viṟaliviṭutūtu* runs as follows: In the southern Pāṇṭiya country, in a town called Tiruvāṭāṉai[107] lived a man called Ātirattiṉam Aiyar with his clever son Cuntaramaiyaṉ. At the tender age of twelve, the boy not only studied Telugu, Tamil, and Sanskrit, but also became a *cōṭacāvatāṉi*, someone skilled in the art of performing sixteen different feats at the same time, such as composing verses, solving mathematical problems, playing chess, etc. He was

104. For a re-assessment of its date (which has hitherto been uncertain), see Appendix 1.

105. On the *tūtu* genre see Āṉantanaṭarācaṉ (1997), Ceyarāmaṉ (1965), Caṇmukam Piḷḷai (1982: 48–60), and Cuntaramūrtti (1980).

106. R. Nagaswamy, in the introduction to his edition of the seventeenth-century *Mūvaraiyaṉ viṟaliviṭutūtu*, gives the year 1600 (Nākacāmi 1982: xiii). However, according to Mu. Aruṇācalam the text may have been composed even before that date (1976: 287–294).

107. The places in the poem are all real and associated with the Ramnad kingdom—often as the locales of important temples. Tiruvāṭāṉai, today located in the northern part of Ramanathapuram District, has an ancient temple celebrated in the verses of the seventh-century Śaivite saint Campantar.

married to a girl named Tuṇaimālai, and both lived a life of domestic bliss, loving each other dearly. One day, while celebrating a temple festival in the town Uttirakōcamaṅkai,[108] Cuntaramaiyaṉ is attracted to visit the house of the prostitute Māṇikkam and gives her all his money and other belongings. A young boy who has gone with him and has witnessed all this instantly runs to Cuntaramaiyaṉ's wife to inform her. Needless to say, wife and husband have an argument, whereupon he leaves their home and takes to roaming around. Burdened by his guilt, he visits many different temples for prayer, and ends up in the town Mutukuḷattūr[109] where he stays for ten days and meets a man named Vētamaiyaṉ. Cuntaramaiyaṉ invites Vētamaiyaṉ to come with him to the famous temple in Tiruviṭaimarutūr, but his new friend dislikes the idea: "Haven't you seen the play of Kōvalaṉ and his wife Kaṇṇaki,[110] how he goes to the prostitute Mātavi and loses all his wealth?" As Tiruviṭaimarutūr is famous for the many prostitutes (*tācis*) who live there, he warns him not to go. Cuntaramaiyaṉ, however, remains unimpressed. Worried about his daredevil friend, Vētamaiyaṉ tells him the story of the young girl Mōkaṉamuttu and how she is instructed in her immoral art by the *tāykkiḻavi*, the "foster-mother" of the dancing girl. Still, the man is determined to go, so both take off and visit the temple in Tiruviṭaimarutūr, where, indeed, Mōkaṉamuttu is dancing in all her alluring splendor. Cuntaramaiyaṉ is completely enraptured, so that after her dance he follows the crowds of men running after her to her house, forgetting everything around him—including his concerned friend Vētamaiyaṉ.

Once he has arrived at the *tāci*'s house, he is first made to pay the "service fee" of 1,750 gold coins. In reward, Mōkaṉamuttu talks sweetly to her new paramour and pleases him as long as he has money. When, before long, all is spent, she tells him to leave. A scuffle ensues which brings the two parties before the village assembly (*panchayat*). After protracted discussions, Cuntaramaiyaṉ leaves the place. Ruined both morally and financially, he again wanders about helplessly. He visits a temple where he sees on the chest of the deity a priceless

108. The old Śiva temple in Uttirakōcamaṅkai, about seven miles southwest of Ramnad town, is praised in the verses of Māṇikkavācakar (ninth century?) and is also a traditional place of worship for the *cētupatis* (see below). See also Thiruvenkatachari (1959, appendix 1).

109. Mutukuḷattūr, about twenty miles west of Ramnad town, is also occasionally mentioned as the birthplace of our poet Caravaṇap Perumāḷ Kavirāyar.

110. The story alluded to is, of course, that of the famous epic *Cilappatikāram*, also current in various folk and dramatized versions.

pendant. He learns from the temple priest that this pendant was given as a gift by Muttuvijaya Rakunāta Civacāmi Cētupati, the ruler of Ramnad and a generous patron. Cuntaramaiyaṉ is so impressed that he thinks that such a generous king must indeed be the ruler of the whole world. Wandering on through the king's fertile country, the opulence and beauty of which are described at length, he finds many other, equally amazing endowments by the *cētupati*. He also meets two poets (*avatāṉis*) in palanquins who, interestingly, identify themselves as Caravaṇap Perumāḷ Kavirāyar and his grandfather with the same name (the grandson being the poet who composed this *viṟaliviṭutūtu*). They have just come from a visit at the Ramnad court where they have obtained the palanquins and various other precious gifts.

Cuntaramaiyaṉ is now determined to visit this gracious king himself, and on his way to the palace he bumps into his old companion Vētamaiyaṉ who encourages him to use his skills as a poet in order to earn some money and revert to a normal life again. Finally, Cuntaramaiyaṉ meets the king sitting in state in his glamorously decorated durbar hall, recites a verse on him, and is instantly showered with the apposite rewards: clothes, a shawl, a ring inlaid with rubies, an elephant, a horse, loads of money, and so forth Now well equipped with money and a positive outlook on his life, the brahmin is anxious to return to his wife and the momentarily forgotten domestic happiness. But fearing that she might not accept him back, he sends a dancing girl as a messenger to achieve reconciliation. To explain the reason for his request, he tells his story to the beautiful *viṟali*.

At this point, it should be mentioned that this slightly meandering plot is a genre convention and, as such, not the invention of our poet. The conventionality becomes clear when we compare our text to the most famous poem belonging to this genre: the *Nākam Kūḷappa Nāyakkaṉ viṟaliviṭutūtu* composed about a century earlier by Cuppiratīpak Kavirāyar, the teacher of the well-known Jesuit missionary Costanzo Giuseppe Beschi (1680–1747).[111] A look at this text suggests that the *Cētupati viṟaliviṭutūtu* is very closely modeled on its predecessor(s), or, in other words, that the genre conventions reach very far. As these conventions first crystallized during the Nāyaka period, it is hardly surprising that we find the typical features of Nāyaka literature, such as a taste for elaborate, ornamental description, and in particular what Narayana Rao et al. have referred to as "hypertrophied eroticism" (1998: 62). For a number of reasons the *viṟaliviṭutūtu* is an "erotic"genre *par excellence*. Not only does the theme of amorous desire and its risks

111. For a discussion of this work, see Shulman (2001: 92–102).

provide the backbone for the story, but throughout the poem the courtly audience is inundated with eulogies on female beauty and explicit details about lovemaking. We may start looking for these right at the beginning of the poem. After the obligatory *veṇpā* stanza to invoke the gods (*kaṭavuḷ vāḻttu*), the poet gets physical with a long description of the *viṟali* who is about to be sent as a messenger. It is indeed a spectacular puranic opening, when we are told that the beauty and art of the anonymous dancing girl unsettle even the gods in heaven who are disturbed in their own musical endeavors:

> Thinking that the new ambrosia which arose that day
> From the ocean [of milk]
> When churning it with the striped serpent strung as a rope and
> The high Mount Meru inserted [as a churning rod],
> In order to please Tirumāl [Viṣṇu], the gods of heaven,
> And the Lord of the gods [Indra],
> Is of inferior quality,
> They cast it aside,
> Disdain the filtered honey
> Which is thought to provoke
> The same intoxication as palm wine,
> Realize that the mango is still unripe, [. . .]
> And thinking that the sugarcane from the press
> Has become useless,
> They throw it away,
> And [instead] procure the milk of Tamil which boils over with music,
> Mix it with the flourishing honey of compassion,
> And add the sweetness of the *maṅkaḷa-rāga* [a musical mode],
> Call forth the *rasa* [aesthetic sentiment] of music and song,
> And exhibit to the ears of the learned
> The liquid *rasa* of ambrosia in whatever musical tunes,
> And as the various flutes which they listen to
> In order to learn themselves the speech of the parrot,
> Stop speaking of all that exists
> And fall silent,
> The white-colored Pārati [Sarasvatī], Nāraṇi [Lakṣmī],

Bhūdevi, Tumpuru and Nāratar [two celestial musicians]
Come forth to appreciate the aesthetic pleasure,
The minds of the excellent connoisseurs are stirred,
Dead trees start blossoming,
Even painted images rear their heads,
All directions become confused,
The learned become enlightened,
Supreme pleasure is being perceived,
And stones melt,
When
Your voice never stammering,
Never covering up the sound of the *vīṇā*,
Never losing the words of your song,
Never failing in the *rāga*,
Never allowing your thoughts to swerve aside,
Never faltering with your slender waist,
Never shaking your pointed breasts,
Never blinking with your eyes
  Which are perhaps victorious arrows
  With sharp tips,
You sing like sugar, o dancing girl!
You are [Indra's] heaven
  With two pointed golden breasts/peaks
To the young men who have set their minds
On thoroughly studying the *kāmaśāstra*!
[. . .]
O flower-chariot bearing the fans
Of royal processions and showing
The playful battle of young people in love
  And drunk with passion!
O goddess granting everyone
The liberating bliss{*mukti*} of seeing
The sacred pavillion of your well-formed buttocks!
  (1–18)[112] [3.18]

112. In what follows, the reference in round brackets is to the stanza(s) of the poem as given in the edition of Cokkaliṅkaṉ (1947) which is the best available edition. The expurgated edition by Cirañcīvi (1958) has to be avoided for obvious reasons. Unfortunately, I have not been able to consult the oldest available edition, which was printed in Madras in 1887 (Caravaṇap Perumāḷ Kavirāyar 1887).

This is just the beginning of what is a truly elaborate praise of the dancing girl continuing through several lines. The poem begins aptly not with ordinary human concerns, but in the realm of the gods, the realm of music, poetry, and pleasure *par excellence*. When the gods hear the dancing girl, they are already in a heightened emotional state in which none of those things which before epitomized sweetness and pleasure can compare to the aesthetic delight of the experience: not the ambrosia of the milk ocean, not filtered honey, not the sweet mangoes, nor sugarcane. The gods prefer a different kind of stimulation, the "milk of Tamil boiling over with music" (*icaip poṅku tamiḻp pāl*). But their own musical efforts are interrupted, outstripped by the dancing girl whose art and accomplishment surpasses everything. The gods abandon their music and come to listen to the girl's beautiful songs which have magical qualities reminding us of Orpheus' famous gift praised in Greek mythology. Dead trees and painted images come alive, stones melt, and everything is saturated with supreme aesthetic pleasure (*iṉparacam*), a cosmic experience indeed. The hyperbole we find here will be the dominant mode throughout the entire poem. Note that the first-person narrator addresses the girl directly. From the observation that her music and dance are sweeter than anything imaginable and superior even to the music of the gods, the narrator quickly comes to focus on her physical charms. All the cliché tropes of Indian erotic poetry are rehearsed here, when the poet elaborates on her waist, breasts, eyes, etc. The young danceuse is also described as an ideal object of the male gaze, almost an "open book" to all the men who wish to pursue the scientific study of pleasure known in Sanskrit as *kāmaśāstra*.[113] But she is more than a static feast for the eyes. Besides the display of her physical beauty, she vividly demonstrates "the battle of young people in love" in her acting and dancing. We may also note that here eroticism is linked to royalty ("the flower-chariot"), a point which we shall take up below.

While throughout the poem the descriptions are elaborate and complex, the language used is rather simple and straightforward, employing notably fewer ambiguities and less rhetorical embroidery than we find in other works of the period. In fact, this is true for the entire work. Although we find a few *yamaka* and *cilēṭai* stanzas, the poet's emphasis is clearly not on sophisticated language use of the kind we saw in the works of Mīṉāṭcicuntaram Piḷḷai and others, but

113. On *kāmaśāstra* and erotic love in classical India in general see Wendy Doniger's and Sudhir Kakar's introduction to their translation of the Sanskrit *Kāmasūtra* (2002) and the literature cited there.

on the opulence and quantity of description. Similarly enthusiastic delineations of female beauty abound in the poem, e.g., when the narrator Cuntaramaiyaṉ sees the *tāci* Mōkaṉamuttu for the first time as she dances in the temple in Tiruviṭaimarutūr:

> At that time, standing near a big golden pavillion,
> I saw her: Mōkaṉamuttu—her tresses swarmed by bees.
> The unique beauty of her bowed forehead,
> The beauty of her eyes shooting forth lances,
> The beauty of her legs, the beauty of her speech,
> The beauty of her garlanded shoulders, of her teeth,
> Of her arms, her chest, her ears, her nose,
> Her breasts—when I had seen all this, I forgot every-
> thing around me.
> I obtained the sight of the elegant cups of her breasts;
> And like wax in a blacksmith's fire, my mind melted
> away. (506–510) [3.19]

Here the effect is achieved by the poetic device of repetition: the word *aḻaku* (beauty) is attached to all parts of her body from top to bottom. But this is only a relatively innocuous prelude to the "act" itself, which is described at impressive length when Cuntaramaiyaṉ comes to cohabit with Mōkaṉamuttu. Unlike other literary genres which contain allusions as erotic elements, the *viṟaliviṭutūtu* explicitly and graphically depicts the sexual act "in all its nakedness" (Nākacāmi 1982: ii). A clipping from the section which, in its entirety, consists of no less than forty-four stanzas (632–76) may suffice. Again, all starts with the gaze:

> She flung the lances of her eyes [at me],
> And she was slightly afraid, bashful,
> Too shy to come closer. Cooing sweetly,
> She disclosed her scented breasts,
> Covered them again, bent her head slightly,
> And then reclined. I touched her rustling
> Colorful saree, seized it fully, and put it on my lap.
> I unfastened her bodice of gold inlaid with gems,
> Embraced her, pinched her cheeks, kissed her,
> Looked at her beggingly, took up some sandal paste
> And anointed her breasts, rubbing gently. I rubbed
> Her nipples on her voluptuous breasts, stretched my
> limbs

And held her with both hands. I tasted the honey
Of her sweet lips. I lay down beside her and
Made her lie down. Reaching for me, she held me tight,
Lay down on my lap, and locking her arms behind my back,
She embraced me. Without saying a word,
She was dazzling, climbing up and moving down.
She pulled up her clothes covering her thighs,
And began the various kinds of love-play.
Her opulent breasts pierced my chest like elephants' tusks.
She revealed all her secret knowledge. She sat on me,
Jumped up and down, grew firm. She whined a little,
Tasted my lips red as *kovvai* flowers, she caressed me,
Gave in, then sulkingly objected. She fed me with betel,
Removed it again, kissed me, looked up, and we both
Lay down. She pulled off my veshti, and truly,
She performed all the amorous sports{*caracam*},
And yielded. I pulled off her saree of tender muslin,
And under it I saw the altar of lust swelling,
And reached for it:
I thought that one may describe it as a cobra's hood
And that this cobra's hood contains the fatal poison!
One may classify it as two halves of a mango fruit;
This fruit, too, left at that, will wither!
One may call it the beautiful hoof of a deer,
But this hoof will not exude and drip with sweet honey!
One may speak of it as a cool lotus flower
Shining beautifully in a garden; This flower, too,
Will fade when the bees hover above! One may earnestly
Compare it to a honey-comb full of honey,
But the sweet honey in it does not always flow!—O man!
One may praise it as a golden cup, but in such a cup
There will not be fine hairs!
One may call it the auspicious love chariot, but for that
Chariot there is not all the time a festival!
One may speak of a pond surrounded by flowers which yield
Rich honey; Such a pond, too, will once dry up entirely!—
Thinking that there is no comparison to this thing, I kissed her
And joined my face to this moon-like face [of hers],

And caressing her back with one hand, I tasted her
breasts,
Touched with my tongue her collyrium eyes,
Ever so softly I pressed the crown of her head
With my finger nails, and—also scratching her navel—
I excelled in love games with my two hands.
Clasping her neck, I wrote "*namacivāya*," left the
Poisonous region, and pressed the region of ambrosia,
I seized her lotus flower hands, her legs,
Put the tip of my tongue into her ears, and held her
[. . .]. (633–659) [3.20]

And so on, and so on. What may perhaps seem unabashed and indecent in its explicitness to a reader of the twenty-first century, and what alarmed nineteenth-century colonial officials and missionaries,[114] was certainly perceived differently in its original context. At the Ramnad court it served various purposes. In its detailed almanac-like description, the above section echoes the specific chapters of the *kāmaśāstra* manuals as compendia of what to do to whom at what time if one wanted to be a proper courtier. But, beyond this implicit didacticism, such overt depictions of *kāma* at work surely entertained a mixed courtly audience as a shared amusement. It is unfortunate that we know nothing about the actual context in which works such as this were recited.

But there is another important constitutive element of the poem besides erotic excess: the praise of the royal patron. After the description of the dancing-girl messenger at the beginning of the poem, we find a short summary of its plot, a frequent element of *pirapantam* works. This directly leads to a portrait of the *pāṭṭuṭait talaivaṉ* in whose honor the work is composed, the royal patron Vijayarakunāta Civacāmi Cētupati. By way of setting the scene, the first-person narrator says:

When I came to Ramnad town{*teṉmukavaiyampati*},
To the region of the man who is like a mother [to his
subjects],

114. The censorship that the colonial state exercised on the "indecent" and "immoral" vernacular literature is briefly discussed in the following chapter. Significantly, Ciraññīvi's edition of the *Cētupati viṟaliviṭutūtu* published in 1958 contains a note that it is an "expurgated edition with reference to the Madras Government G.O. Nos. 1507 of 48 and 3397 of 49 Public General," and the editor consequently curtails the poem to 1,176 instead of 1,245 stanzas.

I saw him:
Who, in his purity of mind, worships the holy feet of Maṅkaḷēcar [Śiva]
In Uttarakōcamaṅkai,
Whose elephants on the battlefield have bloody trunks
From joining in combat the blood-dripping elephants
Of the enemy's army,
He on whose battlefield perished the army of those who do not
Come and place their tribute before him, putting their hands on
His golden crown and praising him,
Whose fame reaches up to the sky,
Who never leaves the path of *dharma*,
The lord of Ramnad,
He who steers Arjuna's chariot [i.e. Kṛṣṇa],
Who is famous for winning again and again the victory of
Straight and righteous words,
The protecting lotus-flower to whom even his enemies bow,
The friend who came as a refuge,
The beautiful one with mountain-like shoulders who has a
Reliable army of four divisions [chariots, elephants, infantry, cavalry],
The king who, knowing his enemies' cunning tricks,
Turned to dust the ramparts of their sevenfold rock fortifications,
The lord of Ramnad who wrote a letter to the Kaliṅkas
Saying that they should pay their tributes daily,
He who is the god of love to the young girls with cup-shaped breasts,
The protector of the *taṉukkōṭi*,[115]
He who possesses the ancient port of Toṇṭi at the pure ocean,
The young crest-jewel of Muttuvijaya Rakunāta Cētupati
Who rules the immensely fertile earth,
The darling of Queen Muttuvīrāyi Nācciyār who shines as the gem of the heavens,

115. The *taṉukkōṭi* or *taṉuṣkōṭi* is the promontory southeast of Ramēcuvaram, the passage to Sri Lanka, also referred to as *cētu*. Hence the hereditary title of the raja as *cētupati*, i.e., "guardian of the *cētu*."

The paramount jewel among kings,
The lord of widespread fame, Vijaya Rakunāta Civacāmi
Cētupati,
The victorious ruler, the sovereign [. . .]. (40–53) [3.21]

This detailed description of the ruler, inserted at the beginning of the poem, to a certain extent echoes the royal genealogies (*meykkīrtti*) found in medieval South Indian inscriptions. It enumerates the various manifestations of royalty by praising the king's devotion to God, his skill in warfare, his righteous rule, his physical beauty, his superior status vis-à-vis other kings, and, in the form of a micro-genealogy, names his parents. This is then followed by the section on "the ten limbs" or ten constituents of a kingdom (*tacāṅkam*). The ten constituents depicted in our poem are the Cētupati's mountain, river, country, town, horse, elephant, garland, war drum, banner, and scepter. The royal mountain, for instance, is delineated in a beautiful vignette:

He [the Cētupati] is the lord of the great southern hill
Potikai, of lasting fame,
Where the dark rain clouds are lingering over the
branches
In flowering groves everywhere full of blossoms
And the crescent moon is slowly wandering by,
Where Kāma with his bow has come searching
For the southern breeze which spreads the scent of
sandal,
Where Indra has come searching for a fragrant grove,
And with which Agastya who spoke of the Southern
Tamil
Reduced the burden[116] of this earth. (56–59) [3.22]

As the mythic mountain Potikai or Potiyam, the abode of Saint Agastya, is said to be located in the southern Pāṇṭiya country where the *cētupatis* now rule, the poet uses it for various mythological allusions. The

116. The allusion is to a well-known myth: On the occasion of Śiva's and Parvatī's wedding on Mount Kailāsa in North India so many gods and celestials assembled that the entire earth became unbalanced, the north sinking under the weight of all the guests and the south rising up. The sage Agastya was sent down to South India and sat on the Potikai mountain in order to provide a counterweight and to restore the balance of the earth. For versions of this myth, see e.g., Shulman (1980: 142f.) and the study by Sivaraja Pillai (1985).

connection between the Cētupati king and Agastya is, of course, not arbitrary. The king is explicitly linked to ancient Tamil tradition, as he rules over the land once inhabited by Agastya. The king's loyalty to the "Southern Tamil,"[117] his erudition and patronage, his own Tamilness are portrayed as an ancient heritage. The dark rainclouds and the flowering groves all point to the beauty, fertility, and opulence of the king's realm and to his largesse. After the *tacāṅkam* section, we find several more panegyric verses; indeed similar eulogistic passages occur again and again throughout the poem. And at the end, when Cuntaramaiyaṉ is on his way to Muttuvijaya Rakunāta Civacāmi Cētupati's court, the audience is again submitted to a description of the wealth of the country and the excellence of Ramnad town (st. 1089–1104). Finally, the focus is on the royal palace and the grandiose durbar with all its dazzling pillars inlaid with rubies, emeralds, and diamonds, where the raja sits in state (st. 1157–1198). Here, the personal beauty of the king is reflected and enhanced by the beauty of his surroundings in a thoroughly aestheticized courtly world.

But let us, for a moment, pause over the description of the king's mountain quoted above. The landscape described is the familiar *locus amoenus* of erotic poetry according to both Tamil and Sanskrit traditions. The dark rainclouds, the flowering groves, the crescent moon, the scent of sandalwood and the south wind are all typical ingredients. This setting for *śṛṅgāra rasa*, the erotic mood, forms an integral part of the *cētupati*'s kingdom. Appropriately inserted into this setting, we find Kāma (or Kāmadeva), the god of love. But the god is only one of several suggestive elements. In contrast to this, the earlier description of the king goes further. By actually equating him with the god of love ("he who is the god of love to the young girls with cup-shaped breasts") it highlights his erotic capacities, and here we find a first link between royal eulogy and eroticism as the other important constitutive element of this poem. The equation is significant: The king *is* Kāma in the sense that he is a paragon of love, and his paramount erotic competence forms an essential part of his royal status that separates him from less powerful people at court. Ultimately, the king's erotic competence and desirability are universal, as the *ulā* poems demonstrate where we see women of all generations fall for the king. This role of the king as the universal lover is one of the signs of his uniqueness as a ruler and hence underscores his claims to royal status. The

117. "Southern Tamil" or "Tamil of the South" (*teṉtamiḻ*) refers to Tamil as a language of the South (of India) and is a standard formulaic expression occurring already in the *Cilappatikāram*.

very plot of the *viṟaliviṭutūtu* is calculated to demonstrate this. The brahmin makes a fool of himself by claiming the privileged access to love outside the domestic one-to-one. Unlike the king who never falls victim to Kāma's arrows, but who is Kāma himself, the brahmin is destroyed by his prurience. The irony and satire of the poem that ridicule the hapless brahmin do not merely say, "This is what happens to you when you fall victim to a prostitute." At a court that was known until late in the nineteenth century for its opulent celebrations of *nautches*, or orgies where *viṟalis* would perform,[118] such a warning would have been too simple. Rather, it seems to say, "This is what happens to you when you try to play king." The poem thus serves to reenact royal status as hierarchically situated above and beyond everybody else at court, including the poet.

This textual strategy is by no means an invention of the nineteenth century. It is built into the *viṟaliviṭutūtu* genre and hence dates back to the Nāyaka period, during which, as we know, erotic excess was a specific prerogative of the king, an important component of royal behavior. This, then, could cause a problem. For if the combination of erotic excess and excessive praise of the king was linked to a specific society at a given historical moment, how are we to make sense of such poetry once the social environment changes? In other words, if we think (as many literary historians tend to) that a poetic genre is linked in very specific ways to the society in which it emerged, one would expect that a different society would "read" or "employ" the same poetry in different ways. That the society in which the nineteenth-century zamindars operated was indeed very different from that of the Nāyakas is a fact which has been detailed at the beginning of the present chapter. Consequently, the observation that nineteenth-century pulavars use earlier genres points to a change in function of these genres. It is my contention, as I have stated above, that the zamindars of this period employed earlier literary styles and traditions in a specific kind of representational practice: the celebration of former glory, or, with Christopher Baker, acts of "ritualized remembrance" (1976: 43). This orientation toward former grandeur and lost splendor has to be seen in connection with other instances of "ritualized remembrance," such as royal processions or festivals. In a rapidly changing social environment which more and more curtailed the zamindars' power and influence, they relied on royal rituals to secure their status, and courtly literature was an essential part of these. It provided a "stable" arena where the ruler could harken back to bygone importance.

118. See Breckenridge (1978: 75).

It is perhaps little wonder that while further changes affected South Indian society during the nineteenth century, the uses of literature also changed further. What was to the zamindars the late reverberation of erstwhile significance was seen as "morally debased" and "detrimental" first by British educationists and later by many others in South Indian society. Ultimately, works such as the *Cētupati viṟaliviṭutūtu* were proscribed and, surviving only in expurgated and bowdlerized editions, gradually faded into oblivion.[119] From the last decades of the nineteenth century onward the zamindars increasingly looked toward other occupations than literary patronage for both entertainment and display of their claim to elevated social status. In particular, the rajas developed an ever-increasing taste for what was unmistakably Western and modern. We remember Ramachandra Tondaiman's interest in Western literature as displayed on Ravi Varma's portrait. Additionally, the medium of the stylized portrait itself, the carefully composed Western-style oil painting, was a sign of being modern as well. And besides literature and painting, there was more. As soon as the silent film arrived in India in the 1870s, the Raja of Ramnad apparently purchased a film projector to screen movies in his palace (Guy 1997: 23). During the early decades of the twentieth century, some of the rajas took to collecting expensive cars or traveling the world and frequenting the salons of Europe's nobility and high society in London, Paris, or Monte Carlo. On one of his trips, Marttanda Bhairava Tondaiman (1875–1928), the Raja of Pudukkottai, met a young woman in Australia, Melbourne-born Molly Fink. He married her in the summer of 1915, scandalizing the press, the colonial government, and his native Pudukkottai with such an unheard-of alliance.[120] Even the literati who had earlier depended on royal patronage now began to ridicule the rajas and their "degenerate mores." In 1913, the famous patriot-poet and social reformer Ci. Cuppiramaṇiya Pārati published a piece of prose fiction titled *Ciṉṉac Caṅkaraṉ katai* ("The Story of Little Shankar"). It was a hilarious satire on court life clearly inspired by his own experience of growing up at the court of the Eṭṭayapuram zamindar.[121] At the beginning of the story, we learn

119. See Venkatachalapathy (1994a, ch. 6) for a discussion of proscription, expurgation and "obscene" literature during the late nineteenth and early twentieth centuries.

120. The story of Molly and the raja is told in vivid detail in Duyker/Younger (1991). Marttanda Bhairava Tondaiman was not unique in his predilection for European women. The story of Jagatjit Singh, Maharaja of Kapurthala, and the Spanish dancer Anita Delgado has recently been retold in a bestselling book by Javier Moro (2007).

121. The *Ciṉṉac Caṅkaraṉ katai* was serialized in Pārati's journal *Ñāṉapāṉu* but has remained a fragment. I have used the separate edition of 1963 (Pāratiyār 1963).

that in Kavuṇṭaṉūr, the zamindari where the protagonist Little Shankar grows up, everything is scarce: water, money, rice, fruit, even flowers. Only of pulavars there is no dearth. Their quarrels and quibbles at the court are described at length. The zamindar Rāmacāmik Kavuṇṭar, whose full name Makārāja Rājapūjita Makārāja Rājaśrī Rājamārttāṇṭa Caṇṭap Piracaṇṭa Aṇṭa Pakiraṇṭa Kavuṇṭāti Kavuṇṭa Kavuṇṭaṉūrātipa Rāmacāmik Kavuṇṭar is intended to ridicule the long customary royal titles, is portrayed as a lazy and profligate ne'er-do-well who neglects his duties in favor of an extravagant lifestyle. Pārati's break with the courtly world and the world of the traditional pulavars could not be more pronounced. With such mockery expressed by those who were earlier drawn to the courts, the rajas' former glory was now vanishing quickly, never to be restored. Before we turn to the new literary tastes and sensibilities that emerged during the nineteenth century under colonial impact, we have to address the changing occupations of the pulavars.

The Pulavar in the Age of Mechanical Reproduction: Changes in Patronage

The traditional modes of literary patronage centered around religious institutions and royal courts continued to exist up to the early twentieth century and in individual cases even longer. But, as one might expect, they did not remain static and unchanged during such a long period which was also a period of momentuous transformations in the wider social sphere. Perhaps the most significant driving force behind these changes in patronage was the increasing impact that the British colonial state exercised in all domains of economic and cultural life, in tandem with the aftereffects of this impact. Already from the 1820s onward, the pulavars felt the wind of change in their face. On the one hand, the major traditional patrons, zamindars, and monasteries, both gradually lost more and more of their economic power and thus their ability to sponsor Tamil literary activities and scholarship. On the other hand, an expanding colonial state machinery offered secure jobs for language teachers and invested in campaigns to foster and reform both Tamil language and literature. Additionally, the activities of religious reformers like Āṟumuka Nāvalar (1822–1879) and Irāmaliṅka Cuvāmikaḷ (1823–1874) led to a transformation of the traditional Tamil Śaivite religious milieu in which the literary works of Mīṉāṭcicuntaram Piḷḷai and others were grounded. While the Tamil Śaiva Siddhānta of the *maṭams* was gradually giving way to neo-Śaivism, the former's literary production was pushed into the background.[122] Thus, as Stuart Blackburn has pointed out, the fact that some time during the 1820s Koṭṭaiyūr Civakkoḻuntu Tēcikar, one of the pulavars we have met above, left the court of king Serfoji of Thanjavur and became Tamil language pundit at the College of Fort St. George in Madras (founded in 1812) was indeed "symptomatic of a shift in Tamil literary culture" (2003: 19).[123] But this shift was not what Blackburn has called a full blown "relocation of Tamil literary culture, from the courts and *matts* to Madras" (ibid., 74). Tamil literary production continued everywhere in the Presidency, and almost all of the works discussed in the present study were not composed in Madras. We may perhaps come closer to historical reality if we speak of an *expansion* of Tamil literary culture. Before the 1820s and 30s, the city of Madras was hardly important in the landscape of Tamil literary production. What was ultimately responsible for its development into the hub of intellectual and cultural activities was a growing educational sector and the explosion of book printing activities during the course of the century.

The newly emerging print culture and a need for Tamil language teachers may be regarded as the two most important factors of change with regard to the pulavars' activities and lifestyles. As both these factors have been examined in the recent work of Stuart Blackburn and A. R. Venkatachalapathy, I will only briefly address them here to further qualify a few points.[124] With the boom of Tamil book publishing after the 1830s, the pulavars entered a new "age of mechanical reproduction."[125] The pulavars' texts now became reproducible in a way they

122. For Āṟumuka Nāvalar's activities as a religious reformer, see Ambalavanar (2006), Rösel (1997: 218–231), Young/Jebanesan (1995), and Bate (2005). For further biographical details, see also Kaṉakarattiṉa Upāttiyāyar (1968), Kailācapiḷḷai (1999), Hellmann-Rajanayagam (1989), Hudson (1992a; 1992b; 1995), Zvelebil (1992: 154–157; 1995: 66f.), and the literature cited there. There is also an interesting biography in verse by Aruṇācalakkavirāyar (1898). The literature on Irāmaliṅka Cuvāmikaḷ is copious. See Raman (2002), Kautamaṉ (2001), and the entry in Zvelebil (1995: 262ff.), all of which cite further literature.

123. For the history of the College of Fort St. George in Madras, see Trautmann (2006; 2009). I discuss the activities of the Tamil pulavars at the College in Ebeling (2009b).

124. See Blackburn (2001; 2003; 2004) and Venkatachalapathy (1994a).

125. The phrase is, of course, borrowed from Walter Benjamin's famous essay, although his original term in German was *Reproduzierbarkeit* (reproducibility) and not *Reproduktion* (the difference is significant). Still, I use the term "reproduction" here, since his essay is better known under this title in the English-speaking world. The original German text of his essay may be found in Opitz (1996). For an English translation, see Benjamin (1992).

Figure 3.1. U. Vē Cāminātaiyar (1855–1942), early twentieth-century portrait.

had never been before. Of course, texts had been circulating in the form of palmleaf manuscripts and the copying of these was a fully-fledged profession in itself, but the possibility of producing books as mass commodities which could be sold and bought led to a set of entirely new occupations and institutions. While some pulavars became publishers themselves, others worked as editors of either older, "classical" texts or contemporary ones. As their task of selecting and editing older literary texts entailed questions of textual criticism as well as canonization, the pulavars were ultimately responsible—in collaboration with Western scholars—for the modernization of entire disciplines, such as Tamil philology and literary history.[126] The most famous editors of Tamil

126. I discuss the modernization of Tamil philology by nineteenth-century pulavars in Ebeling (2009a and 2009b).

"classics" were Rao Bahadur Ci. Vai. Tāmōtaram Piḷḷai (1832–1901),[127] the religious reformer Āṟumuka Nāvalar mentioned above, and, of course, U. Vē. Cāminātaiyar.[128] A considerable number of the printed text editions they produced have still not been superseded today.[129] Āṟumuka Nāvalar even purchased his own printing press in 1849 which he used for the production of teaching materials for his newly established school but also to print his text editions.[130] The pulavars' new book publishing activities also entailed new forms of patronage. The local rulers and zamindars now began to sponsor the printing of books.[131] Ultimately, as A. R. Venkatachalapathy has persuasively demonstrated, traditional patronage with its concomitant institutions of the *ciṟappuppāyiram* and the *araṅkēṟṟam* was gradually replaced by a subscription system in which new social elites, such as colonial administrators, lawyers, advocates, traders, or bankers, contributed to the

127. For his biography and works, see Zvelebil (1992: 174–177; 1995: 645) and Hoole (1997) in English, as well as Rajaruthnam Pillai (1934), Vaiyāpurip Piḷḷai (1968: 229–238), Caṇmukatās (1983), and Iḷaṅkumaraṉ (1991) in Tamil, and the literature cited there. The prefaces to his text editions, which contain important information on the contemporary literary scene, are collected in Tāmōtaram Piḷḷai (1971).

128. The best overview of U. Vē. Cāminātaiyar's life and works is given by Almoneit (1992). Besides his own autobiography (*EC*, translated into English by Zvelebil 1990b and 1994), one may consult Zvelebil (1992: 184–199; 1995: 102f.), Moraes (1955), Vaiyāpurip Piḷḷai (1968: 282–319), Pacupati (1976), and Kācirācaṉ (1987). His text editions are discussed in Colviḷaṅkum Perumāḷ (1981) and Irācu (2003). The International Institute of Tamil Studies has published a useful series of monographs in which his editions are examined in greater detail. For the editions of *Caṅkam* literature, see Cuntaramati (1984). For grammatical works see Nāccimuttu (1986), and for the larger *kāppiyam* works see Kācirācaṉ (1985).

129. As Tiru. Vi. Kaliyāṇacuntara Mutaliyār ('Thiru. Vi. Ka.') famously put it: "Āṟumuka Nāvalar laid the foundations for the publication of ancient Tamil literature; Tāmōtaram Piḷḷai raised the walls; Cāminātaiyar thatched the roof and completed the building" (1969: 160). For a fuller picture of the new text editing and publishing activities of the pulavars, see Zvelebil (1992, ch. 6) and Blackburn (2003, ch. 3).

130. See Ambalavanar (2006: 211f. et passim).

131. A few examples may suffice to illustrate this: The Ramnad kings sponsored some of Āṟumuka Nāvalar's editions (Irākavaiyaṅkār 1951: 45–48), U. Vē. Cāminātaiyar's 1898 edition of the *Maṇimēkalai*, Cantiracēkara Kavirāca Paṇṭitar's anthology of occasional poetry published in 1878 under the title *Taṉippāṭaṟṟiraṭṭu*, and Ciṅkāravēlu Mutaliyār's literary encyclopaedia *Apitāṉa Cintāmaṇi* published in 1910 (see the prefaces to these works). After receiving a copy of Cāminātaiyar's *Puṟanāṉūṟu* edition, in December 1894 Pāṇṭitturait Tēvar sent a versified letter and Rs. 500 for his next publishing venture (*EC* 740–742). A. Cēṣaiyā Cāstiri, the diwan of Pudukkottai, sponsored Tāmōtaram Piḷḷai's 1887 edition of the *Kalittokai* (Tāmōtaram Piḷḷai 1971: 49f.). Mutturāmaliṅkat Tēvar, the zamindar of Ciṟuvayal, contributed to the printing expenses of Cāminātaiyar's *Pattuppāṭṭu* edition (*EC* 659).

financing of printed books.[132] The pulavars' former economy of praise did not vanish entirely, but it was reorganized through praise now circulating in print. *Ciṟappuppāyiram* poems were prefixed to the actual work in printed editions, and when a "classical" text was published new *ciṟappuppāyirams* were provided by the editor's friends and other fellow pulavars. The early title pages, too, reflected what mattered in the economy of praise. Besides the book's title, publisher, place and year of publication, they also contained elaborate details about sponsoring patrons and the scholarly lineages of the book's author, the editor and/or commentator including all the applicable honorary titles. Bold print and different font sizes were used to make sure that the reader would notice these credentials immediately. After 1900, with opportunities for patronage declining further and book authors and editors coming from different social backgrounds, the title pages became simpler and gradually approached the contemporary format of merely including the author's (and/or editor's) name, the book's title, and the publisher's name with all further information shifted to a separate imprint page.

How thoroughly the decline of traditional patronage affected the economy of praise becomes apparent from the following episode in U. Vē. Cāminātaiyar's life (*EC* 720–723). In 1892, he was invited by the raja of Ramnad Pāskara Cētupati to attend the *Navarāttiri* festival celebrated in the Ramnad palace. Before he took leave, the king presented him with a very expensive pair of shawls—a typical gift given to a pulavar in reward of his services and as a token of social distinction. However, rather than keeping the shawls as symbols of honor, Cāminātaiyar sold them for the price of Rs. 300 to the Tiruvāvaṭuturai monastery and used the money to pay back loans which he had taken out to finance the printing of his *Cilappatikāram* edition. Clearly, during earlier times pulavars would not have given away their shawls so easily.

Apart from editing and publishing texts, the pulavars also found new occupations as Tamil language teachers. The newly founded College of Fort St. George in Madras, and after mid-century the new Madras University, as well as an increasing number of high schools and colleges in the mofussil provided welcome opportunities for secure and well-paying positions. Finally, teaching Tamil to Western missionaries and colonial officials as well as assisting in their philological endeavors became important pursuits for the pulavars. We have to mention here in particular Mukavai Irāmāṉucak Kavirāyar (c. 1785–1853) who not

132. See Venkatachalapathy (1994a, ch. 1).

only taught Tamil to W. H. Drew, C. T. E. Rhenius, and George U. Pope, but who also assisted Miron Winslow, who referred to him as "long well known as a leading Munshi [language teacher] in Madras," in the compilation of his dictionary.[133] We know hardly anything about Irāmāṉucak Kavirāyar's life, but there is a charming anecdote which Pope remembered thirty years after the pulavar's death:

> My first teacher of Tamil was a most learned scholar, long dead (peace to his ashes!), who possessed more than any man I have known the *ingenium perfervidum*. He was a profound and zealous Vaishṇavite. I remarked one day a long white line or scar on his neck, where his rosary of huge Elocarpus beads hung, and ventured to ask him (I had to wait on such occasions for the *mollia tempora fandi*!) its history. "Well," said he, "when I was a boy, I could learn nothing. Nothing was clear to me, and I could remember nothing. But I felt my whole soul full of an intense love of learning. So, in despair, I went to a temple of *Sarasvati* (the goddess of learning), and, with a passionate prayer, I cut my throat and fell bleeding at her feet. In a vision she appeared to me, and promised I should become the greatest of Tamil scholars. I recovered, and from that day, by her grace, I found all things easy, and *I am what she said I should be*." I believe he was so; and from that noble enthusiastic teacher I learnt to love Tamil and to reverence its ancient professors. (1992: v, original emphasis)

Whether or not Irāmāṉucak Kavirāyar really was "the greatest of Tamil scholars," his self-confidence was a feature he shared with many of his colleagues who cherished their privileged position in society, their special bond with goddess Sarasvatī, their lives as embodiments of Tamil learning, as guardians of traditional wisdom in a time of change.

133. Winslow (1995: viii). For Irāmāṉucak Kavirāyar, see also Zvelebil (1995: 266) and Subramania Aiyar (1970: 44–48).

4

Toward the Modern Tamil Author

The Colonial Critique of the "Vernacular" and Māyūram Vētanāyakam Piḷḷai (1826–1889) as an Agent of Change

Wenn die Gedichte
einfacher werden
so zeigt das
nicht immer an
daß das Leben
einfach
geworden ist
—Erich Fried[1]

While the pulavars were increasingly drawn toward the new occupations of book publishing and teaching Tamil in the colonial educational system, around mid-century another factor emerged which rendered the pulavars' former lifestyle problematic and less attractive. A public debate arose which severely criticized the aesthetic underpinnings of the pulavars' literary production. This debate was initially begun by British company officials and missionaries who condemned the entire existing body of Tamil literature and its language as "backward," "superstitious," and generally "unfit" to express colonial modernity. They vehemently called for a "new vernacular" and a new literature with "decent" moral content, which could be used in the newly

1. This is Erich Fried's poem "Widerspiegelung" ('Reflection') which could be translated thus: "When the poems / become simpler / this does / not always indicate / that life / has become / simple." See Kaukoreit/Wagenbach (1998: 511).

refurbished educational system. The anatomy of this debate has been examined in Stuart Blackburn's recent work, and there is no need to repeat his arguments here at greater length.[2] A few original voices in the debate will be enough to illustrate its trajectory. In the year 1845, the Governors of the Madras University (who at the time did not yet run a fully-fledged university but a high school), published their 4th Annual Report where we read:

> It is to be observed that the vernacular languages of this Presidency namely Teloogoo, Tamil, Canarese, Malyalum, and Tuluva are almost totally barren of what Europeans deem useful or substantial knowledge. All their ancient, original, valued literary compositions are in *Poetry*. The existing Prose works, very few of which can, we believe, be recommended as exhibiting a correct or sensible style, are (with scarcely an exception) but translations from other Indian Languages, or abridgments and extracts, turned into Prose, from ancient poetical works in the same language. [. . .] As regards the Poetic compositions, their merit by the Native Standard is very different from that of any European compositions. Difficult verbal feats by complex reduplications of the same words with various, and even contrary, meanings—by various alliterations—and by perversely ingenious artifice in the structure of sentences and verses—form the staple of what are considered fine writings. So great and complicated are the difficulties in attaining any thing like a proficiency in this dialectic learning, that many years must elapse before a consummate Vernacular Scholarship can be looked for. At the same time the highest stretch of such Scholarship would hardly reach to the compositions of a prose letter upon business or common events, which would be easily intelligible to any but such profound critics. [. . .] If we turn to the subject-matter of these poetical compositions, it will be found that they chiefly relate to legends, and fictions, as gross, as they are fanciful. Such morality and practical maxims as are taught, are not such as are likely to meet the approbation of European minds, at least—nor indeed of the better portions of the Natives themselves, neither is it to be denied that much is to be found in these works which no other than a depraved

2. See Blackburn (2001) and (2003, ch. 4).

> intellect could tolerate." (*4th Annual Report from the Governors of the Madras University*, 1845, p. 9ff.)

In 1848, George Norton, Advocate General of Madras and later also president of the newly established Madras University, published his pamphlet *Native Education in India; comprising a review of its state and progress within the Presidency of Madras* and wrote in a similar vein:

> Original prose compositions scarce exist at all. Translations and abstracts are meagre and inadequate. What is cultivated among learned Natives, and admired as proficiency in these languages, consists mostly of frivolous and perverse artifices in the construction of words and sentences. The bulk of all Native writing (which are poetical) contain little else than legendary and superstitious nonsense. Better *models* of composition are, therefore, needed—and particularly in prose, and such writings as may convey substantial knowledge, and sounder and more elevated sentiments. A Vernacular Literature has to be created, and to this object primary attention should be given in reference to Vernacular instruction. (1848: 54)

That such convictions were not abstract and inconsequential musings, but that they were actively inculcated into the "native" students becomes apparent from a prize-winning essay by one C. Rungacharry, dated March 29, 1849, which was printed in the same year in the *8th Annual Report from the Governors of the Madras University*. Under the title "What are the advantages to be derived from the Cultivation of English Literature by the nations of India?" we read:

> Turning in the next place to consider the nature of Hindoo literature, we find that with all its beauties it is full of defects. Whatever causes might have acted in producing the character of the Hindoos, it would not be wrong to say that their literature perpetuates it. Their poetry abounds in far fetched similes; hyperbolical expressions, and such other defects which mark a want of accuracy in thought. There is also too much art used in its composition; and accordingly we find that the two great defects of the Hindoo character are want of precision, and a degree of art in all the pursuits of life. Now before these defects are removed, and a degree of nature infused in their works, the literature of the

> Hindoos cannot exercise a beneficial influence upon their character. [. . .] Hence to conclude, the cultivation of English literature by the Hindoos confers two-fold advantages upon them; first, it elevates their character and refines their taste, and secondly it gives an impulse to improvements in their literature. (*8th Annual Report from the Governors of the Madras University*, 1849, pp. 64–66)

In combining a critique of the "vernacular" literature with generalizations on the "Hindoo character," the young man made explicit what many educationists had thought but less frequently openly declared. The direction of the argument, then, is clear. The existing Tamil literature was criticized with regard to both form and content. Tamil poetry was deemed too difficult and artificial ("[d]ifficult verbal feats," "perversely ingenious artifice," "frivolous and perverse artifices in the construction of words and sentences," "far fetched similes; hyperbolical expressions, and such other defects," "too much art"), and its content was declared obnoxious and detrimental ("legends, and fictions, as gross, as they are fanciful," "depraved intellect," "legendary and superstitious nonsense"). What was needed instead was a different medium, viz. prose, which could be employed to convey "useful or substantial knowledge," and "sounder and more elevated sentiments."[3] In short, a "new vernacular literature" had to be created.

The discrepancy between different ideas and presuppositions concerning the uses of literature could hardly be more blatant than here. What the social reformers demanded entailed nothing less than an entirely new social function for elite literary production. For them literature had to be primarily an instrument of education—something that it was clearly not in the traditional universe of the pulavars whose literary production was bound to systems of patronage. We have seen above that the texts produced by the pulavars were used as "instruments" in their economy of praise. The new literature, however, was

---

3. We may add here the voice of the American missionary Miron Winslow (1789–1864). Unlike others, he seems to have thought unusually highly of Tamil poetry, but he also admits the need for prose. In the preface to his *Comprehensive Tamil and English Dictionary* first published in 1862, he wrote: "It is not perhaps extravagant to say, that, in its poetic form, the Tamil is more polished and exact than the Greek, and in both its dialects, with its borrowed treasures, more copious than the Latin. In its fulness and power it more resembles English and German than any other living language. Its prose-style is yet in a forming state, and will well repay the labor of accurate scholars in moulding it properly. Many Natives, who write poetry readily, cannot write a page of correct prose" (1995: vii).

not at all concerned with praise. It was meant to be an educational tool, and in order to be utilizable as such, the content of literature had to be adapted to the rapidly changing social environment. The norms and values of *Western* education had to be cast in indigenous moulds.

To achieve such a far-reaching reform, the Tamil language itself had to be thoroughly refurbished. As Norton declared in his *Speech on Education*, delivered at the opening of Pacheappah's Hall in Madras, on March 20, 1850:

> the main object of a dilligent, a laborious, and a persevering study of the Vernacular languages, is, that they may be enlarged and enriched by a copious infusion of words and phrases to meet advancing knowledge, and increasing ideas, that they may be refined into greater ease and neatness, and that they may be strengthened in power of expression. (1850: 23)

This was best achieved, in his opinion, through a "study of other and superior languages, in combination with that of the Vernacular languages, and also through the substantive knowledge conveyed by those other languages, the treasures of which are to be gradually poured into those of the East" (ibid.). Thus, the reform of the "Vernacular" was envisioned as a major, a "laborious" process. One man who took this new agenda very seriously was the Scottish protestant missionary John Murdoch (1819–1904), who as Stuart Blackburn observes "led a personal campaign against the use of Hindu story literature in government schools in the Madras Presidency" (2003: 136).[4] It was ultimately due to his extended efforts that the *Press and Registration of Books Act* (XXV of 1867) was passed and the office of a "Registrar of Books" was established in Madras—a first step toward state censorship. However, as A. R. Venkatachalapathy has shown in his study of the colonial state's policing of Tamil books and the issues of book registration, the institutionalization of copyright and expurgation (1994a, ch. 6), the role of the colonial state remained strikingly marginal to the world of Tamil publishing. Although a few individual books were proscribed, banned, or expurgated by government order, few individual writers were prosecuted. Perhaps the only exception is the case of patriot-poet Ci. Cuppiramaṇiya Pārati who, in the wake of the Indian Press Act of 1910, was effectively silenced and forced into exile in Pondicherry.

4. For Murdoch's campaign, see Blackburn (2003, ch. 4; 2004: 128–130). For his biography, see Morris (1995).

The harsh critique of the existing Tamil literary production raised by British officials, such as Norton, Murdoch, and others did not only impress Tamil students in the colonial educational system; it also provoked responses on the part of the leading Tamil intellectual elites. Those who were educated in the English language and the whole system of modern Western ideas conveyed by this medium started to second the opinion of the British critics. And what is more, they actually did respond, if hesitantly at first, by creating a "new vernacular literature." One of the earliest of these indigenous responses that is now fully traceable was by Māyūram Vētanāyakam Piḷḷai, an extraordinary writer and intellectual already noted above as one of Mīṉāṭcicuntaram Piḷḷai's good friends. His pioneering contribution to the establishment of a new literary culture forms the subject of this chapter.

As any socio-historical study of literature will attempt to show how texts are created from contexts, we shall begin with a reconstruction of Vētanāyakam Piḷḷai's life history. His biography is in many ways typical of the many English-educated Indians who were employed by the British colonial government all over India. As they began to express their opinion on various social issues and, what is more, to actively pursue agendas of social reform, these men were important agents of change. One may be inclined to see in them typical "filters"[5] corresponding to that new, "hybrid" class of people that Thomas B. Macaulay had called for in his infamous *Minutes on Education* (1835): "a class who may be interpreters between us and the millions whom we govern—a class of persons, Indians in blood and colour, but English in tastes, in opinions, in morals and in intellect."[6] But such a facile classification would seem to gloss over the agency of this new social class, while at the same time grossly overestimating the power of colonial policies. As Rosinka Chaudhuri demonstrates in her invaluable study (2002), colonized middle- and upper-class Indians were not silent, subaltern victims. They actively expressed and implemented their political desires and put their English education to specific uses that were far from dutiful "interpretations" or quiescent mediations between the colonized and the colonizer's cultural strategies. Vētanāyakam Piḷḷai's biography provides us with a view on this new role of social reformer and intellectual that literati took on everywhere

5. The idea that English-educated Indians had to be used in order to spread English reformist plans amongst the masses was known as the "filtration theory." See Viswanathan (1989: 113–117).

6. Quoted in Panikkar (1996: 93).

Figure 4.1. Māyūram Vētanāyakam Piḷḷai (1826–1889), late nineteenth-century portrait.

in India during the course of the century. We will be able to see that literary innovation did also come from the mofussil and was by no means limited to the intellectual circles in the urban metropolis of Madras. We will also see how—under the influence of English education and colonial debates on linguistic and social reforms—a hitherto unprecedented literary consciousness emerged that led to the creation of new forms of writing, new genres and themes.

Māyūram Vētanāyakam Piḷḷai: A Biographical Reconstruction

Samuel Vētanāyakam Piḷḷai was born on Monday, October 11, 1826, in Vēḷāṇkuḷattūr,[7] a village several miles away from the town of Tiruchi-

7. According to the earliest biography of Vētanāyakam Piḷḷai, the name reads "Veḷḷāṉ Kuḷattūr" (Ñāṉappirakācam Piḷḷai 1890: 1).

rappalli (Trichinopoly, Trichy, Tam. Tiruccirāppaḷḷi).[8] Vētanāyakam Piḷḷai's father was the rich landlord Cavarimuttup Piḷḷai, and his mother was Ārōkkiya Mariyammāḷ, the daughter of Mariya Cavariyā Piḷḷai, an influential garrison doctor in the service of the East India Company. Like Mīṉāṭcicuntaram Piḷḷai, they both belonged to the Vēḷāḷar community. However, one of Vētanāyakam's ancestors, Maturanāyakam Piḷḷai, had converted from Śaivism to Catholic Christianity, so that Vētanāyakam was born into a Christian family. An anecdote furnished by Vētanāyakam's biographers explains this conversion. At the age of fifty, Maturanāyakam Piḷḷai was suffering from rheumatic pains. He prayed to his god Kalivarāyaṉ (i.e., Ayyaṉār) to cure him. On the ninth day, Ayyaṉār appeared to him in a dream and told him to travel to Āvūr, one of the places where Catholic missionaries had built a church with the permission of the Toṇṭaimāṉ of Putukkōṭṭai. In this missionary church, Maturanāyakam Piḷḷai prayed to Jesus to cure him and promised to convert to Christianity in case his wish was granted. Thereupon, the missionaries gave him their blessings and an unguent which afforded relief. Thus impressed by the power of Catholicism, Maturanāyakam kept his promise and converted.

Vētanāyakam Piḷḷai's first education was entirely traditional. Until his tenth year, the young boy attended the local village school (*tiṇṇaippaḷḷi*) just like Mīṉāṭcicuntaram Piḷḷai. At the age of eleven, however, Vētanāyakam's life took a decisive turn when he left his hometown for Tiruchirappalli in order to study English with a friend

8. For the following reconstruction of Vētanāyakam Piḷḷai's life, I have examined all the Tamil biographies available to me, viz. Aruṇācalak Kavuṇṭar (1965), Caravaṇapavāṉantar (1970a), Cēcaiyā (1989), Citamparaṉār (1955), Kaviyaḻakaṉ (1981), Louis (1963), Nākacaṇmukam (1964), Naṭarājaṉ (1955), Paktavatcalam (1961), Pāṇṭuraṅkaṉ (1994), and Vimalāṉantam (1970). All of them are obviously based on the short Tamil biography titled *Vētanāyaka Viṟpaṉṉar Carittiram* (with the English subtitle "Life of Mr. S. Vedanayagam Pillay") published in Madras by Vētanāyakam's son Ñāṉappirakācam Piḷḷai one year after his father's death (i.e., in 1890). To the account given in this book, the later biographers have variously added some excerpts from Vētanāyakam's works or some general musings on their high quality and the author's talent. Their primary intention was not to provide an "objective" life history, but rather a eulogy which shows the development of a poetic genius from his infancy and thus serves as a moral *exemplum* for others. I have cross-checked and supplemented the life accounts as given in these biographies with data from other sources, such as orders made by the Madras Government, records of the Madras High Court and the Tamil Nadu Archives, and other contemporary writings, including reviews and obituaries. I have found that the biographies generally do not deviate much from the official records. Exceptions to this will be commented upon in the footnotes. For further accounts of Vētanāyakam Piḷḷai's life and works, see also Marais (1963), Aracumaṇi (1972), Maturam Nampi (1989), Subramaniyam (1992b), and Fernando (1995).

of his father called Tiyākappiḷḷai, who was employed as a translator at the Southern Provincial Court. As already Vētanāyakam's maternal grandfather had been employed by the East India Company, his parents' decision to let the boy study English was certainly made with the prospect of securing for him a similarly lucrative job. Though British presence in South India was, at the time, mainly centred around the city of Madras, its influence had become palpable everywhere in the mofussil. Consequently, the news spread that a good knowledge of English was the "key to success" as it would lead to material well-being and a high social position with influence and power. The common perceptions of the utility of learning languages other than Tamil are reflected in U. Vē. Cāminātaiyar's autobiography. A visitor, who was surprised to hear that the young Cāminātaiyar studied Tamil, asked his father: "Could he not study English? And how about Sanskrit? If he studied English, he would benefit in this world. By studying Sanskrit he would benefit in the other world. If he studies Tamil, he will obtain neither benefit" (*EC* 262).[9] While learning English, however, Vētanāyakam Piḷḷai did not neglect his further studies of Tamil language and literature and, later on, started composing occasional poems in his mother tongue.[10]

On January 4, 1848, at the age of twenty-one, Vētanāyakam Piḷḷai's English studies indeed began to pay off as expected. On that day, he made his first step into what was to become a distinguished (though not unproblematic) career in the service of the East India Company. He was appointed goomastah (a clerk or steward) at the Court of the Principal Sudr Ameen of Tiruchirappalli by Mr. J. Gordon, and subsequently promoted to Criminal Record Keeper.[11] His main task was to translate Tamil papers into English. As did so many other Indian employees, he began his career at the very bottom of the administrative hierarchy, but he seems to have lived up to the system's expectations, as is evident from a letter of reference written by Gordon: "His knowledge of English is far more than is ordinarily possessed by persons serving in the English Departments, in Courts and Cutcherries. He was diligent in his business, and gave me entire

9. On English education in colonial India, see also Viswanathan (1989). A brief sketch focusing specifically on South India is given in Jones (1989: 160–163).

10. The biographies list *Pommaikkaliyāṇam* ("Puppet Marriage") and *Cōpaṉappāṭalkaḷ* ("Congratulatory Songs") as his earliest works. They are now lost. His occasional stanzas were collected posthumously in *TCC* (412–431) and *TPT* 2 (355–415).

11. See G.O. No. 306, 26–39, dated March 17, 1857. For the structure of the legal system in colonial South India, see Paul (1991).

12. Letter dated June 15, 1850, ibid.

satisfaction."[12] Already two years later, on June 11, 1850, Vētanāyakam was appointed as Foujdaree Translator in the Civil and Session Court of Tiruchirappalli by the judge Thomas Ebenezer J. B. Boileau. In this position, he had to face the first major setback in his professional life. The story is a little *tour de force* of colonial administrative adversities and therefore merits to be told in detail. It was Vētanāyakam's regular duty to send English translations of the court proceedings to the Sudder Court.[13] Shortly after Boileau's successor, the judge Thomas Hardwick Davidson,[14] had been transferred from his office in Tiruchirappalli, he died very unexpectedly. At that time, he still had in his possession some documents which Vētanāyakam had translated to be sent to the Sudder Court. When the Sudder Court inquired after the delay, Davidson's successor and Vētanāyakam's new superior George Sullivan Greenway,[15] who Vētanāyakam's biographer Cēcaiyā, obviously feeling strongly about Vētanāyakam's imbroglio, scathingly describes as "a villain without the slightest sense of duty" (1989: 12), blamed his translator. Although one of Vētanāyakam's colleagues wrote to the Sudder Court, testifying that Vētanāyakam was not responsible for the loss, he was dismissed from his office.[16] Shortly after this, the documents were, naturally, discovered in Davidson's house, so that the Sudder Court immediately directed the court in Trichy to duly reinstate Vētanāyakam. However, the now acting judge, George Melville Swinton,[17] who apparently disliked Vētanāyakam Piḷḷai, wrote to the Sudder Court that he did not wish to reinstate him, since he was too frequently ill. The Sudder Court, however, insisted, whereupon Swinton in turn tenaciously refused to comply with the order. Only when the Sudder Court threatened to register a case against him, did Swinton give in, but he also, irate about his defeat, quit his office and sailed back to England in autumn 1853. Before reaching his home, however, Swinton died (of intestinal complications).[18] Ñāṉappirakācam Piḷḷai

13. See the *Hobson-Jobson* dictionary sub "Sudder Court," i.e., "Sudder Adawlut": "ADAWLUT: In 1793 regular courts were established under the British Government, and then the Sudder Adawlut became the chief Court of Appeal for each Presidency, and its work was done by several European (Civilian) Judges" (Yule/Burnell 1994: 4).

14. Thomas Hardwick Davidson, listed in the *Register* of 1852 as "sub judge of Combaconum."

15. George Sullivan Greenway, judge in Trichy according to the *Register* of 1850.

16. This was on 12th June 1852. See G.O. No. 306, 26–39, dated March 17, 1857.

17. George Melville Swinton, assistant judge in Combaconum according to the *Register* of 1853.

18. See also the *Register* of 1854 (vol. 2, p.161, Madras section) which records: "death George Melville Swinton 24th October 1853, Cape of Good Hope."

remarks that this was obviously God's punishment for the injustice Swinton had committed (1890: 13).

The entire affair took one year during which Vētanāyakam had thus been unemployed. Interestingly, it is nowhere mentioned in his official personal dossiers kept by Fort St. George. To make things worse for him, also his father passed away during this period. On July 9, 1853, however, Swinton's successor, the Civil and Session Judge Thomas Inglis P. Harris,[19] appointed Vētanāyakam Piḷḷai again, first as Criminal Record Keeper, and then to his former office of Foujdaree Translator. And not only that. Harris, as before Gordon, later spoke highly about his employee's abilities:

> the Civil and Session Judge desires to record the high sense he entertains of the character and qualifications of Vadanayagom Pillay [sic], as a Public servant in the Civil and Criminal branches of the Department. He has given the Civil and Session Judge the greatest satisfaction in the discharge of his duties, and it will afford him the highest gratification to learn that he has, by his diligence and activity, attained to higher posts than that he now holds, and should it be in the power to promote his future prospects, he assures him that he will gladly do so. The Civil Judge must add that the above servant possesses intimate knowledge of the Regulations and Circular Orders, and is well acquainted with the routine of Judicial business.[20]

It was during this time in Trichy that Vētanāyakam Piḷḷai met Mīṉāṭcicuntaram Piḷḷai for the first time.[21] Vētanāyakam Piḷḷai took the opportunity to discuss the poems he had been composing, and the two immediately became close friends.[22] As both of them were influential members of society, their interaction occasionally entailed more than literary discussions. At one point, the monk who had been appointed by the pontiff of the Tarumapuram monastery to administer

19. Thomas Inglis Parish Harris, Trichy district judge according to the *Register* of 1854.

20. Extract from the Proceedings of the Civil and Session Court of Trichinopoly, under date the 25th September 1855. See G.O. No. 306, 26–39, dated March 17, 1857.

21. See *SMPC* I (149–152).

22. A poem composed by Mīṉāṭcicuntaram Piḷḷai to praise Vētanāyakam Piḷḷai's poetic genius is quoted in Ñāṉappirakācam Piḷḷai (1890: 13) and *SMPC* I (150). This is apparently the earliest token we have of Mīṉāṭcicuntaram Piḷḷai's appreciation of his friend.

the business of the Trichy Rock Fort Temple started to work against the pontiff's will. The Tarumapuram pontiff asked Mīṉāṭcicuntaram Piḷḷai for help who passed the request on to Vētanāyakam Piḷḷai as the court case had to be presented in English. Vētanāyakam Piḷḷai did what he could, and the Tarumapuram *ātīṉam* won the case. As a token of his gratitude, in 1853 Mīṉāṭcicuntaram Piḷḷai composed the *Kuḷattūrkkōvai* we saw in Chapter 2. But this was only the beginning of a long friendship which lasted until Mīṉāṭcicuntaram Piḷḷai's death twenty years later.

Three years after his re-employment and the *araṅkēṟṟam* of the *Kuḷattūrkkōvai,* Vētanāyakam Piḷḷai obtained another opportunity to climb higher on the Company service ladder.[23] In 1856, the Madras Government newly instituted an examination referred to as the "Pleader's Test." Those who passed it were entitled to practice in the Sudder and Mofussil Courts of the Madras Presidency. In February the first examination was held in Kumbakonam by the civil judge George Thomas Beauchamp.[24] Out of thirty-six applicants only three passed. First, T. Muttucāmi Aiyar (1832–1895), a school inspector who later was to become the first Indian judge at the Madras High Court (appointed in 1878).[25] Second was Diwan Bahadur Raghunatha Rao, the famous social reformer who at the time worked as a sheristadar in a district court, and third was Vētanāyakam Piḷḷai. Once he had passed the examination, he did not have to wait long for a job opportunity to come up. On December 8, 1856, Beauchamp wrote to the Sudder Udalut, nominating Vētanāyakam Piḷḷai for the office of Principal Sudr Ameen of Tranquebar (Tam. Taraṅkampāṭi) in Tanjore District, which had become vacant.[26] Both Muttucāmi Aiyar and Raghunatha Rao had been offered the job, but had declined, as they were not impressed by the salary of Rs. 60. Ironically for the two of them, the post was converted to a third class District Munsiff's Court, with a monthly salary of Rs. 100, when Vētanāyakam Piḷḷai was appointed early in 1857 at the young age of thirty.[27] After only a few days, he was transferred as district munsiff to the nearby Cīrkāḻi (Sheally or Cīkāḻi), where he wrote his first book, the *Nītinūl* we will discuss below. In Cīrkāḻi, he

23. The following details have been taken from Parameswaran Pillai (1902: 157–172).

24. George Thomas Beauchamp, judge according to the *Register* of 1856, p.11.

25. For a short biographical sketch of T. Muttucāmi Aiyar, see Buckland (1906: 9), and in greater detail Parameswaran Pillai (1902: 157–172). A slightly different text is found in Parameswaran Pillai (1896: 93–116).

26. See G.O. No. 306, 26–39, dated March 17, 1857.

27. See G.O. No. 518–519, dated May 5, 1857.

often met with Mīṉāṭcicuntaram Piḷḷai who started composing his *Cīkāḻikkōvai*. As we have seen above, the work was premiered in 1859 with Vētanāyakam Piḷḷai presiding over the spectacle.[28]

In 1860, Vētanāyakam Piḷḷai was transferred again, this time to the town of Māyūram (Mayavaram) where he was to remain for the rest of his life. His long connection to this town also earned him the appendix to his name: Māyūram Vētanāyakam Piḷḷai. There he met Mēlakaram Cuppiramaṇiya Tēcikar, at the time junior head and from 1869 onward pontiff of the Tiruvāvaṭuturai monastery. Their friendship is attested by a number of occasional stanzas in which each praises the other according to typical pulavar conventions. The many *taṉippāṭals* and *cīṭṭukkavis* which Vētanāyakam Piḷḷai's biographers were able to collect demonstrate that he was a fully-fledged member of the pulavar community and very actively participated in the economy of praise I outlined in Chapter 2. But he was also an influential member of a wider social group which one may call the nineteenth-century Tamil intellectual elite, a whole network of scholars, literati, and social activists who were in very close contact with each other and who dominated the intellectual and political life in Southern India. Besides Mīṉāṭcicuntaram Piḷḷai and Cuppiramaṇiya Tēcikar one might mention Kōpālakiruṣṇa Pāratiyār (1811–1881), Āṟumuka Nāvalar (1822–1879), Ci. Vai. Tāmōtaram Piḷḷai (1832–1901), Irāmaliṅka Cuvāmikaḷ (1823–1874), U. Vē. Cāminātaiyar, Henry A. Kiruṣṇa Piḷḷai (1827–1900), or Cavarirāyalu Nāyakar.

Since Vētanāyakam Piḷḷai was a man who did not like toadying to his superiors, he did not always put up with their decisions and, as we have seen above, occasionally ran into trouble. A similar incident also provoked the end of his career as a colonial administrator. The Acting Civil Judge of Tranquebar James Henry Nelson (1838–1898), known to posterity mainly for his impressive historical manual *The Madura Country*, apparently had a particularly intense dislike for him.[29] He was involved in a series of allegations against Vētanāyakam Piḷḷai on the occasion of which the latter was forced to retire. John J. Paul, in his detailed study of Vētanāyakam Piḷḷai's dismissal proceedings, remarks that the dismissal was due to a combination of factors: "previous censure by the High Court for his carelessness, his continual disorderly maintenance of the court, his offensive attitude against the higher judicial officer [i.e., Nelson], his worsening physical condition

28. See the discussion above in Chapter 2 and *SMPC* I (168–188).

29. For Nelson's career as both colonial administrator and historian, see Derrett (1961). See also *The India Office List for 1887*, p. 192f.

and finally, the High Court's concerns in warning other Munsifs in the district" (Paul 1983: 23). Vētanāyakam Piḷḷai retired from his work in 1872 with a pension of Rs. 100, after fifteen years as district munsiff, and twenty-four years of service in the colonial administration.[30] For some years he became Municipal Chairman of Mayuram, the town where he had settled. The period after his retirement was the most fruitful with regard to his literary activities, since the majority of his writings, including his two novels, were composed after 1872. But besides his literary work, he also continued his earlier charitable activities, which had made him famous while still in office as munsiff. During the great famine of 1876–1878, he helped people in need in various ways. With his private money he founded a place where gruel was given to the poor for free. As mirrored in his writings (see below), he was also concerned with women's education and he established one of the first girls' schools in his district.

Three years after the publication of his second novel, on the night of Sunday, July 21, 1889, Vētanāyakam Piḷḷai died from dropsy in his house in Mayuram at the age of sixty-two. The leading English-language newspapers *The Hindu* and *The Southern Star* published their obituaries on July 24 and 27 respectively. There, his role as a novelist is not particularly emphasized, but only mentioned amongst his other merits. In the *Hindu*, his contemporaries have the following to say:

> As District Munsiff, he was very popular and discharged his duties with great credit and ability, at a time when Munsiffs of the present type were rare. [. . .] He was an erudite scholar of Tamil and devoted his lifetime to the embellishment of Tamil literature. He was a Tamil novelist and Tamil Poet. His prose and poetical works are read with great avidity by the Tamil-knowing population. The great merit of his works was the purity of expression, and the moral precepts of which they are so full. His ambition was

30. The pension was only secured after protracted litigation. After the initial allegations and the threat to dismiss him, Vētanāyakam Piḷḷai wrote a letter to the High Court on August 27, 1872, in order to request a reconsideration of his case, where we read: "Your generous heart will doubtless feel how hard it is that I should be deprived of my high office on such frivolous grounds, and thus reduced with my large family to a state of beggary, after an honourable career of 24 years. In these circumstances I throw myself on your protection and humbly request that you will be pleased to postpone the matter till the receipt of my explanation and thus save me and my large family from starvation and ruin which stare us in the face" (High Court Administrative Records, Judicial Proceedings, No. 219, dated August 27, 1872). The fascinating details of the case have been examined in detail in Paul (1983).

> to create a good Tamil literature so as to suit the modern taste of his countrymen, in which he attained eminent success. He interested himself very much in the successful administration of the local Municipality, over the Council of which he presided for several years. [. . .] In his death, the Native Community have lost a worthy citizen, a talented Tamil writer, in short, one whose literary attainments and whose earnest longing to improve the social and intellectual condition of his fellow-countrymen have won for him their everlasting gratitude. (Vētanāyakam Piḷḷai 1917: "Select press opinions")

In the *Southern Star*, the Mayuram correspondent wrote:

> He was a pious Christian and a great thinker. A regular student till his last moment. In him we have lost a great Tamil Novelist and a Poet. [. . .] In a word, he was the Oliver Goldsmith of our time. His death was felt here as something more than a public calamity. Men started at the intelligence and turned pale as if they had heard of the loss of a dear friend. (ibid.)

Both obituaries stress Vētanāyakam Piḷḷai's literary achievements, but they also note his significance outside the literary sphere. His death was indeed perceived as "more than a public calamity," not only by the Tamil population everywhere in the Madras Presidency, but also by the British. William Miller (1838–1923), principal and founder of the Madras Christian College,[31] sent a letter of condolence to Vētanāyakam Piḷḷai's son Ñāṉappirakācam Piḷḷai as did the missionary George Mackenzie Cobban who was at the time engaged in translating Vētanāyakam Piḷḷai's first novel into English.[32]

To sum up the discussion of Vētanāyakam Piḷḷai's life, I quote what is perhaps the most imaginative and comprehensive description of his position as an intellectual and cultural mediator. In the words of his biographer P. J. Louis:

---

31. For Miller's biography, see Kandaswamy Chetty (1924), the anonymous pamphlet *A Sketch of the Life of the Honourable The Rev. William Miller* (1894), the Tamil biography Rajaruthnam (1901), and the short sketch by Sharpe (1998).

32. See Vētanāyakam Piḷḷai (1917: "Select press opinions"). For a discussion of Cobban's translation, see the following chapter.

> He was a living embodiment of a lovely compromise between a purely old-time Tamil Pandit and a perverted Anglicised Indian, a High-browed superior official and a small, stooping official, the power-mad men of the officialdom and the self-conscious non-officials, the rich and rank materialists and the religious and fervant devotees, the Englishman and the Indian, the Roman Catholic and the Religious Hindu and the Brahman and the Non-Brahman. He was the common ground and rendezvous of all these diverse elements in society. (1963: 20f.)

Writing for "the moral improvement of the Natives of India": The *Nītinūl* (1859)

Although Vētanāyakam Piḷḷai had been composing occasional stanzas from his early youth, he properly embarked upon what was to become a career as a prolific author in the year 1859, when, aged thirty-three and recently transferred as district munsiff to Cīrkāḻi, he published his first book *Nītinūl* ("The Book of Right Conduct"). Following the usual pulavar practice, the work was immediately received with various *cāṟṟukkavis*. The large number of these, however, was quite extraordinary, for no less than fifty-six poets from all over the Tamil-speaking area sent their congratulatory verses. Vētanāyakam Piḷḷai's friend Mīṉāṭcicuntaram Piḷḷai even composed eleven stanzas (amounting to more than 180 lines), one of the longest *ciṟappuppāyirams* he had ever written.[33] This paratextual mass was in fact so enormous that it was printed as a separate appendix to the work, rather than following the usual practice of placing it at the beginning of the book as prefatory matter. This can be seen as a prime example of the pulavars' economy of praise appearing in print, and it shows clearly that Vētanāyakam Piḷḷai was thought to be a widely respected member of the pulavar community. Spurred by this warm welcome, Vētanāyakam Piḷḷai published a second revised and enlarged edition only a year later which now bore the explanatory English title "Nidinul or A Series of Stanzas on Moral Subjects, the whole being designed to expose vice, to inculcate the practice of virtue, and to point out the relative

33. For a full list of the fifty-six pulavars, see Paktavatcalam (1961: 41–3). Mīṉāṭcicuntaram Piḷḷai's *ciṟappuppāyiram* stanzas have been included in *SMPT* where the Tamil date *tai* month *kāḷayutti* year is given for the poems, which corresponds to January/February 1859 (*SMPT* 5090–5100).

duties of life."[34] The *Nītinūl* is a collection of 600 poems divided into 44 chapters on such varied subjects as "Attributes of God and Piety towards Him," "Character of a False Priest," "Education of Females," "Drunkenness," "On Excess in Sleep," "Characteristics of Dancing Girls or Public Prostitutes," and "Against Cruelty to Animals."[35] Vētanāyakam Piḷḷai's motives for writing this work survive in the form of his preface written in English:

> The want of an ethical work in Tamil, on the principle of the moral writings of English authors, is felt by all those who are interested in the moral improvement of the Natives of India. With a view to supply this desideratum, the author has undertaken to compose the following Poem consisting of 44 chapters, wherein he has endeavoured to convey accurate ideas of God; as well as of moral good and evil—to point out the wide range of social and moral duties incumbent on mankind, together with the grounds on which they are founded—and to exhibit the *amiableness* of virtue, and the *hideousness* of vice [. . .]. (Vētanāyakam Piḷḷai 1860: preface, i; original emphases)

Here, Vētanāyakam Piḷḷai explicitly declares his didactic, social-reformist agenda. Thus, publishing *Nītinūl* was as much a political as a literary move. Vētanāyakam Piḷḷai raised his voice in the contemporary debates on "the moral improvement of the Natives of India" where he was in line with British educationists, such as John Murdoch, George Norton, and others. From the point of view of literary history, he also purposefully contributed to remedy what they perceived as the lack of a "native" literature which could be used to instruct students. To recall George Norton's words: "Better *models* of composition are [. . .] needed—and particularly in prose, and such writings as may convey substantial knowledge, and sounder and more elevated sentiments" (1848: 54; original italics). In its emphasis on moral instruction and its indebtedness to "the best English moralists" (Vētanāyakam Piḷḷai 1860: preface, ii), the *Nītinūl* fitted well into such an educational program. Yet, it was not the much desired prose work, but poetry which the educational reformers had so forcefully condemned. As if

34. I am basing my discussion of the *Nītinūl* on this second enlarged edition (Vētanāyakam Piḷḷai 1860). This is the only historically accurate text, as later editions have been more or less radically abridged and otherwise altered.

35. I am quoting from the book's English table of contents.

preempting this objection, Vētanāyakam Piḷḷai goes on to explain in his preface that he

> has chosen Poetry as the medium of communicating his ideas, as a large majority of Hindoos have a stronger relish for *Poetical* than prosaic works. He has however taken care to compose the verses in a style so simple as to adapt them to the capacity of those whose knowledge of Tamil is only superficial. (Vētanāyakam Piḷḷai 1860: preface, i; original emphasis)

And this adjustment of style reveals the truly innovative character of his work. It meant a deliberate shift away from the elaborate scholarly poetry composed by the pulavars, which was—as we have seen—the typical poetic style of his days. It was also a style which he was well educated in as he had demonstrated, for instance, by his *ciṟappuppāyiram* stanzas for Mīṉāṭcicuntaram Piḷḷai's *Cīkāḻikkōvai* composed in the same year as the *Nītinūl*. His pulavar skills nothwithstanding, Vētanāyakam Piḷḷai obviously wished to transcend the narrow confines of traditional scholarly poetry and thus to reach a much wider audience. A closer look at the poems in the *Nītinūl* shows what this reference to a "simple style" actually means. The poems are quatrains composed in various traditional prosodic structures, such as *viruttam*, *kalitturai*, or *veṇpā* (so words are given in their usual metrical forms), and they do use imaginative similes and imagery. Their simplicity lies in the ordinary language employed and in the absence of complicated *cilēṭai* and other figures of speech which might obscure the direct meaning of a phrase. Thus, the author's agenda to contribute "to the composition of such works which would tend to the moral and intellectual elevation of his countrymen" (ibid., ii) was a stronger incentive for his literary activities than the pulavars' will to stun the audience by their poetic virtuosity. Unlike some of his fellow educationists, Vētanāyakam Piḷḷai did not explicitly ridicule or criticize the pulavars and their works. But he did include a chapter with six poems against "Pedantry and Literary Pride" in the *Nītinūl*, where we read:

> However hard you labor to sing your verses,
> what your imagination has brought forth is nothing new
> but what your predecessors said! Ancient texts
> there are many; it is not you who composed all those,
> nor have you fully understood everything. There are many
> who are better than you—so why do you
> pride yourself, my heart, on your learning? (27.1) [4.1]

What comes across here as a rather general statement about learning or arrogant students may well have been intended to rebuke haughty poets. However, Vētanāyakam Piḷḷai's innovative project of writing simple verses does not seem to have been disapproved of by fully-fledged pulavars, since they so amply publicized their praise in the *cāṟṟukkavis*. In combining a new poetic style with the selection of themes which were very much debated in nineteenth-century South Indian society, e.g., "Education of Females" or "Characteristics of Dancing Girls or Public Prostitutes," Vētanāyakam Piḷḷai was certainly one of the first authors to break with the tradition of scholarly poetry common in his times. He may, from this perspective, be called the first modern Tamil poet—an epithet which usually the famous Ci. Cuppiramaṇiya Pārati (1882–1921) is credited with, two generations later.[36] Yet, the poem quoted above bespeaks the author's awareness of being indebted to a poetic tradition, his innovative break notwithstanding. Similarly, his contemporaries placed his work firmly within the tradition of *nīti* works in Tamil, as becomes apparent from Mīṉāṭcicuntaram Piḷḷai's *cāṟṟukkavis* which connect Vētanāyakam Piḷḷai to Tiruvaḷḷuvar, the legendary author of the *Tirukkuṟaḷ*, the most popular ethical work in Tamil to this date.[37] And the connection is not far-fetched. Even at a general level, the *Nītinūl* deals with four spheres of moral duties also contained in the first two books of the *Tirukkuṟaḷ* (*aṟattuppāl* and *poruṭpāl*): the personal sphere or individual ethics, family or domestic duties, social duties, and the duties of a king. Then, one may observe how the *Nītinūl* takes up various topics, such as the characteristics of God, envy, gambling, falsehood, etc., which are also dealt with in the *Tirukkuṟaḷ*.[38] And finally, Vētanāyakam Piḷḷai himself explicitly quotes from Tiruvaḷḷuvar twice in his book.[39] Thus, while claiming that his work is "indebted to the best English moralists" (Vētanāyakam Piḷḷai 1860: preface, ii), he does not explicitly refer to any of them, but

36. This is not the place to discuss the historical development of Tamil poetry, but we clearly need a more sophisticated analysis than what is offered by most literary histories. A re-assessment would have to include the poetic works of nineteenth-century poets, such as Vētanāyakam Piḷḷai, Taṇṭapāṇi Cuvāmikaḷ (1839–1898), or Irāmaliṅka Cuvāmikaḷ (1823–1874), rather than simply referring to Bharati as the first "modern" Tamil poet.

37. For a discussion of the impact of the *Tirukkuṟaḷ* in nineteenth-century South India, see Blackburn (2000) and Müller (2000).

38. For a detailed discussion of these topics, see Raghupathy (1989, chs. 9 and 10).

39. In chapter 34 "On Excess in sleep," poem 4, he literally quotes from *Tirukkuṟaḷ* 339 "*uṟaṅkuvatu pōluñ cākkāṭu*" (like sleep is death), and in chapter 43 "Characteristics of Dancing Girls or Public Prostitutes," poem 24 he paraphrases *Tirukkuṟaḷ* 913 "Sleeping with a prostitute is like embracing a corpse."

instead locates his book within the "vernacular" tradition, and thus demonstrates how ideas taken from the Tamil literary classics may be modified and developed further to produce a new kind of writing which was entirely unprecedented in his times.

As has been remarked above, what deserves a closer look in terms of innovative contents are those chapters of the *Nītinūl* which deal with hotly-debated social issues of contemporary South Indian society, particularly those on the "Education of Females" or "Characteristics of Dancing Girls or Public Prostitutes." A brief discussion of these chapters will also serve to illustrate some general characteristics of the tone and style that Vētanāyakam Piḷḷai adopts in his book. At times, his message can be rather simple and straightforward, appealing to aesthetic pleasure in the use of clichéd metaphors ("those whose tresses are adorned by soft flowers"), as in the following poem on the "Education of Females" (chapter 9):

> Teaching books on ethics to men, but not
> to those whose tresses are adorned by soft flowers—
> this is like decorating one half of the body
> but leaving the other half without ornament. (9.7) [4.2]

The above argumentative structure of an extended comparison (x is similar to y) is used in many poems throughout the book. The chapter on women's education, with its total of thirteen poems, provides little more than a variation of the idea that it is good to educate women as well as men, for what brings men onto the right path could not do any harm to women (poem 9.1). Moreover, education is considered an embellishment to women (poem 9.10) and to their husbands (9.13). Such arguments are often clothed in rather obvious similes, such as women being like a lamp that gives light in the dark, but that is hidden in a basket as long as they are not educated (poem 9.6). The last poem in this chapter (9.13) has recourse to Hindu mythology and invokes the goddesses Vāṇi (Sarasvatī), Umai (Parvatī), and Kamalai (Lakṣmī) as well as the famous Tamil poetess Auvaiyar as examples of educated females. Then, cleverly elaborating a popular pan-Indian motif, the speaker asks why Sarasvatī, the goddess of learning who is said to reside on the tongues of (learned) men should not equally sit on women's tongues, being female herself. In its uncomplicated, genuine argumentative tone, the chapter on women's education is quite unlike other sections of the *Nītinūl*, where the author does not refrain from employing striking, sometimes even gruesome similes or bitter sarcasm in order to drive home his moral lessons.[40] Yet, in one poem of this chapter, we also come across a more sarcastic tone:

> Those parents who, in fear that she would be spoilt,
> deny her daughter education—they are
> like a husband who effortlessly plucks out
> his wife's eyes, thinking she might see other men. (9.2) [4.3]

Sarcasm and bitter irony are in fact most drastically employed in *Nītinūl*'s chapter 43 "Characteristics of Dancing Girls or Public Prostitutes" ("*Kaṇikaiyar iyalpu*") which portrays the rapacity and evil cunning of prostitutes and the naiveté with which most of their customers approach them. Apparently, Vētanāyakam Piḷḷai wanted the reader not to miss his point, for the chapter contains not less than 40 poems, being surpassed only by the chapters on "Conjugal Affection" and "Attributes of God and Piety towards Him" which contain 48 and 70 poems, respectively. In including a chapter on prostitutes, the author seems to have followed the traditional structure of treatises on *nīti*, such as apparent in the *Tirukkuṟaḷ* or the *Nālaṭiyār* which show clear thematic similarities. The connection becomes most obvious in poem 43.24 which explicitly mentions the name Vaḷḷuvar and paraphrases poem 913 of the *Tirukkuṟaḷ* "Sleeping with a prostitute is like embracing a corpse." In a fashion similar to the older works, the majority of the poems highlight the prostitutes' greed and treacherous charm which may lead men primarily to financial, later to moral ruin.[41] Poem 43.9 illustrates the basic economic laws of dealing with prostitutes: For only one single thing (money), the customer gets a whole range of things in return, such as disease, poverty, lies, murder, theft, etc. The poet also observes how prostitutes have no other god than the man who gives them money (43.36), and he impressively paints their physical charms:

> To eat from other peoples' plates, to wear
> other peoples' clothes, to sleep
> in someone else's bed, no one's mind would bear.
> To swallow the saliva from a prostitute's mouth

40. Despite Vētanāyakam Piḷḷai's sarcasm I would not go as far as Zvelebil who claims that the *Nītinūl* was "striking for its pessimism, bitterness, and Siddha-like hatred of women—the temptress" (1974: 127).

41. See e.g., poems 43.1, 6, 7, 25, 32, and 38.

which is like a spittoon used by many,
 to be shoulder to shoulder with this unclean figure
who has united with many people,
 whose mind could bear this? (43.18) [4.4]

Among the most interesting poems contained in this chapter are those which make use of Hindu mythology in rather unexpected ways. While in his other works, the catholic Vētanāyakam usually claimed that he consciously tried not to denigrate any other religion, it seems that in the often ironical poetry of his *Nītinūl* occasionally he could not abstain from mockery:

One wife joined in marriage her husband's disciple,
 another wife the king of the celestials [Indra],
another wife [her husband's] brothers,
 and they all were hailed as ideal women.
The prostitute, who unites with me, my sons, brothers,
 disciples and the lord of this world,
may be praised as
 the crest-jewel of all these women. (43.26) [4.5]

Here, the notes of ridicule are still muffled, for mythological details are merely hinted at and were not so obvious to the audience. The wife who married her husband's disciple refers to Tārā, the wife of Bṛhaspati, teacher of the Gods. She fell in love with the Moon (Skt. Candra) and had a son with him. The ancient vedic sage (Skt. *ṛṣi*) Gautama's wife Ahalyā coupled with Indra, the king of the gods. And the third line refers to the famous legend of Draupadī who bore five sons to the five Pāṇḍava brothers. All three, Tārā, Ahalyā, and Draupadī are traditionally part of the *pañcakaṉṉiyar*, the five "ideal women."

Poem 43.14 carries the mockery of Hinduism further, this time clearly in a less indirect way. In their directness, the following lines are quite unusual for Vētanāyakam Piḷḷai's otherwise sensitive circumspection:

He who rides a bull [Śiva] ate poison, kicked the god
  of death,
 slew the demon and burnt the city, thus
the Śaivites of this sea[-girded] earth elaborate on his fame.
 If he ate the eye-poison of the dancing girls,
kicked the death of their round breasts, killed the demon
 called chief courtesan and burnt the city
where they live—then also *we*
 would sing his praise. (43.14) [4.6]

The poem alludes to well-known puranic legends about Śiva's destructive undertakings. The theme of the obnoxious dancing girls is then rather forcefully pressed upon the mythology by means of metaphors and similes. Contained in these lines is more than mockery. We discern also the poet's disapproval of the fact that dancing girls are tolerated by, or indeed an integral part of, Hindu traditions. And if Śiva cannot help in solving the problem, another authority has to be invoked.

Once again not mincing matters, poem 43.20 aims to show that the problem of prostitution is similar to theft and murder, so that it requires the attention and action of the colonial government:

Killing murderers and
  keeping thieves in rigorous imprisonment,
our English rulers handle
  and punish those vile people who commit crimes.
By not killing the prostitute,
  whose character brings great evil to a man's soul
and who is the embodiment of all sins,
  alas, what have they allowed her to do in the world!
   (43.20) [4.7]

It becomes clear at this point that Vētanāyakam Piḷḷai's chapter on the dancing girls does more than regurgitate medieval discontent about "wanton women" along the lines of the *Tirukkuṟaḷ*. It also has to be read against the background of the contemporary public debates on *devadāsīs*, nautch girls, and prostitution, which were conducted throughout the entire nineteenth century. In the above lines, the poet does not only implicitly promote what he considers to be the beneficial influences of colonial rule on his society, he also suggests, if in a somewhat exaggerated statement, that prostitution as a crime has to be tackled by government authorities. When his book came out in 1859, his was one of the earliest South Indian voices of what was yet to crystallize as the anti-nautch movement.

To fully understand the importance of Vētanāyakam Piḷḷai's ideas on prostitution, we have to pause here briefly and explore the wider context of the contemporary public debates on the status of women in society, *devadāsīs*, and nautch girls. Victorian attitudes to sexuality and the anxieties sparked by the spread of prostitution back in England[42] as well as missionary zeal to tackle "the 'internal principles

42. For the complexities of Victorian attitudes to sexuality, see Adams (1999) and the literature cited there. In addition, one may look at Levine (1994; 2003) for the construction of the prostitute as a source of venereal diseases in British India.

of depravity' in Indian cultures themselves" (Majeed 1992: 80) were among the primary forces which, during the whole of the nineteenth century, repeatedly triggered extended public discussions on the topic of prostitution in India. These debates focused especially on the status and activities of several originally distinct social groups, mainly the dancing girls or *nautch girls* (or *Rum Johnnies* in contemporary soldiers' parlance), who were secular performers, sometimes attached to zamindar courts (as we have seen above in the discussion of the *Cētupati Viṟaliviṭutūtu*), the *devadāsīs*[43] or temple girls, who performed ritual functions in Hindu temples, and prostitutes in the conventional sense of the term.[44] The distinction between these groups soon became blurred by their critics, since what counted for them was these womens' involvement with what they considered to be licentious behavior. Both the nautch girls and *devadāsīs* performed dances to songs which were overtly expressive of female erotic desires (which usually attracted large audiences), and they both had a privileged status, which set them apart from other Indian women. Already Vētanāyakam Piḷḷai lumped prostitutes and dancing girls together in the English title to chapter 43 of his *Nītinūl*. And what is more, he also used the terms "dancing girls" (*kaṇikaiyar*) and "prostitute(s)" (*vēciyar, vilaimātu* or *poruḷmātu*) interchangeably in his poems. An article of the newspaper *Subodh Patrike* reprinted in the missionary monthly *The Harvest Field* in September 1887 displays their ambiguous social position between aesthetic pleasure and moral deviation which continued to puzzle most of their critics:

> The dancing girl is everywhere. It is she who crowns all merriment at all times. If it is a marriage she gives the finishing stroke to the gaieties of the occasion. If you begin to occupy a house newly built, the ceremony of the day is only brought to a conclusion when the house rings to the noise of her anklets, as the phrase goes. Nay, you cannot treat a

43. A sanskritization of the Tamil term *tēvaraṭiyāḷ* "(female) slave of the god." For a detailed analysis of the lives of *devadāsīs*, their social status, and the changes brought about by reformers, see Srinivasan (1985) who shows how the *devadāsī's* dance was eventually transmogrified into a sanitized and reinvented *Bharatanatyam*. On the *devadāsīs* of South India, see also Kersenboom (1987). On the role of the *devadāsīs* in the reshaping of South India's performing arts see Peterson/Soneji (2008).

44. See Forbes (1998: 181–86) for a discussion about which groups of women were included in the category "prostitute." For a detailed study of prostitution in colonial Madras, see Sundara Raj (1993).

> friend or bid farewell to a departing Anglo-Indian, except by her mediation. It is this importance and this shameful patronage accorded to her that we quarrel with. [. . .] Considered from a pecuniary, social or indeed any other point of view except the moral and religious, her position is far better than that of the millions toiling and moiling members of the Indian womanhood. And there is a freedom and license and an amount of worship of the other sex about her which is specially attractive to minds not open to the light of a high morality. But at the same time, she is the bane of youthful morality. With her rich dress, her trained voice, and the skilful manipulations of her hands and feet, she is the centre of attention to young impressionable minds. (*The Harvest Field*, September 1887: 99)

Interestingly, the above extract highlights the importance and attractions of the dancing girls, but does not spell out clearly what it was that made the institution so despicable. A clearer idea might be gained by Nancy Paxton's characterization of the *devadāsīs* which was in many ways true for the dancing girls in general:

> *Devadasis* could be well educated, highly literate, and culturally sophisticated, since they studied dance and music, and were well versed in both the oral and written sacred traditions. They were often trained to read Sanskrit and other languages, and sometimes they composed and performed their own poetry. *Devadasis* served important ritual functions because they danced in Hindu temples and performed in other religious celebrations, weddings, and other auspicious public events. Unconstrained by the restrictions of purdah, *devadasis* remained unmarried, but were not required to practice chastity. They were exempt from many caste restrictions and were free to engage in sexual relations with any man of the proper caste without public censure. They also escaped the ritual prohibitions defining widowhood. Finally, they were able to inherit property and bequeath it to their biological or adopted daughters. [. . .] In other words, the *devadasi* marked the threshold of several of the most contested boundaries in the colonial imagination that separated the inner from the outer, the private from the public, and the sacred from the sexual. (1999: 85)

And here, the colonial imagination was initially limited to the ideas that British educationists and Christian missionaries voiced about India's present and future, while only later "native" social reformers joined in. The predicament was contained in the question of how to deal with something that was well-established and appealed to the senses but had to be rejected by an imported Victorian rationality. The dancing girl, who had been celebrated in texts of a courtly milieu like Caravaṇap Perumāḷ Kavirāyar's *Cētupati Viṟaliviṭutūtu*, now came in for blame. It was a question of how to cope with "morality in collision with sexuality" (Adams 1999: 130).

Due to their contested social position, the temple and dancing girls were subjected to criticism from various sides, notably from evangelical Christian missionaries who, as Paxton remarks, "began to exert a significant influence on Indian colonial policy in the period between 1820 and 1850" (1999: 87). In the Tamil-speaking area, we come across an extended debate within missionary and social reformers' circles about these stigmatized women during the 1880s. Right from its foundation in 1878, the leading English-language newspaper of the Madras Presidency *The Hindu* attacked the *devadāsī* system. This press campaign, as part of what came to be known as the "anti-nautch movement," was spearheaded by its founding editor Ka. Cuppiramaṇiyam (better known as G. Subramania Iyer, 1855–1916), himself an ardent reformer (Paramarthalingam n.d.: 47).[45] In July 1880, the Wesleyan Methodist minister George Mackenzie Cobban (1846–1905), whose activities in the field of Tamil literature we shall briefly discuss in the following chapter, published a heartrending poem in English titled "The Hindu Temple Girl" in the *Harvest Field*, which describes the pangs of an aging *devadāsī* who bemoans her wasted life and expresses her hope to be finally redeemed by the Christian God. The poem ends with what is presented as a desperate wish uttered by the woman:

> If I could get my girlhood back when I pass away,
> And find, in His great temple, a place to kneel and pray,
> Where even I might blossom, as the flowers I used to weave,
> In my hair on festive days. I could die and would not grieve.
>
> And I would ask this Swami [= the Christian God] to hasten if he can,

45. For a biography of G. Subramania Iyer, see Govindarajan (1969).

> And save the Devadasi, from the cruel wrongs of man
> And rouse the heart of England, as it ne'er yet has been,
> Never to rest till men behold fair India's temples clean
> (Cobban 1880: 11).

Surely, this was more of an ardent missionary's phantasmagoria than a real woman's lament, but it reflects the sense of duty that both the Christian churches and the colonial government felt vis-à-vis their subjects.

Six years later, the same journal printed an article on "Courtesans and their Influence on Hindu Society" by an anonymous "Mysore Thinker." Here, the author is less concerned with the courtesans' state of mind than with the evil influence that they exercise on society: "They tempt young minds to swerve from the path of virtue. [. . .] There are not wanting instances of educated young men who have yielded to them and have gone to ruin" (*The Harvest Field*, January 1886: 209). He further explains that the fact that dancing girls are well educated poses a serious obstacle to reforms of female education:

> No Hindu parent thinks of having his children taught music, because by this acquisition they would in the minds of the people be associated with gay and dissolute women. [. . .] This evil association has made many ignorant Hindus think that female education is necessary only for dancing girls, but not for others. [. . .] These professional women by monopolising music and other feminine accomplishments have prevented honest women from acquiring them. (ibid., 209–11)

The "Mysore Thinker" also points out another "social danger": "Dancing girls bring up poor and orphan girls, and bring them up to a life of infamy" (ibid., 210). He thus points to the fact that, before the colonial establishment of orphanages and female asylums, the *devadāsīs* fulfilled another important social duty by taking into their custody those girls who did not have any other place in society. Further discussions continued much along the same lines and provided repeated calls to action. In September 1888, the *Harvest Field* published a short statement by a missionary correspondent who complained why such illustrious Hindu social reformers as Raghunatha Rao did not address "the dancing girl system" (*The Harvest Field* 1888: 95). He was sure that "[t]he day has come when both European Christians of influence and position and also Native reformers should lay bare the axe at the root of this accursed tree" (ibid., 96). In fact, in the meantime several "native" reformers, such as G. Subramania Iyer or Vētanāyakam Piḷḷai had variously voiced their opinion and condemned prostitution and the evil character of dancing girls. With Vētanāyakam Piḷḷai's *Nītinūl*, already more than twenty years before this missionary's words were written, the nautch girls as the fount of social evil had found their way into Tamil literature. And there were other Tamil authors, too, who took up this sensitive social issue, like Caitāpuram Kācivicuvanāta Mutaliyār (?1806–1871) and Pa. Va. Irāmacāmi Rāju (1852–1897) in their immensely popular stage plays *Ṭampāccāri vilācam* (c. 1867) and *Piratāpa Cantira vilācam* (1877). Vētanāyakam Piḷḷai as well returned to the subject of prostitution in his writings on women's education as we shall see shortly. Let us first return for a moment to the *Nītinūl*.

In the year 1885, more than twenty years after the *Nītinūl* had first appeared in print, Vētanāyakam Piḷḷai asked his younger brother Ñāṉappirakācam Piḷḷai, who worked as a secretary at the Munsiff Courts in Mayuram and Tranquebar and who was a student of Mīṉāṭcicuntaram Piḷḷai, to write a commentary (*urai*) to his book (Vēṅkaṭacāmi 1962: 280f.). We do not know anything about the reasons for this request. Perhaps, as the book was used for Tamil language instruction in schools and colleges, the students needed elucidation of the poetry, despite Vētanāyakam Piḷḷai's original goal to publish simple verses that could be easily understood by all readers. However, it seems also quite likely that by having someone write an *urai* the poet wanted to reinforce the prestige of his book as a classical work, since, in the pulavar tradition, the "classics" were distinguished by such kind of satellite texts. If a text was important, many different scholars would write their commentaries and thus underscore the status of the original text (*mūlam*). Whatever may have been the reason for the *urai*, Vētanāyakam Piḷḷai did not live to see it printed, as it only came out in the year 1892. In subsequent editions, the text of the 1860 edition did not survive unaltered. The currently available editions by Pa. Irāmanāta Piḷḷai (Vētanāyakam Piḷḷai 1969; i.e., the Kaḻakam ed.) and Pā. Aṉparacu (Vētanāyakam Piḷḷai 1994a) have substituted Sanskrit-derived words in a number of the original chapter headings with "pure Tamil" ones and neither of them contains the original number of stanzas.[46] Such alterations have been the fate of Vētanāyakam Piḷḷai's other works, too, with particularly damaging results in the case of his two novels, as we shall see below.

46. Aṉparacu's edition has only 529 stanzas as opposed to the original 600.

Law, Women's Education and Devotional Poetry: Vētanāyakam Piḷḷai's Other Writings

After the publication of his *Nītinūl*, Vētanāyakam Piḷḷai turned to other subjects. In September 1862, he published a digest of case law of the Sudder Court under the bilingual title "A Translation in Tamil of the Rulings of the Sudder Udalut from 1805 to 1861. 1805 *varuṣam mutal* 1861 *varuṣam varaiyil uḷḷa catarkkōrṭṭāravarkaḷiṉ cittāntacaṅkirakam*" (Vētanāyakam Piḷḷai 1862). The book was printed in Madras by the Scottish Press.[47] In his English preface dated September 5, 1862, Vētanāyakam Piḷḷai explains that he found a compilation and translation of the Sudder Court rulings necessary, as the rulings were "interspersed through so many volumes, that even those who are familiar with the English language, and have Copies of those volumes within their reach, experience much difficulty in making themselves at home with the principles and rules laid down therein" (Vētanāyakam Piḷḷai 1962: iii). According to his biographer Ñāṉappirakācam Piḷḷai, he published another Tamil summary of the High Court decisions of the years 1862 and 1863 two years later (Ñāṉappirakācam Piḷḷai 1890: 19).[48] As we learn from chapter 42 of his first novel *Piratāpa Mutaliyār carittiram* (1879), Vētanāyakam Piḷḷai strongly advocated the use of Tamil (instead of English) at law-courts, so his translations may be regarded as a first step into that direction.[49] His contemporaries valued highly the fact that he enriched the Tamil language by coining new legal terms. One of his biographers comments: "Just as he is considered the father of the Tamil novel, he may also be regarded as the father of juridical Tamil" (Pāṇṭuraṅkaṉ 1994: 45). Thus, he contributed to the shaping of Tamil prose as a technical language, while his attempts at literary prose were yet to come.

Seven years later, in 1869, he made another literary-cum-political move when he published two works on the education of women in

47. On June 17, 1863, Vētanāyakam Piḷḷai sent two copies of his new book to the Madras High Court accompanied by a letter in which he requested the "patronage" by the High Court judges and remarked that "the demand for the work has exceeded my expecations." The High Court answered, however, that it was not "the practice of the High Court to recommend the purchase of works of this kind on account of Government." See *Proceedings and Letters of the High Court, Appellate Side, Madras, for the year 1863*, Diary, June 25, No. 3163.

48. This book now seems to be lost.

49. See Vētanāyakam Piḷḷai (1885: 279–290, ch. 42 "*cutēca pāṣāpivirtti. Tamiḻiṉ arumai,*" i.e., "The Advancement of the Vernacular. The Greatness of Tamil"), and see below for further discussion.

one volume: the collection of poems *Peṇmati mālai* ("The Garland of Female Wisdom") and the essay *Peṇ kalvi* ("Women's Education"). While he had already included thirteen poems on this topic in his *Nītinūl,* he now dealt with it in greater detail and thus consciously raised his voice in what was one of the hottest socio-political debates of nineteenth-century India. He states in his English preface:

> At such a time as this when the necessity there is for educating the fair sex of our land, has been fully shown, when the natives of this Presidency have been brought to feel the want of such education, when exertions are put forth in various quarters to establish schools for the education of females, and when the Government have made arrangements for establishing a female Normal School, with a view to educate them most effectually, indeed, no apology is needed to publish a book on the training and education of females. (Vētanāyakam Piḷḷai 1978a: 30)

However, opinions as to extent and methods of educating women were certainly much more divided than they appear in Vētanāyakam Piḷḷai's rather positive and confident statements here. His statements may, in fact, be read as more of a deliberate justification than the author would have us believe. He finds stronger words in the last paragraph of his preface:

> One of the crying evils of the land being the degradation to which females are subjected in their domestic and social life, the writer has dwelt at some length on this evil, and has endeavoured to *convince* the reader, by facts and illustrations, by a reference to the old shastras, etc. of the right that the softer sex of our land have to be treated by their husbands, etc. with greater kindness and regard than what, by the pernicious custom of this country, fall to their lot. (ibid., 31; emphasis added)

So once again, the author followed an educationist agenda and wanted to instruct his readers, but this time he employed *prose* which takes up the bulk of the volume besides his short collection of poems. He characterizes his work thus:

> This book consists of two parts, the first being advice to females, written in Tamil metre, on the manner of behaving

> themselves, with rules and principles to guide them, [. . .] on the characteristics of a good wife as compared with those of a bad one, and on the necessity of educating females [. . .]. The whole of this part [. . .] was originally written for the use of the author's own daughters [. . .]. The second part contains an Essay on Female Education, in writing which, the author endeavoured to draw all illustrations from facts that Hindus are acquainted with, and to show the absurdities of their prejudices and objections in the most agreeable manner possible, without religious bias, and thus to adapt the Essay to the taste of Hindus in general without distinction of class or creed. (ibid., 30f.)

When he published a second edition a year later, in October 1870, he added a second essay titled *Peṇ māṉam* ("Women's Dignity") "on the Social Status of women, the respect due to them, and the manner in which they should be treated" (ibid., 32). He gave the following reason for doing so: "The fact that Hindu women are treated almost like slaves by the generality of Hindu men and that they are not allowed either freedom of speech or freedom of action, has struck the author as such a great social evil, that he has added a Separate Essay on the subject" (ibid.). Although in his English text he used the term "essay," in the Tamil text he referred to these "essays" as *vacaṉakāviyam*. *Vacaṉakāviyam* is also the term he employed for his novels, so that it has often been translated as "prose epic." However, as he used the term for his essays, too, the more general "prose composition" may perhaps be a better rendering.

The argument put forward in *Peṇ kalvi* moves from women's education in particular to education in general as being intimately connected with language competence, i.e., knowledge of Tamil as one's mother tongue. Vētanāyakam Piḷḷai directly addresses the need of prose for the profit of the country:

> In this country, those who have studied foreign languages and do not know their mother tongue {*cuyapāṣai*} obtain distinguished positions. We do not say this with envy. As there are many excellent books on various subjects in foreign languages, like English, French, and others, it is our heartfelt desire that these compatriots write prose compositions in the vernaculars {*cutēcappāṣaikaḷil*}, so that the precious subjects contained in those books may become profitable to the women and men of this country. (ibid., 52) [4.8]

While in his first work, the *Nītinūl*, Vētanāyakam Piḷḷai was still in favor of *poetry*, he now seems to have adopted the idea that prose was the medium of the future. Of course, this echoed the familiar reformist agenda of Norton, Murdoch, and others. Not surprisingly, he went on to argue that the new writing was necessary, as much of the existing literature was of little use to a larger audience:

> The books of this country which are in the form of poetry {*kāviyarūpamāy*} are useless for many. The stanzas of some scholars do not become clear, even if we look at them for the whole day. It is doubtful whether they themselves know the meaning. They may sing on any deity, but will that deity understand the meaning? One should ask that deity. If eminent scholars look at those poems, even they do not know their meaning. The rare words employed in those stanzas are not even found in the dictionary. The commentaries written by certain scholars for certain works or the translations of English books done by some could be Tamil, or unintelligible scribble—one is confused, not knowing whether it is perhaps some other language. It is only by looking at the original text that one can make sense of its commentary. (ibid., 52f.) [4.9]

Read from this perspective, Vētanāyakam Piḷḷai's essays are more than just essays. They also reflect a momentous shift from poetry to prose. They bespeak a change of consciousness, of conscience, and they show how the reform of the "vernacular" was able to influence individual thinking.

Once convinced of the utility and importance of prose for the national destiny, Vētanāyakam Piḷḷai was ready to reiterate his credo in his novelistic writing. In chapter 42 of his first novel *Piratāpa Mutaliyār carittiram*, he lets his female protagonist declare in the midst of a long speech:

> We have to admit that it is a major want that Tamil does not possess prose compositions {*vacaṉakāviyaṅkaḷ*} like English, French and other languages. [. . .] If the European languages had remained without prose compositions, could those countries have attained civilization and high culture? Thus, as long as there are no prose compositions in our own languages, this country will definitely not be properly reformed. (Vētanāyakam Piḷḷai 1885: 287f.) [4.10]

At first sight such lines merely seem to reflect the colonial educationist concern we have discussed above—a theoretical desideratum still far from being brought into action and thus sounding rather hollow. But against the background of Vētanāyakam Piḷḷai's personal development from poetry to prose, we may discern here the ultimate motive behind actual literary practice. We see here the emergence of the "modern author" who writes not to make a living, but because he is convinced that he has something to say that is socially and politically important, who is driven by his reformist agenda, and for whom literature becomes an instrument of social reform. His own confession becomes the much-desired agenda for fellow writers. Envisioning "civilization" (*nākarīkam*) and "high culture" (*naṟpāṅku*) as the ultimate goals, Vētanāyakam Piḷḷai refers to a process of "reform" (*cīrtiruttam*) brought about by those who are educated in European languages and who cast the "precious subjects contained in those [European] books" into Tamil moulds. He himself lived a life doing just this, passing on whatever he thought were the most elevated pieces of knowledge he came across. His story as an author demonstrates how a theoretical reform program crystallized into actual literary activity.

But let us for a moment return to the two essays *Peṇ kalvi* and *Peṇ māṉam*. They are of interest to us here in so far as they already foreshadow the prose style Vētanāyakam Piḷḷai later used in his novels. Lengthy, occasionally verbose hypotactic constructions, ample use of similes, proverbs[50] and rhetorical questions, as well as a heavily sanskritized lexicon form the main characteristics of his prose style. A longer quotation, the beginning of *Peṇ kalvi*, may serve to give an impression of this:

> It is a fact well-known to everyone that the women of this country are dwelling in the darkness of ignorance because they lack education. Although some do recognize the necessity of education for women, many object wrongly, asking what occupation women were to pursue after studying, or maintaining that, if women study, they will not obey their husbands and become spoiled through pride of learning. But is education required merely for an occupation and not to attain faith in God, intelligence and good qualities? Not at all. Just as the water used to irrigate paddy equally serves grass and other plants, as a tank dug for drinking is of use

---

50. For lists of proverbs used in *Peṇ kalvi* and *Peṇ māṉam*, see Kiṟisṭi Merci (1995: appendix, pp. 28–30) and Rācakōpālaṉ (1985: 214f.).

> for bathing and other purposes also, and as a tree which is planted to yield fruits also gives shade, etc.—in the same way, education which is pursued for the improvement of the intellect is also used as an instrument to [obtain an] occupation, so that saying that studying is only for [obtaining an] occupation is equal to saying that the head is made for the cap and not the cap for the head.
>
> As food is for the body, education is highly important for the intellect. Though the Lord has given us a body which grows from day to day, if we ourselves do not search for suitable food and all the things necessary for our health, our body will not grow. Equally, even if God has made us a genius, since whatever natural knowledge we have does not suffice, it is our duty to provide the food called "education" and to improve our intellect. [. . .] As to how our mind is made up, it is moving about in the whole heaven and earth without remaining idle for even a second. It is of such quality that even if we are idle, if we work, we are lying down or if we are sleeping, its roaming does not rest at any time, it feels no tiredness, no fatigue. If this mind does not have education as its protector, there is no doubt that it will roam about like an unreined horse, like a monkey wandering at random, like the flood overflowing the shores, and like a bullock which cannot be bridled it will wander about the whole country and will drag us into evil forests, over hills, rocks, and thorns, and at last will push us into the nether world called hell. Only due to this reason it has become a custom to educate the male children, whether they like to work or not. (Vētanāyakam Piḷḷai 1978a: 27f.) [4.11]

As we do not possess detailed studies on the development of Tamil prose, it is difficult at this point to decide precisely which elements characterize Vētanāyakam Piḷḷai's personal style and which were common to other nineteenth-century prose writers. It may be said, however, that hypotaxis and sanskritization clearly were general characteristics of nineteenth-century Tamil prose—an issue we shall take up below.

In terms of contents, the two essays can be seen as a prose reworking of many of the ideas already contained in the *Nītinūl*. Vētanāyakam Piḷḷai himself makes this clear by often referring to or quoting directly from it. As in the *Nītinūl*, he draws upon examples from Hindu mythology and hagiography, and again prostitutes constitute a topic of major importance taken up repeatedly. Again, he forcefully condemns the abuse of liquor as well as cruelty against animals. But he also mentions several classical Tamil works, such as the *Tirukkuṟaḷ, Nālaṭiyār, Kamparāmāyaṇam,* or *Cīvaka Cintāmaṇi* from which he quotes one stanza to show that Cīvakaṉ's mother was a learned woman. What emerges as his ethic is an interesting, personal amalgamation of Hindu and Christian doctrines. He concedes that eating meat is not forbidden for Christians, but strongly advocates vegetarianism, as "there is no other food in the world which is as unclean and disgusting as meat" (ibid., 121) [4.12]. Similarly, while he amply draws upon Hindu mythology, he repeatedly refers to one "God" in very Christian terms. Westerners and Western concepts are frequently mentioned to illustrate his points. Europeans are mentioned as high-standing moral exemplars, for instance when he argues that female education does not make women unfaithful to their husbands: "European ladies, who know all [branches of] knowledge and have unfailing love and affection for their husbands, demonstrate that what we say is true" (ibid., 30) [4.13]. Or, in a stronger vein: "Not only do we have to sigh before Europe's civilization like a barren woman sighs before a mother who has just given birth, nay, as long as the women are not educated, our country will not be improved" (ibid., 40) [4.14].

In *Peṇ māṉam,* Vētanāyakam Piḷḷai explains that in countries like Europe women who have lost their husbands are allowed to marry again. In the same essay, he condemns brahmins' dowry practices as well as child marriage. More radically than his *Nītinūl,* these essays show Vētanāyakam Piḷḷai as an ardent social reformer. I have called his texts "political," since they have to be seen against the background of the wider, pan-Indian debates about women during the nineteenth century.[51] In the midst of heated debates carried out in the

51. There is a vast and steadily growing literature on this subject, but as usual South India has been less well served. The most important studies for South India are Sita Anantha Raman's history of female education in the Tamil districts (Raman 1996), and Mytheli Sreenivas' study of the conjugal family ideal in colonial South India (Sreenivas 2008). On the widow re-marriage movement in the South, see ch. 2 in Paramarthalingam (n.d.). General discussions of nineteenth-century reformulations of gender issues in India may be found in Forbes (1998) and in the essays contained in Sangari/Vaid (1989) and Sarkar (2001). The essays contained in Tharu/Lalita (1991) also contain precious background information and raise new questions. For debates about widow-burning (or *sati*), see Mani (1999), while the legal position of women during the colonial period is discussed in Nair (1996).

newly founded magazines and newspapers as well as via pamphlets,[52] Vētanāyakam Piḷḷai voiced his opinion on a number of issues: women's education, the evils of prostitution, widow remarriage, brahmin dowry habits, and child marriage. That social reform in general, and questions of female identity in particular, were important to him is also demonstrated by the fact that he addressed these issues again in his novels and even in his songs. In his concerns with women's education and their situation in domestic and public life ("one of the crying evils of the land," ibid.), he was one of the harbingers of the decisive reformations of female identity that took place in nineteenth-century Tamil society.[53]

Like the *Nītinūl*, *Peṇmati mālai*, *Peṇ kalvi*, and *Peṇ māṉam* were often reprinted after their first publication in one volume in 1870. Due to its "wholesome" prose content, the book was soon prescribed for college and university examinations. Apparently, it was read as far away from its original home as England, when it was prescribed for the Senior examination in Tamil at Cambridge University in 1924.[54] I have been able to find several reviews in English.[55] The earliest appeared in Sri Lanka in the *Jaffna Freeman* and was not sparing in its praise: "He describes the inner life of Hindu Females most accurately, and points out most cleverly the evil effects arising from the state of degradation to which they are now subject. We must confess that, although we have seen a number of works in Tamil prose we have not met with such an excellent prose composition as the one we now review."[56] When in 1912 Vētanāyakam Piḷḷai's son V. Ñāṉappirakācam

52. How turbulent debates centering around the social position of women actually were is illustrated by the fact that in October 1884, the *Hindu* newspaper published an announcement that after several weeks of polemic discussion no more readers' comments "on the question of Hindu Widow Marriage" would be printed and that readers should refrain from inundating the newspapers' head office with their letters (*The Hindu*, 13 October 1884).

53. For further discussions of Vētanāyakam Piḷḷai's ideas about women, see Rācakōpālaṉ (1985) and the abridged reissue Irācakōpālaṉ (1999), and Kiṟisṭi (1994).

54. See the preface by Ma.Vē. Tiruñāṉacampantaṉ in Vētanāyakam Piḷḷai (1924).

55. The "Select press opinions" appended to the 1917 edition of *Piratāpa Mutaliyār carittiram* also contain three Tamil reviews (see Vētanāyakam Piḷḷai 1917).

56. The review is quoted in the 1901 edition of the book (Vētanāyakam Piḷḷai 1901). Unfortunately, I have not been able to find the original text of the review. Thus, I have no reliable information regarding its author and date. It must have been published before 1879, as the *Jaffna Freeman* closed down that year. Perhaps it even appeared as early as 1869, since it refers to the first edition of the book which only contained *Peṇmati mālai* and *Peṇ kalvi*.

Piḷḷai published a new edition of the book, it was briefly reviewed in *The Madras Mail* on Thursday, July 11, 1912.[57] On July 24 of the same year, U. Vē. Cāminātaiyar reviewed the book for *The Hindu*:

> The book is written in simple, attractive Tamil, and appeals easily to the imagination of girls [. . .] The telling illustrations of the author will surely create an impression in the minds of young girls, and the nature of the advice given to them in the book is calculated to elevate their morals and ennoble their lives. The versification does not seem to be laboured, and the songs fall most harmoniously on the ear. The book has an educative value, and as such, deserves to be taught to young girls whose formation of character is not among the least considerations of loving parents. (Vētanāyakam Piḷḷai 1917: "Select press opinions," vii)

Despite its obvious and universally acknowledged "educative value," it seems that after the enthusiasm of the 1910s and 1920s other texts were preferred for use in schools, colleges, and universities. The receding attention was certainly influenced by the fact that finally, after half a century, discussions about women's role in society had progressed and Vētanāyakam Piḷḷai's ideas had lost their novelty and immediate relevance. Toward the end of the twentieth century, Vētanāyakam Piḷḷai's essays were known only to a few literary historians and connoisseurs.[58]

The momentous move from poetry to prose we have just outlined did not mean that Vētanāyakam Piḷḷai entirely left the field of poetry. He continued to write verses in a simple style, but in a much more restricted thematic and social sphere. Whereas in his first book he had in his own words "studiously avoided the insertion of any thing likely

57. The full text of this review is reprinted in Vētanāyakam Piḷḷai (1917: "Select press opinions," vi–vii).

58. The book remained in print, however, in the edition of the South India Saiva Siddhanta Works Publishing Society which was republished in 1948, 1950, 1953, 1961 and 1978. Like the same Society's edition of the *Nītinūl*, this edition had suffered the impact of the Tamil purist movement. In the publishers' words: "It has to be noted that, as this book, which is endowed with sweetness, simplicity and natural word order, has an overabundance of foreign language words, in this edition the foreign language words have been removed and Tamil words have been inserted without changing the [author's] intention, [so that] the natural sweet sound of Tamil has been enhanced and the language style has been improved" (Vētanāyakam Piḷḷai 1978b: editors' preface).

to wound the prejudices of any class of men" (Vētanāyakam Piḷḷai 1860: preface, i), he now wrote poems which were overtly Christian in character. In 1873, Vētanāyakam published devotional poetry on Catholic religious themes under the titles *Tiruvaruḷ mālai, Tēvamātā antāti, Tiruvaruḷ antāti,* and *Periya Nāyaki Ammai patikam.*[59] To these was added the *Tēvattōtira mālai,* a collection of 110 *kaṭṭaḷaik kalitturai* stanzas, in 1889.[60] In the same year, he also published a collection of 53 songs on Jesus and the Virgin Mary under the title *Cattiya vētak kīrttaṉaikaḷ,* which was printed at the St. Joseph's Press in Madras.[61] Perhaps not surprisingly, these Christian poems and songs never reached the same popularity as his other works, although they continued to circulate in Catholic parishes during the twentieth century.[62]

The last work that has to be mentioned in this section is Vētanāyakam Piḷḷai's first collection of musical compositions. This collection was published in 1878 under the title *Carva camaya camaracak kīrttaṉaikaḷ* (lit. "Songs on the equality of all faiths"), containing 192 songs in five sections. It stands out from his devotional works listed above in that it does not praise a specifically Christian God, but a personal deity which is common to theistic religions. Although Vētanāyakam Piḷḷai claimed that his songs would appeal to "all faiths," a closer look at their style and content reveals a clear Hindu and Christian bias. He refers to the feet of God (songs 1 and 2) or addresses him in masculine terms as *aiyaṉē* (2) or *pālaṉē* (4). While the first section of the book deals with the praise of God (songs 1 to 138), the second section contains one single song on the famine during the *īcuvara* year (1877–78) we have already seen above. The following sections contain didactic songs (*itōpatēcak kīrttaṉaikaḷ,* songs 140 to 161), employment-related songs (162 to 175), and songs about the

59. See Antōṉi Irācu (1986). According to one editor, the *Periya Nāyaki Ammai patikam* was composed when Vētanāyakam Piḷḷai traveled to Madras in connection with his duties as munsiff. On his way he was invited to the village of Periya Pāḷaiyam, twelve miles from Madras, where he sang these stanzas on the shrine of Virgin Mary (see Vētanāyakam Piḷḷai 1976: 9). The poem is also known as *Periya Nāyaki Ammaṉ patikam.* For an edition of the *Tiruvaruḷ mālai* with a detailed commentary, see Cēcaiyā (1960).

60. This collection of poems was translated into English by G. J. B. Christopher in 1968 (see Christopher 1968). The Tamil original was reprinted in Antōṉi Irācu (1986).

61. See Vētanāyakam Piḷḷai (1889).

62. When visiting the San Thome Cathedral in Chennai in the summer of 2000, I found a pamphlet containing a version of the *Periya Nāyaki Ammai patikam* in which the last line had been altered so as to praise "Our Lady of Mylapore" instead of Mary in Periya Pāḷaiyam. The pamphlet had already been printed in 1987, but was still in circulation (see Aṭaikkalam 1987).

family (176 to 192). According to Kamil Zvelebil, Vētanāyakam Piḷḷai's *kīrttaṉais* were influenced in form by his friend, the poet-composer Kōpālakiruṣṇa Pārati, whom he had met during his time in Mayuram (1974: 114). The songs of this collection quickly became very popular, and they were sung by Tamil communities even outside South India.[63] This popularity is also underlined by the large number of reprints and re-editions which have appeared to date, and by the fact that they still belong to the repertoire of well-trained Carnatic musicians. Several critics have credited Vētanāyakam Piḷḷai for composing songs in the Tamil language at a time when Telugu and Sanskrit were the languages of music in South India.[64] Particularly during the 1940s, his *kīrttaṉais* became instrumental in the so-called "Tamil Icai Movement" (*tamiḻ icai iyakkam*) which sought to revive Tamil musical traditions.[65]

So far, we have covered almost all of Vētanāyakam Piḷḷai's works, and we have seen him as a prolific and multifaceted writer. However, his two novels have been deliberately left out. They are the works which secured Vētanāyakam Piḷḷai lasting fame and recognition until the present day, and they will be examined at some length in the following chapter. For the moment it is important to stress that Vētanāyakam Piḷḷai's personal development, from the poetry of the *Nītinūl* via his essays *Peṇ kalvi* and *Peṇ māṉam* toward his two novels, symbolizes at some level the larger transformation of Tamil elite literary practices during the nineteenth century. On the basis of texts such as Vētanāyakam Piḷḷai's, the emphasis on prose as a vehicle for social reform crystallized toward the end of the century and became the most important driving force behind the bulk of Tamil literary production throughout the twentieth century. Vētanāyakam Piḷḷai's life history illustrates the contexts from which a modern Tamil author could emerge and the influences exerted by Western culture and the colonial state. It also shows how important an individual agent could be in the overall transformational processes, which gradually but decisively came to change the lineaments of Tamil literary culture. To complete the description of Vētanāyakam Piḷḷai as an agent of change, we shall now turn to his two novels—the crowning achievement toward the end of his life.

---

63. See the advertisements for Vētanāyakam Piḷḷai's songs which appeared in July 1887 in the Singapore Tamil newspaper *Ciṅkai Nēcaṉ*.

64. See e.g., Cēcaiyā (1989, ch. 13) or Pāṇṭuraṅkaṉ (1994: 43).

65. On the Tamil Icai Movement, see the short overview in Zvelebil (1995: 640f.), and Nambi Arooran (1975) and Kannan (1983).

5

The Emergence of the Tamil Novel

From the 1850s onward, a new form of narrative called the "novel" emerged in most of India's literary traditions. Manifesting itself first in Bengali and Marathi and moving on to Urdu, Telugu, Hindi, Tamil, and Malayalam, this new genre became increasingly popular in various corners of the subcontinent.[1] Critical comparative scholarship, which seeks to explain the intricacies and diverse processes of this spread, has only begun very recently.[2] One of the reasons why the early Indian novels are still rather poorly understood is that for most Indian literary traditions the socio-cultural processes that lay behind the emergence of the new genre are still far from clear. For a long time, the widespread assumption that the novel was merely an "imported" genre, a form more or less uncritically taken over from English literature, has prevented any serious attempts to describe the specific social conditions in which novels became an integral part of Indian literatures. This assumption partly rests on the problematic term "novel" itself. In its almost uncanny familiarity, the term hardly alerts us to the fact that what was called a "novel" in nineteenth-century India does not necessarily have to conform to what a Western reader of the twenty-first century may think about novels. An anachronistic or otherwise prejudiced view as to what a novel has to be has more than once marred the appreciation of nineteenth-century Indian texts in their own right and has led to subjective value judgments which

1. Though Marathi and Bengali probably produced the earliest Indian novels, this enumeration is not meant in a strictly chronological way. The debates within several of the individual Indian literatures as to which particular work was their "first" novel are still continuing, so that an absolute chronology cannot be given yet. Mukherjee (2002) contains an appendix which is a chronological list of early Indian "narratives," but it is far from complete (Vētanāyakam Piḷḷai's Tamil novels, for instance, are not included at all).

2. A very useful comparative survey of early Indian novels is Mukherjee (2002).

are hardly helpful when we try to explain the emergence of a new genre in the Indian context.

The Tamil novel is no exception to this general misunderstanding. With the twentieth-century Western novel as a model in their minds, critics have often discarded Vētanāyakam Piḷḷai's pioneering novels using labels such as "approximation to a novel" or "longwinded moral tale, weary and unprofitable." But what do we gain by comparing the early Indian novels to, say, their twentieth-century British namesakes? In what follows, I will pursue a different trajectory. I will attempt to describe how the Tamil novel emerged at the intersection of complex social and cultural processes, as an entirely *new* genre influenced by a multiplicity of determinants. One of them, certainly, was the impact of English education and English literature. But the emergence of the novel also has to be seen against the background of public debates within nineteenth-century Tamil society about cultural advancement and the creation of a new "vernacular" language and literature. Stuart Blackburn (2001) has shown how the novel developed out of a growing need for educational texts and for a new language that was capable of rendering the "Modern" in all its manifold aspects. As Meenakshi Mukherjee has pointed out: "The factors that shaped the growth of this genre since the mid-nineteenth century arose as much from the political and social situation of a colonized country as from several indigenous though attenuated narrative traditions of an ancient culture that survived through constant mutation" (1985: 3).

In this chapter, I examine what this means with regard to the Tamil novel. I argue that the earliest Tamil novels emerged as sites of *dialogues* between tradition and modernity, reality and imagination, didacticism and entertainment, the self and the colonial other, the written and the spoken word, and Tamil and English. In the novelistic texts, the boundaries between these dichotomies become fluid and blurred. Drawing upon Mikhail Bakhtin's (1975; 1981) influential theorization of the novel as a genre with dialogical capacities, the early Tamil novels can be regarded as multivocal texts. This multivocality has important consequences. It follows that the novel was not simply "imported" from English into Tamil literature, as Sivapatha Sundaram has maintained (1992: 2995), and that it was not a mere "response to a Western impact" (Das 1991). The analysis presented here takes the first Tamil novel by Vētanāyakam Piḷḷai as a starting point. The view is then expanded to include a second work of his, and a third novel, viz. *Kamalāmpāḷ carittiram* by B. R. Rājam Aiyar. Though *Kamalāmpāḷ carittiram* was not the next novel chronologically after Vētanāyakam Piḷḷai's works, it was definitely one of the most popular and influen-

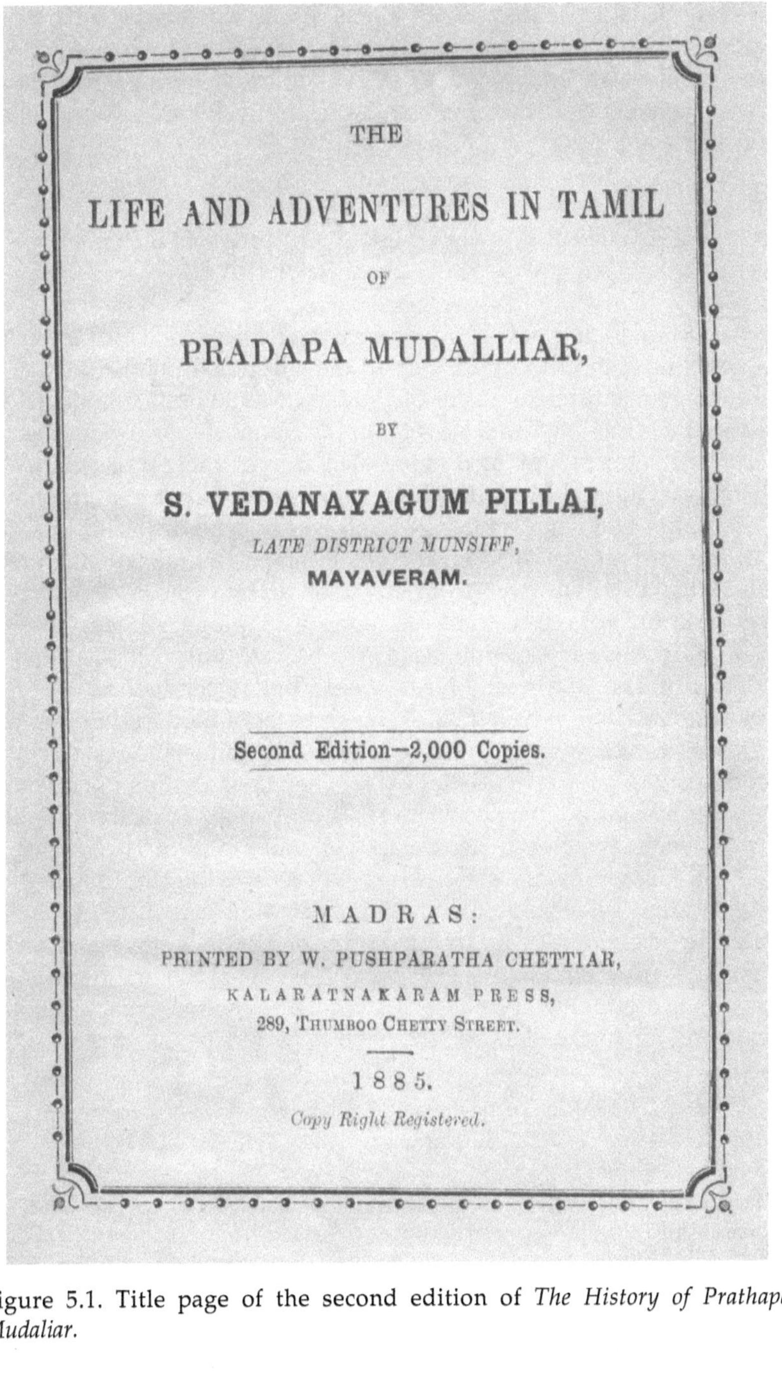

THE

LIFE AND ADVENTURES IN TAMIL

OF

PRADAPA MUDALLIAR,

BY

S. VEDANAYAGUM PILLAI,

LATE DISTRICT MUNSIFF,

MAYAVERAM.

Second Edition—2,000 Copies.

MADRAS:

PRINTED BY W. PUSHPARATHA CHETTIAR,

KALARATNAKARAM PRESS,

289, THUMBOO CHETTY STREET.

1885.

Copy Right Registered.

Figure 5.1. Title page of the second edition of *The History of Prathapa Mudaliar.*

tial early novels.[3] Moreover, as Rājam Aiyar was almost fifty years younger than Vētanāyakam Piḷḷai, a comparison of their works may serve to illustrate how a younger generation of authors responded to and developed further the standards set by Vētanāyakam Piḷḷai's pioneering attempts.

The History of Prathapa Mudaliar (1879): An "approximation to a novel"?[4]

Vētanāyakam Piḷḷai's novel *Piratāpam eṉṉum Piratāpa Mutaliyār carittiram* was published in October 1879[5] with the additional English title "The Life and Adventures in Tamil of Pradapa Mudalliar." It is generally regarded as the first Tamil novel, and as Kamil Zvelebil remarks: "It seems that no amount of digging will uproot the primacy of 'The History of Piratapa Mudaliar' [. . .] as indeed the first genuine novel in the Tamil language" (1986: 2). Well, yes and no. In order to show that "the primacy of 'The History of Piratapa Mudaliar' " is indeed still undisputed, we have to briefly look at two earlier texts which have been unearthed by some "amount of digging." Already in 1875 Tū. Vī. Cēṣaiyaṅkār had published *Ātiyūr avatāṉi caritam* ("Adhiyuravadhani, or The Self-made Man"), a narrative which he had subtitled "An original Tamil novel, delineating pictures of modern Hindu life." It was, however, written in verse. The author himself addresses this fact in his English preface as follows: "The tale is written not in prose after the model of European Novelists, but in an attractive popular form of verse, which our people are generally fond of" (Cēṣaiyaṅkār 1875: 3). Cēṣaiyaṅkār's statement reminds one of the explanation Vētanāyakam Piḷḷai gave for writing poetry instead of prose in the preface to his *Nītinūl*: "a large majority of Hindoos have a stronger relish for *Poetical* than prosaic works" (Vētanāyakam Piḷḷai 1860: preface, i; original emphasis). Cēṣaiyaṅkār obviously knew that at least some of his readers would have expected prose—the medium

3. For a chronological list of the earliest Tamil novels published before 1900, see Appendix 2.

4. Zvelebil (1973: 280).

5. 1876 is often incorrectly given as the year of publication, e.g., in Louis (1963: 18); Subramanian (1978: 91); Varadarajan (1988a: 275), and even in Ñāṉappirakācam Piḷḷai (1890: 25). Although this error has been pointed out repeatedly, namely by Cuntararājaṉ/Civapātacuntaram (1977: 6), Thyagarajan (1978: 63), and Zvelebil (1990a: 163), the wrong year persistently continues to be quoted, e.g., in Fernando (1995: 59), or Cutler (2003: 287, ftn. 34).

which was supposed to bring modernity to Tamil literature. Though not writing prose, it was his declared aim to take part in the reform of the "vernacular," as he explains:

> Conceiving that an original Novel in Tamil delineating pictures of Modern Hindu life would suit the taste of my countrymen, in their present transition stage—a stage in which among other changes, old ideas are giving way to new ones and myths to facts—I have ventured to write and publish this little volume, in the hope that it may perhaps contribute some small extent to that species of Tamil literature which Modern Dravidian scholars aim at building up. (Cēṣaiyaṅkār 1875: 3)

This new Tamil literature should show "Modern Hindu life," hence focus on the here and now. In such a general epistemic move from "myths to facts" what became important was realism. Cēṣaiyaṅkār also emphasizes this point: "The materials are taken from real life, but are glossed over a little poetic varnish [sic], and the language employed is simple and unpedantic" (ibid.).[6] Again, as sixteen years earlier in Vētanāyakam Piḷḷai's *Nītinūl*, the "simple" and "unpedantic" language was an essential characteristic of the new kind of writing which had to be advertised. Such statements tell us a lot about how the newly emerging modern Tamil authors saw themselves and their reformist role in society. Obviously, Cēṣaiyaṅkār himself noted the changes occurring everywhere around him, a "transition stage" of his society, and he responded in what he thought was an appropriate way. Choosing poetry instead of prose was his attempt at a compromise between the educationists' prescriptions and his (imagined) readers' preferences. It is possible that he used the label "novel" mainly for advertising purposes, in order to attract the attention of his readers. At the time, the term "novel" had already become popular with the English-speaking population of South India, which avidly read English

6. The expression "a little poetic varnish" slightly glosses over the fact that this "novel" is very much indebted to older, medieval literary conventions. Besides being written in *kaṇṇis* (couplets), a verse form often employed in *pirapantams* such as the *Cētupati viṟaliviṭutūtu* we have seen above, the text begins with 18 lines of invocatory verse which are clearly a typical *kaṭavuḷ vāḻttu* (though not explicitly marked as such in the printed edition). Moreover, the language incorporates formulae and conventional expressions typical of the earlier *pirapantam* works. Already the first three lines after the invocation make this clear: "*cīr mēvu cōḻat tiru nāṭṭiṭaic ceḻikkum / ēr mēvum ūrkaḷ etilum taṉittu ōṅkum / attiyūr eṉṉum aḻaku talam tāṉilē*" (Cēṣaiyaṅkār 1875: 1, sandhi splits added).

novels imported from Britain. Thus, calling *Ātiyūr avatāṉi caritam* a "novel" may have been intended to signal that, like the English novels, this book provided entertaining and modern reading material. We find what I would argue is a similar instance of this use of the term "novel" when in September 1888 the editor of the Singapore Tamil newspaper *Ciṅkai Nēcaṉ* published a "Comic Dialogue Between a Singaporean and an Indian" (*viṉōta campāṣaṇai, itu ciṅkappūrāṉukkum intiyaṉukkum iṭaiyē naṭantatu*) and gave it the English title "A Novel in Singapore Tamil" with "A Novel" being printed in bold letters.[7] Here also, the label "novel" was an eye-catcher, a sign of something new and interesting, something of contemporary relevance. The author apparently never intended to weave this dialogue into a longer narrative. In any case, the first printed Tamil book that called itself "novel" cannot be counted as belonging to the new Tamil genre which went under the same name, although Zvelebil considers it "a true versified ancestor of the Tamil novel" (1986: 1) without giving further explanations.[8]

The case of the second text which could have been the "first Tamil novel" is slightly more complicated, due to the lack of historical data concerning the book. The Muslim Tamil scholar Tayka Shu'ayb claims that "the first novel produced by the Tamil speaking people" (1993: 104) was a book called *Madīnatu 'n-nuḥās*, a title Shu'ayb translates as "Copper Town," while Torsten Tschacher in his survey of Arabic-Tamil literature points out that "this story from the Arabian Nights is more famous in the West as 'City of Brass' " (2001: 49). The book was probably published in 1858 by the Muslim Tamil writer Sayyid Muḥammad alias Imām al-'Arūs (1816–1898),[9] although we cannot be sure about the date[10] (Shu'ayb, ibid.). It was, however, not written in Tamil, but in Arabic-Tamil (Arwi). According to Shu'ayb, it was only "translated" into Tamil in 1978 (ibid., ftn. 44) or in 1979 (ibid., 785). An edition in the Arabic (as opposed to the Tamil) script apparently did not appear until 1900 in Colombo.[11] In any case, we have

7. See *Ciṅkai Nēcaṉ*, 24 September 1888, p. 48, and the continuation on 1 October 1888, p. 52.

8. For a very brief English summary of the story of *Ātiyūr avatāṉi caritam*, see Zvelebil (1986: 1). The first to unearth this text was, to my knowledge, Pārttacārati (1976) which see for further discussion of the text. See also Zvelebil (1995: 139f.).

9. For Imām al-'Arūs and his works, see Tschacher (2002).

10. As on other issues, too, Shu'ayb's information regarding the date is slightly ambiguous. On p. 104 of his work, he claims that *Madīnatu 'n-nuḥās* was written in 1858, while on p. 632 he attributes it to Imām al-'Arūs' early phase (see Shu'ayb 1993).

11. Unfortunately, I have not been able to find a copy of the book. Therefore, I can only try to assess the information given by Shu'ayb.

no evidence whether the work had any readers at all when it was written. Even if it did, it would have been accessible only to a rather specialized audience which read Arwi, so that its circulation would have been very restricted. Other open questions are in how far Imām al-'Arūs' work was influenced by Arabic and Persian sources and whether a contemporary reading public would have considered the work a "novel," or indeed whether Imām al-'Arūs himself intended to write a "novel."[12] These questions notwithstanding, I would argue, on the basis of limited contemporary reception and of language, that Zvelebil's considering *Piratāpa Mutaliyār carittiram* the "first genuine novel in the Tamil language" remains correct.

Fortunately, we know much more about *Piratāpa Mutaliyār carittiram* and about Vētanāyakam Piḷḷai's objectives for writing something he called "novel." His own views survive in the form of his preface to *Piratāpa Mutaliyār carittiram*, dated August 23, 1879, and written in English. He declares: "My object in writing this work of fiction is to supply the want of prose works in Tamil, a want which is admitted and lamented by all, and also to give a practical illustration of the maxims of morality contained in my former works 'Nidinool,' 'Penmady Malai,' 'Samaras Keerthana,' etc." (Vētanāyakam Piḷḷai 1885: i). He thus refers to both form and content of his new work. The perceived "want of prose works in Tamil," however, expresses much more than a simple concern with literary form. As we have seen above, Vētanāyakam Piḷḷai considered the absence of prose a sign of cultural and civilizational backwardness and thus emphasized the importance of prose for the national destiny. This importance lay in the ability of the novel to reflect the achievements and venerable traditions of a society. By giving "faithful pictures of the national character, domestic life, habits, and manners of the people in Southern India" (Vētanāyakam Piḷḷai 1885: preface, ii), the novel served to refresh the cultural memory of nineteenth-century Tamil society. This concern with a certain kind of "realism," the concern with the actual and real, with contemporary society, was not unique to the Tamil novel. Many early novels similarly attempted to portray their own, contemporary society, to explore ways of transferring social reality into a new kind of literature. In the case of the Telugu novel *Śrīraṅgarāja Caritramu* (1872) by Gōpālakṛṣṇama Ceṭṭi (1832–?), for instance, the English preface tells us that this book is an "attempt to delineate the manners and customs of the Telugus, in their own language" (quoted in Sai Prasad 1991: 93). When in 1886

12. Pī. Mu. Ajmalkāṉ (1985: 79) calls *Madīnatu 'n-nuḥās* a historical novel (without giving further explanations) and also claims that it was the first Tamil novel. He adds that although the novel was written in Arabic script, the language was Tamil.

the American missionary J. Robert Hutchinson translated another early Telugu novel, *Rājaśēkhara Caritramu* (1878) by the famous social reformer Kandukūri Vīrēśaliṅgam Pantulu (1848–1919), into English, he enthusiastically remarked that this novel was "the 'open sesame' before which the door of the Hindu abode flies open, revealing the complete inner life of a representative Hindu family—their home, dress, food, worship, modes of thought and speech, joys and sorrows, loves and hates, hopes and fears" (Viresalingam 1887: iii). Or, as early Urdu novelist Mirzā Muḥammad Hādī Rusvā (1858–1931) remarks in his preface to his novel *Umrāo Jān Adā* (1899): "The most paying and interesting subject of study in this world is what happens to human beings" (quoted in Mukherjee 2002: xi). This new "realism" always entailed the possibility of not only describing reality but also of critiquing, satirizing, subverting it. Writers and critics around the globe have emphasized this special possibility of the novel of saying things that only a novel can say. As Milan Kundera has seen:

> The novel has accompanied man uninterruptedly and faithfully since the beginning of the Modern Era. It was then that the "passion to know," which Husserl considered the essence of European spirituality, seized the novel and led it to scrutinize man's concrete life and protect it against "the forgetting of being"; to hold "the world of life" under a permanent light. That is the sense in which I understand and share Hermann Broch's insistence in repeating: The sole *raison d'être* of a novel is to discover what only the novel can discover. (Kundera 2000: 5)[13]

The novel as possibility, as an *idea*, or as a narrative model came to India at a time when this function of the European novel of holding the world of life under a permanent light was fully developed. The early Indian novelists quickly realized that "novels are not written to narrate life, but rather to transform it, by adding something to it" (Vargas Llosa 1996: 321, modified).[14] As Mario Vargas Llosa describes, the

13. "Le roman accompagne l'homme constamment et fidèlement dès le début des Temps modernes. La «passion de connaître» (celle que Husserl considère comme l'essence de la spiritualité européenne) s'est alors emparée de lui pour qu'il scrute la vie concrète de l'homme et la protège contre «l'oubli de l'être»; pour qu'il tienne «le monde de la vie» sous un éclairage perpétuel. C'est en ce sens-là que je comprends et partage l'obstination avec laquelle Hermann Broch répétait: Découvrir ce que seul un roman peut découvrir, c'est la seule raison d'être d'un roman" (Kundera 1986: 20).

14. "No se escriben novelas para contar la vida sino para transformarla, añadiéndole algo" (Vargas Llosa 1990: 7).

transformation of life through fiction implies a particular structuring: "Real life flows and does not stop, it is incommensurable, a chaos in which each story mingles with all the other stories and thus it never begins or ends. Life in fiction is a *simulacrum* in which that vertiginous disorder becomes order: organization, cause and effect, beginning and end" (ibid., 322, modified).[15] It seems to me that the reason why the novel genre became so popular throughout India was the fact that it was the ideal form of holding a changing Indian world of life under a permanent critical light. We remember would-be novelist Tū. Vī. Cēṣaiyaṅkār speaking of his fellow "countrymen, in their present transition stage—a stage in which among other changes, old ideas are giving way to new ones and myths to facts." In a society in flux, with old certainties being constantly challenged by colonial modernity, intellectuals welcomed a form of discourse in which ways of being in the world could be imagined and examined. As Shivarama Padikkal observes: "As part of the emergence into modernity, the novels created new men and women, and new relationships between them" (1993: 232). The structured worlds of fiction with their reassuring certainties of cause and effect, ending and beginning, provided ways of ordering a messy world of life, of probing into possible worlds, of finding imaginary solutions to real social problems. The sole *raison d'être* of a novel is to discover what only the novel can discover, what cannot be said in other ways (yet). As we shall see in a moment, the early novels were indeed concerned with transforming life, rather than simply narrating it, and they also "provided literary expression for political aspirations that were not yet feasible in the political realm" (ibid., 238).

There is no doubt that Vētanāyakam Piḷḷai saw the novel as an instructing and morally edifying text with the potential to reform and eventually uplift society. As he explicitly states in his preface, the novel presented him with an opportunity to pursue his social reformist agenda which had already induced him to publish his earlier works. Therefore, his *Piratāpa Mutaliyār carittiram* (as well as his second novel) contains many passages, in the form of instructive dialogues or speeches, on edifying topics, such as education, the effects of corruption, the importance of the mothertongue, and the greatness of parents.[16] As Vētanāyakam himself emphasizes in his preface:

15. "La vida real fluye y no se detiene, es inconmensurable, un caos en el que cada historia se mezcla con todas las historias y por lo mismo no empieza ni termina jamás. La vida de la ficción es un simulacro en el que aquel vertiginoso desorden se vuelve orden: organización, causa y efecto, fin y principio" (ibid., 9).

16. To this list could be added the passages on jealousy, slander, telling lies, public and personal hygiene, and child marriage which occur in his second novel *Cukuṇa Cuntari carittiram.*

> The common weaknesses and follies of the world are everywhere ridiculed. I have inculcated piety towards God, and pointed out the relative and social duties of life. I have endeavoured to exhibit the inherent beauty of virtue, and to expose the deformity of vice, in such a manner as to create a love of the one, and a detestation of the other. [. . .] In writing this story, I have not followed the example of those novelists who depict human nature as it is, not as it ought to be, and who thus exhibit bad specimens of humanity which are often mistaken by the young and inexperienced for objects of imitation. (1885: iif.)

In the end, the author has created what S. Sivapatha Sundaram has aptly called "a compendium of morals in the garb of a novel" (1978: 27). Apart from the fostering of Tamil prose and the inculcation of moral values, Vētanāyakam had a third aim. He wanted to "meet the taste of the Hindu readers" (1885: i), to entertain them. Therefore, he also provided what he called "various scenes of humour and pleasantry" or "amusing anecdotes and interesting stories" (ibid.). In fact, the very beginning of the novel is a rather comic account of how the grandfather of the protagonist became diwan at the court of the Nawab of Arcot.[17] Although it is certainly an exaggeration to say that the "desperate attempt to bring out ironically the comic aspects of life as lived by the Tamils is quite obvious *on every page* in the novel" (Satyan 1981: 81, emphasis added), Vētanāyakam's didacticism is quite frequently relieved by humorous interludes. Many critics have seen his humor as a significant characteristic of his novels.[18] Before I examine in greater detail how the objectives that Vētanāyakam Piḷḷai expounds in his preface have shaped the entire novel in both form (e.g., construction of the plot) and content (e.g., selection of themes), let me give a brief synopsis of the plot:

In *Piratāpa Mutaliyār carittiram,* the protagonist Piratāpa Mutaliyār, a "well-educated native gentleman of brilliant parts, wit and humour" (Vētanāyakam Piḷḷai 1885: i), tells the story of his life as a first-person narrator. Piratāpa, his female cousin Ñāṉāmpāḷ and a poor boy called Kaṉakacapai are brought up and educated at home in the town Cattiyapuri. When Piratāpa and Ñāṉāmpāḷ are to get married, the in-laws quarrel about where the two should live and the

17. For a summary of this scene, see Satyan (1981: 81) and Subramanyam (1961: 30).

18. E.g., Dhandayudham (1977: 45) or Patmanāpaṉ (1978: 2).

wedding is canceled. Some time later, Ñāṉāmpāḷ is kidnapped by a tahsildar and rescued by Piratāpa who is then allowed to marry her. Kaṉakacapai is discovered to be really the son of a wealthy man called Tēvarāja Piḷḷai. When Ñāṉāmpāḷ becomes pregnant, another dispute arises about where the grandchild is to stay. Ñāṉāmpāḷ, however, has a miscarriage. Frustrated because of this dispute, Piratāpa decides to secretly go on a journey; Ñāṉāmpāḷ follows him. After having been attacked by robbers, they happen to arrive in Ātiyūr, Kaṉakacapai's home town. There, Tēvarāja Piḷḷai is in trouble, since the government refuses to recognize Kaṉakacapai as his true son. The final verdict goes against Tēvarāja Piḷḷai. Having been witnesses at court, Piratāpa's and Ñāṉāmpāḷ's fathers lose their properties and are sent to prison. Immediately, Piratāpa's mother Cuntara Aṇṇi leads a group of women to petition the Governor of Madras who decides the case to everybody's satisfaction.

While hunting in the forest near Ātiyūr, Piratāpa is carried away by his elephant and left behind. Piratāpa drags himself to the next town called Vikkiramapuri where there is no king and anarchy prevails. There, he is put into prison because of several false charges. Meanwhile, Ñāṉāmpāḷ who has been searching for her husband, dressed as a man for safety reasons, arrives at Vikkiramapuri where its citizens have sent out an elephant with a garland to select a new king. As the elephant puts the garland round Ñāṉāmpāḷ's neck, she is accepted as the new monarch, frees her husband, makes him deputy king, and reforms justice and state administration. As Āṉantavalli, the former king's daughter, desires to marry "king" Ñāṉāmpāḷ and all the people joyfully start preparing the ceremony, Ñāṉāmpāḷ and Piratāpa decide to flee. They return to Ātiyūr, and Ñāṉāmpāḷ sends a letter to Vikkiramapuri, confessing that she is a woman and appointing Āṉantavalli as her successor. Later on, Ñāṉāmpāḷ and Piratāpa travel back home to Cattiyapuri. On the way, Ñāṉāmpāḷ falls ill with smallpox. Already given up for dead, she recovers, however, and all ends well indeed. We read that Ñāṉāmpāḷ's and Cuntara Aṇṇi's heroic fame has spread as far as Europe, so that the Empress (of India, i.e., Queen Victoria) bestows upon them the title "Royal Ladies" and plenty of land.

This is the main story line of the novel. Into this main plot, Vētanāyakam Piḷḷai has inserted a large number of subplots, anecdotes, lectures, and speeches, in order to pursue his aim of instructing his reader. In doing so, he has made use of traditional modes of storytelling. The technique of branching or "emboxed" narrative makes his work structurally similar to the *Pañcatantra* (Sivapatha Sundaram 1978:

27) and other folktales.[19] Mostly, the inserted subtexts do not have any direct connection with the main plot of the novel, apart from being told by one of the characters to the edification of other characters (and the reader). In chapter 2, for example, the protagonist tells several funny childhood anecdotes of his. This chapter is connected to the preceding chapter only by the two introductory sentences "Though I was dull in my studies, I was quite active at playing games. As my childhood pranks will interest the readers, I shall relate them" (George 1993: 987, which see for a translation of the entire chapter 2) [5.2]. The rest of this chapter consists of a string of twenty-one disconnected brief anecdotes which are all complete stories in themselves, frequently beginning with the introductory formula "one day." The following chapter continues Piratāpa's story without making any reference to these "childhood pranks" at all. Similarly, in chapter 29 (titled "Someone spoilt by education"), Tēvarāja Piḷḷai tells Piratāpa and Kaṉakacapai the story of the poor brahmin Aṉantaiyaṉ, without any further motivation except to morally instruct the two. The chapter starts, again providing a self-contained story, thus: "One day, Tēvarāja Piḷḷai said to me and Kaṉakacapai: 'A scholar who knows all the books in English called Bacon says 'A little learning is a dangerous thing.'[20] Therefore, listen to a corresponding story that I know of someone who was educated and dangerous. In Madras there was a poor brahmin called Cuppaiyaṉ' " (Vētanāyakam Piḷḷai 1885: 166f.) [5.3]. By thus embedding subsidiary stories into the main story, Vētanāyakam creates what he calls in his preface a narrative "intermixed with various scenes of humour and pleasantry, and observations of a moral tendency" (Vētanāyakam Piḷḷai 1885: i) or "interspersed with many amusing anecdotes and interesting stories" (ibid., ii). Consequently, the novel becomes a rich multivocal text that incorporates other material to which it attributes new contextual meanings.

It is this particular narrative technique, however, which has provoked dissatisfaction among later scholars, since it runs counter to later, twentieth-century concepts and genre conventions of the novel.

19. Another striking feature of traditional storytelling can be identified in the ending of the novel. It concludes with a valedictory formula typical of oral recitations and performances: "Many people mentioned in this story are leading an entirely happy life till this very moment. May all readers likewise live in good health and everlasting happiness" (Vētanāyakam Piḷḷai 1885: 330) [5.1].

20. The original Tamil can be rendered as "Little education is great danger." I have not been able to identify a similar quotation in the works of Francis Bacon. However, it sounds very much like a famous line (215) from Alexander Pope's *An Essay on Criticism*, which I have therefore used for my translation here.

Some critics consider *Piratāpa Mutaliyār carittiram* badly constructed. Thus, R. E. Asher calls it a "rambling" novel and remarks that "[n]o serious attempt is made [. . .] to bind plot and sub-plots together at any point in the story" (1969: 18),[21] a view to which Kamil Zvelebil (1974: 268) subscribes as well. Satyan (1981: 82) and Shreedharan (1971: 32), calling it a "major flaw," observe that the "narrative flow" is disturbed, while others refer to the novel, in slightly less negative terms, as "loosely structured" (e.g., Subramaniyam 1992a: 3210 and 1992b: 4519) or "not organic in structure" (Dhandayudham 1977: 24). However, quite contrary to Asher's view, Ka. Naa. Subramanyam seems to express a positive opinion, when he states that "[i]n spite of the author's preachiness in places he makes *no false* attempt to integrate the preaching and the story or the characters" (1961: 32; emphasis added).[22]

From this controversy about the construction of *Piratāpa Mutaliyār carittiram* it becomes apparent that the novel has been judged by different standards. Subramanyam is obviously quite content with this "lack" of integration or coherence, while Asher and Zvelebil criticize it. The latter seems to have the mature Western novel in mind as a model, significant characteristics of which are the coherence of the plot and the unity of design. Zvelebil's wholesale dismissal of the novel as "obviously a bad story, entirely unrealistic, a mixture of naive romanticism and moralising, with chains of improbabilities and badly constructed plot" (1974: 268), which he has reiterated in his *Lexicon of Tamil Literature* (1995: 762), betrays this in no uncertain terms. He does not seem to take into account that as a specific horizon of expectations that readers apply to a certain type of text the genre of the novel has in fact been variously reshaped and redefined since its birth in all literatures. The features he criticizes can be seen partly as traces of traditional folk narratives that characterize the first Tamil novel as a multivocal, and in a way a transitional text. In his study on the "pre-history" of the English novel, J. Paul Hunter remarks that the early English novels as well did not always correspond to later concepts of coherence and unity (1990: 24). Furthermore, the interruption of the central narrative flow with illustrative passages or subplots was a technique that many early Indian novelists found attractive. In what many critics call the first proper Hindi novel, Śrīnivāsdās'

21. To avoid confusion it may be worthwhile to state that Asher's article (1969) was reprinted as Asher (1970).

22. See also Irakupati (1999) who discusses the question whether *Piratāpa Mutaliyār carittiram* should be called a novel or not.

Parīkṣāguru ("Trial [is the best] teacher," 1882), the author included not only copious quotations from English writers, Sanskrit classics and other sources, but also a considerable number of didactic chapters which were specially marked so that readers interested purely in the central plot could easily skip them.[23] Similarly, in the case of Bābā Padmanjī's *Yamunāparyaṭan* ("Yamunā's Wanderings," 1857), one of the earliest Marathi novels, "two-thirds of the book is taken up with widow-remarriage propaganda" (Raeside 1970: 85). Moreover, Padmanjī (1831–1906), a Christian convert, wrote the novel with the aim to propagate Christianity. Indeed, some form of didacticism, whether expressed by means of overt lectures or whether implicit in the narrative, is a general characteristic of the early novel throughout India (see Das 1991, ch. 10).

That Vētanāyakam Piḷḷai thought his to be an appropriate structure of a novel becomes evident from a comparison with his second novel *Cukuṇa Cuntari carittiram* where he adheres to the same pattern of inserting subtexts into the main plot. Since Vētanāyakam was a skilled, traditionally educated poet, it would not do him justice to think that he was not concerned with the structure of his work. As his primary aim as a moralist was, however, to educate his reader, he did not put major emphasis on telling a coherent story. Instead, he subordinated the structure of his novel to his didactic aim and composed a plot that would serve as a framework for this. It can even be said that the fact that the entire novel is presented in the form of an autobiography (*carittiram*) is due to this subordination. With regard to eighteenth-century English literature, Hunter points out that "the argument that *lives* are the most effective kind of didactic tool is repeated again and again" (1990: 403, ftn.12, emphasis added). He explains this by referring to the immediacy of life-stories: They give "us back our mundane selves as we might have been in a different body. 'I was born' is our story in some particular identity" (325). Vētanāyakam Piḷḷai must have seen this potential as well and consequently conceived a 'sample life' that the reader could adhere to and identify with. Thus, his "novel attempt of this kind" (Vētanāyakam Piḷḷai 1885: iv) was thoroughly planned and crafted.

But was this what his contemporaries wanted? How did Vētanāyakam Piḷḷai's readers respond to his "novel attempt"? Evidence for contemporary reactions and opinions is scarce. While we have been able to portray Vētanāyakam Piḷḷai's life history in considerable detail,

---

23. *Parīkṣāguru* is discussed in detail by Kalsi (1992) and Dalmia (1999; 2008).

we know very little of his readers. In any case, judgments about the popularity of his novel have to be seen against the background of nineteenth-century literacy. If one wants to believe the 1871 *Census of the Madras Presidency*, out of the entire population of about 31 million people in the Presidency, 5 percent were able to read and write (Cornish 1874: 190). With only 16 out of 10,000 women being literate, the census emphasized the "almost total absence of education amongst the female sex" (ibid.). All in all, the novel must have been very much an enterprise of the male intellectual elite. At least initially, the women for whose education Vētanāyakam Piḷḷai was fighting in so many of his works were not able to read his ideas. Given the absence of other data, we are left with contemporary reviews and print run statistics to gauge Vētanāyakam Piḷḷai's "success" as a novelist. I have not been able to find any reviews of the first edition of *Piratāpa Mutaliyār carittiram*. But already six years after its first publication in October 1879 at the price of 10 annas, a second edition was printed in June 1885[24] with 2,000 copies (for 14 annas), two years before Vētanāyakam Piḷḷai published his second novel *Cukuṇa Cuntari carittiram*. During the months of July to September, the *Hindu* newspaper carried the following advertisement:

> Ready for sale.
> THE LIFE AND ADVENTURES OF
> PRADAPA MUDALLIAR
> A TAMIL NOVEL
> BY
> S. Vedanayagum Pillay,
> Late District Munsiff, Mayaveram
> PRICE 14 ANNAS—POSTAGE 2 ANNAS.
> Apply to the Author.
> Mayaveram.

During mid-August, the price was raised from 14 to 16 annas—a fact which may also point to an increasing demand. Moreover, three extant reviews show that this time *Piratāpa Mutaliyār carittiram* must have been well received by the public. Two months after the book had been released, the *Hindu* published an enthusiastic review on Saturday, 15 August 1885:

---

24. Incorrectly, Cuntararājaṉ/Civapātacuntaram (1977: 6), and Zvelebil (1990a: 163) give the year 1886.

> The book has, no doubt, rare merits, and its popularity has been so great that the first Edition of a pretty large number of copies ran out in a few months, and the second Edition has been just published to meet the increasing demand. It has become a favorite companion of the young and old, and, we dare say, will before long, find its way into every household. Having carefully studied the Tamil selection of the Madras University for several years, we have no hesitation saying that, while Mr. Vedanayagum Pillai's work is in no way inferior in literary merit to any of these Text books, it is far superior in moral tone to the best of them, and is a valuable contribution towards supplying vernacular literature of a wholesome character, which is admittedly one of the greatest wants in this country. Mr. Vedanayagum Pillai is to be congratulated upon the success that has attended his useful publications, and we are glad to find that he has deservedly won the enviable distinction of being styled, "The Addison of the Tamil Land."

While the anonymous reviewer thus commended the novel's "moral tone," he did not refrain entirely from criticism:

> One or two blemishes of the work may here be noticed in the hope of seeing it brought to greater perfection. The author would do well to draw more striking instances of corruption and abuse of power among the officials from the familiar scene around him, instead of roaming the imaginary field. There is no lack of such instances, as they are of every occurence in our own land. With a view to point out the best way of correcting a scene from the Arabian Night's Entertainments which evidently countenances wife-beating so prevalent in this country. This, we think, is very objectionable and cannot be calculated to promote the cause of female education which in his work he so ably advocates. These little blots, it may be expected, will be expunged in a future edition.

Apparently, Vētanāyakam Piḷḷai's readers judged the novel on its moral content and its attention to social issues. The edifying character of the text is also emphasized in the long article which appeared in the *Madras Christian College Magazine* in February 1886:

> In these days when our vernaculars are at a discount the appearance of this Tamil novel should be hailed with joy.

> [. . .] It is [. . .] admirably written, and full of purity of sentiment and sound wisdom. It is an excellent book to place in the hands of our Tamil young men, is calculated to stir their thought on many subjects, and reveal to them the weaknesses of our time. The writer is not afraid to speak aloud his views on important questions both social and political, and as they are the views of one possessing much intelligence, considerable experience as a Government official, added to an intimate knowledge of native social life, they are entitled to a respectful hearing. The story into which all these are woven is full of interest and thoroughly Hindu. [. . .] In short every one should be better for having read it.

Similarly, in the Bangalore missionary magazine *The Harvest Field* (March 1886) the reviewer declares: "This book is an indication of a clear advance both in Tamil thought and literature, for in it the spirit of the West often clothes itself in Tamil speech. It is an eminently healthy and homely book and is well planned and ably written." As is evident, the reviewers commented on various features of the novel, but—unlike twentieth-century literary critics—did not find it "badly constructed." From 1913 onward, the book was indeed "placed in the hands of the Tamil young men," for it was used in schools as an examination text and a model for "Vernacular" prose composition (see Vētanāyakam Piḷḷai 1917: appendix, pp. xff.).

The novel's great popularity and success is also underlined by the fact that it was almost immediately translated into English. Five days after his father's death, Vētanāyakam Piḷḷai's son Ñāṉappirakācam Piḷḷai received a letter of condolence, one among several, by a certain George Mackenzie Cobban (1846–1905). Reverend Cobban, whose poem "The Hindu Temple Girl" we have seen above, was a Wesleyan Methodist minister who served in Madras from 1876 to 1891. He was known as a "singularly effective open-air evangelist" (*Wesleyan Minutes of Conference* 1905: 156) whose Tamil sermons and speeches always attracted a large audience, so that he had "soon attained a remarkable influence over the Hindus" (ibid.).[25] In his letter, Cobban

25. His skills as a rhetorician are referred to in the Bangalore missionary magazine *The Harvest Field*, in the section "Wesleyan Methodist Notes," and in his obituary in the *Wesleyan Minutes of Conference* of 1905. To foster the use of Tamil as a vehicle of Christian ideas he also organized services where "simple Christian songs" were sung in Madras, Blacktown. Cobban's solid command of Tamil is reflected in his translations of the collection of moral maxims *Nālaṭiyār* and the *Tirukkuṟaḷ* which I found among his papers. His translations of poems by the Śaivite saint Paṭṭiṉattup Piḷḷaiyār were published in the *Madras Christian College Magazine*.

says "I wish he could have lived to have seen 'Prathapa Mudaliar's' in English (the 1st hundred pages of which are now printed)."[26] This statement has always been taken as an indication that there actually was a contemporary English translation of *Piratāpa Mutaliyār carittiram*. Cēcaiyā (1989: 114), for instance, mentions Cobban as the author of this translation.[27] The book, however, if it was printed at all, has never been found. In the course of my research, I have discovered amongst other papers of Cobban's a notebook containing his English translation of chapters 30 to 40 of *Piratāpa Mutaliyār carittiram*. As the notebook starts and ends in the middle of a chapter, it seems quite likely that Cobban translated more than just these ten chapters. One chapter (32) from this notebook was published as a specimen in Cobban's review of the novel in *The Harvest Field* (Cobban 1886). Whether any other parts have ever been printed, as Cobban's letter suggests, we will probably never be able to say. What we can prove, however, is that a contemporary English translation did exist.

Due to its lasting popularity, *Piratāpa Mutaliyār carittiram* has had an unusually long history of re-editions and revisions. The third edition was published in 1910, i.e., after the author's death. First alterations to the text were apparently made for the "revised" 5th edition of 1914, when the editor, Vētanāyakam Piḷḷai's son Vī. Ñāṉappirakācam Piḷḷai, corrected misprints together with Mayuram High School pandit Vī. Cuppiramaṇiya Aiyar and added a Tamil preface praising the utility of the text for educational purposes. For the 8th edition of 1917, when 1,500 copies of the novel were printed (price: 1 rupee, and 1 rupee 4 annas for the calico bound version), the Mayuram-based publishers V. G. Arogiaswamy & Brothers, the author's grandsons, added yet another preface, in which they thanked Cuppiramaṇiya Aiyar, who again had "made many revisions and changed mistakes" (Vētanāyakam Piḷḷai 1917: xii), without specifying exactly what he did.

When in 1948 the South India Saiva Siddhanta Works Publishing Company published a new edition of the text, they committed what the critic Ka. Naa. Subramanyam has called an "act of vandalism" (1961: 31). Although they maintained in the preface that they had only "removed the foreign words which the author had used here

---

26. Letter dated 26 July 1889, quoted in the "Select press opinions" section (p. vi) appended to the 1917 edition of *Piratāpa Mutaliyār carittiram* (see Vētanāyakam Piḷḷai 1917).

27. Ñāṉappirakācam Piḷḷai (1890: 6), and hence Cēcaiyā (1989: 114), also mention that an abridged English translation was published by a sheristadar of the Madurai Sub-Court named Makātēvayyar. I have not been able to verify this information.

and there" (Vētanāyakam Piḷḷai 1966: 5), they had, in fact, rewritten the entire novel, replacing every single Sanskrit word by a Tamil equivalent and expurgating various phrases and entire scenes.[28] This bowdlerization, which according to Subramanyam "is rather to be condemned" (1961: 31), bespeaks, on another level, the editors' intention to revitalize a classic. They wanted the text to live on, although in a new garb, since its old one did not suit their purist taste.

As a counterpart to the Saiva Siddhanta edition, Cakti Kāriyālayam brought out an edition in 1957 which was asserted to be unabridged and unchanged, since the editors thought such alterations an "insult" to the author (Vētanāyakam Piḷḷai 1957a: 6). Yet another incident in this history is the publication, in the same year, of a heavily abridged edition prepared by I. Mu. Cuppiramaṇiya Piḷḷai who condensed the novel from 340 to 150 pages. He wanted it to be shorter so as to be more attractive for readers who live in a "fast age" (!) and more easily affordable, and he declared that this condensation would still render the "beauty of the original prose and the author's mastery of language" (Vētanāyakam Piḷḷai 1957b: x). The currently available edition, following the Cakti one in content, is published by the New Century Bookhouse in Madras with the subtitle "The First Tamil Novel" (Vētanāyakam Piḷḷai 1994b).[29] Finally, in 2005 the first complete English translation by Meenakshi Tyagarajan, granddaughter of the novelist A. Mātavayyā (1872–1925), was published by Katha in New Delhi (Vedanayakam Pillai 2005). Thus, this first Tamil novel has been almost constantly in print since its first publication over 130 years ago—an honor not many Tamil novels can claim. All its metamorphoses reflect the changing attitudes and tastes of the reading public, the organic and ever-changing relationship between a text and its readers.

---

28. The most striking case is the omission of a story in chapter 40 that is meant to illustrate injustice. A farmer breaks the legs of a washerman's donkey for having entered his garden. Thereupon, the washerman beats the farmer, and when his pregnant wife tries to interfere, she has a miscarriage and barely survives. The case is brought to court, and the judge decides that the farmer has to carry the clothes for the washerman until the donkey can walk again, whereas the washerman has to cohabit with the farmer's wife until she becomes pregnant again. This story has been excluded from all later editions of the novel ever since. For the original Tamil text of this story, see Appendix 3 [5.4].

29. Another edition that follows the Cakti Kāriyālayam text is Vētanāyakam Piḷḷai (1984).

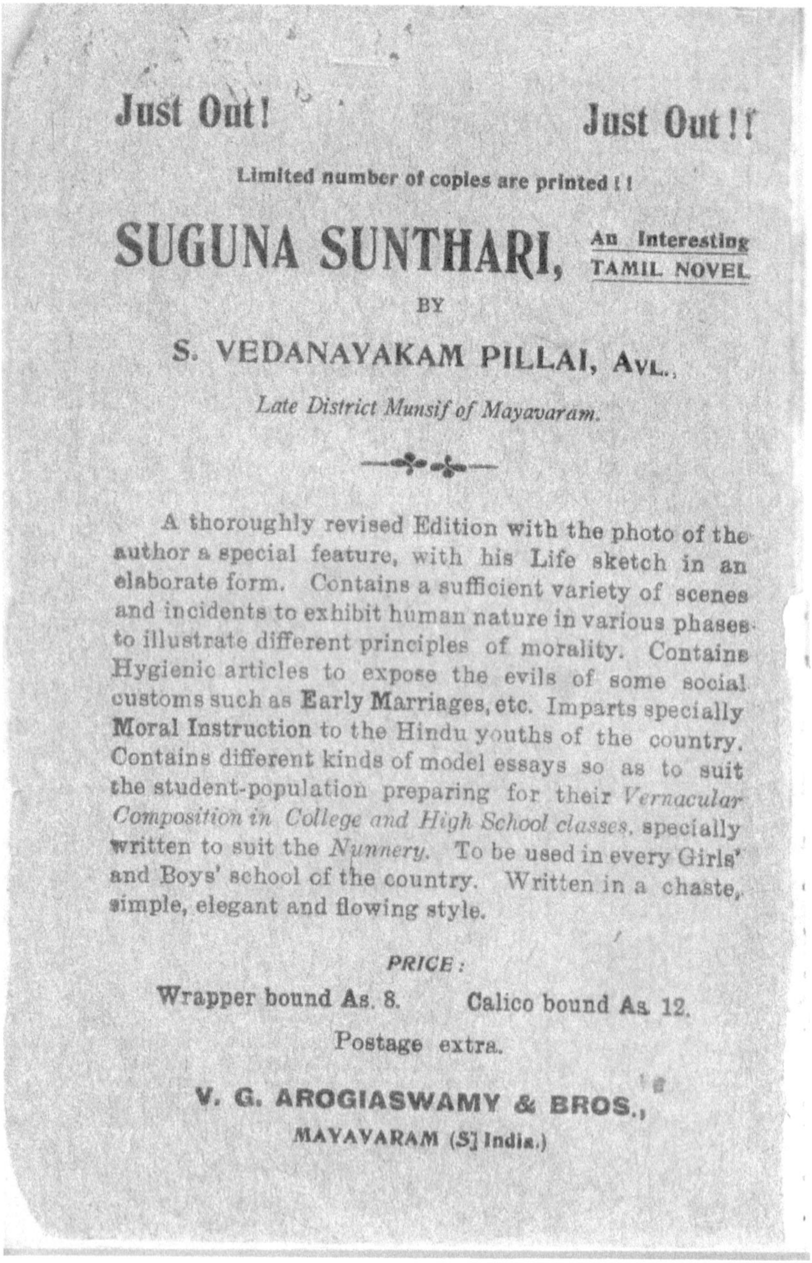

Figure 5.2. Advertisement for a re-edition of *The History of Suguna Sundari*.

The History of Suguna Sundari (1887): A "longwinded moral tale, weary and unprofitable"?[30]

Stimulated by the great success he had with his first novel, Vētanāyakam Piḷḷai wrote a second one, *Cukuṇa Cuntari carittiram*, "The History of Suguna Sundari (lit. "The Well-natured Beautiful One")" referring to the heroine, a princess, which was published in January 1887, two years before his death.[31] When he states in his English preface that this second novel, "although not as large as the former, contains a sufficient variety of scenes and incidents to exhibit human nature in its various phases and to illustrate different principles of morality" (Vētanāyakam Piḷḷai 1887: i), we may suspect that he continues in the same didactic vein. And indeed, as we will see, this second novel is in many respects similar to the first one.

Cukuṇa Cuntari carittiram takes the reader to the imaginary town Pūvaṉacēkaram, where Cukuṇa Cuntari, daughter of king Narātipaṉ and his only descendant, receives her courtly education together with the foundling boy Puvaṉēntiraṉ, allegedly a prince, and the prime minister's son Maturēcaṉ. Ugly and ill-natured Maturēcaṉ becomes jealous of the handsome and intelligent Puvaṉēntiraṉ and in vain devises several evil plans in order to win Cukuṇa Cuntari's heart. When floods destroy the harvest and famine spreads in his country, King Narātipaṉ decides to distribute food to his people. Since all the roads are impassable, some Frenchmen offer balloons for this purpose. While traveling in such a balloon to search for her father, Cukuṇa Cuntari drifts off to another country. It turns out that the king of that country, "Southern Land," has ordered that she be abducted, since he wants to marry her. Hardly fond of the king and his idea, Cukuṇa Cuntari seeks refuge in a nunnery. Meanwhile, Maturēcaṉ's father, the prime minister, tries to kill Puvaṉēntiraṉ, who manages to escape and, disguised as a girl, finally reaches the convent where he meets Cukuṇa Cuntari. In order to be able to take her back to Pūvaṉacēkaram, he accepts an office at the court of the ruler of "Southern Land." Due to his good qualities, he even becomes minister and succeeds in having Cukuṇa Cuntari set free. When the two finally return to their hometown, they find that Maturēcaṉ's father, who has not been able to usurp the throne, is now besieging Narātipaṉ's fortress. A war ensues

30. Dhandayudham (1977: 17).

31. I quote from the first edition throughout. Among the later editions, one may refer to Vētanāyakam Piḷḷai (1957c) since it follows the original text with only minor changes.

in which the usurpers die. Cukuṇa Cuntari is crowned queen, and Puvaṉēntiraṉ is discovered to be the son of the king of Āriyatēca. The wedding of the two leads the story to a happy ending.

The reader will not have missed the striking structural parallels to *Piratāpa Mutaliyār carittiram* in this plot. In both novels two boys and one girl are educated together, and one boy later turns out to be of high descent. After rescuing the heroine who has been kidnapped, the hero marries her. While in *Piratāpa Mutaliyār carittiram* the heroine becomes "king," in *Cukuṇa Cuntari carittiram* the heroine is crowned queen. In both novels the changing of roles by means of disguise plays an important part: Ñāṉāmpāḷ dresses as a man, Puvaṉēntiraṉ as a woman. However, the introduction of antagonists, the villains Maturēcaṉ and his father, is a significant new feature in the second novel, as Pāṇṭuraṅkaṉ has remarked (1994: 73). *Cukuṇa Cuntari carittiram* is also considerably shorter, occupying only about a third of the length of the first novel.

As has been pointed out already, Vētanāyakam Piḷḷai's second novel again contains many subplots and lectures. Just as Kamil Zvelebil states that "the build-up of the plot of Suguna Sunthari is definitely more skilful than the structure of the first novel; the events unfold out of each other in an organic cause-and-effect sequence" (1990a: 148), most scholars consider it better designed. And indeed, the main plot is interrupted less frequently. The subtexts are more directly connected to the main plot, since they are all motivated by the action that takes place.[32] Hence, it is a rather straightforward and linear narrative, and, considering its brevity, "longwinded" (Dhandayudham 1977: 17) is certainly the wrong epithet.

However, literary scholars have emphasized repeatedly that *Cukuṇa Cuntari carittiram* did not have the same success that the author's first novel saw eight years before (e.g., Asher 1969: 19; Cupramaṇiyam 1985: 57).[33] This observation is corroborated by the fact that after its first publication in January 1887 by the St. Joseph

---

32. A speech about the evils of jealousy, for example, is given by the the family guru in front of Maturēcaṉ because he has started to envy Puvaṉēntiraṉ.

33. In their masterful history of the Tamil novel, Pe. Kō. Cuntararājaṉ and Cō. Civapātacuntaram have addressed this widespread dismissal: "Not only did everyone take *Piratāpa Mutaliyār carittiram* as their darling 'first novel' to praise it sky-high, but for some reason they also disregarded the beauty of *Cukuṇa Cuntari*, its good construction, its progress within the novelistic genre and the extent to which it reflects the circumstances of the time. In the history of the novel, *Cukuṇa Cuntari* occupies a pre-eminent place" (Cuntararājaṉ/Civapātacuntaram 1977: 16; my translation).

Press in Madras at the price of 7 annas, a revised second edition only appeared almost three decades later, in October 1914 (V. G. Arogiaswamy & Brothers, price: 8 annas).[34] Consequently, literary critics as well have paid it little attention. Most pronounced is Ka. Naa. Subramanyam's judgment who categorically states that *Cukuṇa Cuntari* is "a moral tale" that "does not deserve serious consideration as a novel" (1961: 31). R. E. Asher tries to find a reason for its lack of popularity, when he suggests that "the success [of the first novel] was not repeated, perhaps because he had packed so much into the first one that he had very little left to say" (1969: 19).[35] However, I would like to suggest another reason. Taking Subramanyam's rather harsh sounding statement seriously, one could say that the reason for the failure of the novel may be that it is, in fact, a traditional *katai* rather than a novel. Regarding *Piratāpa Mutaliyār carittiram,* Vētanāyakam Piḷḷai states that he made Ñāṉāmpāḷ 'king' "with a view to meet the taste of the Hindu readers, who are very fond of kings and queens" (1885: ii). Similarly, to suit the taste of his readers, he wrote his second novel entirely as a "story of kings and queens" (Taṭcaṇāmūrtti 1979: 12). Or as Ka. Kailācapati points out, the novel is actually a "descendant of the 'grandmother's tale' that begins with 'In a town there lived a king' " (1987: 89). The beginning of *Cukuṇa Cuntari carittiram,* though clad in elaborate *kāvya*-style, shows a striking similarity to this traditional folktale opening:

> Slaying the bad and guarding the good without ever departing from the laws of Manu, a king named Narātipaṉ [Skt. "Ruler of Men"] ruled over the entire Dravida country, which had as its capital a town called Pūvaṉacēkaram [Skt. "Crown of the Earth"] that was like the hallowed face of goddess Earth who wears the sea as her girdle. After the king had been childless for a long time, by the grace of the Gods a daughter of surpassing beauty was born to him. Being astoundingly fair and possessing the corresponding good qualities, just as if Beauty herself had come and

34. Moreover, I have not been able to find any contemporary reviews.

35. It may be noted that Vētanāyakam Piḷḷai did in fact occasionally "recycle" material previously used in *Piratāpa Mutaliyār carittiram.* The story that the second minister tells about his education in *Cukuṇa Cuntari carittiram* (1887: 16–19, ch. 2 "How a Poor Child Was Educated") is an elaboration of a remark about the education of Piratāpa's grandfather (1885: 1).

> incarnated as a woman, this child was given the name Cukuṇa Cuntari. (1887: 1f.) [5.5]

Here, the language is that of ornate epics and the sentences are skilfully composed. One may notice how the first sentence reflects in its construction the reader's gradual focusing down from the ocean to the land, to the town, and onto the king, thus ushering the reader into the story.[36] As is evident from this exposition, the narrator unfolds a story of kings and queens that takes place almost entirely in a courtly setting. The story of Puvaṉēntiraṉ, a foundling discovered to be a prince, is a traditional folktale motif. The only overtly "modern" or contemporary elements that Vētanāyakam Piḷḷai has woven into his tale are the English and French characters, the air balloons, and the nunnery. Accordingly, this text was nothing "novel" or progressive for its contemporary readers at all, but a *katai* made of traditional, well-known ingredients.[37] The point of view as well is typical of a traditional narrative. In *Piratāpa Mutaliyār carittiram* Vētanāyakam Piḷḷai has employed a first-person narrator. This produces an effect of immediacy: someone tells his own life-story directly to the reader, and the latter participates closely. Contrary to this, in *Cukuṇa Cuntari carittiram* we find an authorial narrative situation: everything is narrated from the detached, "omniscient" perspective of a mediator who is not involved in the plot. This point of view, involving a greater distance toward the reader, is typical of the traditions of both *kāvya* and *katai*. In creating his second novel, Vētanāyakam Piḷḷai had obviously overestimated his "Hindu readers' " fondness of kings and queens. The text was too removed from the sphere of the contemporary and thus was not greatly appreciated. Although Pe. Kō. Cuntararājaṉ and Cō. Civapātacuntaram emphasize its "progress within the novelistic genre and the extent to which it reflects the circumstances of the time" (1977: 16), I would argue that Vētanāyakam Piḷḷai's second novel was in fact a step backward toward the traditional tale from which the novel meant to emancipate itself.

It must be noted that Vētanāyakam Piḷḷai did not call his works *nāval*, a tamilization of the English term which gained currency later

---

36. Unfortunately, I have not been able to render this effect in the English translation. The original has "*kaṭalaimēkalaiyāka uṭutta pūmitēviyiṉ tirumukamaṇṭalampōṉṟa puvaṉacēkarameṉṉum nakarattai rājatāṉiyāka uṭaiya tirāviṭatēcamuḻumaiyum narātipaṉ eṉṉum aracaṉ* [. . .] *aracākṣiceytuvantāṉ*" (1887: 1).

37. It may be added that in his *Tamil Literature,* M. S. Purnalingam Pillai refers to *Piratāpa Mutaliyār carittiram* as a "romance" but to *Cukuṇa Cuntari carittiram* as a "story" (1985: 342).

on, but *carittiram* (from Sanskrit *caritra*).[38] The *Tamil Lexicon* gives "history" and "biography," i.e., life (hi-)story, as its primary meanings (1926: 1318).[39] And indeed, his two novels are the life-stories of the protagonists Piratāpa Mutaliyār and Cukuṇa Cuntari, respectively. As Dhandayudham (1977: 21–23) and Satyan (1981: 80) argue, the main reason for Vētanāyakam to adopt the term "history" may have been that he wanted to follow the early English novels of Fielding, Richardson and others which had titles like *The History of Tom Jones, The History of the Adventures of Joseph Andrews and of his Friend Mr. Abraham Adams, Clarissa or The History of a Young Lady*, etc. That he was drawing upon English terminology may perhaps also be seen in his use of the term *vacaṉakāviyam* (in chapter 42 of *Piratāpa Mutaliyār carittiram*). Above, I have translated the term loosely as "prose composition," but with regard to a novel it clearly reminds one of the English term "epic in prose"—a term Henry Fielding had employed for his "new species" in his preface to *Joseph Andrews* (1742) (Hunter 1990: 338).[40] There may, however, be more to the deployment of the term *carittiram*. If Vētanāyakam Piḷḷai had simply wanted to present a "story," a piece of fiction, he could have applied the term *katai* (from Sanskrit *kathā*) that was widely used in his times to denote a narrative that was essentially fictitious. But, as has been mentioned above, the *katai* was a traditional form, rooted in folklore,[41] and therefore entirely inadequate to express what was meant as a conscious attempt to publish something *new*, a modern text to shape a modern society. By applying the term *carittiram* to a fictional "biography" instead of the story of a "real," historical person, Vētanāyakam showed the desire to distinguish his work from other kinds of available models of fiction.

Moreover, it has been pointed out that the early English novels generally used the label "history" in their titles to make a claim to

38. Similarly, the titles of the earliest Telugu novels by Narahari Gōpālakṛṣṇama Ceṭṭi (1832–?) and Kandukūri Vīrēśaliṅgam Pantulu (1848–1919) were *Śrīraṅgarāja Caritramu* (1872) and *Rājaśēkhara Caritramu* (1878). On the early Telugu novel, see also Vijayasree (2002), Sai Prasad (1991) and the essays by S. Laxmana Murthy and V. Rangan in Ravindran (2001).

39. That this was the actual usage in nineteenth-century Tamil can be seen from the fact that among the books listed in L. D. Barnett's *Catalogue of the Tamil Books in the Library of the British Museum* all the nineteenth-century works titled *carittiram* are biographies or local histories (see Barnett/Pope 1909 and Barnett 1931).

40. Moreover, in the English preface to the same novel, Vētanāyakam referred to his work as "novel" and "prosaic fiction" (1885: if.).

41. As is evident from the nineteenth-century books bearing this title in Barnett/Pope (1909) and Barnett (1931), e.g., *Mataṉakāmarājaṉ katai, Mariyātairāmaṉ katai*, etc., which are folktales.

truth (Hunter 1990: 403, ftn. 5), and S. V. Subramanian has suggested that, similarly, the early Tamil novelists wanted to give "the impression that [their works] are reconstructed history, and [. . .] not mere fiction" (1984: 66). This brings us back to the question of realism in the works of Vētanāyakam Piḷḷai. How true to reality did he want to be? And how true was he?

On the one hand, it was his declared intention to depict contemporary reality, as is evident from his preface to *Piratāpa Mutaliyār carittiram*: "This work contains faithful pictures of the national character, domestic life, habits, and manners of the people in Southern India [. . .] In the description of the various characters and incidents, I have adhered closely to nature, avoiding the marvellous as well as sentimentalism" (1885: iif.). On the other hand however, in pursuance of his didactic aim he has "represented the principal personages as perfectly virtuous" and designed Piratāpa's father and father-in-law as "types of uneducated native gentlemen in high life" (ibid.). Thus, he created idealized characters or stereotypes which are quite remote from "human nature as it is" (ibid.). Now, this idealization of characters and the representation of reality at the same time seem rather incompatible—at least to many later critics. Hence, R. E. Asher refers to the final product as "brief lifelike scenes in the midst of improbabilities" (1969: 18), and S. Sivapatha Sundaram identifies a "pattern of fantasy mixed with realism" (1978: 28). In the first sentence of *Piratāpa Mutaliyār carittiram*, the narrator specifies the time when the story takes place: "Some time after this country had been taken over by the British rulers, I was born into the lineage of the Toṇṭaimaṇṭala Mutaliyārs in a town called Cattiyapuri" (Vētanāyakam Piḷḷai 1885: 1) [5.6]. As a sharp contrast to this "real" temporal setting, the places of action are the fictitious towns Cattiyapuri, Vikkiramapuri, and Ātiyūr. This contrast illustrates how the novel does not "reconstruct history," but presents a blend of the ordinary and everyday world of fact and event, and the fictional or even fantastic (Ñāṉāmpāḷ becoming a "king") sphere. A similar blend can be found in *Cukuṇa Cuntari carittiram* where the reader is transported into the imaginary "Dravidian" realm of king Narātipaṉ with its "real" French balloons.[42] This is a reality that only the novel could express. The realism of the early Indian novels is often a somewhat precarious realism, a realism in the making, where "old ideas are giving way to new ones and myths

42. Against the background of Robert Caldwell's "proof" of a Dravidian language family in 1856, could this novel be read as a political allegory, when the heroine as the ruler of an imagined "*tirāviṭa tēca muḻumai*" eventually marries the prince of "*āriyatēcam*"?

Figure 5.3. Pi. Ār Rājam Aiyar (1871–1898), late nineteenth-century portrait.

to facts," but not quite. It is a realism modified by didacticism and traditional concepts of storytelling. In the development of the early Indian novel, there are few sudden shifts. Instead, we find very gradual transitions and intertwinings. Other early novelists, like Pi. Ār. Rājam Aiyar or A. Mātavayyā, followed Vētanāyakam Piḷḷai's example and called their novels *carittiram*,[43] but, as we shall see in a moment, the later "histories"' once again rethought and redefined what "realism" could mean in the Tamil novel.

43. Likewise, with *Cukuṇa Cuntari carittiram* Vētanāyakam Piḷḷai also seems to have created the fashion of naming the novel after the heroine. Pi. Ār. Rājam Aiyar, for instance, gave his novel the subtitle *Kamalāmpāḷ carittiram*, although it is in fact rather the story of Muttucāmi Aiyar, as Ashokamitran rightly points out (1986: 92). Other authors followed (see Appendix 2).

The Fatal Rumor or The History of Kamalambal (1893–1895): "Vedanta through fiction"?[44]

In the year 1893, six years after the publication of *Cukuṉa Cuntari carittiram*, and four years after Vētanāyakam Piḷḷai's death, Pi. Ār. Rājam Aiyar started serializing his novel *Āpattukkiṭamāṉa apavātam allatu Kamalāmpāḷ carittiram* ("The Fatal Rumor or The History of Kamalambal") in the new Tamil monthly *Vivēkacintāmaṇi*. Besides the beginning of Rājam Aiyar's novel, the February 1893 issue of *Vivēkacintāmaṇi* also carried an installment of Es. Nārāyaṇacāmi Ayyar's translation of Shakespeare's *A Midsummer Night's Dream* (as *Naṭuvēṉiṟkaṉavu*), one of the earliest Shakespeare translations into Tamil, and an advertisement for U. Vē. Cāminātaiyar's editions of classical Tamil texts, such as *Caṅkam* poems or the voluminous *Cīvakacintāmaṇi* priced at 6 rupees. *Kamalāmpāḷ carittiram* appeared in altogether twenty installments between February 1893 and January 1895.[45] Born as a Smārta brahmin in 1872 in the village Vattalakkuṇṭu in Madurai District, Rājam Aiyar[46] belonged to a younger generation than Vētanāyakam Piḷḷai. After passing his First Arts Examination at the Government School in Madurai in 1887, he attended the Madras Christian College where he earned a BA degree in English Literature. He made his appearance on the literary scene in the early 1890s when he published two reviews of recent literary works, Araṅkanāta Mutaliyār's poem *Kaccik kalampakam* (1889), and the play *Maṉōṉmaṇīyam* (1891) by Pe. Cuntaram Piḷḷai, the philosophical essay "Man, His Littleness and His Greatness," and his *Kamalāmpāḷ carittiram*. From his reviews it becomes clear that he was following the Tamil literary scene with keen attention. In 1896, Rājam Aiyar was appointed editor of the new English journal *Prabuddha Bharata* ("Awakened India") founded by Swami Vivekananda. Using several pseudonyms, Rājam Aiyar wrote a large number of articles for it as well as the unfinished novel *True Greatness or Vasudeva Sastri*. These 850 pages of contributions were

44. Ashokamitran (1986: 91).

45. In the journal, the author's name was given as "Pi. Ār. Civacuppiramaṇiya Ayyar, Pi. Ē. [B.A.]" (see *Vivēkacintāmaṇi*, vol. 10, February 1893, p. 313). Moreover, the first instalment was titled "*Aniyāya apavātam* [unjust/improper slander] *allatu Kamalāmpāḷ carittiram*," which was then changed in the March 1893 issue to "*Āpattukkiṭamāṉa apavātam* [dangerous slander] *allatu Kamalāmpāḷ carittiram*." We do not know whether this was a simple error or a change of mind on Rājam Aiyar's part.

46. Biographical evidence is scarce. For brief and rather idiosyncratic accounts of his life see the "sketch" in Rajam Aiyar (1974: 14–20) in English, and Kastūriraṅka Ayyar (1909) in Tamil.

published in 1905 under the title *Rambles in Vedanta* (see Rajam Iyer 1905; 1974). Also in 1896, *Kamalāmpāḷ carittiram* appeared in book form. Two years later, the "inspired lad of six-and-twenty summers, whose musings and meditations are no mean bequest to posterity" (Rajam Iyer 1974: xv) died from intestinal complications.

His biographer elaborates how as a writer Rājam Aiyar was influenced by both Tamil (Kampaṉ and the mystic Tāyumāṉavar) and English literature (Shakespeare and the Romantic poets) (Rajam Iyer 1974: 14f.). Moreover, Rājam Aiyar devoted himself to Vedānta philosophy. Not only did the majority of his essays in *Prabuddha Bharata* center around this topic, but his *Kamalāmpāḷ carittiram* was also written with the primary aim to propagate Advaita philosophy. As the author solemnly states in his epilogue to the novel: "[T]he story was not my principal goal in writing this 'history.' [. . .] May we all endeavor to reach that divine bliss and pure consciousness, that eternal light and truth which was worshipped in order to produce this little book and in whose name this story is selflessly presented" (Rajam Aiyar 1998: 150f.) [5.7]. While in the first half of the novel action predominates (with instances of robbery, arson, manslaughter, a wedding, and a bullfight), the second half abounds with philosophical reflections and meditations. Consequently, the writer Putumaippittaṉ has remarked that "the first part of *Kamalāmpāḷ carittiram* is a novel, the second part is a dream" (Caṅkaranārāyaṇaṉ 1989: 32). Apart from this, Rājam Aiyar's biographer mentions a second goal: "The novel also aims at popularizing Kamban, the great Tamil poet, by bringing into currency the rich expressions with which he has gifted the Tamil language" (Rajam Iyer 1974: 15).

Rājam Aiyar's objectives are similar to those of Vētanāyakam Piḷḷai, since both use their novels in order to instruct and uplift their readers. However, the essence of the instruction they provide is quite different. The work of the former is made to reflect religio-philosophical truths and deep introspection, whereas the works of the latter mostly contain "practical illustrations," pragmatic secular ideas more related to ordinary everyday life.

The story of *Kamalāmpāḷ carittiram* takes place in the little village Ciṟukuḷam in Madurai District, and it begins with an intriguing invocation of none other than Vētanāyakam Piḷḷai. The protagonist Muttucāmi Aiyar, a wealthy man in Ciṟukuḷam, is married to the virtuous Kamalāmpāḷ, while his brother Cuppiramaṇiya Aiyar is married to Poṉṉammāḷ, a malicious shrew. Upon awakening one fine morning, Muttucāmi calls Kamalāmpāḷ, and the two start a playful argument as she complains about her husband's lack of respect in addressing her. Shrugging off his wife's attempt at self-assertion, Muttucāmi counters by singing a line from Vētanāyakam Piḷḷai's *Peṇmati mālai,* his collection of poems on women's role in society: "Even if she's a Lady, a wife is a servant to her man." Kamalāmpāḷ retorts with aplomb: "He is a man, like you, that Vedanayakam Pillai, isn't he? He can drop dead!" (Rajam Aiyar 1998: 3, modified) [5.8]. That Kamalāmpāḷ immediately recognizes the verse may testify to Vētanāyakam Piḷḷai's fame as a writer of songs. But clearly this is also a nod, however irreverent, to Vētanāyakam Piḷḷai the pioneer novelist whose works Rājam Aiyar must have known well, given his interest in Tamil literature. Also, in this incipit, Rājam Aiyar takes a decisive step away from Vētanāyakam Piḷḷai's *Bildungsroman* style of telling the story "from the beginning," i.e., from the birth of the protagonists. *Kamalāmpāḷ carittiram* begins *in medias res,* with the quarrel between Muttucāmi and his wife, after only two short introductory sentences (fused into one in Stuart Blackburn's English translation): "In Madurai district there is a village named Sirukulam, and in the middle of the main street there is a house known as the 'Big House' " (ibid.) [5.9]. Then, Muttucāmi earns sister-in-law Poṉṉammāḷ's displeasure by not marrying his daughter Lakṣmi to her brother's son, but to a handsome and intelligent boy called Śrīnivācaṉ. Furious about this, Poṉṉammāḷ commences her wicked web of intrigues in order to harm Muttucāmi's family. When the notorious robber Pēyāṇṭi Tēvaṉ breaks into Cuppiramaṇiya Aiyar's house, he is caught, sentenced, and sent to prison. After being released, he kidnaps Muttucāmi's little son Naṭarācaṉ. Moreover, Muttucāmi also has serious trouble with his business. Utterly disconsolate, he leaves home and goes on a long pilgrimage. Evil Poṉṉammāḷ who is still out for revenge starts spreading rumors about Kamalāmpāḷ's infidelity during her husband's absence. Since Muttucāmi believes what he has come to know, he tries to commit suicide in an isolated mandapam in Chidambaram. A *cuvāmi* (ascetic) prevents him from killing himself, makes him his disciple, and takes him to Benares. In the meantime back in Ciṟukuḷam, Cuppiramaṇiya Aiyar dies, having been poisoned by his wife Poṉṉammāḷ. However, once she has fully realized the consequences of her evil deeds, she becomes insane. Searching for Muttucāmi, Kamalāmpāḷ, Lakṣmi and Śrīnivācaṉ finally arrive in Benares as well. There the villain Pēyāṇṭi, reformed in the meantime, sets the kidnapped Naṭarācaṉ free. Muttucāmi regains the wealth he had lost and the family, thus happily reunited, returns to Ciṟukuḷam.

All in all, the plot of *Kamalāmpāḷ carittiram* is quite different from Vētanāyakam Piḷḷai's novels. It can be regarded as more coherent, since Rājam Aiyar has not inserted subtexts in the fashion of Vētanāyakam Piḷḷai's treasuries of speeches and anecdotes. In addition, Rājam Aiyar also uses "real" settings, i.e., the towns of Chidambaram, Madras, and Benares, and his descriptions of backgrounds and events are vivid and show a loving hand.[47] A further important instance of Rājam Aiyar's new realism can be found in the characterizations. In E. M. Forster's famous terms, Rājam Aiyar's characters are "round," psychologically complex and thus closer to real life when compared with the earlier novels *Piratāpa Mutaliyār carittiram* and *Cukuṇa Cuntari carittiram*. Vētanāyakam Piḷḷai drew on earlier literary modes in creating "flat" characters. They are the stereotypes of the epics built around a single quality of either "good" or "bad," and they remain unchanged throughout the story. Their idealized uniformity is reflected in the fact that many of them have symbolic names. For instance, the couple Piratāpa and Ñāṉāmpāḷ, the constellation of "greatness" (*piratāpam*) and "knowledge" (*ñāṉam*), has been interpreted thus: "These two characters are often separated from each other and suffer consequently. Symbolically, it means that one without the other (knowledge without prowess) will not bring happiness to humanity" (Shreedharan 1971: 33). In the second novel, the "good" characters have symbolic names like the heroine "The Well-natured Beautiful One," "Lord of the World" (Puvaṉēntiraṉ), and even the family guru is called Kurucirēṣṭar "First One Among the Teachers." The characters' virtues are hammered home in explicit laudatory enumerations. In chapter 2 (on "Cukuṇa Cuntari's Qualities") we read:

> Just as no man was equal to Puvaṉēntiraṉ, no woman equaled Cukuṇa Cuntari. She was adorned by all the highest qualities. Her chastity, good conduct, humility, patience, truthfulness and purity were beyond the reach of words. Although she was the daughter of the ruler of the world, she knew about the painful hardships of the people. [. . .] She was endowed with a beautiful face, compassionate eyes, a tongue that spoke sweet truth, generous giving hands and passionate *devabhakti* [love for God]. Her beautiful face showed the purity of her soul. The purity of her body showed the purity of her heart. (Vētanāyakam Piḷḷai 1887: 15f.) [5.10]

47. See e.g., his descriptions of a *jalli kaṭṭu* (in chapter 13), or of the group of boys playing on the riverbank in chapter 16.

And with the next sentence the chapter concludes: "Since it is impossible to describe her excellent qualities, we only say this much" (ibid.) [5.11].

In sharp contrast to this, Rājam Aiyar's imaginative characterizations go beyond mere descriptive enumerations. In fact, the virtues of young Lakṣmi seem quite comparable to Cukuṇa Cuntari's qualities, but they are depicted in a strikingly different way:

> Her perfectly formed limbs were not only lovely in their own right but each one of them also revealed the beauty of the others, just as an individual string of the vina not only makes its own sound but also complements the music of the whole instrument. You could no more make a change in Lakshmi's appearance without introducing a blemish than you could insert an extra line or two into the verse of a great poet like Kampan without reducing its aesthetic effect. "If her neck were a little longer," "her leg a bit shorter," "her hands somewhat wider"—all these were as useless and unnecessary to Lakshmi's beauty as case endings to good poetry.[48] [. . .] when Lakshmi spoke, the lovely way her facial expressions shifted to fit her words made one think of a glittering diamond. Her hand movements and changing facial expressions meant that even those standing at a distance could understand her. No matter how much pain she might experience, her wide eyes and high lips showed a firm mind and resolute patience. Those eyes leaping playfully like little fish, the tiny dimples on her cheeks and her gleaming teeth gave her face a remarkable, almost magical power. Although her eyes were cool and soft, when necessary they also had a sharpness that could startle onlookers and bring to mind the saying, "A woman's eyes penetrate body, heart and soul." (Rajam Aiyar 1998: 47f.) [5.12].

Moreover, Rājam Aiyar's characterizations are often implicit, i.e., the characters are described by what they do and how they do it.[49] He exclusively uses "real" names for his characters and makes the

48. Classical Tamil poetry generally uses the case endings common to Modern Tamil rather sparingly, as many of the verses discussed in Chapters 2 and 3 show quite clearly.

49. The slanderous activities of the members of the "Gossip Society," e.g., Suppu and Nagu, are an example of this.

central figures Aiyar brahmins like himself. The reader also gains insights into their psychological condition. Especially the second part of *Kamalāmpāḷ carittiram* is centered around the ponderings and the mental anguish of Muttucāmi Aiyar, depicted through the technique of interior monologue:

> What a horrible day! But who cares? At last this last day of my life is the festival day. Still, what's the point of becoming a sannyasi? Shave my head and beg in the streets—what good's that going to do? Destroy everything—temple and tank—all of it! You survey everything, don't you Mr. Sky, but are you blind, too? Where's your thunder? Why not destroy this worthless world with a single flash of lightning! (Rajam Aiyar 1998: 112) [5.13]

Going through various mental and physical states that the reader can follow closely, Rājam Aiyar's characters develop. Muttucāmi Aiyar and Kamalāmpāḷ are not the same at the end as they are at the beginning of the novel. Pēyāṇṭi Tēvaṉ gives up his profession of a bandit and Poṉṉammāḷ becomes mad. In sum, the mode of characterization in *Kamalāmpāḷ carittiram* can be regarded as innovative in comparison with Vētanāyakam Piḷḷai's novels that utilize traditional techniques of idealization.

Because of the features mentioned above, critics generally agree that Rājam Aiyar's work inaugurated what they call the "Age of Realism" (Dhandayudham 1977: 48) in the history of the Tamil novel. Ka. Naa. Subramanyam, for instance, seems to be rather taken with this new realism when he states that "there are no extraordinary or suspicious incidents at all in this novel" (Cupramaṇiyam 1957: 35). In their enthusiasm, scholars have gone even a step further and, dismissing *Piratāpa Mutaliyār carittiram* and *Cukuṇa Cuntari carittiram* entirely, have emphasized that in fact *Kamalāmpāḷ carittiram* should be regarded as the first Tamil novel.[50]

Further Comparisons

Since Vētanāyakam Piḷḷai and Rājam Aiyar belong to different generations, it is perhaps not surprising that their novels are quite different in both form and content. Well into his fifties and at the end of

50. See e.g., Venkat Swaminathan (1992: 3510) or Tōtāttiri (1977: 32).

his career as a judge, Vētanāyakam Piḷḷai's ideas about his work of prose fiction must have been distinct from those of the young student Rājam Aiyar's views and ambitions. Also, Rājam Aiyar could draw on a wider variety of Western readings that had not yet been available when Vētanāyakam Piḷḷai was educated several decades earlier. Within the framework of an evolutionary historiography of the Tamil novel, Rājam Aiyar's work has been viewed as exhibiting "the rapid progress made in the art of storytelling since the outcome of the first novel by the pioneer Pillai" (Natarajan/Mathialagan 1996: 84). Or as Dhandayudham has it: "The Tamil novel was a tale of wonder in the hands of Vedanayagam Pillai and it began to blaze a tale of real life in the hands of Rajam Iyer" (1977: 50).

Nevertheless, the novels of the two authors are similar in many respects. As has been shown above, both authors regard the novel as a medium for imparting instruction to their readers. At the same time, both authors want to entertain their audience as is evident from the use of humor in the texts. Moreover, they both engage with contemporary political and social themes, albeit presenting different opinions. In *Cukuṇa Cuntari carittiram*, Vētanāyakam Piḷḷai dwells at considerable length on the evils of child marriage, a hotly debated issue in his times.[51] His protest against this practice takes up three entire chapters (55–57) of his novel and culminates in a rather touching "Dialogue between a girl and her mother at a child wedding" (title of chapter 57). Here, a mother explains that the bond of marriage might entail sati to her three-year-old (!) daughter who finally declares: "Only if my husband agrees to commit sati for me as well will I accept the *tāli*. If not, there is no way I am going to accept it. If he ties it anyway, I will cut it off and throw it away" (Vētanāyakam Piḷḷai 1887: 121) [5.14]. Conversely, Rājam Aiyar takes a pronounced stance opposing social reform when his narrator states: "Nowadays some young people think that a woman will only be happy if she marries after the age of twenty, but knowing well the love between Srinivasan and Lakshmi, I cannot agree" (1998: 95) [5.15]. Curiously, both *Cukuṇa Cuntari carittiram* and *Kamalāmpāḷ carittiram* deal with another "social" issue: the effects of slander. Vētanāyakam Piḷḷai who vividly explains in chapter 19 that "just as leftovers we spit into the wind fall back on us, calumny we spread about others will harm ourselves" (1887: 37) [5.16] would certainly have been pleased to see how Rājam Aiyar built his whole novel around this evil.

51. See also Blackburn (1998: 162).

Evidently, all three novels offer a specifically high-class perspective on contemporary society. That a dalit writer would have had a rather different focus becomes apparent from the contemporary Malayalam novel *Sarasvatīvijayam* by Pōttēri Kuññampu (Potheri Kunhambu) that was published in 1892, about a year before the first installments of *Kamalāmpāḷ carittiram* appeared in print.[52] Thematizing his status in society, Kuññampu "celebrates English education for untouchables as a means of escaping subordination" (Menon 1997: 293). The information readers may extract from the three Tamil novels about nineteenth-century Tamil society includes implicit statements about the colonial rulers, the British and French. The colonial "other" is rather awkwardly present in the novelistic texts. Vētanāyakam Piḷḷai's ambivalent attitude toward colonial modernity becomes evident from his deployment of "European" characters and symbols of Western progress in his novels. In *Cukuṇa Cuntari carittiram* he tells "The Story of a European Lady" (chapter 5).[53] In this story, the lady is presented with an aura of obscure alienness. She is set apart from the other passengers, the "natives" who cannot easily understand her clever plans. As part of her obscurity, she has got paper money, a sign of Western modernity, the significance of which is not obvious to the others. At first, she seems to be wicked, trying to escape the situation at someone else's expense, but then she turns out to be well-natured and generous, and above all, more sagacious than all

52. The novel *Sarasvatīvijayam* has recently been translated into English, see Kunhambu (2002). For a critical discussion of this text, see Menon (1997) and, in comparison with other lower-caste Malayalam novels, Menon (2004), which is a revised version of Menon (2002). On the early Malayalam novels and notably the most famous of these, O. Cantu Mēnōn's *Indulēkhā* (1889), see also Panikkar (1996), Arunima (1997; 2004), Kumar (2002), and the essays in Ravindran (2001). *Indulēkhā* is now available in a masterful new translation by Anitha Devasia (Chandumenon 2005).

53. When during a night journey in a mail-coach a man begins to worry about robbers and asks his fellow passengers how he could best hide his ten gold coins, a European lady advises him to put them into his sandals. After some time, a robber does indeed appear and the lady, saying that she has got no money, points at the man with the coins. The robber searches the man and disappears with his loot. Once the robber is gone, the man starts to insult the lady. She, however, says to him and her fellow passengers: "Please come to my house for dinner tomorrow. Then I will tell you the truth." When everybody has assembled, the lady shows them a book: "In this book there is paper money which is worth several thousand gold coins. If I had not told the robber about this man's coins, he would have stolen all the money in my book. Instead of the ten gold coins that this man has lost because of me, I will give him a hundred thousand gold coins." Immediately, everyone is happy, and they celebrate the cleverness and generosity of this lady. For the Tamil text of this story, see Appendix 3 [5.17].

her fellow passengers. This lady is quite mysteriously not what she appears to be, a rather nebulous figure. An Indian woman could not have played this ambivalent role. Another, perhaps even more striking instance of uneasiness about the colonial "other" is the curious appearance of French air balloons, representing the miracle of modern technology, in the middle of fairy tale-like *Cukuṇa Cuntari carittiram*. These balloons symbolize quite clearly Vētanāyakam Piḷḷai's ambivalence. On the one hand, they are used, as the last resort, to distribute food during the famine in King Narātipaṉ's realm. They appear, at a crucial moment, as instruments of succor and salvation. On the other hand, however, a balloon is the ominous vehicle in which the heroine is abducted, and its French pilot is a ruthless villain. The ambiguity which thus ensues may be read as Vētanāyakam Piḷḷai's attempt to demonstrate the potential of Western progress to be beneficial as well as evil. Moreover, the author (who has been dependent on Western authorities throughout his whole life) introduces Western figures of authority into the plot at crucial points. The Governor of Madras has to decide the case about Tēvarāja Piḷḷai's son, and, at the end of the novel, Vētanāyakam Piḷḷai invokes Queen Victoria to emphasize the truth value of his story.

Quite differently, Rājam Aiyar's ironic pen makes Westerners objects of plain mockery. In a beautifully painted episode (chapter 21), he describes the Madras beach, "this seashore of spectacles," as a meeting ground of all the different parts of contemporary society indulging in their leisure activities. There, amidst fishermen, students, young couples, and sannyasis, dallies the colonial "other" as well: "Elsewhere on the beach a group of English women were dressed like peacocks, strutted like swans and chirped like parrots, as they talked and laughed, holding their (or another's) lover's hands" (Rajam Aiyar 1998: 96) [5.18]. In this subtle form of ridicule, Rājam Aiyar's engagement with the 'other' has very much the quality of a clash of cultures. Nevertheless, it has been observed that, on the whole, the author does not seem to take a pronounced anti-colonial stance (Blackburn 1998: 171f.).

Finally, a common characteristic of the three early Tamil novels discussed here is their reference to and inclusion of a variety of pretexts[54] that form part of what could be called the Tamil "cultural heritage." This instance of intertextuality is probably the most obvious feature that characterizes the novels as fundamentally ingesting

54. With the term "pretexts" I refer to a variety of literary and non-literary texts that existed before the first Tamil novels and that influenced them, directly or indirectly.

and multivocal texts. When Stuart Blackburn remarks with regard to *Kamalāmpāḷ carittiram* that "the novel is a steady stream of proverbs, traditional similes, songs and references to folktales" (1998: 173), this is certainly true for *Piratāpa Mutaliyār carittiram* and *Cukuṇa Cuntari carittiram,* as well. The pretexts that the novels draw upon belong to both elite literature and folklore. We can find references to the *Tirukkuṟaḷ,*[55] *Tiruvāymoḻi, Tiruvācakam, Tēvāram,*[56] *Nālaṭiyār,*[57] the poets Kampaṉ[58] and Tāyumāṉavar,[59] and the poetess Auvaiyār,[60] as well as proverbs,[61] allusions to the *katais* of Teṉāli Rāmaṉ[62] or Vikkiramātittaṉ,[63] and the songs of fishermen.[64] The pretexts are sometimes quoted verbatim and their source is given. For instance, all three novels include quotations from the *Tirukkuṟaḷ,* the venerated verse manual of ethics. In all cases the original stanza is given with a reference to the work or its legendary author Tiruvaḷḷuvar,[65] followed by a modern Tamil paraphrase in *Piratāpa Mutaliyār carittiram* and *Cukuṇa Cuntari carittiram.* Sometimes, however, the pretexts are just woven into the novelistic text (verbatim or paraphrased) without indicating their origin, e.g., passages from Kampaṉ in *Kamalāmpāḷ carittiram* and proverbs in all three novels.

Significantly, neither of the two authors could resist taking a sideswipe at the poetic tradition. Rājam Aiyar obviously takes delight in describing the poetic contest between a Paṇṭāram (non-brahmin ascetic) and the clown-pandit Ammaiyappa Piḷḷai. The latter "opening his poetic floodgates" goes on thus:

> He didn't care if the words he used had meaning or not, and he paid no attention to rules of prosody. For him, a verse must have alliteration; without the repetition of sounds

55. In all three novels.

56. In *Kamalāmpāḷ carittiram* (1998: 35).

57. In *Piratāpa Mutaliyār carittiram* (1885: 287).

58. In all three novels.

59. In *Kamalāmpāḷ carittiram* (passim).

60. In *Kamalāmpāḷ carittiram* (16) and *Piratāpa Mutaliyār carittiram* (287).

61. In all three novels.

62. In *Kamalāmpāḷ carittiram* (ch. 7).

63. In *Piratāpa Mutaliyār carittiram* (111).

64. In *Kamalāmpāḷ carittiram* (35).

65. *Tirukkuṟaḷ* 42.2 in *Kamalāmpāḷ carittiram* (ch. 29, Rajam Aiyar 1998: 128), 11.2 in *Piratāpa Mutaliyār carittiram* (Vētanāyakam Piḷḷai 1885: 138), 16.5 and 7.10 in *Cukuṇa Cuntari carittiram* (1887: 22 and 33).

> it wasn't a verse. So he began to throw out all sorts of lyrics. [. . .] In his ecstasy Ammaiyappa Pillai had no idea of where he was going, nor did he stop with these pretty lyrics, but entered into songs embellished with the pathetic fallacy and figures of speech: 'A woman was pining away for her absent lover; night fell and the sun set as usual.' Instead of singing that, however, our poet put it like this: 'Battered by that tempest called a lady's sigh, that kite-like sun descended. Wounded and bloodied in the plunge, it turned the heavens crimson.' He sang many songs in this divine, erotic mode and then sang others that simultaneously describe Spring and compare it to the rainy season. For instance, the rainy season is full of dark clouds and in Spring women have hair like dark clouds. (Rajam Aiyar 1998: 133) [5.19]

In a similarly humorous engagement with the poetic genre, a "half-educated and notoriously dimwitted poet" helps out stupid Maturēcaṉ, eager to win Cukuṇa Cuntari's heart, by composing a praise poem on the beauty of the princess. The delightful passage merits a longer quotation. As an introduction, the narrator remarks to the reader:

> Since we do not wish to print this poem which was full of grammatical mistakes, we will only give a summary that renders its meaning. 'To the great and famous Cukuṇa Cuntari: Although I have not obtained your darshan for some time, the moon of your face keeps shining in the heaven of my heart. Can Āticēṣaṉ who has a thousand tongues[66] describe your beauty? Defeated by your divine face, the moon, its body weak, its interior dark, wanes daily. How can a lotus flower that is born in mud and tasted by bees, that closes itself at night and that withers away, be equal to your face? Since the clouds are not equal to your hair, they are wandering in heaven weeping and shedding floods of tears. How can I compare your eye to an antelope which is a beast with four legs and a tail, or to a stinking fish? The goose, peacock, cuckoo, parrot and mynah which used to roam around the country, are now wandering about in the forest, defeated by your gait, grace

66. The mythological thousand-headed serpent that supports the earth on its hoods and on whom Viṣṇu reclines.

> and speech. Pearls fearing your teeth are hiding in shells in the sea. How can I compare your lips to corals of which everybody says they are red like spittle? Brahma has given you all parts of the body, but he has not given you a waist. Whether he has done this out of forgetfulness or to avert the evil eye,[67] I do not know.'—Maturēcaṉ sent this poem to Cukuṇa Cuntari through her maid. As soon as she had seen it, Cukuṇa Cuntari, who did not know what anger was, became utterly furious. She tore the poem into shreds, threw it at her maid and wrote on a piece of paper 'Just as Brahma forgot to give me a waist, he forgot to give you brains.' She handed it over to the maid and sent her off. After Maturēcaṉ had seen this letter, he realized the mistake he had made and was filled with sorrow. (Vētanāyakam Piḷḷai 1887: 54–56) [5.20]

Note how cleverly Vētanāyakam Piḷḷai avoids the necessity to include a poem in his prose text. Both he and Rājam Aiyar caricature pretentious poets and the susceptibility of the poetic genre to mere bombast and nonsense. They both deal with older, traditional modes of language in order to contrast them to their own new prose. This reflects the struggle of the early novels for respectability in a time when "literature" commonly meant *poetry*, the age-old, venerated "classics," such as the *Tirukkuṟaḷ* or the *Kamparāmāyaṇam*, or the lofty compositions performed by the pulavars. As a new literary form and in order to be more than a mere "story," the novel had to win recognition and claim a place within existing textual traditions.

By thus "ingesting" various pretexts, the early Tamil novel became a veritable "compendium of Tamil literature" (Blackburn 1998: 159). The references to pretexts and their incorporation were significant in that they enabled the early novels to define themselves in dialogue with Tamil literary traditions. True, as practical applications of the "New Vernacular," the language of modernity, the early novels had the potential to overcome "tradition" and to re-fashion elite literary culture. But this was a long process rather than a sudden impulse or disruption caused by a newly "imported" literary form. The novelistic genre emerged gradually, and it was only during the first decades of the twentieth century that it became a mass phenomenon and secured itself a permanent and respected place within Tamil literary

67. This alludes to the common belief that there has to be at least a slight flaw in something that is otherwise entirely perfect in order to avert the evil eye.

production.[68] During the two decades before and after 1900, novels became increasingly important as vehicles of social critique and reform. While initially authors such as A. Mātavayyā (also spelled Mātavaiyār, Madhaviah, 1872–1925)[69] or Ca. Ma. Naṭēca Cāstiri (1859–1906)[70] still experimented with the new Tamil prose and the novelistic genre, an important watershed occurred after 1905, when Tamil fiction began to be produced as a mass commodity. As A. R. Venkatachalapathy has shown, Tamil society was inundated with new texts, and novels became the "art form par excellence of the rising middle class" (2002: 85).[71] The development of the novel during this period has to be seen against the background of continuing socio-political transformations. New social and political movements took over from the "Tamil Renaissance" ideas about the greatness of the Tamil civilization and an interest in language reform, but they also added debates on caste and class inequality.[72] The famous intellectuals and politically active literati Ca. Vētācalam Piḷḷai (1876–1950), the founder of the "pure-Tamil movement" (*taṉittamiḻ iyakkam*) who tamilized his name into Maṟaimalai Aṭikaḷ, and his colleague Vi. Kō. Cūriyanārāyaṇa Cāstiri (1870–1903) alias Paritimāl Kalaiñar, witnessed the emergence of other thoroughly modern genres, such as the short story and nationalist and social-reformist poetry.[73] Va. Ve. Cuppiramaṇiya Aiyar (V. V. S. Aiyar,

---

68. On the development of the Tamil novel into a mass phenomenon during the first half of the twentieth century, see Venkatachalapathy (1997; 2002) and his monograph in Tamil (Vēṅkaṭācalapati 2002). See Raman (2000) for a comparative discussion of constructions of gender and ethnicity in four early novels published between 1879 and 1924, including *Piratāpa Mutaliyār carittiram*.

69. On Mātavayyā and his novels, see Zvelebil (1995: 423–427), Vēṅkaṭarāmaṉ (1999), Kennedy (1980, ch. 1), Parameswaran (1986), Asher (1970; 1972a), Cuntararājaṉ/ Civapātacuntaram (1977: 31–44), Dhandayudham (1977: 55–62), Cupramaṇiyam (1957, ch. 3), and especially the new biography by Sita Anantha Raman (2005). This last book also contains a translation of his novella *Muttumīṉāṭci* ("Muthumeenakshi," 1903). His most popular novel *Patmāvati carittiram* (1898) has been translated into English by one of his granddaughters, Meenakshi Tyagarajan (see Madhaviah 2002).

70. On Naṭēca Cāstiri, see Zvelebil (1995: 487–489), Asher (1970; 1971; 1972a), Blackburn (2003: 165ff.), Cupramaṇiyam (1957, ch. 4), and the literature cited there.

72. There is a considerable literature on the socio-political developments in South India during the early decades of the twentieth century which cannot be listed here in full. See, among others, Hardgrave (1965), Irschick (1969; 1986), Barnett (1976), Pandian (1994), and Vēṅkaṭācalapati (1994).

73. On Maṟaimalai Aṭikaḷ, see Zvelebil (1995: 417f.), Iḷaṅkumaraṉ (2000), Nambi Arooran (1980), Kailasapathy (1979), Vaitheespara (1999), and the literature cited there. On Cūriyanārāyaṇa Cāstiri, see Zvelebil (1995: 219f.). An excellent account of the genesis of the Tamil purist movement is given by Kailasapathy (1979). The development of the Tamil short story is discussed in a masterful study by Kennedy (1980).

1881–1925), the "founder" of the Tamil short story, and above all Ci. Cuppiramaṇiya Pārati (Bharati, 1882–1921), a bright, but short-lived comet on the wide sky of Tamil literature, also have to be mentioned in this connection.[74] After Vētanāyakam Piḷḷai's pioneering attempt to create a new kind of poetry in his *Nītinūl*, Bharati's verses made a significant contribution to the modernization of Tamil poetry, experimenting with new forms, topics and language registers. But all these developments are really the story of the twentieth century which will have to be told elsewhere.

What has to be stressed here in connection with the gradual rise of new genres such as the novel and the short story is the fact that the old literary forms of the pulavars were not displaced overnight. Tamil pulavars continued to compose *pirapantam* works well after the first moments of literary innovation during the second half of the nineteenth century. In fact, they continued to do so throughout the twentieth century. Works such as the *Kaccikkalampakam* (1889) by Pūṇṭi Araṅkanāta Mutaliyār (1844–1893), the *Irācarāca Cētupati orutuṟaikkōvai* (1910) by Ramnad court poet Rā. Irākavaiyaṅkār (1870–1946), Rāya. Cokkaliṅkam's (1898–1974) *Kānti piḷḷaittamiḻ* (1925) on Gandhi, A. Vayinākaram Irāmanātaṉ Ceṭṭiyār's (1885–1944) *Tirupparaṅkiri mummaṇikkōvai* (1934), or Aruḷ Cellaturai's *Iyēcupirāṉ piḷḷaittamiḻ* (1985) on Jesus Christ all attest to the continued interest in traditional forms.[75] But, as opposed to earlier times, such "neo-classical" *pirapantams* were now no longer part of the literary mainstream. They became increasingly anachronistic, remnants of a bygone literary era, such as writing a Shakespearean sonnet would be in the year 2010. Novels, short stories, and modern poetry had come to stay, and those genres that used to be the norm around 1800 had become rare exceptions after 1900.

74. On V. V. S. Aiyar, see Zvelebil (1995: 753–756), Kennedy (1980, ch. 2), and Padmanabhan (1980) in English, and Maṇi (1993) and Celvam (2000) in Tamil. A large amount of work has been done already on Bharati. For a first orientation, see the long entry in Zvelebil (1995: 201–209), and Subrahmanian (2000).

75. The *Irācarāca Cētupati orutuṟaikkōvai* was edited by Mu. Caṇmukam Piḷḷai many years after the poet's death (see Caṇmukam Piḷḷai 1984). Cellaturai's *Iyēcupirāṉ piḷḷaittamiḻ* is discussed in Richman (1997, ch. 7).

6

Epilogue

As we have seen in the preceding chapters, the colonization of Tamil literature—the transformation of the entire system of Tamil elite literary production and consumption during the course of the nineteenth century—consisted of a set of gradual, interdependent, and complex processes operating at a variety of levels. While British colonial presence increasingly destabilized the old institutions and mechanisms of literary patronage described in Chapters 2 and 3, pulavars found new occupations as book publishers, editors, and language teachers, often in the emerging colonial metropolis of Madras which developed into a literary and cultural hub where Indians and Westerners interacted with growing intensity. With the ever-increasing spread of the printed book, the pulavars' earlier economy of praise was inscribed into print culture through elaborate title pages which highlighted the scholarly lineage and credentials of a book's editor or author and through the inclusion of *ciṟappuppāyiram* praise poems in the books (as we have seen in the case of Vētanāyakam Piḷḷai's *Nītinūl*). The shift from a culture of palmleaf manuscripts to a print culture led to a number of new practices and institutions: a growing book market, libraries, journals, and magazines, and an increasing number of readers who began to participate in what may be called a new public sphere. These new readers as well as the new authors, like Vētanāyakam Piḷḷai or Rājam Aiyar, belonged to a new social elite that was increasingly thoroughly educated in Western culture and that looked at their own society through the lenses of both Indian traditions and Western modernity. Literature, and the novel in particular, became a medium through which contemporary socio-political concerns were debated. The public debates I have referred to above as the colonial critique of the Tamil language and Tamil literature led to new tastes, condemning earlier literature as "obscene" and "backward," new literary forms, such as the novel, new themes, such as the role of women in society, prostitution, or the possibility of a Tamil nation, and a new language, modern

Tamil prose. At the same time, scholars and intellectuals increasingly engaged with what they discovered about their past. The edition and re-assessment of classical Tamil texts, in particular of the ancient Tamil heritage of *Caṅkam* poetry, was combined with the new disciplines of epigraphy and archaeology to systematically write a history that was uniquely Tamil. This "Tamil Renaissance" led to a wider sense of cultural self-esteem vis-à-vis the West and North India, and it paved the way for the explicit anti-colonial stance we find in the works of politically active authors, such as Va. Ve. Cuppiramaṇiya Aiyar or Cuppiramaṇiya Pārati.

What might the particular case of Tamil literature tell us about the larger question of "literature and/under colonialism"? At this point, I am skeptical about larger generalizations. Certainly, the case of Tamil shows that the moments of intensified cultural exchange entailed by colonialism may produce a number of shifts and changes. One may expect new genres, themes, ideas, narrative modes, new social groups providing writers and readers, new modes of consumption (such as silent reading vs. public recitation), and new media, such as printed books and journals. There may also be epistemic "adjustments," changes in the realm of the imagination and in ways of looking at and being in the world. Concomitantly, discourses about literature (literary history, aesthetics, philology, literary criticism) may be transformed. All this can be found in the case of other Indian literatures and even in other colonized literatures in different times and places. But the finer details of nineteenth-century Tamil literature laid out above should demonstrate the need to study the manifold social processes underlying the colonization of a given literary tradition in detail *before* we attempt any simple generalizations about East and West, colonizer and colonized, agency and subjection. In the case of many literary traditions in India, and elsewhere, their transformation under colonial influence may look similar, at first glance, to what we found in Tamil. In my analysis above I have frequently alluded to parallel phenomena and developments in other Indian languages. But we need many more case studies, grounded in the analysis of actual texts and life histories, to be able to generalize systematically and to draw larger connections from our data. Every region responded differently to the challenges of colonial modernity, and it is my contention that these regional differences have not been sufficiently recognized in the writing of the history of colonialisms in India and elsewhere. For India, David Washbrook has recently pointed out that "the pasts of the South (and to some degree, the West) of the subcontinent have been very much marginalized from the history of what is usually understood to be 'the whole' [of India]. [. . .] We may now need not only a different and more plural history of India, but also of colonialism in the nineteenth century" (2007: 332; 351). Attempts to write comparative histories of the novel in India, in fact, the history of the novel as a global phenomenon, present a case in point.[1] In many literary cultures in South and Southeast Asia, the novel emerged as a new form under Western colonial influence. Tamil, Hindi, Bengali, Marathi, Burmese, Vietnamese, and Indonesian/Malay all present comparable scenarios. Like their Indian namesakes, early Vietnamese or Indonesian novels were produced by a new colonial, Western-educated elite and they focused precisely on the challenges of modernity's impact on indigenous traditions. The very popular early Vietnamese novel *Tố Tâm* ("Pure Heart," the name of the female protagonist, written in 1922, published in 1925) by Hoàng Ngọc Phách (1896–1973) tells the story of the tragic love affair of the young couple Tố Tâm and Đạm Thủy who are not allowed to marry. Like the heroine of Alexandre Dumas' *La Dame aux Camélias* (1848), which inspired Hoàng Ngọc Phách's novel attempt, Tố Tâm dies, heartbroken, of tuberculosis. Her lover Đạm Thủy, an aspiring writer, is portrayed as caught between indigenous traditions and Western modernity, eager to compare the new Western disciplines he is studying in school with the "Asian *Weltanschauung*" and to use his mother tongue to formulate a modern morality for his country.[2] Similarly, the two early Indonesian novels *Sitti Noerbaja* (the name of a girl, 1922) by Marah Roesli (1889–1968) and *Salah Asoehan* ("Wrong Upbringing," 1928) by Abdoel Moeis (?1883–1959) both tell the tragic stories of young couples struggling to navigate between traditional social norms and modern Western modes of being in the world to which they are exposed within the colonial situation.[3] Like the Tamil examples we have seen, these Southeast Asian novels were written under the impact of colonialism, in order to explore new possible worlds, to create and interrogate new, modern identities and sensibilities. But while it is easy to spot similarities and parallels, the colonialisms of British India, French Indochina, and the Dutch

1. Both Das (1991) and Padikkal (1993) contain numerous useful insights into the history of the novel in India, but both are ultimately marred by overgeneralizations.

2. *Tố Tâm* is not available in English but has been translated into French (Phách 2006). For the history of the Vietnamese novel, see Thanh (1991).

3. For a discussion of *Sitti Noerbaja* see Foulcher (2002), and for *Salah Asoehan* see Foulcher (2005). Both cite further secondary literature. The stimulating essays in Foulcher/Day (2002) show the great potential of a dialogue of Postcolonial Studies and Indonesian philology or area studies.

East Indies were very different in countless aspects. To give only one example from the literary sphere: While the role of the state in the Tamil publishing world was marginal, censorship, banning, press control, and other means of government regulation were far more effective in North India. The colonial government of the Dutch East Indies had a special government publishing house, Balai Poestaka, which controlled the publication and distribution of reading materials with great vigilance.[4] Comparative studies should thus proceed from an intimate knowledge of the individual situations upward, as it were, rather than downward from larger generalizations or theoretical speculations which are then simply grafted onto local realities. The gulf between theorization and actual regional practices has for too long marred the possibility of a fruitful dialogue between Postcolonial Studies and the individual philologies.

Another obvious area of further comparative research on literature and colonialism is the study of colonial translation practices. Not only how works of South or Southeast Asian literatures were translated into Western languages, but also the reverse process. The translation and appropriation of Western literature—of Shakespeare's plays, of G. W. M. Reynolds' popular novels, of *Robinson Crusoe*, the *Count of Monte Cristo*, or *Sherlock Holmes*—into the languages of the colonized was always an important moment in the colonization of literatures and promises crucial insights into processes of epistemic confrontation within the literary "contact zone."[5] When Doris Jedamski observes for colonial Indonesia that "the business of translation and adaptation was not innocent of the power relations of colonialism; in fact, the circulation of these [translated] texts in colonial society opened up a counter-canonical discourse right under the colonizer's gaze" (2002: 45), this could certainly be shown to be valid for other colonized regions too. But all these questions belong to future research.

---

4. For censorship in North India, see Barrier (1974). For a detailed study of the Balai Poestaka and of the colonization of Indonesian literature in general, see Jedamski (1992). A short overview of the activities of the Balai Poestaka in English is Fitzpatrick (2000).

5. The existing body of literature on the question of colonialism and translation shows how much more could be done. See e.g., Trivedi (1993) and Bassnett/Trivedi (1999). On Shakespeare in India see Trivedi/Bartholomeusz (2005). Arangasamy (1994) deals specifically with Shakespeare in Tamil appropriations which begin in 1870 with Vi. Vicuvanāta Piḷḷai's *Vēṉis Varttakaṉ*, a translation of *The Merchant of Venice*. Tamil versions of Reynolds' novels, such as Āraṇi Kuppucāmi Mutaliyār's (1866–1925) "translation" of *The Mysteries of London* as *Irattiṉapuri irakaciyam* (1916ff.), would merit in-depth study. On the translation of European novels, such as of *Robinson Crusoe*, the *Count of Monte Cristo* or *Sherlock Holmes*, into Malay, see Jedamski (2002).

Elsewhere, too, further qualifications regarding nineteenth-century Tamil literature will have to be made. As I have stressed in the Introduction, I consider the preceding pages nothing but a preliminary attempt at a re-assessment of the poets and authors of the period discussed here. Much is still missing, even unknown. A fuller treatment would have to consider a larger number of texts (in particular the pre-modern compositions of the pulavars which we are currently just beginning to understand), forgotten or marginalized authors, and also the question of how modern Tamil drama emerged during the nineteenth century. Similarly, the fascinating stories of the recovery of Classical Tamil literature and the birth of Tamil philology will one day have to be told in detail. Finally, despite many scholarly attempts, we still possess only a rudimentary knowledge of the long-term historical development of both Tamil poetry and prose. Much indeed is yet before us. But my task is done, for now, if I have succeeded in demonstrating why nineteenth-century Tamil literature, as a crucial moment in Tamil's long literary history, still merits our attention today and why it should be more widely read, translated, and appreciated.

APPENDIX 1

The Dating of the *Cētupati viṟaliviṭutūtu* Revisited

A look at the available secondary literature shows that the date of the work is controversial, not least due to the fact that we know of two poets with the name Caravaṇap Perumāḷ Kavirāyar, both patronized by the Ramnad court. Standard accounts of Tamil literature[1] firstly list Aṭṭāvatāṉam Caravaṇap Perumāḷ Kavirāyar alias Periya Caravaṇap Perumāḷ Kavirāyar (i.e., "C.P.K. the Elder"), and secondly his grandson Tuvātrīm Tacāvatāṉam[2] Caravaṇap Perumāḷ Kavirāyar alias Ciṟiya Caravaṇap Perumāḷ Kavirāyar (i.e. "C.P.K. the Younger"). The existence of these two poets is corroborated by late nineteenth-century book titles which mention in their ornate explications a Tuvātrīm Tacāvatāṉam/Catāvatāṉam Caravaṇap Perumāḷ Kavirāyar as the son of Makāśrī Aruṇācalak Kavirāyar and grandson (*pauttirar*) of Irāmanātapuram Camastāṉavittuvāṉ Makāśrī Cōṭacāvatāṉam Caravaṇapperumāṭ Kavirāyar.[3] While the grandfather is supposed to have lived during the late eighteenth to early nineteenth centuries, the grandson is placed in the nineteenth century, his year of death being fixed as 1888 (or 1886).[4] But here the general agreement ends. The birthplace of both poets is variously given as Nallūr or Mutukuḷattūr,

1. See e.g., Zvelebil (1995: 124f.); Irākavaiyaṅkār (1928: 36–38); Paḻaniyappaṉ/Paḻani (1984: 342– 44); Civakāmi (1994: 308f.); Vēṅkaṭacāmi (1962: 219f., 272f.); Vimalāṉantam (1987: 496).

2. We also find the title Catāvatāṉam, one version perhaps being a confusion of syllables.

3. See various editions of *Irāmāyaṇavaṇṇam* in the catalogue of the Roja Muthiah Research Library, Chennai.

4. Vēṅkaṭacāmi (1962: 219), and hence Zvelebil (1995: 124), have 1886, while Civakāmi (1994: 308), Paḻaniyappaṉ/Paḻani (1984: 344) and Ceyarāmaṉ (1983: 96) have 1888. Needless to say, no one gives a source for their date.

and while Zvelebil (1995: 124) and Nākacāmi (1982: xiv) attribute the *Cētupati viṟaliviṭutūtu* to C.P.K. the Elder, Civakāmi (1994: 309), Ceyarāmaṉ (1983: 96), and both of the two editions of the text available to me (Cokkaliṅkaṉ 1947: 121, commentary on stanza 1041; and Cirañcīvi 1958: 198) attribute it to his grandson. Kamil Zvelebil even provides us with the date 1776 for the text, but Nākacāmi dates it to 1770. Unfortunately, neither of them lets us know how they arrived at their dates. Perhaps with a view to evade controversy, a number of sources do not list the *Cētupati viṟaliviṭutūtu* at all as a work of either of the two poets.[5]

A very early source of literary history that mentions Periya Caravaṇap Perumāḷ Kavirāyar is Simon Casie Chitty's *The Tamil Plutarch*, a collection of short sketches in English on various poets that was first published in 1859. As this book is close to the actual date of the poet, one may at least hope to find a fairly accurate account, but the reader is disappointed to find the misleading statement that the poet's patron Mutturamalinga Setupati "ascended the musnud [throne] at Ramnad in A.D. 1795" (Casie Chitty 1982: 97). However, as the historians of the Ramnad court tell us, Muttурāmaliṅka Cētupati ruled first from 1762 until 1773 when he was defeated by the joint forces of the British armies and the Nawab of the Carnatic. In 1780 he was restored by the Nawab until he was again deposed in 1795 and sent as a state prisoner to Madras.[6] After this erroneous date given by Casie Chitty (and repeated in several later literary histories), obviously no one has felt the need to either look at the genealogy of the Ramnad kings or to examine the *Cētupati viṟaliviṭutūtu* itself.

Fortunately, the poem does provide several clues to its dating. First of all, the poem repeatedly speaks of its *pāṭṭuṭait talaivaṉ* Vijayarakunāta Civacāmi Cētupati as the son of King Muttuvijaya Rakunāta Cētupati and Queen Muttuvīrāyi Nācciyār (e.g. in stanzas 50–52, 160). Then, it also calls him the son of Muttuccellac Cētupati's sister (*marukaṉ*, st. 153) and the brother of the wife (*maittuṉaṉ*) of Maharaja Rāmacāmi (st. 156). Now, both editors of the text state that there was no *cētupati* with the name Civacāmi, and therefore take him to be merely an important courtier (see Cokkaliṅkaṉ 1947: ix; Cirañcīvi 1958: 198). But here, we need to remember that *cētupati* is not necessarily the exclusive title for the ruler, but also a family title. The five names/titles the poem mentions may now be checked

5. Viz. Irākavaiyaṅkār, Paḻaniyappaṉ/Paḻani, and Vēṅkaṭacāmi.

6. See Thiruvenkatachari (1959: 52–55). A similar account (with dates varying by one or two years) is given by Sewell (1884: 227–232).

with the annals of the Ramnad court. And here we find one Queen Muttuvīrāyi Nācciyār, chief wife of Raja Aṇṇācāmi Cētupati alias Muttuvijaya Rakunāta Cētupati(!) who ruled from 1812 to his death in 1820, and sister of both Muttuccella who was the manager of the royal estate from 1830 to 1845, and of Rāmacāmi who briefly ruled as raja in 1830 when he also died.[7] As a strategic move in a dispute about the royal succession in Ramnad, Muttuvīrāyi Nācciyār adopted a courtier as her son (probably in 1845), and he was called Civacāmi.[8] Due to protracted litigations, he did not become the zamindar, but he obtained a village, a convenient monthly allowance, and a lump sum of Rs. 50,000; and when Muttuvīrāyi Nācciyār died, he inherited her villages. He himself passed away in 1862.[9]

As the kinship descriptions given in the poem do exactly correspond with Muttuvīrāyi Nācciyār and her relatives, we may take her adopted son Civacāmi as our *pāṭṭuṭait talaivaṉ* Vijayarakunāta Civacāmi Cētupati. If we further suppose that the *Cētupati viṟaliviṭutūtu* was composed—as was customary—during the patron's lifetime (or even commissioned by him), we arrive at a *terminus ante quem* of the year 1862. We may thus safely date the poem to the first half of the nineteenth century and thus ascribe it to Ciṟiya Caravaṇap Perumāḷ Kavirāyar, i.e., the grandson.

All further fine-tuning relies on heavier conjecture, but it is possible if we now look at the date for the poet. If he really died in 1886/1888, and if we suppose an average lifetime of 60 years for people of nineteenth-century South India, the poet could have been born around 1826/1828. From all we know about Tamil literary traditions, to compose a sophisticated poem, such as the *viṟaliviṭutūtu*, would take several years of poetic training, so that the poet could have been not much younger than twenty at the time he wrote his masterpiece. This would yield a *terminus a quo* of c. 1846. Additionally, the kinship relations mentioned in the poem only existed in this form after the adoption of Civacāmi in 1845. Thus, we arrive at an estimated date between 1845 and 1862. And that is probably all we can do, unless we can find further documents which provide us with more details. The evidence discussed above, however, certainly places the work in the first half of the nineteenth century, which is sufficiently precise for the purposes of the present study.

7. I am indebted here to the genealogical details provided in Pamela Price's study of the Ramnad court (Price 1996).

8. Price (1996: 63, et passim).

9. Price (1996: 68).

APPENDIX 2

Chronological Table of the Earliest Tamil Novels Published Before 1900

The following table has been compiled on the basis of Cuntararājaṉ/Civapātacuntaram (1977; abbreviated in the Notes as CC followed by the page number/s), Dhandayudham (1977; D) and Zvelebil (1995; Z), and completed/corrected using the Tamil catalogues of the India Office Library, Barnett/Pope (1909; BP), Barnett (1931; B), and Gaur (1980; G), as well as the online catalogue of the Roja Muthiah Research Library, Chennai (http://www.lib.uchicago.edu/e/su/southasia/rmrl-catalog.html, abbreviated as RM) and the two Madras Government catalogues *Classified Catalogue of the Public Reference Library, consisting of books registered from 1867 to 1889 at the Office of the Registrar of Books, Old College, Madras* (1894; Reg1) and *Classified Catalogue of Books Registered from 1890–1900 at the Office of the Registrar of Books* (1962; Reg2). Titles not listed in Cītālaṭcumi (1985) are marked "nv." The table is as comprehensive as current research allows.

Year	Author	Title	Notes
1879	S. Vētanāyakam Piḷḷai	*Piratāpa Mutaliyār carittiram*	See Chapter 5.
1885	Cittilevvai Mukammatu Kācim Maraikkār	*Acaṉ Pē carittiram*	Original Title: *Acaṉpēyuṭaiya katai*. Colombo: Muslim Friend Press. First Sri Lankan Tamil novel. 2nd ed. Madras: St. Joseph Printing Press, 1890. New edition (Maraikkār 1974) with introduction by Es. Em. Kamālutīṉ, vii+170 pp. Author (1839–1899) was publisher of the weekly "Muslim Friend" (*Muslim Nēcaṉ*) and proctor at the Sri Lankan Supreme Court. See Z 443; CC 20f.; Zvelebil (1990a); Samy (2000: 109).
1886	Ti. Kō. Nārāyaṇacāmi Piḷḷai	*Viṉōta carittiram*	Referred to in D 71 as "not extant," but might still be recovered. Listed in Reg1; nv.
1887	S. Vētanāyakam Piḷḷai	*Cukuṇa Cuntari carittiram*	See Chapter 5.
1892	Ti. Kō. Nārāyaṇacāmi Piḷḷai	*Māmi marukiyar vāḻkkai*	Perhaps not a novel? See CC 42; Z 482; nv.
1893	Cu. Vai. Kurusvāmi Carmā	*Pirēmakalāvatyam*	Madras: Star of India Press. Also *Pirēmakalāvatīyam*. 2nd ed. Parampakkuṭi, 1908, in B 103. New edition (see Kurusvāmi Carmā 1980), viii+292 pp. See D 51ff.; CC 21ff.; Reg2; Zvelebil (1990a).

1893–1895	Pi. Ār. Rājam Aiyar	*Kamalāmpāḷ carittiram*	First serialized. Published in book form in 1896. See Chapter 5.
1894	Ca. Ma. Naṭēca Cāstiri	*Tāṉavaṉ eṉṟa pōlīs nipuṇaṉ kaṇṭupiṭitta atputa kuṟṟaṅkaḷ (Tales of an Indian Detective)*	Perhaps rather a collection of short stories than a novel. 2nd ed. Madras, 1914, in B 237. New edition by Cīṉi. Vicuvanātaṉ (see Naṭēca Cāstiriyār 1994), 320 pp. See CC 52ff.; Z 487ff.; Reg2; Asher (1971).
1895	Ti. Ta. Caravaṇamuttu Piḷḷai	*Mōkaṉāṅki. Oru katai*	Madras: Hindu Union Press, 384 pp. First Tamil historical novel. Listed in BP 306. Author was from Trincomalee (Sri Lanka) and became librarian at Presidency College, Madras. See CC 27ff.; Z 123; D 244; Zvelebil (1990a).
1896	Ma. Ve. Naṭarāja Aiyar	*Ñāṉapūṣaṇi*	Madras: Star of India Press, i+192 pp. Listed in Reg2; BP 213. See D 68f.; CC 46; Z 486.
1897	Vi. Kō. Cūriyanārāyaṇa Cāstiri	*Mativāṇaṉ. Putuvatu puṉaintatōr centamiḻk katai*	First serialized in the monthly *Ñāṉapōtiṉi*. Published in book form in Madras, 1902 (see BP 361). New edition (see Cūriyanārāyaṇa Cāstiri 1963), 122 pp. See D 66ff.; CC 69f.; Z 219f.
1897	Na. Palarāmayyar	*Līlai*	Serialized in the monthly *Ñāṉapōtiṉi*. Author was a student of Cūriyanārāyaṇa Cāstiri. See CC 71; Z 510; nv.

(Continued on next page)

Year	Author	Title	Notes
1897	Rājātti Ammāḷ	*Ñāṉappirakācam*	See CC 46; Z 599; nv.
1897	Ca. Rāmacāmi Aiyaṅkār	*Kamaliṉi*	2nd ed. Madras: Scottish Press, 1902, 166 pp. See CC 46; D 234; Z 602.
1897	Ti. El. Turaicāmi Aiyar	*Kuṇapūṣaṇi*	2nd ed. Madras: P. Cuppiramaṇiya Mutaliyār, 1902, 152 pp., listed in G 381. See Reg2.
1898	Ci. Arumaināyakam	*Mīti Iruḷ*	See CC 44ff.; Z 65; nv.
1898	Ci. Ē. Cuppiramaṇiya Aiyar	*Kaṟpiṉ Vijayam*	See CC 46; Z 197; nv.
1898	Pi. Ci. Kōvintacāmi Rājā	*Marakatavalli*	First serialized in a journal in Madras. Published in book form Madras: Thomson & Co., 1902. Author was a clerk in the office of the Collector of Aṉantappūr. See CC 67ff.; D 242.
1898	A. Mātavayyā	*Patmāvati carittiram*	Listed in Reg2. See Chapter 6.
1898	?	*Kōmakaḷ*	See CC 46; nv.
1899	A. K. Kōpālacāri	*Jīvaratnam*	I follow the information in Reg2. Author listed in Cītālaṭcumi (1985: 385) is Tirumayilai Irāmaliṅka Mutaliyār (Madras: Citty Press, 160 pp.). BP 271 also lists him as the author of a two-volume edition of 1900/1901. See D 71; CC 69; Z 264f.; Reg2.

I have not included in this list the two novels *Kamalam* and *Cakuṇā* by the female author Kirupā Cattiyanātaṉ (Krupabai Satthianadhan, 1862–1894), since they were originally written in English, not in Tamil. Coming from Ahmedabad to Madras in order to study at Madras Medical College, Cattiyanātaṉ wrote two novels, *Saguna: A Story of Native Christian Life* (1887–88) and *Kamala: A Story of Hindu Life* (1894), which were posthumously translated into Tamil by Father Samuel Paul from Tirunelveli and published in 1896.[1] A short note on the publication of *Saguna* appeared in *The Harvest Field* (July 1889, p. 28). R. Dhandayudham argues that Cattiyanātaṉ's works have to be mentioned in the Tamil context, because, on the one hand, she was the first female writer introduced to the Tamil reading public, and on the other hand, her novels depict the lives of South Indian Hindu and Christian families (1977: 69). Moreover, the two novels appear to have been quite popular, since, as the Tamil translator points out in his preface, Queen Victoria herself had read them and had asked for more works of the same author (ibid.). Both novels have recently been re-edited by Chandani Lokugé (1998a; 1998b) with useful introductions citing further literature. See also the discussion of *Saguna* in Tharu/Lalita (1991: 275–281).

The other novel I have not listed above is a book titled *Lalitāṅki* which, according to Zvelebil (1995: 486), was published in 1899 by Ma. Ve. Naṭarāja Aiyar (d. 1908), author of the novel *Ñāṉapūṣaṇi* and editor of the popular journal *Lōkōpakāri*. For his biography see Irāmacāmip Pulavar (1960c: 6–11) and Samy (2000: 186). While I have not found an 1899 edition anywhere, BP 213 and RM (RMRL database no. 021598) list a novel titled *Lalitāṅki* by this author (Vaijayanti Acciyantiracālai, 1902, 102 pp., nv). According to Mu. Paḻaṉiyappaṉ (2003: 45), this novel was originally written by the female author Vicālāṭci Ammāḷ (1881–?1915), but published in 1902 under Naṭarāja Aiyar's name. If this is true, it is not clear what to make of Zvelebil's early date.

1. According to Cuntararājaṉ/Civapātacuntaram (1977: 31) and Lokugé (1998a: xv) both translations were published in 1896, but the translation of *Saguna* listed in BP 139 is dated 1898. I have not been able to examine the actual book to determine which year is correct. In 1898, also a German translation of *Kamala* was published (Satthianadhan 1898).

APPENDIX 3

Original Tamil Texts Quoted and Annotations

This appendix contains the original Tamil versions of all the quotations from Tamil primary sources not already incorporated into the main text. The texts are given in the order in which they appear above and may be identified by the serial number in square brackets (the first number indicates the chapter). Sandhi splits and annotations are provided whenever deemed necessary, in which cases two versions of the text are given. Occasionally, punctuation marks have been inserted into the sandhi-split version to guide the reader. Due to considerations of space, quotations from Tamil secondary literature which I have translated in the main text are not included here. My correction of typographical and other errors in a source is marked by angle brackets < > in the text with the original corrupt reading listed and explained after "Corr." below the text.

Chapter 2

[2.1] (*SMPT* 5088):

tēṉaruvi pāyuñ cirāmalaiyi leṉṟumamar
ñāṉamutaṟ kaṉpi ṉayampayappa – mēṉmaipeṟuñ
cupparā yappulavaṉ colliyaveṇ pāmālai
yeppoḻutum vāḻkaviṉi tē.

tēṉ aruvi pāyum cirāmalaiyil eṉṟum amar
ñāṉa mutaṟku aṉpiṉ nayam payappa – mēṉmai peṟum
cupparāya pulavaṉ colliya veṇpā mālai
eppoḻutum vāḻka iṉitē.

[2.2] (*SMPT* 272):
tēṉāṭcic ceñcoṟpiḷ ḷaittamiḻaic ceytaḷittāṉ
mīṉāṭci cuntaravēḷ mēṉmaiyōṉ – vāṉāṭcik
kāvaiyaki lāṇṭavammai kātaṟ kaṭalmūḻka
nāvalariṉ pūṟa nayantu.

tēṉ āṭci cem col piḷḷaittamiḻai ceytu aḷittāṉ
mīṉāṭcicuntara vēḷ mēṉmaiyōṉ – vāṉ āṭci
kāvai akilāṇṭa ammai kātal kaṭal mūḻka
nāvalar iṉpūṟa nayantu.

Note:
kāvai = *tiruvaṉaikkā* (see also *SMPC* I: 65, ftn.).

[2.3] (*SMPT* 1685):
vātavū rutittannā ṭirukkōvai yuraitta māṇikka vācakarē cirapuratti linnā
ḷātavaṉiṟ ṟōṉṟimī ṉāṭcicun taraṉeṉ ṟarumpeyarpūṇ ṭorukōvai
yaṟaintaṉaṉkā ḻikkē
yētamiṟil laikkōvai yāyuvatiṉ mūtta teṉṉiṉuṅkaṟ paṉainayatti likkōvai
muṉṉām
mūtaṟiñar vaikalumpā ṭappāṭa vākkiṉ mutumaikoḷvā reṉavulaka moḻiyu-
moḻi meyyē.

vātavūr utittu annāḷ tirukkōvai uraitta māṇikkavācakarē cirapurattil innāḷ
ātavaṉiṉ tōṉṟi mīṉāṭcicuntaraṉ eṉṟu arum peyar pūṇṭu oru kōvai
aṟaintaṉaṉ kāḻikkē.
ētam il tillaikkōvai āyuvatiṉ mūttatu eṉṉiṉum kaṟpaṉai nayattil ikkōvai
muṉṉām.
"mūtu aṟiñar vaikalum pāṭa pāṭa, vākkil mutumai koḷvār" eṉa ulakam
moḻiyum moḻi meyyē.

Notes:
1. Meter: *eṇcīrkkaḻineṭilaṭi āciriyaviruttam.*
2. *kāḻi* = *cīrkāḻi.*
3. This and the following stanzas are also included in *TCC* (424–427) and Ñāṉappirakācam Piḷḷai (1890: 49–53, henceforth *NP*) where we occasionally find variant readings. I have listed them whenever they entail morphological, lexical and/or semantic changes, i.e., I have not included mere metrical or phonological variations. *TCC*, *NP*: 3 *yāyukattiṉ.*

[2.4] (*SMPT* 1686):
tiruvamarkō vaiyaimakiḻntu vātavū raraittaṉpāṟ cērttuk koṇṭa
poruvilcitam paranātaṉ piṉṉumorkō vaikkācai pūṇṭaṉ ṉārai

maruvucira purattīṉṟu mīṉāṭci cuntarappēr vaḻaṅkik kāḻik
korukōvai ceyvittāṉ citamparanā taṉcēyeṉ ṟuraittaṉ meyyē.

tiru amar kōvaiyai makiḻntu vātavūrarai taṉ pāl cērttukkoṇṭa
poru il citamparanātaṉ, piṉṉum or kōvaikku ācai pūṇṭu aṉṉārai
maruvu cirapurattu īṉṟu mīṉāṭcicuntara pēr vaḻaṅki kāḻikku
oru kōvai ceyvittāṉ citamparanātaṉ cēy eṉṟu uraittal meyyē.

Notes:
1. Meter: *aṟucīrkkaḻineṭilaṭi āciriyaviruttam.*
2. *cirapuram = cīrkāḻi.*
3. *TCC, NP:* 2 *paranāta ṉiṉṉumōrkō vaikkācai pūṇṭaṉ ṉāṉai.*

[2.5] (*SMPT* 1687):
piramapurat tīcarmēṉ mīṉāṭci cuntaramāl peṭpiṟ ceyta
varamuṟukō vaiyaikkēṭpōr makiḻuvarañ cuvaṉṟamiyēṉ vaḷḷi ṉiṟkēṭ
ṭaravaracu ciramacaikkiṟ ṟaraiyacaiyum varaiyacaiyu macaiyu māḻi
maramacaiyu maṉaiyacaiyu maṉṉuyire lāmacaintu varuntu meṉṟē.

piramapurattu īcar mēl mīṉāṭcicuntara māl peṭpiṉ ceyta
varam uṟu kōvaiyai kēṭpōr makiḻuvar. añcuvaṉ tamiyēṉ, vaḷḷiṉil kēṭṭu
aravu aracu ciram acaikkil, tarai acaiyum, varai acaiyum, acaiyum āḻi,
maram acaiyum, maṉai acaiyum, maṉṉuyir elām acaintu varuntum eṉṟē.

Notes:
1. Meter: *aṟucīrkkaḻineṭilaṭi āciriyaviruttam.*
2. *piramapuram = cīrkāḻi.*

[2.6] (*SMPT* 1692):
taṇtamiḻuṉ pāluṇara vācaikū raṉantaṉ ṟaṉamīya vakaiyiṉṟi niṉcēṭa ṉākik
koṇṭaṉaṉan nāmamē yakattiyaṉṟāṉ ṟaṉṉaik kūṭāma luṉaimēvik kulāvutami ḻataṉai
yaṇṭalariṉ muṉintataṉāṟ ṟamiḻmuṉiva ṉeṉumpē raṭaintaṉaṉā taliṉakilat tiyāvaruṉai nikarvār
vaṇṭamartār mīṉāṭci cuntaravē ḷēnī vaḷappuṟavak kōvaicoliṉ viyappavarā raiyā.

taṉ tamiḻ uṉ pāl uṇara ācai kūr aṉantaṉ taṉam īya vakai iṉṟi niṉ cēṭaṉ āki
koṇṭaṉaṉ annāmamē, akattiyaṉ tāṉ taṉṉai kūṭāmal uṉai mēvi kulāvu tamiḻ ataṉai
aṇṭalariṉ muṉintataṉāl tamiḻ muṉivaṉ eṉum pēr aṭaintaṉaṉātaliṉ akilattu yāvar uṉai nikarvār?
vaṇṭu amar tār mīṉāṭcicuntara vēḷē, nī vaḷa puṟavam kōvai coliṉ viyap-pavar ār, aiyā?

Notes:
1. Meter: *eṇcīrkkaḻineṭilaṭi āciriyaviruttam.*
2. *puṟavam* = *cīrkāḻi.*
3. *TCC, NP*: 3 *muṉintatāṟ;* 4 *kōvaicolli ṉevarviyappā raiyā.*

[2.7] (*SMPT* 1697):
vitiyetiri larimutalōr pukalpukali yīcarē viṇṇōr maṇṇōr
tutipotipal pāmālai peṟṟiruppīr mīṉāṭci cunta rappēr
matimutiyaṉ kōvaiyaippōṟ peṟṟīrko likkāḻi vaippi ṉīti
yatipatinā meṉavaṟivīr nammuṉṉañ cattiyamā vaṟaiku vīrē.

viti etir il ari mutalōr pukal pukali īcarē viṇṇōr maṇṇōr
tuti poti pal pāmālai peṟṟiruppīr, mīṉāṭcicuntara pēr
mati mutiyaṉ kōvaiyaippōl peṟṟīrkol? ikkāḻi vaippil nīti
atipati nām eṉa aṟivīr, nam muṉṉam cattiyamā aṟaikuvīrē.

Notes:
1. Meter: *aṟucīrkkaḻineṭilaṭi āciriyaviruttam.*
2. *pukali* = *cīrkāḻi.*

[2.8] (*SMPT* 1700):
taṇṭamiḻmun nīrparuki mīṉāṭci cuntarappērt tarumak koṇṭa
ṟoṇṭarkaḷcūḻ cirapurattiṟ poḻikōvai yeṉumamutat tūya māri
maṇṭalamum viṇṭalamuṅ karaipuraṇṭu tiraicuruṇṭu varuta ṉōkki
yaṇṭartoḻum pukaliyiṟai tōṇiyuṟṟā ṉakṭiṉṟē lamiḻntu vāṉē.

taṇ tamiḻ munnīr paruki mīṉāṭcicuntara pēr tarumakkoṇṭal
toṇṭarkaḷ cūḻ cirapurattil poḻi kōvai eṉum amuta tūya māri
maṇ talam-um viṇ talam-um karai puraṇṭu tirai curuṇṭu varutal nōkki
aṇṭar toḻum pukali iṟai tōṇi uṟṟāṉ akṭu iṉṟēl amiḻntuvāṉē.

Notes:
1. Meter: *aṟucīrkkaḻineṭilaṭi āciriyaviruttam.*
2. *cirapuram, pukali* = *cīrkāḻi.*
3. *TPTC* (137): 4 *amiḻu vāṉē.*

[2.9] (*SMPT* 1690):
paṉṉūlu māyntāyntōr payaṉuṟā tuḷamvaruntum pāva līrē,
naṉṉūlōr mīṉāṭci cuntaramā lorukōvai naviṉṟāṉ kāḻik,
kannūlu ḷorupāvi lōraṭiyi lorucīrai yāyvī rāyi,
ṉennūluṅ kaṟṟavarā yikaparamum peṟṟavarā yilaku vīrē.

pal nūlum āyntu āyntu ōr payaṉ uṟātu uḷam varuntum pāvalīrē,
nal nūl ōr mīṉāṭcicuntara māl oru kōvai naviṉṟāṉ kāḻikku!
annūluḷ oru pāvil ōr aṭiyil oru cīrai āyvīrāyiṉ
ennūlum kaṟṟavarāy ikaparamum peṟṟavarāy ilakuvīrē.

Notes:
1. Meter: *aṟucīrkkaḻineṭilaṭi āciriyaviruttam.*
2. *āyvīr-āy-iṉ*: lit. "if you become those who research."

[2.10] (*SMPT* 1693):
iṉpāviṟ kōvaicoṉṉa mīṉāṭci cuntarappē riṟaiva yāṉu
muṉpāviṟ kavicolvē ṉeṉkavipārp pōritaimīṇ ṭōrā tāṉṟōr
muṉpācco ṉūlkaḷaiyē tutipparuṉpā vuṇarvōrkaṇ muṉṉōr nūlaip
piṉpākac coliveṟuppar nallavaṉī yōyāṉō pēcu vāyē.

iṉ pāvil kōvai coṉṉa mīṉāṭcicuntara pēr iṟaiva, yāṉum
uṉ pāvil kavi colvēṉ. eṉ kavi pārppōr itai mīṇṭu ōrātu, āṉṟōr
muṉpā col nūlkaḷaiyē tutippar. uṉ pā uṇarvōrkaḷ, muṉṉōr nūlai
piṉpāka coli veṟuppar, nallavaṉ nīyō yāṉō pēcuvāyē.

Notes:
1. Meter: *aṟucīrkkaḻineṭilaṭi āciriyaviruttam.*
2. *uṉ pāvil* could also be read as 'like your verse.'
3. *TCC, NP, TPTC* (136), *TPT* 2 (396): 2 *pōrataimīṇ*; 4 *nallavaṉā ṉōnīyō.*

[2.11] (*SMPT* 1694):
viṇṇēṟu mātavaṉēr mīṉāṭci cuntaravil vēḷē nīco
leṇṇēṟu kōvaiyiṉaip pukaḻayāṉ ṟiṟamillē ṉeṉiṉu muṉcīr
maṇṇēṟum vāṉēṟu matiyiṉarta nāvēṟum vakaiyā luṉṉaik
kaṇṇēṟu mēvāmaṟ kaṟaiyēṟu meṉpukaḻuṅ kaikkoḷ vāyē.

viṇ ēṟum mātavaṉ nēr mīṉāṭcicuntara vil vēḷē, nī col
eṇ ēṟu kōvaiyiṉai pukaḻa yāṉ tiṟam illēṉ eṉiṉum, uṉ cīr
maṇ ēṟum vāṉ ēṟum matiyiṉar tam nā ēṟum vakaiyāl uṉṉai
kaṇṇēṟu mēvāmal kaṟaiyēṟum eṉ pukaḻum kaikkoḷvāyē.

Notes:
1. Meter: *aṟucīrkkaḻineṭilaṭi āciriyaviruttam.*
2. *vil vēḷē* may refer to Kāmadeva with his sugarcane bow, but also to Murukaṉ who is described as having a bow in *Caṅkam* literature.

[2.12] (*SMPT* 1704):
tēmāri poḻipotumpart tirukkāḻi yiṟaimuṉ ṟikaḻāṇṭu cittārtti tiṅkaḷpāt tirattiṟ
pūmāri curarpoḻiyac celvarpalar kūṭip poṉmāri mikappoḻiyap pulavarkuḻān tutittup
pāmāri naṉipoḻiyap palliyaṅkaṇ muḻaṅkap palampuriya nalampuriyum valampurimaṇ ṭapattut
tūmāri yeṉappukalik kōvaiyaimī ṉāṭci cuntarappēr mativallō ṉaraṅkēṟṟi ṉāṉē.

tēṉ māri poḻi potumpar tiru kāḻi iṟai muṉ tikaḻ āṇṭu cittārtti tiṅkaḷ pāt-tirattil
pū māri curar poḻiya celvar palar kūṭi poṉ māri mika poḻiya pulavar kuḻām tutittu
pā māri naṉi poḻiya pal iyaṅkaḷ muḻaṅka palam puriya nalam puriyum valampuri maṇṭapattu
tū māri eṉa pukali kōvaiyai mīṉāṭcicuntaram pēr mati vallōṉ araṅkēṟṟiṉāṉē.

Note:
Meter: *eṇcīrkkaḻineṭilaṭi āciriyaviruttam.*

[2.13] (Paḻaniccāmi 1908: 2):
utittatiṉa mutaṟciṟitu muṇarviṉṟi veṟimēṟkoṇ ṭuḻalu mūmaṉ
vitittapala kalaiyumika viritturaicey tiṭappukunta vitamē yokkum
katittavaṭa moḻippaṭiciṅ kāraraca mañcariyaik kaṭalcūḻ pāriṟ
ṟutittatamiḻvalarkketiryāṉcolvaleṉattoṭaṅkiyatōrtuṇivutāṉē.

utitta tiṉam mutal ciṟitum uṇarvu iṉṟi veṟi mēṟkoṇṭu uḻalum ūmaṉ
vititta pala kalaiyum mika viritturai ceytiṭa pukunta vitamē okkum
katitta vaṭamoḻi paṭi ciṅkāraracamañcariyai kaṭal cūḻ pāril/pāriṉ
tutitta tamiḻ valarkku etir yāṉ colval eṉa toṭaṅkiyatu ōr tuṇivu tāṉē.

[2.14] (*SMPT* 155):
poṅkumalai nīrparuku morumaniva ṉamarnaṟum potiyat tirunteḻuntu
-puṉṉaivī yiṉṟā taḷaintaviḷa meṉciṟu pututteṉṟal vantarumpa
veṅkumoḷir centaḻa larumputē māvaṭa reḻiṟkāvai yampatiyiṉmē
-vempirāṭ ṭikkiyā ṉuraiceypiḷ ḷaikkaviyi teṉpō lirukkumeṉṉiṟ
ṟaṅkumū tarivuṭaiya cāṉṟō ruṟunteyva caivaneṟi yoḻuku vōriṉ
-caṅkattu meypporu ḷuṇarttu nūl pukaluvatu tāṉkēṭ ṭeḻuntu tīmpāl
ceṅkumuta vāyoḻuka mantaman tacceṉṟu tērumak kaḻakamuṟṟōr
-ciṟumaṭalkai paṟṟiyoru ciṟukuḻavi kuḻaruñ ciṟappiṉuk kokkumaṉṟē.

poṅkum alai nīr parukum oru maṉivaṉ amar naṟum potiyattu iruntu eḻuntu
puṉṉai vīyiṉ tātu aḷainta iḷa meṉ ciṟu putu teṉṟal vantu arumpa
eṅkum oḷir cen taḻal arumpu tē mā aṭar eḻil kā_vaiyam_patiyiṉ mēl
em pirāṭṭikku yāṉ urai cey piḷḷaikkavi itu eṉ pōl irukkum eṉṉiṉ
taṅkum mūtu aṟivuṭaiya cāṉṟōr uṟun teyva caiva neṟi oḻukuvōriṉ
caṅkattu meypporuḷ uṇarttu nūl pukaluvatu tāṉ kēṭṭu eḻuntu tīm pāl
ceṅ kumuta vāy oḻuka manta manta ceṉṟu tērum akkaḻakamuṟṟōr
ciṟu maṭal kai paṟṟi oru ciṟu kuḻavi kuḻarum ciṟappiṉukku okkum aṉṟē.

[2.15] (*TPT* 752):
nallainakar āṟumuka nāvalarpi ṟantilarēl
collutami ḻeṅkē curutiyeṅkē – ellavarum
ēttupurā ṇākamaṅka ḷeṅkēpra caṅkameṅkē
āttaṉaṟi veṅkē yaṟai.

nallai nakar āṟumuka nāvalar piṟantu ilarēl,
collu tamiḻ eṅkē? curuti eṅkē? – ellavarum
ēttu purāṇa ākamaṅkaḷ eṅkē? piracaṅkam eṅkē?
āttaṉ aṟivu eṅkē? aṟai!

[2.16] (*TPT* 753):
vētamvali kuṉṟiyatu mētakuci vākama vitaṅkaḷvali kuṉṟiṉavaṭaṟ
cūtaṉmoḻi mūvaṟupu rāṇamvali kuṉṟiyatu collariya caivacamayap
pōtamvali kuṉṟiyatu poṟpotiya māmuṉi pukaṉṟamoḻi kuṉṟiyatunam
nātaṉiṇai ñālamicai nāṭariya vāṟumuka nāvalara ṭaintapoḻutē.

vētam vali kuṉṟiyatu, mētaku civākama vitaṅkaḷ vali kuṉṟiṉa, aṭal
cūtaṉ moḻi mū-aṟu purāṇam vali kuṉṟiyatu, collu ariya caiva camayap
pōtam vali kuṉṟiyatu, poṉ potiya mā muṉi pukaṉṟa moḻi kuṉṟiyatu, nam
nātaṉ iṇai(yai), ñālam-micai nāṭu ariya āṟumuka nāvalar aṭainta poḻutē.

[2.17] (*TPT* 756):
kāmōti vaṇṭar kaṭimalarttēṉ kūṭṭutalpōl
nāmōtu centamiḻiṉ naṉṉūl palatokutta
tāmō tarampiḷḷai cālpeṭuttuc cāṟṟavevar
tāmō taramuṭaiyār taṇṭamiḻccen nāppulavīr.

kā mōti vaṇṭar kaṭi malar tēṉ kūṭṭutal pōl
nām ōtu cem tamiḻiṉ nal nūl pala tokutta
tāmōtaram piḷḷai cālpu eṭuttu cāṟṟa, evar
tāmō taram uṭaiyār, taṇ tamiḻ cem nā pulavīr?

[2.18] (*EC* 382):
ilakkaṉa meykkarai māttirai yāmiv vaḷavumiṉṟi
malakkaṇ viḷaipiṇi yāṟpalar māyntaṉar maṇṭuminnōy
vilakka varuḷpuri mummala nōykeṭa vittakaṉā
nilakka ṇuṟaicup piramaṇi yāṉanta niṉmalaṉē.

ilakkaṇam meykku arai māttirai yām, ivvaḷavum iṉṟi
malakkaṇ viḷai piṇiyāl palar māyntaṉar. maṇṭum innōy
vilakka aruḷ puri mummala nōy keṭa vittakaṉā
nilakkaṇ uṟai cuppiramaṇiya āṉanta niṉmalaṉē.

Note:
TPTC (125): 3 *vittakaṉāy;* 4 *nilakkaṇamar cuppiramaṇi.*

[2.19] (*SMPC* I: 312f.):
1. *kuṟaḷ veṇpā*
pērāḷā ñāṉap pirakāca vaḷḷaleṉum
cīrāḷā vikkaṭitan tēr.

2. *viruttam*
uṟuvaliyi ṉiṭaṅkoṇṭu vaṉappamainta nāṟkāli oṉṟu vēṇṭum
maṟuvaṟunāṟ kāliyeṉal yāṉaiyaṉṟu kutiraiyaṉṟu vallē ṟaṉṟu
kaṟuvakalpāṟ pacuvaṉṟā livaiyellā miyaṅkutalcey kaṭaṉmēṟ koḷḷum
peṟupavarpā liyaṅkātu vaittaviṭat tēyirukkap peṟṟa tāmē.

3.
attakaiya toṉṟaṉuppi ṉatilamarntu mikkacukam aṭaivēṉ yāṉum
uttamanaṟ kuṇattiluyar nīyumiku cīrttiyaiyā oḷirā niṟpai
vittakamaṟ ṟakṭevvā ṟiruppataṟku miṭaṅkoṭuttal vēṇṭu mēya
cuttamiku mataṉaivaru pavaṉpālē yaṉuppiṭutal tūya tāmē.

1.
pēr āḷā ñāṉappirakāca vaḷḷal eṉum
cīr āḷā ikkaṭitam tēr.

2.
uṟu valiyiṉ iṭam koṇṭu vaṉappu amainta nāṟkāli oṉṟu vēṇṭum.
maṟu aṟu nāṟkāli eṉal yāṉai aṉṟu kutirai aṉṟu val ēṟu aṉṟu
kaṟuvu akal pāl pacu aṉṟu āl ivai ellām iyaṅkutal cey kaṭaṉ mēṟ koḷḷum
peṟupavar pāl iyaṅkātu vaitta iṭattē irukka peṟṟatu-āmē.

3.
attakaiyatu o<u>n</u><u>r</u>u a<u>n</u>uppi<u>n</u> atil amarntu mikka cukam aṭaivē<u>n</u> yā<u>n</u>um
uttama nal kuṇattil uyar nīyum miku cīrttiyaiyā oḷirāni<u>r</u>pai
vittaka ma<u>r</u><u>r</u>u a<u>k</u>tu evvā<u>r</u>u iruppata<u>r</u>kum iṭaṅkoṭuttal vēṇṭum mēya
cuttam mikum ata<u>n</u>ai varupava<u>n</u>-pālē a<u>n</u>uppiṭutal tūyatu-āmē.

[2.20] (*SMPT* 4611):
kāṭci
po<u>n</u>pūtta kañcamu mēnte<u>l</u>i <u>n</u>īlamum pūntaḷavun
te<u>n</u>pūtta kōṅkamum pāṅkamar kāntaḷuñ cērakkoṇṭu
ma<u>n</u>pūtta centami <u>l</u>āyvēta nāyaka mālkuḷantaik
ko<u>n</u>pūtta mālvarai vāyvirai vāyor koṭini<u>n</u><u>r</u>atē.

po<u>n</u> pūtta kañcamum ēntu e<u>l</u>il nīlamum pūm taḷavum
te<u>n</u> pūtta kōṅkamum pāṅku amar kāntaḷum cēra koṇṭu
ma<u>n</u> pūtta centami<u>l</u> āy vētanāyaka māl kuḷantai
ko<u>n</u> pūtta māl varai vāy, virai vāy, or koṭi ni<u>n</u><u>r</u>atē.

Note:
pāṅku amar kāntaḷ may be read as "the *kāntaḷ* residing on the side{*pāṅku*} [of the *kōṅkam*]." However, as all the other flowers have "beauty" as their epithet, I prefer the reading "the *kāntaḷ* in which beauty{*pāṅku*} resides."

[2.21] (Cōmacuntarā<u>n</u>ār 1970: 6) = *Tirukkōvaiyār* 1:
tiruvaḷar tāmarai cīrvaḷar kāvika ḷīcartillaik
kuruvaḷar pūṅkumi<u>l</u> kōṅkupaiṅ kāntaḷkoṇ ṭōṅkuteyva
maruvaḷar mālaiyor valliyi <u>n</u>olki ya<u>n</u>anaṭaivāyn
turuvaḷar kāma<u>n</u><u>r</u>a<u>n</u> ve<u>n</u><u>r</u>ik koṭipō<u>n</u> <u>r</u>oḷirki<u>n</u><u>r</u>atē.

tiru vaḷar tāmarai cīr vaḷar kāvikaḷ īcar tillai
kuru vaḷar pūm kumi<u>l</u> kōṅku paim kāntaḷ koṇṭu ōṅku teyva
maru vaḷar mālai or valliyi<u>n</u> olki a<u>n</u>a naṭai vāyntu
uru vaḷar kāma<u>n</u> ta<u>n</u> ve<u>n</u><u>r</u>ikkoṭi pō<u>n</u><u>r</u>u oḷirki<u>n</u><u>r</u>atē.

[2.22] (*SMPT* 4612):
aiyam
viṇṇula kōviti naṇṇula kōtiru mēvu<u>r</u>umāl
kaṇṇula kōvara voṇṇula kōtaṇ kaṭaluṭutta
maṇṇula kōpo<u>r</u>aip pūṇvēta nāyaka vaḷḷalve<u>r</u>pi
laṇṇula kōtivar po<u>n</u>naṭi tōytava mā<u>r</u><u>r</u>iyatē.

viṇ ulakō, viti naṇṇu ulakō, tiru mēvu uṟu māl
kaṇṇu ulakō, aravu oṇṇu ulakō, taṇ kaṭal uṭutta
maṇ ulakō, poṟai pūṇ vētanāyaka vaḷḷal veṟpil
aṇṇu ulaku ōtu ivar poṉ aṭi tōy tavam āṟṟiyatē.

[2.23] (*SMPT* 4613):
tuṇivu
pūveṉṟa mēṉiyim maṅkaiyeṉ ṉāmakaḷ pūmakaḷē
kāveṉṟa ceṅkait talavēta nāyakak kāḷai taṉpāṟ
ṟāveṉ ṟaṭaiyalar pōlvā ṭuvakuḻaṟ ṟāmanammai
vāveṉ ṟaḻaippaṉa pōṉṟimai yāniṟkum vāṭkaṇkaḷē.

pū veṉṟa mēṉi immaṅkai eṉṉā makaḷ pū makaḷē.
kā veṉṟa ceṅkait tala vētanāyaka kāḷai taṉ pāl
"tā!" eṉṟu aṭaiy_al_ar pōl vāṭuva kuḻal tāmam. "nammai
vā!" eṉṟu aḻaippaṉa pōṉṟu imaiyāniṟkum vāḷ kaṇkaḷē.

Note:
ceṅkaittalam: lit. "the palms{*talam*} of his fair{*cem*} hands."

[2.24] (*SMPT* 4614):
kuṟippaṟital
kayalārtam pēṭṭuk kiṟavūṭṭi yaṉṉaṅ kaḷikkuñcennel
vayalār kuḷantai varuvēta nāyaka vaḷḷalveṟpi
liyalā rivarkaṇ maruḷaru ṇōkka miraṇṭunalku
mayalār viṭamu mamiḻtunal kāḻiyi ṉāymaṉamē.

kayal ār tam pēṭṭukku iṟavu ūṭṭi aṉṉam kaḷikkum cem nel
vayal ār kuḷantai varum vētanāyaka vaḷḷal veṟpil
iyal ār ivar kaṇ maruḷ aruḷ nōkkam iraṇṭum nalkum
mayal ār viṭamum amiḻtum nalku āḻiyiṉ āy maṉamē.

[2.25] (*SMPT* 4615):
irantupiṉiṟṟaṟkeṇṇal
viḻiyē yevarkku maṉavēta nāyaka vēḷkuḷantaip
poḻiyēr varaiyiṭat tañcēṉeñ cēyuṭ poru tuyaraṅ
kaḻiyē yirappumo rēruṭait tamma karappiṉavar
paḻiyē yeṉaṟerin tāyirap pāmivar pāṅkaruṟṟē.

viḻiyē evarkkum aṉa vētanāyaka vēḷ kuḷantai
poḻil ēr varaiyiṭattu, añcēl neñcē, uḷ poru tuyaram
kaḻiyē! irappum or ēr uṭaittu amma, karappiṉ avar
paḻiyē, eṉal terintāy! irappām ivar pāṅkaruṟṟē.

Note:
In line 2 the final *l* of *poḻil* is elided to make up the *etukai*.

[2.26] (*SMPT* 4616):
irantupiṉṉilainiṟṟal
kaṇiceytiṇ ṭōṇeṭu mālvēta nāyakak kāmaṉveṟpiṟ
paṇicey tiṟattamain tēṉkoṭuṅ kāmap pacitaṇiya
maṇicey kuḻaṟṟiru vaṉṉīrnuṅ kovvaiccev vāyamiḻta
maṇiceynum malkuṟ ṟaṭamūḻki yuṇṇa vaḷittiṭumē.

kaṇi cey tiṇ tōḷ neṭu māl vētanāyaka kāmaṉ veṟpil,
paṇi cey tiṟattu amaintēṉ. koṭuṅ kāma paci taṇiya
maṇi cey kuḻal tiru aṉṉīr, num kovvai cevvāy amiḻtam,
(m)aṇi cey num alkul taṭam mūḻki, uṇṇa aḷittiṭumē.

Note:
taṭam: a *cilēṭai* on "width, expanse" and "temple tank."

[2.27] (*SMPT* 4617):
muṉṉilaiyākkal
tōṟṟiya kalvik kaṭalvēta nāyaka tuṅkaṉveṟpiṟ
pōṟṟiya vāyat toṭucuṉai mūḻkiyum pūkkaḷkoytuñ
cāṟṟiya vūca lukaittunaṉ ṟāṭa ṟaṇantaṭiyē
ṉāṟṟiya mātava mōtaṉi niṉṟa taṟaikutirē.

tōṟṟiya kalvi kaṭal vētanāyaka tuṅkaṉ veṟpil,
pōṟṟiya āyattoṭu cuṉai mūḻkiyum, pūkkaḷ koytum,
cāṟṟiya ūcal ukaittum, naṉṟu āṭal taṇantu, aṭiyēṉ
āṟṟiya mā tavamō, taṉi niṉṟatu aṟaikutirē.

Notes:
1. *ākkal* in the *kiḷavi 'muṉṉilaiyākkal'* is causative, i.e., lit. "Bringing [his body] in front of her."
2. The epithet *cāṟṟiya* for *ūcal* perhaps shows the restrictions of the rhyme scheme here, as there is no reason for the swing to be 'praised.'
3. Perhaps one may also read *naṉṟu āṭal* here separately as 'dancing nicely'?

[2.28] (*SMPT* 4618):
vaṇṭōccimaruṅkaṇaital
kāraṇi kaṟpakaṅ kaṟṟōrcin tāmaṇi kalvikkaṭa
ṉāraṇi cintaip pukaḻvēta nāyaka naṇpaṉveṟpil

vāraṇi vaṇṭiṉaṅ kāṇaṭu nīṅkavim mātaraimpāṟ
ṟāraṇi yāṇṭu matuvuṇ ṭirutta ṟakātumakkē.

kār aṇi kaṟpakam kaṟṟōr cintāmaṇi kalvi kaṭal
nār aṇi cintai pukaḻ vētanāyaka naṇpaṉ veṟpil,
vār aṇi vaṇṭu iṉaṅkāḷ, naṭu nīṅka, immātar aimpāl
tār aṇi āṇṭu matu uṇṭu iruttal takātu umakkē.

[2.29] (*SMPT* 5048):
talaimakaḷōṭu irunta talaimakaṉ kārpparuvam kaṇṭu makiḻntu colliyatu
cilaiyāka vāynta nutalivaḷ cantaṉac cēṟaṇinta
mulaiyākam vimma muyaṅkiṉam yāmpoṉ muḻumaṉaipoṉ
malaiyāka vāḻkuḷat tūrvēta nāyaka vaḷḷalceṅkait
talaiyāka mēvutal pōṟpoḻi vāḻiya taṇmukilē.

cilaiyāka vāynta nutal ivaḷ cantaṉa cēṟu aṇinta
mulai ākam vimma muyaṅkiṉam yām poṉ muḻu maṉai poṉ
malaiyāka vāḻ kuḷattūr vētanāyaka vaḷḷal cem kai
talaiyāka mēvutal pōl poḻi vāḻiya taṇ mukilē.

Chapter 3

[3.1] (*EC* 24):
pattuppai muttuppai vajrap patakkamum
paipaiyāp paṇattaik koṭuttavar pōlap
pāṭiṉa pāṭṭukkum āṭṭukkum nīreṉṉaip
pacappiṉa tēpōtum palaṉaṟi vēṉkāṇum.

Notes:
1. The final *kāṇum*, lit. "See!," may be treated as an expletive.
2. *palaṉ aṟivēṉ*: lit. "now I understand the effect."

[3.2] (*EC* 26):
pattuppai muttuppai vajrap patakkamum
parintu koṭuttu mikaccukan tantupiṉ
pañcaṇai mītiṉiṟ koñci viḷaiyāṭi
rañcitamum aṟinta makarājaṉē.

[3.3] (Paḻaniccāmi 1908: 47):
kaṅkaṅkulavu katirvēlāṉ kaṉakamēru karuṇaimukil
poṅkamperuteṉ putuvaivaḷar poṉṉuccāmi pūpaṉeṉak

keṅkuntiṟalkūr kaviccinka meṉumōrpeyariṭ ṭeḻilvaḷamai
taṅkumpukaḻmē lāṅkalaiyun tantēyeṉaiyā tarittaṉaṉē.

kaṅkam kulavu katir vēlāṉ kaṉaka mēru karuṇai mukil
poṅkam peṟu teṉ putuvai vaḷar poṉṉuccāmi pūpaṉ eṉakku
eṅkum tiṟal kūr kavicciṅkam eṉum ōr peyar iṭṭu eḻil vaḷamai
taṅkum pukaḻ mēlām kalaiyum tantē eṉai ātarittaṉaṉē.

[3.4] (Cāminātaiyar 1932: 337f.):
oṇṇutalpeṟu miṅkilīṣmā
  torutti lukmaihāṇ ṭeṉṟāḷ
ōtiṉēṉavaḷ pāṇirēkaikaṇ
  ṭutaviṉāḷinta mēkalai.

[3.5] (*TPT* 2: 651; see also *TPTC* 169):
orukaiyilē aṉṉam orukaiyilē coṉṉam
varukaiyilē caṉmāṉa vārttai – perukupukaḻc
cīmāṉām eṅkaḷ civappirakā cattiruvak
kōmāṉuk kuḷḷa kuṇam.

oru kaiyilē aṉṉam, oru kaiyilē coṉṉam,
varukaiyilē caṉmāṉa vārttai – peruku pukaḻ
cīmāṉām eṅkaḷ civappirakāca tiru
akkōmāṉukkuḷḷa kuṇam.

[3.6] (*TPT* 2: 687; see also *TPTC* 186):
cuntarañcēr muttu cuvāmimāl kaittalamum
antarañcēr maṅkulumop pāṉatē – cantatamum
naṉṟupata muṇṭākki nāṭṭiṟ kaliyakala
niṉṟukaṉa kampeyya lāl.

cuntaram cēr muttucuvāmi māl kai talamum
antaram cēr maṅkulum oppāṉatē – cantatamum
naṉṟu patam uṇṭākki, nāṭṭil kali akala
niṉṟu kaṉakam peyyalāl.

Note:
TPTC : 2 *pāṉatuvē;* 4 *vaṉṟukaṉa kam.*

[3.7] (*TPT* 2: 558; see also *TPTC* 163f.):
kārār mukilai mayiliṉa nōkkiṭuṅ kātalittē
ērār cakōra matiyiṉai nāṭiṭu mēya mullait

tārār puyappoṉṉuc cāmi makīpaniṉ cālpilaku
cīrār vacaṉac cuvainōk kiṭumeṉ ciravaṇamē.

kār ār mukilai mayiliṉam nōkkiṭum, kātalittē
ēr ār cakōram matiyiṉai nāṭiṭum, mēya, mullait
tār ār puya poṉṉuccāmi makīpa, niṉ cālpu ilaku
cīr ār vacaṉac cuvai nōkkiṭum eṉ ciravaṇamē.

[3.8] (*TPT* 2: 343; see also *TPTC* 111):
kaikkār nititaru tēṉucintāmaṇi kaṉṉaṉ kārtti
kaikkār nikarala vāṅkoṭai yōṉpoṉṉu cāmikaṭak
kaikkār varaiyiṟ pavaṉivan tāṉkaṇṭu mālkoḷkāri
kaikkār tuṇaipuri vāriṟa vātu karuṇaiceytē.

kai kār niti taru tēṉu cintāmaṇi kaṉṉaṉ kārttikai
kār nikar ala ām koṭaiyōṉ poṉṉucāmi kaṭam
kai kār varaiyil pavaṉi vantāṉ kaṇṭu māl koḷ kārikaikku
ār tuṇai purivār iṟavātu karuṇai ceytē.

Note:
The first line could also be constructed as "*kai kār, niti taru tēṉu*,"
i.e., "the strong{*kai*} (black) rain cloud, *kāmadhenu* giving riches" or
"*kai kār, niti taru, . . .*," i.e., "the strong{*kai*} (black) rain cloud, the
kalpaka tree{*taru*} [bestowing] wealth."

[3.9] (*TPT* 2: 350; see also *TPTC* 114):
eṅkun tampuka ḻōṅka vaḷittamū vēḻu vaḷḷalka ḷumiva ṉīkaiyāl
taṅkun taṅkumi vaṟkē pukaḻeṉac cāṟṟuñ caṟkuṉa ṉāmpoṉṉu cāmimā
taṅka mēṟkoṭu pōntaṉa ṉōrtiṉañ cārum vītiyiṟ kaṇṭār mayalkoṭu
caṅkun taṅkalai yuntari yātuḷan taḷarntu nāṇamun tāmiḻan tārkaḻē.

eṅkum tam pukaḻ ōṅka aḷitta mū ēḻu vaḷḷalkaḷum ivaṉ īkaiyāl
taṅkum taṅkum ivaṟkē pukaḻ eṉa cāṟṟum caṟkuṉaṉ ām poṉṉucāmi
mātaṅkam mēl koṭu pōntaṉaṉ ōr tiṉam cārum vītiyil kaṇṭār mayal koṭu
caṅkum tam kalaiyum tariyātu uḷam taḷarntu nāṇamum tām iḻantārkaḻē.

[3.10] (*TPT* 2: 685; see also *TPTC* 185f.):
virumpa vaṉitaiyarcūḻ vēḻmuttu cāmī
varumpavaṉi taiyalkaṉ ṭuṉmālē – poruntinitan
tākamikun tāḻvaṉaiyun tāṉaiyiḻan tāḻkaraiyun
tēkamaṟan tāḻcolavan tēṉ.

virumpa vaṉitaiyar cūḻ vēḷ muttucāmī,
varum pavaṉi taiyal kaṇṭu, uṉ mālē – porunti nitam
tākam mikuntāḷ, vaṉaiyun tāṉai iḻantāḷ, karaiyum
tēkam maṟantāḷ cola vantēṉ.

[3.11] (*TPT* 2: 686; see also *TPTC* 186):
intiravil vāṇutalāḷ eppoḻutum maiyalkoṇṭē
intiravil vantaḻalai yīntataṉāl – cantatamum
vāṭimuttu cāmi makipatiyai nīyaḻaittu
vāṭiyeṉṟāḷ cēra varuvāy.

intiravil vāḷ nutalāḷ eppoḻutum maiyal koṇṭē
intu iravil vantu aḻalai īntataṉāl – cantatamum
vāṭi muttucāmi makipatiyai nī aḻaittu
vāṭi eṉṟāḷ cēra varuvāy.

[3.12] (*TPT* 2: 353; see also *TPTC* 116):
māṉēcaran toṭutta mataṉaṅkam viḻitterittōṉ māṉma larkkō
māṉēcā tavarparavum paraṉaṉpaṉ cētupati maṉṉaṉ vāyil
māṉēca rāmpoṉṉu cāmivaḷḷa leṉṉaiyavar maruvi nalla
māṉēca rākumvakai nīpurintā livvulakil vāḻu vēṉē.

māṉē, caram toṭutta mataṉ aṅkam viḻittu erittōṉ, māl malar kōmāṉ
ēcātavar paravum paraṉ aṉpaṉ, cētupati maṉṉaṉ vāyil
māṉēcar ām poṉṉucāmi vaḷḷal, eṉṉai avar maruvi nalla
māl nēcar ākum vakai nī purintāl ivvulakil vāḻuvēṉē.

Notes:
1. What I translate as "My girl!" is lit. "O doe!."
2. Line 2 *māṉēcar*: a tamilization of the English word "manager."
3. *TCC* (371), *TPTC* (116): 3 *maruva.*

[3.13] (*TPT* 2: 683; see also *TPTC* 185):
kōmakaṉē yiṅkuṉ koṭaikkeṉ koṭaiyatikam
vāmamuttu cāmi makipālā – nīmuṉ
orukait taṉaṅkoṭuttāl uṇmaivait tippōtē
irukait taṉaṅkoṭuppēṉ yāṉ.

kōmakaṉē, iṅku uṉ koṭaikku eṉ koṭai atikam
vāmam muttucāmi makipālā – nī muṉ

oru kai taṉam koṭuttāl uṇmai vaittu ippōtē
irukai taṉam koṭuppēṉ yāṉ.

[3.14] (Cāminātaiyar 1932: 303, st. 15):
taṅkupeṟun tiṟalvīrar cēṉaikkā valarkaḷoṭu tāṉu mōrpāl
maṅkaiyarcē ṉāpatiyāyc cēvittu varumataṉaṉ mataṉa valli
eṅkaḷuyar tañcainakarc carapōji maṉṉavaṉṟa ṉeḻilai nōkkit
tuṅkumaṉat tiṭaikkātal koṇṭiṭumuṉ malarvāḷi corintiṭ ṭāṉē.

taṅku peṟum tiṟal vīrar cēṉaikkāvalarkaḷoṭu tāṉum ōr pāl
maṅkaiyar cēṉāpatiyāy cēvittuvarum mataṉaṉ, mataṉavalli
eṅkaḷ uyar tañcai nakar carapōji maṉṉavaṉ taṉ eḻilai nōkki
tuṅku maṉattiṭai kātal koṇṭiṭu muṉ, malarvāḷi corintiṭṭāṉē.

[3.15] (Irāmacāmi Piḷḷai 1952: 9):
aruḷē vaṭivāṉ tirucceṅkōṭ, ṭartta nārī curaṉaiyeṅka
  ḷammai periya nāyakiyai, yatta ṉūram pikaiyaiyaṉpar
maruḷē tavira varuṅkūvai, malaivē lavaṉaip paṇintucelvam
  vaḷarkkum pukaḻvē ḷukkuṟicci, maṉṉaṉ parañcai nakarkkatipaṉ
poruḷē poḻiyum viḷiyakulap, puyaliṅ kitanañ cayacāmi
  putalva ṉeṉumvē lappatiṭa, puruṭaṉ pavaṉip polivukaṇṭa
teruḷē yuḷapeṇ kaḷilorucit, tiṉimāl kaṉiyat taṉittutitta
  ceḻuñcan tiraṉaic cakiyāmaṟ, ciṭuttāḷ palacoṟ ṟoṭuttāḷē.

aruḷē vaṭivu_ām tirucceṅkōṭṭu arttanārīcuraṉai, eṅkaḷ
  ammai periya nāyakiyai, attaṉūr ampikaiyai, aṉpar
maruḷē tavira varum kūvai malai vēlavaṉai paṇintu, celvam
  vaḷarkkum pukaḻ vēḷukkuṟicci maṉṉaṉ, parañcai nakarkku atipaṉ,
poruḷē poḻiyum iṉiya kula puyal, iṅkitaṉ, nañcayacāmi
  putalvaṉ eṉum vēlappa tiṭa puruṭaṉ pavaṉi polivu kaṇṭa
teruḷē uḷa peṇkaḷil oru cittiṉi māl kaṉiya, taṉittu, utitta
  ceḻum cantiraṉai cakiyāmal ciṭuttāḷ, pala col toṭuttāḷē.

Note:
aṉpar maruḷē tavira: lit. "so that the confusion of the devotees ceases," since *tavir-tal* is intransitive.

[3.16] (Irāmacāmi Piḷḷai 1952: 5):
kārkoṇṭa — vutāraṉkaṉa
    pērkoṇṭa — kupēraṉ
  kaṅkākula — tuṅkaṉpo
    ṉalaṅkāratu — raṅkaṉ
pārkoṇṭa — narēcaṉ kuṇa
    nērkoṇṭa — vulācaṉ

palavaṇṭami — laṟiyunturai
nalavaṇṭiṭai — ceṟiyun
tārkoṇṭa — puyattāṉmika
vērkoṇṭa — ceyattāṉ
tarunañcaya — tīraṉpeṟa
varumiṉpa — kumāraṉ
cīrkoṇṭatol — pukaḻāṉmuti
yōrkoṇṭaco — likaḻāṉ
cīlappaṇi — tāṉēpuṉai
vēlappa — pūmāṉē.

kār koṇṭa utāraṉ, kaṉa
pēr koṇṭa kupēraṉ,
kaṅkā kulatuṅkaṉ,
poṉ alaṅkāra turaṅkaṉ,
pār koṇṭa narēcaṉ, kuṇam
nēr koṇṭa ulācaṉ,
pala val tamiḻ aṟiyum turai,
nala vaṇṭiṭai ceṟiyum
tār koṇṭa puyattāṉ, mika
vēr koṇṭa ceyattāṉ,
taru nañcaya tīraṉ peṟa
varum iṉpa kumāraṉ,
cīr koṇṭa tol pukaḻāṉ,
mutiyōr koṇṭa col ikaḻāṉ,
cīla paṇi tāṉē puṉai
vēlappa pūmāṉē.

[3.17] (Irāmacāmi Piḷḷai 1952: 7):
malarmātaima ṇampūciya
maṇimārpati ṉumpā
makaḷaittiru vataṉattiṉu
makiḻkoṟṟavai taṉaimā
nilamētoḻa nimirtōḷiṉu
neṟiyāṉiṟu viyacīr
nītitturai kūvaikkiri
nēyakkuka ṉirutāḷ
vilakātoḷir maṉavāṉmaḻai
miṭaicōlaikaḷ puṭaicūḻ
vēḷaippati vēlappa
vinōtapra puṭīkaṉ
palavāḻviṉu makavāṉikar
paricēpeṟu taliṉāṟ

paravuñcuka maruvumpukaḻ
pakaikoñcamu milaiyē.

malar mātai maṇam pūciya
maṇi mārpatiṉum
pāmakaḷai tiru vataṉattiṉum
makiḻ koṟṟavai taṉai
māṉilamē toḻa nimir tōḷiṉum
neṟiyāl niṟuviya cīr
nīti turai kūvaikkiri
nēya kukaṉ iru tāḷ
vilakātu oḷir maṉavāṉ maḻai
miṭai cōlaikaḷ puṭai cūḻ
vēḷai pati vēlappa
vinōta prapuṭīkaṉ
pala vāḻviṉum makavāṉ nikar
paricē peṟutaliṉāl
paravum cukam maruvum pukaḻ
pakai koñcamum ilaiyē.

[3.18] (Cokkaliṅkaṉ 1947: st. 1–18):
tirumālum poṉṉulakat tēvarkaḷum tēvar
perumāṉum iṉpam peruka – varicēr (1)

vaṭaaravam pūṭṭineṭu mantarattai nāṭṭip
puṭaviati rattirukum pōtu – kaṭalil (2)

puṭaipaṭṭu eḻuntuvanta puttamiḻtam annāḷ
kaṭaippaṭṭa teṉṟu kaṭatti – vaṭi iṭṭa (3)

tēṅkuḻampaik kaḷḷuveṟi cērnta teṉa akaṟṟi
māṅkaṉikkum koñcam vaṭukkāṭṭip – pūṅkuyilai (4)

āṅkōtu ciṉṉameṉṟum ālaik karuppamoḻi
tāṅkōtu paṭṭateṉṟum taḷḷivaittup – pāṅkilicai (5)

poṅkutamiḻp pālvāṅkip pūṅkaruṇait tēṉkalantu
maṅkaḷarā kappākiṉ mattittuc – caṅkītak (6)

kāṉa racameḻuppik kaṟṟōr cevikkamuta
pāṉaracam eṉṉa icaip paṇkāṭṭit – tāṉorupāl (7)

kiḷḷaimoḻi vantukaṟkak kēṭkum kuḻalvakaikaḷ
uḷḷatellām pēcātu oḻittuviṭa – veḷḷainiṟap (8)

pāratiyum nāraṇiyum pārmakaḷum tumpuruvum
nāratarum vantu nayamkēṭpac – cāramuḷḷa (9)

pattarmaṉam tāṉurukap paṭṭamara mumtaḻaiyac
cittiramum kūṭac ciram acaikka – etticaiyum (10)

viṇṭurukak kaṟṟaṟintōr meyyuruka iṉparacam
kaṇṭurukak kallum karainturukat – toṇṭaicaṟṟum (11)

vikkāmal vīṇaiyicai miñcāmal pāṭiyacol
tikkāmal rākam citaiyāmal – pakkattil (12)

cittam kalaiyāmal ciṟṟiṭaitaḷ ḷāṭāmal
kuttu mulaiyum kuluṅkāmal – kattimuṉai (13)

vellampō eṉṉum viḻiyimaiyum kōṭṭāmal
vellampōl pāṭum viṟaliyē! – vallamaiyāy (14)

maṉmatanūl pārkkum matiyuḷḷa vāliparkkuc
coṉṉa mulaikkōṭṭuc corkkamē! – ennāḷum (15)

kākam paṟavāta kāmak kaṭalnaṭuvē
nāka cuṉaikāṭṭum nāyakamē! – mōkaveṟi (16)

ērkāṭṭum kāmat tiḷaiyōr viḷaiyāṭṭup
pōrkāṭṭum ālavaṭṭap pūntērē! – yārum (17)

varicait tirunitampa maṇṭapattaik kaṇṭu
tericikka muttitarum tēvē! [. . .] (18)

[3.19] (Cokkaliṅkaṉ 1947: st. 506–510):
[. . .] annēram (506)

mākaṉaka maṇṭapattil vantuniṟkum pōtukaṇṭēṉ
mōkaṉamut teṉṉumoru moykuḻalai – ēkanūtal (507)

villaḻakum pāyntaviḻi vēlaḻakum kālaḻakum
collaḻakum mālaiyiṭṭa tōḷaḻakum – pallaḻakum (508)

kaiyaḻakum mārpaḻakum kātaḻakum mūkkaḻakum
meyyaḻakum kaṇṭavuṭaṉ meymaṟantēṉ – oyyārac (509)

ceppumulai kaṇṭu tericittēṉ tīvāyil
oppumulai vāymeḻukāy uḷḷuṭaintēṉ [. . .] (510)

[3.20] (Cokkaliṅkaṉ 1947: st. 633–659):
[. . .] vēlviḻiyai (633)

vīciṉāḷ añcimaṉam veṭkiṉāḷ kiṭṭavarak
kūciṉāḷ koñcam kuṉukiṉāḷ – vāca (634)

mulaiyait tiṟantāḷpiṉ mūṭiṉāḷ caṟṟē
talaiyaik kaviḻntāḷpiṉ cāyntāḷ – kalakaleṉa (635)

vaṉṉak kalaipiṭittēṉ vārimaṭi mītuvaittēṉ
coṉṉamaṇik kaccaviḻttēṉ – tōḷkoṭittēṉkaṉṉattaik (636)

kiḷḷiṉēṉ muttamiṭṭēṉ keñciṉēṉ cantaṉattai
aḷḷiṉēṉ koṅkaiyiṉmēl appiṉēṉ – meḷḷa (637)

varuṭiṉēṉ kōtiṉēṉ vaḷḷamulaik kāmpai
neruṭiṉēṉ nīṭṭi nimirntēṉ – irukaiyāl (638)

kaṭṭip piṭittēṉ kaṉiyatarat tēṉuṇṭēṉ
kiṭṭap paṭuttēṉ kiṭattiṉēṉ – eṭṭiyeṉai (639)

maṟkaṭṭuk kaṭṭiṉāḷ vantumaṭi mēṟpaṭuttāḷ
piṟkaṭṭāyk kaiyiṟukap piṉṉiṉāḷ – coṟkaṭṭāy (640)

miṉṉiṉāḷ mēlēṟi vīḻntāḷ toṭaikkalaiyai
maṉṉiṉāḷ līlai vakaitoṭuttāḷ – eṉmārpil (641)

vaḷḷat taṉakkōṭṭu vāraṇattaip pāyaviṭṭāḷ
kaḷḷat taṉattaiyellām kāṭṭiṉāḷ – uḷḷēṟit (642)

tavviṉāḷ mīṟiṉāḷ caṟṟē ciṇuṅkiṉāḷ
kovvaiyitaḻ uṇṭāḷ kuṇukiṉāḷ – ovviṉāḷ (643)

ūṭiṉāḷ tampalattai uṇṇak koṭuttāḷkai
āṭiṉāḷ muttiṭṭāḷ aṇṇāntāḷ – cōṭāka (644)

mallāntāḷ eṉcō maṉaiyumurin tāḷcaracam
ellāntāṉ ceytāḷ iṇaṅkiṉāḷ – callā (645)

urukkattuc cēlai urintuviṭṭēṉ uḷḷē
parukkumma pīṭameṭṭip pārttēṉ – karuttil itai (646)

nākapaṭam eṉṟē navilalām maṟṟumanta
nāka paṭattilē nañcuṇṭē! – cēkaramāy (647)

māṅkaṉiyai nērāy vakukkalām akkaṉiyum
tūṅki vaṭuppaṭṭuc cōrumē! – pāṅkāṉa (648)

māṉkuḷampaic collalām māṟāmal akkuḷampil
tēṉkuḷampu tattaḷittuc cintātē! – kāṉciṟakkum (649)

taṇṭā maraippūvaic cāṟṟalām appūvum
vaṇṭārac cōrntu vataṅkumē! – koṇṭāṭi (650)

oppākat tēṉṟāṭṭai ōtalām ākilatil
eppōtum centēṉ eḻumpātē! – appappā! (651)

taṅkavaḷḷam ākumeṉṟu cāṟṟalām avvaḷḷattil
eṅkum ciṟurōmam illaiyē! – maṅkaḷamāyc (652)

ceṉṟuvarum ciṅkārat tēreṉalām attērukku
eṉṟum tiruviḻā illaiyē! – naṉṟāyttēṉ (653)

peṟṟirukkum pūñcuṉaiyaip pēcalām accuṉaiyum
vaṟṟiyoru kālam vaṟaṇṭiṭumē! – paṟṟi (654)

ituvē itaṟkiṇaiyeṉ ṟeṇṇi muttamiṭṭu
matimukattō ṭēmukattai vaittu – mutukaiyoru (655)

kaiyāl taṭavik kaḻuvimulai yumcuvaittu
maiyār viḻikaḷainā vāltaṭavi – eyyāmal (656)

uccinakam vaittaḻutti untiyilum kīṟiyiru
kaiccaracam mīṟik kaḻuttaṇaittu – vaiccu (657)

namacivaya eṉṟeḻuti nañcunilai taḷḷi
amut nilaikaṇ ṭaḻuttik – kamalamalark (658)

kaikōttuk kālkaḷpiṉṉik kātilnuṉi nāvaiviṭṭu
meyyōṭu kaṭṭi [. . .] (659)

[3.21] (Cokkaliṅkaṉ 1947: st. 40–53):
teṉmukavai yampatiyil cērntuvum – aṉṉaiyaṉṉa (40)

vaṉtikku vantatuvum maṅkaimaṅka ḷēcaraṭi
vantikkum tūya maṉattāṉai – muntamaril (41)

cinturattam cinturattaic cēramaru vārtaḷattaic
cinturatta kaiccin turattāṉai – vantukappam (42)

kāṇavaittup poṉmuṭimēl kaiyaivaittup pōṟṟātār
tāṇaiyattai veṉṟa taḷattāṉaic – cēṇulavum (43)

pērāṉait taṉmanilai pērāṉait teṉmukavai
ūrāṉai arccuṉaṉtēr ūrntāṉai – nērāṉa (44)

ceñcolnava rañcitace yampeṟutu rantaraṉai
añcalari ṟaiñcucara ṇāmpuyaṉait – tañcameṉṟu (45)

vantavarca kāyaṉvicu vācacatu raṅkataḷa
tantrapuya mantaraca vuntaraṉait – tantiramāy (46)

ettaḷappup pārkkumoṉṉār ēḻucuṟṟuk kaṟkōṭṭaik
kottaḷattait tūḷākkum kōmāṉai – nittanittam (47)

kappamiṭac collik kaliṅkarukkuc cīṭṭeḻuti
ōppamiṭum teṉmukavai ūrāṉaic – ceppumulait (48)

taiyalarkku vēḷait taṉukkōṭi kāvalaṉait
tuyyakaṭal toṇṭit tuṟaiyāṉaic – ceyyavaḷa (49)

mētiṉiyāḷ muttu vijaya rakunāta
cētupati celvac cirōmaṇiyai – mātaraci (50)

viṇmaṇiyāy vantamuttu vīrāyi nācciyār
kaṇmaṇiyai maṉṉavarci kāmaṇiyai – eṇṇupukaḻ (51)

nātaṉ vijayaraku nāta civacāmi
cētu patiyai jeyapatiyai – ātipaṉaik (52)

kaṇṭatuvum [. . .] (53)

[3.22] (Cokkaliṅkaṉ 1947: st. 56–59):
[. . .] – eṅkumalar (56)

kontūrum pūñcōlaik kompellām kārmēkam
vantūrap piḷḷai matiyūrac – cantūrum (57)

teṉṟalkāl tēṭic cilaimāraṉ vantirukka
maṉṟalkā tēṭimaka vāṉirukkat – teṉ tamiḻaip (58)

paṉṉukumpaṉ ippūmi pārattuk kāyirukka
maṉṉupukaḻt teṉpotiya māmalaiyāṉ – [. . .] (59)

Chapter 4

[4.1] *Nītinūl* 27.1:
eṉṉa nīvarun tikkavi pāṭiṉum
eṭuttakaṟ paṉaimuṉṉōr
coṉṉa tēyalāl nūtaṉa moṉṟilait
toṉmainūl palavākum
muṉṉan nūlelān tantava ṉīyalai
muṟṟuṇarn taṉaiyallai
uṉṉiṉ mikkavar palaruḷār kalviyāl
uḷḷamē cerukkeṉṉē.

[4.2] *Nītinūl* 9.7:
nītinūṉ maintarkku nikaḻtti meṉmalar
ōtiyarkku ōtiṭā toḻittaṉ meyyiṉil
pātiyai yēyalaṅ karittup pātimey
mītiṉi laṇiyiṉṟi viṭuttal okkumē.

[4.3] *Nītinūl* 9.2:
peṇmakaḷ keṭuvaḷeṉ ṟañcip peṟṟavaṉ
uṇmainū lavaṭkuṇart tāmai taṉmaṉaik
kaṇmaṟu puruṭaraik kāṇu meṉṟatai
eṇmaiyāyt tavaṉpaṟit teṟital okkumē.

[4.4] *Nītinūl* 43.18:
oruvaṉuṇṭa kalattuṇṇa voruvaṉuṭai
yiṉaiyuṭukka voruvaṉ ṟūṅkum
tiruvamaḷi tuyilamaṉam poruntātu
palareccañ cērpa ṭikkam

poruvuvē ciyarvāyec cilaiyuṇṇap
palapēraip puṇarnta cuttam
uruvukoṇṭa taṉaiyavartōḷ cēravē
yevarkkumaṉa moṉṟuṅ kollō.

[4.5] *Nītinūl* 43.26:
orumātu taṉṟuṇaivaṉ cīṭaṉaimaṟ
ṟorumātav vumpar kōṉai
orumātu cōtararai varaiccērntu
kaṉṉiyareṉ ṟuyarpēr koṇṭār
arumaiyā vemaiccēyar cōtararcī
ṭaraiyimpark karacaic cērum
poruṇmātak kaṉṉiyark kelāñcirō
maṇiyeṉṉap pukala lāmē.

[4.6] *Nītinūl* 43.14:
viṭamuṇṭāṉ kūṟṟutaittāṉ alakaiveṉṟāṉ
puramerittāṉ viṭaiyō ṉeṉṉak
kaṭalulakiṟ caivaravaṉ pukaḻvirippār
kaṇikaiyarkaṭ kaṭuvai yuṇṭu
kuṭamulaiyāṅ kūṟṟutaittut tāykkiḻavi
yeṉumpēyaik koṉṟaṉ ṉārvāḻ
iṭameṉṉum puramerittā ṉeṉilyāmum
avaṉpukaḻai yiyampu vōmē.

[4.7] *Nītinūl* 43.20:
kolaiñartamaik kolai ceytu kaḷvaraiveñ
ciṟaiyiliṭṭuk kuṟṟam ceyyum
pulaiñaraittaṇ ṭittaṭakku nammiṅki
līcumaṉṉar puruṭa rāvikku
ulaivaikkun taṉmaiyaḷāyp pātakame
lāntiraṇṭō ruruvāy vanta
vilaimātaik kollāma lulakamicai
yātuceya viṭuttā rammā.

[4.8] (Vētanāyakam Piḷḷai 1978a: 52):
intat tēcattil anniya pāṣaiyaik kaṟṟukkoṇṭu cuyapāṣai teriyāmaliruppavarkaḷukku pirapalamāṉa uttiyōkaṅkaḷ kiṭaikkiṉṟaṉa. ataṟkāka nām poṟāmai koḷḷa villai. iṅkilīs pirāṉcu mutaliya anniyapāṣaikaḷil palaviṣayaṅkaḷaippaṟṟi arumaiyāṉa aṉēkak kirantaṅkaḷirukkiṉṟamaiyāl anta pāṣaikaḷaip paṭikkiṟa intat tēcattār antak kirantaṅkaḷiluḷḷa arumaiyāṉa poruḷkaḷ intat tēca stirīkaḷukkum puruṣarkaḷukkum upayōkamākum poruṭṭuc cutēcap pāṣaikaḷil vacaṉa kāviyaṅkaḷ eḻutavēṇṭumeṉpatē nammuṭaiya maṉōratamāyirukkiṉṟatu.

[4.9] (Vētanāyakam Piḷḷai 1978a: 52f.):
kāviyarūpamāyirukkiṟa intat tēcattuk kirantaṅkaḷ aṉēkarukku appirayōcaṉa-māyirukkiṉṟaṉa. cila vitvāṉkaḷuṭaiya pāṭalkaḷai nām nāḷ muḻuvatum pārt-tālum arttam viḷaṅkavillai. avarkaḷukkuttāṉ payaṉ teriyumō teriyatō atuvuñ cantēkam. avarkaḷ entat teyvattiṉ mēlē pāṭiyirukkiṟārkaḷō, antat teyvattukkut-tāṉ arttan teriyumō? teriyātō? antat teyvattaik kēṭkavēṇṭum. antak kavikaḷai ciṟanta vitvāṉkaḷiṭattiṟ kāṭṭiṉālum avarkaḷukkum poruḷ teriyavillai. antap pāṭalkaḷiṟ pirayōkikkappaṭṭa arumpataṅkaḷ akarātiyilum akappaṭavillai. cila nūlkaḷukkuc cila vitvāṉkaḷ ceytirukkiṟa uraikaḷum cila iṅkilīṣ pustakaṅkaḷukkuc cilar ceytirukkiṟa moḻi peyarppukaḷum tamiḻō piramalipiyō? allatu vēṟeṉṉa pāṣaiyō veṉṟu teriyāmal piramikkum paṭiyāyirukkiṟatu. mūlattaip pārttu anta uraikku arttañ ceyyavēṇṭiyatāyirukkiṟatu.

[4.10] (Vētanāyakam Piḷḷai 1885: 287f.):
iṅkilīṣ, pirāṉcu mutaliya pāṣaikaḷaip pōlat tamiḻil vacaṉakāviyaṅkaḷ illāmal-iruppatu peruṅ kuṟaiveṉpatai nām oppukkoḷḷukiṟōm. [. . .] *airōppiya pāṣaikaḷil vacaṉakāviyaṅkaḷ illāmalirukkumāṉāl antat tēcaṅkaḷ nākarīkamum naṟpāṅkum aṭaintirukkakkūṭumā? appaṭiyē nammuṭaiya cuyapāṣaikaḷil vacaṉakāviyaṅkaḷ illāmalirukkiṟavaraiyil intat tēcam cariyāṉa cīrtiruttam aṭaiyā teṉpatu niccayam.*

[4.11] (Vētanāyakam Piḷḷai 1978a: 27f.):
intat tēcattup peṇkaḷ kalvi yillāmaiyāl aññāṉa iruḷil āḻntirukkiṟārka ḷeṉpatu yāvarukkun terinta viṣayamāyirukkiṉṟatu. peṇkaḷukkuk kalvi āvaci-yameṉpataic cilar oppukkoṇṭālum, anēkar peṇkaḷ paṭittu eṉṉa uttiyōkañ ceyyappōkiṟārkaḷeṉṟum, avarkaḷ paṭittāl, puruṣarukkaṭaṅki naṭavāmal vittiyā karvattiṉāl keṭṭuppōkiṟārkaḷeṉṟum turākṣēpañ ceykiṟārkaḷ. teyva paktiyum vivēkamum naṟkuṇaṅkaḷum uṇṭāvataṟkākak kalvi kaṟpatē yal-lātu uttiyōkamē ceyvataṟkākavō? allavē. nellukkiṟaikkiṟa taṇṇīr, pulmu-taliya pūṇṭukaḷukkum upayōkamāvatu pōlavum pāṉattukkāka veṭṭukiṟa kuḷam snāṉa mutaliyavaṟṟiṟkum utavukiṟatupōlavum, paḻattukkāka vaik-kum virukṣam niḻalmutaliyavaṟṟiṟkum upayuttamāvatu pōlavum, put-tiyiṉ apivirttikkākap paṭikkappaṭuṅkalvi uttiyōka mutaliyavaṟṟiṟkum cātaṉamākiṟatē tavira, paṭippataṟku uttiyōkamaṭṭuṅ kāraṇameṉṟu col-vatu kullāvukkākat talaiyēyallāmal, talaikkākak kullā allaveṉṟu colvataṟkuc camāṉamāyirukkiṉṟatu.

carīrattukku ākāram eppaṭiyō appaṭiyē kalviyāṉatu puttikku mikavum āvaciyamāyirukkiṉṟatu. nāḷukku nāḷ vaḷarkiṉṟa carīrattaic cuvāmi namakkuk koṭuttiruntālum ataṟkut takunta ākāraṅkaḷaikkoṭuttuc caukkiyattukkaṭutta kāriyaṅkaḷai yellām nāmē tēṭikkoḷḷāviṭṭāl, carīram vaḷaramāṭṭātē, appaṭiyē kaṭavuḷ nammai ñāṉātmāvākac ciruṣṭittiruntālum, nammuṭaiya cupāvañāṉam evvaḷavum pōtāmaliruppatāl kalvi eṉkiṟa ākārattaik koṭuttup puttiyai apivirtti ceyyavēṇṭiyatu nammuṭaiya kaṭamaiyā yirukkiṟatu. [. . .]

nammuṭaiya maṉam eppaṭippaṭṭateṉṟāl, oru kaṇappoḻutāyiṉum cummāyirāmal pūmaṇṭalam, ākāca maṇṭalam muḻuvatum cañcarittukkoṇṭirukkiṉṟatu. nām cummāyiruntālum, vēlaiceytālum, paṭuttiruntālum, nittirai ceytālum, taṉṉuṭaiya cañcārattukku eppōtum ōyvillai, taṉakkuk kaḷaippumillai, iḷaippumillai eṉṉum ittaṉmaiyatu. ippaṭippaṭṭa maṉattukkuk kalvi yeṉkiṟa tuṇaivaṉillāviṭṭāl, kaṭivāḷamillāta kutirai pōlavum kaṇṭapaṭi tiriyuṅ kuraṅku pōlavum karai kaṭanta veḷḷam pōlavum, kaṭṭukkaṭaṅkāk kāḷaipōlavum atu tēcamellān tirintu nammait turkkuṇamākiya kāṭṭilum, mēṭṭilum, kallilum, muḷḷilum, iḻuttu, muṭivil narakameṉkiṟa pātāḷattil, taḷḷiviṭu meṉpataṟku evvaḷavum cantēkamillai<,> intak kāraṇattaip paṟṟiyē āṇ piḷḷaikaḷ uttiyōkañ ceyya virumpiṉālum virumpāviṭṭālum, avarkaḷukkup paṭippippatu vaḻakkamākiṉṟatu.

Corr. comma added.

[4.12] (Vētanāyakam Piḷḷai 1978a: 121):
ulakattil māmsattaippōl acuciyum aruvaruppum uḷḷa patārttam vēṟoṉṟum illaiyē.

[4.13] (Vētanāyakam Piḷḷai 1978a: 30):
nām ippaṭic colvatu uṇmai yeṉataṟku ellāk kalviyum uṇarntu puruṣarkaḷ mēl māṟāta nēcamum aṉpumuḷḷa airōppiyastirīkaḷ cākṣikaḷāyirukkiṟārkaḷ.

[4.14] (Vētanāyakam Piḷḷai 1978a: 40):
piḷḷai peṟṟavaḷaip pārttu malaṭi perumūccu viṭṭatupōl, yūrōp tēcattu nākarīkattaip pārttu, nām perumūccu viṭavēṇṭiyatēyallāmal peṇkaḷ kalvi kallātavaraiyil nammuṭaiya tēcam tiruntavē māṭṭātu.

Chapter 5

[5.1] (Vētanāyakam Piḷḷai 1885: 330):
intac carittirattilē pirastāpikkappaṭṭa palarum inta nimiṣam varaiyil oru kuṟaivum illāmal cukajīvikaḷā yirukkiṟārkaḷ. appaṭiyē itai vācikkiṟavarkaḷ ellārum vaccira carīrikaḷāy nittiya maṅkaḷamāy vāḻntirukkak kaṭavārkaḷ.

[5.2] (George 1993: 987) = (Vētanāyakam Piḷḷai 1885: 9):
nāṉ paṭippu viṣayattil mantamā yiruntālum, viḷaiyāṭukiṟa viṣayattil atika muyaṟci uḷḷavaṉāka iruntēṉ. eṉṉuṭaiya pālliya cēṣṭaikaḷ yāvarukkum viyappāyirukkumāṉatāl, avaikaḷai aṭiyil vivarikkiṟēṉ.

Note:
The first sentence is missing in M. Tyagarajan's translation (Vedanayakam Pillai 2005: 15).

[5.3] (Vētanāyakam Piḷḷai 1885: 166f.):
orunāḷ tēvarājapiḷḷai eṉṉaiyuṅ kaṉakacapaiyaiyumpārttu "iṅkilīṣil cakala cāstira paṇṭitarākiya pēkkaṉ eṉpavar 'aṟpappaṭippu āpattu' eṉṟu collukiṟār. ataṟku aṉukuṇamāka eṉakkutterinta oru aṟpap paṭippāḷiyiṉ carittirattaik kēḷuṅkaḷ" eṉṟu ceppaluṟṟār. ceṉṉai nakarattil cuppaiyaṉ eṉṟu peyarkoṇṭa oru ēḻaippirāmaṇaṉ iruntāṉ.

[5.4] (Vētanāyakam Piḷḷai 1885: 266f.):
oru vaiciyaṉuṭaiya kaṟittōṭṭattil oru vaṇṇaṉuṭaiya kaḻutai pukuntu mēyntapaṭiyāl antak kaḻutaiyai vaiciyaṉ aṭittu, noṇṭiyākkiṉāṉ. ataṉāl vaṇṇaṉukkuk kōpam uṇṭāki, vaiciyaṉaip piṭittut tontaravu ceyya yattaṉittapōtu pūraṇa karppiṇiyāyirunta vaiciyaṉuṭaiya peṇcāti kuṟukkēvantu maṟittāḷ. avaḷai vaṇṇaṉ eṭṭi utaittapaṭiyāl avaḷuṭaiya karppañ citaintu, avaḷ piḻaittatu perum putumaiyākiviṭṭatu. intac caṅkatikaḷaiyellām vicāritta atikāri iruvarukkum potuvākat tīrmāṉañ ceytāṉ. eppaṭi yeṉṟāl, vaiciyaṉaippārttu, "nī kaḻutaikkālai oṭittapaṭiyāl antak kāl svastamākiṟavaraiyil kaḻutaikkup patilāka vaṇṇaṉukku nī vastirañ cumakkavēṇṭum" eṉṟu tīrmāṉittāṉ. piṟaku atikāri vaṇṇaṉaippārttu, "vaiciyaṉuṭaiya pattiṉikkuc cūl uṇṭākiṟavaraiyil avaḷōṭu nī cērntirukkavēṇṭum" eṉṟu tīrmāṉittāṉ.

[5.5] (Vētanāyakam Piḷḷai 1887: 1f.):
kaṭalaimēkalaiyāka uṭutta pūmitēviyiṉ tirumukamaṇṭalampōṉṟa puvaṉacēkarameṉṉum nakarattai rājatāṉiyāka uṭaiya tirāviṭatēcamuḻumaiyum narātipaṉ eṉṉum aracaṉ tuṣṭanikrakam ciṣṭaparipālaṉañ ceytu, manunītitavaṟāmal aracākṣiceytuvantāṉ. avaṉukku vekukālam piḷḷaiyillāmaliruntu, piṟaku kaṭavuḷatu aṉukkirakattāl atirūpacauntariyamāṉa oru peṇkuḻantai piṟantatu. aḻakutāṉē oru peṇṇākavantu avatārañceytatupōl ati aṟputamāṉacuntaramum ataṟkēṟṟa cukuṇaṅkaḷum poruntiyiruntamaiyāl antakkuḻantaikkuc cukuṇacuntari yeṉṟu peyariṭṭārkaḷ.

[5.6] (Vētanāyakam Piḷḷai 1885: 1):
intattēcam iṅkilīṣ turaittaṉattār cuvātīṉamākic cilakālattiṟkuppiṉpu cattiyapuri eṉṉum ūrilē, toṇṭaimaṇṭala mutalimār kulattilē nāṉ piṟantēṉ.

[5.7] (Rajam Aiyar 1998: 150f.) = (Rājamayyar 1994: 329f.):
iccarittira meḻutuvatil eṉakkuk kataiyē mukkiya karuttaṉṟu. [. . .] enta teyvattait toḻutu icciṟu kirantamāṉatu iyaṟṟappaṭṭatō, enta cuyampirakācamāṉa tivya tējōrūpattiṉ poruṭṭu ikkataiyaiyāṉatu niṣkāmiyamāka arppikkap paṭukiṟatō, anta tivviya, maṅkaḷa, kuṇātīta paripūraṇa caccitāṉanta svarūpattai nāmaṉaivarum muyaṟcittu aṭaivōmāka.

[5.8] (Rajam Aiyar 1998: 3) = (Rājamayyar 1994: 2):
'turaimakaḷāṉālum pāri uriyavaṉukkavaḷ ūḻiyakkāri' eṉṟu caṅkītam pāṭat toṭaṅkiṉār. ataik kēṭṭa ammāḷ: 'uṅkaḷaippōl avaṉ oru puruṣaṉ tāṉē, vētanāyakam piḷḷaiyām, kariyāvāṉ. [. . .].'

Note:
The original verse, Vētanāyakam Piḷḷai's *Peṇmati mālai* 87, runs *'turaimakaḷāṉālum pāri koṇṭa uriyavaṉukkava ḷūḻiyakkāri.' turaimakaḷ* may be read as both 'lady, queen' or 'European woman.'

[5.9] (Rajam Aiyar 1998: 3) = (Rājamayyar 1994: 1):
maturai jillāvil 'ciṟukuḷam' eṉṟa oru kirāmam uṇṭu. anta kirāmattiṉ naṭutteruviṉ mattiyil 'periya vīṭu' eṉṟu peyaruḷḷa oru vīṭu iruntatu.

[5.10] (Vētanāyakam Piḷḷai 1887: 15f.):
puvaṉēntiraṉukkuc camāṉamāṉa puruṣarkaḷ eppaṭiyillaiyō appaṭiyē cukuṇacuntarikkuc camāṉamāṉa peṇkaḷ oruvarumillai. avaḷ uttamakuṇaṅkaḷaiyellām āparaṇamāka uṭaiyavaḷ. avaḷuṭaiya kaṟpuneṟiyum, cīlamum, aṭakkamum, poṟumaiyum<,> vāymaiyum, tūymaiyum, vācāmakōcaram. avaḷ maṇṭalātipaṉuṭaiya makaḷāyiruntum ēḻaikaḷuṭaiya kaṣṭaniṣṭūraṅkaḷaiyellām aṟivāḷ. [. . .] avaḷ aḻaku kuṭikoṇṭamukattaiyuṭaiyavaḷ. karuṇai kuṭikoṇṭakaṇk aḷaiyuṭaiyavaḷ. cattiyamum iṉcolluṅkuṭikoṇṭanāvaiyuṭaiyavaḷ, īkaikuṭikoṇṭa karattaiyuṭaiyavaḷ. teyvapakti kuṭikoṇṭa cintaiyaiyuṭaiyavaḷ. avaḷuṭaiya aka aḻakai muka aḻakukāṭṭum. avaḷuṭaiya hīrtaya cuttattait tēkacuttaṅkāṭṭum.

Corr. <,> instead of <.>. Note that Vētanāyakam Piḷḷai consistently writes *hīrtayam* for the modern *hirutayam* or *irutayam.*

[5.11] (Vētanāyakam Piḷḷai 1887: 16):
avaḷuṭaiya maṅkaḷakuṇaṅkaḷai varṇippatu acāttiyamākaiyāl ivvaḷavōṭē niṟuttiṉōm.

[5.12] (Rajam Aiyar 1998: 47f.) = (Rājamayyar 1994: 93–95):
avaḷuṭaiya aḻakāyamainta aṅkaṅkaḷ cevvaiyāy curuti kūṭṭiya vīṇaiyiṉ cantikaḷ taṉittaṉi taṅkaḷ nātattai toṉikkiṟatumaṉṟi maṟṟa taṉtikaḷuṭaiya nātattaiyum eppaṭi cōpikkac ceykiṉṟaṉavō atu pōlat taṉittaṉi tattam aḻakāl viḷaṅkiyatum tavira maṟṟuḷḷa aṅkaṅkaḷiṉ aḻakaiyum eṭuttuk kāṭṭiṉa. teyvīkap pulavarkaḷākiya kampar mutaliyōruṭaiya kavikaḷil eppaṭi uḷḷa patattai eṭuttu vēṟu entap patam pōṭṭālum racam kuṟaintu pōmō atupōla leṭcumiyiṉuṭaiya aṅkaṅkaḷil etaiyum ciṟitu māṟ ṟiṉālum aḻakukkuk kuṟaivē tavira virttikiṭaiyatu. 'kaḻuttu ciṟitu nīṇṭiruntāl naṉṟ<āy>irukkum' 'kāl ciṟitu kuṟukik kai ciṟitu peruttiruntāḷ,' eṉṟippaṭi āl um eṉṟa vikutip pirayōkaṅkaḷukku iṭam kiṭaiyātapaṭi avaḷuṭaiya aṅkaṅkaḷiṉamaippu avvaḷavu aḻakāyirukkum. [. . .] laṭcumi <pēcum pōtu avaḷuṭaiya vārttaikaḷiṉ karuttukkut takkapaṭi avaḷuṭaiya mukakkuṟi> aṭikkaṭi

aḻakāy māṟuvatu, takatakaveṉṟu palavitamāyp pirakācikkum vayirakkallai ñāpakapaṭuttum. avaḷ pēcumpōtu avaḷuṭaiya kaikāl ceyyum apiṉayattālum mukattil uṇṭākum vēṟupāṭālum tūraniṟpavarkaḷ kūṭa avaḷ karuttai aṟiyalām. avaḷuṭaiya uyarnta utaṭukaḷum vicālamāṉa kaṇkaḷum evvaḷavu tuṉpam vantālum pārāṭṭātu cahikkakkūṭiya tiṭa cittattaiyum poṟumaiyaiyum kāṭṭi niṉṟaṉa. tuḷḷi tuḷḷi viḻum mīṉkaḷ pōlac calikkum avaḷuṭaiya kaṇkaḷum, avaḷuṭaiya kaṉṉaṅkaḷil uṇṭākum cuḻikaḷum, avaḷuṭaiya aḻakāṉa palvaricaiyum avaḷ mukattiṟku ōr apūrvamāṉa vacīkara caktiyai uṇṭu paṇṇiṉa. avaḷuṭaiya kaṇkaḷiṉ tōṟṟam veku aritāṉa kuḷircciyaiyum mirutut taṉmaiyaiyum uṭaiyatāṉālum, tēvaiyāṉa kālattuk kaṇṭōraik kalakkattakka 'uṭaliṉuyiraiyum-uṇarvaiyu naṭuvupōyuruvu <mātarviḻi>' eṉṟa laṭcaṇattiṟkup poruntiya oru kūrmaiyāṉa pārvaiyum avaikaḷukku uṇṭeṉṟu niṉaikka iṭamiruntatu.

Corr. <*naṉṟākayirukkum*>, <*pēcum pōtu avaḷuṭaiya mukakkuṟi*>, <*matarviḻi*> to restore original text. The currently available editions Rājamayyar (1990 and 1994) introduce a large number of mistakes into the text which I correct here and below on the basis of the *Urtext.*

[5.13] (Rajam Aiyar 1998: 112) = (Rājamayyar 1994: 232):
naṉṟāyp poḻutu viṭintatu iṉṟaikku; pōkaṭṭum, eṉ āyucukkuk kaṭaici nāḷākavāvatu irukki<ṟa>tēyallāvō; nalla nāḷtāṉ. canniyācamum āccu kaḻutai-yumāccu. moṭṭaiyaṭittuk koṇṭu ūrilē piccaiyeṭuttukkoṇṭu appaṭiyāvatu yāraik kāppāṟṟavēṇṭum? kōvileṉṉa kuḷam eṉṉa? ellāvaṟṟaiyum neruppai vaittuk koḷuttuk kaḻutaiyai. kaṇkaḷ niṟainta ākāyamē, uṉakkumā kaṇ teri-yavillai. uṉatu iṭiyōcaikaḷ eṅkē oḷintu viṭṭaṉa? inta vīṇiḻavukaḷai oru iṭiyil takartteṟiyamāṭṭāyā!

Corr. <*irukkitēyallāvō*>, missing syllable added.

[5.14] (Vētanāyakam Piḷḷai 1887: 121):
puruṣaṉ eṉṉōṭukūṭa uṭaṉkaṭṭai yēṟaccammatittāltāṉ nāṉ tālikaṭṭik koḷvēṉ. allātēpōṉāl tāli kaṭṭikkoḷḷa māṭṭavē māṭṭēṉ. avaṉ kaṭṭiṉālum aṟuttu eṟintu viṭuvēṉ.

[5.15] (Rajam Aiyar 1998: 95) = (Rājamayyar 1994: 195):
namakkuḷ taṟkālattil <cila ciṟuvarkaḷ stirīkaḷ> irupatu vayatukku mēṟpaṭṭu maṇam ceytāltāṉ puruṣaṉuṭaṉ cukittu vāḻakkūṭum eṉṟu niṉaikkiṟārkaḷ. śrīnivācaṉ leṭcumi ivarkaḷuṭaiya nēcattai naṉṟāy aṟinta eṉakku appaṭit tōṉṟavillai.

Corr. <*cilar, stirīkaḷ*>, restores original reading.

[5.16] (Vētanāyakam Piḷḷai 1887: 37):
kaṭuṅkāṟṟukku etirēniṉṟu nāmkāṟiyumiḻkiṟa ucciṣṭam nammēlē tirumpiviḻukiṟatupōla nāmpiṟarmēṟ collum nintaṉai nammaiyē cārukiṉṟatu.

[5.17] (Vētanāyakam Piḷḷai 1887: 38–40):
cilavaruṣaṅkaḷukku muṉ oruvarukkoruvar aṟimukamillāta palapērkaḷ oru añcal vaṇṭiyiṉ mēlē ēṟikkoṇṭu pala ūrkaḷukkup payaṇampōṉārkaḷ. vaḻiyil irākkālam camīpittatāl cōrapayattaik kuṟittup pēcikkoṇṭupōṉārkaḷ. appoḻutu orukaṉavāṉ taṉkai vacatti liruntapattut taṅkanāṇayaṅkaḷai yeppaṭip pattirappaṭuttavē ṉeṉṟu maṟṟavarkaḷai nōkkiccoṉṉāṉ. avaṉukkuc camīpattilirunta oruturaicāṉi, "avaikaḷai ummuṭaiya pātarakṣaiyil vaittup pattirappaṭuttalāmē<"> yeṉṟāḷ. avaṉ appaṭiyē antattaṅkanāṇayaṅkaḷaip pāta rakṣaiyilvaittu maṟaittāṉ. piṟaku caṟṟu nērattukkuḷ orutiruṭaṉvantu, paṇappaikaḷaik koṭukkumpaṭi kēṭṭāṉ. appōtu antatturaicāṉi "eṉṉiṭattil paṇamillai. atō antat turaiyiṉuṭaiya pātarakṣaikaḷaic cōtittāl pattut taṅkanāṇayaṅkaḷ akappaṭum" eṉṟāḷ. avaṉ antappaṭicōtittu, akappaṭṭa taṅkanāṇayaṅkaḷaik kavarntukoṇṭu pōyviṭṭāṉ. avaṉpōṉapiṟaku antat turaicāṉiyai antakkaṉavāṉ vāyilvantapaṭi tūṣittāṉ. uṭaṉē antastirī avaṉaiyum maṟṟavarkaḷaiyum nōkki, "nīṅkaḷ tayaiceytu nāḷaikku eṉvīṭṭilviruntu cāppiṭuvīrkaḷāṉāl uṅkaḷukku uṇmaiyaitterivikkiṟēṉ," eṉṟāḷ. antappaṭi maṟunāḷ campiramamāy avarkaḷellōrum viruntuṇṭa piṟaku, antatturaicāṉi taṉkaiyilirunta pustakattaik kāṭṭi, "anēka āyiran taṅkanāṇayam matippuḷḷa kaṭitanāṇayaṅkaḷ intappustakattilirukkiṉṟaṉa. antattiruṭaṉukku intatturaiyiṉiṭa miruntataṅka nāṇayaṅkaḷai nāṉ terivikkāmaliruntāl avaṉ intap pustakattiluḷḷa kaṭita nāṇayaṅkaḷai yellām kavarntukoṇṭu pōyiruppāṉ. intatturai eṉṉālē iḻanta pattuttaṅka nāṇayaṅkaḷukkup patilāy nūṟu taṅka nāṇayaṅkaḷ koṭukkiṟēṉ. avar vēṇṭā meṉṟālum nāṉviṭamāṭṭēṉ" eṉṟucolli nūṟutaṅka nāṇayaṅkaḷai avarukkuk koṭuttāḷ. uṭaṉē ellārum paramacantōṣamaṭaintu, antastirīyiṉuṭaiya cāmarttiyattaiyum utārakuṇattaiyum pukaḻntu koṇṭāṭiṉārkaḷ" eṉṟāḷ.

Corr. missing <"> inserted.

[5.18] (Rajam Aiyar 1998: 96) = (Rājamayyar 1994: 198):

māṉiṉam varuvapōṉṟu mayiliṉan tirivapōṉṟum
mīṉiṉa miḷirvapōṉṟu miṉṉiṉa miṭaivapōṉṟum

pommeṉap pukunta <āṅkilēya> mātarkaḷ tōkai pōṉṟa uṭaiyum, aṉṉampōṉṟa naṭaiyum, kiḷḷai pōṉṟa moḻiyuṅ koṇṭu taṅkaḷuṭaiya (allatu piṟaruṭaiya) nāyakarkaḷōṭu kai kōrttu<,> uraiyāṭi nakaiyāṭiṉār orucār.

Corr. *<āṅkilēyē>*, <.>, restores original reading.

[5.19] (Rajam Aiyar 1998: 133) = (Rājamayyar 1994: 288f.):
arttamō arttamillaiyō atu avarukku laṭciyamēyillai. ilakkaṇa vitiyaik kavaṉittē kaṭṭi varukiṟatillai; emakam tirupukkuk kuṟainta pāṭṭu avar apippirāyattil pāṭṭēyillai. [. . .] *ammaiyappapiḷḷaikku irunta āvēcattil eṅkē pōkiṟōm, varukiṟōm, eṉkiṟa niṉaivukūṭa illai. avar veṟum cittirakkavikaḷuṭaṉ niṟuttāmal utpirēṭcai mutaliya alaṅkārak kavikaḷilēyum pukuntuviṭṭār. oru stirī virakatāpattiliruntāḷām. appoḻutu nāḻikaiyāy viṭṭatāl cūriyaṉ taṉ*

vaḻakkappaṭi kiramamāka astamittāṉ. appaṭic colvataṟkup patilāka namatu vitvāṉ 'cūriyaṉākiya kāṟṟāṭiyāṉatu anta stirīyiṉuṭaiya perumūccākiya caṇṭamārutattāl aṭippaṭṭuk kīḻē viḻuntatu. viḻuntu mēlellām kāyampaṭṭu irattam vantatāl ākāyamellām cevvāṉamāyviṭṭatu' eṉṟu tivyamāṉa ciṅkāra racattōṭu kūṭiya pāṭṭukaḷ aṉēkam pāṭiṉār. iṉṉum vacantakālattai varṇikkumpōtu vacanta kālam kār kālattaiyottatu eṉṟu pāṭiṉār. ēṉeṉṟāl kārkālattil mēkaṅkaḷ niṟaintirukkum. vacanta kālattilum stirīkaḷuṭaiya kūntalkaḷākiya mēkaṅkaḷuṇṭu.

[5.20] (Vētanāyakam Piḷḷai 1887: 54–56):
ilakkaṇa vaḻukkaḷ niṟainta antakkaviyaip piracurañ ceyya namakkup piriya millāmaiyāl, ataṉ poruḷaimaṭṭum oruvāṟu curukkic<colluvōm>.
"makimaitaṅkiya pukaḻviḷaṅkiya cukuṇacuntari kāṇka.
"cilanāḷāy uṉṉuṭaiya taricaṉam eṉakkuk kiṭaikkā maliruntapōtilum uṉṉuṭaiya mukamākiya cantiraṉ eṉṉuṭaiya hīrtayamākiya ākāyattil eññāṉṟum pirakācittuk koṇṭirukkiṉṟatu. uṉṉuṭaiya aḻakai varṇikka āyiram nāvuṭaiya āticēṣaṉāluṅ kūṭumā? uṉṉuṭaiya tirumukattukkut tōṟṟuppōyc cantiraṉ meyveḷuttu, uḷḷaṅkaṟuttu nāḷtōṟun tēyntupōkiṟāṉ. appaṭiyirukkac cēṟṟilēpiṟantu, matukaraṅkaḷāl cuvaikkappaṭṭu, iravilēkuvintu vāṭippōkiṟa tāmaraimalar uṉ mukattukku eṅṅaṉañ camāṉamākum? mēkaṅkaḷ uṉṉuṭaiya kūntalukkuc camāṉamākāmaiyāl jalappira vākamāyk kaṇṇīrvaṭittu aḻutukoṇṭu, ākāyattilētirintukoṇ ṭirukkiṉṟaṉa. nālukālōṭum oruvālōṭuṅ kūṭiyamirukajantuvākiya māṉaiyum turnāṟṟamuḷḷa mīṉaiyum uṉkaṇṇukku eppaṭi oppuccolvēṉ. nāṭṭilē cañcarittuk koṇṭirunta aṉṉamum mayiluṅ kuyiluṅ kiḷiyum pūvaiyum uṉṉuṭaiya naṭaikkuñ cāyalukkum moḻikkun tōṟṟuppōyk kāṭṭilē cañcarikkiṉṟaṉa. muttukkaḷ uṉṉuṭaiya pallukkuppayantu, cippikkuṭ pukuntu, kaṭalil oḷintukoṇṭē yirukkiṉṟaṉa. ellārun tuppu, tuppu, eṉṟucollukiṟa pavaḷattai uṉṉuṭaiya itaḻukku nāṉ eppaṭi oppuraippēṉ. piramā uṉakkuccakala avayavaṅkaḷaiyum paṭaittu, iṭaiyaip paṭaikkāmal viṭṭu viṭṭatu maṟatiyiṉālō allatu tiruṣṭiparikārattukkākavō teriyavillai" eṉpatutāṉ.

maturēcaṉ antakkaviyai oru caki vacamāyc cukuṇacuntariyiṭam aṉuppiṉāṉ. ataippārtta uṭaṉē kōpameṉpataiyē aṟiyāta cukuṇacuntarikkup piramātamāṉa kōpamuṇṭāki, antak kaviyaikkiḻittu, ataikkoṇarntavaḷ talaimēlē viṭṭeṟintu, orutuṇṭukkākitattil "piramā eṉakku iṭaiyaippaṭaikka maṟantu viṭṭatu pōla uṉakkupputtiyaip paṭaikka maṟantuviṭṭāṉ," eṉṟu eḻuti, accakikaiyilē koṭuttaṉuppiṉāḷ. antalikitattaik kaṇṇuṟṟapiṉpu maturēcaṉ tāṉ ceytatu picakeṉṟuṇarntu, mikavum cintāk kirāntaṉāṉāṉ.

Corr. for <*colluvām*>, since Vētanāyakam Piḷḷai does not use the old *-ām* ending elsewhere.

Glossary

Although unfamiliar terms are generally explained in the text when they are first used, the following glossary contains a list of recurrent words for quick reference. T = Tamil, E = colonial English or "Anglo-Indian" usage as described by Yule/Burnell (1994) and Lewis (1999), M = Malayalam, S = Sanskrit.

anna	(E) Indian unit of currency. 16 annas = 1 rupee.
aṉṉatāṉam	(T) lit. "the giving of rice/food." The public distribution of food by a wealthy donor.
araṅkēṟṟam	(T) lit. "ascending the podium." The first public recitation of a literary work before a larger audience.
ātīṉam	(T) a central Hindu religious institution (monastery) that administers subordinate *maṭams* and temples.
ātīṉavittuvāṉ	(T) leading poet-scholar of an *ātīṉam*.
avaiyaṭakkam	(T) lit. "addressing/appeasing the assembly [of fellow poets]." Verse in which the poet apologizes for the shortcomings of his work, comparable to the *captatio benevolentiae* in classical Western rhetorics.
calico	(E) cotton cloth.
camastāṉavittuvāṉ	(T) court poet.
Caṅkam literature	(T) the oldest extant corpus of Tamil poetry (c. 100 BCE to 250 CE).

cāṟṟukkavi	(T) see *ciṟappuppāyiram.*
chattram	(E) home for pilgrims and traveling high-caste Hindus.
choultry	(E) see chattram.
cilēṭai	(T) Skt. *śleṣa*. A kind of pun ("double entendre" or paronomasia).
ciṟappuppāyiram	(T) lit. "special preface," also called *cāṟṟukkavi* "praise poem." A kind of congratulatory verse written for and prefixed to someone else's poetic composition.
cittirakkavi	(T) lit. "picture poem." Skt. *citrakāvya*. Poem in which the lines or syllables are arranged so as to fit into a fanciful picture or diagram (*cittiram*) if written down.
cīṭṭukkavi	(T) epistolary poem or versified letter.
dewan	(E) prime minister of an Indian state or manager of a zamindari.
Foujdaree translator	(E) translator employed for criminal as opposed to civil cases in the colonial legal system.
kōvai	(T) a Tamil poetic genre.
maṭakku	(T) see *yamakam*.
maṭam	(T) Skt. *maṭha*. A kind of Hindu monastery.
mofussil	(E) hinterland, the rural localities as opposed to the metropolis.
munsiff	(E) rank of an Indian civil judge.
murajapam	(M) prayer ceremony.
mutt	(E) see *maṭam*.
pirapantam	(T) Skt. *prabandha*. A group of genres or "hypergenre" of Tamil poetry.
poligar	(E) Tam. *pāḷaiyakkārar*. An Indian local ruler or native king.
pulavar	(T) Tamil poet-scholar, Tamil pundit.

raiyat	(E) wealthy peasant.
rudrākṣa beads	(S) the berries of Elaeocarpus Ganitrus strung up and used for religious purposes (often compared to a rosary).
sandhi	(S) change in the appearance (and pronunciation) of words when they are joined in a phrase or sentence.
Sarasvatī	(S) goddess of learning and the arts.
sheristadar	(E) head legal officer.
śleṣa	(S) see *cilēṭai.*
sthalapurāṇa	(S) see *talapurāṇam.*
Sudder Court/ Sudder Udalut	(E) court of appeal in the colonial legal system.
Sudr Ameen	(E) rank of an Indian civil judge.
tahsildar	(E) the chief revenue officer of the subdivision (taluk) of a district.
talapurāṇam	(T) Skt. *sthalapurāṇa* or *mahātmya.* A temple myth or a text containing the localized legends of a particular sacred place explaining its foundation.
taṉippāṭal	(T) an occasional poem or "solitary stanza."
tiripu	(T) a technique in Tamil poetry.
tulābhāram	(S/M) also *tulāpuruṣadānam.* Weighing the body of the raja against an amount of gold to be distributed to brahmins.
Vēḷāḷar	(T) landowning non-brahmin caste in South India.
viṟaliviṭutūtu	(T) lit. "dancing-girl sent [as] messenger." A Tamil poetic genre.
yamakam	(T) Skt. *yamaka.* A poetic technique.
zamindar	(E) Indian landholder paying taxes to the British.
zamindari	(E) the estate of a zamindar.

References

All items (including the transliterated Tamil sources) are sorted in the order of the English alphabet. A publication year in brackets [ ] indicates the year of the first edition.

Archival Records

(Madras Government Orders, Colonial Administrative Papers, Missionary Papers, etc.)

4th Annual Report from the Governors of the Madras University, for 1845. Madras: Minerva Press, 1845.

8th Annual Report from the Governors of the Madras University, for 1848–49. Madras: Christian Knowledge Society Press.

Classified Catalogue of the Public Reference Library, consisting of books registered from 1867 to 1889 at the Office of the Registrar of Books, Old College, Madras. Madras: Printed by the Superintendent, Government Press, 1894.

G.O. No. 306, 26–39, dated March 17, 1857.

G.O. No. 518–519, dated May 5, 1857.

High Court Administrative Records, Judicial Proceedings, No. 219, dated August 27, 1872.

Madras Record Office. *Classified Catalogue of Books Registered from 1890–1900 at the Office of the Registrar of Books.* Reprint. Government of Madras, 1962.

Proceedings and Letters of the High Court, Appellate Side, Madras, for the year 1863, Diary, 25th June, No. 3163.

The India Office List for 1887. London: Harrison and Sons, 1887.

Wesleyan Minutes of Conference 1905.

Periodicals

(Tamil and English)

Ciṅkai Nēcaṉ. Singapore.
The Harvest Field. Bangalore.
The Hindu. Madras.
Madras Christian College Magazine. Madras.
Vivēkacintāmaṇi. Madras.

Sources in Tamil

Ajmalkāṉ, Pī. Mu. 1985. *Tamiḻakattil muslimkaḷ. Pōrccukīciyar varukaikku muṉpum piṉpum*. Ceṉṉai: Millat Piriṇṭars.

Aḻakapparācu, Ta. 1983. "Kātal ilakkiyaṅkaḷ," in: Cuppiramaṇiyaṉ/ Pakavati (1983: 117–148).

Aḻakiyacokkanātap Piḷḷai, V. 1868. *Muttucuvāmiya Piḷḷai pēriṟ kātaṟ pirapantam*. Tirunelvēli: Muttamiḻākara accukkūṭam.

Āṉantanaṭarācaṉ, A. 1997. *Tamiḻil tūtu ilakkiya vaḷarcci*. Aṇṇāmalainakar: Aṇṇāmalaip palkalaikkaḻakam.

Antōṉi Irācu, Ā. Pi., ed. 1986. *Māyūram nītipati Vētanāyakariṉ ceyyuḷ nūlkaḷ*. Tirucci: Ārōkkiyam patippakam.

Aracumaṇi, Pulavar. 1972. *Nakaiccuvai Nāyakam*. Ceṉṉai: Acōkaṉ patippakam.

Aṟivuṭainampi, Ma. Cā. 1994. *Tañcai marāṭṭiya maṉṉar vaḷartta tamiḻ ilakkiyam. Pakuti 1*. Tañcāvūr: Tamiḻp palkalaikkaḻakam.

Āṟumuka Nāvalar, ed. 1963 [1851]. *Naṉṉūl kāṇṭikai urai*. Ceṉṉai: Āṟumuka Nāvalar Accakam.

Aruṇācalakkavirāyar, Civakāci. 1898. *Yāḻppāṇattu Nallūr Śrī-la-Śrī Āṟumukanāvalar carittiram*. Ceṉṉai: Alpīṉiyaṉ accukkūṭam.

Aruṇācalak Kavuṇṭar, Ku. 1965 [1952]. *"Māyūram muṉisīp" Vētanāyakam Piḷḷai*. Ceṉṉai: Allied Publishing Company.

Aruṇācalam, Mu. 1976. *Tamiḻ ilakkiya varalāṟu. Patiṉāṟam nūṟṟāṇṭu—mūṉṟām pākam*. Tiruccirrampalam: Kānti vittiyālayam.

———, ed. 1943. *Kūḷappa Nāyakkaṉ kātal*. Ceṉṉai: Cakti kāriyālayam.

Aṭaikkalam, Ā. Jō. 1987. *Māyūram viṟpaṉṉar Vētanāyakar iyaṟṟiyaruḷiya Mayilai Aṉṉai patikam*. Cennai: Tōmaip Pērālayam.

Caktivēl, Cu. 1997. *Itaḻiyal*. Ceṉṉai: Maṇivācakar patippakam.

Cāminātaiyar, U. Vē., ed. 1898. *Maṇimēkalai mūlamum . . . Vē. Cāminātaiyar eḻutiya arumpatavuraiyum*. Ceṉṉai: Jūpili Accukkūṭam.

———, ed. 1926. *Śrī Mīṉāṭcicuntaram Piḷḷaiyavarkaḷ pirapantattiraṭṭu.* 2nd revised and enlarged edition. Ceṉṉapaṭṭaṇam: Kamarṣiyal Accukkūṭam.

———, ed. 1932. *Koṭṭaiyūr Śrī Civakkoḻuntu Tēcikar pirapantaṅkaḷ.* Ceṉṉai: Kēsari Accukkūṭam.

———. 1933. *Tiruvāvaṭutuṟaiyātīṉattu Makāvittuvāṉ Tiricirapuram Śrī Mīṉāṭcicuntaram Piḷḷaiyavarkaḷ carittiram. Mutaṟ pākam.* Ceṉṉai: Kēsari Accukkūṭam.

———. 1936a. *Kaṉam Kiruṣṇaiyar.* Ceṉṉai: Kēcari Accukkūṭam.

———. 1936b. *Kōpālakiruṣṇa Pāratiyār (kīrttaṉaṅkaḷuṭaṉ).* Ceṉṉai: Kēcari Accukkūṭam.

———. 1940. *Tiruvāvaṭutuṟaiyātīṉattu Makāvittuvāṉ Tiricirapuram Śrī Mīṉāṭcicuntaram Piḷḷaiyavarkaḷ carittiram. Iraṇṭām pākam.* Ceṉṉai: Liparṭṭi Accukkūṭam.

———. 1943 [1885]. *Śrī Mattiyārccuṉa māṉmiyam.* Ceṉṉai: Kapīr Accukkūṭam.

———. 1957 [1940]. *Niṉaivu mañcari. Mutaṟ pākam.* Ceṉṉai: Kapīr Accukkūṭam.

———. 1996 [1929]. *Caṅkattamiḻum piṟkālattamiḻum.* Ceṉṉai: U. Vē. Cāminātaiyar Nūlnilaiyam.

———. 2000 [1950]. *Eṉ carittiram.* Ceṉṉai: U. Vē. Cāminātaiyar Nūlnilaiyam.

———. 2005. "Uṭaiyār pāḷaiyam," in: Pacupati, Ma. Vē., Ñā. Mēkalā, and Cā. Cāyrāmaṉ, eds. *Ṭākṭar U. Vē. Cā. avarkaḷiṉ urainaṭai nūlkaḷ.* vol. 2. Ceṉṉai: U. Vē. Cāminātaiyar Nūlnilaiyam. pp. 221–246.

Cāmpacivaṉ, Ca. 1961. *Nāvalar nālvar.* Ceṉṉai: Teṉṉintiya Caivacittānta Nūṟpatippuk Kaḻakam.

Campantaṉ, Mā. Cu. 1987. *Tamiḻ itaḻiyal varalāṟu.* Ceṉṉai: Tamiḻar Patippakam.

Caṅkaranārāyaṇaṉ, Es. 1989. "Rājamayyariṉ 'Kamalāmpāḷ carittiram'," in: Mōkaṉ, Irā, ed. *Nāval vaḷarcci.* Ceṉṉai: Maṇivācakar Patippakam. pp. 15–34.

Caṇmukam, Ce. Vai, ed. 1975. *Cuvāminātam.* Aṇṇāmalainakar: Aṇṇāmalaip palkalaikkaḻakam.

Caṇmukam Piḷḷai, M. 1982. *Ciṟṟilakkiya vakaikaḷ.* Ceṉṉai: Maṇivācakar Nūlakam.

Caṇmukam Piḷḷai, Mu. 1984. *Irācarāca Cētupati oruturaikkōvai. Cētucamattāṉa makāvittuvāṉ Rā. Irākavaiyaṅkār pāṭiyatu.* Citamparam: Maṇivācakar Patippakam.

Caṇmukatās, Maṉōṉmaṇi. 1983. *Ci. Vai. Tāmōtaram Piḷḷai—ōr āvyu nōkku.* Yāḻppāṇam: Muttamiḻ Veḷiyīṭṭukkaḻakam.

Cantiracēkara Kavirāca Paṇṭitar, Ti, ed. 1878. *Taṉippāṭaṟṟiraṭṭu. Mutaṟ pākam*. Ceṉṉai: Kalāratnākaram accukkūṭam.
Caravaṇapavāṉantar. 1970a. *Muttamiḻ vittakar. Vētanāyakam Piḷḷaiyiṉ vāḻkkai viḷakkam*. Tūttukkuṭi: Tamiḻ ilakkiyak kaḻakam.
Caravaṇapavāṉantar, Cuvāmi. 1970b. *Paḻaṉi Māmpaḻak Kavicciṅka Nāvalar. Icaip pērurai*. Ceṉṉai: Visvakarma Puttaka Veḷiyīṭṭuk Kuḻu.
Caravaṇap Perumāḷ Kavirāyar, A. 1887. *Viṟaliviṭu tūtu*. [Ceṉṉai]: Cuntaravilāca accukkūṭam.
Cauntarapāṇṭiyaṉ, Es. 1988. *Tamiḻil avaiyaṭakkap pāṭalkaḷ*. Ceṉṉai: Stār Piracuram.
Cēcaiyā, Mā, comm. 1960. *Māyūram Vētanāyakaṉāriṉ Tiruvaruḷ mālai*. Maturai: Tēnopili Accakam.
Cēcaiyā, Mā. 1989. *Mutal tamiḻ nāvalāciriyar nītipati Vētanāyakar*. Ceṉṉai: Vāṉati Patippakam.
Celvam, Kō. 2000. *Va.Vē.Cu. Aiyar*. Pututilli: Cākittiya Akkātemi.
Celvarācaṉ, Cillaiyūr. 1967. *Īḻattil tamiḻ nāval vaḷarcci*. Ceṉṉai: Aruḷ nilaiyam.
Cēṣaiyaṅkār, Tū. Vī. 1875. *Ātiyūr avatāṉi caritam*. Madras: Sreedhara Press.
Cētuppiḷḷai, Rā. Pi. 1964. *Kālṭuvel Ayar caritam*. Ceṉṉai: Paḻaṉiyappā Piratars.
Cevvantināta Tēcikar, ed. 1939. *Civacampup pulavar pirapantat tiraṭṭu. Mutaṟ pākam*. Cuṉṉākam: n.p.
Ceyarāmaṉ, Na. Vī. 1965. *Tūtu ilakkiyaṅkaḷ*. Citamparam: Maṇivācakar Nūlakam.
———. 1966. *Ulā ilakkiyaṅkaḷ*. Citamparam: Maṇivācakar Nūlakam.
———. 1981. *Pāṭṭiyalum ilakkiya vakaikaḷum*. Ceṉṉai: Ilakkiyap Patippakam.
———. 1983. *Ciṟṟilakkiyap pulavar akarāti*. Ceṉṉai: Pāri Nilaiyam.
Chandrewarnam Mudaliyar, A. Santiagopulle. 1875. *The Kathácintámani. A Series of Narratives in Tamil, edited for the use of the members of the Civil Service*. Colombo.
Cīṉivācaṉ, Araṅka. 1984. *Kāvaṭiccintum kaviñaṉ varalāṟum*. Ceṉṉai: Cēkar patippakam.
———. 1988. *Koṭṭaiyūr Civakkoḻuntu Tēcikar iyaṟṟiya Carapēntira pūpāla kuṟavañci nāṭakam*. Ceṉṉai: Aintiṇaip patippakam.
Ciṅkāravēlu Mutaliyār, Ā. 1910. *Apitāṉa Cintāmaṇi*. Ceṉṉai: Vaijayanti Accuyantiracālai.
Cirañcīvi, ed. 1958. *Mūṉṟu kātal pirapantaṅkaḷ. Kūḷappa Nāyakkaṉ Kātal, Viṟali viṭu tūtu, Cētupati viṟali viṭu tūtu*. Ceṉṉai: Pirēmā Piracuram.

———. 1981a. *Cētupatikaḷ varalāṟu*. Ceṉṉai: Apirāmi Papḷikēṣaṉs.

———. 1981b. *Putukkōṭṭai camastāṉa varalāṟu*. Ceṉṉai: Apirāmi Papḷikēṣaṉs.

Citamparaṉār, Cāmi. 1955. *Muṉcīp Vētanāyakam Piḷḷai*. Ceṉṉai: M. D. Nākapūṣaṇam and Son.

Cītālaṭcumi, Vē. 1985. *Tamiḻ nāvalkaḷ (akara varicai)*. Ceṉṉai: Ulakattamiḻārāycci Niṟuvaṉam.

Civakāmi, Ca. 1994. *Pattoṉpatām nūṟṟāṇṭut tamiḻ ilakkiyam*. Ceṉṉai: Ulakattamiḻārāycci Niṟuvaṉam.

Civaliṅkarājā, Es., and Carasvati Civaliṅkarājā. 2000. *Pattoṉpatām nūṟṟāṇṭil yāḻppāṇattut tamiḻkkalvi*. Koḻumpu/Ceṉṉai: Kumaraṉ puttaka illam.

Cokkaliṅkaṉ, Rāya, ed. 1947. *Cētupati viṟaliviṭu tūtu*. Kāraikkuṭi: Ilakkiyap Patippakam.

Colviḷaṅkum Perumāḷ, Pū. 1981. *Ṭāktar U.Vē.Cā. patippuppaṇi—ōr āyvu*. Maturai: Vañcikkō patippakam.

Cōmacuntaraṉār, Po. Vē, ed. 1970. *Tirukkōvaiyār. Paḻaiya uraiyum putiya viḷakkamum*. Ceṉṉai: Kaḻakam.

Cuntaramati, Kuḷōṟiyā. 1984. *U.Vē.Cā. caṅka ilakkiyap patippukaḷ*. Ceṉṉai: Ulakattamiḻārāycci Niṟuvaṉam.

Cuntaramūrtti, I. 1980. "Tūtu," in: Cuppiramaṇiyaṉ/Vijayalaṭcumi (1980: 307–340).

Cuntararācaṉ, Cē. 1996. *Ulakak kiṟittuvat tamiḻt toṇṭar*. Ceṉṉai: Pāri Nilaiyam.

Cuntararājaṉ, Pe. Kō, and Cō. Civapātacuntaram. 1977. *Tamiḻ nāval: nūṟāṇṭu varalāṟum vaḷarcciyum*. [Tamil Novel: A Century of Growth.] Madras: Christian Literature Society.

Cuppiramaṇiyaṉ, Ca. Vē. 1980. *Pirapantatīpam*. Ceṉṉai: Tamiḻp patippakam.

Cuppiramaṇiyaṉ, Ca. Vē, and Ra. Vijayalaṭcumi, eds. 1980. *Tamiḻ ilakkiyak koḷkai 7*. Ceṉṉai: Ulakattamiḻārāycci Niṟuvaṉam.

Cuppiramaṇiyaṉ, Ca. Vē, and Annie Thomas, eds. 1982. *Pirapantatīpikai*. Ceṉṉai: Ulakattamiḻārāycci Niṟuvaṉam.

Cuppiramaṇiyaṉ, Ca. Vē, and Kē. Pakavati, eds. 1983. *Tamiḻ ilakkiyak koḷkai 8*. Ceṉṉai: Ulakattamiḻārāycci Niṟuvaṉam.

Cuppiramaṇiyappiḷḷai, Nā, comm. 1939. *Palavittuvāṉkaḷ pāṭiya taṉippāṭaṟṟiraṭṭu. Iraṇṭām pākam*. Ceṉṉai: Irattiṉa Nāyakar Saṉs.

Cupramaṇiyam, Ka. Nā. 1957. *Mutal aintu tamiḻ nāvalkaḷ*. Ceṉṉai: Amuta Nilaiyam.

———. 1985. *Nāval kalai*. Ceṉṉai: Kalaiñāṉ Patippakam.

Cūriyanārāyaṇa Cāstiri, Vi. Kō. 1963 [1897]. *Mativāṇaṉ. Putuvatu puṉaintatōr centamiḻk katai*. Maturai: Vi. Cū. Cuvāminātaṉ.

Iḷaṅkumaraṉ, Irā. 1985. *Ilakkiya vakai akarāti*. Citamparam: Maṇivācakar patippakam.

———. 1991. *Tamiḻ vaḷartta Tāmōtaraṉār*. Ceṉṉai: Teṉṉintiya Caivacittānta Nūṟpatippuk Kaḻakam.

———. 2000 [1995]. *Maṟaimalai Aṭikaḷ*. Pututilli: Cākittiya Akkātemi.

Irācakōpālaṉ, Ca. 1999. *Vētanāyakar pōṟṟiya peṇmai*. Ceṉṉai: Aṉpup patippakam.

Irācu, Ce. 2003. *U. Vē. Cā. patippup paṇiyum paṉmuka māṭciyum*. Ceṉṉai: Ulakattamiḻārāycci Niṟuvaṉam.

Irākavaiyaṅkār, Mu. 1951 [1948]. *Centamiḻ vaḷartta tēvarkaḷ*. Tiruccirāppaḷḷi, Ceṉṉai: T.G. Kōpāl Piḷḷai.

Irākavaiyaṅkār, Rā. 1928. *Cētunāṭun tamiḻum*. 2nd ed. Maturai: Tamiḻ ccaṅkamuttirācālai.

Irakupati, Ṭi. Jē. 1999. "Piratāpa Mutaliyār carittiram—nāvalā?," in: Iḷavaracu, Irā. and A.A. Maṇavāḷaṉ (eds.). *Poruḷ putitu*. Ceṉṉai: Ulakattamiḻārāycci Niṟuvaṉam. pp. 11–14.

Irāmacāmi Piḷḷai, Ce. Re., comm. 1952. *Māmpaḻak Kaviccińka Nāvalar iyaṟṟiya cantiravilācam*. Ceṉṉai: Teṉṉintiya Caivacittānta Nūṟpatippuk Kaḻakam.

Irāmacāmippulavar, Cu. A. 1953. *Tamiḻp pulavar varicai. Nāṉkām puttakam*. Ceṉṉai: Teṉṉintiya Caivacittānta Nūṟpatippuk Kaḻakam.

———. 1955a. *Tamiḻppulavar varicai. Eḻām pustakam*. Ceṉṉai: Teṉṉintiya Caivacittānta Nūṟpatippuk Kaḻakam.

———. 1955b. *Tamiḻppulavar varicai. Eṭṭām pustakam*. Ceṉṉai: Teṉṉintiya Caivacittānta Nūṟpatippuk Kaḻakam.

———. 1955c. *Tamiḻppulavar varicai. Pattām pustakam*. Ceṉṉai: Teṉṉintiya Caivacittānta Nūṟpatippuk Kaḻakam.

———. 1955d. *Tamiḻppulavar varicai. Patiṉōṟām pustakam*. Ceṉṉai: Teṉṉintiya Caivacittānta Nūṟpatippuk Kaḻakam.

———. 1955e. *Tamiḻppulavar varicai. Paṉṉiraṇṭām pustakam*. Ceṉṉai: Teṉṉintiya Caivacittānta Nūṟpatippuk Kaḻakam.

———. 1956a. *Tamiḻppulavar varicai. Patiṉmūṉṟām pustakam*. Ceṉṉai: Teṉṉintiya Caivacittānta Nūṟpatippuk Kaḻakam.

———. 1956b. *Tamiḻppulavar varicai. Patiṉāṉkām pustakam*. Ceṉṉai: Teṉṉintiya Caivacittānta Nūṟpatippuk Kaḻakam.

———. 1956c. *Tamiḻppulavar varicai. Patiṉaintām pustakam*. Ceṉṉai: Teṉṉintiya Caivacittānta Nūṟpatippuk Kaḻakam.

———. 1958a. *Tamiḻppulavar varicai. Patiṉāṟām pustakam*. Ceṉṉai: Teṉṉintiya Caivacittānta Nūṟpatippuk Kaḻakam.

———. 1958b. *Tamiḻppulavar varicai. Patiṉeṭṭām pustakam*. Ceṉṉai: Teṉṉintiya Caivacittānta Nūṟpatippuk Kaḻakam.

———. 1958c. *Tamiḻppulavar varicai. Pattoṉpatām pustakam*. Ceṉṉai: Teṉṉintiya Caivacittānta Nūṟpatippuk Kaḻakam.
———. 1958d. *Tamiḻppulavar varicai. Irupatām pustakam*. Ceṉṉai: Teṉṉintiya Caivacittānta Nūṟpatippuk Kaḻakam.
———. 1959. *Tamiḻppulavar akaravaricai. Mutaṟ pakuti*. Ceṉṉai: Teṉṉintiya Caivacittānta Nūṟpatippuk Kaḻakam.
———. 1960a. *Tamiḻppulavar akaravaricai. Mūṉṟām pakuti*. Ceṉṉai: Teṉṉintiya Caivacittānta Nūṟpatippuk Kaḻakam.
———. 1960b. *Tamiḻppulavar varicai. Irupattiraṇṭām pustakam*. Ceṉṉai: Teṉṉintiya Caivacittānta Nūṟpatippuk Kaḻakam.
———. 1960c. *Tamiḻppulavar varicai. Irupattumūṉṟām pustakam*. Ceṉṉai: Teṉṉintiya Caivacittānta Nūṟpatippuk Kaḻakam.
———. 1962. *Tamiḻp pulavar akaravaricai. Iraṇṭām tokuti. Mutaṟ pakuti*. Ceṉṉai: Teṉṉintiya Caivacittānta Nūṟpatippuk Kaḻakam.
———, ed. 1964a. *Taṉippāṭal tiraṭṭu. Iraṇṭām pakuti*. Ceṉṉai: Teṉṉintiya Caivacittānta Nūṟpatippuk Kaḻakam.
———, ed. 1964b. *Taṉippāṭal tiraṭṭu. Mūṉṟām pakuti*. Ceṉṉai: Teṉṉintiya Caivacittānta Nūṟpatippuk Kaḻakam.
———, ed. 1964c. *Taṉippāṭal tiraṭṭu. Nāṉkām pakuti*. Ceṉṉai: Teṉṉintiya Caivacittānta Nūṟpatippuk Kaḻakam.
———. 1965 [1953]. *Tamiḻp pulavar varicai. Aintām puttakam*. Ceṉṉai: Teṉṉintiya Caivacittānta Nūṟpatippuk Kaḻakam.
Irāmaiyā, Mā. 1978. *Malēciya tamiḻ ilakkiya varalāṟu*. Cēlam: Puraṭcip paṇṇai.
Irāmaliṅkam Piḷḷai, Ve. 1977. *Eṉ katai*. Ceṉṉai.
Jagannathan, Kee. Vaa., ed. 1950. *Three Tamil Operas. 1. Madana Sundara Prasada Santana Vilasam, 2. Pandya Keli Vilasa Natakam, 3. Pururava Natakam*. Tanjore: Saraswathi Mahal Library.
Jāṉ Ammaiyār, Lū. 1967. "Carapēntira pūpāla kuṟavañci," in: *Ciṟṟilakkiyac coṟpoḻivukaḷ*. vol. 3. Tirunelvēli: Teṉṉintiya Caivacittānta Nūṟpatippuk kaḻakam. pp. 275–292.
Kācirācaṉ, Es. Ṭi. 1987. *U.Vē.Cā. oru tamiḻ vāḻvu*. Ceṉṉai: Ulakattamiḻārāycci Niṟuvaṉam.
Kācirācaṉ, Irā. 1987. *U.Vē.Cā. kāppiyap patippukaḷ*. Ceṉṉai: Ulakattamiḻārāycci Niṟuvaṉam.
Kailācapati, Ka. 1987. *Tamiḻ nāval ilakkiyam*. (Studies in the Tamil Novel). Ceṉṉai: New Century Book House.
Kailācapiḷḷai, Ta. 1999 [1916]. *Ārumuka Nāvalar carittiram*. Citamparam: Śrī Ārumuka Nāvalar caivappirakāca vittiyācālai aṟakkaṭṭaḷai.
Kaliyāṇacuntaraṉār, Tiru. Vi. 1969 [1944]. *Tiru. Vi. Ka. vāḻkkaik kuṟippukkaḷ*. Ceṉṉai: Teṉṉintiya Caivacittānta Nūṟpatippuk Kaḻakam.

Kamāl, Es. Em. 1987. *Viṭutalaip pōril cētupati maṉṉar*. Ceṉṉai: New Century Book House.
———. 1989. *Māvīrar Marutupāṇṭiyar*. Irāmanātapuram: Ṣarmiḷā.
———. 1992. *Maṉṉar Pāskara Cētupati*. Irāmanātapuram: Ṣarmiḷā.
———. 1997. *Cīrmiku Civakaṅkai cīmai*. Civakaṅkai: Pacumpoṉ māvaṭṭa kalai, ilakkiya varalāṟṟu āyvu maiyam.
———. 2001. *Maṟavar cīmai māvīraṉ Mayilappaṉ*. Irāmanātapuram: Ṣarmiḷā.
———. 2002. *Cētupati maṉṉar kalveṭṭukkaḷ*. Irāmanātapuram: Carmiḷā.
———. 2003. *Cētupati maṉṉar varalāṟu*. Irāmanātapuram: Carmiḷā.
Kamāl, Es. Em., and Nā. Mukammatu Cerīpu. 1984. *Irāmanātapuram māvaṭṭam. Varalāṟṟu kuṟippukaḷ*. Paramakkuṭi: Leṉiṉ camūka varalāṟṟu ārāycci niṟuvaṉam.
Kaṉakarattiṉa Upāttiyāyar, Vē. 1968. [1882]. *Śrīlaśrī Nallūr Āṟumukanāvalar carittiram*. Yāḻppāṇam: Nāvalar nūṟṟāṇṭu viḻāc capaiyiṉar.
Kaṇapatip Piḷḷai, Mu. 1967. *Īḻanāṭṭiṉ tamiḻc cuṭarmaṇikaḷ*. Ceṉṉai: Pāri nilaiyam.
Kantacāmikkavirāyar, Mu. Rā., ed. 1908. *Taṉicceyyuṭcintāmaṇi. Mutaṟ pākam*. Maturai: Vivēkapāṉu Acciyantiracālai.
Kastūriraṅka Ayyar, A. S. 1909. *Rājam Aiyar caritai*. Ceṉṉai: General Publications.
Kautamaṉ, Rāj. 2001. *Kaṇmūṭi vaḻakkam elām maṇmūṭippōka . . .! Ci. Irāmaliṅkam (1823–1874)*. Ceṉṉai: Tamiḻiṉi.
Kaviyaḻakaṉ. 1981. *Tamiḻ vaḷartta periyār: Vētanāyakam Piḷḷai*. Maturai: Cōmu puttaka nilaiyam.
Kiṟisṭi, Liṉṭā. 1994. "Vētanāyakam Piḷḷaiyiṉ nāvalkaḷ—Oru peṇṇiya nōkkut tiṟaṉāyvu," in: Caṇmukacuntaram, Cu., ed. *Peṇṇiyamum kalai ilakkiya piratikaḷum*. Bangalore: Kāvya. pp. 69–77.
Kiṟisṭi Merci, Em. 1995. *Vētanāyakarum avaratu nūlkaḷum*. unpublished Ph.D. thesis. Tirunelveli: Manonmaniam Sundaranar University.
Kiruṣṇacāmi, Vē. 1974. *Tamiḻil talapurāṇa ilakkiyam*. Nākarkōvil: Kiruṣṇā Accakam.
Kiruṣṇaṉ, Pa. 1984. *Tamiḻ nūlkaḷil tamiḻ moḻi tamiḻ iṉam tamiḻ nāṭu*. Ceṉṉai: Iḷantamiḻar Patippakam.
Kōvintarāca Mutaliyār, Kā. Ra., ed. 1966. *Nāṟkavirāca Nampi iyaṟṟiya akapporuḷ viḷakkam paḻaiya uraiyuṭaṉ*. Tirunelvēli: Teṉṉintiya Caivacittānta Nūṟpatippuk kaḻakam.
Kulēntiraṉ, Ñāṉa, and Kē. Pi. Kiṭṭappā, eds. 1994. *Nāṭṭiya pāṭṭicai: Tañcai carapēntira pūpālak kuṟavañci*. Tañcāvūr: Tamiḻp palkalaikkaḻakam.

Kurusvāmi Carmā, Cu. Vai. 1980 [1893]. *Pirēmakalāvatyam*. Ceṉṉai: Vāṉavil Piracuram.
Kurumūrtti, Piramīḻā. 2003. *Kōpālakiruṣṇapāratiyār*. Pututilli: Cākittiya Akkātemi.
Makāliṅkam, Ci. 2002. *Tirukkayilāya paramparait Tiruvāvaṭutuṟai ātīṉam varālaṟṟuc curukkam (A Short History of the Thiruvavaduthurai Adheenam Mutt)*. Tiruvāvaṭutuṟai: Tiruvāvaṭutuṟai ātīṉam Caracuvati Makāl Nūlnilaiya Āyvu Maiyam.
Maṇi, Pe. Cu. 1993. *Va.Vē.Cu. Aiyar araciyal—ilakkiya paṇikaḷ*. Ceṉṉai: Ulakattamiḻārāycci Niṟuvaṉam.
Māṇikkam, Va. Cupa, ed. 1974. *Tamiḻppulavar varalāṟṟuk kalañciyam. Pakuti I.* Aṇṇāmalainakar: Aṇṇāmalaip palkalaikkaḻakam.
Maṉōkaraṉ, Mī. 1994. *Marutupāṇṭiya maṉṉarkaḷ (1780–1801)*. Civakaṅkai: Aṉṉam.
Maraikkār, Cittilevvai Mukammatu Kācim. 1974 [1885]. *Acaṉpē carittiram*. Tiruccirāppaḷḷi: Jamāl Mukamatu Kallūri.
Mātavaṉ, Vē. Rā. 1983. "Cittirakkavikaḷ," in: Cuppiramaṇiyaṉ/Pakavati (1983: 149–245).
Mātavaṉ, Vē. Irā, ed. 1994. *Vaṇṇaccarapam Taṇṭapāṇi Cuvāmikaḷ iyaṟṟiya Vīrakēraḷamputūr Navanītakiruṭṭiṉaṉ kalampakam*. Tañcāvūr: Pāvai Veḷiyīṭṭakam.
Mātavaṉ, Vē. Rā. 1995. *Tamiḻil talapurāṇaṅkaḷ*. 2 vols. Tañcāvūr: Pāvai Veḷiyīṭṭakam.
———. 2000. *Perumpulavar Mīṉāṭcicuntaram Piḷḷai*. Ceṉṉai: Maṇivācakar Patippakam.
Maturam Nampi. 1989. *Viṟpaṉṉar Vētanāyakar. Ōr tiṟaṉāyvu*. Virukāvūr: Kītāñcali nilaiya veḷiyīṭu.
Mīṉāṭcicuntaram Piḷḷai, Ti. 1970. *Tirunākaikkarōṇappurāṇam (kuṟippurai mutaliyaṉa)...Ampalavāṇatēcika cuvāmikaḷ... veḷiyiṭappeṟṟatu*. Tiruvāvaṭutuṟai: Tiruvāvaṭutuṟai ātīṉam.
Mōkaṉaraṅkaṉ, Kō. 1991. *Tāttāvukku Tāttā. Makāvittuvāṉ Mīṉāṭcicuntarampiḷḷai vāḻkkai varalāṟu*. Ceṉṉai: Mīṉā Kōpāl Patippakam.
Murukēcak Kavirāyar, Pa. 1866. *Śrīmatu Ulakanātacuvāmi carittira akaval, pañcarattiṉamālai, cintu, āṉantakkaḷippu*. Madras: Lyceum Press.
Muttappaṉ, Paḻa. 1983. *Cintu ilakkiyam*. Ceṉṉai: Ulakattamiḻārāycci Niṟuvaṉam.
Muttuccāmi, Em., ed. 1994. *Cētupati centamiḻt tiraṭṭu*. Ceṉṉai: Murukālayam.
Muttuvīrak Kavirāyar, Pu. 1968. *Caṅkara Nārāyaṇar kōyil Kōmatiyampikaip piḷḷaittamiḻ*. Ceṉṉai: Teṉṉintiya Caivacittānta Nūṟpatippuk Kaḻakam.

Muttuvīra Upāttiyāyar. 1889. *Muttuvīriyam*. Madras: Albinion Press.
Nāccimuttu, Ki. 1986. *U. Vē. Cā. ilakkaṇap patippukaḷ*. Ceṉṉai: Ulakattamiḻārāycci Niṟuvaṉam.
Nākacāmi, Irā., ed. 1982. *Mūvaraiyaṉ viṟali viṭutūtu*. Ceṉṉai: U. Vē. Cāminātaiyar Nūlnilaiyam.
Nākacaṇmukam. 1964. *Vētanāyakam Piḷḷai*. Ceṉṉai: Vairam patippakam.
Nākarācaṉ, Karu. 1980. "Vilācam," in: Cuppiramaṇiyaṉ/Vijayalaṭcumi (1980: 223–258).
———. 1983. *Cilēṭai ilakkiyam*. Kāraikkuṭi: Meyyammai Patippakam.
Nallaiyāpiḷḷai, Mu, ed. 1882. *Yāḻppāṇattu mayilvākaṉappulavar iyaṟṟiya puliyūryamakavantāti*. no place.
Ñāṉacikāmaṇi, Vī., ed. 1998. *Mīṭpukkaviñar Kiruṣṇapiḷḷaiyiṉ taṉ varalāṟu*. Ceṉṉai: Kiṟistava Ilakkiyac caṅkam.
Ñāṉappirakācam Piḷḷai, Ca. 1890. *Life of Mr. S. Vedanayagam Pillai. Vētanāyaka Viṟpaṉṉar Carittiram*. Ceṉṉai: Arc. Cūcaiyappar Acciyantiracālai.
Naṭarājaṉ, Vī. Pa. 1955. *Mētai Vētanāyakam*. Maturai: Maṇip patippakam.
Naṭēca Cāstiriyār, Paṇṭita. 1994 [1894]. *Tāṉavaṉ eṉṟa pōlīs nipuṇaṉ kaṇṭupiṭitta atputa kuṟṟaṅkaḷ*. Ceṉṉai: Śrī Puvaṉēsvari patippakam.
Olaganatha Pillay, L. 1964 [1925]. *A Descriptive Catalogue of the Tamil Manuscripts in the Tanjore Maharaja Sarafoji's Saraswathi Mahal Library, Thanjavoor*. vol. 1. Tanjore: Saraswathi Mahal Library.
Pacupati, Ma. Vē. 1976. *U. Vē. Cā. vāḻvum tamiḻt toṇṭum*. Kāraikkuṭi: Poṉṉaḻakammai Nūlakam.
Pākkiyamaṇi, E. 1999. *Vētanāyaka cāttiriyār paṭaippukaḷ oru tiṟaṉāyvu*. Nākarkōvil: Cutaṉ Patippakam.
Paktavatcalam, Ke. 1961. *Vētanāyakar*. Ceṉṉai.
Pālacuppiramaṇiyaṉ, Ku. Ve. 1998. *Āyvuk kaḷaṅkaḷ*. Tañcāvūr: Umā Nūl Veḷiyīṭṭakam.
Paḻaniccāmi, M. P., ed. 1908. *Mu. Māmpaḻakkavicciṅka Nāvalaravarkaḷ iyaṟṟiyaruḷiya pirapantattiraṭṭu. Mutaṟ pākam*. Maturai: Vivēkapānu Acciyantiracālai.
Paḻaniyappaṉ, Pe., and U. Paḻani.1984. *Tamiḻppulavar varalāṟṟuk kalañciyam. Pakuti II*. Aṇṇāmalainakar: Aṇṇāmalaip palkalaikkaḻakam.
Paḻaniyappaṉ, Mu. 2003. *Viṭutalaikku muntaiya peṇkaḷiṉ nāvalkaḷ*. Ceṉṉai: Ti Pārkkar.
Palarāma Aiyar, Na. 1939. *Cittira kavi viḷakkam,. . .Vi.Kō. Cūriyanārāyaṇa Cāstiriyār amaittatu*. Matarās: Vi. Cū. Cuvāminātaṉ.

Pāṇṭitturait Tēvar, Po. 1905. *Civañāṉacuvāmikaḷ mītu iraṭṭaimaṇi mālai.* Maturai: Tamiḻc caṅkam pavar piras.

Pāṇṭuraṅkaṉ, A. 1994. *Vētanāyakam Piḷḷai.* Pututilli: Cākittiya Akkātemi.

Paramacivāṉantam, A. Mu. 1966. *Pattoṉpatām nūṟṟāṇṭiṉ tamiḻ urainaṭai vaḷarcci.* Ceṉṉai: Tamiḻ Eḻuttāḷar Kūṭṭuṟavuc caṅkam.

Pāratiyār, Makākavi. 1963. *Ciṉṉac Caṅkaraṉ katai.* Ceṉṉai: Aṟivālayam.

Pārttacārati, Je. 1976. "*Ātiyūr avatāṉi pāṭṭu nāṭōti ilakkiyattil oru tiruppam.*" *Pulamai* 2.3 (July–September): 267–84.

Patmanāpaṉ, Nīla. 1978. "Piratāpa Mutaliyār carittiram," in: Irājacēkaraṉ, Irā., ed. *Tamiḻ nāval 50 pārvai.* Mēlaiyūr, Pūmpukār: Pattiṉi Kōṭṭap Patippakam. pp. 1–3.

Rācakōpālaṉ, Ca. 1985. *Vētanāyakarum peṇmaiyum.* Ceṉṉai: Oḷip patippakam.

Rājamayyar, Pi. Ār. 1990. *Kamalāmpāḷ carittiram.* Tirucci: Intirā patippakam.

———. 1994. *Āpattukkiṭamāṉa apavātam allatu Kamalāmpāḷ carittiram.* Ceṉṉai: Niyū Ceñcuri Puk Havus (New Century Book House).

Rajaruthnam, T. A. 1901. *The Life of The Hon. The Rev. Dr. William Miller [. . .] in Tamil.* Madras: Thompson & Co.

Rajaruthnam Pillai, T. A. 1934. *The Life of Rao Bahadur C.W. Thamotharam Pillai [. . .] in Tamil.* Madras: Munisawmy Mudalliar.

Rakunātaṉ. 1980. *Camutāya ilakkiyam.* Maturai: Mīṉāṭci puttaka nilaiyam.

Tamiḻaraci, Irā. 1980. "Cilēṭai," in: Cuppiramaṇiyaṉ/Vijayalaṭcumi (1980: 129–154).

Tāmōtaram Piḷḷai, Ci. Vai. 1971. *Tāmōtaram. Ci. Vai. Tāmōtaram Piḷḷai eḻutiya patippuraikaḷiṉ tokuppu.* Yāḻppāṇam: Kūṭṭuṟavut tamiḻnūṟ patippu viṟpaṉaik kaḻakam.

Taṇṭapāṇi Tēcikar, Ca., ed. 1965. *Śrī Mīṉāṭcicuntaram Piḷḷaiyavarkaḷ iyaṟṟiya Tiru Amparppurāṇam.* Ceṉṉai: U. Vē. Cāminātaiyar Nūlnilaiyam.

Taṭcaṇāmūrtti, Pi. 1979. *Nāval āyvu.* Tirunelvēli: Ilañciyār Patippakam.

Tiṇṇappaṉ, Cupa., 1993. *Ciṅkappūril tamiḻ moḻiyum ilakkiyamum.* Tēvakōṭṭai: Tēn Vaḷḷiyammai Patippakam.

Tiṇṇappaṉ, Cupa. and Ē. Ār. Ē. Civakumāraṉ. 2003. *Ciṅkappūrt tamiḻ ilakkiya varalāṟu. Oru kaṇṇōṭṭam.* Ciṅkappūr: Kaḷaikal maṉram, Ciṅkappūr tēciya palkalaikkaḻakam.

Tirumurukaṉ, Irā. 1991. *Cintu ilakkiyam.* Tañcāvūr: Tamiḻp palkalaikkaḻakam.

Tōtāttiri, Es. 1977. "Kamalāmpāḷ carittiram," in: Vāṉamāmalai, Nā. (ed.). *Tamiḻ nāvalkaḷ—oru matippīṭu*. Ceṉṉai: New Century Book House. pp. 16–34.
Vaiyāpurip Piḷḷai, Es. 1968 [1949]. *Tamiḻc cuṭar maṇikaḷ*. Ceṉṉai: Pāri Nilaiyam.
Vēṅkaṭācalapati, Ā. Irā. 1994. *Tirāviṭa iyakkamum vēḷāḷarum. Cuyamariyātai iyakkak kaṭṭam, 1927–1944*. Ceṉṉai: South Asian Books.
———. 2002. *Nāvalum vācippum. Oru varalāṟṟup pārvai*. Nākarkōvil: Kālaccuvaṭu Patippakam.
Vēṅkaṭacāmi, Mayilai Cīṉi. 1962. *Pattoṉpatām nūṟṟāṇṭil tamiḻ ilakkiyam*. Ceṉṉai: Cānti Nūlakam.
Vēṅkaṭarāmaiyā, Kē. Em. 1984. *Tañcai marāṭṭiya maṉṉarkāla araciyalum camutāya vāḻkkaiyum*. Tañcāvūr: Tamiḻp palkalaikkaḻakam.
———. 1987.*Tañcai marāṭṭiya maṉṉar varalāṟu (Mackenzie Manuscript D 3180)*. Tañcāvūr: Tamiḻp palkalaikkaḻakam.
Vēṅkaṭarāmaṉ, Cu. 1999. *A. Mātavaiyā*. Pututilli: Cākittiya Akkātemi.
Vētanāyakam Piḷḷai, S. 1860. *Nidinul, or A Series of Stanzas on Moral Subjects*. Second edition, revised and enlarged. Vepery: SPCK Press.
———. 1862. *A Translation in Tamil of the Rulings of the Sudder Udalut from 1805 to 1861. 1805 varuṣam mutal 1861 varuṣam varaiyil uḷḷa catarkkōrṭṭāravarkaḷiṉ cittāntacaṅkirakam*. Madras: Scottish Press.
———. 1885. *Piratāpa Mutaliyār carittiram*. Second edition. Madras: W. Pushparatha Chettiyar, Kalaratnakaram Press.
———. 1887. *Suguna Sunthari. A Tamil Novel. Cukuṇa Cuntari carittiram*. Madras: M. S. Yaga Pillai, St. Joseph's Press.
———. 1889. *Christian Lyrics in Tamil*. [= *Cattiya Vētak kīrttaṉaikaḷ*]. Madras: St. Joseph's Press.
———. 1901. *Penmadimalai, Penkalvi, Pen Manum*. Madras: Thondaimandalam Press.
———. 1917. *Piratāpa Mutaliyār carittiram*. 8th edition. Mayavaram: V. G. Arogiaswamy & Brothers.
———. 1924. *Peṇkalvi [. . .] Ma. Vē. Tiruñāṉacampantap Piḷḷai ceyta tiruttattōṭum arumpata viḷakkattōṭum*. Yāḻppāṇam: Taiyalnāyaki Acciyantiracālai.
———. 1957a. *Piratāpa Mutaliyār carittiram*. Ceṉṉai: Cakti Kāriyālayam.
———. 1957b. *Piratāpa Mutaliyār carittiram. Curukka patippu*. Ceṉṉai: Umātēvaṉ Company.
———. 1957c. *Cukuṇa Cuntari carittiram*. Ceṉṉai: Cakti Kāriyālayam.
———. 1966. *Piratāpa Mutaliyār carittiram. Putiya patippu*. Ceṉṉai: Caivacittānta Nūṟpatippuk Kaḻakam.

———. 1969. *Nītinūl uraiyuṭaṉ*. comm. by Pa. Irāmanāta Piḷḷai. Ceṉṉai: Caivacittānta Nūṟpatippuk Kaḻakam.

———. 1976. *Periyanāyaki Ammaṉ patikam, Tēvamātā antāti, Taṉippāṭalkaḷ cila . . .Māṇikka mālai*. Ceṉṉai: Es. Mikkēl.

———. 1978a. *Peṇmati mālai. Peṇ Kalvi. Peṇ māṉam*. Tiruccirāppaḷḷi: Tamiḻ Ilakkiyak Kaḻakam.

———. 1978b. *Peṇ kalvi*. Ceṉṉai: Caivacittānta Nūṟpatippuk Kaḻakam.

———. 1984. *Piratāpa Mutaliyār carittiram*. Ceṉṉai: Vāṉavil piracuram.

———. 1994a. *Nītinūl virivāṉa teḷivāṉa uraiyuṭaṉ*. comm. by Pā. Aṉparacu. Ceṉṉai: Caracu Patippakam.

———. 1994b. *Piratāpa Mutaliyār carittiram (mutal tamiḻ nāval)*. Ceṉṉai: Niyū Ceñcuri Puk Havus (New Century Book House).

Vimalāṉantam, Matu. Ca. 1970. *Tāyakam tanta nāyakam*. Maturai: Mīṉāṭci puttaka nilaiyam.

———. 1987. *Tamiḻ ilakkiya varalāṟṟuk kalañciyam. Tokuti 1*. Ceṉṉai: Aintiṇai Patippakam.

Sources in Other Languages

Adams, James Eli. 1999. "Victorian Sexualities," in: Tucker, Herbert F., ed. *A companion to Victorian literature and culture*. Oxford: Blackwell. pp. 125–138.

Ali, Daud. 1996. *Regimes of Pleasure in Early India: A Genealogy of Practices at the Cola Court*. Unpublished PhD dissertation. Chicago: University of Chicago.

———. 2004a. *Courtly Culture and Political Life in Early Medieval India*. Cambridge: Cambridge University Press.

———. "Notes Towards Understanding Secular Processions in Medieval South India." *NewKOLAM* 9&10. <http://www.fas.nus.edu.sg/journal/kolam/vols/kolam9&10/ali.htm>.

Almoneit, Ute. 1992. *U. V. Cāminātaiyar (1855–1942) und die klassische Tamil-Literatur. Untersuchungen zur Lebens- und Wirkungsgeschichte eines bedeutenden Tamil-Gelehrten nebst Auszügen aus seinen Schriften*. Unpublished MA dissertation. Cologne: University of Cologne.

Ambalavanar, Devadarshan Niranjan. 2006. *Arumuga Navalar and the Construction of a* Caiva *Public in Colonial Jaffna*. Unpublished PhD dissertation. Cambridge, Mass.: Harvard University.

Amur, G. S. 2001. *Essays on Modern Kannada Literature*. Bangalore: Karnataka Sahitya Academy.

Anonymous. 1894. *A Sketch of the Life of the Honourable The Rev. William Miller by a Former Student*. Madras: Hoe & Co.

———. 1901. *Christian Friedrich Schwartz, der 'Königspriester' von Tandschāur*. Leipzig: Verlag der Evangelisch-Lutherischen Mission.

Appadurai, Arjun. 1990. "Topographies of the self: praise and emotion in Hindu India," in: Lutz, Catherine A. and Lila Abu-Lughod, eds. *Language and the politics of emotion*. Cambridge: Cambridge University Press. pp. 92–112.

———. 1993. "Number in the Colonial Imagination," in: Breckenridge/van der Veer (1993: 314–339).

Apparao, Gurajada. 2007. *Girls for Sale. Kanyasulkam. A Play from Colonial India*. Translated from Telugu by Velcheru Narayana Rao. Bloomington: Indiana University Press.

Arangasamy, Palany. 1994. *Shakespeare in Tamil Versions. An Appraisal*. Thanjavur: Muthamizh Nilayam.

Arnold, David. 1986. "Cholera and Colonialism." *Past and Present* 113: 118–151.

———. 1993. *Colonizing the Body. State Medicine and Epidemic Disease in Nineteenth-Century India*. Berkeley: University of California Press.

Arunachalam, Mu. 1974. *An Introduction to the History of Tamil Literature*. Tiruchitrambalam: Gandhi Vidyalayam.

Arunima, G. 1997. "Writing culture: Of modernity and the Malayalam novel." *Studies in History* 13.2: 271–290.

———. 2003. "Face Value: Ravi Varma's portraiture and the project of colonial modernity." *Indian Economic and Social History Review* 40.1: 57–79.

———. 2004. "Glimpses from a Writer's World: O. Chandu Menon, His Contemporaries, and Their Times." *Studies in History* 20.2: 189–214.

Asher, R. E. 1969. "The Tamil Renaissance and the Beginnings of the Tamil Novel." *Journal of the Royal Asiatic Society*: 13–28. [reprinted as Asher (1970)].

———. 1970. "The Tamil Renaissance and the Beginnings of the Tamil Novel," in: Clark (1970: 179–204).

———. 1971. "Pandit S. M. Natesa Sastri (1859–1906), Pioneer Tamil Novelist," in: id., ed. *Proceedings of the Second International Conference Seminar of Tamil Studies, 1968, Madras*. vol. 2. Madras: International Association for Tamil Research. pp. 107–115.

———. 1972a. "Aspects de la littérature en prose dans le sud de l'Inde." *Bulletin de l'École Française d'Extrême-Orient (BEFEO)* 59: 123–188.

———. 1972b. *Some Landmarks in the History of Tamil Prose. The Dr. R.P. Sethu Pillai Silver Jubilee Commemoration Endowment Lectures, 1967–68*. Madras: University of Madras.

Ashokamitran. 1986. "A landmark in spite of . . . : B. R. Rajam Aiyar and his 'Kamalambal Charitram' ," in: Narasimhaiah, C. D. and C. N. Srinath, eds. *The Rise of the Indian Novel*. Mysore: Dhvanyaloka. pp. 86–92.

Baker, Christopher J. 1975. "Temples and Political Development," in: Baker, C. J. and D. A. Washbrook. *South India: Political Institutions and Political Change 1880–1940*. Delhi: Macmillan India. pp. 69–97.

———. 1976. "Tamilnad Estates in the Twentieth Century." *The Indian Economic and Social History Review* 13.1: 1–44.

———. 1978. "Introduction," in: Baskaran, S. Theodore. *The Message Bearers: The Nationalist Politics and the Entertainment Media in South India 1880–1945*. Madras: Cre-A. pp. 1–20.

Бахтин, М. М. 1975. *Вопросы литературы и эстетики*. Москва: Художественная литература.

Bakhtin, M. M. 1981. *The Dialogic Imagination*. Austin: University of Texas Press.

Balasubramanian, C. 1980. *A Study of the Literature of the Cēra Country (up to 11th Century A.D.)*. Madras: University of Madras.

Banerjee, Sumanta. 1998. *The Parlour and the Streets. Elite and Popular Culture in Nineteenth-Century Calcutta*. Calcutta: Seagull Books.

Barnett, L. D. and G. U. Pope. 1909. *A Catalogue of the Tamil Books in the Library of the British Museum*. London: British Museum.

Barnett, L. D. 1931. *A Supplementary Catalogue of the Tamil Books in the Library of the British Museum*. London: British Museum.

Barnett, Marguerite Ross. 1976. *The Politics of Cultural Nationalism in South India*. Princeton: Princeton University Press.

Barrier, N. Gerald. 1974. *Banned. Controversial Literature and Political Control in British India, 1907–1947*. Columbia: University of Missouri Press.

Bassnett, Susan, and Harish Trivedi (eds.). 1999. *Postcolonial Translation. Theory and Practice*. London: Routledge.

Bate, Bernard. 2005. "Arumuga Navalar, Saivite sermons, and the delimitation of religion, c. 1850." *Indian Economic and Social History Review* 42.4: 469–484.

Bayly, Christopher A., ed. 1990. *The Raj. India and the British 1600–1947*. London: National Portrait Gallery Publications.

———. 1999 [1996]. *Empire and Information. Intelligence Gathering and Social Communication in India, 1780–1870*. New Delhi: Foundation Books.

Bayly, Susan. 1989. *Saints, Goddesses and Kings. Muslims and Christians in South Indian society, 1700–1900*. Cambridge: Cambridge University Press.

Benjamin, Walter. 1992. *Illuminations*. Edited with an introduction by Hannah Arendt. Translated by Harry Zohn. London: Fontana Press.

Benton, Catherine. 2006. *God of Desire. Tales of Kāmadeva in Sanskrit Story Literature*. Albany: State University of New York Press.

Bes, Lennart. 2001. "The Setupatis, the Dutch, and other bandits in eighteenth-century Ramnad (South India)." *Journal of the Economic and Social History of the Orient* 44.4: 540–574.

Beythan, Hermann. 1943. *Praktische Grammatik der Tamilsprache in Umschrift*. Leipzig: Otto Harrassowitz.

Bhatia, Nandi. 2004. *Acts of Authority/Acts of Resistance. Theater and Politics in Colonial and Postcolonial India*. Ann Arbor: The University of Michigan Press.

Bhattacharya, Tithi. 2005. *The Sentinels of Culture. Class, Education, and the Colonial Intellectual in Bengal (1848–85)*. New Delhi: Oxford University Press.

Blackburn, Stuart. 1998. "Afterword—Rajam Aiyar and 'The Fatal Rumour': Making the Novel Familiar," in: Rajam Aiyar (1998: 157–175).

———. 2000. "Corruption and Redemption: The Legend of Valluvar and Tamil Literary History." *Modern Asian Studies* 34.2: 449–482.

———. 2001. "The Tale of the Book: Storytelling and Print in Nineteenth-century Tamil," in: Dwyer, Rachel and Christopher Pinney (eds.). *Pleasure and the Nation. The History, Politics and Consumption of Public Culture in India*. New Delhi: Oxford University Press. pp. 115–138.

———. 2003. *Print, Folklore, and Nationalism in Colonial South India*. New Delhi: Permanent Black.

———. 2004. "The Burden of Authenticity: Printed Oral Tales in Tamil Literary History," in: Blackburn/Dalmia (2004: 119–145).

Blackburn, Stuart, and Vasudha Dalmia, eds. 2004. *India's Literary History. Essays on the Nineteenth Century*. New Delhi: Permanent Black.

Boehmer, Elleke. 2005 [1995]. *Colonial and Postcolonial Literature. Migrant Metaphors*. Second revised edition. Oxford: Oxford University Press.

Bourdieu, Pierre. 1998. *Practical Reason. On the Theory of Action*. Stanford: Stanford University Press.

Breckenridge, Carol Appadurai. 1978. "From Protector to Litigant: Changing Relations Between Hindu Temples and the Raja of

Ramnad," in: Stein, Burton, ed. *South Indian Temples. An Analytical Reconsideration.* New Delhi: Vikas. pp. 75–106.

Breckenridge, Carol A., and Peter van der Veer, eds. 1993. *Orientalism and the Postcolonial Predicament. Perspectives on South Asia.* Philadelphia: University of Pennsylvania Press.

Bronner, Yigal. 2010. *Extreme Poetry. The South Asian Movement of Simultaneous Narration.* New York: Columbia University Press.

Buck, David C., and K. Paramasivam, trans. 1997. *The Study of Stolen Love. A Translation of Kaḷaviyal eṉṟa Iṟaiyaṉār Akapporuḷ with Commentary by Nakkīraṉār.* Atlanta: Scholars Press.

Buckland, C. E. 1906. *Dictionary of Indian Biography.* London: Swan, Sonnenschein & Co.

Bugge, Henriette. 1994. *Mission and Tamil Society. Social and Religious Change in South India (1840–1900).* Richmond: Curzon.

Burnell, Arthur C. 1874. *Elements of South-Indian Palaeography from the Fourth to the Seventeenth Century A.D.* London: Trübner & Co.

Caldwell, Robert. 1849. *The Tinnevelly Shanars.* Madras.

———. 1856. *A Comparative Grammar of the Dravidian or South Indian Family of Languages.* London: Harrison. [2nd ed. 1875, 3rd ed. 1913].

———. 1881. *A Political and General History of Tinnevelly.* Madras: Government Press.

Casie Chitty, Simon. 1982 [1946]. *The Tamil Plutarch.* 2nd revised ed. New Delhi: Asian Educational Services.

Chakrabarty, Dipesh. 2001 [2000]. *Provincializing Europe. Postcolonial Thought and Historical Difference.* New Delhi: Oxford University Press.

———. 2002. *Habitations of Modernity. Essays in the Wake of Subaltern Studies.* New Delhi: Permanent Black.

Chandra, Sudhir. 1979. "Literature and Changing Social Consciousness." *The Indian Historical Review* 6.1–2: 209–229.

Chandrewarnam Mudaliyar (1875), see Tamil section.

Chandumenon, O. 2005. *Indulekha.* Translated from the Malayalam by Anitha Devasia. New Delhi: Oxford University Press.

Chatterjee, Sudipto. 1995. "*Mise-en-*(colonial-)*Scène*: The Theatre of the Bengal Renaissance," in: Gainor, J. Ellen. (ed.). *Imperialism and Theatre. Essays on World Theatre, Drama and Performance 1795–1995.* London: Routledge. pp. 19–37.

Chaudhuri, Rosinka. 2002. *Gentlemen Poets in Colonial Bengal. Emergent Nationalism and the Orientalist Project.* Calcutta: Seagull Books.

Chengalvaraya Pillai, V. S. 1966 [1904]. *History of the Tamil Prose Literature.* Madras: South India Saiva Siddhanta Works Publishing Society.

Chevillard, Jean-Luc. 2004. "Avant-propos: Horizons des études tamoules," in: Chevillard, Jean-Luc and Eva Wilden, eds. *South-Indian Horizons. Felicitation Volume for François Gros on the occasion of his 70th birthday*. Pondicherry: Institut Français and EFEO. pp. xxi–xxix.

Christopher, G. J. B., trans. 1968. *Mayuram Vedanayakam Pillai's Deva Thothira Malai (A Garland of Hymns). A metrical translation into English*. Madras: V.G. Arokiasamy Pillai.

Clark, T. W., ed. 1970. *The Novel in India: Its Birth and Development*. London: Allen and Unwin.

Cobban, George Mackenzie. 1880. "The Hindu Temple Girl." *The Harvest Field* (July 1880): 9–11.

———. 1886. "A Chapter from the First Tamil Novel." *The Harvest Field* (March 1886): 267–273.

Cohn, Bernard S. 1987 [1984]. "The Census, Social Structure and Objectification in South Asia," in: id. *An Anthropologist Among the Historians and Other Essays*. New Delhi: Oxford University Press. pp. 224–254.

———. 1992. "The Transformation of Objects into Artifacts, Antiquities and Art in Nineteenth-Century India," in: Stoler Miller (1992: 301–329).

———. 1996. *Colonialism and Its Forms of Knowledge. The British in India*. Princeton: Princeton University Press.

Collingwood, R. G. 1972 [1940]. *An Essay on Metaphysics*. Chicago: Henry Regnery Company.

Cooper, Frederick, and Ann Laura Stoler. 1997. "Between Metropole and Colony: Rethinking a Research Agenda," in: id., eds. *Tensions of Empire. Colonial Cultures in a Bourgeois World*. Berkeley: University of California Press. pp. 1–56.

Cornish, W. R. 1874. *Report on the Census of the Madras Presidency 1871*. Madras: Government Gazette Press.

Curtius, Ernst Robert. 1963. *European Literature and then Latin Middle Ages*. Trans. from the German by Willard R. Trask. New York: Harper & Row.

Cutler, Norman J. 1987. *Songs of Experience. The Poetics of Tamil Devotion*. Bloomington and Indianapolis: Indiana University Press.

———. 2003. "Three Moments in the Genealogy of Tamil Literary Culture," in: Pollock (2003a: 271–322).

———. 2008. "Four Spatial Realms in *Tirukkōvaiyār*," in: Selby, Martha Ann and Indira Viswanathan Peterson, eds. *Tamil Geographies. Cultural Constructions of Space and Place in South India*. Albany: State University of New York Press. pp. 43–58.

Dalmia, Vasudha. 1997. *The Nationalization of Hindu Traditions. Bhāratendu Hariśchandra and Nineteenth-Century Banaras*. New Delhi: Oxford University Press.

———. 1999 [1998]. "A novel moment in Hindi: *Parīkshā guru*," in: id. and Theo Damsteegt (eds.). *Narrative Strategies. Essays on South Asian Literature and Film*. New Delhi: Oxford University Press. pp. 169–184.

———. 2008. "Merchant Tales and the Emergence of the Novel in Hindi." *Economic and Political Weekly* (August 23, 2008): 43–60.

Das, Sisir Kumar. 1991. *A History of Indian Literature. Vol. 8. 1800–1900: Western Impact and Indian Response*. New Delhi: Sahitya Akademi.

Dayanandan Francis, T. 1998 [1978]. *Vedanayagam Sastriyar and Krishna Pillai*. Chennai: Christian Literature Society.

Derrett, J. D. M. 1961. "J. H. Nelson: A Forgotten Administrator-Historian of India," in: C. H. Philips, ed. *Historians of India, Pakistan and Ceylon*. London: Oxford University Press. pp. 354–372.

D'haen, Theo. 2002. " 'White man's burden': De Engelse koloniale literatuur," in: id., ed. *Europa buitengaats. Koloniale en postkoloniale literaturen in Europese Talen*. 2 vol. Amsterdam: Uitgeverij Bert Bakker. vol. 1, pp. 377–413.

Dhandayudham, R. 1973. "The Development of Tamil Short Story in Malaysia." *Journal of Tamil Studies* 3: 7–16.

———. 1977. *A Study of the Sociological Novels in Tamil*. Madras: University of Madras.

Dirks, Nicholas B. 1982. "The Pasts of a *Pāḷaiyakārar*: The Ethnohistory of a South Indian Little King." *Journal of Asian Studies* 41.4: 655–683.

———. 1987. *The Hollow Crown. Ethnohistory of an Indian Kingdom*. Cambridge: Cambridge University Press.

———. 1989. "The Invention of Caste: Civil Society in Colonial India." *Social Analysis* 25: 42–52.

———. 1993. "Colonial Histories and Native Informants: Biography of an Archive," in: Breckenridge/van der Veer (1993: 279–313).

———. 1997. "The Policing of Tradition: Colonialism and Anthropology in Southern India." *Comparative Studies in Society and History* 39.1: 182–212.

———. 2001. *Castes of Mind. Colonialism and the Making of Modern India*. New Delhi: Permanent Black.

Dodson, Michael S. 2007. *Orientalism, Empire, and National Culture. India, 1770–1880*. New York: Palgrave Macmillan.

Doniger O'Flaherty, Wendy. 1973. *Śiva. The Erotic Ascetic*. Oxford: Oxford University Press.

———. 1975. *Hindu Myths. A Sourcebook Translated from the Sanskrit.* London: Penguin Books.
Doniger, Wendy, and Brian K. Smith, trans. 1991. *The Laws of Manu.* London: Penguin Books.
Doniger, Wendy, and Sudhir Kakar, trans. 2002. *Vatsyayana Mallanaga. Kamasutra. A new, complete English translation of the Sanskrit text.* Oxford: Oxford University Press.
Dossal, Marriam. 1991. *Imperial Designs and Indian Realities: The Planning of Bombay City, 1845–1875.* New Delhi: Oxford University Press.
Droste, Heiko. 2001. "Habitus und Sprache: Kritische Anmerkungen zu Pierre Bourdieu." *Zeitschrift für historische Forschung* 28.1: 95–120.
Dubois, J. A. 1817. *Description of the Character, Manners, and Customs of the People of India; and of their Institutions, Religious and Civil.* Translated from the French Manuscript. London: Longman.
———. 1825. *Mœurs, institutions et cérémonies des peuples de l'Inde.* Paris: Merlin.
Duyker, Edward, and Coralie Younger. 1991. *Molly and the Rajah. Race, Romance and the Raj.* Sylvania: Australian Mauritian Press.
Dwyer, Rachel. 2001. *The Poetics of Devotion. The Gujarati Lyrics of Dayārām.* Richmond: Curzon Press.
Eaton, Richard. 2000. "(Re)imag(in)ing Other^{2}ness: A Postmortem for the Postmodern in India." *Journal of World History* 11.1: 57–78.
Ebeling, Sascha. 2009a. "Tamil or 'Incomprehensible Scribble'? The Tamil Philological Commentary (*urai*) in the Nineteenth Century," in: Wilden, Eva, ed. *Between Preservation and Recreation. Tamil Traditions of Commentary.* Pondicherry: Institut Français and EFEO. pp. 281–312.
———. 2009b. "The College of Fort St George and the Transformation of Tamil Philology during the Nineteenth Century," in Trautmann (2009: 233–260).
Edney, Matthew H. 1990. *Mapping an Empire. The Geographical Construction of British India, 1765–1843.* Chicago: University of Chicago Press.
Fernando, L. 1995. "Vedanayagar and Tamil Culture." *Indian Church History Review* 29.1 (June): 56–70.
Fitzpatrick, Elizabeth B. 2000. "Balai Pustaka in the Dutch East Indies: Colonizing a Literature," in: Simon, Sherry and Paul St-Pierre, eds. *Changing the Terms. Translating in the Postcolonial Era.* Ottawa: University of Ottawa Press. pp. 85–108.

Forbes, Geraldine. 1998 [1996]. *Women in Modern India.* [= The New Cambridge History of India vol. IV.2]. New Delhi: Foundation Books.

Foulcher, Keith. 2002. "Dissolving into the elsewhere: Mimicry and ambivalence in Marah Roesli's 'Sitti Noerbaja' ," in: Foulcher/ Day (2002: 85–108).

———. 2005. "Biography, History and the Indonesian Novel: Reading *Salah Asuhan.*" *Bijdragen tot de Taal-, Land- en Volkenkunde* 161.2/3: 247–268.

Foulcher, Keith, and Tony Day, eds. 2002. *Clearing a Space. Postcolonial readings of modern Indonesian literature.* Leiden: KITLV Press.

Frenz, Margret. 2000. *Vom Herrscher zum Untertan. Spannungsverhältnis zwischen lokaler Herrschaftsstruktur und der Kolonialverwaltung in Malabar zu Beginn der britischen Herrschaft (1790–1805).* Stuttgart: Franz Steiner Verlag.

———. 2003. *From Contact to Conquest. Transition to British Rule in Malabar, 1790–1805.* New Delhi: Oxford University Press.

Frykenberg, Robert E. 1999. "The Legacy of Christian Friedrich Schwartz." *International Bulletin of Missionary Research* 23.3: 130–132.

Ganapathi Pillai, W. E. 1890. *Ettaiyapuram past and present.* Madras.

Gaur, Albertine. 1980. *Second Supplementary Catalogue of Tamil Books in the British Library.* London: The British Library.

Gehring, A. 1906. *Erinnerungen aus dem Leben eines Tamulenmissionars.* Leipzig: Verlag der Evangelisch-Lutherischen Mission.

George, K. M., ed. 1993. *Modern Indian Literature: An Anthology.* Vol. 2: Fiction. New Delhi: Sahitya Akademi.

Ghosh, Anindita. 2006. *Power in Print. Popular Publishing and the Politics of Language and Culture in a Colonial Society.* New Delhi: Oxford University Press.

Gover, Charles E. 1873. "Pyal Schools in Madras." *Indian Antiquary* 2: 52–56.

———. 1983 [1871]. *The Folk-Songs of Southern India.* Madras: South India Saiva Siddhanta Works Publishing Society.

Govindarajan, S. A. 1969. *G. Subramania Iyer.* New Delhi: Publications Division.

Grafe, Hugald. 1990. *The History of Christianity in Tamilnadu from 1800 to 1975.* Erlangen: Verlag der Ev.-Luth. Mission.

Graul, Karl. 1853. "Die tamulische Bibliothek der ev.-luth. Missionsanstalt zu Leipzig. I. Der Catalog." *Zeitschrift der Deutschen Morgenländischen Gesellschaft (ZDMG)* 7: 558–568.

———. 1854–1865. *Bibliotheca Tamulica*. Tomus I–IV. Leipzig.
———. 1857. "Die tamulische Bibliothek der ev.-luth. Missionsanstalt zu Leipzig. III. Übersetzung von Nampi's Akapporul Vilakkam." *Zeitschrift der Deutschen Morgenländischen Gesellschaft (ZDMG)* 11: 369–395.
———. 1865. *Indische Sinnpflanzen und Blumen zur Kennzeichnung des indischen, vornehmlich tamulischen Geistes*. Erlangen: Andreas Deichert.
Griffin, Dustin. 1996. *Literary Patronage in England, 1650–1800*. Cambridge: Cambridge University Press.
Guha Thakurta, Tapati. 1986. "Westernisation and Tradition in South Indian Painting in the Nineteenth Century: The Case of Raja Ravi Varma (1848–1906)." *Studies in History* 2.2: 165–195.
Guruswamy, Sridharam K. 1976. *A Poets' Poet. Mahavidwan Sri Meenakshisundaram Pillai of Tiruchirappalli*. Madras: U. V. Swaminatha Iyer Library.
Guy, Randor. 1997. *Starlight, Starbright. The Early Tamil Cinema*. Chennai: Amra Publishers.
Habermas, Jürgen. 1991. *Structural Transformation of the Public Sphere: An Inquiry into a Category of Bourgeois Society*. Massachusetts: MIT Press.
Hardgrave, Robert L. 1965. *The Dravidian Movement*. Bombay: Popular Prakashan.
Hellmann-Rajanayagam, Dagmar. 1989. "Arumuka Navalar: Religious reformer or national leader of Eelam." *Indian Economic and Social History Review* 26.2: 235–257.
Hemingway, F. R. 1906. *Tanjore (Madras District Gazetteers)*. Madras: Government Press.
Hickey, W. 1988 [1873]. *The Tanjore Mahratta Principality in Southern India*. New Delhi: Asian Educational Services.
Hikosaka, Shu and G. John Samuel (eds.). 1992. *Encyclopaedia of Tamil Literature. Volume 2*. Madras: Institute of Asian Studies.
Hikosaka, Shu, and G. John Samuel, eds. 1996. *Encyclopaedia of Tamil Literature. Volume 3*. Madras: Institute of Asian Studies.
Hiltebeitel, Alf. 1998. "Conventions of the Naimiṣa Forest." *Journal of Indian Philosophy* 26: 161–171.
Hogan, Patrick Colm. 2000a. *Colonialism and Cultural Identity. Crises of Tradition in the Anglophone Literatures of India, Africa, and the Caribbean*. Albany: State University of New York Press.
———. 2000b. *Philosophical Approaches to the Study of Literature*. Gainesville: University Press of Florida.

———. 2004. *Empire and Poetic Voice. Cognitive and Cultural Studies of Literary Tradition and Colonialism.* Albany: State University of New York Press.

Hoole, S. Ratnajeevan H. 1997. *C.W. Thamotharampillai, Tamil Revivalist: The Man Behind the Legend of Tamil Nationalism.* Colombo: International Centre for Ethnic Studies.

Howes, Jennifer. 2003. *The Courts of Pre-Colonial South India. Material Culture and Kingship.* London, New York: RoutledgeCurzon.

Hudson, D. Dennis. 1970. *The Life and Times of H. A. Krishna Pillai (1827–1900).* Unpublished PhD thesis. Claremont: Claremont Graduate School.

———. 1992a. "Arumuga Navalar and the Hindu Renaissance Among the Tamils," in: Jones, Kenneth W., ed. *Religious Controversy in British India. Dialogues in South Asian languages.* Albany: State University of New York Press. pp. 27–51.

——— 1992b. "Winning Souls for Siva: Arumuga Navalar's Transmission of the Saiva Religion," in: Williams, Raymond Brady (ed.). *A Sacred Thread. Modern Transmission of Hindu Traditions in India and Abroad.* Chambersburg: Anima Publications. pp. 23–51.

———. 1995. "Tamil Hindu Responses to Protestants: Nineteenth-Century Literati in Jaffna and Tinnevelly," in: Kaplan, Steven, ed. *Indigenous Responses to Western Christianity.* New York: New York University Press. pp. 95–123.

———. 2000. *Protestant Origins in India. Tamil Evangelical Christians, 1706–1835.* Grand Rapids, Michigan: William B. Eerdmans.

Hunter, J. Paul. 1990. *Before Novels: The Cultural Contexts of Eighteenth-Century English Fiction.* New York and London: W. W. Norton & Company.

Inden, Ronald. 1986. "Orientalist Constructions of India." *Modern Asian Studies* 20.3: 401–46.

———. 1990. *Imagining India.* Oxford: Blackwell.

Ingalls, Daniel H. H. 1989. "Ānandavardhana's Devīśataka." *Journal of the American Oriental Society* 109.4: 565–575.

Irschick, Eugene F. 1969. *Politics and Social Conflict in South India. The Non-Brahman Movement and Tamil Separatism, 1916–1929.* Berkeley: University of California Press.

———. 1986. *Tamil Revivalism in the 1930s.* Madras: Cre-A.

———. 1994. *Dialogue and History. Constructing South India, 1795–1895.* Berkeley: University of California Press.

Jagannathan (1950), see Tamil section.

Jakobson, Roman. 1960. "Linguistics and Poetics," in: Sebeok, Thomas A. (ed.). *Style in Language*. New York: Wiley. pp. 350–377.

———. 1972. "Co je poezie?," in: Stempel, Wolf-Dieter, ed. *Texte der russischen Formalisten. Band II.* München: Wilhelm Fink Verlag. pp. 392–417.

James, Gregory. 2000. *Colporuḷ. A History of Tamil Dictionaries*. Chennai: Cre-A.

Jedamski, Doris. 1992. *Die Institution Literatur und der Prozeß ihrer Kolonisation. Entstehung, Entwicklung und Arbeitsweise des Kantoor voor de Volkslectuur/Balai Poestaka in Niederländisch-Indien zu Beginn dieses Jahrhunderts*. Münster: Lit Verlag.

———. 2002. "Popular literature and postcolonial subjectivities: *Robinson Crusoe, The Count of Monte Christo* and *Sherlock Holmes* in colonial Indonesia," in: Foulcher/Day (2002: 19–47).

Jeyaraj, Daniel. 1996. *Inkulturation in Tranquebar. Der Beitrag der frühen dänisch-halleschen Mission zum Werden einer indisch-einheimischen Kirche (1706–1730)*. Erlangen: Verlag der Ev.-Luth. Mission.

Jeyaraj, Daniel, ed. 1999. *Christian Fredrick Schwartz. His Contributions to South India*. Chennai: Gurukul Lutheran Theological College and Research Institute.

Jones, Kenneth W. 1989. *Socio-religious Reform Movements in British India*. [= The New Cambridge History of India vol. III.1]. Cambridge: Cambridge University Press.

Joshi, Priya. 2002. *In Another Country. Colonialism, Culture, and the English Novel in India*. New York: Columbia University Press.

Kadhirvel, S. 1977. *A History of the Maravas, 1700–1802*. Madurai: Madurai Publishing House.

Kailasapathy, K. 1968. *Tamil Heroic Poetry*. Oxford: Oxford University Press.

———. 1979. "The Tamil Purist Movement: A Re-Evaluation." *Social Scientist* 7.10: 23–51.

Kalki. 2008. *Sivakamiyin Sabadam. Sivakami's Vow*. Trans. by P. S. Sri. New Delhi: Sahitya Akademi.

Kalsi, A. S. 1992. "*Parīkṣāguru* (1882): The First Hindi Novel and the Hindu Elite." *Modern Asian Studies* 26.4: 763–790.

Kamesvara Aiyar, R. V. 1902. *Sir A. Seshiah Sastri*. Madras: Srinivasa, Varadachari & Co.

Kandaswamy Chetty, O. 1924. *Dr. William Miller*. Madras: Christian Literature Society for India.

Kannan, K. 1983. "Tamil Isai Movement," in: Subramanian, S. V. and A. N. Perumal, eds. *Heritage of the Tamils: Art & Architecture*. Madras: International Institute of Tamil Studies. pp. 116–124.

Kapp, Dieter B. 1975. "Der Strībhedavarṇana-Khaṇḍa in der Padumāvatī des Malik Muḥammad Jāyasī." *Indo-Iranian Journal* 16.3: 183–221.

———. 2003. "Zwei neuindoarische Frauentypologien." *Traditional South Asian Medicine* 7: 144–161.

Karthik Narayanan, C. V., trans. 1999–2003. *Kalki. Ponniyin Selvan. Parts I–V*. 6 volumes. Chennai: Macmillan India.

Katten, Michael. 2005. *Colonial Lists/Indian Power. Identity Formation in Nineteenth-Century Telugu-speaking India*. New York: Columbia University Press.

Kaukoreit, Volker, and Klaus Wagenbach, eds. 1998. *Erich Fried. Gesammelte Werke. Gedichte 2*. Berlin: Wagenbach.

Kaviraj, Sudipto. 1995. *The Unhappy Consciousness. Bankimchandra Chattopadhyay and the Formation of Nationalist Discourse in India*. New Delhi: Oxford University Press.

Kawashima, Koji. 1998. *Missionaries and a Hindu State. Travancore 1858–1936*. New Delhi: Oxford University Press.

Kennedy, Richard Stanton. 1980. *Public Voices, Private Voices. Manikkoti, Nationalism and the Development of the Tamil Short Story, 1914–1947*. Unpublished PhD dissertation. Berkeley: University of California.

Kersenboom, Saskia C. 1987. *Nityasumaṅgalī. Devadasi Tradition in South India*. Delhi: Motilal Banarsidass.

King, Christopher R. 1994. *One Language, Two Scripts. The Hindi Movement in Nineteenth-Century North India*. New Delhi: Oxford University Press.

Kohl, Thomas, ed. 2002. *Abbé Jean Antoine Dubois. Leben und Riten der Inder. Kastenwesen und Hinduglaube in Südindien um 1800*. Bielefeld: Reise Know-How Verlag Peter Rump.

Kumar, Udaya. 2002. "Seeing and Reading: The Early Malayalam Novel and Some Questions of Visibility," in: Mukherjee (2002: 161–192).

Kundera, Milan. 1986. *L'art du roman*. Paris: Gallimard.

———. 2000. *The Art of the Novel*. New York: HarperCollins (Perennial).

Kunhambu, Potheri. 2002. *Saraswativijayam*. Translated from the Malayalam by Dilip Menon. New Delhi: The Book Review Literary Trust.

Lal, Mohan, ed. 1992. *Encyclopaedia of Indian Literature*. Delhi: Sahitya Akademi.

Lehmann, Arno. 1961. "The German Contribution to Tamil Studies." *Tamil Culture* 9.2: 109–115.

———. 1964. "Karl Graul, the Nineteenth Century Dravidologist." *Tamil Culture* 11.3: 209–225.
Leonard, John G. 1970. *Kandukuri Viresalingam, 1848–1919. A Biography of an Indian Social Reformer*. Unpublished PhD dissertation. Madison: University of Wisconsin.
Levine, Philippa. 1994. "Venereal Disease, Prostitution, and the Politics of Empire: The Case of British India." *Journal of the History of Sexuality* 4.4: 579–602.
———. 2003. *Prostitution, Race, and Politics. Policing Venereal Disease in the British Empire*. New York: Routledge.
Lewis, Ivor. 1999 [1991]. *Sahibs, Nabobs and Boxwallahs. A Dictionary of the Words of Anglo-India*. New Delhi: Oxford University Press.
Lokugé, Chandani, ed. 1998a. *Saguna. The First Autobiographical Novel in English by an Indian Woman, by Krupabai Satthianadhan*. New Delhi: Oxford University Press.
———. 1998b. *Kamala. The Story of a Hindu Life by Krupabai Satthianadhan*. New Delhi: Oxford University Press.
Loomba, Ania. 1998. *Colonialism/Postcolonialism*. London: Routledge.
Louis, P. J. 1963. *Vedanayagar—A Good Poet*. Tiruchirappalli: St. Joseph's Ind. School Press Dept.
Madhaviah, A. 2002. *Padmavati*. translated by Meenakshi Tyagarajan. New Delhi: Katha.
Majeed, Javed. 1992. *Ungoverned Imaginings: James Mill's History of British India and Orientalism*. Oxford: Clarendon Press.
Mangharam, Parsram, ed. 2003. *Raja Ravi Varma. The Painter Prince (1848–1906)*. Bangalore: Parsram Mangharam.
Mani, Lata. 1999. *Contentious Traditions. The Debate on Sati in Colonial India*. New Delhi: Oxford University Press.
Mantena, Rama Sundari. 2002. *Vernacular Futures. Orientalism, History, and Language in Colonial South India*. Unpublished PhD dissertation. Ann Arbor: University of Michigan.
———. 2005. "Vernacular Futures: Colonial philology and the idea of history in nineteenth-century south India." *Indian Economic and Social History Review* 42.4: 513–534.
Manuel, Indra. 1997. *Literary Theories in Tamil (With Special Reference to Tolka:ppiyam)*. Pondicherry: Pondicherry Institute of Linguistics and Culture.
Marais, F. 1963. "Vedanayagam Pillai." *Tamil Culture* 10.2: 31–41.
Masillamani, Mary. 1969. "H. A. Krishna Pillai's Contribution to Tamil Literature," in: Thani Nayagam (1969: 224–231).
Meenakshisundaram, K. 1974a. *The Contribution of European Scholars to Tamil*. Madras: University of Madras.

———. 1974b. "The Literary Renaissance of the South." *Indian Literature* XVII.1,2: 155–165.

Mehrotra, Arvind Krishna, ed. 2003. *An Illustrated History of Indian Literature in English*. New Delhi: Permanent Black.

Menon, C. Karunakara. 1903. *A Critical Essay on Sir Seshia Sastri*. Madras: Minerva Press.

Menon, Dilip M. 1997. "Caste and colonial modernity: Reading *Saraswativijayam*." *Studies in History* 13.2: 291–312.

———. 2002. "No, not the Nation: Lower Caste Malayalam Novels of the Nineteenth Century," in: Mukherjee (2002: 41–72).

———. 2004. "A Place Elsewhere: Lower-caste Malayalam Novels of the Nineteenth Century," in: Blackburn/Dalmia (2004: 483–515).

Metcalf, Thomas R. 1994. *Ideologies of the Raj*. [= The New Cambridge History of India vol. III.4]. Cambridge: Cambridge University Press.

Mitchell, Lisa. 2005. "Parallel languages, parallel cultures: Language as a new foundation for the reorganisation of knowledge and practice in southern India." *Indian Economic and Social History Review* 42.4: 445–467.

———. 2009. *Language, Emotion, and Politics in South India. The Making of a Mother Tongue*. Bloomington: Indiana University Press.

Mitter, Partha. 1994. *Art and Nationalism in Colonial India 1850–1922. Occidental Orientations*. Cambridge: Cambridge University Press.

Mohanavelu, C. S. 1993. *German Tamilology. German contributions to Tamil language, literature and culture during the period 1706–1945*. Madras: South India Saiva Siddhanta Works Publishing Society.

Mohapatra, Pragati. 1997. *The Making of a Cultural Identity. Language, Literature and Gender in Orissa in Late Nineteenth and Early Twentieth Centuries*. Unpublished PhD dissertation. London: University of London, School of Oriental and African Studies.

Moraes, Francis. 1955. "Dr. Swaminatha Aiyar, Editor and Writer." *Tamil Culture* 4.1: 40–52.

Moro, Javier. 2007. *Passion India*. New Delhi: Full Circle Publishing. [Spanish original published as *Pasión India*, Barcelona: Editorial Seix Barral, 2005.]

Morris, Henry. 1995 [1906]. *The Life of John Murdoch LL.D. The Literary Evangelist of India*. Madras: Christian Literature Society.

Müller, Srilata. 2000. "Antiquity and Sacred Writing: Tamil Literary Histories in the late 19th to early 20th Centuries." *NewKOLAM* 5&6. <http://www.fas.nus.edu.sg/journal/kolam/vols/kolam 5&6/3HistArtIcon/Antiqu&SacrWriting.htm>.

Muilwijk, Marina. 1996. *The Divine Kuṟa Tribe. Kuṟavañci and other Prabandhams*. Groningen: Egbert Forsten.
Mukherjee, Meenakshi. 1985. *Realism and Reality. The Novel and Society in India*. Delhi: Oxford University Press.
———. 2000. *The Perishable Empire. Essays on Indian Writing in English*. New Delhi: Oxford University Press.
———, ed. 2002. *Early Novels in India*. New Delhi: Sahitya Akademi.
Murdoch, John. 1968 [1865]. *Classified Catalogue of Tamil Printed Books*. Madras: Tamil Development and Research Council, Govt. of Tamilnad.
Murugan, V., and M. Mathialagan, eds. 1999. *A Dictionary of Tamil Literary and Critical Terms*. Chennai: Institute of Asian Studies.
Muttucumaraswamy, V. 1992. *Some Eminent Tamils. Writers and Other Leading Figures (19th to 20th Centuries)*. s.l. [Colombo?]: Department of Hindu Religious and Cultural Affairs.
Naim, C. M. 1991. "Poet–audience interaction at Urdu musha'iras," in: Shackle, Christopher (ed.). *Urdu and Muslim South Asia. Studies in Honour of Ralph Russell*. Delhi: Oxford University Press. pp. 167–173.
Nair, Janaki. 1996. *Women and Law in Colonial India. A Social History*. New Delhi: Kali for Women.
Nair, Savithri Preetha. 2005. "Native Collecting and Natural Knowledge (1798–1832): Raja Serfoji II of Tanjore as a 'Centre of Calculation.' " *Journal of the Royal Asiatic Society* 15.3: 279–302.
Nambi Arooran, K. 1975. "The Beginnings of the Tamil Icai Movement." *Journal of Tamil Studies* 7: 54–61.
———. 1980. *Tamil Renaissance and Dravidian Nationalism, 1905–1944*. Madurai: Koodal Publishers.
Narayana Rao, Velcheru, and David Shulman. 1998. *A Poem at the Right Moment. Remembered Verses from Premodern South India*. Berkeley, Los Angeles, London: University of California Press.
———. 2002. *Classical Telugu Poetry. An Anthology*. New Delhi: Oxford University Press.
Narayana Rao, Velcheru, David Shulman, and Sanjay Subrahmanyam. 1998 [1992]. *Symbols of Substance. Court and State in Nāyaka Period Tamilnadu*. Delhi: Oxford University Press.
Naregal, Veena. 2001. *Language Politics, Elites, and the Public Sphere. Western India under Colonialism*. New Delhi: Permanent Black.
Natarajan, S., and M. Mathialagan. 1996. "Āpattukkiṭamāṉa apavātam," in: Hikosaka/Samuel (1996: 84–85).
Nehring, Andreas. 2003. *Orientalismus und Mission. Die Repräsentation der tamilischen Gesellschaft und Religion durch Leipziger Missionare 1840–1940*. Wiesbaden: Harrassowitz Verlag.

Nelson, James Henry. 1868. *The Madura Country: A Manual*. Madras: Asylum Press.

Neumayer, Erwin, and Christine Schelberger, eds. 2005. *Raja Ravi Varma. Portrait of an Artist. The Diary of C. Raja Raja Varma*. New Delhi: Oxford University Press.

Nørgaard, Anders. 1988. *Mission und Obrigkeit. Die Dänisch-hallische Mission in Tranquebar 1706–1845*. Gütersloh: Gütersloher Verlagshaus Gerd Mohn.

Norton, George. 1848. *Native Education in India; comprising a review of its state and progress within the Presidency of Madras*. Madras: Pharoah and Co., Athenaeum Press.

———. 1850. *Speech on Education, delivered at the opening of Pacheappah's Hall in Madras, on the 20th March 1850*. Madras: Pharoah and Co., Athenaeum Press.

Oddie, G. A. 1981. "The Character, Role and Significance of Non-Brahmin Saivite Mutts in Tanjore District in the Nineteenth Century." Unpublished paper presented at the Seventh European Conference on Modern South Asian Studies, School of Oriental and African Studies, London, 7–11 July 1981. [published with changes as Oddie (1984)].

———. 1984. "The Character, Role and Significance of Non-Brahmin Saivite Mutts in Tanjore District in the Nineteenth Century," in: Ballhatchet, Kenneth, and David Taylor, eds. *Changing South Asia. Religion and Society*. Hong Kong: Asian Research Service. pp. 37–49.

Olaganatha Pillay (1964), see Tamil section.

Oldenberg, Veena Talwar. 1984. *The Making of Colonial Lucknow, 1756–1877*. Princeton: Princeton University Press.

Opitz, Michael, ed. 1996. *Walter Benjamin. Ein Lesebuch*. Frankfurt am Main: Suhrkamp.

Orr, Leslie C. 2004. "Processions in the medieval South Indian temple: Sociology, sovereignty and soteriology," in: Chevillard, Jean-Luc and Eva Wilden (eds.). *South-Indian Horizons. Felicitation Volume for François Gros on the occasion of his 70th birthday*. Pondicherry: Institut Français and EFEO. pp. 437–470.

Orsini, Francesca. 2002. *The Hindi Public Sphere 1920–1940. Language and Literature in the Age of Nationalism*. New Delhi: Oxford University Press.

Ortmann, Christina, and Hedda Ragotzky. 1990. "Minnesang als 'Vollzugskunst': Zur spezifischen Struktur literarischen Zeremonialhandelns im Kontext höfischer Repräsentation," in: Ragotzky, Hedda, and Horst Wenzel, eds. *Höfische Repräsentation. Das Zeremoniell und die Zeichen*. Tübingen: Niemeyer. pp. 227–257.

Osterhammel, Jürgen. 1997. *Colonialism. A Theoretical Overview*. Princeton: Markus Wiener Publishers.
Padikkal, Shivarama. 1993. "Inventing Modernity: The Emergence of the Novel in India," in: Niranjana, Tejaswini, P. Sudhir, and Vivek Dhareshwar, eds. *Interrogating Modernity. Culture and Colonialism in India*. Calcutta: Seagull. pp. 220–241.
———. 2002. "Colonial Modernity and the Social Reformist Novel: Reading *Indira Bai* (1899)," in: Mukherjee (2002: 212–226).
Padmanabhan, R. 1980. *V.V.S. Aiyar*. New Delhi: National Book Trust.
Pandian, M. S. S. 1994. "Notes on the Transformation of 'Dravidian' Ideology: Tamilnadu, c. 1900–1940." *Social Scientist* 22.5–6: 84–104.
Pandiyaji, Ramanatha Sivasankara, and S. A. Venkataram Aiyangar. 1896. *Celebration of the Navaratri Festival at Ramnad in 1892* (The Miniature Hindi Excelsior Series, English Number IV). Madras: Adyar Theosophical Society Library, 1892.
Panikkar, K. N. 1996. "Creating a New Cultural Taste: Reading a Nineteenth-century Malayalam Novel," in: R. Champakalakshmi and S. Gopal, eds. *Tradition, Dissent and Ideology. Essays in Honour of Romila Thapar*. Delhi: Oxford University Press. pp. 89–108.
Paramarthalingam, C. n.d. *Religion and Social Reform in Tamilnadu*. Madurai.
———. 1995. *Social Reform Movement in Tamilnadu in the 19th Century with Special Reference to St. Ramalinga*. Madurai: Rajakumari Publications.
Parameswaran, Uma. 1986. "A. Madhaviah 1872–1925: An Assessment." *Journal of Commonwealth Literatures* 21.2: 222–239.
Parameswaran Pillai, G. 1896. *Representative Men of Southern India*. Madras: Price Current Press.
———. 1902 [1897]. *Representative Indians*. 2nd ed. London: W. Thacker & Co.
Parthasarathi, J. 1990. "Akam Poetry," in: Samuel, G. John, ed. *Encyclopaedia of Tamil Literature. Volume 1*. Madras: Institute of Asian Studies. pp. 149–162.
Paul, John J. 1983. "Stages and Actors in the Drama of Indian Law: The Dismissal Proceedings of Munsif Vedanayagam Pillai (1826–1889)." Unpublished paper presented at the Twelfth Annual Conference on South Asia, University of Wisconsin–Madison, 4–6 November, 1983.
———. 1991. *The Legal Profession in Colonial South India*. Bombay: Oxford University Press.

Paxton, Nancy L. 1999. *Writing under the Raj: gender, race, and rape in the British colonial imagination*. Piscataway: Rutgers University Press.

Peabody, Norbert. 2001. "Cents, Sense, Census: Human Inventories in Late Precolonial and Early Colonial India." *Comparative Studies in Society and History* 43.4: 819–850.

———. 2003. *Hindu Kingship and Polity in Precolonial India*. Cambridge: Cambridge University Press.

Percival, Peter. 1854. *The Land of the Veda. India briefly described in some of its Aspects, physical, social, intellectual and moral*. London: George Bell.

Peterson, Indira Viswanathan. 1998. "The Evolution of the *Kuṟavañci* Dance Drama in Tamil Nadu: Negotiating the 'Folk' and the 'Classical' in the *Bhārata Nāṭyam* Canon." *South Asia Research* 18.1: 39–72.

———. 1999a. "The Cabinet of King Serfoji of Tanjore: A European Collection in Early Nineteenth-Century India." *Journal of the History of Collections* 11.1: 71–93.

———. 1999b. "Science in the Tranquebar Mission Curriculum: Natural Theology and Indian Responses," in: Bergunder, Michael, ed. *Missionsberichte aus Indien im 18. Jahrhundert*. Halle: Franckesche Stiftungen. pp. 175–219.

———. 2002. "*Bethlehem Kuṟavañci* of Vedanayaka Sastri of Tanjore: The Cultural Discourses of an Early Nineteenth-Century Tamil Christian Poem," in: Brown, Judith M., and Robert E. Frykenberg, eds. *Christians, Cultural Interactions, and India's Religious Traditions*. Grand Rapids, Michigan: William B. Eerdmans. pp. 9–36.

———. 2003a. *Design and Rhetoric in a Sanskrit Court Epic. The* Kirātārjunīya *of Bhāravi*. Albany: State University of New York Press.

———. 2003b. "Tanjore, Tranquebar, and Halle: European Science and German Missionary Education in the Lives of Two Indian Intellectuals in the Early Nineteenth Century," in: Frykenberg, Robert E., ed. *Christians and Missionaries in India. Cross-Cultural Communication since 1500*. Grand Rapids, Michigan: William B. Eerdmans. pp. 93–126.

———. 2004. "Between Print and Performance: The Tamil Christian Poems of Vedanayaka Sastri and the Literary Cultures of Nineteenth-century South India," in: Blackburn/Dalmia (2004: 25–59).

———. 2008. "The Drama of the Kuṟavañci Fortune-teller: Land, Landscape, and Social Relations in an Eighteenth-century Tamil

Genre," in: Selby, Martha Ann and Indira Viswanathan Peterson, eds. *Tamil Geographies. Cultural Constructions of Space and Place in South India.* Albany: State University of New York Press. pp. 59–86.

Peterson, Indira Viswanathan, and Davesh Soneji, eds. 2008. *Performing Pasts. Reinventing the Arts in Modern South India.* New Delhi: Oxford University Press.

Phách, Hoàng Ngọc. 2006. *Un cœur pur. Le roman de Tố Tâm.* traduit du vietnamien, présenté et annoté par Michèle Sullivan et Emmanuel Lê Ốc Mạch. Paris: Gallimard.

Pillay, K. K. 1957. "The Western Influence on Tamil Prose." *Tamil Culture* 6.3: 159–175.

Pinch, W. R. 1999. "Same Difference in India and Europe." *History and Theory* 38.3: 389–407.

Pinto, Rochelle. 2007. *Between Empires. Print and Politics in Goa.* New Delhi: Oxford University Press.

Pollock, Sheldon. 1995. "In Praise of Poets: On the History and Function of the *kavipraśaṃsā*," in: Channakeshava, B., and H. V. Nagaraja Rao, eds. *Ānanda Bhārati. Dr. Krishnamoorthy Felicitation Volume.* Mysore: D. V. K. Murthy. pp. 443–457.

———, ed. 2003a. *Literary Cultures in History. Reconstructions from South Asia.* Berkeley: University of California Press.

———. 2003b. "Introduction," in: Pollock (2003a: 1–36).

Pope, George Uglow. 1893. *The Nāladiyār or Four Hundred Quatrains in Tamil.* Oxford: Clarendon Press.

———. 1992 [1886]. *The Sacred Kurral of Tiruvalluva Nayanar.* (Reprint). New Delhi: Asian Educational Services.

———. 1995 [1900]. *The Tiruvāçagam or 'Sacred Utterances' of the Tamil Poet, Saint, and Sage Māṇikka-Vāçagar.* (Reprint). New Delhi: Asian Educational Services.

———. 1997. *Tamil Heroic Poems.* (Reprint). Chennai: International Institute of Tamil Studies.

Pratt, Mary Louise. 1992. *Imperial Eyes. Travel Writing and Transculturation.* London: Routledge.

Price, Pamela G. 1996. *Kingship and Political Practice in Colonial India.* Cambridge: Cambridge University Press.

Pritchett, Frances W. 1994. *Nets of Awareness. Urdu Poetry and its Critics.* Berkeley: University of California Press.

Purnalingam Pillai, M. S. 1985 [1929]. *Tamil Literature.* 2nd enlarged ed. Thanjavur: Tamil University.

Radhakrishna Aiyar, S. 1916. *A General History of the Pudukkottai state.* Pudukkottai: Sri Brihadamba State Press.

Raeside, I. M. P. 1970. "Early Prose Fiction in Marathi," in: Clark (1970: 75–101).

Rahman, Munibur. 1983. "The musha'irah." *Annual of Urdu Studies* 3: 75–84.

Rajagopal, Vakulabharanam. 2004. *Self and Society in Transition. A Study of Modern Autobiographical Practice in Telugu*. Unpublished PhD dissertation. Madison: University of Wisconsin.

———. 2005. "Fashioning Modernity in Telugu: Viresalingam and His Interventionist Strategy." *Studies in History* 21.1: 44–77.

Rajam Aiyar, B. R. 1998. *The Fatal Rumour. A Nineteenth-century Indian Novel*. Translated from the Tamil and with an Afterword by Stuart Blackburn. New Delhi: Oxford University Press.

Rajam Iyer, B. R. 1905. *Rambles in the Vedanta*. Madras: Thompson.

———. 1974. *Rambles in Vedanta*. Reprint. Delhi: Motilal Banarsidass.

Rajarigam, D. 1958. *The History of Tamil Christian Literature*. Madras: Christian Literature Society.

Rajaruthnam (1901), see Tamil section.

Rajaruthnam Pillai (1934), see Tamil section.

Rajayyan, K. 1969. *A History of British Diplomacy in Tanjore*. Mysore: Rao and Raghavan.

———. 1974. *The Rise and Fall of the Poligars of Tamilnad*. Madras: University of Madras.

———. 1982. *History of Tamil Nadu 1565–1982*. Madurai: Raj Publishers.

Rajendran, N. 1994. *The National Movement in Tamil Nadu, 1905–14. Agitational Politics and State Coercion*. Madras: Oxford University Press.

Ramachandran, C. N. 2001. " 'Yes, But . . .': Response to Colonialism and Early Kannada Novels," in: Ravindran (2001: 25–48).

Ramachandran, T. N., trans. 1989. *Tirukkovaiyar*. Thanjavur: Tamil University.

Raman, Bhavani. 1999. *The Emergence of the Public Arena in Nineteenth-Century Tamil Nadu*. Unpublished MPhil dissertation. New Delhi: Jawaharlal Nehru University.

Raman, Sita Anantha. 1996. *Getting Girls to School. Social Reform in the Tamil Districts, 1870–1930*. Calcutta: Stree.

———. 2000. "Old Norms in New Bottles: Constructions of Gender and Ethnicity in the Early Tamil Novel." *Journal of Women's History* 12.3: 93–119.

———. 2005. *A. Madhaviah. A Biography. Muthumeenakshi. A novella translated from Tamil by Vasantha Surya*. New Delhi: Oxford University Press.

Raman, Srilata. 2002. "Departure and Prophecy: The Disappearance of Irāmaliṅka Aṭikaḷ in the Early Narratives of His Life." *Indologica Taurinensia* 28: 179–203.
Ramanujan, A. K. 1996 [1985]. *Poems of Love and War*. Delhi: Oxford University Press.
Ramaswami Aiyar, M. S. 1932. *Gôpâlakrishna Bhârati (Author of Nandan Charitram)*. Madras: Kabeer Printing Works.
Ramaswamy, Sumathi. 1997. *Passions of the Tongue: Language Devotion in Tamil India, 1891–1970*. Berkeley: University of California Press.
Ramnarayan, Akhila. 2006. *Kalki's Avatars. Writing Nation, History, Region and Culture in the Tamil Public Sphere*. Unpublished PhD dissertation. Columbus, Ohio: Ohio State University.
Ramusack, Barbara N. 2004. *The Indian Princes and Their States*. [= The New Cambridge History of India, vol. III.6]. Cambridge: Cambridge University Press.
Ravindiran, V. 1996. "The Unanticipated Legacy of Robert Caldwell and the Dravidian Movement." *South Indian Studies* 1.1: 83–110.
Ravindran, Sankaran, ed. 2001. *The Early Novels in the South Indian Languages*. Calicut: University of Calicut.
Raychaudhuri, Tapan. 2002 [1988]. *Europe Reconsidered. Perceptions of the West in Nineteenth-Century Bengal*. New Delhi: Oxford University Press.
Rege, Josna E. 2004. *Colonial Karma. Self, Action, and Nation in the Indian English Novel*. New York: Palgrave Macmillan.
Richman, Paula. 1997. *Extraordinary Child. Poems from a South Indian Devotional Genre*. Honolulu: University of Hawaii Press.
Rösel, Jakob. 1997. *Die Gestalt und Entstehung des tamilischen Nationalismus*. Berlin: Duncker & Humblot.
Roy, Tapti. 1995. "Disciplining the Printed Text: Colonial and Nationalist Surveillance of Bengali Literature," in: Chatterjee, Partha, ed. *Texts of Power. Emerging Disciplines in Colonial Bengal*. Minneapolis: University of Minnesota Press. pp. 30–62.
Russell, Ralph, ed. 1972. *Ghalib. The Poet and his Age*. New York: Barnes and Noble.
Ryerson, Charles A. 1988. *Regionalism and Religion. The Tamil Renaissance and Popular Hinduism*. Madras: Christian Literature Society.
Sadasivan, D. 1974. *The Growth of Public Opinion in the Madras Presidency (1858–1909)*. Madras: University of Madras.
Sai Prasad, A. B. 1991. "A Critical Study of Early Social Novels and Novelists in Telugu." *Journal of the Institute of Asian Studies* IX.1: 91–104.
Said, Edward W. 1978. *Orientalism*. New York: Pantheon.

———. 1994 [1993]. *Culture and Imperialism*. London: Vintage.
Samy, A. Ma. 2000. *History of Tamil Journals (19th Century)*. Chennai: Navamani Pathippakam.
Sangari, Kumkum and Sudesh Vaid. 1989. *Recasting Women. Essays in Colonial History*. New Delhi: Kali for Women.
Sankara Menon, T. C. 1997 [1974]. *Chandu Menon*. New Delhi: Sahitya Akademi.
Sarkar, Tanika. 2001. *Hindu Wife, Hindu Nation. Community, Religion and Cultural Nationalism*. New Delhi: Permanent Black.
Satthianadhan, Krupabai. 1898. *Kamala. Eine Geschichte aus dem Hinduleben*. autorisierte Übersetzung. Leipzig: H.G. Wallmann.
Satthianadhan, Samuel. 1894. *History of Education in the Madras Presidency*. Madras: Srinivasa, Varadachari & Co.
Satyan, R. 1981. "Three Pioneer Indian Novelists." *Indian Literature* 24.4 (July–August): 78–84.
Schirmer, Walter F., and Ulrich Broich. 1962. *Studien zum literarischen Patronat im England des 12. Jahrhunderts*. Köln and Opladen: Westdeutscher Verlag.
Schmitthenner, Peter L. 2001. *Telugu Resurgence. C. P. Brown and Cultural Consolidation in Nineteenth-century South India*. New Delhi: Manohar.
Schnepel, Burkhard. 1997. *Die Dschungelkönige. Ethnohistorische Aspekte von Politik und Ritual in Südorissa/Indien*. Stuttgart: Franz Steiner Verlag.
Sears, Laurie J. 1996. *Shadows of Empire. Colonial Discourse and Javanese Tales*. Durham: Duke University Press.
Seetha, S. 2001 [1981]. *Tanjore as a Seat of Music (during the 17th, 18th and 19th Centuries)*. Madras: University of Madras.
Seshadri, K. 1979. "Setupatis' Contribution to Tamil Culture." *Journal of Tamil Studies* 15: 40–43.
Sewell, Robert. 1884. *Lists of Inscriptions, and Sketch of the Dynasties of Southern India*. Madras: Government Press. (appendix 1)
Sharpe, Eric J. 1998. "Miller, William," in: Anderson, Gerald H., ed. *Biographical Dictionary of Christian Missions*. New York: Macmillan. p. 459.
Shortt, John. 1867–1870. "Habits and Manners of Maravar Tribes of India," in: *Memoirs Read Before the Anthropological Society of London*, vol. III, pp. 201–15.
Shreedharan. 1971. "The First Tamil Novel." *Indian Writing Today* 15.V.1: 31–33.
Shu'ayb, Tayka. 1993. *Arabic, Arwi and Persian in Sarandib and Tamil Nadu. A Study of the Contributions of Sri Lanka and Tamil Nadu to*

Arabic, Arwi, Persian and Urdu Languages, Literatures and Education. Madras: Imāmul 'Arūs Trust.

Shulman, David D. 1980. *Tamil Temple Myths. Sacrifice and Divine Marriage in the South Indian Śaiva Tradition*. Princeton: Princeton University Press.

———. 1985. *The King and the Clown in South Indian Myth and Poetry*. Princeton: Princeton University Press.

———. 2001. *The Wisdom of Poets. Studies in Tamil, Telugu, and Sanskrit*. New Delhi: Oxford University Press.

———. 2001a. "Poets and Patrons in Tamil Literature and Literary Legend," in: Shulman (2001: 63–102).

———. 2001b. "From Author to Non-Author in Tamil Literary Legend," in: Shulman (2001: 103–128).

———. 2002. "*Tirukkōvaiyār*. Downstream into God," in: id. and Guy G. Stroumsa, eds. *Self and Self-Transformation in the History of Religions*. Oxford: Oxford University Press. pp. 131–149.

———. 2004. "Notes on *Tillaikkalampakam*," in: Chevillard, Jean-Luc, and Eva Wilden, eds. *South-Indian Horizons. Felicitation Volume for François Gros on the occasion of his 70th birthday*. Pondicherry: Institut Français and EFEO. pp. 157–176.

Sivapatha Sundaram, S. 1978. "Pioneers of the Tamil Novel: New Discoveries." *Indian Literature* 21.4 (July–August): 25–39.

———. 1992. "Novel (Tamil)," in: Lal (1992: 2995–2999).

Sivaraja Pillai, K. N. 1985 [1930]. *Agastya in the Tamil Land*. New Delhi: Asian Educational Services.

Spiegel, Gabrielle M. 1990. "History, Historicism, and the Social Logic of the Text in the Middle Ages." *Speculum* 65: 59–86.

———. 1993. *Romancing the Past. The Rise of Vernacular Prose Historiography in Thirteenth-Century France*. Berkeley: University of California Press.

Spivak, Gayatri Chakravorty. 1999. *A Critique of Postcolonial Reason. Toward a History of the Vanishing Present*. Cambridge, Mass.: Harvard University Press.

Sreenivas, Mytheli. 2008. *Wives, Widows, and Concubines. The Conjugal Family Ideal in Colonial India*. Bloomington: Indiana University Press.

Srinivasa Aiyangar, M. 1982 [1914]. *Tamil Studies*. Delhi: Asian Educational Services.

Srinivasan, Amrit. 1985. "Reform and Revival: The Devadasi and Her Dance." *Economic and Political Weekly*, 20, 44, 2 November: 1869–76.

Srinivasan, C. K. 1944. *Maratha Rule in the Carnatic*. Annamalainagar: Annamalai University.

Stark, Ulrike. 2007. *An Empire of Books. The Naval Kishore Press and the Diffusion of the Printed Word in Colonial India*. New Delhi: Permanent Black.

Stein, Burton. 1984. "Mahānavami: Medieval and Modern Kingly Ritual in South India," in: id. *All the King's Mana. Papers on Medieval South India*. Delhi: Oxford University Press. pp. 1–67.

Stoler Miller, Barbara, ed. 1992. *The Powers of Art. Patronage in Indian Culture*. Delhi: Oxford University Press.

Subrahmanian, N. 1979. "Social and Religious Reform Movements in Tamilnad in the Nineteenth and Twentieth Centuries," in: Sen, S. P., ed. *Social and Religious Reform Movements in the Nineteenth and Twentieth Centuries*. Calcutta: Institute of Historical Studies. pp. 331–344.

———. 1981. *An Introduction to Tamil Literature*. Madras: Christian Literature Society.

———. 1984. *History of Tamilnad (A.D. 1565–1984)*. 3rd. ed. Madurai: Ennes Publications.

———. 2000. *Psychobiography of C. Subramania Bharati*. Udumalpet: Ennes Publications.

Subrahmanyam, Sanjay. 2001. *Penumbral Visions. Making Polities in Early Modern South India*. New Delhi: Oxford University Press.

Subramania Aiyar, A. V. 1969. *Tamil Studies. First Series*. Tirunelveli: The author.

———. 1970. *Tamil Studies. Second Series*. Tirunelveli: The author.

Subramanian, K. R. 1988 [1928]. *The Maratha Rajas of Tanjore*. New Delhi: Asian Educational Services.

Subramanian, P. 1978. "Tamil Literature in the Nineteenth Century: A Sociological Study." *Journal of Tamil Studies* 13: 87–96.

Subramanian, S. V. 1984. "Novels in Dravidian Languages (History & Trends)." *Journal of Tamil Studies* 26: 65–81.

Subramaniyam, V. K. 1992a. "Piratapa Mudaliyar Charittiram," in: Lal (1992: 3209- 3210).

———. 1992b. "Vedanayagam Pillai," in: Lal (1992: 4519).

Subramanyam, Ka. Naa. 1961. "The First Three Novels in the Tamil Language." *Quest* 30 (July–September): 29–32.

Sundara Raj, M. 1993. *Prostitution in Madras. A Study in Historical Perspective*. Delhi: Konark Publishers.

Suntharalingam, R. 1974. *Politics and Nationalist Awakening in South India, 1852–1891*. Tucson: The University of Arizona Press.

Tamil Lexicon. Madras: University of Madras, 1926ff.
Tavakoli-Targhi, Mohamad. 2001. "Orientalism's Genesis Amnesia," in: id. *Refashioning Iran. Orientalism, Occidentalism and Historiography*. New York: Palgrave. pp. 18–34.
Thangiah, A. Arul. 1952. "Dr. G.U. Pope—Tamil's Ambassador." *Tamil Culture* 1.1: 52–61.
Thanh, Hoang Ngoc. 1991. *Vietnam's Social and Political Development as Seen through the Modern Novel*. New York: Peter Lang.
Thani Nayagam, Xavier S., ed. *Proceedings of the First International Conference Seminar of Tamil Studies, Kuala Lumpur, Malaysia, April 1966*. vol. 2. Kuala Lumpur: University of Malaya.
Tharu, Susie, and K. Lalita, eds. 1991. *Women Writing in India. 600 B.C. to the Present. Vol. I: 600 B.C. to the Early 20th Century*. Delhi: Oxford University Press.
Thirumavalavan, G. 1991. *Political, Social and Cultural History of the Cholas as Gleaned from Ulā literature*. Thiruvathipuram: Ezhilagam.
Thirunavukkarasu, K. D. 1971. "The Evolution of Nationalism as an Ideology in Tamil Literature." *Annals of Oriental Research* 23.2: 1–14.
Thiruvenkatachari, S. 1959. *The Setupatis of Ramnad*. Karaikudi: Dr. Alagappa Chettiar Training College.
Thompson, M. S. H. 1961. "News and Notes—Dr. Caldwell." *Tamil Culture* 9.4: 416–419.
Thyagarajan, J. 1978. "Tamil Writing: A Coming of Age?" *Indian Literature* 21.6 (Nov.–Dec.): 63–70.
Trautmann, Thomas R. 1999a. "Hullabaloo about Telugu." *South Asia Research* 19.1: 53–70.
———. 1999b. "Inventing the History of South India." in: Ali, Daud, ed. *Invoking the Past. The Uses of History in South Asia*. New Delhi: Oxford University Press. pp. 36–54.
———. 2006. *Languages and Nations. The Dravidian Proof in Colonial Madras*. Berkeley: University of California Press.
———, ed. 2009. *The Madras School of Orientalism. Producing Knowledge in Colonial South India*. New Delhi: Oxford University Press.
Trivedi, Harish. 1993. *Colonial Transactions. English Literature and India*. Calcutta: Papyrus.
Trivedi, Poonam, and Dennis Bartholomeusz, eds. 2005. *India's Shakespeare. Translation, Interpretation, and Performance*. Newark: University of Delaware Press.
Tschacher, Torsten. 2001. *Islam in Tamilnadu: Varia*. [= Südasienwissenschaftliche Arbeitsblätter, Band 2]. Halle (Saale): Institut für Indologie und Südasienwissenschaften der Martin-Luther-Universität Halle-Wittenberg.

———. 2002. *Die Hadya-Mālai des Sayyid Muḥammad "Imām al-'Arūs." Untersuchungen zu Inhalt und Kontext eines Arwi-Prabandha.* Unpublished MA dissertation. Cologne: University of Cologne, Germany.

Tulpule, Shankar Gopal. 1979. *Classical Marāṭhī Literature.* Wiesbaden: Harrassowitz.

Vadivelu, A. 1984a [1903]. *The Aristocracy of Southern India.* Vol. 1. Delhi: Mittal Publications.

———. 1984b [1908]. *The Aristocracy of Southern India.* Vol. 2. Delhi: Mittal Publications.

Vaitheespara, Ravindiran. 1999. *Caste, Hybridity and the Construction of Cultural Identity in Colonial India. Maraimalai Adigal and the Intellectual Genealogy of Dravidian Nationalism, 1800–1950.* Unpublished PhD dissertation. Toronto: University of Toronto.

van der Veer, Peter. 1998. "The Global History of 'Modernity.' " *Journal of the Economic and Social History of the Orient* 41.3: 285–294.

Varadarajan, Mu. 1988a. *History of Tamil Literature.* translated from Tamil by E. Sa. Visswanathan. Delhi: Sahitya Akademi.

———. 1988b. "Tamil," in: Nagendra, ed. *Indian Literature.* Delhi: Prabhat Prakashan. pp. 1–53.

Vargas Llosa, Mario. 1990. *La verdad de las mentiras. Ensayos sobre literatura.* Barcelona: Editorial Seix Barral.

———. 1996. *Making Waves.* Ed. and Trans. John King. London: Faber and Faber.

Vedanayakam Pillai, Mayuram. 2005. *The Life and Times of Pratapa Mudaliar.* Trans. Meenakshi Tyagarajan, with an Afterword by S. Ebeling. New Delhi: Katha.

Venkat Swaminathan. 1992. "Rajam Iyer," in: Lal (1992: 3510f.).

Venkatachalapathy, A. R. 1994a. *A Social History of Tamil Book Publishing.* Unpublished PhD dissertation. New Delhi: Jawaharlal Nehru University.

———. 1994b. "Reading Practices and Modes of Reading in Colonial Tamil Nadu." *Studies in History* 10.2: 273–290.

———. 1995. "Coining Words: Language and Politics in Late Colonial Tamilnadu." *South Asia Bulletin, Comparative Studies of South Asia, Africa and the Middle East* 15.2: 120–129.

———. 1997. "Domesticating the novel: Society and culture in inter-War Tamil Nadu." *Indian Economic and Social History Review* 34.1: 53–67.

———. 1999. "Songsters of the Cross-roads: Popular Literature and Print in Colonial Tamilnadu." *South Indian Folklorist* 3.1: 49–79.

———. 2002. "Fiction and the Tamil Reading Public: The Inter-War Period," in: Mukherjee (2002: 81–98).

Venkataraman, M. S., trans. 2003. *Kalki's Parthiban Kanavu (Dream of Parthiban)*. New Delhi: Macmillan India.

Venkata Rao, N. 1978. *The Southern School in Telugu Literature*. Madras: University of Madras.

Venugopal, Sabapathy. 1999. *Malaysian Tamil Novels Before Independence*. Kuala Lumpur: University of Malaya Press.

Vijayasree, C. 2002. "The Birth of a Genre: Telugu Novel in the Nineteenth Century," in: Mukherjee (2002: 99–116).

Vimalachandra, Arumukam. 1969. "The American Contribution to the Development of Tamil Language in Ceylon," in: Thani Nayagam (1969: 338–349).

Vinson, Julien. 1861. *Littérature tamoule ancienne: Le Râmâyana de Kamban*. Pondichéry: Saligny, imprimeur du Gouvernement.

———. 1894. *Les Français dans l'Inde. Dupleix et Labourdonnais. Extraits du journal d'Anandarangappoullé (1736–1748)*. Paris: Leroux.

———. 1900. *Légendes bouddhistes et jaïnas*. 2 vols. Paris: Maisonneuve.

———. 1986 [1903]. *Manuel de la langue tamoule (Grammaire, textes, vocabulaire)*. New Delhi: Asian Educational Services.

Viresalingam, K. 1887. *Fortune's Wheel. A Tale of Hindu Domestic Life*. Trans. J. Robert Hutchinson. London: Elliot Stock.

Visswanathan, E. Sa. 1984. "Some Major Trends in Tamil Literature up to the First Half of the Twentieth Century." *Journal of Tamil Studies* 26: 36–52.

Viswanathan, Gauri. 1989. *Masks of Conquest. Literary Study and British Rule in India*. London: Faber and Faber.

Vithiananthan, S. 1969. "Tamil Literature and Scholarship: The Pioneer Work of Christians in Ceylon," in: Thani Nayagam (1969: 330–337).

Waghorne, Joanne Punzo. 1989. "From Robber Baron to Royal Servant of God? Gaining a Divine Body in South India," in: Hiltebeitel, Alf, ed. *Criminal Gods and Demon Devotees. Essays on the Guardians of Popular Hinduism*. Albany: State University of New York Press. pp. 405–426.

———. 1994. *The Raja's Magic Clothes. Re-Visioning Kingship and Divinity in England's India*. Pennsylvania: Pennsylvania State University Press.

Wagoner, Phillip B. 2003. "Precolonial Intellectuals and the Production of Colonial Knowledge." *Comparative Studies in Society and History* 45.4: 783–814.

Walker, Benjamin. 1995 [1968]. *Hindu World. An Encyclopedic Survey of Hinduism*. Vol. 2. New Delhi: Indus.

Washbrook, David. 1991. " 'To each a language of his own': language, culture, and society in colonial India," in: Corfield, Penelope J., ed. *Language, History and Class*. Oxford: Blackwell. pp. 179–203.

———. 1997. "From Comparative Sociology to Global History: Britain and India in the Pre-History of Modernity." *Journal of the Economic and Social History of the Orient* 40.4: 410–443.

———. 1998. "The Global History of 'Modernity'—A Response to a Reply." *Journal of the Economic and Social History of the Orient* 41.3: 295–311.

———. 2004. "South India 1770–1840: The Colonial Transition." *Modern Asian Studies* 38.3: 479–516.

———. 2007. "Towards a History of the Present: Southern Perspectives on the Nineteenth and Twentieth Centuries," in: Chakrabarty, Dipesh, Rochona Majumdar, and Andrew Sartori, eds. *From the Colonial to the Postcolonial. India and Pakistan in Transition*. New Delhi: Oxford University Press. pp. 332–357.

White, Hayden. 1975. "The Problem of Change in Literary History." *New Literary History* 7.1: 97–111.

Wilpert, Gero von. 1989. *Sachwörterbuch der Literatur*. 7th ed. Stuttgart: Alfred Kröner.

Winslow, M. 1995 [1862]. *A Comprehensive Tamil and English Dictionary*. New Delhi: Asian Educational Services.

Worswick, Clark, and Ainslie Embree, eds. 1976. *The Last Empire. Photography in British India, 1855–1911*. New York: Aperture.

Wyatt, J. L., ed. 1894. *Reminiscences of Bishop Caldwell*. Madras: Addison & Co.

Yesudhas, D. 1969. "*The Pilgrim's Progress* and *Iratcaniya Yaattirikam*," in: Thani Nayagam (1969: 232–236).

Young, R. F., and S. Jebanesan. 1995. *The Bible Trembled. The Hindu-Christian Controversies of Nineteenth-Century Ceylon*. Vienna: De Nobili Research Library, University of Vienna.

Yule, H., and A. C. Burnell. 1994 [1886]. *Hobson-Jobson. A Glossary of Colloquial Anglo-Indian Words and Phrases, and of Kindred Terms, Etymological, Historical, Geographical and Discursive*. Delhi: Rupa & Co.

Zvelebil, Kamil V. 1973. *The Smile of Murugan. On Tamil Literature of South India*. Leiden: E.J. Brill.

———. 1974. *History of Tamil Literature*. Wiesbaden: Otto Harrassowitz.

———. 1975. *Tamil Literature*. [= *Handbuch der Orientalistik*, ed. by B. Spuler, 2. Abteilung, 2. Band, 1. Abschnitt]. Leiden/Köln: E. J. Brill.

———. 1986. "The First Six Novels in Tamil." *Journal of Tamil Studies* 30: 1–14.

———. 1990a. "The First Six Novels in the Tamil Language," in: Offredi, Mariola, ed. *Language versus Dialect: Linguistic and Literary Essays on Hindi, Tamil and Sarnami*. New Delhi: Manohar Publications. pp. 142–169.

———, trans. 1990b. *The Story of My Life. An Autobiography of Dr. U. V. Swaminatha Iyer. English Version. Part 1*. Madras: Institute of Asian Studies.

———. 1992. *Companion Studies to the History of Tamil Literature*. Leiden: E. J. Brill.

———, trans. 1994. *The Story of My Life. An Autobiography of Dr. U. V. Swaminatha Iyer. English Version. Part 2*. Madras: Institute of Asian Studies.

———. 1995. *Lexicon of Tamil Literature*. Leiden: E. J. Brill.

Index

Acan Pē carittiram, 258
Acanpēyuṭaiya katai. See *Acan Pē carittiram*
Āccāpurattalapurāṇam, 120
Agastya, 67, 69, 75, 80, 155, 156
Ahmad, Aijaz, 7
Aiyar, V. V. S. *See* Cuppiramaṇiya Aiyar, Va. Ve.
akam poetics, 89, 90n81, 91, 91n83, 92n85, 93–95, 99, 100, 115n15, 129, 135, 136
Akapporuḷ viḷakkam, 24n57, 90n81, 92n83, 92n84, 98n91, 115n15
Akilāṇṭanāyaki piḷḷaittamiḻ, 62, 64, 75
Aḻakiyaccokkanātap Piḷḷai, 34n3, 134, 137, 139, 144n102
alaṃkāra, in Tamil. *See* figures of speech in Tamil
Alaṅkārak kōvai, 123n44
Ali, Daud, 140
alkul, 97, 273
Ampalavāṇa Tēcikar, 61, 62
Amparppurāṇam, 46, 48, 49, 51, 52, 57, 88
anācikam (a poetic technique), 51
Anand, Mulk Raj, 8
Āṉantapārati Aiyaṅkar, Umaiyammāḷpuram, 120
Āṉantaraṅkap Piḷḷai, 24n54
aṇi. *See* figures of speech in Tamil
Aṇṇāmalai Reṭṭiyār, Ceṉṉikuḷam, 129, 130
aṉṉatāṉam (public distribution of food), 60, 134, 295
antāti (a poetic technique; genre named after that technique), 39, 40, 53, 56, 89, 13
Āṇṭiyappap Piḷḷai, 130
Āpattukkiṭamāṉa apavātam. See *Kamalāmpāḷ carittiram*
Apitāṉa Cintāmaṇi, 162n131
Appadurai, Arjun, 73
Appaiya Nāyakkar, Kaṉṉivāṭi Malaiyāṇṭi, 132n84
Araṅkanāta Mutaliyār, Pūṇṭi, 232, 245
araṅkēṟṟam (public premiere of a literary work), 70, 73, 76–79, 84, 85, 86, 162, 176, 295
Ariyilūr, 132
Arumaināyakam, Ci., 260
Āṟumuka Nāvalar, 3, 22, 36, 60, 80, 83n69, 101n92, 159, 160n122, 162, 177
Aruṇācalakkavi, 120
Aruṇācalak Kavirāyar, Makāśrī, 160n122, 253
Arunachalam, Mu., 18
Aruṇakiriyantāti, 43
Aṟuvakai ilakkaṇam, 55
Arwi (Arabic Tamil), 15n30, 210, 211
ātīṉam. *See* monasteries, Śaiva
Ātiyūr avatāṉi caritam, 208, 210
aṭṭanākapantam (a form of *cittirakkavi*), 49

avaiyaṭakkam (addressing the assembly [of fellow poets]), 73, 74–76, 295
avatārikai (explanatory comment), 77

Bacon, Francis, 216
Baker, Christopher, 58, 103n1, 104, 106, 108, 123n41, 157
Bakhtin, Mikhail M., 27, 28, 30, 31, 206
Balai Poestaka, 250
Bayly, Christopher A., 20n38, 26
Beauchamp, George Thomas, 176
Bengali, colonial writing in, 8
Bengali novel, 205, 205n1, 249
Benjamin, Walter, 160n125
Beschi, Costanzo Giuseppe, 25, 147
Bharati. *See* Cuppiramaṇiya Pārati, Ci.
Bhaskara Sethupati. *See* Pāskara Cētupati
Blackburn, Stuart, 2n3, 8n15, 13n21, 15, 16, 19, 31, 160, 166, 169, 206, 234, 240, 241, 243
Boehmer, Elleke, 4, 6, 6n9
Boileau, Thomas Ebenezer J. B., 174
book publishing, nineteenth-century Tamil. *See* publishing, nineteenth-century Tamil
Bourdieu, Pierre, 60, 73n61, 112
Bower, H., 14n23
Broch, Hermann, 212
Bronner, Yigal, 43n15, 54, 67
Bunyan, John, 36n7
Burmese, novel in, 249
Burnell, Arthur Coke, 23, 23n52, 295

Caemmerer, August Friedrich, 24
Caivamañcari, 126n55
Cakuṇā. See *Saguna, A Story of Native Christian Life*
Caldwell, Robert, 23, 230n42
Cāminātaiyar, Uttamatāṉapuram Vēṅkaṭarāmaṉ (U. Vē.)
  as editor and publisher, 22, 119, 120, 162, 163, 232
  as friend of Vētanāyakam Piḷḷai, 177
  autobiography of, 34n3, 35, 37n9, 39, 86, 112, 113, 128, 129, 131, 162n128, 173
  biography of his teacher Mīṉāṭcicuntaram Piḷḷai, 35, 36n6, 56, 57, 60, 61n49, 63, 70–72, 77, 78, 81, 85, 87n76, 87n77, 102, 122
  on *kōvais, 100, 101n92*
  on patronage in Cēṟṟūr, 133n91
  on patronage in Pudukkottai, 107, 121, 122n37
  portrait of, 161
  review of *Peṇ kalvi*, 201
Camuttiravilācam, 128n64, 141, 142
Caṅkam literature, 18, 22, 54, 89–91, 93n86, 100, 101n92, 135–137, 162n128, 232, 248, 267, 295
Caṅkaramūrttikavirāyar, Irācapāḷaiyam, 131
Caṅkara Nārāyaṇakkōyil Kōmatiyammaip piḷḷaittamiḻ. See *Caṅkara Nārāyaṇakkōyil Kōmatiyampikaip piḷḷaittamiḻ*
Caṅkara Nārāyaṇakkōyil Kōmatiyampikaip piḷḷaittamiḻ, 129
Caṅkaranārāyaṇakkōyil tiripantāti, 129n67
Cantiracēkara Kavirāca Paṇṭitar. *See* Cantiracēkara Kavirāyar, Tillaiyampūr
Cantiracēkara Kavirāyar, Tillaiyampūr, 124, 126, 136, 137, 138, 162n131
Cantiravilācam, 125, 128n64, 129n65, 130n72, 131n81, 132n87, 138, 141, 142, 143
Cantu Mēnōn, O., 239n52
Capāpati Nāvalar, 60
Capāpati Mutaliyār, Kāñcipuram, 71
Capāpati Mutaliyār, Puracai Aṣṭāvatāṉam, 87n77
captatio benevolentiae. See *avaiyaṭakkam*

Caraca Callāpamālai, 123n43
Carapēntira pūpāla kuṟavañci nāṭakam, 119, 120, 140
Carapēntirar caṉṉirōka cikiccaikaḷ, 119
Carapēntirar vaittiyam, 119
Carapēntirar vaittiya muṟaikaḷ, 119
Carapōji. *See* Serfoji II, King
Caravaṇak Kavirāyar, Vayalcēri, 128
Caravaṇamuttu Piḷḷai, Ti. Ta., 259
Caravaṇap Perumāḷ Kavirāyar, Aṭṭāvatāṉam, 125, 253, 254
Caravaṇap Perumāḷ Kavirāyar, Tuvātrīm Tacāvatāṉam, 30, 124–126, 128, 145, 253, 255
See also *Cētupati viṟaliviṭutūtu*
carittiram (history) as genre, 229–231
cāṟṟukkavi (praise poem). See *ciṟappuppāyiram*
caruppatōpattiram (a form of *cittirakkavi*), 47, 48
Carva camaya camaracak kīrttaṉaikaḷ, 202
Casie Chitty, Simon, 254
Caṭākkara Cārappatikam, 123n43
Caṭakōpa Aiyaṅkār, 132n86
Cattiyanātaṉ, Kirupā, 261
Cattiya vētak kīrttaṉaikaḷ, 202
Cavarirāyalu Nāyakar, 177
Cēkkiḻār piḷḷaittamiḻ, 36, 76n64
Cellaturai, Aruḷ, 245
censorship, 97n90, 149n112, 153n114, 158, 169, 223, 250, 250n4
Centamiḻ (journal), 126n55, 127
Cēṟṟūr, 130, 131, 133
Cēṟṟūr Muttuccāmitturai kuṟavañci, 131
Cēṟṟūr paḷḷu, 132
Cēṣaiyā Cāstiri, A., 121, 162n131
Cēṣaiyaṅkār, Tū. Vī., 208–210, 213
Cētupati dynasty, 122–128, 144–159, 253–255
Cētupati viṟaliviṭutūtu, 30, 126, 144–159, 190, 209n6
new dating of, 253–255
Chakrabarty, Dipesh, 2n3, 9
Chandu Menon, O. *See* Cantu Mēnōn, O.
Chatterjee, Bankimchandra, 8
Chaudhuri, Rosinka, 7, 8n12, 170
Chennai. *See* Madras
Chidambaram, 40, 41, 64–66, 72, 89, 94, 234, 235
child marriage, debates on, 20, 199, 200, 213n16, 238
Christian College, Madras. *See* Madras Christian College
Christian missionaries. *See* missionaries, Christian
Christian Tamil literature, 14n23, 15n30, 202
Cīkāḻikkōvai, 64, 100, 177, 182
Cilappatikāram, 24n54, 146n110, 156n117, 163
cilēṭai (double entendre; *śleṣa*), 41, 43–45, 53, 54, 65–67, 81, 82, 94, 125, 128n64, 139, 142, 150, 182, 273, 296, 297
cilēṭaiveṇpā (a literary genre), 53
Ciṅkai Nēcaṉ (newspaper), 203n63, 210
Ciṅkāravēlu Mutaliyār, 162n131
Ciṉṉaccāmi Pāratiyār. *See* Citampara Pāratiyār, Maḻavarāyaṉēntal
Ciṉṉac Caṅkaraṉ katai, 158, 159
Ciṉṉattampi Paṇṭiyaturai, Caṅkilivīrappa, 131n81
ciṟappuppāyiram (special preface; praise poem), 74, 128, 247, 296
as source for literary history, 117n16
definition, 62, 63
for *Cantiravilācam*, 129n65, 130n72, 131n81, 132n87
for *Cīkāḻikkōvai*, 62–73, 182
for *Nītinūl*, *180*
in printed books, 162, 163
poetics of, 62–73
Ciṟiya Caravaṇap Perumāḷ Kavirāyar. *See* Caravaṇap Perumāḷ Kavirāyar, Tuvātrīm Tacāvatāṉam

ciṟṟilakkiyam (minor literature). See *pirapantams*
Ciṟuvayal, 132, 162n131
Citamparam. *See* Chidambaram
Citamparam Piḷḷai, 36, 37, 45, 66, 102
Citampara Pāratiyār, Maḻavarāyaṉēntal, 122
citrakāvya (picture poetry). See *cittirakkavi*
Cittilevvai Mukammatu Kācim Maraikkār. *See* Maraikkār, Cittilevvai Mukammatu Kācim
cittirakkavi (picture poem), 46–52, 125, 296
cīṭṭukkavi (epistolary poem), 73, 81–83, 177, 296
Civacampup Pulavar, Uṭuppiṭṭi, 127
Cīvakacintāmaṇi, 24n54, 74, 87n77, 101n92, 199, 232
Civakāmi, Ca., 15n28, 60, 89, 126, 127n59, 13, 132n88, 254
Civakāmiyiṉ capatam, 18n34
Civakaṅkai. *See* Sivagangai
Civakiri, 131n81, 132
Civakirikkumarakkaṭavuḷ piḷḷaittamiḻ, 130
Civakkoḻuntu Tēcikar, Koṭṭaiyūr, 92n83, 92n84, 98n91, 118–120, 140, 160
Civappirakācat Tiruvaṇātatturai, 133
Civatattuvacitāniti, 130
Civavākkiyam, 24n57
Cobban, George Mackenzie, 179, 190, 191, 221, 222
Cokkaliṅkaṉ, Rāya., 149n112, 245, 254
Cokkaliṅka Nāyakar varukkakkōvai, 132n88
Cōḻa dynasty, 18, 106n3, 139
College of Fort St. George, 23n49, 25n62, 118n22, 160, 163
Colombo, 210, 258
colonialism, 4, 4n6, 5, 11, 16, 248–250
colonial knowledge, 10, 10n17, 11, 15
Comparative Literature, 6, 9
Conrad, Joseph, 3, 6
contact zone, 5, 6, 9, 250
Count of Monte Cristo, The, 250
Cukuṇa Cuntari carittiram, 213n16, 218, 219, 225–228, 231n43, 232, 233, 235–243, 258
  editions of, 226, 227
  plot summary, 225, 226
  See also *carittiram*
Cuntaram Piḷḷai, Rao Bahadur P., 21, 232
Cuntaratācat Tēvar, 131
Cuntarēcuvara Aiyar, 127
Cuppaiya Nāvalar, Vēmpattūr Muttuvēṅkaṭa, 56n38
Cupparāya, 63
Cupparāya Ceṭṭiyār, Cōṭacāvatāṉam, 87n77
Cuppiramaṇiya Aiyar, Ci. ē., 260
Cuppiramaṇiya Aiyar, Va. Ve., 244, 248
Cuppiramaṇiyam, Ka. *See* Subramania Iyer, G.
Cuppiramaṇiya Pārati, Ci. 130, 158, 169, 183, 245, 248
Cuppiramaṇiya Tēcikar, Mēlakaram, 61n49, 81, 82, 102, 177
Cuppiramaṇiya Tēcikar, Vēḷūr, 61, 131
Cuppiratīpak Kavirāyar, 144n102, 147
Cūriyanārāyaṇa Cāstiri, Vi. Kō., 46n21, 80, 81n68, 244, 259
Curzon, Viceroy Lord. *See* Lord Curzon, Viceroy
Cutēcamittiraṉ, 20
Cutler, Norman, 36n6, 91, 94, 95n89, 100
Cuvāmi Kavirāyar, Kalliṭaiyūr, 55
Cuvāminātam, 55

Dalmia, Vasudha, 8n15, 13n21, 31
Dame aux Camélias, La, 249

Damodaram Pillai, C. V. *See* Tāmōtaram Piḷḷai, Ci. Vai.
dancing girls. See *devadāsīs*
Dänisch-hallesche Mission. *See* Danish Halle Mission
Danish Halle Mission, 5n7, 14n23
Davidson, Thomas Hardwick, 174
Delgado, Anita, 158n120
devadāsīs, 187–192
  See also *Cētupati viṟaliviṭutūtu*
Dharmapuram. *See* Tarumapuram monastery
Dirks, Nicholas, 121, 103n1
Divyaprabandha. See *Nālāyirativviyap pirapantam*
Doniger, Wendy, 41n13, 150n113
drama, birth of modern Tamil, 21, 251
Drew, W. H., 164
Dubois, Jean Antoine, 23, 24n53
Dumas, Alexandre, 249
Dupuis, Louis Savinien, 24, 24n55
Dutt, Michael Madhusudan, 8

economy of praise, 29, 62, 73–84, 87, 101, 112, 133, 137, 163, 168, 177, 180, 247
Edward II, King, 108
Ellis, Francis Whyte, 23, 23n49
Eṉ carittiram, 35
English
  and Tamil language, 14, 20, 21, 26, 30, 138, 139, 193, 206, 209, 228, 277
  education in, 26, 170, 171, 172, 173, 173n9, 206, 232, 239
  Indian writing in, 8, 294, 295, 261
epistolary poem. See *cīṭṭukkavi*
eroticism
  colonial critique of, 187–192
  in court literature, 113, 135, 144–159
  See also prostitution; *devadāsīs*
Eṭṭaiyapuram. *See* Eṭṭayapuram
Ettappa Nayakar Bahadur, Sri Rajah Jagavira Rama Venkateswara, 108
Eṭṭayapuram, 108, 130, 141, 158
E. V. R. *See* Periyar
expurgation of texts. *See* censorship

Fabricius, Johann Philipp, 25
Fatal Rumour, The. See *Kamalāmpāḷ carittiram*
figures of speech in Tamil, 39, 46, 53, 54, 81, 142, 182
  See also *cilēṭai; maṭakku; tiripu; yamakam*
Fink, Molly, 158
Forster, Edward Morgan, 3, 6, 235
Foucault, Michel, 17
Fried, Erich, 165

Gōpālakṛṣṇama Ceṭṭi, Narahari, 211, 229n38
Gordon, J., 173–175
Gover, Charles E., 23, 38, 39
Graul, Karl, 24, 24n57
Greenway, George Sullivan, 174
Guruswamy Sharma, S. V. *See* Kurusvāmi Carmā, Cu. Vai.

Harris, Thomas Inglis P., 175
Harvest Field, The (missionary magazine), 188–191, 221, 222, 261
Hindi novel, 217, 249
Hindu, The (newspaper), 20, 58, 178, 190, 200n52, 201, 219
Hinduism
  and Tamil Renaissance, 22n44
  See also monasteries, Śaiva
History of Prathapa Mudaliar, The. See *Piratāpa Mutaliyār carittiram*
History of Suguna Sundari, The. See *Cukuṇa Cuntari carittiram*
Hogan, Patrick Colm, 9n16
Hunter, J. Paul, 217, 218, 229, 230
Husserl, Edmund, 212
Hutchinson, J. Robert, 212

Imām al-'Arūs, 210, 211
Indonesian novel, 249, 250n4
Indulēkhā, 239n52
Irācarāca Cētupati oruturaikkōvai, 245
Irācarācēcuvari patikam, 126n55
Iraiyaṉār Akapporuḷ, 54, 63n51, 64n52, 90n81, 115n15
Irākavaiyaṅkār, Rā., 245
Irāmacāmikkavirāyar, 131
Irāmacāmi Rāju, Pa. Va., 14n24, 192
Irāmaccantirat Toṇṭaimāṉ. *See* Ramachandra Tondaiman, of Pudukkottai
Irāmacuvāmi Pāratikaḷ, Puṉalvēli, 129
Irāmaliṅka Cuvāmikaḷ, 159, 160n122, 177, 183n36
Irāmaliṅkam Piḷḷai, Ve. *See* Nāmakkal Kaviñar
Irāmaliṅka Mutaliyār, Tirumayilai, 260
Irāmaliṅkat Tēvar, 132
Irāmanātaṉ Ceṭṭiyār, A. Vayinākaram, 245
Irāmāṉucāccāriyār, Caṭakōpa, 83n69
Irāmāṉucak Kavirāyar, Mukavai, 83n69, 163, 164
Irāmāyaṇavaṇṇam, 126
Iraṭcaṇiya yāttirikam, 36n7
Irattiṉapuri irakaciyam, 250n5
Irschick, Eugene, 10n17, 11n19
Iṭapa vākaṉakkīrttaṉai, 120n27
Iyēcupirāṉ piḷḷaittamiḻ, 245

Jagatjit Singh, 158n120
Jakobson, Roman, 53
Jaṉavinōtiṉi, 20
Jedamski, Doris, 250
Jeyaraj, Daniel, 5n7
Jīvaratnam, 260
journalism
  rise of Tamil, 15, 20, 26, 127, 158, 169, 190, 191, 232, 247, 248, 250
  See also publishing, nineteenth-century Tamil

Kaccik kalampakam, 232, 245
Kaccik Kalyāṇaraṅka Uṭaiyār, 113, 131
Kacciraṅkappa Uṭaiyār, 131
Kācivicuvanāta Mutaliyār, Caitāpuram, 14n24, 192
Kalittokai, 162n131
Kaliyāṇacuntara Mutaliyār, Tiru. Vi., 162n129
Kalki (Ra. Kiruṣṇamūrtti), 18, 18n34
Kallaṇai vaipavakkīrttaṉai, 120n27
Kallāṭam, 86, 87
Kaḻukumalai ōreḻuttantāti, 126
Kaḻukumalai paḷḷu, 130
Kaḻukumalai tiripantāti, 130
Kāmadeva (god of love), 69, 95, 138, 140, 155–157, 267
Kamala, A Story of Hindu Life, 261
Kamalam. See *Kamala, A Story of Hindu Life*
Kamalāmpāḷ carittiram, 206, 231n43, 232–237, 238–243, 259
  plot summary, 233, 234
  See also *carittiram*
Kamaliṉi, 260
Kampaṉ, 24n54, 38, 46, 75n63, 199, 233, 236, 241, 243
Kamparāmāyaṇam. *See* Kampaṉ
Kaṇam Kiruṣṇaiyar, 103, 113, 131
Kaṇapati Kavirāyar, 122n37, 131
Kāñci Ñāṉappirakācar monastery, 60
Kannada
  as classical language, 22n45
  literature of the nineteenth century, 8n15
Kantacāmikkavirāyar, 131
Kantacāmikkavirāyar, Mukavūr, 131
Kantacāmippulavar, Cevaṟkuḷam, 130, 130n72
Kantacāmippulavar, Vācutēvanallūr, 129, 129n70
Kaṇṭatēvip purāṇam, 34n3
Kantavarukkac canta veṇpā, 126
Kānti piḷḷaittamiḻ, 245

Kaṟpiṉ Vijayam, 260
Karuttamuttup Piḷḷai, 130
Karuvai mummaṇikkōvai, 129n67
Karuvaiyantāti, 129n67
Katācintāmaṇi, 38n10
kātal (a literary genre), 34n3, 56, 89, 127, 140, 144
kaṭavuḷ vāḻttu (invocatory stanza), 62, 74, 148, 209n6
Kaṭikaimuttup Pulavar, 128n64, 141
Kāvaṭiccintu, 129
kavipraśaṃsā (praise of poets), 84
Kāyakappiriyā, 123n43
Kayaṟkaṇṇimālai, 126
kiḷavi (poetic situation), 91, 92n83
kiḷavittalaivaṉ (hero of the narrative), 94, 95, 100, 115, 144
King Solomon's Mines, 3
Kipling, Rudyard, 6
Kiruṣṇaiyar, Tirumāṉūr A., 132
Kiruṣṇamūrtti, Ra. *See* Kalki
Kiruṣṇa Piḷḷai, Henry A., 36n7, 37n9, 177
Kiruṭṭiṇakkavi, 120
Kōmakaḷ, 260
Kōmatiyantāti, 129n67
kōmūttiri (a form of *cittirakkavi*), 47
Kōpālacāri, A. K., 260
Kōpālakiruṣṇa Pāratiyār, 72, 177
Kōṭīccurakkōvai, 92n83, 92n84, 98n91, 119
Kōṭīccurarulā, 120
kōvai (a literary genre), 56, 64–70, 89–91, 92n84, 92n85, 98, 100, 101, 115n15, 296
  See also *Cīkāḻikkōvai*; *Kuḷattūrkkōvai*; *Tirukkōvaiyār*
Kōvintacāmi Rājā, Pi. Ci., 260
Krishnamurthy, R. *See* Kalki
Krishna Pillai, Henry A. *See* Kiruṣṇa Piḷḷai, Henry A.
Kūḷappa Nāyakkaṉ kātal, 144n102, 147
Kuḷattūrkkōvai, 29, 90–101, 115, 116, 119, 176
Kuṇapūṣaṇi, 260
Kundera, Milan, 212
Kunhambu, Potheri. *See* Kuññampu, Pōttēri
Kuññampu, Pōttēri, 239
Kuṉṟaic cilēṭaiveṇpā, 126
Kuppucāmi Mutaliyār, Āraṇi, 250n5
kuṟavañci (a literary genre), 14, 56, 119, 124, 131, 132n88, 139, 140, 142, 143
Kurucāmi Nāyuṭu mītu marutavilācam, 131
Kurusvāmi Carmā, Cu. Vai., 258
Kuṭantaittiripantāti, 34n3
Kutiraimalaip patikam, 130

Lalitāṅki, 261
Līlai, 259
literacy in Tamil during nineteenth century, 19, 85, 86, 219
little kings, 103n1
  See also poligars
locus amoenus topos, 76, 116, 156
Lōkōpakāri (journal), 261
Loomba, Ania, 5, 9
Lord Curzon, Viceroy, 3

Macaulay, Thomas B., 170
Madhaviah, A. *See* Mātavayyā, A.
Madīnatu 'n-nuḥās, 210, 211n12
Madras, 14, 16, 20, 36, 62, 126, 160, 171, 173, 235
Madras Christian College, 80, 179, 220, 232
Madras Mail, The (newspaper), 201
Madras Presidency, 13, 14, 20n37, 20n38, 38, 103, 169, 176, 190, 219
Madras University, 163, 166–168, 220
Madurai, 36, 59, 60, 128, 232–234
Madurai Tamil Sangam, 126n55, 127
Mahābhārata, Tamil version of, 38n10
mahātmya (temple myth). See *talapurāṇam*
Makāliṅkaiyar, Maḷavai, 62

Makaravantāti, 126
Malayalam
literature of the nineteenth century, 8n15
novel in, 205, 239
Malay novel, 249
Malaysia
Tamil literature in, 13
Māmi marukiyar vāḻkkai, 258
Māmpaḻak Kavicciṅka Nāvalar, 41n14, 42, 51, 71, 74, 75, 84, 114, 124, 125, 128n64, 132n88, 134, 138, 141
See also *Cantiravilācam*
Māṇikkavācakar, 64, 65, 94
Maṇimēkalai, 24n54, 162n131
Maṅkaḷāmpikai piḷḷaittamiḻ, 34n3
Maṉōṉmaṇīyam, 21, 232
Maraikkār, Cittilevvai Mukammatu Kācim, 258
Maṟaimalai Aṭikaḷ, 244
Marakatavalli, 260
Maratha rulers in Thanjavur. *See* Thanjavur, Maratha court in
Marathi, 8n14
in Thanjavur, 14, 117, 118n20
novel in, 205, 205n1, 218, 249
See also Thanjavur, Maratha court in
Marttanda Bhairava Tondaiman, 158
Maruṅkāpuri, 125n47, 132
Marutanāyakam Piḷḷai, 45
Marutappatēvar, Irutayālaya 128, 129, 130, 131n81
Marutūr veṇpā, 120n27
maṭakku (a poetic technique). See *yamakam*
maṭam. *See* monasteries, Śaiva
Mataṉacuntarappiracāta cantāṉa vilāca nāṭakam, 120n28
Mātavayyā, A., 223, 231, 244, 260
Mativāṇaṉ, 259
Maturaic Campanta Maṭattut Tampirāṉ, 134, 135
Maturaiccilēṭaivēṇpā, 126
Maturai Mīṉāṭciyammaṉ Cōmacuntarakkaṭavuḷ pēril aṭimaṭakkāciriyaviruttam, 126
Maturainirōṭṭakayamakavantāti, 53
Maturai Tamiḻc Caṅkam. *See* Madurai Tamil Sangam
Maturaiyamakavantāti, 126
Mayilvākaṉappulavar, Mātakal, 40
Meenakshisundaram Pillai, T. *See* Mīṉāṭcicuntaram Piḷḷai, Ti.
Merchant of Venice, The, 250n5
Meykaṇṭacāttiram, 45, 61
Midsummer Night's Dream, A, 232
Miller, Rev. William, 179
Mīṉāṭcicuntarak Kavirāyar, Mukavūr, 130, 131
Mīṉāṭcicuntaram Piḷḷai, Ti., 29, 34n3, 115, 118n22, 127, 150, 170
and *akam* poetics, 90–101
and Kōpālakiruṣṇa Pāratiyār, 72
and the Tiruvāvaṭuturai monastery, 57–62, 101, 102
araṅkēṟṟam of works by, 76–79
as editor of classic texts, 86, 87
avaiyaṭakkam poem by, 75, 76
birth, 36
cilēṭai poem by, 43–45
ciṟappuppāyiram poems by, 63, 64
ciṟappuppāyiram poems by Vētanāyakam Piḷḷai for, 64–70
cittirakkavi poems by, 46–51
cīṭṭukkavi (epistolary) poem by, 82, 83
death, 101, 102
education as pulavar, 37–55
first meeting with Vētanāyakam Piḷḷai, 175
in Pudukkottai, 122
marriage, 45
portrait of, 35
themes of his works, 87–90
U. Vē. Cāminātaiyar's biography of, 35
See also *Amparppurāṇam*, *Kuḷattūrkkōvai*

Mīṉāṭciyammaipiḷḷaittamiḻ, 43
missionaries, Christian, 10, 13, 14n23, 23–25, 26n63, 30, 118, 153, 163, 165, 168n3, 169, 172, 179, 190–192, 212, 221
See also *Harvest Field, The* (missionary magazine)
Mīti iruḷ, 260
modernity, 2, 21, 26, 30, 33, 102, 108, 165, 209, 213, 239, 243, 247–249
definition, 2n3
Moeis, Abdoel, 249
Mohanangi. See *Mōkaṉāṅki*
Mōkaṉāṅki, 259
monasteries, Śaiva, 34, 35, 57–62, 85, 86, 102, 159, 295, 296
See also Tiruvāvaṭuturai monastery; Tarumapuram monastery
Mousset, Louis Marie, 24
Mukherjee, Meenakshi, 205n1, 205n2, 206, 212
Muppāṟṟiraṭṭu, 120n27
Murdoch, John, 169, 170, 181, 196
Murukaraṉupūti, 123n43, 130
Murukēcak Kavirāyar, Paṉaiyañcēri, 122
musha'ira, 84
Muslim Nēcaṉ (newspaper), 258
Muslim Tamil literature, 15, 210
Muthumeenakshi. See *Muttumīṉāṭci*
mutts. *See* monasteries, Śaiva
Muttucāmi Aiyar, T., 176
Muttucāmippiḷḷai, Irācavallipuram, 130
Muttuccāmit Tēvar, 131
Muttucuvāmi Piḷḷai, 134, 137, 139
Muttumīṉāṭci, 244n69
Mutturāmaliṅka Cētupati, 123–126, 254
Mutturāmaliṅkat Tēvar, 132, 162n131
Muttuveṅkiṭa Cuppayyar. *See* Piccuvaiyar, Cilēṭaippuli Vēmpattūr
Muttuvīrak Kavirāyar, Puḷiyaṅkuṭi, 129
Muttuvīrappap Piḷḷai, 127n61
Muttuvīrappūccayaturai, Raṅkakiruṣṇa, 132n88
Muttuvīra Vāttiyār, Uṟaiyūr, 45, 54, 131n81
Muttuvīrāyi Nācciyār, 154, 254, 255
Muttuvīriyam, 45, 54, 90n81, 131n81
Mutukuḷattūr, 146, 253
Mysteries of London, The, 3, 250n5

Naiṭatam, 17, 43
Nālaṭiyār, 23n48, 185, 199, 221n25, 241
Nālāyirativviyappirapantam, 24n57
Nāmakkal, 132
Nāmakkal Kaviñar, 132n89
Nampiyakapporuḷ. See *Akapporuḷ viḷakkam*
Ñāṉapāṉu (magazine), 20, 158n121
Ñāṉapōtiṉi (monthly magazine), 259
Ñāṉappirakācam, 260
Ñāṉappirakācam Piḷḷai, Ca., 82, 83, 172n8, 174, 175n22, 179, 192, 193, 200, 201, 221, 222, 264
Ñāṉapūṣaṇi, 259
Naṉṉūl, 38, 83, 84, 126
Nantaṉār carittirak kīrttaṉaikaḷ, 72
Narayan, R. K., 8
Nārāyaṇa Aiyaṅkar, 127
Nārāyaṇacāmi Ayyar, Es., 232
Nārāyaṇacāmi Nāvalar, 120
Nārāyaṇacāmi Nāyakar, Peṉṉelūr, 64
Nārāyaṇacāmi Piḷḷai, Ti. Kō., 258
Nārāyaṇakkavi, 120
Narayana Rao, Velcheru, 34, 110, 144n103, 147
Naregal, Veena, 11
Naṭarāja Aiyar, Ma. Ve., 259, 261
Naṭēca Cāstiri, Ca. Ma., 244, 259
Natesa Sastri, S. M. *See* Naṭēca Cāstiri, Ca. Ma.
Naṭuvēṉiṟkaṉavu, 232

nationalism, 16, 20, 21n42, 23n46
nautch girls. See *devadāsīs*
Navarāttiri festival, 107, 121, 163
Nāyaka period, 34, 103, 105, 106, 109n6, 110, 117n17, 134, 147, 157
Nelson, James Henry, 23, 23n50, 59, 177
nirōṭṭakam (a poetic technique), 51, 53
Nītinūl, 176, 180–192, 193, 194, 196, 198–200, 201n58, 203, 208, 209, 245, 247
Nītipōtakaveṇpā, 123n43
Norton, George, 167, 169, 170, 181, 196
novel
  earliest Tamil novels, list of, 257–261
  rise of the novel in India, 6, 205, 206, 211–213, 249
  rise of the novel in Tamil, 4, 13, 15, 16, 18, 21, 30, 205–245, 247
  See also *carittiram*; Hindi; Kannada; Malayalam; Telugu

occasional poem. See *taṉippāṭal*
Oddie, Geoffrey, 58n43, 60
ōlai. *See* palmleaf manuscript

Padmanjī, Bābā, 218
Pākavata tacamaskanta nāṭakam, 120n27
pāḷaiyakkārar. *See* poligars
Pālapōtam, 123n43
Palarāmayyar, Na., 259
palmleaf manuscript, 22, 37, 46, 77, 78, 81, 84–86, 161, 247
Paṉacait tiripantāti, 126
Pañcalaṭcaṇat tirumukavilācam, 128
Pañcatantra, 215
Paṉṉūṟṟiraṭṭu, 126n55
Pāṇṭikkōvai, 64n52, 115n15
Pāṇṭitturait Tēvar, 123, 126, 127, 162n131
Pāṇṭiya kēḷī vilāca nāṭakam, 120n29
Pārata ammāṉai, 120n30
Pāratiyār. *See* Cuppiramaṇiya Pārati, Ci.
Pāratiyār. *See* Kōpālakiruṣṇa Pāratiyār
Parīkṣāguru, 218
Paritimāl Kalaiñar. *See* Cūriyanārāyaṇa Cāstiri, Vi. Kō.
Pārttipaṉ kaṉavu, 18n34
Pāskara Cētupati, 107, 126, 127, 131n81, 163
Passage to India, A, 3
Patmāvati carittiram, 244n69, 260
patronage, literary, 4, 21, 29, 30, 34n3, 111n9, 112, 247
  monasteries as patrons, 57–62, 87, 159, 160
  zamindars and local kings as patrons, 1, 71, 87, 88, 103–163, 253, 254
pāṭṭiyal treatises, 56
Pattuppāṭṭu, 162n131
pāṭṭuṭait talaivaṉ (hero of the composition), 94, 99, 100, 115, 115n15, 116, 119, 141, 144, 153, 254, 255
Paul, John J., 177, 178
Peṇ kalvi, 194–201, 203
Peṇ māṉam, 195, 197, 199, 200, 203
Peṇmati mālai, 194, 200, 211, 234
Percival, Peter, 16, 17, 18, 24, 24n58
Periya Caravaṇap Perumāḷ Kavirāyar. *See* Caravaṇap Perumāḷ Kavirāyar, Aṭṭāvatāṉam
Periya Nāyaki Ammai patikam, 202
Periya Nāyaki Ammaṉ patikam. See *Periya Nāyaki Ammai patikam*
Periyapurāṇam, 36
Periyar, 4
Peterson, Indira Viswanathan, 46, 48n25, 118
Phách, Hoàng Ngọc, 249
philology, Tamil, 25, 161, 163, 248, 251

Piccupāratikaḷ. *See* Piccuvaiyar, Cilēṭaippuli Vēmpattūr
Piccuvaiyar, Cilēṭaippuli Vēmpattūr, 53, 127, 128, 129, 130
Piccuvaiyar, Kalpōtu, 131
Pilgrim's Progress, The, 36n7
piḷḷaittamiḻ (a literary genre), 56, 62, 75, 76n64, 89, 130, 245
Pirammāṉantayōki carittiram, 120n31
Pirapākaramālai, 123n43
pirapantams (category of literary genres), 34n3, 62, 64, 116
  definition, 55, 56, 296
  in the twentieth century, 245
  overview of nineteenth-century, 55–57, 88–90
Pirapantatīpam, 90n81
Pirapantatīpikai, 56n38
Piratāpa Cantira vilācam, 14n24, 192
Piratāpa Mutaliyār carittiram, 193, 196, 208–223, 226–230, 235, 237–243, 258
  editions of, 200n55, 219, 222, 223
  English translations of, 221, 222, 223
  plot summary, 214–215
  See also *carittiram*
Pirēmakalāvatyam, 258
Pirēmakalāvatīyam. See *Pirēmakalāvatyam*
poligars, 103–105, 296
Pollock, Sheldon, 27, 85
Poṉṉampalam Piḷḷai, 133, 133n91, 134
Poṉṉiyiṉ Celvaṉ, 18n34
Poṉṉuccāmit Tēvar, 42, 51, 114, 115n14, 123–127, 134–138
Pope, Alexander, 216n20
Pope, George Uglow, 14n23, 23, 23n48, 164, 257
Postcolonial Studies, 4n6, 7, 9, 10n17, 249n3, 250
Prabuddha Bharata (journal), 232, 233
Pratt, Mary Louise, 5
Presidency College, 16, 24n58, 259
press. *See* journalism
Price, Pamela, 103n1, 105, 107n4, 110, 115n14, 123, 255n7
printing press
  in Tamil, 19, 20, 26, 162
  See also publishing, nineteenth-century Tamil
prose
  development of modern Tamil, 20, 21, 26, 193–198, 211, 221, 248
  Vētanāyakam Piḷḷai, as author of, 30, 178, 181, 193–203, 208, 211, 214, 223, 229, 238, 243
prostitution, 146, 151, 185–192, 200, 247
  See also *devadāsīs*
public sphere, 20, 20n38, 247
publishing, nineteenth-century Tamil, 19, 20, 28, 45, 85, 86, 160–163, 165, 169, 247, 250, 257–261
Pudukkottai, 1, 2, 3, 103n1, 107, 121, 122, 158, 162n131, 172
pulavars (poet-scholars), 15, 16, 21, 29, 30, 36, 180, 245, 247, 296
  as authors, 55–57, 84–87, 95, 100
  as publishers and editors, 159–164, 165
  monasteries as patrons of, 57–62
  traditional education of, 37–55
  zamindars and local kings as patrons of, 103–163
  See also economy of praise
Puliyūryamakavantāti, 40
Puṟanāṉūṟu, 23n48, 162n131
Pūraṇap Piramāṉanta Yōki, 120
Puṟapporuḷveṇpāmālai, 23n48, 24n57
Pure Tamil Movement, 80, 244
pūrttiviḻā (concluding ceremony), 78
Puvaṉēntiraṉ ammāṉai, 126
pyal school. See *tiṇṇaippaḷḷi*

Racikarañcaṉam, 123n43
Raghunatha Rao, Diwan Bahadur, 176, 191

Rājam Aiyar, Pi. Ār., 30, 206, 208, 231, 247, 259
as novelist, 232–243
biography, 232, 233
portrait, 231
See also *Kamalāmpāḷ carittiram*
Raja Rao, 8
Rājaśēkhara Caritramu, 212, 229n38
Rājātti Ammāḷ, 260
Rāmacāmi Aiyaṅkār, Ca., 260
Rāmacāmi Nāyakkar, Ī. Vī. *See* Periyar
Ramachandra Tondaiman, of Pudukkottai, xxiv, 1–3, 121, 158
Ramalinga Swami. *See* Irāmaliṅka Cuvāmikaḷ
Ramanujan, A. K., 93, 136
Ramaswamy, Sumathi, 14n27, 23n46, 127n56
Rāmāyaṇa, Tamil. *See* Kampaṉ
Rambles in Vedanta, 233
Ramnad, 42, 71, 103n1, 104, 105, 107, 108, 110, 114, 122–128, 136, 145–147, 153, 154, 156, 158, 162n131, 163, 245, 253–255
Ravi Varma, Raja, 2, 3, 121, 158
reading practices, 21, 22, 248
registration of books, 169
Reynolds, George William MacArthur, 3, 250
Rhenius, Carl Theophilus Ewald, 14n23, 164
Richman, Paula, 138, 245n75
Rider Haggard, Sir Henry, 3, 6
Robinson Crusoe, 250
Roesli, Marah, 249
Rusvā, Mirzā Muḥammad Hādī, 212

Saguna, A Story of Native Christian Life, 261
Śāhāji, King, 118n20
Said, Edward, 6, 7
Śaiva Siddhānta, Tamil. See *Meykaṇṭacāttiram*
Salah Asoehan, 249
Sangam literature. See *Caṅkam* literature
Sanskrit, 14, 22, 53, 54, 57, 60, 61, 67, 74, 79, 98, 107, 117, 121, 124, 125, 138, 203, 229
Sarasvatīvijayam, 239
sati (widow burning), 20, 199n51, 238
Satthianadhan, Krupabai. *See* Cattiyanātaṉ, Kirupā
Sayyid Muḥammad. *See* Imām al-'Arūs
Schwartz, Christian Friedrich, 118
Sears, Laurie J., 7, 7n11
Serfoji II, King, 117n17, 118, 119, 120, 140, 141, 160
Sethupati dynasty. *See* Cētupati dynasty
Shakespeare, William, 3n5, 233, 245
translations into Tamil, 232, 250, 250n5
Sherlock Holmes, 250
Shulman, David, 34, 39, 75n63, 104n1, 109n6, 110, 128, 139n96, 144
silent reading. *See* reading practices
Singapore
Tamil literature in, 13, 203n63, 210
Sitti Noerbaja, 249
Sivagangai, 103n1, 107n4, 122–128
Sivaji II, King, 120
śleṣa (double entendre). See *cilēṭai*
social reform, 4, 21, 26, 30, 168, 170, 181, 190, 197, 200, 213, 238, 244
See also women
Southern Star, The (newspaper), 178, 179
Spiegel, Gabrielle M., 27, 28
Spivak, Gayatri Chakravorty, 6, 17
Sri Lanka
Tamil literature in, 13, 101n92, 200, 258, 259
Srinivasa Aiyangar, M., 17n33, 33, 52
Śrīnivāsdās, 217, 218

Śrīraṅgarāja Caritramu, 211, 229n38
śṛṅgāra rasa, 116, 135, 156
Śṛṅgārarasamañjarī, 74, 125
sthalapurāṇa (temple myth). See *talapurāṇam*
Subrahmanyam, Sanjay, 11n19, 34, 110, 144n103
Subramania Iyer, G., 20, 190, 192
Sundaram Pillai, P. *See* Cuntaram Piḷḷai, Rao Bahadur P.
Suryanarayana Sastri, V. G. *See* Cūriyanārāyaṇa Cāstiri, Vi. Kō.
Swaminatha Iyer, U. V. *See* Cāminātaiyar, U. Vē.
Swinton, George Melville, 174, 175

tacāṅkam (ten constituents of the kingdom), 155, 156
Tagore, Rabindranath, 8
talapurāṇam (temple myth), 34n3, 46n23, 55–57, 88, 89n78, 129, 297
Tales of an Indian Detective. See *Tāṉavaṉ eṉṟa pōlīs nipuṇaṉ kaṇṭupiṭitta atputa kuṟṟaṅkaḷ*
Tamil language
  colonial critique of, 16, 30, 165–171, 247
Tamil literature
  colonial critique of, 16, 165–171
Tamil Plutarch, The, 254
Tamil Renaissance, 22, 244, 248
Tāmōtaram Piḷḷai, Ci. Vai., 22, 80, 81, 81n68, 121n35, 162, 177
Ṭampāccāri vilācam, 14n24, 192
Tāṉavaṉ eṉṟa pōlīs nipuṇaṉ kaṇṭupiṭitta atputa kuṟṟaṅkaḷ (Tales of an Indian Detective), 259
Tañcaip peruvuṭaiyārulā, 119
Tañcāvūr. *See* Thanjavur
taṉippāṭal (occasional poem), 79–81, 117n16, 122, 123n43, 123n44, 125, 126n51, 127n61, 129n70, 131n79, 131n81, 133, 177, 180, 297
taṉittamiḻ iyakkam. *See* Pure Tamil Movement
Taṉiyūrp purāṇam, 34n3
Tanjore. *See* Thanjavur
Taṇṭapāṇi Cuvāmikaḷ, 55, 129, 183n36
Tāṇṭavarāya Tampirāṉ, 61, 131
Taṇṭiyalaṅkāram, 46, 126
Tarumapuram monastery, 58, 60, 130, 175, 176
Tēcikappirapantam, 120n27
Telugu
  as classical language, 22n45
  at Maratha court in Thanjavur, 14, 117, 188n20
  literature of the nineteenth century, 8n15, 53n31, 79n67, 203
  novel in, 205, 211, 212, 229n38
temple myth. See *talapurāṇam*
Teṉkācaip paḷḷu, 130
Tēvamātā antāti, 202
Tēvāṅka purāṇam, 125
Tēvāram, 57, 59, 241
Thanjavur, Maratha court in, 14, 29, 110, 117–120, 128, 140, 160
Thiru. Vi. Ka. *See* Kaliyāṇacuntara Mutaliyār, Tiru. Vi.
Tiṉavarttamāṉi, 20, 24n58
tiṇṇaippaḷḷi (verandah or *pyal* school), 37, 38, 39, 172
Tiricirapuram. *See* Tiruchirappalli
tiripu (a poetic technique), 42, 43, 46, 53, 125, 297
Tiruccirāmalaiyamakavantāti, 41, 62
Tirucculiyal ōreḻuttantāti, 126
Tiruchirappalli, 36, 63, 64, 45, 90, 171, 172–176
Tirukkamavak Kavirāyar, 129
Tirukkaṇṇapuram purāṇam, 120n32
Tirukkōṭṭiyūrp paḷḷu, 132n88
Tirukkōvaiyār, 64–66, 94, 95, 100
Tirukkuṟaḷ, 23n48, 23n49, 24n56, 24n57, 38, 57, 96, 97, 100, 183, 185, 187, 199, 221n25, 241, 243
Tirukkuṭantaippurāṇam, 34n3, 78

Tirumalaivēluppulavar, Eṭṭiccēri. *See* Vērkavirāyar, Tirumalai
Tirunākaikkarōṇappurāṇam, 46n23, 77n66
Tirunāḷaippōvār, 72
Tiruñāṉacampantar, 46
Tiruñāṉacampantar monastery, 60
Tirunelveli, 34n3, 128, 144n102, 261
Tirunelvēli Ceṅkōl monastery, 60
Tiruppaiññīlittiripantāti, 62
Tiruppaṉantāḷ monastery, 60
Tirupparaṅkiri mummaṇikkōvai, 245
Tirupparaṅkirippatikaṅkaḷ, 130
Tirupperunturaippurāṇam, 78, 86n75
Tiruppuvaṉappurāṇam, 130
Tiruttillaiyamakavantāti, 41
Tirutturuttip purāṇam, 34n3
Tiruvācakam, 23n48, 57, 102, 241
Tiruvaḷḷuvar. *See* Tirukkuṟaḷ
Tiruvaṉaikkāttiripantāti, 62
Tiruvaruḷ antāti, 202
Tiruvaruḷ mālai, 202
Tiruvāṭāṇai antāti, 131n82
Tiruvātavūrarpurāṇam, 65
Tiruvāvaṭuturai monastery, 57–62, 81, 126, 131, 132n84, 163, 177
Tiruvāymoḻi, 241
Tiruviṭaimarutūr noṇṭināṭakam, 120n27
Tiruviṭaimarutūrppurāṇam, 120
Tiruvūṟaippatiṟṟuppattantāti, 56
Tiyākarāca Ceṭṭiyār, Pūvaḷūr, 57, 60, 87, 88
Tolkāppiyam, 54, 90n81, 92n83
Tô Tâm, 249
translation, colonial practice of, 250
Trautmann, Thomas R., 10, 23n49
Travancore, 3n5, 106, 121
Trichinopoly. *See* Tiruchirappalli
Trichy. *See* Tiruchirappalli
Trincomalee, 259
Tschacher, Torsten, 15n30, 210
Tulukkāṇattammai patikam, 126
tuṟai (poetic situation), 91
Tuṟaicaiyamakavantāti, 41
Turaicāmi Aiyar, Ti. El., 260
Turaicāmi Reṭṭiyar, 132n89
Turaiciṅka Tēvar, 127, 128
Tūtukkaṇṇi, 130n72

ulā (a literary genre), 56, 89, 116, 139, 139n96, 140, 143, 156
Umrāo Jān Adā, 212
Uṟaiyūrppurāṇam, 88
Urdu novel, 205, 212
Ūṟṟumalai, 128, 132n87
Uṭaiyārpāḷaiyam, 113, 131
Utāracōtaṉai mañcari, 130
Uttararāmāyaṇa kīrttaṉai, 120n27

Vaḷḷimaṇamālai, 123n43
Varadarajan, Mu., 19
Vargas Llosa, Mario, 212, 213
Varma, Raja Ravi. *See* Ravi Varma, Raja
Vaṭappaḻani vaṇṇamañcari, 129n70
Vedānta, 24n57, 232, 233
Vēḷāḷar (non-brahmin caste group), 34n3, 36, 143, 172, 297
Vēḷāḷar paḷḷu, 130
Vēlappak Kavuṇṭar, 125, 141, 143
Vēḷukkuṟicci, 132, 141, 143
Vēṉis Varttakaṉ, 250n5
Vēṅkaṭacāmi, Mayilai Cīṉi, 15n28, 122
Venkatachalapathy, A. R., 14n27, 15, 19, 34n3, 70, 76, 160, 162, 169, 244
Vēṟkavirāyar, Tirumalai, 132n87
Veṟimaṅkaipākak Kavirāyar, 132n88
vernacular. *See* Tamil language
Vētācalam Piḷḷai, Ca. *See* Maṟaimalai Aṭikaḷ
Vētanāyaka Cāstiri, 118
Vētanāyakam Piḷḷai, Māyūram, 4, 29, 30, 36, 54n33, 170, 234, 247, 258
  and the *Kuḷattūrkkōvai*, 90–101, 115
  as first modern poet, 183
  as novelist, 206–231, 237–245. See also *Cukuṇa cuntari carittiram*; *Piratāpa Mutaliyār carittiram*

birth, 171, 172
ci͟rappuppāyiram poems by, 64–70
death, 178, 179
education, 172, 173
epistolary poem by, 81
legal career of, 173–180
on law, 193
on women's issues, 184–187, 193–201
portrait of, 171
religious songs by, 202, 203
See also *Cukuṇa cuntari carittiram; Nītinūl; Piratāpa Mutaliyār carittiram*
Vicākapperumāḷ Aiyar, Tiruttaṇikai, 83n69
Vicālāṭci Ammāḷ, 261
Vicuvanāta Piḷḷai, Vi., 250n5
Vietnamese novel, 249
vilācam (a literary genre), 139–141, 141n97, 143
See also *Camuttiravilācam; Cantiravilācam*
Villiyappa Piḷḷai, 127, 128
Vilvava͟nappurāṇam, 130
Vi͟nōta carittiram, 258
Vinson, Julien, 17n33, 24, 24n54
Vīracāmi Aiyaṅkar, Eṭṭaiyapuram, 127
Vīraiccilēṭaiveṇpā, 129n67
Vīrai navanīta kiruṭṭiṇacāmi patikam, 129n67
Vīrai navanīta kiruṭṭiṇa͟n piḷḷaittami͟l, 129n67
Vīraittalapurāṇam, 129n67
Vīraiyantāti, 129n67
Vīrakēraḷamputūr Navanītakiruṭṭiṇa͟n kalampakam, 129
vi͟raliviṭutūtu (a literary genre), 18, 98, 145, 297
See also *Cētupati vi͟raliviṭutūtu*
Vīrava͟nap purāṇam, 34n3
Vīrēśaliṅgam Pantulu, Kandukūri, 212, 229n38
Viruttaparācariyam, 130
Vivēkacintāmaṇi (journal), 232
Vivekananda, Swami, 232
V. V. S. Aiyar. *See* Cuppiramaṇiya Aiyar, Va. Ve.

Waghorne, Joanne Punzo, 1n1, 109n7, 121
Wagoner, Phillip, 10, 11
Washbrook, David, 12, 14, 248
White, Hayden, 28
Winslow, Miron, 24, 164, 168n3
women
in Tamil literature, 89, 116, 119, 137, 140, 142, 156, 185n40, 186, 187, 215, 242
education of, 30, 178, 184, 191, 192, 193–200, 219
social position of, 20, 187, 188, 199n51, 201, 213, 234
widow re-marriage, 20, 199n51, 200, 218
See also child marriage; prostitution; sati

yamakam (a poetic technique), 39, 40, 41, 43, 46, 53, 81, 125, 138, 142, 150, 296, 297
yamakavantāti (a literary genre), 40, 41, 53
Yamunāparyaṭan, 218
Ya͟naimēla͟lakar noṇṭiccintu, 120n27

zamindars (landholders), 29, 34n3, 58, 102, 188, 297
as patrons of literature, 1f., 87, 103–163
colonial critique of, 158, 159
courtly rituals of, 106–111
emergence of, 103–106
scandals and ridicule, 158, 159
Ziegenbalg, Bartholomäus, 25
Zvelebil, Kamil V., 16n31, 22, 55, 185n40, 203, 208, 210, 211, 217, 226, 253, 254, 257, 258, 259, 261

www.ingramcontent.com/pod-product-compliance
Lightning Source LLC
Chambersburg PA
CBHW030126240426
43672CB00005B/35
9781438432007